The Hardball Times Baseball Annual 2009

Featuring contributions by THT's staff writers:
Richard Barbieri • Sal Baxamusa • Brian Borawski
John Brattain • Craig Brown • Matthew Carruth • Derek Carty
Mike Fast • David Gassko • Brandon Isleib • Josh Kalk •
Dave Studenmund • Steve Treder • Tuck • John Walsh • Victor Wang

With additional contributions by guest writers:
Joe Posnanski • Craig Wright • John Dewan • Rob Neyer
Tim Marchman • Tom Tango • Rich Lederer • Don Malcolm
Phil Birnbaum • Will Leitch • Mitchel Lichtman • Craig Calcaterra
Sean Smith • Roel Torres • Jack Marshall • Greg Rybarczyk
Anthony Giacalone • Eric Seidman • Corey Seidman • Colin Wyers

Produced by Dave Studenmund
Edited by Joe Distelheim, Bryan Tsao, Carolina Bolado and Ben Jacobs

The Hardball Times Baseball Annual 2009

New articles daily at www.hardballtimes.com

Edited by Joe Distelheim, Bryan Tsao, Carolina Bolado, and Ben Jacobs
Stats developed by Dave Studenmund and Bryan Donovan
Cover design by Tom Wright
Typesetting by Dave Studenmund

Published by: ACTA Sports
                 5559 W. Howard Street
                 Skokie, IL 60077
                 1-800-397-2282
                 info@actasports.com
                 www.actasports.com

ISBN: 978-0-87946-368-7
ISSN: 1940-4484
Printed in the United States of America by Hess Print Solutions.
Year: 15 14 13 12 11 10 09 08
Printing: 10 9 8 7 6 5 4 3 2 1

What's Inside

What's Inside (cont.)

Welcome to Our Book

The Hardball Times began as a website devoted to baseball writing, but we also had the quaint notion of writing a book, putting our thoughts and ideas in print. In the tradition of great baseball writers of the past (and present!), we settled on an Annual format: *The Hardball Times Baseball Annual*. For over four years now, we've generated enough baseball verbiage to produce a website that is updated daily and a book that runs nearly 400 pages. Allow me one brief moment of pride in that.

The first *Annual* consisted of a few original articles, reprinted articles from the site and stats. When we started working with ACTA Sports on the second *Annual*, we dropped the reprints and expanded our pool of writers to include guest writers, friends from the Blogosphere, and others. In fact, we began to think of the *Annual* as not just a THT publication, but a publication that represents the Internet's best baseball writers and thinkers. It's a formula that's worked well.

But we're always looking to improve. So we surveyed our readers last summer, asking them what they liked and didn't like about the *Annual*. The response informed the book you now hold in your hands.

Don't worry. We haven't changed the basic formula at all. As usual, you'll find four sections of writing: a review of the 2008 season, general baseball commentary, historical essays and analytic articles. You'll also find our insightful 2008 statistics and graphs in the second half of the book.

But there is now more writing than ever before: 40 brand new baseball essays, 25 percent more than in the past. Plus, we've reached out to even more writers, and our list looks like an All-Star team of the very best writers practicing their craft right now, such as Joe Posnanski, Rob Neyer, Tim Marchman and Craig Wright (to name a few). We also reformatted our season reviews and dropped the leaderboards from our stats.

Yes, 'tis a far better *Annual* than we have ever created before. Don't believe me? Take a look for yourself.

Interesting things happen when you ask a variety of authors to submit their meandering baseball thoughts. Those thoughts come together in unexpected ways. Of course, several people wanted to write about the Tampa Bay Rays, so we coordinated their efforts into an overview of how the Rays got so good, and how they compare to similar teams in history.

There's going to be quite a Hall of Fame election in five years, and Joe Posnanski takes a peek in his crystal ball to see what the outcome will be. Mike Piazza will be part of that class, and legendary sabermetrician Craig Wright has contributed his own Piazza piece, writing from the perspective of an insider who worked for the Dodgers when Piazza was learning his craft in the minors. Craig's essay fits nicely with an article about catcher development and usage from Tom Tango.

Craig also contributed a fantastic article about how well Honus Wagner played in his old age, coinciding with a player aging analysis from Phil Birnbaum. John Dewan looks at the best fielding teams of 2008, while Sean Smith looks at the best fielders of the "Retrosheet era."

And for some reason, Pete Rose crops up several times in these pages. Go figure.

Our perennial features return intact. Tuck has contributed a number of "toons" that appear randomly throughout the book. John Burnson has contributed his "playing time constellations," which appear after the stats.

Oh, and there are lots of stats. The usual counting stats that we all know and love are contained herein, as well as some sabermetric stats like Base Runs and Pitching Runs Created. And we're justifiably proud of our Batted Ball stats, which are thoroughly explained in the Stats Intro. Plus, there is a Glossary to explain everything else.

This sort of thing doesn't happen without a lot of hard work by a lot of people. Particular thanks go to David Appelman of Fangraphs for supplying WPA stats and John Burnson of *HEATER Magazine* for the constellations. Our friends at Baseball Info Solutions and ACTA Sports—John Dewan, Steve Moyer, Damon Lichtenwalner, Greg Pierce, Charles Fiore and Andrew Yankech—have been wonderful business partners for several years now. Bryan Donovan continues his masterly work creating THT's statistics and Steve Treder contributed 30 terrific Stat Facts to the *Annual*.

So many Internet sites and blogs support THT that I can't name them all. But a few like Inside The Book, Baseball Think Factory, Baseball Reference, Fangraphs, Ballhype—even big guys like ESPN, Fox Sports and old friend Baseball Prospectus—must be mentioned. My apologies to the hundreds of sites I just neglected.

The biggest expression of gratitude goes to our four editors: Bryan Tsao, Joe Distelheim, Carolina Bolado and Ben Jacobs. I have no idea why they work so hard for so little. Must be the glory.

Happy Baseball,

Dave Studenmund

The 2008 Season

In the past, a *THT Annual* division review consisted of a pennant race graph followed by a recap of the season. This year, we're trying something a little different.

Each article still begins with the pennant race graph, but we've also added a few tables that fill in the divisional story. That allows the accompanying article to be more commentary than reportage.

For instance, Steve Treder looks in-depth at the major disappointments in the NL West. Matthew Carruth examines how each team in the AL West evaluated their potential and talent. Craig Brown lists the way each team in the AL Central defied preseason predictions.

We think you'll find these articles more interesting, but we also want to make sure you get the most out of the tables. So here is a brief description of each one.

The first table is pretty simple; it lays out the number of runs scored and allowed by each team per game as well as the number of projected wins each team would have accrued based simply on the difference between their runs scored and allowed. Among baseball analysts, these are called "Pythagorean Wins" and the "run differential." Here's the AL East table:

Run Scoring			
Team	RS/G	RA/G	PWins
BAL	4.9	5.5	72
BOS	5.2	4.3	96
NYA	4.9	4.5	87
TB	4.8	4.1	92
TOR	4.4	3.8	93
Average	4.8	4.5	88

If run differential were king, the Red Sox would have won the division (96 projected wins).

The second table...

Win Contributions			
	WPA		Bball
Team	Bat	Start	Pen	Field
BAL	-3.3	-4.5	-4.7	-1.6
BOS	6.0	5.5	2.6	0.4
NYA	0.6	-0.9	8.3	-1.8
TB	5.3	1.4	9.3	1.4
TOR	-2.9	4.6	3.3	4.3
Average	1.1	1.2	3.7	0.5

...is pretty straightforward once you understand it. It lists the "win contributions" of each team's components. We use Win Probability Added (WPA, defined in the Glossary) to apportion win credit between the offense, starting pitching and bullpen. Since this version of WPA doesn't split out credit for fielders, we have a separate column that translates John Dewan's plus/minus team fielding components into fielding wins (see John's "Fielding Breeds Winning" article).

Each figure is expressed as a number of wins above or below average. For example, the division champion Rays' bullpen was fantastic, contributing nine wins more than average. WPA puts more weight on late innings of close games, so it tends to give more credit to bullpens. The best way to read this table is to compare each component across teams (say, Boston's bullpen vs. Toronto's bullpen) instead of within teams (Boston's bullpen vs. its offense).

The tables in the middle of each page need no explanation. The first table lays out the division's record against other divisions, and the second one lists the transactions that had the biggest impact on the race.

The table at the top of the third column shows how the teams performed against each other during the year. Once again, here is the AL East version:

Head-to-Head Records						
Team	BAL	BOS	NYA	TB	TOR	TOT
BAL		6	7	3	6	22
BOS	12		9	8	9	38
NYA	11	9		11	9	40
TB	15	10	7		11	43
TOR	12	9	9	7		37

You find wins by reading across the table and losses by reading down the table. For example, the Blue Jays were 12-6 against the Orioles.

The last table lists the top five individual batters and pitchers in the division. Batters are ranked by Base Runs (BR is our preferred run estimator—see Colin Wyers' article in this *Annual* for an explanation) and we also include each batter's On Base Percentage (OBP) and Slugging Percentage (SLG).

Pitchers are ranked by Pitching Runs Created (PRC—which is essentially Base Runs for pitchers; see our Glossary for a definition). We also include each pitcher's ERA and strikeouts per game (K/G).

American League East View

by John Brattain

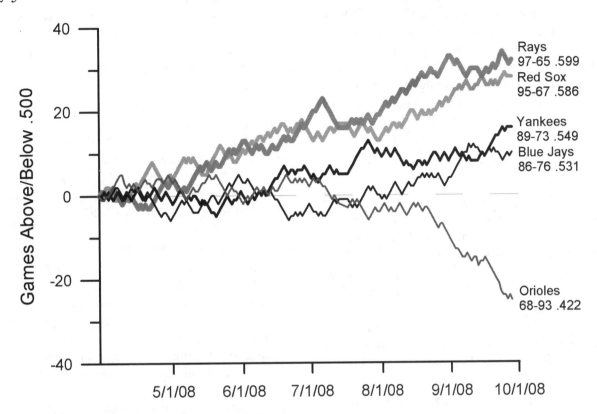

Run Scoring

Team	RS/G	RA/G	PWins
BAL	4.9	5.5	72
BOS	5.2	4.3	96
NYA	4.9	4.5	87
TB	4.8	4.1	92
TOR	4.4	3.8	93
Average	4.8	4.5	88

Win Contributions

Team	WPA			Bball
	Bat	Start	Pen	Field
BAL	-3.3	-4.5	-4.7	-1.1
BOS	6.0	5.5	2.6	1.7
NYA	0.6	-0.9	8.3	-4.5
TB	5.3	1.4	9.3	2.0
TOR	-2.9	4.6	3.3	3.2
Average	1.1	1.2	3.7	0.3

Play Against Other Divisions

Division	W	L	Win%
AL Central	109	77	.586
AL West	94	79	.543
NL East	16	11	.593
NL Central	31	26	.544
NL West	5	1	.833
Total	255	194	.568

Key Transactions

TB	Picked up Bartlett, Garza, Percival in offseason
TB	4/12: Brought up Longoria from minors
NYA	6/16: Wang out for year
NYA	7/20: Posada out for year
BOS	7/31: Manny traded for Bay

Head-to-Head Records

Team	BAL	BOS	NYA	TB	TOR	TOT
BAL		6	7	3	6	22
BOS	12		9	8	9	38
NYA	11	9		11	9	40
TB	15	10	7		11	43
TOR	12	9	9	7		37

Top Performances

Hitters	Tm	OBP	SLG	BR
Youkilis	BOS	.390	.569	120
Markakis	BAL	.406	.491	114
Huff	BAL	.360	.552	113
Abreu	NYA	.371	.471	105
Damon	NYA	.375	.461	104

Pitchers	Tm	ERA	K/G	PRC
Halladay	TOR	2.78	7.5	140
Lester	BOS	3.21	6.5	114
Matsuzaka	BOS	2.90	8.3	101
Burnett	TOR	4.07	9.4	100
Shields	TB	3.56	6.7	97

A tombstone once had as an epitaph: "I expected this but not just this soon."

It's also the sentiment surrounding the Tampa Bay Rays; most acknowledged they were a team on the rise and would likely be bona fide contenders in 2009 or 2010 at the latest. However, they had their coming out party a little earlier than most expected. Also, it was probably thought that the Rays' first taste of October baseball would come via the wild card—I mean, c'mon, we could see them overtaking the Yankees or the Red Sox if the winds blew right, but not both.

Oops.

Just goes to show you …

What exactly?

Well, the AL East was both a proving ground and a myth-busting phenomenon, where baseball truisms came to the fore yet certain bits of "conventional wisdom" were thoroughly debunked.

To begin with, the Rays' success proved once again that money in and of itself isn't necessary to field a competitive club. Indeed, the $200 million New York Yankees finished eight games back and out of the play-offs while the Rays, with about 20 percent of their payroll, finished atop the East with the second-best record in the American League.

Many try to discount the Rays' success by stating that any club with a decade's worth of early first-round draft picks would eventually be good. They neglect to mention that the Kansas City Royals and Pittsburgh Pirates have had a bushel of top draft picks and remain very much themselves (although some glimmers of hope are starting to emerge).

The Rays had to identify the talent to draft and ultimately get them to sign (not to be assumed in the Scott Boras era of draft shenanigans) and finally polish their minor league jewels to the point where they could be productive big leaguers.

Regardless, the Rays weren't simply a team put together in that fashion. Like all successful teams, they made astute trades (getting Scott Kazmir from the Mets, Matt Garza and Jason Bartlett from the Twins, Dioner Navarro from the Dodgers, Dan Wheeler from the Astros, J.P. Howell from the Royals and Grant Balfour from the Brewers), made solid pick-ups off the "scrap heap" (Eric Hinske, Carlos Pena) and found talent wherever they could (Akinori Iwamura).

That's 10 key players acquired "the old-fashioned way," with scouting and not throwing money at the shiniest bauble in the free agent market.

Yes, they had some nice chits to trade because of their draft positioning, but it still takes skill to parlay that into useful talent and not chaff.

Another thing the Rays accomplished was to poke a big hole in "it's not fair that teams have to compete in the AL East with the Yankees and Red Sox." Believe it or not, the Toronto Blue Jays have been demonstrating the same thing in recent years.

In 2008, the Blue Jays were 18-18 against the (fiscal) beasts of the East; they were 17-19 in 2007 and 20-17 in 2006, giving them a three-year mark of 55-54 versus the Red Sox and Yankees. The Jays' difficulty comes against teams with losing records. The Blue Birds are 132-121 (.520) against teams with winning records and 124-109 (.532) against clubs with losing marks. They've owned Baltimore over that span (32-22), which means that absent the O's recent travails Toronto has been only five games over .500 against losing clubs.

Toronto can compete in the AL East; they just haven't fattened their record against second-division patsies. Regardless, both the Rays and the Jays have demonstrated that the alleged unfairness of playing in the East simply does not exist. In 2000, had they won just 11 of their final 20 games the Jays would have finished tied for the division lead; they won just seven—three against the Yankees.

Of course, you still need "luck" (defined as the breaks that come from normal mathematical variance falling in your direction).

One of the most remarkable aspects to the Rays' season is that their five main starters: Kazmir, James Shields, Garza, Edwin Jackson and Andy Sonnanstine, made 153 of their starts. The Rays were tied for fifth in starter ERA in MLB in 2008; of the teams ahead of them, Toronto (3.72 ERA) had its top five starters go 139 times, the Cubs (3.75 ERA) 130, the Brewers (3.86 ERA) 132, the Dodgers (3.87 ERA) 135 and the Diamondbacks (3.95 ERA) 141.

Compare that with the sport's five worst starting staffs: Seattle (5.07 ERA) 120, Colorado (5.14 ERA) 122, Pittsburgh (5.36 ERA) 125, Texas (5.51 ERA) 110 and Baltimore (5.51 ERA) 116.

Another random variation working in the Rays' favor was their success in one-run games. Tampa Bay was 29-18 in such contests.

While we're on the subject of potentially deceiving records, the Baltimore Orioles again spent the early part of the baseball season wondering if somehow the front office had caught lightning in a bottle.

What we saw in reality is that a team will ultimately play to its true level, given a big enough sample size.

In 2007, the Orioles raised some eyebrows by winning 11 of their first 18 games. Last season, they almost finished April in first place by opening the season 6-1. By the end of both seasons, they finished within hailing distance (both ways) of 70 wins.

I was asked both times, on various radio shows, about the O's. Were all the preseason prognosticators wrong? Was this team a lot better than initially thought? The answer was a simple no. It took no great insight to make such a statement because of the power of the sample size. Given enough time, a team will play to its true talent level. Even among the mainstream media it is understood that a team "is never as good as it is when it is playing well nor as bad as it is when it is playing poorly." The 97-win Rays of 2008 endured a seven-game losing streak; the 70-win Rays of 2004 enjoyed a 12-game winning streak.

A team that opens or closes a season on a tear is often misjudged. The Orioles were not as good as their 6-1 start indicated, nor as bad as their 1-11 finish indicated. The last two years, the rebuilding O's had the talent of about a 70-win team and finished in the neighborhood. Yes, a degree of random chance might net a team a few more wins or losses due to one-run games in a given season, but if the talent level remains unchanged, it will revert to its normal level—"water seeks its own level."

A quick look at the rest of the AL East for examples of: "never as good as it is when it is playing well nor as bad as it is when it is playing poorly."

- Rays (97 wins): At one point they won 15 of 18 and were on a seven-game winning streak and followed that up with a seven-game losing streak.
- Red Sox (95 wins): In May they had five- and seven-game winning streaks, along with skids of losing six-of-eight and five-of-six.
- Yankees (89 wins): They won just 5-of-16 in late July/early August but won 12-of-14 in September.
- Blue Jays (86 wins): They had a seven-game losing streak in June and a 10-game winning streak in late August/early September.

In each case you could find articles in the media during these periods and read examples of unbridled optimism or soul-crushing pessimism—but each case was only the normal ebb and flow of a season.

The division also saw the truth in a lot of what is said about pitching. We know the various drills: you can never have too much pitching; young pitchers will break your heart, Baseball Prospectus' axiom that "there is no such thing as a pitching prospect," etc.

The Yankees came into the year with a seemingly solid rotation with Andy Pettitte and Mike Mussina as the veterans, Philip Hughes and Ian Kennedy the kids, and Chien-Ming Wang the innings-eating ace. They had some decent fallbacks that could fill in over short stretches in Darrell Rasner (who was averaging six innings per start and had a 3.64 ERA in June), Ross Ohlendorf, a big righty with decent command (minor league BB/9 of 2.32), and Mexican Leaguer Alfredo Aceves.

The Red Sox had a nice mix of youth and experience in Josh Beckett, Curt Schilling, Jon Lester, Daisuke Matsuzaka, Clay Buchholz and Tim Wakefield.

The Blue Jays were also sick with young pitching, having seen Dustin McGowan, Shaun Marcum and Jesse Litsch make major strides in 2007; if any of them faltered there were some intriguing arms in David Purcey, Ricky and Davis Romero, Brett Cecil and Indy Leaguer Scott Richmond just behind them.

The Yankees lost Wang, Kennedy and Hughes to a combination of injury and ineffectiveness. Schilling, who was trying to rehab his shoulder, opted for surgery, and Buchholz never really got on track. The Jays lost both McGowan and Marcum to major surgery and Litsch (and Marcum) saw time in the minors.

While the Jays plugged holes from within, the Yankees gave a shot to Sidney Ponson and the Red Sox traded for Paul Byrd and started Bartolo Colon.

It also demonstrated that young pitchers will break your heart as Hughes, Kennedy, McGowan, Marcum and Buchholz all were derailed at some point both this year and next. The Red Sox and Jays, especially, looked absolutely stacked in pitching depth only to find out the truth that one can never have too much.

Conventional wisdom states that pitching and defense win championships. However, the Toronto Blue Jays conclusively demonstrated that you still have to hit. Toronto led the majors with one of the best staff ERAs in two decades (3.49), had the best rotation and bullpen in the AL (3.72 and 2.94) and one of the best defensive units in the league.

The Jays finished fourth in the AL East at 86-76.

Toronto had a below league average batting average, (.264/.267), OBP (.331/.335) and SLG (.399/.420) and was second in the loop in hitting into double plays (150), including a staggering number with the bases loaded late in close games. The Blue Jays lost 20 times when holding the other side to three or fewer runs—among those, there were 12 games that could be described as outstanding pitching efforts (defined as two or fewer runs over nine innings or three or less in extra innings). The Jays lost two 10-inning games where they held the opposition to three runs, and had 12-inning losses in which they allowed one and three runs. They had seven other losses in which they were beaten despite allowing two or fewer runs.

Toronto had 143 opportunities in those 20 games (with runners in scoring position) and managed just 14 hits (.097).

Toronto was to a degree a victim of bad luck (as discussed earlier), but they did demonstrate that pitching and defense only gets a team so far—clubs ignore this at their own peril.

The Yankees demonstrated that a team tries to artificially extend (read: keep throwing money at problems as they crop up) its success cycle at its own risk. The Yankees are an old team with an aging lineup, several holes/question marks in the rotation and not much in the bullpen behind Mariano Rivera. The team defense is unreliable and there's not a lot of help in the minors.

It finally caught up with them this year.

Should the Yankees blow a wad in the free agent market this offseason, they'll add a lot of older, expensive pieces that will be difficult to move in trades and cost them a lot of draft picks.

If indeed 2008 wasn't an aberration, then the Yankees will again reinforce the axiom that there is no substitute for a strong player development program. Money's biggest benefit isn't in developing talent; it is retaining that talent. The Rays demonstrated that to put together a quality team requires brains, savvy and luck, not throwing money around and hoping the results will work out.

Finally, we learned a valuable lesson in the whole Manny Ramirez fiasco in Boston: the importance of the complete player and the value of skills not directly linked with hitting. Ramirez is a no-doubt, first-ballot Hall of Famer, but the Boston Red Sox were undeniably a better team with Jason Bay.

Some of that can be attributed to simply not having the distraction of the whole circus surrounding Ramirez, but it went far deeper than that.

Ramirez enjoyed yet another terrific season, batting .332/.430/.601 with 37 home runs, good for a 164 OPS+, yet Bay was no slouch either, posting a line of .286/.373/.522 with 31 home runs for a 134 OPS+. Looking back 20 years from now, many may say that the Red Sox would have been better off with Manny than Bay in left field. Yet, their numbers with the Red Sox...

- .299/.398/.529, 20 home runs, 136 OPS+ (Ramirez)
- .293/.370/.527, nine home runs, 128 OPS+ (Bay)
  ...tell a different story.

Also, a degree of Ramirez's value was eroded by his historically inept defense, comatose base running and whatever disruptions and distractions he caused for the team.

Bay, on the other hand, is a much superior player to Ramirez in the other aspects of the game. Ramirez batted .347/.473/.587 in July (his best month in Boston last season), but the club won just 11 games. In August, with Bay in left field, the Red Sox were 18-9.

The biggest difference between the two months was the man in left field—obviously not all of the swing can be attributed to the switch but, by the same token, it had a notable effect. While providing close to the same amount of offense as Ramirez, Bay converted more balls hit to left field into outs and did a better job on the basepaths (of note, while not a prolific base stealer, Bay has only been nabbed four times in his last 50 attempts since 2005; Ramirez has attempted 68 steals in his career and been caught 31 times).

Although we may need a larger sample size to know for certain, it appears the Red Sox's acquisition of a better all-around player over a first-ballot Hall of Fame bat improved the team. Being able to rake will always be coveted, but there is a difference between a great hitter and a great player.

In all, the AL East aptly separated the wheat from the chaff with respect to conventional baseball wisdom.

American League Central View

by Craig Brown

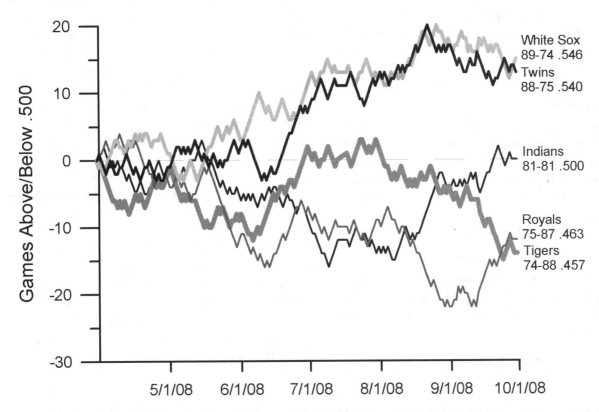

Run Scoring			
Team	RS/G	RA/G	PWins
CHA	5.0	4.5	90
CLE	5.0	4.8	85
DET	5.1	5.3	78
KC	4.3	4.9	72
MIN	5.1	4.6	90
Average	4.9	4.8	83

Play Against Other Divisions			
Division	W	L	Win%
AL East	77	109	0.414
AL West	91	83	0.523
NL East	5	1	0.833
NL Central	17	13	0.567
NL West	36	18	0.667
Total	226	224	0.502

Head-to-Head Records						
Team	CHA	CLE	DET	KC	MIN	TOT
CHA		11	12	12	9	44
CLE	7		11	10	8	36
DET	6	7		7	7	27
KC	6	8	11		6	31
MIN	10	10	11	12		43

Win Contributions				
	WPA			Bball
Team	Bat	Start	Pen	Field
CHA	-2.3	4.6	5.2	-2.5
CLE	-0.9	6.0	-5.1	1.7
DET	-1.2	-1.5	-4.4	-4.3
KC	-6.7	-3.9	4.5	-3.9
MIN	4.6	-0.3	2.2	-2.4
Average	-1.3	1.0	0.5	-2.3

Key Transactions	
CHA	Picked up Quentin, O. Cabrera in offseason
DET	Many prospects for M. Cabrera, Reneteria, Willis
MIN	Traded Santana for prospects in offseason
DET	6/10: Willis sent to minors
CLE	7/7: Dealt Sabathia to MIL
MIN	8/1: Recalled Liriano from minors

Top Performances				
Hitters	Tm	OBP	SLG	BR
Sizemore	CLE	.374	.502	122
Morneau	MIN	.374	.499	118
Cabrera	DET	.349	.537	109
Quentin	CHA	.394	.571	102
Granderson	DET	.365	.494	98
Pitchers	Tm	ERA	K/G	PRC
Lee	CLE	2.54	6.9	139
Danks	CHA	3.32	7.3	106
Greinke	KC	3.47	8.1	98
Meche	KC	3.98	7.8	94
Buehrle	CHA	3.79	5.8	91

The AL Central in 2008 figured to be a dog fight between two teams. The two had some quality arms and were so loaded on offense that they would take turns running circles around the rest of the division and would easily rise to the top of the pile. They were so evenly matched that 162 games might not be enough to settle the division. This one would almost certainly go down to the wire.

Wait ... you thought we were talking about Cleveland and Detroit?

For sure, it was a crazy season in which all expectations in the AL Central were turned on their heads. Where up was down and left was right. Cats and dogs, living together. If you made the mistake thinking something was a certainty, it was likely the exact opposite happened.

Each team defied expectations in one way or another.

Preseason prediction number one: The Tigers have such a potent offense, they could shatter the record for runs scored in a season held by the 1931 Yankees (1,067).

Maybe not break the record, but they certainly had a great chance at scoring more than 1,000 runs. At least that was the conventional wisdom when Detroit snagged third baseman Miguel Cabrera (along with starter Dontrelle Willis) in early December in exchange for a package of prospects that included outfielder Cameron Maybin and starter Andrew Miller. The 2007 version of the Tigers offense scored 887 runs and conventional wisdom held that by adding one of the top bats in the game in Cabrera, Detroit would only improve.

But conventional wisdom isn't always wise. The Tigers scored 821 runs, still a quality number, but a decline of 66 from just a year ago.

Cabrera did his part. With 85 runs scored, 127 RBIs and 37 home runs, he generated over 100 Base Runs. Cabrera began the year at third base, but by mid-April he moved across the diamond to first, where he remained for the rest of the season. His line of .292/.349/.537 was an offensive upgrade over Sean Casey (.296/.353/.393), who started most of the games at first for the Tigers the previous year. However, it was the only position where the Tigers saw improvement from 2007.

Gary Sheffield again received most of the team's plate appearances as a DH, but at age 39 you have to wonder how much is left in the tank. He had a respectable 2007 season in which he hit .265/.378/.462 for an OPS+ of 120. In November, he underwent surgery to clean up his shoulder and doctors found that he had a torn labrum. He was back by spring training, but was continually hampered by soreness. It didn't help that he tore a tendon on his left ring finger in the third game of the season and spent time on the DL with a strained oblique. Injuries, soreness and general old age conspired to sap Sheffield of his power and productivity, dropping him to .225/.326/.400 and an OPS+ of 91 with 19 home runs. It was his lowest OBP and slugging since he hit .194/.277/.320 in 50 games for Milwaukee in 1991.

After hitting .363/.434/.595 and finishing as runner-up in the AL MVP balloting in 2007, it was going to be difficult for Magglio Ordonez to top what was the best year of his career. Certainly, there would be some drop in production; the hope in Detroit was he wouldn't have a drastic decline. While .317/.376/.494 with 21 home runs is still quite productive, it was a far cry from 2007.

The Tigers got off to a horrible start, losing their first seven games by a combined score of 44-15, and were four games out of first place by the end of the first week of the season. They briefly rallied in June, winning 18 of 22 to move their overall record to two games above .500 and pulling to within 4.5 games of first. If they were going to make their move, that was the time. But they couldn't build on their momentum and packed it in in September, losing 12 of 13 at one point, and finished in the cellar of the Central.

It turned out that Jim Leyland could have penciled in the entire lineup from that record-setting Yankees team from '31, and he still couldn't have managed this team to the postseason.

The Tigers' bullpen was its Achilles heel. Start with Fernando Rodney (4.26 ERA, 3.81 FIP, 9.6 K/G in '07) and Joel Zumaya (4.28 ERA, 4.40 FIP, 7.2 K/G) out for the first two and a half months, putting the Tigers without two of their key setup men. Then add an ineffective Todd Jones as the closer and it's easy to see why the Tigers stumbled so badly. They lost 13 games in which they held the lead entering the eighth inning, a stinging indictment of a bullpen that collectively posted a 4.65 ERA, the third-worst in the AL.

A disappointing season for a team that fancied itself a contender.

Note: FIP stands for Fielding Independent Pitching and is defined in the Glossary.

Preseason prediction number two: The Twins Opening Day starter is Livan Hernandez. If that's the best they can do, their rotation is going to be horrible.

Faced with the prospect of losing ace Johan Santana to free agency after the 2008 season, the Twins took the proactive route and shipped him to the New York Mets for a bucketful of prospects. That came on the heels of letting Carlos Silva depart via free agency to Seattle and after trading Matt Garza to Tampa for Delmon Young. The offseason shuffling saw the Twins lose more than 500 innings from their starting rotation of 2007, including more than 210 from Santana.

While the Twins had some young arms percolating in the minors, they still felt the need to pursue another starter in the free agent market. Signed to a $5 million deal before the opening of spring training, Hernandez was supposed to supply the "veteran leadership" that was thought to be lacking with the departures of Santana and Silva. The fact Hernandez was known as an "innings eater" was thrown in for good measure. What the Twins bought for their trouble was a starter who averaged around six innings per start while posting a 5.48 ERA, a strikeout rate of 3.5 K/G and a 1.63 WHIP.

Following Hernandez at the front of the rotation was Boof Bonser. While Bonser's strikeout rate was down to 5.7 K/G as a starter (compared to the previous season's 7.1 K/G) his real problem was the fact he couldn't get hitters out with runners on base. The opposition tagged him for a .313 average with runners on and .303 when they were in scoring position. His 4.31 xFIP suggests he was a bit unlucky and while his 5.93 ERA may suggest otherwise, Bonser wasn't any worse than his previous two seasons in the Twins rotation. He lasted 12 starts before being banished to the bullpen.

While Hernandez and Bonser were struggling, Nick Blackburn (4.05 ERA, 103 ERA+), Scott Baker (3.45 ERA, 121 ERA+), Kevin Slowey (3.99 ERA, 105 ERA+) and Glen Perkins (4.41 ERA, 95 ERA+) all showed they were more than capable as major league starters. While all four were between 24 and 26 years old, they did not let age become a factor (or an excuse).

On Aug. 1, the Twins had seen enough poorly eaten innings that they released Hernandez and replaced him by calling up Francisco Liriano from the minors. Liriano, whose velocity was down and struggled in his return to the majors with an 11.32 ERA in his first three starts following Tommy John surgery, was a different pitcher after his exile to Triple-A. In 11 starts from

early August to the end of the year, Liriano threw 65.2 innings with a 2.74 ERA and a strikeout rate of 8.2 K/G. While Minnesota's record in his starts was only 6-5, it should be noted that in three of the five losses, Liriano surrendered two or fewer runs with the bullpen twice blowing leads. It's odd that Minnesota's offense failed given that they had the most potent offense in the division, scoring 892 runs. Joe Mauer (.328/.413/.451) won his second batting title in three years and Justin Morneau (.300/.374/.499) provided the power.

However, starting pitching was the story and in games through Aug. 2, Twins starters had a 4.53 ERA with a strikeout ratio of 5.4 K/G and a walk ratio of 2.0 BB/G. In games from Aug. 3 (the return of Liriano to the rotation) to the end of the season, the Twins rotation posted a 3.91 ERA with a strikeout rate of 6.2 K/G and walk rate of 2.3 BB/G.

Perhaps if the Twins had moved faster on returning Liriano to the rotation, they might not have needed that 163rd game.

Preseason prediction number three: Cliff Lee is a fifth starter.

After posting a 6.29 ERA in 20 appearances last season (16 starts and four relief appearances after he was banished to the bullpen) Lee entered spring training needing to pitch well to be named the fifth starter. While his 5.27 spring ERA wasn't great by any stretch of the imagination, it was enough to hold off Aaron Laffey and Jeremy Sowers to clinch the final spot in the Indians' rotation.

Lee made his first start on April 6 against the A's and went 6.2 innings while allowing just one unearned run. In his next start, he threw eight innings of two-hit ball against the same A's and followed that with another eight-inning, two-hit performance against the Twins. Then he went the full nine in shutting out Kansas City on three hits. Through his first four starts spanning 31.2 innings, Lee had 29 strikeouts against two walks and an ERA of 0.28.

As you read in Mike Fast's article in the Analysis section of the *Annual*, the key to Lee's success was new-found control. After walking 3.3 batters per nine innings in '07, Lee lived in the strike zone so much this year he practically built a house. His walk rate was 1.4 BB/G, the best such rate among qualifiers. He added about 1.5 mph to his fastball (average speed 91.5 mph) and the uptick in velocity made his off-speed pitches that much snappier. Bolstered by an improved sinker, Lee suddenly became a groundball pitcher with a 1.3

GB/FB ratio, the first time in his career he trended away from the flyball side of the equation. The result was a 2.54 ERA and 3.69 xFIP in over 220 innings. Basically, Lee reinvented himself.

Improved control, better velocity, more grounders and fewer home runs all added up to new hardware as Lee will likely win the AL Cy Young award.

Not bad for a fifth starter.

Preseason prediction number four: The White Sox are a solid team, but in a rough-and-tumble division, they will do no better than .500.

While the Tigers made the offseason headlines with their acquisition of Cabrera, the South Siders made a trade that was just as key to their success in '08 when they sent minor league first baseman Chris Carter to Arizona for outfielder Carlos Quentin. After a couple cups of coffee for the Diamondbacks during which Quentin hit just .230/.316/.425 with 14 home runs in 395 at-bats, he was deemed surplus in a Diamondbacks organization with plenty of young offensive talent.

Sometimes, a change of address will do wonders. Quentin homered in his fifth at-bat for the Sox and then went on a power surge, slamming eight out of the park in his first 27 games while posting a .620 slugging percentage. Nothing could stop him, except for a freak injury where he broke his wrist after tapping it against his bat. He finished the season with 36 home runs and a batting line of .288/.394/.571, finishing second in the league in homers and slugging, and fourth in on-base percentage.

Quentin was the youthful leader of a veteran-heavy lineup in which six regulars hit 21 or more home runs. Jermaine Dye, Jim Thome and Paul Konerko have been through a few pennant chases. As a team, the Sox bashed 235 home runs, the most in the majors.

However, offense wasn't the whole story of the Chicago success.

It took some time, but a pair of trades Kenny Williams executed after the 2006 season finally paid dividends—and in a big way. The Sox traded away pitchers Brandon McCarthy and Freddy Garcia, who have since been plagued with injuries, making just eight combined starts in 2008. While the short-term results weren't promising, the long view saw the

return net Chicago the foundation of a rotation that had a 4.09 ERA, the best mark among their rivals in the Central.

Lefty John Danks delivered a complete turnaround from his disastrous 2007 debut with the White Sox. In cutting his walk rate from 3.5 BB/G in '07 to 2.6 BB/G, Danks curbed his wildness. He also added about two mph to his fastball, began mixing it with a cutter and let his infielders earn their keep as he posted a 1.2 GB/FB ratio. He finished with a 3.32 ERA, the fifth-best mark in the AL and an xFIP of 3.96.

Then there was Gavin Floyd, who won only once in '07 after he bounced between the rotation, the bullpen and the minors. Finally left alone, he made 33 starts and topped 200 innings for the first time in his career at any level. While his strikeout (6.3 K/G in '07 and 6.3 K/G in '08) and walk rates (2.4 BB/G in '07 and 3.1 BB/G in '08) were largely static, his success was predicated on limiting opposing hitters to a .246 AVG.

The Sox were a combined 40-26 in starts made by their young duo, with Floyd picking up the win in Chicago's makeup game against Detroit and Danks winning his start in the one-game playoff against Minnesota.

Preseason prediction number five: The Royals have improved, but once again they will struggle to escape the basement of the division.

One out of five puts us at the Mendoza line in predictions, meaning the Royals were about the only sure thing in a topsy-turvy Central division.

On Aug. 29, the Royals were 56-78 and solidly in last place, nine games behind the disappointing Tigers. However, a finishing kick that saw Kansas City win 19 of its final 28 games combined with a Detroit team that was less than interested gave the Royals just enough juice to squeak past the team many picked to win the division.

The two teams were within a half game of each other at the end of the regular season. But the Tigers' makeup game on Monday to (possibly) settle the division title also decided who would finish in last. The Tigers fell 8-2 to the Sox, giving fourth place to the Royals and moving them out of the cellar for the first time since 2003.

American League West View

by Matthew Carruth

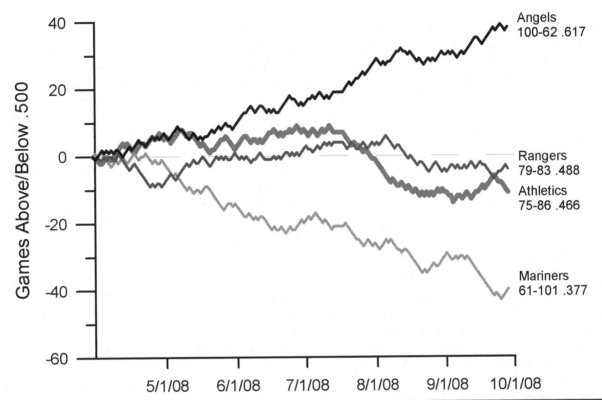

Run Scoring

Team	RS/G	RA/G	PWins
LAA	4.7	4.3	88
OAK	4.0	4.3	76
SEA	4.1	5.1	67
TEX	5.6	6.0	75
Average	4.6	4.9	77

Win Contributions

Team	WPA			Bball
	Bat	Start	Pen	Field
LAA	6.3	6.0	6.7	-0.6
OAK	-6.9	-2.7	4.0	2.8
SEA	-8.1	-6.3	-5.6	-0.8
TEX	0.6	-4.8	2.2	-4.0
Average	-2.0	-2.0	1.8	-0.6

Play Against Other Divisions

Division	W	L	Win%
AL East	79	94	.457
AL Central	83	91	.477
NL East	23	22	.511
NL Central	3	3	.500
NL West	13	8	.619
Total	201	218	.480

Key Transactions

SEA	Traded Jones, others for Bedard in offseason
LAA	Signed FA Torii Hunter in offseason
OAK	Traded Haren and Swisher in offseason for Smith, Eveland, others
SEA	7/5: Bedard out for season
OAK	July: Traded away Harden, Blanton for many
LAA	Picked up Teixeira from ATL 7/29

Head-to-Head Records

Team	LAA	OAK	SEA	TEX	TOT
LAA		10	14	12	36
OAK	9		10	7	26
SEA	5	9		8	22
TEX	7	12	11		30

Top Performances

Hitters	Tm	OBP	SLG	BR
Hamilton	TEX	.371	.530	116
Ibanez	SEA	.358	.479	109
Kinsler	TEX	.375	.517	105
Guerrero	LAA	.365	.521	96
Suzuki	SEA	.361	.386	94

Pitchers	Tm	ERA	K/G	PRC
Santana	LAA	3.49	8.8	113
Hernandez	SEA	3.45	7.8	95
Saunders	LAA	3.41	4.7	87
Duchscherer	OAK	2.54	6.0	82
Lackey	LAA	3.75	7.2	76

This was not, as it turned out, an exciting year for the AL West. According to CoolStandings.com, the Angels surpassed the 90 percent likelihood mark for winning the division by July 28, just 104 games into the season. At that time, they held an 11.5-game lead over the Rangers and were 12 games over the free-falling Athletics. The lack of any semblance of a competitive division made the pennant race uneventful, but despite that, there was no shortage of worthy stories.

In last season's AL West review, Sal Baxamusa wrote, "An early poor performance caused Texas to take a long-term view. If Oakland ('but for the injuries') and Seattle ('we won almost 90 games') conclude they are at the cusp of contention, they could make franchise-crippling mistakes." These two teams took almost diametrically opposite approaches over the following 12 months, with Seattle deciding to go for it and Oakland trading some of its best players while still in the playoff race. Seattle certainly made execution mistakes, but was it a mistake to conclude they were at the cusp of contention?

The 2007 Mariners finished the season with 88 wins, despite a bevy of core metrics, including a Pythagorean record of 79-83, that indicated that they were more of a .500 team. However, while the strong performance by the Mariners during 2007 was a fluke, which detractors correctly pointed out, a message often lost was that the 2007 Angels were lucky as well.

The Angels' Pythagorean win total in 2007 was 90 compared to their 94 actual wins. In last year's Annual, Mitchel Lichtman calculated the projected win totals of each team, based on the actual playing time and under-lying performances of the players.

Team	Projected 2007 wins
OAK	84
LAA	82
TEX	80
SEA	80

Seattle ended up in last place, but notice how close all four teams were. By this measure, it was the Angels, not the Mariners, who most overperformed their talent. Given those parameters, four games behind in talent, it appears the Seattle brass made a justifiable decision to go for the playoffs.

Before the Mariners even made a single move, the Angels were already close to done. On Nov. 19, the Angels traded Orlando Cabrera to the White Sox for pitcher Jon Garland. At the time, it looked like the Angels anticipated making a play for Miguel Cabrera or possibly Alex Rodriguez to fill the gap in the left side of their infield. The problem was that the Angels did not have a capable replacement for Cabrera, and Garland was overvalued due to a low ERA but poor strikeout and groundball rates. Some analysts would claim that the Angels had voluntarily made themselves worse.

Two days later, the Angels decided that their horrid signing of Gary Matthews Jr. in the prior offseason was a sunk cost, kicked him out of center field and handed the job to Torii Hunter at the cost of a five-year, $90-million contract. That signing would be it for Anaheim however, as Rodriguez stayed with New York and the Tigers landed Cabrera. All told, it was a quiet winter for the Angels. On the surface, that wouldn't seem bad given their 2007 finish, but as mentioned, there were reasons to be skeptical that the Angels were far better than their division counterparts. Still, the important aspect of the winter for them was that they retained their depth in the minors.

Contrast that to the Seattle Mariners' offseason, which got started around the winter GM meetings in December. Believing that their starting pitching cost them the division in 2007, the Mariners went into the winter determined to upgrade that area. This tunnel vision, a hallmark of Bill Bavasi's tenure, proved disastrous.

They began by cutting ties with the wrong starter, letting Jeff Weaver (who wasn't good but was incredibly unlucky in 2007) go while retaining Horacio Ramirez (who was both unlucky and terrible), only to later cut Ramirez before the season started at a cost of a few hundred thousand dollars.

Meanwhile, the Mariners also not only refused arbitration to Jose Guillen, they actively paid him $500,000 to go away. The official reason offered was that they didn't want to risk the chance of Guillen accepting arbitration. Jose Guillen signed a three-year, $36 million contract with the Kansas City Royals on Dec. 4. The Mariners either managed to misjudge the market so completely that they thought a player who went on to get $12 million a year might accept arbitration (possible given their incompetence level) or there was (steroids) some other (steroids) reason (steroids) they wanted to make sure Jose Guillen would no longer be a Mariner.

A fortnight after the conclusion of the winter meetings, the Mariners announced the signing of Carlos Silva to a four-year, $48 million contract, an outrageous price for a pitcher who at his best was never more than a middle of the rotation option. Befitting the Mariners' front office M.O., no other team was even close to that figure for Silva's services, but as they have done time

(Jarrod Washburn) and time (Jose Vidro) again, the Mariners front office spent far more than was needed to fill a hole with veteran talent. It was like having a nail hole in a wall that you decide needs to be covered, and instead of just getting some spackle and paint, you went out and bought an "original" Matisse from some person in a van out behind a local art school. Sure, you covered the nail hole, but there were cheaper solutions. If they deemed it necessary to splurge, why not at least splurge on talent instead of mediocrity?

Two months later and after 10 weeks of rumors, Erik Bedard was officially traded to the Mariners for a package of young talent good enough to start your own team. In one fell swoop, the Mariners wiped out their security blanket of talent close to the majors. Moreover, the Mariners gambled all of that on a pitcher known for his awesome curveball and fragility. Adding Bedard gave the Mariners the front line talent in the rotation to match up with the Angels; the difference was that Los Angeles possessed a safety net, while the Mariners were relying on every important player to stay healthy.

The Angels came to lean heavily on that depth even before the season began, as Kelvim Escobar went down for the season and John Lackey was set to miss at least a month. Lackey and Escobar combined to form an underrated pitching duo in 2007, so their loss was a substantial blow that had more people moving the Mariners ahead of the Angels. However, it only took two games for the Mariners to suffer their own injuries as J.J. Putz and Bedard (gasp) both ended up on the trainer's table, and neither player fully recovered in 2008. Right away, the one thing the Mariners could not afford happened twice, exposing their lack of depth. Without Putz, their bullpen quickly fell apart. While the Angels held onto an 18-11 record through April, the Mariners struggled to 13-15 and their season was already hanging by a thread.

An 8-20 record in May unceremoniously snapped that thread, and the Mariners found themselves in last place with their hopes for a postseason berth in 2008 crushed. Meanwhile, the Angels posted a 15-13 record and were back atop the division standings, a position they didn't yield the rest of the year. Instead, the Mariners found themselves in a different race: a race to the bottom for the first overall draft pick in 2009. Entering the final series of the season, the Mariners held a one-game "lead" over the Washington Nationals for that coveted first pick, but the two teams went opposite ways that weekend: Seattle swept Oakland while the Phillies swept Washington, propelling the Mariners

to the second spot and a 61-101 record. The Mariners' 2008 payroll was comfortably above $100 million while losing 101 games. The sheer size of financial folly they provided makes it a wonder that they weren't the team based in Washington, D.C.

Back in Anaheim, the Angels kept on cruising, never facing much of a threat from either Oakland or Texas. With the division all but wrapped up early, they quickly turned their sights to October at the trade deadline, dealing Casey Kotchman to Atlanta for Mark Teixeira. Sure it was an upgrade (and it was a huge one for 2008), but with Teixeira a free agent after the season, it appeared that the Angels were dumping Kotchman's future (and others) in hopes of getting better production in the playoffs. No matter how it turned out (Teixeira had 15 postseason at-bats), it provided an interesting debate amongst analysts.

The only team to offer any challenge to Los Angeles during the year was Oakland, much to many people's surprise. A majority of analysts roundly dismissed Oakland at the start of the season. The trading of Nick Swisher and Dan Haren had most expecting the Athletics to dwell in the cellar. Those who saw Oakland's pitching and defense as being enough to overcome a dismal offense were few and far between. However, 30 games into the season, those people looked like visionaries as the Athletics stood at 18-12 and in first place.

The Athletics hung around in May and June, and entered July just a few games behind the Angels, but a major part of their success was due to Rich Harden's dominance. Everyone knew Harden had immense talent; it was staying healthy that was his problem. Since Billy Beane had already established 2008 as a rebuilding year during the winter, Beane was likely wary of delaying this rebuild on the hope that Harden remained healthy. Instead, he took the opportunity to deal Harden at peak value and procured a haul of prospects from the Cubs. A week later, Beane added Joe Blanton to the departed list, trading him to Philadelphia for more minor league talent.

Did those trades kill Oakland's season? It sure seemed like it as the A's went just 2-19 over a span from July 12 to August 8, but seven of those losses were of the one-run variety and the main culprit was the offense. For the month of July, the A's scored just 3.44 per game but only allowed 4.36 runs per game, still above average. So it's hard to say the loss of Harden and Blanton affected the A's so much as their bad hitting talent finally caught up to them.

As bad as July was, August was even worse as the A's offense regressed even further, scoring just 82 runs in 30 games. Even worse, the run prevention finally regressed, allowing 5.4 runs per game. For an entire month, the Athletics averaged giving up in nine innings what took them 18 to score. It's no wonder they posted a 10-20 record in the month. They rebounded in September and for what was a rebuilding season, the Athletics were hugely successful and showed they deserve attention in the 2009 and 2010 seasons.

On July 24, the Rangers and Athletics swapped places in the division for good. It marked Oakland's descent and left the Rangers in a place they hadn't been in the division in some time: second place. Entering their first season without Teixeira at first base, the Rangers planned to give Ben Broussard a run at the job but quickly moved on when he got off to a slow start. Other positions of change were center field and designated hitter, where the Rangers moved from Kenny Lofton and Sammy Sosa to younger options. Seizing an opportunity, the Rangers moved prized pitching prospect Edinson Volquez to the Reds for breakout hitter Josh Hamilton, while snagging Milton Bradley on a one-year deal after injury concerns dimmed his value.

Bradley was healthy and ready from the get-go, posting a .912 OPS in April and getting better from there. Hamilton himself was no slouch with a .970 OPS in the first month of play, providing the Rangers with formidable offensive power in the middle of the order. Despite the offensive output from those two, the Rangers did not get off to a good start for the season, dropping the opening series to Mariners, with bad pitching and defensive miscues aplenty. At the conclusion of April, they stood at an abysmal 10-18, 7.5 games out of first, and while the offense was fine, it certainly wasn't a juggernaut nor enough to overcome the staggering 6.32 runs the team was allowing per game.

The Rangers opened May with a bang, though, winning their first three games and 12 of their first 16 to level their record at 22-22 and make up five games in the division. They finished May with a 19-10 record, a ramped-up offense and improved defense, outscoring their opponents by an average of 1.34 runs a game. Through June and July, the Rangers circled in a holding pattern around a .500 record, never dropping more than two games below that mark and never getting higher than four games above. Despite the best efforts of Ian Kinsler, with his near 1.000 OPS during that span, and the emergence of Chris Davis, who burst on the scene with a similar performance, the Rangers just couldn't overcome their abysmal pitching and dropped 8.5 games further back of the Angels during those two months. The Rangers never came close to the Angels from then on, falling apart in August and finishing the year with a 79-83 record and yet another season spent around the .500 mark. Overall, they scored an MLB-best 901 runs and allowed a staggeringly bad 967 to score.

With 2008 a snoozer, how does 2009 look? Obviously a lot will change with the winter's moves, but there are some general outlines we can look at. Notably in Seattle, where a new front office enters and may change the talent gap in the management teams of the AL West. Jack Zduriencik faces many difficult decisions on players such as 2009 free agents Adrian Beltre and Erik Bedard, and some easy ones, like dumping Jarrod Washburn on whoever's interested.

In 2008, Oakland took the opportunity to stock up an ark full of young talent, which bodes extremely well for their future. However, 2009 might still be too soon for them to compete for a postseason berth. Don't be surprised, though, if the Athletics ride good defense and solid but unspectacular pitching to another surprisingly competitive start.

The Rangers put together the most potent offense in baseball in 2008 and most of it should be back for another go in 2009. Their defense is a problem, especially up the middle with Kinsler and Michael Young, but they certainly hit enough to overcome that. The pressing issue is the pitching. Even with an adjustment for the ballpark, the Rangers' rotation was epically bad and the bullpen did them no favors either. Given that the Rangers have yet to show any coherent plans in the past on how to build a good staff, they could remain limited by this handicap for years to come.

The Angels are going to need to have their touted young hitters stay on the field and produce. Howie Kendrick is a fantastic talent, but he needs to stay off the disabled list and log 100-plus games so that they aren't forced to turn to the likes of Sean Rodriguez. Ignoring for the moment the key question of whether Teixeira will be back, the Angels also have to be wary of Vladimir Guerrero's production as he's entering the decline phase. On the pitching side, getting Escobar and Lackey back should help in the rotation, but both are free agents after 2009 and the bullpen without Francisco Rodriguez might be a liability. Still, the Angels have plenty of payroll room in a winter ripe with talent. Given the state of the rest of the division, they will likely enter 2009 as the favorites once again.

National League East View

by John Walsh

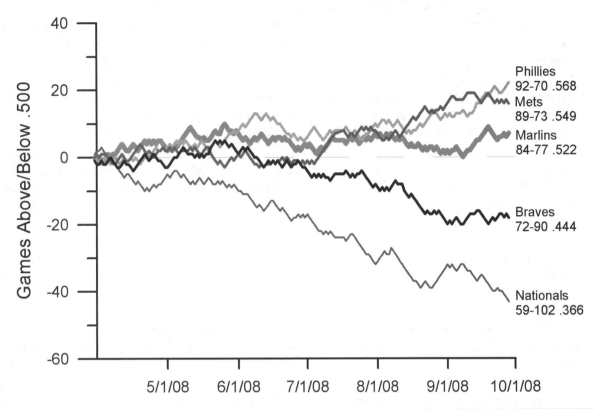

Run Scoring

Team	RS/G	RA/G	PWins
ATL	4.4	4.9	78
FLA	4.8	4.8	81
NYN	4.9	4.4	89
PHI	4.9	4.2	93
WAS	4.0	5.2	62
Average	**4.6**	**4.7**	**81**

Win Contributions

Team	WPA Bat	WPA Start	WPA Pen	Bball Field
ATL	-6.4	-1.0	-1.6	0.9
FLA	6.9	-4.0	0.7	1.8
NYN	6.7	3.9	-2.6	2.6
PHI	3.5	-0.8	8.3	4.4
WAS	-11.9	-7.3	-2.3	2.5
Average	**-0.2**	**-1.8**	**0.5**	**2.4**

Play Against Other Divisions

Division	W	L	Win%
AL East	11	16	.407
AL Central	1	5	.167
AL West	22	23	.489
NL Central	94	109	.463
NL West	89	80	.527
Total	**217**	**233**	**.482**

Key Transactions

PHI	Picked up Brad Lidge in offseason
NYN	Traded prospects for Santana
NYN	6/13: Alou out for season
ATL	6/3: Smoltz out for season
ATL	Swapped Teixeira for Kotchman on 7/29
NYN	8/3: Wagner out for season

Head-to-Head Records

Team	ATL	FLA	NYN	PHI	WAS	TOT
ATL		10	11	4	6	31
FLA	8		8	10	14	40
NYN	7	10		11	12	40
PHI	14	8	7		12	41
WAS	12	3	6	6		27

Top Performances

Hitters	Tm	OBP	SLG	BR
Howard	PHI	.339	.543	120
Ramirez	FLA	.400	.540	120
Beltran	NYN	.376	.500	117
Wright	NYN	.390	.534	117
Reyes	NYN	.358	.475	116

Pitchers	Tm	ERA	K/G	PRC
Santana	NYN	2.53	7.9	135
Hamels	PHI	3.09	7.8	114
Nolasco	FLA	3.52	7.9	98
Moyer	PHI	3.71	5.6	84
Pelfrey	NYN	3.72	4.9	80

It's *deja vu* all over again. Let's see, the Phillies win the division, the Mets head into the last day of the season needing a win to reach the playoffs. They lose. To the Marlins. The season ends with Phillies fans rejoicing as their team goes to the playoffs and Mets fans despairing of another blown September lead.

Now, normally at this point I'd write about 2,000 words recapping the NL East Division in 2008—give you my insights, such as they are, on the race, the teams, the players who were good and the ones who weren't. You know, an NL East Division Review. But the season just ended and you already know all this stuff, so this year, I'm taking a different approach. I'm going to focus on a couple of issues from the division that I think are interesting: (1) how the Phillies outperformed the Mets and won the division crown and (2) the abundance of MVP-caliber position players in the division.

Before tackling those two topics, though, here is a super-condensed version of what went down in the NL East this year (for posterity's sake).

This was a three-team race until mid-August, when the Marlins faded a little and the Phils and Mets battled it out until the last week of the season. The Phillies and Mets were evenly matched on offense; in fact, both teams scored 799 runs on the season. The Phils had the better pitching, though, especially, as I will examine below, in the bullpen.

The Florida Marlins were the surprise of the division with 84 wins, an improvement of 13 games over 2007. Their offense ranked fifth in the National League, which they achieved by avoiding glaring holes: six of their eight regulars had an OPS+ of 110 or more, and a seventh was nearly average at 93. The Fish's most notable characteristic was the power displayed by its quartet of infielders; Mike Jacobs (32), Dan Uggla (32), Jorge Cantu (29) and Hanley Ramirez (33) combined for the impressive total of 126 home runs.

The Atlanta Braves lost 90 games for the first time in 18 seasons and finished their third straight season out of the money, after reaching the playoffs 14 years in a row. In their defense, the Braves were beset by injuries in 2008 (their two best pitchers, Tim Hudson and John Smoltz suffered season-ending injuries) and their run differential (25 fewer runs scored than allowed) was more typical of a 78-84 record.

As for the Washington Nationals, my mother used to tell me if you can't say anything nice about somebody, don't say anything at all. Well, Cristian Guzman had an unexpectedly good year with the bat, and 24-year-old Elijah Dukes put up a nice line of .264/.386/.478 in limited playing time. I guess I should stop here.

So the Phillies finished three games ahead of the Mets. Why? We already saw their offenses were similar—the Mets' was a bit better, because they played in a tougher park for hitters—so the difference was in the pitching. Once you account for park effects, the two starting rotations were about equal. The big difference was in the teams' bullpens. As every Mets fan knows, the Mets bullpen was the main culprit in the team's failure to reach the postseason.

The Phillies had the top relief corps in the NL with an ERA of 3.19. Closer Brad Lidge continued his comeback from the nightmare that was 2006 (when Lidge delivered an unsightly 5.26 ERA), posting a 1.95 ERA and notching 41 saves without blowing a single one. The Phillies also got fabulous work from a group of relievers who weren't exactly household names: J.C. Romero, Ryan Madson, Chad Durbin and Clay Condrey. The worst ERA of that group, a pretty-good 3.27, belonged to Condrey.

The Mets, on the other hand, ranked 13th in the NL in reliever ERA. It's hard to reach the postseason with such a lousy bullpen. This year's NL playoff teams ranked first, second, fourth and eighth in bullpen ERA. Closer Billy Wagner was his usual self—when he was healthy. In 47 innings, the little lefty struck out 52 and walked only 10. He surrendered just 32 hits, for an ERA of 2.30 and a WHIP of 0.89. Those are all great numbers, except one: the 47 innings pitched. Wagner threw his last pitch of the season on Aug. 2, and from then on the rest of the Mets bullpen was rather like an airplane crew whose pilot has just suffered a fatal in-flight heart attack.

The Mets tried to do *something* to avoid disaster by acquiring Luis Ayala from the Nationals in mid-August, but Ayala did not turn out to be the solution. On the contrary, he registered an ERA of 5.40 in 16.2 innings for the Mets. Mets fans will remember his key role in two excruciating late-inning losses: to Atlanta on Sept. 14 (the Braves scored five runs in the ninth) and a 9-6 loss to the Cubs 10 days later, with the difference being a three-run bomb surrendered by the Mets' ersatz closer in the 10th inning.

Since the NL East title came down to who had the better bullpen, should we blame the Mets' front office for not putting together a top-notch 'pen, while the Phillies did just that?

I say no. Because, you can't look only at what happened, but what might have been expected to happen when these bullpens were put together. The following tables show the performance of the top six relievers (by innings pitched) for the two teams along with their THT preseason projections, i.e. a prediction on how they could be expected to do based on past performance and age.

Phillies Bullpen Projection and Performance

	Preseason Projection		Actual Performance	
	IP	ERA	IP	ERA
Lidge	70	3.76	69	1.95
Romero	59	4.28	59	2.75
Madson	70	4.41	83	3.05
Durbin	126	5.09	88	2.87
Condrey	73	4.88	69	3.26
Seanez	68	4.57	43	3.53
Total	466	4.58	411	2.87

Mets Bullpen Projection and Performance

	Preseason Projection		Actual Performance	
	IP	ERA	IP	ERA
Wagner	72	2.84	47	2.30
Feliciano	68	3.31	53	4.05
Smith	54	3.53	63	3.55
Heilman	82	3.16	76	5.21
Schoeneweis	64	3.83	57	3.34
Sanchez	36	3.62	58	4.32
Total	376	3.34	355	3.91

Note that every single Phillies reliever in this table beat his ERA projection and not by a little. These guys *destroyed* their projections. The Mets' top relievers, on the other hand, were somewhat worse than we should have expected: 3.91 ERA against a projection of 3.34.

So, given what was known before the season started (i.e. the player projections), it's fairly clear that the better bullpen was assembled in New York and not 100 miles down the road in Philadelphia. Of course, if Philadelphia's front office saw something in these particular players indicating they would pitch better than expected, I tip my cap to them. But I doubt that's the case.

Another key point is that the Phillies got more innings out of their top six relievers than the Mets did, 411 to 354.2. Those missing innings were taken by the bottom of the Mets 'pen, who had an ERA of 5.19 in 138.2 innings. Note that the bottom of the Phillies bullpen wasn't any better: their ERA was 5.34, but they were needed in only 71 innings.

I can say with confidence that had the Phillies relievers simply met their projections, they would not have won the division.

This division had an abundance of position players who had MVP-type seasons—in fact I reckon five players from the division should be in the MVP discussion. The mainstream media have, for the most part, included two NL East players in their MVP discussions. There's one problem, though: neither of these two media-promoted players are among the five who should be considered for the award! Talk about barking up the wrong tree.

The Phillies' Ryan Howard not only has often been brought up in the MVP discussions, I think the big first baseman could well win the award (by the time you read this, you'll know whether he did or not). Looking at the traditional stats, Howard does not seem like a bad candidate: a .251 batting average, 48 home runs and 146 RBIs. The home run and RBI numbers both led the major leagues in 2008.

But dig down past these traditional numbers, and you start to see some serious flaws in Howard's game. By now we know that the single most important offensive statistic is on-base percentage: if you had to choose one player from among 10 and could only be given one stat for each player, you'd want to know the players' OBP. Of the 70 NL players who qualified for the batting title this past season, Ryan Howard (.339) ranked 47th in OBP. Yes, the man who many are hyping as the league's most valuable player ranked in the *bottom third* in the league in the most important offensive statistic.

The Win Shares statistic, developed by Bill James and tabulated at the Hardball Times web site, combines offensive and defensive contributions into a single overall number. It's a useful, if not a perfect stat (none is). Ryan Howard accumulated 25 Win Shares in 2008, a very good total. He ranked 12th (tied) in Win Shares in the National League this season. Don't like Win Shares? Baseball Prospectus' VORP statistic estimates offensive contributions (in runs) over and above a replacement-level player at the same position. Ryan Howard's VORP was 35 in 2008, good for 30th in the NL.

Consider also the fact that Howard plays the least-demanding position on the field and by most accounts plays it poorly. Evaluating defensive performance is notoriously difficult, but most estimates of Howard's defensive ability range from below average to truly terrible.

Of course, Howard has prodigious power and those 48 home runs are extremely valuable. Still, even in slugging percentage, the most direct measure of power, Howard did not rank first or second in the league—his .543 SLG put him in sixth place. Ryan Howard happened to hit a lot of home runs and drive in a lot in a good-but-not-great offensive season. There are several, as we shall see, better candidates for MVP.

Carlos Delgado had a real Jekyll-and-Hyde season. On the morning of July 1, the Mets' first baseman woke up in the midst of the worst season of his career. His batting line stood at a miserable .228/.307/.419. Mets fans were starting to call for Delgado to be benched or even released outright.

Fast forward to September: Delgado has turned his season around, batting .313/.396/.617 after July 1. The mainstream media is filled with articles about MVP candidate Carlos Delgado. It's true that the Delgado love train lost some steam when the Mets did not reach the playoffs; still there never was any justification for mentioning Delgado as a viable MVP winner in the first place.

Sure, he had a great second half. Sure, he helped the Mets get back in the race against the Phillies. Sure, he had several key hits to give the Mets improbable victories in August and September. But you know what? He also made numerous key outs contributing to all those Mets losses in May and June. And as we say in this biz: every game counts the same. So, while Delgado's hot bat lifted the Mets out of the doldrums from July onward, his cold bat was a major reason they were in those doldrums in the first place.

Delgado's overall numbers do not suggest an MVP-caliber performance. He ranked, in the NL, 17th in Win Shares, 26th in VORP, 34th in OBP, 13th in SLG and 22nd in OPS. Like Howard, he plays a non-demanding defensive position, although he doesn't play it as badly as Howard. No, Delgado doesn't really belong in the MVP discussion—and with the Mets golfing in October, I don't think he'll win the award, although he will get some votes.

So, who are the five NL East players who really should be in the discussion? Carlos Beltran, Hanley Ramirez, Chase Utley, David Wright and Jose Reyes. I don't have the space to make a case for each of these here, but I will comment on the two who don't quite get their fair share of praise.

I'm beginning to think Hanley Ramirez is the most underrated player in the game, just edging out Chase Utley for the title. A 24-year-old shortstop who hits 30 home runs and OBP's .400? I'll take him, thanks. Ramirez has had some defensive issues in the past, but this year's performance indicates a big step forward in the field. Ramirez has improved his game significantly in the two years since his (fabulous) rookie season. On average, position players improve up until age 28 or so, so how scary-good is Ramirez going to be in 2012?

Utley is not quite as, I dunno, flashy? exciting? athletic? as Ramirez, but he's a fabulous player, too. Couple his .292/.380/.535 batting line with solid defense (some systems rate him very highly) at a premium position and you have an MVP candidate. One reason Utley is underrated is that he's really good at many things, rather than otherworldly great at one thing or two. (I'm looking at you, Ryan Howard.) More than 100 runs and 100 RBIs, but not in the top three in either category. Thirty home runs, not 50. A modest total of 14 stolen bases, but an excellent success rate (88 percent). Utley grounded into five fewer double plays than the average player with the same opportunities. He led the league in HBP by a huge margin (27 to 15, the next-highest total). These things don't necessarily make the headlines, but add them up and Chase Utley is an MVP-caliber player.

I don't want to slight the three Mets superstars, Carlos Beltran, David Wright and Jose Reyes. All three of them had fabulous seasons that are worthy of serious MVP consideration. Beltran, who sometimes flies a little under the radar, led the division in Win Shares. I don't have space to cover their individual seasons here, but that's not because they weren't excellent.

These five players represent an extraordinary concentration of talent in the NL East, finishing third through seventh in Win Shares in the NL in 2008. Of course, the man who actually deserves to win the NL MVP award this year (every year, it seems) does not play in the NL East and so doesn't appear in this article. The NL Central View will have something to say about Albert Pujols.

National League Central View

by Josh Kalk

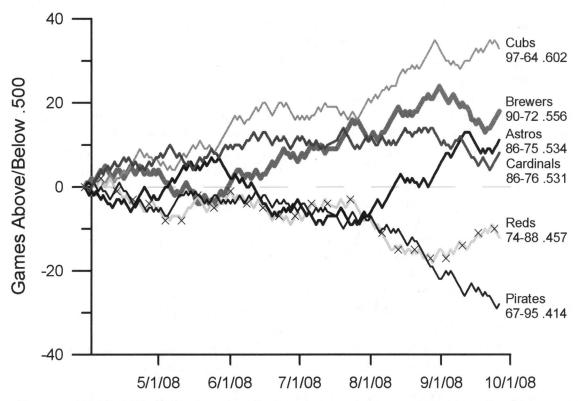

Run Scoring

Team	RS/G	RA/G	PWins
CHN	5.3	4.2	99
CIN	4.3	5.0	71
HOU	4.4	4.7	77
MIL	4.6	4.3	87
PIT	4.5	5.5	67
STL	4.8	4.5	86
Average	4.7	4.7	81

Win Contributions

	WPA			Bball
Team	Bat	Start	Pen	Field
CHN	7.7	6.9	1.9	-1.6
CIN	-2.7	-4.7	0.4	-2.0
HOU	2.6	-2.7	5.5	1.3
MIL	6.5	1.8	0.7	2.6
PIT	-2.8	-11.9	0.7	-3.0
STL	5.0	1.9	-1.9	3.9
Average	2.7	-1.5	1.2	0.2

Play Against Other Divisions

Division	W	L	Win%
AL East	26	31	.456
AL Central	13	17	.433
AL West	3	3	.500
NL East	109	94	.537
NL West	112	88	.560
Total	263	233	.530

Key Transactions

MIL	7/7: Mega deal for CC Sabathia
CHN	7/8: Cubs picked up Rich Harden
PIT	Traded Nady and Bay for LaRoche, others in late July
STL	7/30: Carpenter attempted short comeback
HOU	8/10: Carlos Lee out for season
CIN	8/11: Swapped Dunn to ARI
STL	8/17: Izzy out for season

Head-to-Head Records

Team	CHN	CIN	HOU	MIL	PIT	STL	TOT
CHN		8	8	9	14	9	48
CIN	7		3	10	6	5	31
HOU	9	12		7	8	7	43
MIL	7	8	8		14	10	47
PIT	4	9	8	1		10	32
STL	6	10	8	5	7		36

Top Performances

Hitters	Tm	OBP	SLG	BR
Pujols	STL	.462	.653	133
Berkman	HOU	.420	.567	128
Ludwick	STL	.375	.591	110
McLouth	PIT	.356	.497	109
Fielder	MIL	.372	.507	104

Pitchers	Tm	ERA	K/G	PRC
Dempster	CHN	2.96	8.1	113
Sheets	MIL	3.09	7.2	100
Sabathia	MIL	1.65	8.8	98
Volquez	CIN	3.21	9.5	97
Oswalt	HOU	3.54	7.1	92

After a down year in 2007, the National League Central stood tall in 2008. Four teams topped the 85-win-mark and the division hosted four of the six best records in the league. The Cubs paced the league and the Brewers won the wild card. If the Astros or Cardinals had been in the NL West, they would have won the division. Despite both playoff teams bowing out early, fans from all six teams had something to be happy about this year.

Besides sporting the best record in the league, the Cubs scored the most runs in the league, gave up the second-fewest runs and had the best run differential. This was a complete team with a strong lineup, bench, rotation, and bullpen. At the helm was the surprising steady hand of Lou Piniella, who mixed and matched to perfection. He was able to keep the ship afloat when star players like Alfonso Soriano and Carlos Zambrano were hurt. When Kosuke Fukudome sputtered in the second half, Piniella went to a platoon with Mark DeRosa. When rookie Felix Pie struggled, the Cubs added Jim Edmonds, who showed he still had a little left. Don't think Piniella had it in for rookies, though; he handed over the pitching staff to rookie catcher Geovany Soto.

The lineup may not have had a MVP-caliber player, but the Cubs got good production out of everyone. Derrek Lee's power numbers were down a bit but a .361 OBP made up for that. Ryan Theriot hit .307 and had way more walks that strikeouts. Aramis Ramirez reinvented himself at the plate and drew more walks than ever before. Geovany Soto was third on the team in home runs and had one of the best seasons by a rookie catcher in years. Reed Johnson and Jim Edmonds were pulled off the scrap heap and combined to make a formidable center field platoon. The theme of the offense was patience: the Cubs drew more walks than any other team in the league, up from 15th in the league in 2007.

The rotation was led by starter-turned-closer-turned-starter Ryan Dempster. Carlos Zambrano, who had a history of mental breakdowns, had a very even-keeled season despite seeing the disabled list and missing a start in September. He even threw a no-hitter. Midseason addition Rich Harden was able to stay healthy and produced an ERA under two for the Cubs. Ted Lilly and Jason Marquis were among the best back-end starters in all of baseball.

The bullpen featured starter-turned-closer Kerry Wood, who generally stayed healthy and converted 34 of 40 saves. Super setup man Carlos Marmol was lights out during much of the year. While he did appear to tire a bit during the middle of the season, he finished the year with 87 innings and a 2.68 ERA while leading the league in holds. If Wood can't close games for the Cubs in the next few years, Marmol should have no problem filling the role. Piniella did a great job of managing the rest of the bullpen.

While Cubs fans will certainly be disappointed with how the year finished, from the first game to the last, no team was better or more consistent than the Cubs. With the largest payroll in the division and most of their key players under contract, expect them to again be at, or near, the top of the heap in 2009.

If the Cubs were the most consistent team in 2008, the Brewers played the role of Jekyll and Hyde. After starting out 20-24 on May 19, they surged from last place to catch the Cubs for a tie for first on July 26. They proceeded to get swept by the Cubs at home in a four game series and then, a month later, were swept in a four game series by the Phillies. That meltdown cost Ned Yost his job with just twelve games to play. They fell two and a half games behind the Mets for the wild card with seven to play, but finished 6-1 to make the playoffs.

Part of the reason for the Brewers' ups and downs was their reliance on the home run. The Brew Crew slugged 198 homers, good for third in the league, but because their on-base percentage was a paltry .325 (10th in the league), they were just middle of the pack in runs scored. Ryan Braun followed up his rookie of the year campaign with a solid sophomore year including 37 dingers but a .335 OBP. Prince Fielder only managed 34 home runs, down from 50 in 2007, but he took his share of walks and led the team with a .372 OBP. Corey Hart was voted in as the last NL All Star, but he slumped in the second half and posted a mediocre .759 OPS. He did show off his power and speed, collecting his second straight 20/20 year. J.J. Hardy showed the power he had last year was no fluke by belting 24 this year. But Hardy's keystone mate Rickie Weeks once again disappointed hitting a meager .234.

The rotation can be summed up in two words: CC Sabathia. After a shrewd trade early in July to maximize the number of his starts, Sabathia was the best pitcher in the league. Teaming with Ben Sheets, they provided the league's best one-two punch until Sheets injured his elbow late in the season. Left hander Manny Parra, technically not a rookie due to DL time in 2007, pitched like a front line starter before tiring at the end of the year. Yovani Gallardo blew out his ACL on May 1st but gritted out the inning and another after the injury.

He healed very quickly and came back to start a key game against the Pirates at the end of the year. Dave Bush started the year very slowly, but after one start in Triple-A he came back and was the Brewers' second-best pitcher in the second half.

The bullpen was more of a mess with 2007 closer Derrick Turnbow and early 2008 closer Eric Gagne both blowing up early in the year. Turnbow was sent to Triple-A and then to the DL while Gagne also spent time on the DL. Salomon Torres filled in as the closer and at least held down the role. Almost all of the key players in the Brewers' bullpen are free agents this offseason, so expect to see a completely different group in 2009.

The Astros weren't picked by anyone to contend. After a hot May, they fell back under .500 and it was assumed they would compete with the Reds and the Pirates for fourth place in the division. Outside of Lance Berkman, their offense wasn't scoring runs and their rotation was less than effective. The anchor of their staff, Roy Oswalt, was having a particularly hard first half of the season. But the Astros clicked in the second half of the year.

Oswalt pitched like the ace he is, going 10-2 with a 2.24 ERA after the All-Star break. In a surprising move, the team traded for veteran Randy Wolf who was solid down the stretch with a 3.57 ERA. Wandy Rodriguez came off the DL and posted a 3.54 ERA. In the bullpen, newly acquired closer Jose Valverde led the league in saves after a rocky start, and the team got steady production out of setup man Doug Brocail.

Offensively, things weren't quite as good. The team ended with only 712 runs, 11th in the league, which is unacceptable in the ballpark in which they play. Berkman cooled to a .986 OPS, and when Carlos Lee went on the DL in early August the Astros lost a key bat in the lineup. Shortstop Miguel Tejada aged two years after the Astros traded for him, and he played like it. Outfielder Michael Bourn showed his speed, swiping 41 bases, but posted a horrendous OBP of .288. Hunter Pence's sophomore campaign did not match his great rookie year, but he's likely to rebound in 2009. Free agent Kazuo Matsui posted decent numbers when in the lineup.

While the Astros made a late charge, the Cardinals fought the Cubs and Brewers for much of the season despite a roster that appeared lackluster. While there is some truth to that, don't be fooled. These Cardinals can play. Although manager Tony La Russa and pitching coach Dave Duncan deserve a lot of credit for tweaking the roster when needed, this is a team that has plenty of players.

Offensively they scored the second-most runs in the division and were again led by Albert Pujols who again posted a 1.100 OPS despite again playing through injuries. Backing up Pujols was a mix-and-match outfield that La Russa used perfectly last season. After being injured much of his career, Ryan Ludwick played a full season and broke out in a big way, tying with Pujols for the team lead in home runs with 37. Rick Ankiel not only had a very solid year at the plate, but he played a very solid center field after working his way back up as a corner outfielder. Troy Glaus had a nice resurgence after a few lean years in Toronto raising his OBP to .372.

The pitching was a mix and match of retreads that other teams had given up on. Kyle Lohse led the team in wins and was rewarded with a nice four-year contract after signing in spring training. Todd Wellemeyer was the latest bullpen-to-starter project for Duncan and he responded with an ERA of 3.71. Alumnus Braden Looper, who was a convert last year, pitched well again. Adam Wainwright was the ace of the staff but a midseason injury limited him to only 20 starts.

The other two what-ifs, Chris Carpenter and Mark Mulder, both returned in the middle of the year and both promptly re-injured themselves after throwing a combined 17 innings. Carpenter looked good, but he was shut down due to more shoulder problems. Still, Carpenter could be back by spring training next year. If he can somehow stay healthy, the arm still has it and he could provide a huge lift.

The Reds suffered through another year of sub-.500 baseball, but fans in Great American Ballpark at least got to watch a very interesting team. The team hovered only a handful of games below .500 into July and some wondered if management would be sellers at the trading deadline. New general manager Walt Jocketty, who took over for Wayne Krivsky at the end of April, smartly did sell and was able to bring in some good young talent for Adam Dunn and Ken Griffey Jr.

On the field, the Reds trotted out some very high ceiling young talent in Joey Votto, Jay Bruce, and Edinson Volquez. Losing Josh Hamilton's bat in return for Volquez stings a little, but hitting hasn't really been the Reds' problem in the last few years. While the youngsters shined, many of the Reds veterans had poor performances. Brandon Phillips posted a .754 OPS though he did play stellar defense at second. Jeff Keppinger managed only a .656 OPS after an injury-marred 2007. In the rotation, mainstays Bronson Arroyo and Aaron Harang both had difficultly keeping their ERAs under 5.00, and Harang went 6-17 for the year.

If some of these veterans can get back to their 2007 form the future looks bright for the Reds. Volquez, Harang, Arroyo, and Johnny Cueto could be one of the best rotations in the NL Central next year. An offense led by Bruce and Votto should score a decent amount of runs if guys like Edwin Encarnacion and Ryan Freel play to their potential. What Jocketty will do with manager Dusty Baker will be one of the biggest stories this offseason. Baker made some curious moves at best last year and it was Baker who endorsed Corey Patterson and gave him 366 at-bats.

The Pirates also seem to be moving in the right direction under new general manager Neal Huntington and manager John Russell. While many people didn't notice, Russell did a lot of things right this year. He committed to Nate McLouth and Ryan Doumit and was rewarded with breakout seasons from both of them. Doumit, who had been jerked around in previous years, found a home wearing the tools of ignorance. Doumit's throwing arm wasn't great, but he more than made up for it with his .858 OPS.

Huntington did what previous general manager Dave Littlefield didn't: he unloaded veteran players for young talent at the trading deadline. Jason Bay and Xavier Nady weren't going to be a part of the next good Pirates team, but Brandon Moss and Jeff Karstens very well could be. He also cut bait on the previous administration's biggest gaffe, Matt Morris. While the Pedro Alvarez eventual signing might set a bad precedent, he is exactly what the Pirates farm system needs: high-ceiling talent. Huntington may have paid a steep price, but he recognized the need and addressed it.

The NL Central produced the best baseball in the senior circuit in 2008 and the teams at the bottom clearly improved themselves. While it may take a few years for the Pirates to fully rebuild, they appear to finally be on the right path. The Reds could top the .500 mark as soon as next year. This will put more pressure on the teams at the top in 2009, but the Cubs, Brewers, Cardinals, and Astros all have a solid core to build around. Look for several teams from the division to compete for the wild card in 2009.

National League West View

by Steve Treder

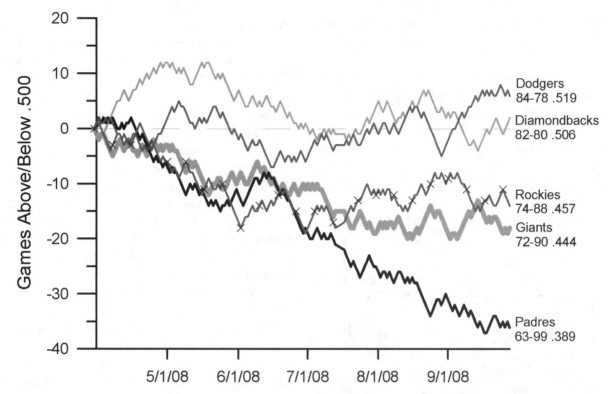

Run Scoring			
Team	RS/G	RA/G	PWins
ARI	4.4	4.4	82
COL	4.6	5.1	74
LAN	4.3	4.0	87
SD	3.9	4.7	68
SF	4.0	4.7	68
Average	4.3	4.6	76

Play Against Other Divisions			
Division	W	L	Win%
AL East	1	5	.167
AL Central	18	36	.333
AL West	8	13	.381
NL East	80	89	.473
NL Central	88	112	.440
Total	195	255	.433

Head-to-Head Records						
Team	ARI	COL	LAN	SD	SF	TOT
ARI		15	8	10	11	44
COL	3		8	9	11	31
LAN	10	10		11	9	40
SD	8	9	7		5	29
SF	7	7	9	13		36

Win Contributions				
	WPA			Bball
Team	Bat	Start	Pen	Field
ARI	-1.0	3.2	-1.2	1.1
COL	-3.8	-3.7	0.5	-2.2
LAN	2.0	-0.8	1.8	-1.0
SD	-9.6	-4.2	-4.3	1.3
SF	-5.9	-1.2	-2.0	-0.5
Average	-3.7	-1.3	-1.0	-0.3

Key Transactions	
SF	Let Barry Bonds go
ARI	Prospects to OAK for Haren in offseason
LAN	Rafael Furcal on DL starting 5/6
LAN	Traded for Manny Ramirez on 7/31
ARI	Picked up Adam Dunn on 8/11

Top Performances				
Hitters	Tm	OBP	SLG	BR
Gonzalez	SD	.361	.510	124
Giles	SD	.398	.456	102
Ethier	LAN	.375	.510	98
Holliday	COL	.409	.538	95
Drew	ARI	.333	.502	91
Pitchers	Tm	ERA	K/G	PRC
Lincecum	SF	2.62	10.5	143
Haren	ARI	3.33	8.6	112
Webb	ARI	3.30	7.3	108
Billingsley	LAN	3.14	9.0	103
Cain	SF	3.76	7.7	98

Remember your Greek mythology? Sisyphus was the guy who was condemned by the gods to roll a big heavy boulder up a steep hill, and just when he was about to reach the top, the boulder would slip from his grasp and roll all the way back down to the bottom, forcing Sisyphus to begin his exhausting task again. The poor fellow was condemned to repeat this agonizing frustration for eternity.

It hasn't exactly been eternity yet for the NL West, but the division's competitive progress over the past several years has been all too Sisyphean. Consider the following table, which presents the regular-season winning percentage of the NL West against all extra-division opponents (the NL East, the NL Central, and inter-league) for the past 10 seasons:

Year	vs. NLE	vs. NLC	vs. AL	Total
1999	.536	.481	.514	.507
2000	.543	.563	.431	.538
2001	.531	.576	.431	.535
2002	.579	.533	.511	.545
2003	.421	.543	.583	.506
2004	.444	.478	.478	.465
2005	.422	.453	.368	.426
2006	.469	.535	.467	.499
2007	.568	.547	.436	.536
2008	.473	.440	.333	.433

We see that through the early years of this decade, the NL West was an extremely competitive division, clearly the best in the National League, and as often as not getting the best of AL opponents as well. But the slide beginning in 2003 was swift and steady, landing the NL West at the bottom of the hill in 2005, not just the worst division in baseball that season, but the worst division ever in a non-strike-shortened season.

Well, the NL West picked itself up, dusted itself off, and got busy pushing that big rock. Up the arduous incline it went, gaining significant improvement in 2006, and in 2007 attaining a lofty footing that was virtually identical to that of 2000 or 2001.

Only to see, in 2008, the boulder slipping loose again, and heavily tumbling down, down, down, all the way down to the gloomy depths of 2005. Again.

The Tumble of 2008

How exactly is it that a division containing five different teams pulls off such a spectacular collective pratfall? Well, obviously it ain't easy. It pretty much has to be one of those cases in which just about everything that can go wrong, does go wrong.

Only one of the five NL West teams in 2008 encountered a season that wasn't a distinct disappointment. And that team, the San Francisco Giants, finished 72-90; the only reason their season wasn't a distinct disappointment is that they were the one team in the division that everyone expected to be lousy. And everyone was right: the Giants were lousy.

Every other team in the division slogged through a disappointing year in 2008. Yes, that includes the division champ Dodgers: sure, they won the crown, but come on, 84-78? That's definitely inferior to the record they were anticipating coming into the season, and in no other division in baseball would they have been sniffing postseason qualification. Moreover, the Dodgers were able to squeak into the division title only by virtue of acquiring Manny Ramirez at the trade deadline and having him hit impossibly well the rest of the way; without Manny's just-in-time contribution of 18 Win Shares in the final two months, the Dodgers' 2008 season would have been far more disappointing than it was.

The Diamondbacks? After a 90-72 campaign to win the division in 2007 and adding Danny Haren in the offseason to one of the better young rosters in the game, their 82-80 2008 season must have been disappointing in the extreme. Though not as disappointing as that of the Rockies, who were the '07 NL Wild Card champ and pennant winner, only to flounder to 74-88. And that bellyflop wasn't as humiliating as the one performed by the Padres, who tied the Rockies at 89-73 in the 2007 regular season, before laying their colossal 63-99 egg in 2008.

But just as team performance is nothing more than the aggregation of individual player performances, the performance of an entire division is still nothing more than the aggregation of individual player performances—just more of them. Which is to say that when a five-team division sees its aggregate winning percentage drop by 100 points in a single year, there must have been a whole lot of truly disappointing individual player performances.

So just who led the parade?

10. Troy Tulowitzki, Rockies

It could certainly be the case that the 22-year-old Tulowitzki was hitting somewhat over his head in 2007 and was bound to come back to earth to some degree. And clearly, missing almost two months with a quadriceps injury didn't do him any favors in 2008.

But it must be remembered that it was before going down with the injury that Tulowitzki's hitting was unbelievably ghastly—.152/.226/.238, in fact. Upon his return, over the second half the big young shortstop seemed finally to be picking up where he left off in 2007. But for the '08 Rockies, that was too late.

9. Omar Vizquel, Giants

It would be one thing if the ultra-veteran Vizquel was in the final year of a long-term deal, and the Giants were keeping him on for one last season despite his distinct offensive decline in 2007. But, no, GM Brian Sabean took the proactive step of offering the 41-year-old shortstop a new one-year deal for 2008.

Oops. Vizquel twisted a knee in spring training and upon his return demonstrated that his bat speed was utterly a thing of the past. His injury and subsequent offensive futility would force the Giants to experiment with rookie shortstops—what a concept for a rebuilding team!—and one of them, Emmanuel Burriss, didn't look too bad. But they could have figured that out without investing $5 million and 300 plate appearances to get a .192 GPA from Vizquel.

8. Todd Helton, Rockies

Much of the discussion of Helton in recent years has focused on his massive contract and the fact that as he advances into his 30s he hasn't delivered the kind of superstar performance that such a contract would seem to warrant. But still, the fact is that heading into 2008, the fewest Win Shares Helton had produced in any season since 1999 was 23; while no elite superstar, he was a consistent, durable, all-around top-drawer first baseman.

But in 2008, the 34-year-old Helton, plagued by a bad back, was limited to just 83 games of mediocre hitting, and his Win Share total plunged to eight. Among the reasons the Rockies fell apart in '08, getting so little from Helton looms large.

7. Josh Bard, Padres

He was no star, but Bard was a solid, productive-hitting catcher for San Diego in 2006-2007. (His throwing was another story.) But 2008 was a complete disaster, with two trips to the DL, and he hadn't been hitting a lick (.200/.278/.262 in late May) even before he got hurt. As a consequence, the Padres' catching in 2008 became just one of several black holes sucking energy out of the roster.

6. Jeff Francis, Rockies

Though he wasn't blowing anyone away, Francis had been a consistently dependable starter in 2006 and 2007, indeed emerging in the Rockies' breakout season as the closest thing to an ace on their no-name pitching staff. Then came '08.

Francis's decline in effectiveness was problematic enough, with his FIP jumping from 4.12 to 4.79, but a tender shoulder inhibited his durability as well, limiting him to a non-ace-like 24 starts and 144 innings. The Colorado rotation could little afford the stress, as manager Clint Hurdle would scramble, with nine different pitchers making at least five starts.

5. Barry Zito, Giants

Well, then, let's say this for the Giants' $126-million man: he just kept taking the ball every fifth day and marching out there to the mound.

But exactly why San Francisco manager Bruce Bochy was determined to keep handing it to Zito is an excellent question. Yes, it's true that Zito improved after his cataclysmically awful 2008 start—at 0-6 in six starts, with a 7.53 ERA, how could he not?—but it isn't as though he found an effective plateau. The old "Quality Starts" stat is a low bar, yet it remained persistently beyond Zito's reach: never, all season long, did he manage to put together as many as three in a row.

Thus, faithfully taking that ball, Zito walked the third-most batters in the league, posted the third-worst ERA among qualifiers, allowed the second-most runs, and led the league in losses. All this for only $14.5 million! Plus five more years to go on the contract!

4. Eric Byrnes, Diamondbacks

Speaking of, um, interesting contracts ... are you sure this guy and Arizona GM Josh Byrnes aren't related?

To be fair, Byrnes the ballplayer had presented back-to-back solid all-around seasons in 2006 and 2007. But that's all they were: solid all-around seasons, hardly top-star stuff, and moreover he was going on 32 and had a history of inconsistency. So, $30 million with a no-trade clause for three years? Seriously?

Well, if there was to be any doubt that it was a bad deal—for Byrnes the general manager, that is—Byrnes the ballplayer immediately put it to rest, delivering a woeful .205 GPA and a grand total of two—count 'em, two—Win Shares in 52 games before going on the shelf with a bad hamstring for the rest of 2008. It's difficult to imagine a less helpful contribution from the Byrnes boys to the Diamondbacks' effort to defend the division flag.

3. Brad Penny, Dodgers

And things seemed to be going so well!

Nobody ever questioned Penny's stuff, but his career had been checkered with injuries and inconsistency, and the stardom he seemed destined to reach remained elusive. And then in 2007, at the age of 29, it finally all came together: a career-high 208 innings, third in the league with an ERA+ of 151, a 16-4 win-loss record, third in the NL's Cy Young Award voting. At last, Penny was the strong-as-a-bull ace we'd been expecting.

And in 2008 Penny began right where he'd left off: as of May 2, he was 5-2 with a 3.19 ERA. But then, look out, the cable snapped on the Brad Penny elevator; in his next eight starts, he went 0-7 with an 8.52 ERA. By June 14, Penny's season totals stood at 5-9, 5.88. So much for the ace thing.

Just a handful of appearances, and a couple of long DL stints nursing a sore shoulder, would comprise the remainder of Penny's 2008 season. The Dodgers' pitching resources were sufficient to allow them to fill the void; rookie Clayton Kershaw in particular rose to the occasion. But few u-turns have ever been as sudden and dizzying as the 2008 Brad Penny humdinger.

2. Khalil Greene, Padres

He'd been a quirky sort of player with all-too-apparent flaws—injury-proneness, along with a swing-for-the-fences-no-matter-what approach at the plate—nonetheless when the complete package was considered, Greene through 2007 had been a distinct asset to the Padres. The positives—being an exceptionally sure-handed shortstop with serious extra-base power—delivered a whole lot of counterweight.

But not in 2008. The sure-handed shortstop part of Greene's game was still in evidence, but his batting stroke skipped town without a trace. Greene's strikeout rate (immodest to begin with) leapt from .194 in 2007 to .236 in 2008, and meanwhile his home runs dropped from a rate of 12.2 percent of his fly balls to 7.5 percent. The deadly combination of less contact and less pop served to send Greene's GPA plummeting from .270 to .219.

Yet disconcerting as this circumstance was, Greene managed to make it worse. As of late July, he still

had time to salvage his season to some degree, but no. Instead Greene decided to smack a storage chest with his left hand, injuring himself badly enough to be finished for the year. Padres management, which had already been fruitlessly attempting to trade Greene, was understandably less than amused. The entire bad-to-worse episode served as an apt symbol for San Diego's wretched 2008.

1. Andruw Jones, Dodgers

Nobody, but nobody, slipped on a banana peel quite the way Andruw did in 2008. Indeed this one isn't just the No. 1 fall-on-the-keister of 2008, this is an all-timer. To find something comparable to the pratfall of Mr. Jones, one must ardently dust off the record books. This is Zoilo Versalles or even Steve Blass territory that Andruw has entered.

View this disaster from any angle you please; each vista is every bit as ugly as the last. For instance, the decline from 2007 to 2008 is bad enough (.246 GPA to .181), but then consider that 2007 was itself a very bad year for Jones; his .299 GPA of 2006 was far more typical of his established level of performance.

Consider Win Shares: Jones had dropped from his customary 25 in 2006 to 16 in 2007. That was bad. But the evaporation to zero, that's right, goose-egg 2008 Win Shares in 75 games, well that's something else again.

So, just what the heck happened here? How could it be that a durable and consistent star, a guy who seemed to be heading to Cooperstown on cruise control, suddenly became a sub-replacement-level performer at age 31?

Well, nobody exactly knows, of course. But two obvious suspects present themselves: first, Jones struggled with knee trouble throughout 2008, undergoing arthroscopic surgery and spending much of the year on the DL; and second, he's been carrying a significant proportion of excess weight for many years, creating a general-body strain that shouldn't be dismissed. And these two issues are hardly unrelated; the latter has caused many of us for several years to fear the emergence of something like the former.

But, again, nobody, least of all Jones himself, knows for sure. The world is a complicated and constantly surprising place. But whatever it is that happened, it was something extraordinary: in the entire long history of this sport, we've almost never seen anything comparable to this.

The Postseason View

by Sal Baxamusa

You might not know it from the endless—though often valid—complaints about the length of the games, frequent off-days, late start times, and poor broadcasting, but 2008 was probably the best postseason since 2004. Consider:

- The Twins stormed back in the final week of the season to force a one-game playoff with the White Sox, but the South Siders won a 1-0 thriller to capture the AL Central crown.

- The Cubs and the Angels, who paced their respective circuits in wins, were dispatched in the division series.

- Last year's champions, the Red Sox, were edged in the ALCS by last year's cellar-dwellers, the Rays. B.J. Upton, who hit only nine homers in the regular season, clubbed seven in 16 postseason games.

- Postseason mainstay Manny Ramirez hit .520/.666/1.080 for the Dodgers but the Phillies won the NLCS in five games.

- Despite the Phillies needing only five games to defeat the Rays in the World Series, we were treated to three one-run games, including a walkoff; the first World Series home run by a pitcher since 1974; and disastrous weather that suspended the eventual clincher for two days.

The postseason is great because it selects, more or less, the best teams in baseball and gives us a month of those teams playing each other. And, despite using B-list celebrities like Bon Jovi and Dane Cook in the advertising campaigns and the woeful TV contracts that lead to bizarre scheduling, the playoffs really are the showcase event for Major League Baseball. It's great that baseball is capitalizing on the drama and the unpredictability that comes with short-series baseball.

All the emphasis on the postseason does have a sad side effect: The regular season, the 162-game marathon that is the essence of baseball, has become somewhat marginalized. The postseason is all about clutch and small sample size. That's why it's so exciting—anything can happen. But the do-or-die emphasis on short-series baseball detracts from regular season achievements. A team can dominate the regular season, but a three-game playoff pratfall will render the whole season meaningless. Media storylines, comments by players and management, and even fan reactions confirm this.

Don't believe me? The day after the 100-win Angels were ousted from the playoffs by the Red Sox, an Angels blogger reportedly spotted some Angels "fans" returning unworn merchandise to the team store. No reason to bask in the glory of the best record in the majors if your team stinks for a few games in October, right?

Imagine if the Rays, easily the best story in the baseball even before the playoffs started, had been bounced by the Red Sox in the ALCS. It almost happened, and in dramatic fashion to boot. Tampa Bay's plucky division title—beating back the two behemoths of the AL East—would have been forgotten, rendered meaningless because an inexperienced young team choked under the pressure of the postseason. That storyline was avoided only because they won.

That's not to say that the postseason has some great moral failing and that we should eliminate the playoffs in favor of a thousand-game regular season. No, all this buildup is just to say that the postseason is really, really random. As Oakland's polarizing general manger Billy Beane once said, "My s--- don't work in the playoffs."

It's not that Beane can't build a team particularly suited for postseason glory—nobody can. The best way to tilt the scales in your favor is to have a very good team, and even that doesn't get you all that far. Consider: a 100-loss team would win a best-of-five series against a 100-win team some 13 percent of the time. And teams in the postseason tend to be more evenly matched than that; a 100-win team playing an 85-win team, which is about as big a mismatch as you will find in the playoffs, will result in an upset fully one-third of the time in a best-of-five series.

Why? It can be plain old dumb luck, like Evan Longoria's well-struck fly ball getting caught in the wind in Game 3 of the World Series. It can be bad baseball from players who are usually good, like Mike Cameron's shaky defense in the NLDS. Over time, Longoria will get a wind-assisted homer to make up for the one that turned into an out and Cameron will make all the routine plays in center and then some. It's not a value judgment to say that the outcome of the postseason is heavily influenced by luck. It is, as a cliché-spouting athlete might say, what it is.

But just because the postseason is unpredictable, it doesn't absolve managers or players of guilt for their poor decisions. In fact, it is doubly important for a manager or player to put his team in a position to win in the postseason. Sometimes that means changing in-game strategy, like using your ace reliever for multiple innings. Sometimes that means changing nothing, and using the same approach that got you to the playoffs. Managerial decision-making is the subject of many post-season postmortems, and they usually deal with bullpen management (as in, why did Tampa skipper Joe Maddon allow the Red Sox to rally in Game 5 of the ALCS on the strength of two homers by left-handed hitters while his three lefty relievers sat in the bullpen?).

Although not necessarily as egregious as the paren-thetical Maddon example, there were two strange pitching decisions that exemplified the bizarre mental gymnastics that must occupy a manager's brain in October.

In the eighth inning of Game 2 of the ALDS and an off-day to follow, Boston manager Terry Francona entrusted Justin Masterson with a one-run lead. Master-son faced one hitter, allowing a Chone Figgins triple with nobody out, before being lifted for the Boston ace closer, Jonathan Papelbon. Makes sense, right? Man on third, nobody out—bring in your best strikeout pitcher. But if Francona was prepared to lean on Papelbon for six outs after the triple, why didn't he do so before the triple?

Facing elimination, Milwaukee interim manager Dale Sveum trotted out Jeff Suppan in Game 4 of the NLDS. After he was predictably cuffed around by the Phillies, the Brewers turned to Yovani Gallardo to try to salvage their season. Gallardo was clearly the better pitcher. If the Brewers were comfortable using Gallardo on short rest for long relief, why not just let him start, even if only an abbreviated start? Gallardo was not being saved to start a possible Game 5, since CC Sabathia was ready to take the ball. Instead, the game was allowed to get out of hand and Gallardo was reduced to mop-up duty.

I don't think baseball managers are dumb, but their decisions often lack the logical consistency that would make their actions explicable. It's as if Ralph Waldo Emerson had been watching a game of baseball when he made his observation about foolish consistencies being the hobgoblins of little minds.

Even more interesting are the decisions that didn't come with the requisite second-guessing. This postsea-son saw some bizarre decisions even before the games were played. Exhibit A: Nick Swisher, the boisterous Chicago outfielder-cum-first baseman. Swisher had a pretty poor year by his standards, seeing his OPS+ drop from .836 in 2007 to .742 in 2008. His "decline"

was mostly a fluky-low batting average (.219), but his secondary skills remained mostly intact.

Even if we accept that Swisher's low batting average was "real," a player's performance data—including his batting average—over the past year is not representative of his true skill. Countless analysts have confirmed that, and by appropriately considering a player's stats over the past several years and throwing in some regression to the mean, we can compute any player's "true talent" at any given time. The simplest process by which to do this is the "Marcel," a projection system stewarded by noted baseball analyst Tom Tango. In Swisher's case, even taking into account his poor (or possibly unlucky) 2008 season, his true talent OPS as of October 2008 was about .800. That's more than 50 points higher than his OPS during the season!

But, probably due to his "bad" year, Swisher was relegated to cheerleader status, appearing in three of the four ALDS games—once each as a starter, pinch hitter and defensive replacement. And nary a word of outrage! Swisher was sacrificed at the altar of small sample sizes so that the White Sox could run guys like Brian Anderson, Dewayne Wise and Ken Griffey Jr. onto the field. The true talent OPSes for that fearsome troika? .703, .727 and .797. Only Griffey was even in Swisher's arena as a hitter. Anderson and Wise had demonstrated incompetence with the bat for long enough that they were clearly inferior to Swisher.

White Sox manager Ozzie Guillen played the hot hand (or, equivalently, didn't play the cold hand). That was the wrong decision. That Wise hit a home run in Game 1, or that Swisher managed only a single base hit in four at-bats doesn't change that fact. Benching or playing a (not obviously injured) slumping or streaking player is almost always the wrong decision, since cold and hot streaks have essentially zero predictive value. The better player is whichever one has the best projec-tion, Marcel or otherwise, on any given day (platoon issues duly considered).

That's not meant to pick solely on Guillen, who is generally a good manager. Across town, Lou Piniella made a head-scratcher of his own. Gifted with Rich Harden, who at the time was—on a rate basis—one of the best pitchers in baseball, Piniella decided to hold him back for Game 3 of the NLDS. Harden had been boasting a mid-90s fastball and some kind of impos-sible-to-hit offspeed ghost pitch. Pitching him in the third game of a best-of-five series eliminated the possi-bility of his return in Games 4 and 5. It was like Piniella said, "Thanks, but I prefer to play with a handicap."

It would be one thing if Piniella had had Harden pitch Game 2 and tabbed Carlos Zambrano as the Game 1 starter. At least that would have made Harden a candidate for a Game 5 start, and it would be semi-defensible given Zambrano's status as longtime team ace. Instead, with a big division lead that gave him all of September to set up his postseason rotation, Piniella tabbed Ryan Dempster as his Game 1 starter.

Dempster made the reliever-to-starter switch in 2008 after spending four years in the Cubs' bullpen and responded with a great year: 200-plus innings, sub-3.00 ERA. More importantly, Dempster had a very good Fielding Independent Pitching (FIP) mark of 3.50. FIP is a THT statistic that evaluates pitchers independently of their defense by considering only a pitcher's rate of strikeouts, walks and home runs allowed. FIP generally is considered a more accurate measure of pitcher's quality than his ERA.

While Dempster may have had a very good year even by advanced metrics like FIP, we must again consider that a player's performance in 2008 is not his true talent. A Marcel projection suggests that Dempster had a 3.60 true talent FIP, and that's giving him a bunch of extra credit for his good years as a reliever. His true talent FIP at the time was probably closer to over 4.00 as a starter, which is about where Zambrano was. Harden blew them both away with a true talent FIP of 3.20. Over a typical start, that's a half-run difference, or approximately the difference between a 100-win team and an 88-win team.

As it turned out, the Dodgers swept the Cubs in the first round, so Piniella's rotation order didn't end up costing his team. But given the information available at the time, starting Dempster in Game 1 was kind of nuts. (Okay, that's not strictly true. Maybe Piniella knew something about Harden's health. But Harden's postseason MRI was clean, and there was no reason to believe that he was injured going into the NLDS. Moreover, since both Harden and Dempster are right-handed, there weren't any significant platoon reasons to favor one over the other.)

Want more examples? Angels manager Mike Scioscia put lefty Joe Saunders (true talent 4.11 FIP) in the playoff rotation and relegated the superior righty Jered Weaver (true talent 3.72 FIP) to the bullpen. In addition to Weaver being a better pitcher than Saunders, Red Sox hitters positively murdered left-handed pitching in 2008. There's almost no question that Weaver was a better option than Saunders and his hilariously low true talent 5.3 K/9.

Scioscia also started Gary Matthews Jr. in Game 1 of the ALDS, but then banished him to the bench after an 0-for-3 game and some misplays in right field. If Matthews was the right guy in Game 1, what changed that made him the wrong guy the very next day? And if he wasn't the right guy in Games 2 through 4, what business did he have starting Game 1?

Probably the two most important lessons of sabermetrics are (1) some numbers are more telling than others and (2) numbers are misleading if not taken in the context of their sample size and regressed to the mean. All of these moves (and it is by no means an exhaustive list) reflect the belief that much information can be gleaned using either garbage stats, like batting average and ERA; a small sample of data, like one season or even a single game; or both. For anybody who thinks that sabermetrics is dead, I submit that the parade of objectively questionable-to-terrible moves made by managers suggests otherwise.

It is possible, I suppose, that managers become managers because they have a magical ability to learn more about a player in one evening than an army of analysts can learn in several years. It seems unlikely, though. Instant punditry ought to be left to columnists and talking heads, and managers should be charged with maximizing their team's chances to win.

Of course, in the postseason happenstance and luck can make even good decisions look foolish. Having suitably scolded the poor decisions, it is worth noting the good decisions that were rewarded with goat horns. There were a number of these, but my favorites are good baserunning decisions that end with the runner taking the jog of shame back to the dugout.

The World Series saw two of these in the first two games. In Game 1, Shane Victorino attempted to tag up on a short fly ball to Rays center fielder Upton. Victorino is a speedy guy, but a perfect one-hop bullet and a nifty tag by Dioner Navarro nailed Victorino at the plate. In the very next game, Rocco Baldelli tried to score from second on a single to right, but Jayson Werth's throw beat him to the plate. Despite bowling over Phillies catcher Carlos Ruiz, Baldelli was out. Did Victorino and Baldelli let their World Series nerves get the better of them? Or were their aggressive attempts at the extra base calculated risks that just didn't work out?

This is the sort of question that is perfectly analyzed by Win Probability. Win Probability describes, given the score, inning, base occupancy and number of outs the likelihood of a game being won or lost. Naturally, late-and-close situations tend to have a greater impact on a team's chances of winning.

For example, had Victorino not attempted to score, the Phillies would have had a 2-0 lead with the bases loaded and two out in the second inning. That's a Win Probability of 72 percent—teams in that situation win about seven times out of 10. Had Victorino scored successfully, the Win Probability would have been 78 percent. Since he was out, the Win Probability dropped to 66 percent. Using these numbers, we can calculate the "break-even point," which is the success rate at which Victorino should be indifferent to trying to score.

Without getting into the mathematical details, the break-even point in this situation was about 45 percent. That means that if Victorino thought that he had a better than even chance of being safe, then trying to score was the right move—regardless of the eventual outcome. Given Victorino's speed and the fact that it took a very good throw to nail him, trying to score was almost certainly the correct choice.

Going through the same analysis in Baldelli's case, the breakeven point was again about 50/50. Given Werth's average arm, Baldelli (or his third base coach) made the correct percentage play. That both Victorino and Baldelli were thrown out doesn't change the fact that they made pretty good decisions to head for home. Given a hundred chances, they are probably safe half of the time. There weren't afforded a hundred chances, though, and it was their bad luck that they made the right move and still got burned.

In the vein of luck, the Angels were one of the luckiest (or most clutch, take your pick) teams in baseball this year. By Batting Runs Above Average, as tracked on Fangraphs.com, the Angels pitched and hit like a 89-win team; they actually won 100 games. (Just as an aside, magic bullpen pixie dust accounted for only 4.3 of the 11-win discrepancy. Clutch starting pitching accounted for 2.2 wins and clutch hitting for the remaining 4.4.) So it seems karmic, if not particularly fair to Angels fans, that three baserunning decisions that led to disastrous results in the ALDS against the Red Sox were, at the least, defensible if not downright smart.

In Game 1 of the ALDS, with the Angels down by one run in the bottom of the eighth, Vlad Guerrero was gunned down at third base trying to advance from first on a bloop fly ball down the right field line. Vlad was widely panned for his "poor" baserunning and it was implied that Scioscia's aggressive philosophy was to blame. But was it a bad decision for Guerrero to try to advance?

Using Win Probability to analyze the situation as before, the break-even point for that decision is 66 percent. If Guerrero thought that he had a two-thirds chance of being safe, then trying for the extra base was the right thing to do. Given that the fielder Kevin Youkilis had to find the ball in short right field, grip it, turn, and fire a strike to third base, Vlad's gambit seemed reasonable.

He could be faulted for having hesitated as he rounded second base, but not really for his decision to try for the extra base. Just because he was thrown out, it doesn't mean it was the wrong decision at the time. These sorts of things tend to even out over time—time that isn't afforded teams in the playoffs. Vlad was out, and he won't get two more chances.

Late in Game 3 of the ALDS, Torii Hunter tried to stretch a leadoff single into a double with the score tied at 4. As in Vlad's situation, it turns out that the break-even point was about 66 percent. Hunter, like Guerrero, must have thought he had a two-thirds chance of being safe. Losing a baserunner late in a tie game hurts, but it wasn't a bad idea to force the defense to make the play in that situation. It took a fortunate bounce and a good throw for Red Sox left fielder Jason Bay to nail Hunter. Again, Hunter's maneuver was a reasonable gamble, but one that didn't work out.

And finally, in Game 4 of the ALDS and with the Angels facing elimination, they tried to bring home the winning run on a suicide squeeze in the ninth inning. With the speedy Reggie Willits on third and Erick Aybar at bat, Boston reliever Manny Delcarmen pounded the inner part of the plate, perhaps expecting a squeeze attempt. With the count 2-0, the squeeze was on and Willits broke from third as Aybar stabbed at the ball.

In a tie game in the ninth inning, a runner on third and one out results in a win 68 percent of the time. A successful squeeze bumps that up to 83 percent, and a botched squeeze knocks that down to 40 percent. As with the two other plays, the squeeze needed to have a two-thirds chance of success. While it is difficult to guess what a batter's "true" bunting skill is, Aybar presumably is a good bunter. He had nine sacrifice bunts and nine bunt hits in 29 bunt attempts. Players of his skill set—light-hitting glovemen—tend to be good bunters, and Aybar's lack of strikeouts suggests at least decent bat control. The runner at third base, Willits, is one of the fastest runners in the AL. The corner infielders were a first baseman pressed into duty at third and an outfielder pressed into duty at first. With the count 2-0 and the top of the order coming up, a buntable fastball seemed likely. And, had the Angels taken the lead, their probability of winning may have been even higher than 83 percent given that they would have inserted their very good closer Francisco Rodriguez. In all, there were a lot of factors working in the Angels' favor. A two-thirds probability of success seemed realistic.

Unfortunately for the Angels, Aybar whiffed on the bunt attempt and Willits was hung out halfway between third and home. It was seen as the ultimate failure of Scioscia's small ball, force-the-action, play-for-one-run philosophy. The schadenfreude brigade used variations on the phrase "live by the sword, die by the sword" to describe the Angels' failure. Small ball is still overrated, but as a percentage play, the squeeze was certainly defensible.

None of the three plays went in the Angels' favor, and in a series as tight as the Sox-Angels ALDS—three of the four games were decided in the final inning—it isn't hyperbole to think that with a little better luck, the Angels might have won. Even good, or at least defensible, decisions do not guarantee playoff success.

The final bit of decision-making is yet to come. Clubs ought to focus on areas of need demonstrated over the full season rather than divining what, based on their playoff experiences, they need to get into the next round. The Cubs, for example, need not worry that Alfonso Soriano and Aramis Ramirez (combined 5-51 over the 2007-2008 playoffs) are holding their team back from postseason glory. That the Rays slugged nearly .500 in the playoffs doesn't exempt them from looking to upgrade their offense.

Fortunately, many of this year's postseason teams are run by smart management teams, and this sort of over-reaction is unlikely to drive teams' decision-making. It is, however, an absolute certainty that some media and fans will be convinced that their club needs some kind of overhaul based on postseason performance. This sort of thing was endemic earlier in the decade when the Yankees were repeatedly bounced out of the play-offs in the early rounds. Still, it wasn't uncommon to hear fans in The Hub opine that Tim Wakefield should never be allowed to start another postseason game after Boston's ALCS loss.

The coda to all of this—and I say this knowing that I am invoking the wrath of Phillies Phanatics who waited nearly 30 years for a championship—is that the best team quite obviously did not win the World Series. By almost any non-superficial measure, the best team in the majors in October 2008 was almost certainly the Boston Red Sox.

But it's not an injustice that the Red Sox didn't win the championship, nor is it an indictment of the 2008 World Champion Phillies. It's a validation of a playoff process which was not designed to make the best team the prohibitive favorite. It's a validation of the playoff process—the one all 30 teams agreed upon—that favors tension, uncertainty and clutch performance. Philadelphia won when it counted. It didn't make the Phillies the best team, it made them World Champions. If you're a fan, why would you care about anything else?

Commentary

Ten Things I Learned This Year

by Dave Studenmund

As I write these words, the regular season has been extended by at least one day, just as it was in 2007. The tarps have been permanently pulled over the fields in two New York ballparks. The Rays have qualified for the postseason—the last of MLB's 30 teams to make it to October. The Cubs, having posted their best winning percentage in over 60 years, will try to break their 100-year postseason curse.

By the time you read these words, you'll know the outcome of the postseason and the final destiny of the Rays and Cubs, among others. Actually, given how long it usually takes me to write, I'll probably know the World Series champ by the end of this piece, too. Still, this was a typical baseball season, filled with surprising plays, games and insights. There's a lot to talk about while we wait for the postseason drama to play out.

Youth is Rampant

Major league baseball is getting younger. This isn't exactly news; the average age of major league players has been heading down the last two years. But MLB took a major turn toward adolescence in 2008. In fact, the change from 2007 to 2008 was the biggest one-year age decrease in major league history.

Here's a table of the biggest one-season changes in Win Shares age since 1900. Win Shares age is simply the average age of major league players, weighted by the number of Win Shares each player accrued. (Win Shares is a metric that measures overall player impact. You can read more about it in our Glossary.)

Year	Age	Previous Year's Age	Diff
2008	27.7	28.8	-1.08
1909	27.4	28.4	-1.01
1946	29.4	30.2	-0.80
1948	28.7	29.1	-0.39

I included only four years in the table because the top two years, maybe three, blow away the competition. Of course, 1946 marked the return of World War II veterans to the national pastime; the only time you might say that "veterans" made anything younger. Even so, 1946 is pretty far behind the top two years. For sheer impact,

only 1909—the year that featured the emergence of Eddie Collins and Tris Speaker building on the recent successes of Ty Cobb and Walter Johnson (perhaps the greatest emergence of top talent ever in one short period)—compares to 2008.

One of the biggest factors behind the 2008 youth movement was the retirement (forced or otherwise) of some of the game's greatest talents: Barry Bonds, Roger Clemens, Mike Piazza, etc. In fact, these simultaneous exits will make the Hall of Fame voting five years from now *very* interesting, a topic Joe Posnanski explores a little later in the *Annual*.

As the old guys faded into the figurative Iowa cornfield, the youth of America took over. Of course, the Rays helped lead this charge of youth by winning 97 games with an average Win Shares age of 25.8 years, making them the third-youngest team in the majors. But the trend was ubiquitous: 24 of the 30 major league teams got younger this year. In fact, the Giants turned 3.5 years younger in 2008 (compared to 2007), thanks to Bonds' exile and the great success of Tim Lincecum.

The Twins won 88 games with an average age of 25.5 years (the youngest team in the majors), a decline of 2.6 years from 2007. The Cardinals, Dodgers and Red Sox all "de-aged" 1.9 years. It was just an all-out youth movement. Good teams, bad teams and mediocre teams all got younger in 2008 at a pace unprecedented in major league history.

Yet No One Seems to Believe in Young Teams

In the beginning of the season, everyone was charmed by the Rays, but it seemed like people kept expecting the Yankees to reclaim their usual high ranking in the division and, when that failed to happen, they expected the Red Sox to take over. The Rays were fun, but they didn't gain full respect. Many baseball writers and commentators seemed to think they eventually would fold in the competitive AL East.

Didn't happen. The Rays rolled and rolled and nothing stopped them on their way to a 97-65 record and the AL East title. Why did the "mainstream media" (whoever they are) take so long to recognize the Rays were real?

Well, first of all, teams with great records early in the year tend to do worse in the latter part of the year. That's called "regression to the mean" when statisticians talk. You can see it in this table of all teams' records since 1960, in which I've grouped teams by their record as of July 1:

7/1 Win%	Teams	Average Winning Percentages		
		1-Jul	End of Year	Diff
.250-.350	32	.323	.372	.049
.350-.450	220	.412	.433	.021
.450-.550	525	.502	.502	.001
.550-.650	247	.589	.568	-.021
.650-.750	24	.680	.624	-.056

Under "Average Winning Percentages," the July 1 is the average winning percentage of all teams in that category as of July 1 (duh). The End of Year column is their record over the entire year (including games before July 1) and "Diff" is the diff between the two. As the table shows, the best records get worse, the worst records get better and the average stay average.

The story becomes more telling when you take each team's record from the previous year into account. After all, the Rays were 66-96 in 2007—a 31-game improvement from one year to the next isn't impossible, but it's not very common. Only three teams have posted bigger one-year gains in 162-game seasons.

That kind of changes the statistical dynamic. Here's a table of teams that were playing at a .543 clip or better as of July 1 (.543 is the winning percentage of an 88-win team over a full season, which seems to be the going rate for playoff teams), grouped by their winning percentage the previous year:

Previous Year Win%	Teams	Average Winning Percentages		
		1-Jul	EOY	Diff
.350-.450	32	.576	.539	-.037
.450-.550	156	.587	.556	-.031
.550-.650	113	.600	.588	-.012

As you can see, teams that did poorly in the previous year had a bigger drop in the second half of the year than teams that had performed well the previous year.

So this was the extra-damning thing about the Rays. They were playing well (good records tend to get worse) and they had a bad year in 2007 (teams that played poor-

ly in the previous year really tend to get worse). Yes, the Rays were young, and young teams tend to improve, but there were a lot of other factors to overcome in the minds of the masses.

So I guess I can't be overly critical of those Tampa Bay critics. There was some underlying rationale behind their disbelief. But the Rays have put all doubts to rest in the postseason, defeating the White Sox and Red Sox. The word is out: They belong.

The Angels Made Recording History

The best regular season record in 2008 belonged to the Los Angeles Angels of Anaheim, the only team to hit the magical, and very round, number of 100 wins. A remarkable record, really, because the Angels' offense managed to score only 765 runs—a little less than the average American League team.

Yes, 'twas pitching that drove the machine. The Angels allowed only 697 runs all year, the lowest total … no, the second-lowest … no, um … well, let's see. Actually, four American League teams had better pitching (and fielding) than the Angels; the Blue Jays, Rays, Athletics and Red Sox all gave up fewer runs than the Angels.

So how did LA of A manage to win 100 games? Well, one of the "luck" stats that people tend to cite is a team's record in one-run games. The Angels were 31-21 in one-run games last year. Good, but not great; five teams were better.

But if you expand your definition of close games to include two-run contests, you find that the Angels were 61-28 (in one- and two-run contests), which was the best record last year and (get this) the 10th-best record in major league history. The Angels won 30 two-run ballgames last year, the most in major league history (the 1992 Braves also won 30, but they lost 11; the 2008 Angels lost just seven).

Of course, one of the keys to the Angels' success was the guy in the bullpen, name of Francisco Rodriguez, who managed to save 62 games and blow away Bobby Thigpen's previous record of 57. A strong bullpen is one of the key ingredients for winning close ballgames, but the weird thing is that bullpen success isn't *predictive* of success in close games. It's a baseballian enigma.

Baseball analysts like me calculate something called the "Pythagorean formula," which is a fancy way of saying we estimate the number of games a team "should" have won based on the number of runs it scored and allowed. Published by Bill James in the

1980s and enhanced by several statisticians since, it's a pretty accurate tool.

The Angels outperformed their Pythagorean formula by almost 12 wins, which is the second-biggest variance in major league history. The record for Pythagorean variance (12.9 wins) was set by the 1905 Tigers.

Four of the 10 largest Pythagorean variances of the last 108 years have been set in the last four years. Are we just feeling "lucky" these days, or is something else going on?

Bullpen Usage Rant No. 2,478

Rich Lederer has penned an article in the *Annual* about the bullpen, the save statistic and Francisco Rodriguez's new record. I don't have much to add to Rich's insights, but I do want to point out the sort of thing that drives me nuts.

Tom M. Tango has developed a wonderful stat called Leverage Index (LI), which measures the relative criticality of each game situation. An average situation has a Leverage Index of 1.0, but it can vary quite a bit. As an example: In the top of the seventh, with a runner on first and a tie score, the LI is 2.4. The same situation in the top of the ninth has an LI of 3.4. Two innings add a point of impact, because the home team will have less time to respond to, say, a home run by the batting team.

Turns out that an LI of three (three times more critical than the average situation) is a pretty good cutoff point for "critical situations." About 3 percent of all plays last year had an LI of 3.0 and above. Sixty percent of games had at least one play with an LI of 3.0 or higher.

So who faced the most batters when with an LI of at least three? It was that Angels reliever.

Pitcher	Team	LI>3	Save Ops
Rodriguez, F	LAA	100	69
Wilson, B	SF	84	47
Torres, S	MIL	83	35
Gregg, K	FLA	81	38
Cordero, F	CIN	71	40

There is a nice correlation between appearances in high leverage situations and save opportunities. In general, pitchers who have the most save opportunities also face the most batters when LI is three or more.

There are a few exceptions on some teams, however. Here are three teams on which the leader in save opportunities wasn't the leader in high-leverage appearances:

Team	Pitcher	LI > 3	Save Ops
Detroit	Rodney, F	42	19
	Jones, T	26	21
San Diego	Bell, H	53	7
	Hoffman, T	30	34
NY Mets	Heilman, A	47	8
	Wagner, B	31	34

If you're like me (and why wouldn't you be?) you're probably not surprised to see that Trevor Hoffman and Todd Jones didn't lead their teams in high-leverage situations.

But check out the Mets. Aaron Heilman faced more high-leverage situations than closer Billy Wagner! That's Aaron Heilman, of the 5.21 ERA. Yes, I know that Wagner was on the disabled list for virtually all of August and September, but Heilman led Wagner in high-leverage situations even prior to Aug. 1 (28-25).

Heilman has been a fine pitcher in the past, but he fell apart in 2008. The Mets were slow to realize this, but they didn't have a lot of other options and Wagner's lack of flexibility handicapped them further. When closers can't pull out of their one-inning-with-a-lead-only rut, as Wagner seemingly can't, the team is crippled.

The White Sox are Heavy, Man, Heavy

David Gassko has a great article in the *Annual* about the size of players in major league history, and how short and tall players have performed relative to each other over the years. But if you take a look around any major league spring training camp these days, my guess is you'll see a lot of great big guys.

David does a smart thing in his analysis. He uses height as a proxy for size. That's smart, because weight statistics are very unreliable, even for players in the recent past. Weight statistics for players in the 1920s? Fuggedaboutit.

Or not. Damn the statistics, I say, full spreadsheet ahead. I was curious about weight trends, so I tallied up the weight data from Retrosheet and Baseball Info Solutions (for the last three years) to see if I could figure out the heaviest team in baseball history. To calculate my BMI (Baseball Mass Index), I used the weight of each player and, um, weighted it by the number of at-bats he had each year (as a percentage of team at-bats).

According to my very loose translation of bad data, the heaviest batting team of all time has been (drum-roll, please) ... the 2008 Chicago White Sox.

Yep, the ChiSox averaged 220 pounds—and that's including the Cuban Beanpole, Alexei Ramirez. The Big Sox included Jim Thome (255 pounds), Jermaine Dye (245) and AJ Pierzynski (240). Even infielder Juan Uribe weights 225, and I didn't include 275-pounder Bobby Jenks because he's a pitcher.

The second-largest batting team of 2008 (and the team that initially got me interested in the subject) was the Washington Nationals, who averaged 215 pounds. Unfortunately (or not), 298-pound Dmitri Young and 268-pound Willy Mo Pena didn't get enough at-bats to vault the Nats to the top of the list. That's right. They didn't pull their weight.

As I said, these data are deeply untrustworthy (case in point: Walt Goldsby, who played in the 1800s, reportedly weighed 1,658 pounds), so take this with a grain of salt. But Dmitri Young appears to be the second-heaviest player of all time, behind 322-pound Walter Young (who played first base for the Orioles several years ago). And don't forget 295-pound Jumbo Brown, a reliever from the 1930s, who ranks as the third-heaviest player of all time.

Last trivia point before you go totally insane: the Orioles of 1991 and 1992 were mighty heavy too, ranking at the top of the list of teams before 2000. Remember Chris Hoiles, Randy Milligan and Sam Horn? The shortstop was a pretty big guy, too.

Albert Pujols is an Incredible Hitter

Remember that hot start by Chipper Jones? Three months into the season, he was batting .394/.485/.630 and Atlanta fans (and others) were on a .400 watch. He didn't make it, of course, but he sure sizzled through June.

And remember how Manny sizzled for LA? During his time on the left coast, he batted .396/.489/.743. Amazing numbers, although spread over only 229 plate appearances.

So let's do this: let's combine Chipper's stats through the end of June and Manny's stats from the beginning of July until the end of the season (Manny wasn't too shabby in Boston the month of July, either). Then, let's compare that line to a single player, say, the first baseman of St. Louis, Albert Pujols. Take a look at the bottom of the page.

Virtually the same number of runs, RBIs and home runs, though Pujols has more doubles. The only thing separating King Albert from our merged superstar is 13 singles. Manny and Chipper were great for half seasons and received a lot of publicity for it. Albert was great all year long. That's called perspective.

Confession: I totally stole this idea from The Book Blog (www.insidethebook.com).

Streaky Teams

Which team would you guess was the streakiest last year? Perhaps the Dodgers, who had to click off a number of September wins to take the division title? Or the Indians, who were white-hot at the end of the year? Maybe Houston, with that August surge?

Wrong. The streakiest team last year was the Kansas City Royals. Don't believe me? Take a look at their game graph in the back-of-the-book statistics. They lost 12 games in a row in late May (that tends to happen when you play the Red Sox, Blue Jays and Twins in a row), then won 11 of 12 against National League competition in June. Lost a bunch in August; won a bunch in September.

By the way, there were three 12-game streaks last year—all losing streaks—by the Royals, Nationals and Mariners.

Using some simple probability theory, a team with KC's record is expected to have about 82 "runs"—a switch from a win or loss in the previous game to the opposite in the next game—during the season. KC had only 68. As statisticians say, that is significant at the 95 percent probability level.

The least streaky team in the majors last year was the Florida Marlins. Probabilistically, the Marlins "should" have had 81 runs last year, but they actually had 92 (once again significant at the 95 percent level). Their only real streak came in September, when they were drifting out of the NL East race. Nine wins in a row against the

	AB	R	H	2B	HR	RBI	BA	OBP	SLG
Manny/Chipper	516	102	200	32	37	115	.388	.485	.665
Albert	524	100	187	44	37	116	.357	.462	.653

Phillies, Astros and Nationals put them 4.5 games out of the wild card slot, but they lost the next four games to effectively end their pennant chances.

Among the postseason qualifiers:

Streaky: White Sox, Brewers

Not Streaky: Red Sox, Angels

Average Streakiness: Rays, Cubs, Phillies, Dodgers

There's no particular pattern here. Successful teams can be streaky or not. Just thought you'd like to know.

The Astros' Streak

Really, I told you all that just so I could write about the most awesome streak of the year. On July 26, the Houston Astros were languishing in the National League Central basement and roundly criticized for picking up pitcher Randy Wolf in a trade. Well, guess what. From July 27 (Wolf's first start with his new team) until Sept. 11 (forever a chilling date, even in a baseball column), the Astros went 33-11, the best 44-game streak in the majors last year.

Unfortunately, Hurricane Ike struck land on the 12th, postponing a couple of key games against the Cubs (which eventually were played in Milwaukee, just up the lake from Chicago) and the Astros' pennant chances were blown away.

Houston was only three games behind Milwaukee on the 11th, but the Brewers turned it on and the Astros were 6-8 the rest of the month. Regardless of the final outcome, it was a remarkable run by Houston.

These are the heroes of the Houston streak, ranked by WPA (that's Win Probability Added—read about it in the Glossary) contribution to the team during the 44 games:

Lee, Carlos	1.76
Oswalt, Roy	1.68
Berkman, Lance	1.63
Valverde, Jose	1.53
Hawkins, LaTroy	1.21
Blum, Geoff	1.11

Yeah, Carlos Lee led the Astros in WPA during this streak even though he didn't play after Aug. 9. Lee was seriously hot at the time of his injury, and his broken pinky was a significant blow to the Astros' season.

The Wolf transaction made the Houston headlines, but the Astros' pickup of Latroy Hawkins from the Yankees on July 30 was quite a steal for the 'Stros.

Hawkins posted a 0.43 ERA in 21 innings for Houston and picked up 1.2 WPA during their streak.

And Geoff Blum? The erstwhile infielder batted only .261/.302/.539 as Houston surged, but he delivered three of the six biggest blows of the streak:

- Sept. 2: Blum hit a two-run home run in the top of the 11th off Kerry Wood to beat the Cubs.

- Aug. 2: Blum hit a pinch-hit two-run single in the bottom of the ninth off Billy Wagner (Wagner's last game) to tie the game. The Astros won in extra innings.

- Aug. 19: Blum hit a two-out, three-run home run in the top of the sixth to break up a tie game with the Brewers. Houston went on to win, 5-2.

You probably knew about Oswalt's and Berkman's contribution to The Streak—they're the Astros' stars, after all. But give Hawkins and Blum some love, too.

The Clutchiest Batter of the Year

Wouldn't you like to know how other batters performed in the clutch last year? Since we've already picked apart pitcher performance using Leverage Index, let's turn around and do the same thing for batters. Turns out there were two batters who stood out last year when the game was critical.

The Phillies' Pat Burrell had 21 plate appearances in high-leverage situations (LI over 3) and he rose to the challenge, particularly in the first three months of the season. Altogether, he hit three singles, four doubles and a home run. He also walked four times and was hit by a pitch, winding up with a .500 batting average, .620 OBP and .938 slugging percentage in the most critical situations.

But our award for clutchiest player of the year goes to the Dodgers' Andre Ethier. Ethier came to bat 26 times when the game's Leverage Index was higher than three. Here's what he did:

- Singled seven times

- One double, two triples and a home run

- Five walks and a HBP

- Made nine outs, including six strikeouts

That's a .550 batting average, .653 OBP and .950 slugging percentage. His biggest blow might have been a triple in the top of the eighth against the Padres to tie the game. The Dodgers eventually won the game and increased their NL West lead to 2.5 games at a critical time in the pennant race.

Special credit goes to Mark Teixeira, who had eight plate appearances in high-leverage situations during his brief time with the Angels. He was splendiferous, with three singles, three home runs and a sacrifice fly. There was more than one reason the Angels won all those close games.

In the End, it was the Phillies' Year

But once you got past all the trends, the drama and the angst (have I mentioned the Cubs?), there was one team left in major league baseball, one team standing tall in the cold rain. The Phillies conquered the high-profile Mets, CC Sabathia's Brewers, Manny's Dodgers and the hot young Rays to take home the Commission-er's Trophy (can't they come up with a catchier name for the trophy that goes to the World Series winner?).

The postseason was sort of a coming-out party for Cole Hamels, who proved on the national stage that he is an ace, winning both the NLCS and World Series MVP trophies. But the real story to the Phillies' season, the biggest difference between this year's team and last year's, was their bullpen ace Brad Lidge.

K-Rod may have gotten the record and all the hype, but Lidge was the best reliever in baseball this past season. He didn't blow a single save, didn't lose a game. His WPA (5.37) led all major league relievers and he continued to dominate in the postseason, with seven saves in nine games, yielding only six hits and one run in nine innings.

Not too long ago, Lidge was a pariah in Houston, giving up a huge home run to Albert Pujols in the 2005 postseason, temporarily losing his closer role in 2007 and being subsequently traded to the Phillies. To add injury to insult, he tore his knee in Spring Training. I don't know if Brad Lidge is haunted by the ghosts of his past, but his exorcism of those ghosts was the Phillies' triumph.

You wonder, however, if the lasting image of this year's World Series will be the sight of players bundled against the cold and "hydroplaning" when they slid into second base. All year long, baseball tried to fight the elements. MLB moved a game to Milwaukee to avoid Hurricane Ike. They played a minor league game in Des Moines even though the town was evacuated due to flooding. There was literally no one there.

Give it up, guys. You can't fight Mother Nature. Either shorten the season or require every team to build a domed stadium. We aren't interested in snowballs and soaked uniforms. It's baseball we love, played on green grass on a sunny day.

The Annotated Year in Baseball

by Richard Barbieri

On our site each week, I look back at events from the past week in baseball history. When I write those columns, I have the whole of history to look back on. Nonetheless, it is possible simply to reflect on the past year and find news that's worthy of another look. Some of these events you probably remember, others might not even have registered. Whether big news or small, all connect to the past in one way or another.

November 2007: *General managers approve instant replay.*

This was not a unanimous decision; the general managers voted collectively with 80 percent in favor of instituting a replay system. It was also a nonbinding vote, and one that seems in hindsight almost naïve. A major league spokesman characterized the process by which baseball made its moves as "glacial" and doubted that such a system would be place for the 2008 season.

Of course, a few blown home runs calls later, things changed. After both Carlos Delgado and Alex Rodriguez were robbed of home runs on mistaken calls, the system was put into place. A-Rod, apparently doomed to be linked to oddities as well as his greatness, was the first player to have a home run put under review, one that stood up.

December 2007: *"Mitchell Report" released.*

Officially titled—deep breath here—"Report to the Commissioner of Baseball of an Independent Investigation into the Illegal Use of Steroids and Other Performance Enhancing Substances by Players in Major League Baseball," this was the culmination of baseball's investigation of performance enhancing drugs in the sport.

All said, 89 players were listed in the report, some of note (Roger Clemens, of course) but the majority were substantially mediocre players. For every Barry Bonds or Eric Gagné, there were several Matt Francos, Matt Carreons or Jim Parques. This isn't an absolution of anyone involved with the report—the use of PEDs is rightly banned—but people would do well to remember that when questioning the feats of All-Stars, it is much more likely to be the guy on the bench, the fourth outfielder or mop-up man who is on the juice.

January 2008: *Jose Lima signs with Kia Tigers.*

Yes, that's Kia like the Korean car company, which means that yes, it's a Korean team. This one can probably be filed in the "how the mighty have fallen" department. As recently as 2004, Lima was throwing a shutout against the eventual National League pennant winners in the playoffs. Just a few years before that, in 1999, Lima won 21 games for the Astros.

After 2005 and 2006, when Lima's ERA clocked in at 6.99 and 9.87, he spent 2007 in the Mexican League. Apparently no longer able to find a job on this continent, Lima went to Korea. The Kia Tigers might be called the Yankees of the Korean League, although lately they have fallen on tough times. Signing Lima was no help as he soon found himself pitching terribly once more and demoted to the minor leagues. In the Korean leagues! Lima was released, and spent the rest of the year with the Camden Riversharks for whom he posted an ERA of nearly five.

I think it is safe to say that Lima Time is over.

February 2008: *Mariners acquire Erik Bedard.*

About 10 days before the Mariners and Orioles consummated this deal, the Mets and Twins made an even bigger deal, which landed Johan Santana in New York. Both the Mets and Mariners had missed the playoffs in 2007 and both were hoping to acquire an ace to put them over the top in 2008.

While neither team succeeded in making the playoffs this season, the two trades could not have gone any differently. Santana—despite winning just 16 games—was probably the best pitcher in the National League. He led the league in ERA and innings, and finished second in strikeouts. The Mets missed the playoffs by just one game, and won 89. Bedard meanwhile, went 6-4 for Seattle, and made only 15 starts. Because of an injury, he last appeared on July 4. The Mariners lost 101 games.

Making a big trade can sometimes pay off, and even when it doesn't carry a team to October it can be a successful move. As the Mariners proved, however, such a move can also spell disaster.

March 2008: *Kaz Matsui returns to Astros' lineup.*

Missing a few games in spring training is hardly the end of the world. Many players do it as a matter of habit—Mariano Rivera for one hasn't traveled to a Yankees spring road game in years. Nonetheless, Matsui's return to the lineup was just temporary. His problem would end up requiring surgery.

I won't get into what exactly the symptom was, except to say that it involved his rear end. But I will use this as an interesting note on the challenges foreign players face. Matsui's initial diagnosis was hemorrhoids, a word which apparently—in the words of Astros' GM Ed Wade—"carries negative connotations in Japan."

So foreign players have to deal with being away from their family and friends and with living in a strange country where they may not speak the language. On top of all that, even something as simple as the diagnosis of hemorrhoids can cause people in one's home country serious concern. It's a tough life.

April 2008: *Tigers win game.*

Now this may not seem like much of an event. Although the Tigers were a last place team in 2008—quite a fall from their 2006 season—they did win 74 games, including 13 in April. But it took the Tigers eight tries to finally win a game in April, and that did not come until April 9. By then, the team picked by many (including yours truly) to win the AL Central was already five games back.

Of course, as bad starts go, the Tigers' was really nothing. The 1988 Baltimore Orioles would not sympathize with the Tigers; they lost 21 straight games to open the year. Manager Cal Ripken Sr. was fired after the first six games, a change which made no difference. Replacement Frank Robinson then lost the next 15.

Broadcaster Jon Miller, whose Sisyphean ordeal of calling the O's every night made him a source of national interest, bemoaned that he and his partner had become "curiosities," comparing them to figures in a wax museum. In an attempt to put the misery in greater words than his own, Miller resorted to reading Dickens' *Great Expectations* on the air.

So while the Tigers and their fans doubtless have nothing kind to say about the beginning of their 2008 season, at least they can look 20 years in the past and remember how much worse things can get.

May 2008: *Barry Zito loses seventh straight game.*

Last year in this space I discussed Carl Pavano and the "All-Bust" starting rotation. That inglorious company included names like Mike Hampton and Jaime Navarro. This year, a new name can be added to the list: Barry Zito. Starting in 2001, Zito pitched six straight seasons of at least 213 innings, was never worse than league average in ERA and won the Cy Young award in 2002.

Unfortunately for the Giants, all that came while Zito was with the cross-town A's. Before the 2007 season, San Francisco signed Zito to a massive, seven-year $126 million deal. Since then, Zito has neither topped 200 innings nor been better than league average, and he's frequently been simply terrible. He lost his first seven starts of 2008 and led the league in losses. The Giants have five years left at more than $20 million. Zito could turn things around, but for now it looks like a new member of the All-Bust rotation is in place.

June 2008: *Jackie Robinson receives new Hall of Fame plaque.*

The Hall of Fame in Cooperstown sometimes is referred to as home of the immortals. But common belief would have it that once a player is inducted into the Hall, that's the end of the road. A plaque honors his career accomplishments, he gives a little speech on an induction weekend (assuming he is alive to see it) and that's that.

But like any other institution, the Hall of Fame is alive and subject to keeping up with the times. Sometimes, such as the controversy involving appearances by the left-leaning stars of *Bull Durham,* this is to the Hall's detriment. But it can also be to the Hall's benefit.

Such was the case when the Hall of Fame unveiled a new plaque for Jackie Robinson, giving the trailblazing Brooklyn Dodger a more complete history, as well as putting his common baseball name on the plaque. While the Hall does change plaques when factual errors are discovered, changes like the one for Robinson are rare. Yet if any player was to merit such an honor, it is hard to argue with Jackie Robinson being that player.

July 2008: *Mariano Rivera throws 1,000th career inning.*

Since 1901, just over 1,000 pitchers have thrown 1,000 or more innings. While not an unsubstantial number, especially given the context of the huge number of innings thrown in early baseball, it is not all that many innings. Logically, such a list consists mostly of starters.

Of those 1,000 pitchers, only 127 appeared in relief in two-thirds of their games. If you up the percentage to 90, only 56 pitchers managed the feat.

One of those pitchers is Rivera, arguably the greatest pitcher ever. Rivera is the all-time leader in ERA+, and 17th in ERA. His career walks per nine innings are 11th all-time, and combined with his hits per nine innings (ninth, all time) that gives him the third best WHIP in history. Now, some of this does come from Rivera's advantage of being a reliever. Nonetheless, it is clear that Rivera is in rare company among the elite pitchers of all time. As his career winds to an end, fans should make sure to see him.

August 2008: *Tom Glavine undergoes surgery.*

It is a popular pastime among the media to declare that whichever pitcher is the most recent winner of 300 games will surely be the last pitcher to win 300 games. This has been going as far back as Early Wynn, who won his 300th game in 1963.

For now, the "last" 300-game winner is Tom Glavine, who sits on 305, good for 21st all-time. Glavine's dual elbow and shoulder surgery prevented him from reaching an even higher win total—he needs only three wins to jump into the top 20—but of course could not undo his accomplishment.

At this moment, Randy Johnson (295) and Mike Mussina (270) seem the most likely pitchers to reach 300, although both are said to be considering retirement. After those two, it seems unlikely that any pitcher will win 300 for at least a decade. But if history teaches us nothing else, it is that one should never rule out a possibility. So whether Glavine keeps his title, or the Big Unit or the Moose become the next last man to 300, I will go on record here that someday another 300-game winner will come. But he'll be the last.

At least until the next one.

September 2008: *Texas Rangers eliminated from playoffs.*

Unfortunately for the Rangers, this marked their ninth straight year without a playoff appearance. But while nine years without a playoff appearance isn't great for a franchise, it isn't too bad. Ask the Kansas City Royals, who haven't been to October in 22 years. But the Rangers' streak happens to coincide exactly with the career of Michael Young, who has now played 1,216 games without appearing in the playoffs.

Now that is not altogether a terrible number; many players have appeared in more. The active leader in 2008 was Damion Easley, who has now played 1,706 games without making the playoffs. Easley also has the misfortune of missing the playoffs on the last day of the season two years in a row. But for Michael Young, the forecast is perhaps much worse.

Next year will be the first of a five-year, $80 million contract between Young and the Rangers. If Young were to continue playing 155 games a season and the Rangers to continue their ineptitude, by the time his contract expires in 2013, he would have played nearly 2,000 games without reaching October. Were he to reach 2,000 games and never see October, he would be just the 14th player to do so. That's not company Young is hoping to reach, I am sure.

October 2008: *Rays open playoffs.*

So this one is cheating a little, but only a little. The Tampa Bay Rays opened their playoff campaign against the Chicago White Sox, who they were destined to play once it became clear the Boston Red Sox would take the American League wild card. Nonetheless, Tampa did not play Chicago because of the prohibition on intra-division rivalries in the first round, but because they did not have the best record in the American League—the Angels did. (And a lot of good it did them.)

This means that Tampa Bay could not go from having the worst record in the league (as the Rays had in 2007, 66-96) to having the best. But that's okay. Only one team in history has done it. In 1889, the Louisville Colonels went 27-111 in the American Association. The next season, they made a remarkable turnaround to 88-44. So the challenge remains open.

Somehow, I don't see either the Seattle Mariners (61-101) or Washington Nationals (59-102) making such a turnaround. But if it happens, I'll be here to write about it.

The Year in Pointlessness

by Will Leitch

We can find ourselves, sometimes, so far deep inside the game of baseball that we forget it's supposed to be *fun*. Fortunately, there's always enough off-the-field weirdness to remind us that no matter how seriously we take the great game, its participants and those who cover it always will make sure they remind us of how silly they can truly be.

Here's a look at a season's worth of goofiness and malfeasance.

April

Before the first game at the new Nationals Park, lame-duck President George W. Bush throws out the first pitch. Afterward, he visits in the booth with ESPN broadcasters Joe Morgan and Jon Miller. Typically, when luminaries like the President chat with the announcers, they leave after half an inning, which makes sense, considering the fact that running the country is, you know, a lot of work. But our Prez, exhausted and happy to have a night away from it all, insists on chatting with Morgan and Miller for a full inning and a half, talking about the Nationals infielders, Jeff Francoeur's spring training injury and pretty much anything that doesn't involve the Al-Anbar Province, the economy or the election.

After the inning and a half, Miller, somewhat concerned about the state of our country, asks, "You sure you don't need to go?" The President sighs and says, yeah, he should probably get back to work, and then, once again, curses Bud Selig for not letting him be baseball commissioner like he always wanted. He wouldn't have called the All-Star Game a tie, that's for darned sure.

After an offseason that ensured he'd never play baseball again—or, for that matter, ever be able to discuss his buttocks on national television again (mercifully)—Roger Clemens' reputation takes another hit. Country music singer Mindy McCready confesses that she carried on a 10-year affair with the now-disgraced pitcher. The affair began when Clemens saw her in a Fort Myers bar while drinking with his Red Sox teammates, and it was "love at first sight." Which wouldn't be all that bad, had Clemens not been married at the time and (more to the point) McCready not been 15 years old. As might be expected from someone whose formative years involved occasionally lying next to Roger Clemens, McCready's life has been an unhappy one, with Oxycontin addictions, abusive husbands and a suicide attempt. She has also won only three Cy Youngs.

May

It wouldn't be a year in review without the joyous human being that is Ozzie Guillen. The White Sox manager drew the ire of the Association for Women in Sports Media for an unusual motivational gimmick. To show how the White Sox need to keep playing hard, or something, he installed two inflatable sex dolls in the clubhouse (in full view of reporters). Said *The National Post* in Toronto: "Bats were circled around the two naked female dolls, one of whom had a bat inserted in its backside to prop it up. Each wore a sign over her breasts, one saying "Let's Go White Sox" and the other reading "You've Got to Push," the *National Post* in Toronto reported.

Guillen defended himself: "I'm sure it wasn't done to disrespect anyone ... A lot of worse things happen in the clubhouse ... If people got their feelings hurt because of that ... they don't really know much about baseball." He was forced to remove the dolls, but, as of press time, there was no word on the potential removal of the bats.

They're not booing, they're saying, "beeee-rrrrrr." Because of his inconsistent play in left field, Alfonso Soriano had been feeling the wrath of angry Cubs fans tired of watching him play the position as if he were wearing eel slippers on ice. Rather than work on Soriano's play (or at least get him some spikes), the Cubs announced that anyone who booed Soriano would be tossed from Wrigley Field.

The *Chicago Tribune* reported: "A Cubs official offered protection for Soriano, instructing left-field bleacherites before Monday's game that any profane or inappropriate comments made toward Soriano would result in their immediate ejection." No fans end up being thrown out of the game, and Soriano, his delicate psyche protected to live another day, actually improves in the outfield. Probably got some spikes.

June

Every catcher with a bone to pick with an umpire has thought about it, but it took Georgia high school catcher Matt Hill to actually do it. After arguing with the home plate ump over a few calls during the Class AAA state championship series, Hill, waiting for a pitch to home plate, ducked out of the way and let the pitch smack the umpire right in the mask. Hill denied it was on purpose, but anyone who saw the video could plainly see otherwise.

Gordon College had been planning to offer Hill a scholarship but pulled it in the wake of the incident. (Rick Reilly of *ESPN The Magazine* ended up writing his first non-golf column for the magazine about the incident.) Hill still hasn't spoken publicly about the incident, but the rest of us now have a clear alternative explanation for Mike Piazza's "abilities" behind the plate throughout his career.

At the end of the 2007 season, the New York Mets suffered one of the worst—if not *the* worst—collapses in baseball history. Despite the bloodlust of New York media (and, you know, logic), manager Willie Randolph kept his job. Until June, anyway, when, for reasons unbeknownst to anyone, Mets general manager Omar Minaya decides to fire Randolph in the middle of the night, after flying across the country to Anaheim, following a win. (It was the first game after the start of a road trip, so he easily could have taken care of the firing without the plane fare.)

Despite a similar collapse at the end of 2008, Minaya extends the contract of then-interim manager Jerry Manuel, though he saves himself trouble by doing it in Queens. But if Minaya ends up in Southern California, it would be wise for Manuel to turn his cell phone off.

July

In one of those truly disturbing pieces of trash gossip, it turns out that Yankees third baseman Alex Rodriguez has been sneaking around with aging, atrophying pop magistrate Madonna. (At least according to their publicists.) A-Rod's wife reportedly responds by hanging out with Lenny Kravitz, which is, somehow, worse than sleeping with a woman who's almost 50 years old and hasn't had a hit record in more than a decade.

Rodriguez is taunted by Red Sox fans but is undaunted, and after the season ends, is said to accompany Madonna on a trip to the private vacation compound of Jerry Seinfeld. This presumably set off a dinner conversation the likes of which has not been seen since Dorothy Parker and the Algonquin Round Table. Both Rodriguez and Madonna are now going forward with divorces. You're stuck with this crap for the next eight years, New Yorkers.

You have to go to the minor leagues to see a true wild baseball fight anymore—somehow, the alleged "fisticuffs" among the Rays and Red Sox never quite meets the minimum entrance requirements—and the Dayton Dragons and the Peoria Chiefs give us a great one. (In real life, it is unlikely that a Chief, no matter how many crossbows he brought with him, could handle a group of dragons.)

So many players were ejected in the melee—which included a closeup fastball to the sternum and a veritable cornucopia of dramatically misplaced haymakers—that several players had to be allowed to come back in the game so that there'd be enough players to finish it. One was not second baseman Gian Guzman, who broke his leg in the scramble, proving once again that baseball players are not hockey players and can actually be injured in fights.

August

After years of alternately tormenting and titillating Red Sox fans, Manny Ramirez finally burns his last bridge and is traded to the Los Angeles Dodgers right before the deadline. (Boston is forced to accept Jason Bay, a quieter, less streaky, cheaper, more cost-controlled version of Manny, in return.) Ramirez commences, as expected, hitting the bejeezus out of the ball the rest of the season, but the Dodgers still go as far in the playoffs as the Red Sox do. (Not quite as far, actually.) Ramirez then, as planned, files for free agency in the offseason, and the Red Sox move on with their lives. Rather than dealing with Manny every season, they now have a rotating circle of fratty white guys named Jed, Kevin and Dustin. Some consider this an upgrade. Most of them live in Boston.

For years, Yankee Stadium—the old one—has had a strange rule: During the singing of "God Bless America," the stadium actually chains off aisles so that you can't leave your seat. They really do this. In August, a man named Bradford Campeau-Laurion left for the restroom before the song started. This was a mistake.

He told Deadspin, "My right arm was twisted violently behind my back and I was informed that I was being escorted out of the stadium. A second officer then joined in and twisted my left arm, also in an excessively forceful manner, behind my back. I informed them they were violating my First Amendment rights and that I had done nothing wrong, with no response from them. I was sitting in the Tier Level, and of course this is the highest level of the stadium and I was escorted in this painful manner down the entire length of the stadium. About halfway down, I informed them that they were hurting me, repeated that I had done nothing wrong, and that I was not resisting nor talking back to them. One of them said something to the effect that if I continued to speak, he would find a way to hurt me more. When we reached the exit of the stadium, they confiscated my ticket and the first officer shoved me through the turnstiles, saying 'Get the hell out of my country if you don't like it.'"

This is not quite the "joke" you were expecting in this spot, but, you know, we kind of felt we should mention it. We won't miss this place at all.

September

For a pointless afternoon game in mid-September against the Nationals, the Florida Marlins draw 600 fans, a number that's probably higher than were actually there. (According to a head count by both teams' managers.) This would be more upsetting if there were not just 300 more people in St. Petersburg for a Rays game just a couple of nights later. The Marlins have won two World Series, by the way. Just to remind you.

After throwing out all the undesirables, Yankee Stadium finally closes its doors in a pointless Sunday night game against the Baltimore Orioles. The Yankees win. Everyone moves on to go next door, to a stadium that's almost an exact replica of the old place, only somehow *more* expensive. (As of press date, there were still five luxury boxes at the new Yankee Stadium at the bargain price of $600,000. Run, don't walk.)

October

For the first time in World Series history, an inning of a game is played by men wearing flippers. Despite a torrential downpour—in which fans in the upper deck reported not being able to see a thing, like they were watching a Fog Bowl—Game 5 of the World Series between the Phillies and the Rays (the Rays made the World Series! Really!) continues into the sixth inning. When B.J. Upton scores the tying run before the game is mercifully suspended, announcers Joe Buck and Tim McCarver keep referring to his "hydroplaning." This is not, in fact, the correct usage of this term, but you're used to that.

The game is delayed two days, and the two teams play the most exciting three and a half innings of baseball in recent memory, ending in a Phillies victory that inspires fans to flip over cars and set things on fire. Deadspin editor A.J. Daulerio, a Phillies fan who was drunk for about three months after the win, reported this sighting: "On my way home last night, I had a bizarre conversation with some drunk guys on South Street who wanted to know where they could get tattoos. I told them to keep heading east on South and they said. "We don't want tattoos from no mooks" and I said "I don't know what that means but it sounds kind of racist. However, if you want tattoos, you should head east till you hit like 4th or 3rd" and then they said "She thinks mooks is racist!...Nah nah, we just don't want to get tattoos from pompous fags." At which point, I said, "Well, I don't really know about that either, but if you want a tattoo, you should head east until 3rd or 4th" Then, they tore a sign off a building and broke it.'

Go Phillies!

The 2008 Pujols Awards

by John Brattain

On Jan. 8, 2008, an article on the Hardball Times web site opened with the words: Welcome to the inaugural edition of "The Pujols Awards."

This award is designed to honor (or snark on) the various do-gooders and the ne'er-do-wells involved with the game of baseball. The various heroes of the week will be given an "Albert"—named after the always-superb Albert Pujols. As we know, he is well on his way to the Hall of Fame. His seemed a good name for an award.

Meanwhile, the zeros of a given week will be bestowed with a "Luis." Luis Pujols was a nondescript backup catcher with the Astros, Rangers and Royals with a career line of .193/.240/.260. (That translates into an OPS+ of 44). In 850 career at-bats, he hit six home runs and grounded into 26 double plays. It is nothing personal against Luis Pujols, you understand; it's just that he has the misfortune of sharing a last name with somebody on track to become one of baseball's all-time greats.

As the season wore on, new awards were added: On March 14, commissioner Bud Selig's actions in the aftermath of the Mitchell Report inspired the following:

> You may think you have the authority to do it, but if there were an honest bone in your body you would realize that you have no moral authority to do so. The sins of the players are misdemeanors compared to yours. You should judge accordingly and listen to Mitchell's recommendation.
>
> In honor of Bud's level of depravity, I am adding a new dimension to the Pujols Awards. Every week that goes on where he doesn't implement Mitchell's suggestion of amnesty he gets "The Bud." If he suspends one more player based on the Mitchell Report, "The Bud" becomes a permanent feature (although he'll cease to receive them weekly since he'll be permanently "honored" by the award's existence).

Selig did implement Mitchell's recommendations, so a change was made on April 18:

> Well, "The Bud" is kaput. Before you start tossing around party favors and cueing up Kool and the Gang's "Celebration," bear in mind that we're talking about the award and not the commissioner. Bud Selig finally wised up and implemented George

> Mitchell's recommendation not to punish players named in his report.
>
> I am a man of my word.
>
> There is a void, however (besides the one between my ears), and we need to recognize the worst of the worst. I gave this a few seconds hard thought and decided that the new award should recognize those who demonstrate short-sightedness, small thinking, diminutive moral standing, undersized intellectual capacity, and stunted mental and emotional development, those who have stooped so low that they could get their nose hairs caught in their own fly with YKK imprinted on the skin between their nostrils.
>
> This isn't for garden-variety chuckleheadedness—it's for giving I.D. advocates a living example to claim that natural selection is bogus simply by virtue of their continued existence.
>
> Now, who could fit such a description? Who? Who? Who? Who? Who? For the love of God …WHO???
>
> Well, after receiving the criteria from the one side of my brain, the other side of my brain had an epiphany. Angels descended from on high, bathing me in golden light announcing with a trumpet flourish…
>
> (trumpet flourish)
>
> …and a voice that sounded like thunder reverberated with "Thou shalt call thy new award … THE SAMSONS!!!'"

Finally, on May 2, following a suggestion from a reader (wishing to be be identified only as "Jake") that disputed the award of a Luis:

> Then (Jake) dropped a comment in passing that caught my attention … here it is in full: "haha, okay, point taken—still I'm not sure if it's worthy of a Luis. Maybe a Manny being Manny award?"
>
> I felt I had struck gold.

So, here we are. It's time to wrap up the 2008 "Pujols Awards" with the best of the best and worst of the worst. On Aug. 27, I asked readers to vote, ranking the various persons who were nominated for The Albert, The

Luis, The "Manny being Manny" and The Samson (nee "The Bud"). Unfortunately, the reader input just wasn't there. What was received will be used as we recap who shone like stars and who sucked like black holes; who sped like an F1 and who sucked like an F5, who basked in the limelight and who asked for a nightlight.

The Alberts

We have four finalists for the Albert: Josh Hamilton, Marvin Miller, Jamie Moyer and oddly enough, Albert Pujols himself.

Josh Hamilton

A first round draft pick of the Tampa Bay Rays in 1999 and highly touted prospect, Hamilton fell into a trap that sadly claims too many young people: substance abuse. Fortunately, Hamilton was able to extract himself from the iron grip of crack cocaine. He also managed to resurrect his promising career in 2007, posting an OPS+ of 131 in 90 games while hitting 19 homers for the Cincinnati Reds. Traded to the Texas Rangers for Edinson Volquez, Hamilton captured the nation's imagination with a breakout 32 homer, 138 OPS+ season that included a memorable performance in the All-Star Game's home run derby in Yankee Stadium.

Marvin Miller

If anyone deserves a spot in Cooperstown for his positive contributions to the game of baseball, it's the fomer executive director of the Major League Baseball Players Association, Marvin Miller. However, voting for the Hall often has been more about politics than excellence, as evidenced by the induction of those with a far smaller footprint in the sands of the game than him.

Bill Baer of the Phillies blog "Crashburn Alley" (http://crashburnalley.com/) wrote in his nomination of Miller at the end of May:

"For sending a well-deserved middle finger to the Baseball Writers Association of America and the baseball Hall of Fame. Miller wrote a letter requesting that his name be taken off ... ballots following three failures to get nominated in 2003 and 2007, and again recently. There's nothing you can do but give a standing ovation to Miller for not pulling any punches":

The antiunion bias of the powers who control the hall has consistently prevented recognition of the historic significance of the changes to baseball brought about by collective bargaining. As former executive director (retired since 1983) of the players'

union that negotiated these changes, I find myself unwilling to contemplate one more rigged veterans committee whose members are handpicked to reach a particular outcome while offering the pretense of a democratic vote. It is an insult to baseball fans, historians, sports writers and especially to those baseball players who sacrificed and brought the game into the 21st century. At the age of 91, I can do without farce.

Miller may never be given his rightful place in the Hall of Fame but the Hall needs Miller far more than he needs the Hall.

Jamie Moyer

In 1992, Moyer looked like he was finished as a big league player, having gone unsigned by every major league team. He had a career 34-54 record with a 4.56 ERA (in 1991 Moyer posted a 5.74 ERA when league average was 3.69). His was a common story ... someone just not good enough to compete at the sport's highest levels.

In 1993, the Baltimore Orioles took a flyer on the 30-year-old southpaw, and he responded with a 12-9, 3.43 ERA (130 ERA+) campaign. Fifteen years later, on May 21, 2008, Moyer won his 200th game since the season in which he turned 30. He's added 12 more to that total since and is now among the top 10 in baseball history in wins since that point of their careers.

Every other pitcher in the top 10 is in the Hall of Fame or a mortal lock. He has more wins since the season he turned 30 than ageless wonders Roger Clemens, Greg Maddux and Nolan Ryan. He has pitched 3,046.2 innings over that span and is 212-131, 4.10 ERA. Since the season in which he turned 40, Moyer is 82-60, 4.29 ERA in 1,224 innings.

With three innings in 2009, he will tie Cy Young for fifth place in post-40 innings pitched and with 122.1 innings next season will be third in baseball history in that category. After age 40, he is third in wins and fourth in winning percentage in modern history. He is 10th in ERA among the over-40 set during the expansion era, but has more innings pitched than any among the top 10 except Phil Niekro, Hoyt Wilhelm and Nolan Ryan (and will pass Ryan with 47.2 innings next season).

Since he was traded to the Phillies in August 2006 and began pitching home games in hitter-friendly Citizens Bank Park, Moyer is 35-21 with a 4.31 ERA in 447 innings. From July 1 to the end of the season in 2008,

Moyer averaged six innings per start and was 9-1 with a 3.28 ERA.

Adding to the luster of his career is that he has won the NL East division-clinching game the last two seasons in, respectively, the final and penultimate games of the year, and posted a 0.79 ERA in those contests.

As amazing as it may seem, he may hang around the Hall of Fame ballot for quite some time and may even make it should he add a couple of years of similar work.

Albert Pujols

While he should win the NL MVP this season, his actions off the field (See: Weeks 14, 19-20, and July of the Pujols Awards on the web site) demonstrate that his excellence does not end when he is not between the white lines. Whether it's being a team leader by treating rookies well, his concern for other (teams') players' well-being or giving high school athletes a memorable experience, the Cardinals' first baseman consistently demonstrates that his gifts do not end with his hand-eye coordination or his fast-twitch muscles.

Winner: Jamie Moyer.

Runner up: Albert Pujols.

Honorable mention: While he is not officially a finalist, I received a torrent of late nominations for CC Sabathia. After acquiring Sabathia, the Brewers went 40-32 but CC was 11-2 (1.72 ERA) over his 16 starts. When the Brewers started to scuffle, Sabathia pitched on three days rest three straight times and threw 21.2 innings of 0.83 ERA ball, culminating in a complete game win against the Cubs on the season's final day, giving the Brewers the NL Wild Card. It also gave Sabathia the major league lead in complete games with 10.

The Luis

Here is where things get tough. Where does one even begin narrowing the field? Well, we did manage to whittle down the list to four finalists:

Elijah Dukes

Most stressed out parents (is there any other kind?) have probably threatened to "kill" their kids at some point. Generally, "kill" is synonymous with grounding, revocation of some privilege or losing video games for a period of time. In Elijah Dukes' world, threatening to kill your children means just that. Dukes' now notorious threat: *"It's on, dawg. You dead, dawg.... Your kids too, dawg. It don't even matter to me who is in the car with you*

(and it gets worse, even with every-few-words expletives deleted)" is proof that he should look into getting a restraining order against natural selection.

He should have been a candidate for the Samson, but alas, his transgressions predated the creation of the award.

The New York Mets

Another tidal wave of last minute (heck, last *second*) nominations pushed the New York Mets into the finals, having lost a playoff berth at home for the second season in a row against the Florida Marlins.

On Sept. 10, the Mets were 3.5 games up on the Philadelphia Phillies in the NL East. In 2007; they were up seven games with 17 to play. Since those points in those seasons, the Mets are 12-22. Over those same stretches, the Phillies are 25-7. While it's easy to talk of Mets collapses, it should not be forgotten that the Phillies played exceptionally well and as much can be said about that as any lack of clutch ability on the part of the Metropolitans.

Regardless, it is hard not to feel bad for fans of the team—no fans should have to experience that kind of heartbreak two seasons in a row.

Jim Pohlad

Pohlad stated about Johan Santana: "It's about what each party wants, and it's different in some cases. There's loyalty and wanting to stay in Minnesota, and it varies from player to player." It is nice to see he has his father's sense of avarice. The Pohlads were so loyal to Minnesota that they threatened for years to either relocate the club or contract it if they did not receive several hundred million dollars of corporate welfare.

Not content with being among the richest people in America, he now implies that a person who would have spent 13 years in professional baseball honing his skills, who had suffered the aches and pains and ups and downs that come with the territory only to become one of the few that actually get to the point where they could test the market and see what their skills are worth, should now subsidize him out of a sense of loyalty to a fan base that he himself never demonstrated?

Uh huh.

When his magical left arm wears down, you can bet that fans will show him little loyalty and will clamor for his de facto firing so someone else can have his job.

Stop listening to the misguided media or greedy wealthy people looking for a subsidy from the working man. It is bad enough the locals gave the Pohlads a fortune in free money—now they have the gall to ask a man from Venezuela to spot them a few million that would not be put back into the roster but rather right back into their bank accounts.

Ugh.

MLB and the media

I think most can agree that Barry Bonds is not the most pleasant sort. I think it is obvious that folks wanted him out of the game. In time it will be revealed whether collusion occurred in this instance, but regardless, Major League Baseball blew it with Bonds on two counts:

If MLB officials wanted him out so badly, they should have had the courage of their convictions and made a statement by suspending him and presenting their evidence for their actions for public scrutiny. Have a hearing, give the man baseball's version of due process and let it be known that playing in the major leagues is a privilege and certain actions will simply not be tolerated.

Baseball has employed some disagreeable cranks over the years and taken flyers on some pretty desperate players in attempts to win. While clubs made a lot of noise about Bonds' age (see: Jamie Moyer above), health (see: Moises Alou), legal issues (irrelevant in 2008) or his general character (see: Elijah Dukes above) a number of teams gave either collusion or a misguided sense of PR a higher priority than winning ballgames. It may have made a difference to a lot of clubs' postseason chances, including the Mets, Twins and Blue Jays.

Teams were afraid that signing Bonds would turn off the fan base? He packed ballparks both home and away in 2007 but would empty them in 2008?

The media made it easier for teams to just say no by indirectly threatening to disrupt the clubhouse of any team employing him—after all, it was the media members themselves saying that his presence would create a media circus. Chances are good they could make this prediction come true. Bonds brought a lot of this upon himself, but neither MLB nor the media have acquitted themselves well. It's a shame that the one group is allowed to stand in judgment of the other.

Even we fans aren't completely innocent. Where was our sense of outrage when we flocked en masse to watch him chase Hank Aaron? Now that we have received what

we wanted, we choose to find our conscience? Nobody came out of this smelling like a rose, but only one man paid the price for the transgressions of so many.

Winner: Elijah Dukes.

Runner-up: Those amazing Mets (again).

The Manny being Manny

There were only two finalists in this category. Not surprisingly, one of them was the Man(ny) himself.

Mariah Carey

She can throw a tantrum, she can throw a hissy fit, but can she throw a baseball? Mariah Carey was invited to throw out the first pitch in a game in Tokyo and appeared in a getup that most hookers would be hard pressed to top. It was amazing that she could even breathe let alone throw, and now the credit crisis isn't the only instance of mass suffering America has inflicted on the folks of the Land of the Rising Sun in the last 65 years.

Evidently she misunderstood and imagined her ears told her that folks associated her with being "a classic pitch" so often that she felt qualified to deliver the first "skank ball" in the history of the game. The aftermath was not pretty: There were unconfirmed reports that the remains of Kenesaw Mountain Landis emerged from his eternal repose, lurched himself to the right field position at Safeco Field and did his impression of Thich Quang Duc in protest.

Her fashion designer should be tried for crimes against humanity.

Manny Ramirez

Joseph Lavalle will go down in history as the man who cast the tie-breaking vote in a category decided by a single vote. His nomination of Ramirez's high-fiving a fan before completing a double play earlier this season put him over the top over the inventor of the "skank ball."

Winner: Manny Ramirez.

Runner-up: Mariah Carey

The Samsons

Without a doubt, this was the most hotly contested final among readers. When it comes to creating the stench of a just-opened exhumed casket, few are as proficient as the movers and shakers of major league baseball. Our lower than the low include:

Scott Boras

If one thing came out of the whole Pedro Alvarez debacle, it was this: It wasn't about the best interests of Alvarez but rather Scott Boras. The difference he was seeking between what was initially agreed to by Pittsburgh draft choice Alvarez and the total Boras wanted to renegotiate for could be made up by the Vanderbilt star reaching the major leagues six months earlier—close to the development time lost by Boras' gambit.

However, the difference between negotiating the second highest and highest bonus in the draft is of immeasurable value to Boras. After all, why go through all the headaches that retaining Boras can cause if you can get as good or better money with other representation, with only a fraction of the grief and hits to your reputation?

Scott Boras put his own career and interests—in this case, his ongoing battle to dismantle the draft—ahead of his client, a naïve kid from Washington Heights, N.Y.

His Samson doesn't end there, either.

What has to be remembered is precisely why the New York Yankees won 22 of 29 pennants between 1936-64, a run of dominance that almost killed off the American League. The Yankees had access to the best amateur talent on an annual basis. Their revenues allowed them to outbid every other AL team in signing the best and brightest prospects. The only thing that could keep a top amateur out of the organization's grasp was (1) New York's scouting department missed him or (2) the youngster simply did not care to play for the Yankees.

The Yankees' hold on the AL was broken in part by the introduction of the draft.

Now Boras wants to return to the good old days when the richest clubs could always have first dibs on the best talent; from 1936-64 they had it through the lack of a draft and the ability to buy the best players from cash-strapped teams. Boras' dream is to allow that through free agency and no draft. It doesn't matter to Boras that his dream could ruin competitive balance, just so long as he can become still wealthier—it's all good to him.

Stephen Lenhart submitted the following on Boras:

Scott Boras has to be the Luis Pujols of the year, for agreeing to sign client Pedro Alvarez to the Pirates at a $6 million bonus and then demanding that the contract be renegotiated. It's a gross breach of contract (verbal contracts are legally binding), which, if it were to set a precedent, would seriously undermine the ability of players and teams to make deadline deals over the phone, thousands of miles from each other, where there may be little ability to sign physical documents to certify the terms of the contract.

Sad as it is to say, I can't say it would be all bad if the talented Mr. Alvarez lost a year of professional playing time as a result of this—he doesn't deserve it, but a message needs to be sent that this sort of behavior is unacceptable, and if you choose to work with an agent that conducts himself in this fashion, you may be the loser.

The Washington Nationals

Probably one of the most disturbing trends of modern society is how such a sizeable chunk of taxes paid by the citizenry isn't used for the public well being, but rather simply funnelled by various parties into the pockets of the wealthiest people in the country. Professional sports, sadly, has been no exception to this trend—what is worse is that not only do they not feel any remorse over the fact that they're depriving the average person (especially children) of essential services such as education and health care just to pad their bottom lines, *they actually feel they're entitled to it!*

The media like to speak of the attitude of entitlement on the part of professional athletes, but it is nothing in comparison to the attitudes of those owning the clubs. This was no more obvious than in the case of the Washington Nationals. After getting more than $600 million in public money to build Nationals Park, plus the right to keep the revenues generated by the facility, the Nats started to use the park and collect those juicy revenues from luxury seating and overpriced concessions and various shops within the building.

Then, claiming that the ballpark that they didn't pay for but get to make money on wasn't completed in time, not only are they not paying their rent ($3.5 million ... a little more than what they're paying Chad Cordero on the 60-day DL), they're demanding $100,000 a day in damages dating back to the beginning of March.

Evidently the team thought the park was sufficiently complete to open to the paying public. What the Nationals are saying is that it was complete enough to begin earning profits, but not complete enough that they're obligated to pay rent. It was complete enough to be able to use all the new revenue steams, but so incomplete that they feel they've suffered more than $21 million in monetary damages.

Of course, the team expects the taxpayers—many of whom have no interest in the Nats—to pick up the tab. So what if it means cuts to schools or health care. I coined a little ditty in May about this:

Take me out to the Bud-park

Take me out to get screwed

We built their park with rev-en-ue streams

It's just the start of our get-ting reamed

Since they root-root-root through our pockets

If they miss a dime it's a shock

For it's one, two, three hundred clams

At the old Bud-park!

Mike Ilitch and Detroit politicians

"Every prostitute receives a fee, but you give gifts to all your lovers, bribing them to come to you from everywhere for your illicit favors. So in your prostitution you are the opposite of others; no one runs after you for your favors. You are the very opposite, for you give payment and none is given to you."

—Ezekiel 16:33-34

About 2,600 years ago, an old Hebrew man must have had a vision of Mike Ilitch's relationship with Detroit politicians. Former Mayor Kwame Kilpatrick and his predecessor Dennis Archer played the role of the shekel-dispensing whores to their owner Ilitch and made up an unholy trinity consisting of The Plotter, The Bum and the Sorry Half-wit.

If they get their way, all that will come of the corner of Michigan and Trumbull is another vacant lot. However, in Ilitch's eyes an empty space holds no threat to his financial empire, whereas he wanted to make sure that nobody with a capitalistic bent (verboten in Ilitch's monopolistic domain known as Detroit) could put a minor league/independent league team in the ballyard.

Politicians, ideally, should be serving the public interest and a good, honest entrepreneurial spirit is good for all. As we outlined in the section regarding the Nationals, however, it seems politicos are more beholden to their corporate masters, as can be seen in taxing the gentry and forwarding the proceeds to their overlords.

Throughout the year, I described many team owners as insatiable fiscal succubi as their greed destroys what is precious to so many just so they can have even more than they already possess. The fact is that people who pledged to serve the needs of the electorate in reality serve only those whose contributions finance their elections to office, where they can enjoy the privilege of being the conduit between taxpayer and billionaire that funnels billions to these black holes of avarice.

What makes the situation in Motown so disgusting is that the city picked up a large chunk of Comerica Park's tab for Ilitch, paid Ilitch about $400,000 a year to maintain (read: allow to rot) Tiger Stadium after the team left and now will gladly pick up the tab to destroy a landmark if nobody commits to developing/saving part of the park.

Winner: (Tie) Washington Nationals and Mike Ilitch and Detroit politicians.

Honorable mention: Bill Bavasi

Aaron Whitehead of Somerset, Kentucky and owner of the blog "The Whiz Kid's Baseball Wisdom" (http://whizball.blogspot.com/) submitted the following:

But the worst part of this whole tragedy (The Mariners) has been management's response. Manager John McLaren chewed the team out yesterday, and team president Chuck Armstrong tore into the coaching staff (Armstrong refused to specify his comments for the record). McLaren's outburst is understandable, especially since the team's disappointment puts his ass on the line.

But the most despicable of all was general manager Bill Bavasi, who ordered the players to sit in front of their lockers and take responsibility for the team's poor play. Here's how the espn.com report describes it:

"Before McLaren went off, Bavasi ordered each of the 25 Mariners players to sit at his locker immediately after the game to take full responsibility publicly for having the worst record in the major leagues despite a $117 million payroll that is just below the richest in baseball."

Who in the hell does Bill Bavasi think he is to make 25 baseball players take responsibility for his incompetence? Bill, did Carlos Silva force you to sign him to a stupid contract? Did Miguel Batista? Was Mark Lowe or Brad Wilkerson responsible for hiring the obviously overmatched McLaren as interim manager and then keeping him on the job after a dismal 2007 finish?

The full article is at: http://whizball.blogspot.com/2008/06/i-am-ozzie-hear-me-roar.html.

There you have it: the best, the worst, the funniest and the sleaziest of the 2008 baseball season. Thanks to all who contributed. A special shout out goes to Bill Baer of Crashburn Alley and Baseball Digest Daily and eTrueSports' Frank Coffey, who were the top two submitters of nominations.

Where the Devil did These Rays Come From?...

by Steve Treder

No one in the world saw this coming.

Oh, sure, most observers understood that the 2008 Tampa Bay Rays were likely to be better than their 2007 edition, and some even predicted that they would, for the first time, break the .500 barrier. Perhaps they'd even be on the fringes of contention. But nobody anticipated that the '08 Rays would be *this* good.

And nobody should be faulted for this. Because, come on, not only were the 2007 Rays really lousy—66-96, last place and deserving it, with a Pythagorean record of 67-95—but this was an organization that had never produced anything *but* lousy teams. In the team's entire 10-year history, Tampa Bay never had lost fewer than 91 games, finishing last in nine of those seasons, delivering an average record of 65-97. For a team with such a record to suddenly bust out to a 97-65 performance, not just winning its division but doing so by surpassing the Yankees and the Red Sox, whose combined payrolls outrank the GDP of most medium-sized countries, isn't the sort of thing one can be expected to have seen coming.

Which raises the question: Just how far out of the ordinary was the dramatic arrival of the 2008 Rays?

Let's find out.

I searched the record book (well, actually it was Baseball Reference, but you know what I mean) and identified every team since 1900 that performed a feat comparable to that of the '08 Rays.

I calculated improvement in raw wins and losses, winning percentage and position in the standings, looking at the difference between the current year and each of the previous five seasons. The reason for including the seasons previous to the most recent year is that it removes from consideration teams that were bouncing back from an isolated bad year or two. To balance the significance of single-year improvement and improvement over a sustained period, I double-weighted the difference between the current year and the most recent year.

After exhaustively searching, I whittled the list down to the ballclubs in history that pulled off the very most significant improvements. Where do our boys from Tampa-St. Pete rank on the all-time Most Surprising list?

Wins and Losses

First, let's consider the placement of the Rays regarding improvement in wins and losses. Check it out: We see that the Rays rank at the very top, *numero uno*, of this list. No team in history has ever pulled off an improvement in raw wins and losses as out-of-nowhere as the 2008 Tampa Bay Rays:

Improvement in Wins and Losses

Rank	Team	W-L
1.	2008 TAMPA BAY RAYS	31.4
2.	1969 New York Mets	30.5
3.	1991 Atlanta Braves	29.6
4.	1914 Boston Braves	29.5
5.	1912 Washington Senators	29.3

That's right, in this regard the devilish-no-more 2008 AL East champs outdid both the 1969 "Miracle Mets" and the 1914 "Miracle Braves," along with every other contender. How come nobody's been calling these guys the "Miracle Rays"?

Percentage

But the sheer total of wins and losses might be a bit misleading, given that the length of the regular season schedule hasn't been constant throughout history, and strikes have shortened seasons from time to time as well. So instead of raw wins and losses, next let's compile the list of the all-time greatest teams on the basis of improvement in winning percentage:

Improvement in Winning Percentage

Rank	Team	Pct.
1T.	2008 TAMPA BAY RAYS	.194
1T.	1914 Boston Braves	.194
3.	1912 Washington Senators	.192
4.	1969 New York Mets	.188
5.	1991 Atlanta Braves	.183

The 1914 Braves are able to match the 2008 Rays on this metric, but no one has ever topped them.

Position in Standings

All right, then how about improvement against competitors in the standings? Certainly moving from last to first in a five-team division isn't quite as difficult or unusual as leaping from the bottom to the top of a larger aggregation, such as a six-team division, or an eight-team or 10-team league. How do our Floridian friends measure up on that scale?

Improvement in Position in Standings

Rank	Team	Pos.
1.	1969 New York Mets	8.2
2.	1967 Boston Red Sox	7.8
3.	1967 Chicago Cubs	6.4
4T.	1912 Washington Senators	5.1
4T.	1958 Pittsburgh Pirates	5.1
4T.	1991 Minnesota Twins	5.1
7.	1991 Atlanta Braves	5.0
8.	1914 Boston Braves	4.8
9.	1944 St. Louis Browns	4.7
10.	1993 Philadelphia Phillies	4.5
11.	1934 Detroit Tigers	4.2
12.	1984 Chicago Cubs	4.1
13.	2008 TAMPA BAY RAYS	4.0
14.	1939 Cincinnati Reds	3.8
15.	1990 Pittsburgh Pirates	3.6

Ah, here the Rays aren't quite so miraculous. I've expanded the list here to show the top 15 teams, and we see that our Rays drop all the way down to 13th, while the '69 Mets—benefitting from making their leap in the same season the league went from a single 10-team configuration to a six-team-division arrangement—score top honors.

Still, while Tampa Bay falls back, let's not forget that the Rays' performance on this metric is the 13th-best of all time; their standings improvement has been one of the greatest in history.

Total Improvement

So let's put it all together, combining the wins-losses, percentage and position improvements into an aggregate comparison. I've counted the average rank in wins-losses and percentage together, and then averaged that total against the position in the standings.

Here we see the top 10 Most Surprising list:

Rank	Team	W+Pct Rank	Pos Rank	Total Rank
1	1969 New York Mets	3	1	4
2	1912 Washington Senators	4	5	9
3	1914 Boston Braves	2.75	8	10.75
4	1991 Atlanta Braves	4	7	11
5	1967 Chicago Cubs	11	3	14
6	2008 TAMPA BAY RAYS	1.25	13	14.25
7	1934 Detroit Tigers	6.25	11	17.25
8	1967 Boston Red Sox	16	2	18
9	1993 Philadelphia Phillies	8.75	10	18.75
10	1958 Pittsburgh Pirates	14	5	19

Alas, our Rays remain eclipsed, placing sixth on the all-time list. Not having had the opportunity to finish worse than fifth place in their division has proven to be their undoing in this comparison—though one certainly got the feeling, in watching the pre-2008 Tampa Bay ball clubs, that they could have finished a whole lot worse than fifth if just given the chance.

And in any case, what this exercise vividly demonstrates is that the sudden improvement of the 2008 Rays was indeed something very rare. Only a very few ball clubs in the long history of the sport have achieved any better.

Who Were These Guys?

It's worth taking a closer look at those few ball clubs that out-surprised the Rays.

I suspect everyone is at least reasonably familiar with the No. 1 team on the list, the 1969 New York Mets. One of the most famous ballclubs of all time, the significance of their ugly-duckling-into-swan transformation from laughingstock to World Champion was amplified by taking place in media-saturated New York, and in the television age.

The '69 Mets had just one superstar in Cy Young Award-winner Tom Seaver, but Tom Terrific's supporting cast was strong, led by fellow starting pitcher Jerry Koosman, ace reliever Tug McGraw, defensive whiz center fielder Tommie Agee and heavy-hitting left fielder Cleon Jones. The team was deftly managed by the calm, sure Gil Hodges, cleverly platooning at several positions.

But almost none of us are familiar with the 1912 Washington Senators; before undertaking this study, I sure wasn't. Their obscurity is assured by a host of "nots": not in New York, not in the television age, not even in the radio age. What's more, they were not a pennant winner in their breakthrough season of 1912, finishing in second place, at 91-61.

But this 91-61 performance was a 28-game improvement over 1911. Moreover, since the creation of the franchise in 1901 they'd never come close to finishing .500, and had been in last place or next-to-last every season since 1903. The 1912 blossoming came with the arrival of dynamic manager Clark Griffith (who would later become owner of the franchise), and especially the phenomenal pitching of 24-year-old fastballing sensation Walter Johnson. He catapulted into superstardom with 33 wins, leading the league in ERA, strikeouts and almost everything else.

The "Miracle" 1914 Boston Braves not only won the pennant after having finished last in four of the previous five years, but also after having been in last place as late as July 18 of 1914. They topped that off with another stunner in the World Series, sweeping Connie Mack's heavily-favored Athletics, the World Series champs in three of the previous four years.

The Braves were a team without a superstar; the only Hall of Famers on their roster were second baseman Johnny Evers and shortstop Rabbit Maranville, both very fine ballplayers but dubiously deserving of Cooperstown. Appropriately, manager George Stallings received enormous credit for the team's success; for the rest of his life he would be known as "The Miracle Man."

The Braves of 1991, by now in Atlanta, are likely well-remembered. This team had been patiently built by Bobby Cox as the general manager since 1985; Cox had moved to the field manager role in mid-1990, with John Schuerholz taking over as GM that fall. The '91 Braves were paced by MVP third baseman Terry Pendleton (signed as a free agent in one of Schuerholz' first moves), center fielder Ron Gant, and 25-year-old ace pitcher Tom Glavine, achieving the first of his five 20-game-winning seasons. This Atlanta team, in last place in 1988, 1989 and 1990, got as far as the 10th inning of the seventh game of the 1991 World Series before finally succumbing to the Twins in a 1-0 shutout by Jack Morris, one of the greatest Game 7s in history.

For the 1967 Chicago Cubs, it was the manager who was seen as the primary ingredient of breakout success: Leo "The Lip" Durocher, who'd taken over the team a year earlier after a decade-long absence from the managerial ranks. The Cubs didn't win the pennant in 1967—as every Cubs fan is only too aware, they still haven't found a way to pull that off since 1945—but their 87-74, third-place finish was far and away the best the franchise had achieved in more than 20 years. The '67 Cubs' best player, third baseman Ron Santo, is not in the Hall of Fame, but three other key contributors to their success are: ace pitcher Ferguson Jenkins, left fielder Billy Williams and first baseman Ernie Banks.

Might there be something about the 2008 Tampa Bay ball club that's similar to these other tremendous improvers, not just in the scale of their leap, but in the construction of their roster?

Why don't we first consider a very basic issue …

Age

Let's examine these all-time great improvers from the standpoint of how much youth they feature in the lineup. Using the Batting Age and Pitching Age stats as calculated by Baseball Reference:

Team	B Age	Rank	P Age	Rank
1969 Mets	25.9	1/12	25.8	3/12
1912 Senators	25.9	2/8	25.7	3/8
1914 Braves	25.7	1/8	25.2	3/8
1991 Braves	28.0	3/12	27.1	3/12
1967 Cubs	27.6	6/10	25.1	1/10
Average	26.6	2.6/10	25.8	2.6/10
2008 RAYS	27.0	2/14	27.5	3/14

Isn't this interesting: a clear and consistent similarity is apparent. They're all very young teams, in both halves of the inning. In only one of the instances (the 1967 Cubs' hitting) is one of these teams anything but younger than its league norm, and the '67 Cubs were just barely above it—while deploying a pitching staff that's the youngest of all we see.

And this pattern is strongly replicated by the '08 Rays, one of the youngest teams in baseball today.

So youth seems to trump experience in the makeup of these suddenly good ball clubs. In what other ways might these teams exhibit some distinctive traits?

Hitting/Pitching/Fielding

Well, now, how about about this. All of the top-five teams in the next table turn out to be variations on a distinct theme: these aren't big-hitting teams; their success is a function of pitching and defense. And look how closely that pattern is matched by the 2008 Tampa Bay Rays: a decent-hitting team, but nothing special in

Team	OPS+	Rank	ERA+	Rank	DER	Rank
1969 Mets	93	10/12	122	1/12	.728	1/12
1912 Senators	93	4/8	125	1/8	.678	3/8
1914 Braves	99	5.5/8	104	2/8	.703	4/8
1991 Braves	104	3/12	112	2/12	.713	1/12
1967 Cubs	102	6/10	102	5/10	.717	2/10
Average	98	3/10	113	1/10	.708	2.2/10
2008 RAYS	103	5/14	114	2.5/14	.708	1/14

that regard, while presenting outstanding pitching and outstanding fielding.

Matthew Carruth's companion article in this book examines in detail the manner in which Rays GM Andrew Friedman and field manager Joe Maddon made run prevention (specifically focusing on defense up the middle, and the bullpen) the No. 1 priority for 2008. It seems they were on to something significant.

Okay, let's consider one final aspect of these teams.

Manager

Manager	Age	Tenure	Prior career
Hodges	45	2nd yr	1 team, 5 yrs, 0 pennants
Griffith	42	1st yr	3 teams, 11 yrs, 1 pennant
Stallings	46	2nd yr	3 teams, 4+ yrs, 0 pennants
Cox	50	1st full yr	2 teams, 8 yrs, 1 division title
Durocher	61	2nd yr	2 teams, 16 yrs, 3 pennants, 1 WS
Maddon	53	3rd yr	2 teams, 51 interim games, 0 titles

There isn't complete consistency here. Durocher is the outlier: significantly older than the rest, and the only one considered a star manager at the time he was hired (though not having been offered a manager's job in 10 years had dimmed his luster). But otherwise, Durocher conforms to a pattern: none were rookie managers, and all achieved the rags-to-riches breakthrough quickly, within their first or second year of tenure except Maddon, who's done it in his third season in Tampa Bay.

In terms of interpersonal style, there isn't a clear conclusion to draw. Few managers have been more fiery than Durocher, and few more stoic than Hodges. Between those temperamental poles, the rest fall at various points along the spectrum: Cox isn't as volatile as Durocher, but has his tempestuous side; Stallings,

whose other nickname was "Gentleman George," was closer to Hodges in manner; and Griffith, widely admired for his intelligence and integrity, was neither quiet nor raucous.

For his part, Maddon is definitely on the easygoing side, and more cerebral than emotional.

Lessons

First of all, if the team you root for is a tail-ender punching bag year after year—well, I hate to have to break it to you, but you're in deep doo-doo in more ways than one. Not only are you getting drubbed today, but history distinctly shows that the likelihood of your team suddenly busting out as a champ overnight is extremely low.

It happens once in a while, but the sort of "worst to first" blossoming along the lines of what Tampa Bay performed in 2008 is very rare. Inasmuch as the Rays' performance specifically ranks as the sixth most surprising since 1900, it's reasonable to conclude that we can expect to see something like this about once every 15 or 20 years. Those aren't good betting odds.

But if your ball club does endeavor to pull off a Rays-like longshot leapfrog maneuver, history provides a few suggestions as to how to go about it. If your manager has been in place for more than two or three years, replacing him might be in order, as it seems that the environment-altering effect of a new or fairly new manager is important. This new manager shouldn't be a rookie, but it also seems best that he still has something to prove in his managerial career. Whether his style leans toward back-patting or butt-kicking doesn't appear to be a crucial factor.

As for mode of play, it would seem that the key is to be found in run prevention more than run generation. The few teams that have been such sensational surprises have stifled rather than bludgeoned opponents, and the team displaying the single most extraordinary improvement in history—the 1969 Mets—was the most extremely pitching-and-fielding-oriented of this select bunch. Obviously, every ball club should always be striving to improve in every facet of its game, but facing reality is often a function of setting priorities and sticking to them. A maxim for a team seeking to beat long odds might be that the best offense is a good defense.

And finally, having a very young team is also crucial in overcoming those daunting probabilities. This one might seem rather obvious, given that young players are far more likely than veterans to make dramatic year-to-year improvement. Moreover, agile youngsters tend to play defense better than heftier, slower veterans, and fine fielding is at the heart of these out-of-nowhere cases.

Yet though the youth-is-essential concept might be obvious, consider how often it is that we see the GM of a long-suffering franchise attempting—or at least being pressured by local media—to enact a "quick fix" improvement through the importation of "proven veteran" talent, especially of the slow-footed power-hitting mode. Such a blueprint is vividly not what the 2008 Tampa Bay Rays followed in achieving their stunning overnight success.

...And How Did They Get Here?

by Matthew Carruth

It's a fascinating look into great management. The 2007 Rays suffered from two massive black holes: their bullpen and their defense. Luckily, those are the two easiest areas to address in major league baseball. Defensive specialists almost universally fly under the radar because good fielding remains criminally undervalued. And far too much stock is put on experience in bullpens, leading to opportunities using converted starters and minor league relievers.

The 2007 Rays managed to have a defense so bad that it eclipsed even the horribleness of the Florida Marlins, who sometimes seemed to be playing the wrong sport entirely. To fix that problem, the Rays made several comprehensive moves. The management moved B.J. Upton, who couldn't handle ground balls, to center field, where his superior speed was of more benefit. Akinori Iwamura moved to the vacant second base position and made room for Evan Longoria, a defensive whiz in his own right, at third. Finally, general manager Andrew Friedman addressed shortstop by shipping prized outfield prospect Delmon Young (and a few others) to Minnesota for starter Matt Garza and shortstop Jason Bartlett, who has an excellent glove.

Almost overnight, the Rays had upgraded the fielding at three infield positions and in center field. It's no fluke that the Rays went from 107 plays below average (according to John Dewan's measurement in the 2008 *Annual*) in 2007 to a positive 34 plays made in the field in 2008 according to this year's findings (see John's article in this *Annual*).

Stop and really consider that for a second. The Rays went from 107 plays below average to 34 above in a single year. That's a difference of 141 plays. The difference between a play made and not made is about 0.8 runs. Therefore, by defense alone, the Rays improved themselves by 113 runs. One hundred and thirteen runs! Manager Joe Maddon said in his now famous "nine equals eight" line that he wanted to see nine more wins from the pitching, from the hitting and from the defense. Well, the defense exceeded its quota.

For the bullpen, the most egregious offenders in 2007 were tossed overboard along with the Devil moniker. Gone from prominent roles were Casey Fossum (5.81 Fielding Independent Pitching), Tim Corcoran (5.92), Shawn Camp (4.98), Juan Salas (6.27), Chad Orvella (10.51), Brian Strokes (5.85) and Jay Witasick (6.32). In came J.P. Howell, Troy Percival and more innings for Grant Balfour. But beyond those three was some better management by Maddon, who avoided giving too many innings to relievers who were hurting the team (aside from Jason Hammel).

Long story shorter, the Rays vastly improved their defense (their biggest weakness in 2007) and jettisoned the worst parts of their bullpen (their second biggest weakness). They imported some new bullpen faces. One of their strategies, a quality approach exemplified by Howell, was to convert starters to relievers.

The 2008 Rays bullpen posted a +10.75 Win Probability Added as a group, the single highest mark in baseball. In fact, according to measurements called tRA at StatCorner.com, the Rays' bullpen was 53 runs more valuable in 2008 than in 2007. Add the 113 runs from defense above and you have 166 runs of improvement on the run prevention side of the ledger. As you'll note from Steve Treder's piece, a dramatic emphasis on enhancing run prevention combined with a young team is pretty much the blueprint for one-year turnarounds.

If Friedman had stopped right there, that would have been a fine enough improvement for one winter, more than enough to get the Rays out of the cellar (remember, they finished 2007 with the worst record in baseball) and around the .500 mark. After all, the 2007 Rays had a run differential of -162 runs, so an addition of 166 runs brings them to break-even.

But those 166 runs don't include the addition of Matt Garza to a 2007 rotation that consisted of James Shields (awesome), Scott Kazmir (incredibly awesome), a bunch of flotsam (incredibly bad) and Andy Sonnanstine. Nobody seemed to appreciate Sonnanstine's performance last year because of an almost unheard-of amount of bad luck. Although he posted a 5.85 ERA, his core performance was very good, as indicated by his 4.35 FIP and 4.42 xFIP.

The rotation improvement meant that even though Kazmir had a mediocre year (for him) with a curiously plunging groundball rate, it was more than offset by Garza and Sonnanstine (who employed a strategy of never throwing pitches outside the strike zone). Furthermore, it meant that instead of a bunch of starts going to Jae Seo, Edwin Jackson, Fossum, Hammel and Howell, the Rays' only wasted starts went to Jackson, who has not yet produced an ounce of good results in six years in the major leagues.

The Rays used other principles and maneuvers to build their roster. Notably, they made shrewd use of the disabled list and were keen on picking up useful depth pieces on the cheap. What they did not do, however, was just rely on a stockpile of talent secured from picking high in the draft year after year, as some pundits would have you believe. Courtesy of the wonderful Cork Gaines at Rays Index, we have a nifty picture of how the core 2008 roster was acquired.

How the Rays Acquired Their Roster

Player	How Acquired
Rocco Baldelli	Draft (1-2000)
B.J. Upton	Draft (1-2002)
Evan Longoria	Draft (1-2006)
Carl Crawford	Draft (2-1999)
Jason Hammel	Draft (10-2002)
Andy Sonnanstine	Draft (13-2004)
James Shields	Draft (16-2000)
Shawn Riggans	Draft (24-2000)
Cliff Floyd	Free Agent
Trever Miller	Free Agent
Troy Percival	Free Agent
Akinori Iwamura	Free Agent
Carlos Pena	Free Agent
Eric Hinske	Free Agent
Juan Salas	International Free Agent
Ben Zobrist	Trade
Chad Bradford	Trade
Dan Wheeler	Trade
Dioner Navarro	Trade

How the Rays Acquired Their Roster

Player	How Acquired
Edwin Jackson	Trade
Gabe Gross	Trade
Grant Balfour	Trade
J.P. Howell	Trade
Jason Bartlett	Trade
Justin Ruggiano	Trade
Matt Garza	Trade
Scott Kazmir	Trade
Willy Aybar	Trade

There's not a lot of first-round talent in there. And just in case you want to claim that the Rays must have used all those fabulous high picks to fund those delicious trades, that's demonstrably untrue as well. As it turns out, the only first-round pick used in a trade was Young, sent packing in the Garza trade. The other members of their rotation came from trades and late-round draft picks. While Longoria and Upton certainly paid heavy dividends in 2008, the minor league pickups of Carlos Pena and Eric Hinske and the bullpen built almost entirely out of trades highlight their enlightened decision making.

So where did all those first round drafts go? Well, thank goodness for Cork Gaines, who gives us this status of the Rays' last 10 first-round draft picks as of September 2008. Consider that, in chronological order, the Rays chose first, sixth, third, second, first, fourth, eighth, third, first and first, and one could argue that this represents a somewhat spotty record of picks. Josh Hamilton never contributed anything to Tampa and the pitchers haven't done much to help yet. Of course, it's not a terrible slate of first round picks either, but the main point is that these 10 consecutive top-10 overall picks are not what built the 2008 Rays into a powerhouse.

The Rays' Last Ten First-Round Draft Picks

Year	Player	Status
1999	Josh Hamilton	Lost in Rule 5 Draft
2000	Rocco Baldelli	Spent most of season on DL
2001	Dewon Brazelton	Out of baseball
2002	B.J. Upton	25-man roster
2003	Delmon Young	Traded to Twins
2004	Jeff Niemann	Currently in Triple-A
2005	Wade Townsend	Currently in Triple-A
2006	Evan Longoria	25-man roster
2007	David Price	Postseason roster
2008	Tim Beckham	Playing in Short-Season A

So where did all these winter moves leave the Rays in the minds of analysts? Well, the Vegas odds didn't put much stock in them, opening their season win line in the low 70s, which was a laughably easy call to take the over on. Even the most pessimistic of sensible projection systems had the Rays as near a .500 team and some were quite a bit more aggressive. Notably, Baseball Prospectus' PECOTA pegged the Rays as an 88-win team. Here at THT, the feelings were mixed but most picked them to finish either third or fourth in a tough AL East division.

The Rays didn't exactly light the world on fire in April. After getting shut out by the White Sox 6-0 on the 20th, Tampa had an 8-11 record and was in a familiar place, last, in the AL East. However, the Rays would close April with a bang, winning seven of their final eight games and ending up in a crowded pack near the top of the division.

May certainly didn't start well either, with a three-game sweep at the hands of the Red Sox in Fenway sucking out the momentum from the end of April. The Rays would quickly recover once they came back home, though, finishing 13-3 in home games during May, including series wins over the Angels, Yankees, Orioles, Rangers and White Sox. All told, the Rays ended May with a 34-22 record and found themselves leading the division by a game.

By a quirk in the schedule, Tampa started another month with a trip up to Fenway. The result was the same: a three-game sweep by the Red Sox. However, the Rays would finish June with a satisfactory 16-10 record and were back atop the division. Each passing day brought them more and more coverage as the media kept wondering when they would fade.

It wasn't going to happen. The Fourth of July triggered the resurgence of Carlos Pena, who had gotten off to a slow start. But he turned his .778 OPS before the All-Star break into a .978 OPS after, a transformation that helped the Rays during some rough patches. July also meant it was time to play the Red Sox again. This time it was home in Tampa and again the home team held serve as the Rays swept the Sox out of town. After taking the first three from the Royals immediately after, the Rays had a whopping five-game lead in the East. At that point, Cool Standings gave the Rays an 84 percent probability of making the playoffs, but still the predominant vibe from the media was disbelief.

That disbelief seemed founded when an extra-innings loss to the Royals that ended the Rays' seven-game winning streak touched off a seven-game losing streak that was halted only by the All-Star break. The Rays were now out of first place. With a four-day layoff between games, the young team had to sit through a number of stories dismissing their second-half chances.

This Rays came out of the break taking their first two series and reclaimed first place. In fact, Tampa wouldn't drop any series the rest of July nor a single one in August, posting an obscene 21-7 mark in that month that left them 33 games over .500 and 5.5 games up in the division. The media had wondered whether the Rays were for real. The Rays had answered the question.

September wasn't a spectacular month for the Rays, who went only 13-12, but they did enough to hold off Boston for the division crown. A postseason berth was all but assured by the time they entered the month anyway, as Tampa held an eight-game lead over the wild card leader. All in all, the Rays, like so many other teams in 2008, enjoyed tremendous success at home, 57-24 at Tropicana Field in Tampa, but were just 40-41 away from it. They played only about .500 against division mates Toronto, Boston and New York, but they feasted on the Orioles, with a 15-3 record.

Tampa entered the playoffs for the first time in 2008 and what a way to have done it, going from the majors' worst record in 2007 to its third best, a 31-game improvement. The players will get their credit, and Maddon has been widely and rightfully praised. But don't forget the front office management that assembled the team. And not just Friedman (though he deserves a lot of credit). Add senior vice president Gerry Hunsicker and president Matthew Silverman, as well as controlling owner Stu Sternberg, who put those people in their roles.

Below them are the myriad analysts the Rays have hired. It's been a collective effort that has done a marvelous job of turning around what was a short time ago one of baseball's most inept franchises.

Trades of the Midseason

by Rob Neyer

Baseball writers have short memories.

Most of them, anyway. When midseason acquisitions CC Sabathia and Manny Ramirez both shattered all reasonable expectations with their new teams, the scribes rushed to judgment. But were they really the greatest midseason acquisitions *ever*? When considering other candidates, some of the scribes' memories stretched all the way back to 1998 (Randy Johnson) or 1993 (Fred McGriff), and a few of the old timers even recalled those prehistoric days of 1984, when Rick Sutcliffe began the season in the American League and wound up as the National League's Cy Young Award winner.

Contending teams began making big trades long before 1984. It's obvious that Manny being Manny and CC being CC were incredibly important in their teams' dramatic runs to the postseason. But lest we fall prey to the common fallacy of thinking that what we *just saw* is the greatest, the most special, it's worth taking a deeper look at the history of midseason trades.

Granted, it's worth noting that midseason trades today are not what they used to be. Today, teams often trade good players because they feel that they have to; if they don't trade them, they'll lose them to free agency and receive nothing but a couple of draft picks (at best). This is a fairly recent phenomenon, though. Prior to the early 1990s, contending teams weren't making midseason trades for good players having good seasons; typically, they were making trades for good players having lousy seasons, which is quite a different thing.

Sutcliffe is a great example. In 1983 with the Indians, he made the All-Star team and won 17 games. But in 1984 he got off to a crummy start: 4-5 with a 5.15 ERA in 15 starts. Going back much further, we find Chicago Cubs right-hander Grover Cleveland "Pete" Alexander, who was acquired by the Cardinals on waivers in 1926. Alexander wasn't actually pitching poorly—he was 3-3 with a 3.46 ERA—but he'd shown up drunk a few times, and manager Joe McCarthy was at the end of his rope, so the future Hall of Famer was deemed expendable.

But this doesn't make Sutcliffe or Alexander or any of the pre-McGriff midseason acquisitions any less great.

So today we're going way back, as far as we can, to come up with lists of the greatest ever. And we're looking for three things. To qualify, a player must (1) have joined his new team after April, (2) played particularly well for his new team, and (3) made some sort of a difference in the pennant race (or in the battle for a postseason berth in the wild card era), with his team coming out on top (and preferably in a close race).

We'll start with the pitchers.

The Cardinals probably wouldn't have won the National League pennant without **Pete Alexander** in 1926, but that's not even the half of it, because they probably wouldn't have won the World Series without him, too. If you're reading this, you probably know that Alexander struck out Tony Lazzeri in Game 7 to preserve the Cardinals' tenuous lead. But what's easily forgotten is that Alexander also beat the Yankees 6-2 in Game 2 and 10-2 in Game 6, both of them complete games.

Four years after picking up Alexander, the Cardinals traded for **Burleigh Grimes**, and the similarities are striking. Both Alexander and Grimes wound up in the Hall of Fame. Both were in their late 30s. Both pitched roughly 150 innings after joining the Cardinals. Both posted ERAs right around 3.00. And both were key factors in the Cardinals winning the National League pennant by two games.

Two real differences though: (1) Relative to their leagues, Grimes actually pitched much better than Alexander had, and (2) whereas Alexander won two World Series games and saved another, Grimes lost both of his starts (though he didn't pitch poorly in either of them).

Hank Borowy debuted in the majors as a Yankee in 1942 and became one of the great wartime pitchers, going 67-32 with a 2.66 ERA from '42 through '45. In each of his first two seasons, the Yankees reached the World Series; in his third, he went 17-12, but the Yankees failed to win the pennant for only the second time since 1935. In his fourth, the Yankees sold him to the Cubs on July 27 for roughly $100,000.

At the time, the Yankees were in third place, four games behind the first-place Tigers. They finished the season 6.5 games out. After Borowy won Game 1 of the World Series for the Cubs, Yankees general manager Larry MacPhail said, "Borowy had his chance with us and he failed." According to *The New York Times*, "Previously MacPhail had said that Borowy lacked staying power and couldn't finish a game after July 4. With the Cubs, the right-hander ... finished 11 games and had an 11-2 record for an overall performance of 21-7."

Down the stretch, Borowy beat the second-place Cardinals three times. In the World Series, he tossed a Game 1 shutout against the Tigers, got hit hard in Game 5 (and lost), came back the next day in relief to earn the victory with four scoreless innings, and then—thanks to a decision that's been second-guessed ever since—started Game 7 and was knocked out in the first inning.

Was MacPhail a mad genius? Even if they'd kept Borowy, it seems unlikely that the Yankees would have won the pennant. And after 1945, Borowy was never again worth anywhere near $100,000. We shouldn't discount the possibility that MacPhail (1) knew how good his team really was, and (2) knew what would happen in 1946 when all those young men came back from the service.

When the Brooklyn Dodgers purchased **Sal Maglie** from the Cleveland Indians in 1956 it was big news, as Maglie—"the Barber"—had perhaps been the Dodgers' most hated mound opponent. Would his new teammates accept him? Would the famously partisan Ebbets Field fans cheer for him? All questions were answered fairly quickly by Maglie himself, who tossed a three-hit shutout in his second start with Brooklyn and wound up going 13-5 as a Dodger.

Did Maglie make a difference? The Dodgers just *barely* won the National League pennant: one game ahead of the Milwaukee Braves, two ahead of Cincinnati. Maglie started against the Braves five times; the Dodgers won four of them. He started against the Reds six times; the Dodgers won four of those games, too.

And that was before the World Series. Maglie started Game 1 and beat Whitey Ford and the Yankees 6-3 with a complete game. He went the distance again in Game 5, but was on the wrong end of Don Larsen's perfect game.

In 1967, the "Impossible Dream" Red Sox finished with a one-game lead in perhaps the greatest pennant race ever, with four teams within two games of first place heading into the season's last two days. Obviously, in that sort of pennant race *anything* might have made the difference, so it's safe to say that if Boston hadn't traded for **Gary Bell** on June 4 they wouldn't have won.

Bell had been an All-Star with the Indians in 1966, but he got off to a bit of a slow start in '67 and didn't get along particularly well with new manager Joe Adcock. (Granted, Bell wasn't the only one.)

At the time, the Red Sox were in fourth place, four games out. The year before, the Red Sox had finished ninth in the 10-team American League. Nevertheless, upon Bell's arrival, manager Dick Williams said, "I think this gives us a shot at the pennant." It's not clear, more than 40 years later, whether or not anyone took him seriously. But of course Williams was right. Bell went 12-8 with a 3.16 ERA after joining the club, and though 3.16 was not all that special in '67, considering how the final standings looked it's fair to say that Bell did make a difference (if not necessarily *the* difference). In the World Series, he was knocked out of Game 3 early but saved Game 6 with two innings of scoreless relief.

Big left-hander **Woody Fryman**, off to a 4-10 start with the Phillies in 1972, was plucked off waivers by the Tigers in early August; every National League team had passed, and most of the American League teams, too. But Fryman slid right into Detroit's rotation, went 10-3 down the stretch, and became one of manager Billy Martin's favorites. As Martin later wrote, "He was a country boy, a tobacco grower, and his arm hurt him badly, but he'd say, 'Just give me the ball, and I'll do the job for you,' and he did just that." Fryman started the fifth (and deciding game) of the American League Championship Series against the A's and pitched a four-hitter but lost 2-1.

You might actually remember **Rick Sutcliffe**. If you were following baseball in 1984, it's hard to forget a guy who went 16-1 and paced the Chicago Cubs to their first postseason appearance in nearly 40 years. What you might have forgotten is that Sutcliffe continued his amazing run in the National League Championship Series, tossing a six-hit shutout against the Padres in Game 1. But Game 5 didn't go so well. The Cubs got off to a quick 3-0 start, but they wouldn't score again and Sutcliffe couldn't hold the lead, giving up two runs in the sixth and four more—thanks in part to a pair of Leon Durham errors—in the seventh.

Doyle Alexander will always be held up as the best *and* the worst of midseason acquisitions. The best, because he went 9-0 with the Tigers and was the obvious difference as they finished two games ahead of the Blue Jays in 1987; in his last eight starts, Alexander gave up eight runs. The worst, because to get Alexander from the Braves, the Tigers gave up John Smoltz. After the trade, Alexander won 29 games; Smoltz has won 210, saved 154, and is probably heading for Cooperstown in a few years.

As great as **Randy Johnson** was after joining the Astros in 1998, they obviously didn't *need* him, as they finished with a huge lead in their division. On the other hand, when they got him they couldn't have known that; Johnson first pitched (and won) for Houston on Aug. 2, giving the Astros a modest 4.5 game lead over the second-place Cubs.

Johnson pitched well in the Division Series against the Padres but lost both games anyway. Also, in exchange for the Big Unit, the Astros gave up a great deal of talent: Freddy Garcia, Carlos Guillen and John Halama. (Houston did gain a couple of draft picks after the Diamondbacks signed Johnson as a free agent, but neither of the draftees reached the majors.)

Not much needs to be said about **CC Sabathia**, perhaps. In 17 starts with Milwaukee, he went 11-2 and could have done even better, as he posted a 1.65 ERA and never allowed more than four runs in one game. On the last day of the season, he beat the Cubs 3-1 to clinch the Brewers' first postseason berth since 1982. I do hope it's not indelicate to mention that he didn't survive the fourth inning in his only postseason start. Or that the Brewers, to pry Sabathia from the Indians in the first place, had to give up four young players, including top prospect Matt LaPorta.

Well, that's all of them (or rather, all of them I could find). Here are the same pitchers with some numbers, systematically; the last two columns list the Win Shares for each pitcher and where his team finished in the standings (or in the case of Sabathia, in the Wild Card standings) . . .

Player	Team	Year	IP	W-L	ERA	ERA+	WS	Finish
P Alexander	StL (N)	1926	148	9-7	2.91	134	12	2
B Grimes	StL (N)	1930	152	13-6	3.01	167	16	2
H Borowy	Chi (N)	1945	122	11-2	2.13	171	14	3
S Maglie	Bro	1956	191	13-5	2.87	138	16	1
Gary Bell	Bos	1967	165	12-8	3.16	110	11	1
W Fryman	Det	1972	114	10-3	2.06	153	11	+ ½
R Sutcliffe	Chi (N)	1984	150	16-1	2.69	144	16	+ 6 ½
D Alexander	Det	1987	117	9-0	1.53	278	12	2
R Johnson	Hou	1998	84	10-1	1.28	321	11	+12 ½
CC Sabathia	Mil	2008	132	11-2	1.65	262	16	1

I'm not going to try to rank these guys, as it's hard enough to pick the No. 1 guy; besides, such banal exercises are beneath you and me both. But I think it's fair to suggest that Sabathia is the best since the Red Baron, who was the best since the Barber, who was the best since Ol' Pete.

Now let's turn to the hitters. Before running through the serious candidates, I'd like to dispense with a couple of also-rans quickly. In 1914, the Boston Braves traded for third baseman **Red Smith**, who immediately went on the greatest two-month run of his life. He was as miraculous as anyone, but the Miracle Braves won the pennant by 10.5 games and would have been fine without Smith. (What's more, he got hurt just before the World Series and didn't play an inning of the Braves' sweep of the Athletics.) Similarly, **Red Schoendienst** played brilliantly for the 1957 Milwaukee Braves after joining them in mid-June. But the Braves cruised to the pennant (and Schoendienst didn't do much in the Series).

So we'll start with **Billy Southworth**, just enshrined in the Hall of Fame last summer. That's not the only interesting thing about Southworth. For one thing, he was acquired by the Cardinals in 1926—in a trade with the Giants—just a few days before the Cards picked up Pete Alexander, and one could argue that Southworth played just as big a role in the club's pennant run as the old lefty did. And like Alexander, Southworth played brilliantly in the World Series; in Game 2 he busted things wide open with a three-run homer in the seventh inning. What's more, the deal gets a ton of extra credit because this was the beginning of Southworth's long association with the franchise. After taking over as manager in the 1940s, he led the Redbirds to three pennants and two World Championships.

Now, fast-forward to 1964. There's an odd thing about **Lou Brock**: Everyone knows the Cubs traded Brock to the Cardinals for Ernie Broglio, because that deal's gone down as one of the most lopsided ever (and remains a symbol of the Cubs' longstanding woes). But what nobody seems to remember or mention is that in addition to giving the Cardinals a future Hall of Famer, the deal gave the Cardinals the National League pennant and their first World Championship since 1944.

How good was Brock after joining the Cardinals on June 15? In 103 games, he batted .348 and posted a 146 OPS+; over the rest of his long career, he never batted higher than .314 or finished with an OPS+ better than 128. In the one season in which his team absolutely needed Lou Brock at his best, that's exactly what he was.

I suspect that **Tony Gonzalez** is the least famous player we'll consider, but just because we've forgotten him doesn't mean we shouldn't remember him. Gonzalez, for years a fine-hitting outfielder with the Phillies, found himself exiled to San Diego after the '68 season, via the expansion draft. But Gonzalez got off to a lousy start in the Padres' inaugural campaign. On June 13 they traded him to Atlanta for three younger (and as it turned out, lesser) players. In his second game with the Braves, Gonzalez hit two homers—for the first and only time in his career—and he never really stopped hitting all summer long. The Braves finished the season with a three-game lead over the second-place Giants, and without Gonzalez that lead certainly would have been smaller (though probably not non-existent). The Braves were swept by the Mets in the first-ever National League Championship Series, but Gonzalez collected five hits (including a home run) in 14 at-bats, and he scored four times.

Perennial .300 hitter **Bill Madlock** got off to a .261 start with the Giants in 1979 and became expendable. So the Pirates got Madlock (and two other players) on June 28 in a six-player deal, and of course he became that .300 hitter again. Better than .300, actually. With the Pirates making up a big deficit in the second half of the season, Madlock batted .328, practically dead on his career average entering the season. And Madlock's arrival not only got his bat into the lineup; it also got Rennie Stennett's bat *out* of the lineup, which helped just as much. The Pirates finished two games ahead of the Expos in the National League East, then climaxed their run by coming back from a 3-1 deficit in the World Series.

Rickey Henderson returned to the Oakland Athletics (his original team) three times, but the first time, in 1989, was definitely the best. Off to a lousy start (for him) with the Yankees, Rickey went to the A's on June 21 in exchange for three Oakland prospects. His bat came around, and he stole 52 bases in 85 games. As things turned out, the A's really didn't need Henderson to win their division; they finished seven games ahead of the second-place Royals. But Rickey gets a super-sized dollop of extra credit for what happened that October. In a five-game ALCS, he destroyed the Red Sox, reaching base 13 times and stealing eight bases. And in the Athletics' four-game, earthquake-interrupted sweep of the Giants in the World Series, he reached base 11 times.

If you'd asked me a few months ago to name the greatest midseason acquisition, I'd have said **Fred McGriff** in 1993. Not because he is, necessarily, but because I simply didn't know any better. McGriff made a big impression on me in 1993. When McGriff played in his first game with the Braves after the Padres traded him for three prospects—none of whom wound up doing anything as major leaguers, by the way—his new club was nine games behind the first-place Giants. By the end of the season, McGriff had driven home 55 runs in 68 games and the Braves had won 104 games to beat out the Giants by one game.

In the summer of 2004, everybody wanted to know who would end up with **Carlos Beltran**, because he obviously wasn't going to be remain a Royal for long. The Astros won the sweepstakes. And Beltran, while he did play brilliantly for the Astros that season, saved his real heroics for after the MVP ballots had been submitted. In the Division Series, Beltran hit four homers, scored nine runs and drove in nine; in the NLCS against the Cardinals, Beltran hit four more homers, scored 12 runs and drove in five. The Astros lost that series in seven games though, depriving Beltran of the chance to set a new postseason home-run record. (Instead he's tied for the record with Barry Bonds, who did have the benefit of the World Series when he hit eight homers in 2002.)

You remember **Manny Ramirez**, right? The toast of Los Angeles? Drove in 53 runs in 53 games? Magically turned Andre Ethier into the second coming of Ted Williams? Oh, and scored nine runs, drove in 10 in the postseason? Yeah, that guy. By now, he might be the National League's reigning Most Valuable Player. How does he measure up?

Player	Team	Year	G	R	RBI	OPS+	WS	Finish
B Southworth	StL (N)	1926	99	76	69	123	15	2
Lou Brock	StL	1964	103	81	44	146	22	1
Tony Gonzalez	Atl	1969	89	51	50	124	15	3
Bill Madlock	Pit	1979	85	48	44	129	13	2
R Henderson	Oak	1989	85	72	35	150	20	7
Fred McGriff	Atl	1993	68	59	55	163	16	1
Carlos Beltran	Hou	2004	90	70	53	134	18	1
M Ramirez	LA (N)	2008	53	36	53	213	19	2

For me, the competition here comes down to four players—Brock, McGriff, Beltran and Ramirez—and who you like depends on ... well, on *what* you like. Do you like two months of near-Bondsian hitting? That's Manny Ramirez. Do you like three full months of brilliance followed by one of the greatest postseasons that we've ever seen? That's Carlos Beltran. Do you like a slugger whose team went 49-17 after he showed up and beat out a 103-win team in the standings? That's Fred

McGriff. Do you like a leadoff man who propelled his team to one of the more exciting first-place finishes in National League history *and* remained with that team throughout the remainder of a long, Hall of Fame career *and* was acquired in exchange for (as things turned out) practically nothing? That's Lou Brock.

As I write this—shortly before the World Series—there's a great deal of speculation about the National League's Most Valuable Player Award. With the best hitters (Albert Pujols and Lance Berkman) missing the playoffs and the Mets and their many candidates falling just short, the door has opened wide for Manny Ramirez and CC Sabathia. Now, I'll be honest with you—I think it's preposterous to suggest that a player who wasn't in the league for even half the season could have been that league's *most* valuable player.

But there *is* precedent for a midseason acquisition—even one who opened the season in the other league—drawing support from the award voters.

- In 1945, Hank Borowy finished sixth in National League MVP balloting, picking up one first-place vote.

- In 1956, the scribes were *terribly* impressed with Sal Maglie, who finished second in National League MVP balloting (behind teammate Don Newcombe) and second in Cy Young balloting (also to Newcombe; this was the first year of the Cy Young, and the voters apparently hadn't yet decided to treat pitchers differently than hitters).

- In 1964, Lou Brock finished 10th in NL MVP balloting and picked up one first-place vote.

- In 1979, Bill Madlock finished 19th in the MVP balloting and picked up one first-place vote.

- In 1984, Rick Sutcliffe finished fourth among NL MVP candidates and was the unanimous Cy Young choice.

- In 1987, Doyle Alexander finished fourth in the Cy Young balloting; it was a distant fourth, but he did pick up one first-place vote.

- In 1989, Rickey Henderson finished ninth in the American League MVP voting.

- In 2004, Carlos Beltran finished 12th in the National League's MVP vote.

I may have missed a few, but I will suggest that precedent is very clear on this matter. Only two midseason acquisitions have fared particularly well in award voting, and both of them—Maglie and Sutcliffe—joined their new clubs well before the All-Star break. I'll not be surprised if Sabathia and Ramirez garner some first-place votes. Ramirez, especially. Enough first-place votes to actually win an award, though? You already know. But I will also suggest that if Ramirez or Sabathia does win a major award, the voters have established a shiny new precedent, one they'll spend many years grappling with.

Fielding Breeds Winning

by John Dewan

Can a team win without defense? Maybe if that team's name is the New York Yankees. Otherwise it's pretty hard. Here are the Yankee team plus/minus totals over the last six seasons.

New York Yankees Defense

Year	Plus/Minus	Wins
2003	-48	101
2004	-83	101
2005	-164	95
2006	-67	97
2007	-42	94
2008	-75	89

Quite simply, the Bronx Bombers lived up to their name and overwhelmed their lack of defense with their potent offense. They came in first or second in scoring in the majors in four of those years. But you know what? They didn't win a world championship and only got into the World Series once (2003).

For the mere mortals of baseball, defense almost always pays off. This year the best defensive team in MLB, the Philadelphia Phillies, played in the World Series against another one of the best defensive teams, the Tampa Bay Rays. The Phillies had a +74 plus/minus figure as a team and the Rays were third best in the American League at +34 (Toronto +53, Oakland +47). Aside from the Colorado Rockies, who had a -3 last year, every team in the World Series in the last five years has had a positive plus/minus figure. World Series teams (including the Rockies) have averaged a +35 in those five years.

Six years ago the Yankees were in the Series (2003) and had a -48. The Marlins won with a defense that was below average that year as well, a -43.

Team Defense of World Series teams

Year	Winner	+/-	Loser	+/-
2003	Marlins	-43	Yankees	-48
2004	Red Sox	+13	Cardinals	+38
2005	White Sox	+52	Astros	+50
2006	Cardinals	+65	Tigers	+15
2007	Red Sox	+13	Rockies	-3
2008	Phillies	+74	Rays	+34

Last year in these pages we talked about how team speed correlates strongly with team defense. It played out that way once again this year, as the Phillies also had the highest baserunning gain in baseball (+114, from *The Bill James Handbook 2009*) as well as the best defense. The Rays were fifth in the AL in base running (+36) to go along with their third-place finish in defense.

Here are the individual starters and their defensive plus/minus figures for the 2008 world champion Phillies, the top defensive team in all of baseball:

- 1B Howard +1 (ranked 12th in MLB)
- 2B Utley +47 (ranked first, by a wide margin)
- 3B Feliz +7 (ranked 12th)
- SS Rollins +23 (ranked first)
- LF Burrell -20 (ranked 34th, the only defensive weak spot on the team)
- CF Victorino +10 (ranked seventh)
- RF Werth +2 (ranked 15th)

(Note: rankings at each position are based on the 35 major leaguers who played the most innings at that position.)

Every Phillies player except for Burrell was positive, but it was the double play combination of Chase Utley and Fielding Bible Award winner Jimmy Rollins that really excelled. In addition to the title of Best Team Defense of 2008, the Phillies also win the Best Infield Defense award. Their total of +78 for their infield by itself holds off a nicely balanced infield defensive display by the St. Louis Cardinals (three-time Fielding Bible Award winner Albert Pujols +20, Adam Kennedy +19, Troy Glaus +6, Cesar Izturis +19). The Cards infield was +68 overall.

In the outfield, the New York Mets were baseball's best. Their +75 easily beat the +44 posted by the Cleveland Indians and San Diego Padres outfield trios. The Mets were led by repeat Fielding Bible Award winner Carlos Beltran with +24 in center field. Left field and right field were manned by committee, and an awesome defensive committee it was. Ryan Church only started 81 games in right field, but he was the next most regular outfielder after Beltran. He scored a +11. Endy Chavez split time between left field and right field and was sensational with +9 in 54 total games (13 starts) in left field and +10 in 41 starts (60 total games) in right. Fernando Tatis played about the same amount of time as Chavez but was just average with +3 in left and -3 in right. Four other players logged between 165 and 249 innings in left field and all did well: Marlon Anderson +5, Nick Evans +5, Daniel Murphy +5 and Angel Pagan +1.

Description of the 2008 Team Totals and Rankings

On the next page, team defensive totals and rankings are broken into four groups: Plus/Minus, Ground DP, Bunts and Throwing. In the columns under the heading Plus/Minus I've broken down the data further into three groupings: Middle Infield (second base and shortstop), Corner Infield (first and third base), and Outfield (left, center and right). The next three main column headings are associated with one of those same position groupings. Ground DP tells you how often the team turned double plays given their opportunities (ground ball with a man on first and fewer than two outs) and primarily applies to the middle infielders, though all GDPs are included in these team totals. Bunts apply primarily to the corner infielders, though all bunts are included in the team totals, regardless of who fielded them. You'll see letter grades based on the traditional system in schools of A through F, so you can get an idea of how well a team performed on bunts. The entire bunt grading system is described in *The Fielding Bible*. Throwing applies to outfielders only.

The Plus/Minus System

My book *The Fielding Bible* goes into great length describing the new fielding system we developed at Baseball Info Solutions—the Plus/Minus System. (The new edition, *The Fielding Bible—Volume II* comes out in February 2009.) Video Scouts at Baseball Info Solutions review video of every play of every major league game and record detailed information on each play, such as the location of each batted ball, the speed, the type of hit, etc. Using this in-depth data, we're able to figure out how each player compares to his peers at his position. For example, how often does Derek Jeter field that softly batted ball located 20 feet to the right of the normal shortstop position, compared to all other major league shortstops?

A player gets credit (a "plus" number) if he makes a play that at least one other player at his position missed during the season, and he loses credit (a "minus" number) if he misses a play that at least one player made. The credit is directly related to how often players make the play. Each play is considered individually and receives its own score. Sum up all the plays for each player at each position and you get his total plus/minus for the season. A total plus/minus score near zero means the player is average. A positive score is above average, and a negative score is below average. Chase Utley turned in the highest total in 2008 with +47. That means he made 47 more plays than the average MLB second baseman would make if he had the same types of batted balls to handle that Utley had.

The Bill James Handbook 2009 has the final plus/minus leader boards (and trailer boards) for the 2008 season, plus the announcement of the third annual Fielding Bible Awards (which, just for the record, come out each year *before* the Gold Gloves!).

The Manny Adjustment

After the release of *The Hardball Times Baseball Annual* and *The Bill James Handbook* last year we put "The Manny Adjustment" into the plus/minus system. This adjustment came about because of parks with high outfield walls like the Green Monster in Fenway and the Baggie in the Metrodome. This is a specific adjustment to the calculation of plus/minus numbers for outfielders. In this adjustment, we eliminate from consideration all balls that hit an outfield wall that are too high on the wall and out of reach of the defender (in the same way that we remove home runs hit over the wall). The effect was to improve plus/minus numbers for Manny Ramirez and other outfielders who play in parks with high outfield fences. In 2007, Manny had a -38 before the adjustment and a -24 afterwards. It's still a very poor performance reflecting Manny's ineptitude as a defender, but it's not as incredibly atrocious as -38. As a result, Manny is no longer the three-year trailer in left field. His three-year plus/minus figure of -68 "improves" to second worst. Pat Burrell takes over the dubious distinction of having the worst plus/minus figure over the last three years in left field at -73.

Team Totals and Rankings - 2008

Team	PLUS/MINUS					GROUND DP				BUNTS				THROWING				
	Middle Corner					GDP								Opps To	Extra			
	Infield	Infield	Outfield	Total	Rank	Opps	GDP	Pct	Rank	Opps	Score	Grade	Rank	Advance	Bases	Kills	Pct	Rank
Philadelphia Phillies	+71	+7	-4	+74	1	338	127	.376	22	45	.559	B-	10	407	181	26	.445	1
St Louis Cardinals	+43	+25	-3	+65	2	330	135	.409	11	37	.634	A-	3	458	218	20	.476	7
Toronto Blue Jays	+7	+45	+1	+53	3	293	111	.379	21	35	.499	C	24	374	186	21	.497	12
Oakland Athletics	-4	+27	+24	+47	4	273	142	.520	1	34	.529	C+	17	426	212	19	.498	13
Milwaukee Brewers	+24	-5	+25	+44	5	374	132	.353	25	68	.504	C+	23	386	194	14	.503	17
New York Mets	-21	-11	+75	+43	6	341	113	.331	29	47	.640	A-	2	462	234	20	.506	18
Washington Nationals	+1	+5	+35	+41	7	310	119	.384	19	39	.549	B-	14	478	258	11	.540	28
Tampa Bay Rays	-12	+32	+14	+34	8	303	134	.442	8	45	.622	B+	4	389	200	19	.514	23
Florida Marlins	+17	-26	+39	+30	9	313	100	.319	30	54	.512	C+	20	445	227	20	.510	19
Boston Red Sox	+16	+19	-6	+29	10	299	119	.398	15	42	.577	B	7	427	227	14	.532	27
Cleveland Indians	-11	-5	+44	+28	11	330	159	.482	2	47	.447	C-	27	499	232	23	.465	3
Houston Astros	-18	+26	+14	+22	12	296	120	.405	12	30	.532	C+	16	401	198	20	.494	11
San Diego Padres	-16	-7	+44	+21	13	324	127	.392	17	53	.692	A+	1	442	246	14	.557	29
Arizona Diamondbacks	+6	-28	+41	+19	14	324	114	.352	26	52	.513	C+	19	417	213	13	.511	21
Atlanta Braves	+23	+25	-33	+15	15	390	132	.338	28	35	.557	B-	12	418	206	13	.493	9
San Francisco Giants	-11	-8	+10	-9	16	283	104	.367	23	53	.607	B+	6	441	230	12	.522	25
Los Angeles Angels	+1	+27	-38	-10	17	315	141	.448	4	31	.555	B-	13	428	227	16	.530	26
Seattle Mariners	-23	+34	-25	-14	18	336	138	.411	10	44	.572	B	8	516	244	20	.473	6
Los Angeles Dodgers	-12	+11	-15	-16	19	362	124	.343	27	50	.613	B+	5	469	234	19	.499	15
Baltimore Orioles	-37	-20	+38	-19	20	368	142	.386	18	44	.473	C	25	518	233	24	.450	2
Chicago Cubs	+6	-6	-27	-27	21	266	97	.365	24	49	.558	B-	11	369	184	17	.499	14
Cincinnati Reds	+2	-10	-26	-34	22	340	130	.382	20	50	.567	B-	9	439	207	18	.472	5
Colorado Rockies	+21	-13	-44	-36	23	359	144	.401	14	43	.535	C+	15	513	267	15	.520	24
Minnesota Twins	-13	-21	-6	-40	24	327	142	.434	9	28	.511	C+	21	475	232	23	.488	8
Chicago White Sox	-13	+3	-31	-41	25	311	138	.444	6	37	.435	D+	28	445	227	10	.510	19
Pittsburgh Pirates	+13	-5	-58	-50	26	391	157	.402	13	68	.524	C+	18	512	256	15	.500	16
Kansas City Royals	-4	-24	-37	-65	27	301	134	.445	5	32	.467	C-	26	490	276	15	.563	30
Texas Rangers	-21	-39	-6	-66	28	361	160	.443	7	44	.506	C+	22	555	274	19	.494	10
Detroit Tigers	-8	-33	-31	-72	29	341	153	.449	3	36	.411	D+	30	513	263	13	.513	22
New York Yankees	-29	-32	-14	-75	30	280	110	.393	16	36	.419	D+	29	453	213	21	.470	4

Team Totals and Rankings - 2007

Team	PLUS/MINUS					GROUND DP				BUNTS				THROWING				
	Middle Corner					GDP								Opps To	Extra			
	Infield	Infield	Outfield	Total	Rank	Opps	GDP	Pct	Rank	Opps	Score	Grade	Rank	Advance	Bases	Kills	Pct	Rank
Toronto Blue Jays	+56	+25	+16	+97	1	348	148	.425	8	22	.461	C-	30	418	203	18	.486	9
New York Mets	+15	+11	+42	+68	2	319	110	.345	29	54	.622	B+	2	407	219	16	.538	27
Kansas City Royals	+25	+24	+14	+63	3	296	139	.470	1	25	.466	C-	26	460	234	21	.509	21
Atlanta Braves	-5	+4	+62	+61	4	334	123	.368	27	59	.529	C+	17	449	204	21	.454	1
Detroit Tigers	0	+29	+15	+44	5	297	125	.421	10	24	.515	C+	19	470	229	18	.487	10
Arizona Diamondbacks	+19	-18	+43	+44	5	330	141	.427	6	41	.562	B-	10	416	211	18	.507	19
Chicago Cubs	+3	+13	+23	+39	7	303	117	.386	26	61	.534	C+	14	402	194	26	.483	8
St Louis Cardinals	-17	+58	-11	+30	8	338	135	.399	22	35	.734	A+	1	497	243	18	.489	12
Oakland Athletics	+14	+8	-1	+21	9	318	135	.425	9	33	.480	C	22	465	250	12	.538	26
San Diego Padres	0	-6	+25	+19	10	326	128	.393	24	68	.607	B+	4	434	238	14	.548	28
Cleveland Indians	+5	-9	+22	+18	11	335	137	.409	17	49	.530	C+	16	474	240	14	.506	18
Philadelphia Phillies	+25	-2	-5	+18	11	341	137	.402	21	55	.589	B	6	478	218	29	.456	2
Boston Red Sox	+3	+14	-4	+13	13	278	117	.421	11	31	.577	B	8	378	192	13	.508	20
San Francisco Giants	+1	+46	-34	+13	13	328	130	.396	23	63	.618	B+	3	442	220	9	.498	15
Minnesota Twins	+14	+16	-23	+7	15	298	127	.426	7	29	.469	C-	25	428	204	18	.477	6
Texas Rangers	-9	-14	+25	+2	16	366	143	.391	25	37	.470	C	24	495	261	19	.527	24
Washington Nationals	-33	-8	+40	-1	17	318	132	.415	14	55	.580	B	7	474	254	13	.536	25
Colorado Rockies	+46	-16	-33	-3	18	346	156	.451	4	44	.518	C+	18	465	233	12	.501	17
Los Angeles Angels	+8	+27	-40	-5	19	296	135	.456	3	30	.465	C-	27	460	228	17	.496	14
Baltimore Orioles	+3	-5	-6	-8	20	333	135	.405	19	49	.462	C-	28	520	269	19	.517	23
Milwaukee Brewers	-5	-41	+36	-10	21	298	124	.416	13	51	.545	B-	12	489	244	14	.499	16
Los Angeles Dodgers	-8	-20	+14	-14	22	338	142	.420	12	46	.593	B	5	447	265	9	.593	30
New York Yankees	-20	+17	-39	-42	23	333	153	.459	2	39	.462	C-	29	463	218	25	.471	4
Pittsburgh Pirates	-4	-18	-26	-48	24	369	164	.444	5	52	.575	B	9	527	260	21	.493	13
Houston Astros	-5	-17	-28	-50	25	334	114	.341	30	52	.547	B-	11	438	243	18	.555	29
Seattle Mariners	-11	-14	-28	-53	26	339	140	.413	16	34	.472	C	23	502	238	16	.474	5
Cincinnati Reds	+7	-29	-41	-63	27	319	132	.414	15	49	.490	C	21	482	235	17	.488	11
Florida Marlins	-54	-44	+18	-80	28	346	127	.367	28	56	.530	C+	15	554	267	26	.482	7
Chicago White Sox	-38	-15	-29	-82	29	345	139	.403	20	55	.536	C+	13	528	271	15	.513	22
Tampa Bay Devil Rays	-51	-17	-39	-107	30	314	128	.408	18	49	.491	C	20	546	256	24	.469	3

There's No Success Like Failure: The Mitchell Report

by Craig A. Calcaterra

I haven't seen the report yet, but I'm proud I did it . . . I'm just happy it will be out there and we can move on.

—Allan Huber Selig Jr., Dec. 13, 2007

Say what you will about the Mitchell Report—and I will in a moment—but if those words by Commissioner Selig are to be taken at face value, it was a wild success. Baseball has certainly moved on, as have the public and the press. Indeed, during his annual All-Star break question-and-answer session with the Baseball Writers Association of America in New York last summer, Selig was asked about everything from maple bats to high gas prices, but there was nary an inquiry about performance-enhancing drugs.

It was old news, it seemed—news that broke on Dec. 13, 2007 and then quickly became irrelevant. If it weren't for the headline-grabbing follies of Roger Clemens and his legal team, the whole affair would have died completely before pitchers and catchers reported the following February.

That, I believe, was the very point of the Mitchell Report in the first place. Despite his announcement in March of 2006 that former Sen. George Mitchell was tasked with "following the evidence wherever it may lead," and that Mitchell's investigators should "take it as far as they want to go," everything about the report itself suggests that it was intended to constitute the narrowest of inquiries.

Mitchell made no effort to discover the pre-Jose Canseco history of steroids in baseball. He made little effort to look beyond the scope of previously existing law enforcement investigations into PED use. While so much of his effort was spent on the "who" of steroid use (i.e. his now-famous list of users), he was relatively uninterested in the what, where, when, why and how of it all. Instead of plowing the depths of performance-enhancing drugs in baseball, the investigation that culminated in the Mitchell Report was an exercise in plucking the lowest hanging fruit, and as we sit here today, we really don't know much about the Steroid Era beyond the names of the fewer than 100 players who happened to choose a drug dealer of whom George Mitchell became aware. Of course, given how much hysteria attached to the subject during its media heyday, maybe that's a good thing.

But as we embark on the 2009 season, I think it's important to look back at some of those things we've forgotten, to document on the printed page just how curious a beast the Mitchell Report truly was and how, despite great sound and fury, it ultimately signified nothing.

The public has an insatiable curiosity to know everything, except what is worth knowing.

—Oscar Wilde

On page 14 of the "Summary and Recommendations" section which kicked off the report, Mitchell tried to peg the beginning of the Steroid Era. Not surprisingly, he began with a guy everyone hated already:

> *Reports of steroid use in Major League Baseball began soon after the widely publicized discipline of Canadian sprinter Ben Johnson at the Summer Olympic Games in September 1988. Jose Canseco of the Oakland Athletics was the subject of the first media speculation about his use of steroids, and Boston Red Sox fans taunted him for his alleged steroids use during the 1988 American League Championship Series.*

It's curious that Mitchell pretended that steroids did not exist before the late '80s and seemingly had no interest in digging beyond Canseco. This is especially true in light of the fact that Mitchell himself notes on page 28 of his very own report that as early as 1973 anabolic steroids were prominently mentioned in an in-depth congressional investigation into the use of illegal and dangerous drugs in sports, including professional baseball. Indeed, the 1973 report concluded that "the degree of improper drug use—primarily amphetamines and anabolic steroids—can only be described as alarming." Jose Canseco, it should be noted, was nine years old in 1973.

Did Mitchell ever try to talk to Brian Downing, a guy who totally reshaped his body and experienced a dramatic power spike in the early '80s? How about Tom House, who has actually admitted that he experimented with steroids in the 1970s? Nope. Mitchell is happy naming Jose Canseco—a none-too-bright guy who seems to lack ambition—as the mastermind and birth father of an era.

Why Canseco? I suppose partly because it was the announcement of Jose's book in the summer of 2002 and its subsequent publication that thrust steroids into the spotlight, and naming him in the Mitchell Report would make for a nice set of bookends. I also suppose that if you were to name someone like Tom House as an early steroid user, it might raise questions about the guys *he* worked and played with, just as so many Oakland A's later came under suspicion in Canseco's wake. Like, say, a guy who credited House with helping him get into "the best shape of his life." No, it would not do to have a living legend like Nolan Ryan, who said those words about House during his Hall of Fame induction ceremony, associated with steroids.

But let us not be too hard on Mitchell for wanting to name Jose Canseco as patient zero in the steroid epidemic. After all, Jose himself has tried to take credit for it on numerous occasions, and it would be a shame to deprive the poor guy of the only thing he'll ever truly be remembered for. What this little example does do, however, is illustrate how uncurious and incomprehensive George Mitchell was when compiling his report.

Judge a man by his questions, rather than by his answers.
—Voltaire

While both Mitchell and the media were all too willing to characterize the report as a "thorough" and "comprehensive" investigation into steroid use in baseball, much of it was a basic stenography job in which Mitchell related the results of three previously existing investigations: (1) the BALCO investigation; (2) the investigation and prosecution of trainer/lackeys Kirk Radomski and Brian McNamee; and (3) the investigation of Signature Pharmacy by the Albany, N.Y. district attorney's office. If you were a player unlucky enough to have been a client of one of those sources, you found yourself mentioned in the Mitchell Report. If you bought from some other drug dealer—like, say, the kind that *doesn't* accept the credit cards and personal checks seemingly favored by these institutions (i.e., every other drug dealer on the planet)—you basically skated.

And make no mistake, there were no doubt plenty of players who used different dealers. Mitchell himself notes that during baseball's 2003 trial testing program alone, some 93 positive tests came back. What's more, pages 234-238 of the Mitchell Report itself detail the extensive and elaborate system by which steroids are created and distributed *outside* of the context of places like BALCO and Signature Pharmacy. It was a network, Mitchell notes, that resulted in tens of millions of

doses of steroids being seized in a single government operation.

However, the Mitchell Report, which purports to span more than a decade, has only 89 names, all of whom were Radomski, McNamee, BALCO or Signature Pharmacy customers. Sure, I suppose it's *possible* that those places served the majority of PED-using players in the game, but it's far more likely that the Mitchell Report's famous 89 represented only the tip of the iceberg. But more than the mere lack of names of other players who likely used, the Mitchell Report's lack of comprehensiveness is evidenced by its profound lack of curiosity about the very nature of PED use in baseball.

I submit to you that if people truly wanted to know how steroids have impacted the game, they'd want to know more than merely who used. They'd want to know why they used, and when they started, and what incentives and disincentives existed that promoted or deterred the spread of PEDs in the game. Questions such as:

- How often did people actually use?
- Were the primary users people who got hurt and were trying to come back more quickly? Stars who wanted to blast their way into the Hall of Fame? Minor leaguers who wanted to become major leaguers?
- When did users actually start using? High school? College? In the minors? After making The Show?
- Was drug use a personal thing? Specifically, did guys decide on their own, based on their own personal experiences to use steroids, or was it a peer pressure thing in which certain clubhouses promoted a "steroid culture?"
- How did players connect with their dealers? By word of mouth, or did the dealers seek out their customers?
- Were the people who *didn't* use steroids choir boys who had moral objections, or did fear of the dangers of steroids and/or a belief that they simply didn't need them inform their decision making?

The answers to any or all of these questions would have been more useful—though far less salacious—than the mere list of names the Mitchell Report provided, but Mitchell didn't seem to want to go there. Why? Probably because answering those questions would have required a lot more cooperation from the players, and that kind of cooperation was not forthcoming. But despite George Mitchell and the media's insistence that the lack of cooperation was borne of the players' culture of secrecy, there was way more going on than your typical closing of ranks.

If we do not hang together, we will all hang separately.

—Benjamin Franklin

Before he began formally naming names, Mitchell made a point of explaining just how uncooperative the players were over the course of his investigation:

> *From the outset, my objective in this investigation has been "to gather facts," to prepare a report that is thorough, accurate, and fair, and to "provide those whose reputations have been, or might be, called into question by these allegations a fair opportunity to be heard." Each player mentioned in this report, and others not mentioned, was provided that fair opportunity; each was invited to meet with me, with his personal lawyer and a lawyer from the Players Association if he so chose, so that I could provide him with information about the allegations against him and give him the opportunity to respond. Most players declined to meet with me.*

And indeed, much of the public response in the year and change since the Mitchell Report dropped has taken the form of "hey, the named players had a chance to be heard, so screw them if they now complain about the strength and validity of the evidence against them." And on some level I understand and sympathize with that. Dealing with unions, especially this one, is a tough racket, and there can be no disputing that the Players Association had no intention of helping the good senator.

But it didn't have to be that way. Mitchell—with the help of Major League Baseball and his former congressional colleagues who were signaling their interest in becoming involved years before the report was completed—could have created an atmosphere in which the answers to the questions set forth in the previous paragraph could have been answered. Anonymity could have been granted. Amnesty and limited immunity deals could have been brokered. Easy? Of course not, but no effort to encourage cooperation was ever made.

Instead, Mitchell waded into things with federal agents on one side of him and an implied threat of subsequent congressional investigations on the other. There was no talk of being interested in information as opposed to scapegoats. There was no talk of granting players anonymity for cooperating. There was no talk of immunity from prosecution or amnesty from league sanction. There was nothing other than a former senator and current member of a team's ownership group with a nebulous mandate and a public expectation that names would be named.

I am an attorney, and I can tell you, I would never allow my client to talk to anyone under such uncertain circumstances, even if I was certain of his innocence. People I know have gone to jail based on the odd conversational tangents that can occur during such interviews. The common response of "well, he'd talk if he didn't have something to hide" is a nonstarter concocted by people who don't understand what the Fifth Amendment and, more broadly speaking, the concept of self-incrimination is all about. The point of all of this is to remind ourselves that Mitchell was far less interested in obtaining information about the scourge of steroids in baseball than he was in hanging a sample of players out to dry.

The sad postscript to all of this is that, at the end of the day, Mitchell and Major League Baseball did, in essence, grant everyone immunity. The Mitchell Report contained a strong exhortation that no retrospective discipline be meted out, and by January and February of 2008, Selig was publicly stating that he was inclined to look forward instead of back. To date, no player named in the Mitchell Report has received discipline from Major League Baseball, and with the exception of the wounds Clemens has inflicted upon himself via his reckless litigation tactics, no player first-named as a PED user in the Mitchell Report has faced criminal investigation or prosecution.

It's not whether you win or lose; it's how you place the blame.

—Oscar Wilde

Determining the effects of steroids on a batted or pitched ball, let alone figuring out how they may have impacted stats and/or game outcomes, is way above my pay grade. Studies that have attempted to quantify the effect of steroids—most have found some moderate uptick in the stats of Mitchell Report players—have all been criticized to greater or lesser degrees. Some of these criticisms note that the researchers may have been too conservative in identifying a given player's "steroid years," which could have the effect of attributing offensive spikes to steroids when, in fact, the player was juicing back when he was terrible too. Others have noted that much if not all of the aggregate improvement of steroid-using players is attributable to Barry Bonds, and that even the extent of Bonds' steroid years varied depending on who you believed.

Others still have noted what I noted above, and that's that, by definition, the George Mitchell All-Stars were drawn from a pool of guys who simply had the misfortune of buying from one of three or four already-identified sources, and that as such, we're not exactly dealing with a representative sample of major leaguers, juicers or otherwise.

But I'll leave all of that to the statisticians and researchers. What does strike me, however, is that whatever you can say about them statistically, the 89 players named in the Mitchell Report don't, for the most part, *look* like what we'd expect from steroid users. For every Todd Hundley, whose steroid use appeared to correspond with the sort of rise in power numbers that the public assumes always accompanies steroid use, there are many more Hal Morrises and Chuck Knoblauchs, whose "steroid years" were far worse than their career averages. For every Roger Clemens, whose toughness and durability are now attributed to steroid-fueled workout and recovery regimes, there are many more Rondell Whites and Lenny Dykstras who, if anything, became more fragile as the steroid era wore on.

The point of all of this? That for all of the press about Mitchell's revelations, the Mitchell Report raised far more questions than it answered, not just about who used, but when, why, and to what end. I have very little faith that the 89 men named in the Mitchell Report are anything close to exhaustive, and I believe that they don't constitute a representative sample. At present, there is no official effort to figure out if that is the case, and I would not advise holding one's breath until one is undertaken.

A yawn may not be polite, but at least it is an honest opinion.

—Anonymous

According to MLB Advanced Media President Bob Bowman, the day the Mitchell Report was released on MLB.com was nowhere near the biggest traffic day in the site's history. Indeed, during an interview with Biz of Baseball's Maury Brown, Bowman said "(i)t was not even *close* to the highest traffic day for mlb.com. The traffic was up substantially, but we've had days where we had 11 million visitors during the season during a regular day, and we didn't get anywhere near that on the day of the Mitchell Report. We were in the six million-range."

I suppose the lesson here was that while steroids in baseball is an important issue for the chattering classes, your average fan is far more interested in seeing replays of a shortstop turn a slick double play in August than he is in reading about a left fielder sticking a syringe in his right buttock. This is underscored by the fact that there was a collective yawn at 86 of the 89 players named in the Mitchell Report. No sportswriters wrote about how they felt betrayed by Larry Bigbie or contested the legitimacy of Josias Manzanillo's accomplishments. The biggest story about Brian Roberts in 2008 surrounded speculation that he might be traded to the Cubs, not that he was named as a steroid user in the Mitchell Report.

The only two players whose steroid use has received and, to some extent, continues to receive considerable attention are Barry Bonds and Roger Clemens. Given that he broke Hank Aaron's record, got indicted, and served as the subject of the seminal book on steroids in baseball, Bonds would have been in the headlines anyway. If Clemens had gone the Andy Pettitte route and made a quiet mea culpa instead of suing his accuser, his involvement in all of this would have faded from memory with the cold winter winds just like Pettitte's did.

There is much I did not learn.

—George Mitchell, *Report to the Commissioner of Baseball of an Independent Investigation Into the Illegal Use of Steroids and Other Performance Enhancing Substances by Players in Major League Baseball.*

The Mitchell Report contained many facts, but very few answers. It certainly didn't provide anything approaching a comprehensive look at how steroids came to baseball, what they meant to baseball, and what, exactly, baseball was to do with all of this new information after Dec. 13, 2007.

That is not to say that the Mitchell Report was a failure. To the contrary, it did what it was intended to do, and that was to serve as the signpost marking the end of the Steroids Era. It gave the teeming masses what they wanted: blood in the form of many named-names, while assiduously ensuring that not too many rocks were turned over and not too many apple carts were upset. It highlighted baseball's dirty past in a way that allowed people to believe that it was all in the past. Indeed, the offenses listed were mostly old news. Many if not most of the players named in the report were out of the game by the time it was published or soon will be. Ahh, sweet closure!

At least that is how the Mitchell Report has come to be received, lo these many months later, and that seems to be good enough for Major League Baseball, the Players Association, most of the fans, and most of the media.

Is it good enough for you?

I would like to thank Pete Toms, who was the first to suggest to me that, just maybe, the whole point of the Mitchell Report was to end the conversation about steroids in baseball rather than inform it. I would also like to thank Baseball Think Factory's resident libertarian and Orioles fan David Nieporent for pointing out that there were more interesting questions to be asked about steroids in baseball than merely who used them.

The Ethics of Baseball

by Jack Marshall

The ethical dilemmas and controversies of baseball reveal a great deal, not only about the sport itself, but about the nature of competition, and American society. This is why the explosion of a major ethics issue in Major League Baseball, such as the use of performance-enhancing drugs by star players, becomes a source of debate and commentary, not just within the sport itself, but on editorial pages, Sunday morning news shows and business journals.

Baseball—notwithstanding the propaganda steadily produced by NASCAR and the NFL—really is the national pastime, both in its influence on American culture and its traditional connection to basic American virtues and values. The resolution of ethics controversies in the sport often has impact, positive and negative, on national attitudes and values. Culture, after all, is a society's verdict about what matters and what doesn't, and how it chooses to conduct itself. Baseball both reflects and influences American culture.

Cultures create themselves, in part, through the conduct of publicly visible role models and leaders. Major league baseball players, as baseball analyst and philosopher Bill James is fond of pointing out, are professional heroes. Shoeless Joe Jackson's corruption, Pete Rose's lies, Steve Howe's drug use and Barry Bonds' cheating all created a real danger: that conduct our culture had rightfully rejected would gain a stronger foothold in American society as a whole.

For this reason, the ethics of baseball is important beyond its influence on the game itself. To the extent possible, America's game ought to be a *good* game, embodying positive values and played by athletes worthy of being role models and heroes. Those who deny this deny the significance of culture itself. And they are wrong.

Baseball's Values

Major league baseball is a profession as well as a sport, and like all professions, it has evolved a unique hierarchy of values. In medicine, the prime value is the welfare of the patient. In law, it is zealous representation of the client and preserving client confidences. Professional baseball has two primary values: winning the game, which is what ethicists call a "non-ethical" consideration (that is, a practical objective motivated by a desire for results that have tangible benefits, rather than principle alone); and winning the right way.

That reverses the order of the values in amateur sports, in which, as Grantland Rice wrote, "how you play the game" takes top priority. "Winning the right way" embraces key ethical considerations, such as preserving the integrity of the sport, demonstrating competence, diligence, honesty, dignity, courage, loyalty and sacrifice, and upholding baseball's stature and reputation in the national culture as a whole.

Once baseball began to take hold of the nation's imagination in the years following World War I, the sport's leadership recognized that it had to live up to its role as the forge of national heroes and role models. Although society, industry and politics were riddled with corruption, baseball had to be purged of it. The Chicago "Black Sox" were banished in the aftermath of baseball's worst ethics scandal: the fixing of the 1919 World Series. Shortly thereafter, the game banned the institutionalized cheating represented by the surreptitious doctoring of baseballs to make them dive and sail past puzzled batters. Baseball was going to be a clean, gambler-free, no-spitballs-allowed sport worthy of America's youth.

But because baseball has always reflected the culture as much as it influences it, many of American society's most unethical practices stayed entrenched in the sport for a long time. Baseball banned blacks from playing Major League Baseball in 1887, following the national Jim Crow attitudes in the wake of Reconstruction, undeniably unethical conduct that was hardly recognized as such at the time. But baseball later took a leadership role in the name of American virtues, with high-profile athletes like Bob Feller, Ted Williams and Hank Greenberg enlisting to fight in World War II. After the war, baseball struck a major blow against the racial segregation it had helped entrench, thanks to the vision of Branch Rickey and the courage of Jackie Robinson.

In other ethical matters, baseball sometimes lagged behind. The labor movement had made great strides in allowing workers to get fair value for their work, but baseball maintained an oppressive labor system that treated rare athletic talent as chattel until an arbitration decision by Peter Seitz disassembled it in 1976. Recreational drugs invaded baseball, along with the rest of

America, in the 1960s and baseball took a belated stand against them in the '70s. Steroids infested the game in the '90s, and baseball began to act aggressively against chemical cheating by 2006.

Sometimes ahead of the curve and sometimes behind it, Major League Baseball has consistently, if not always successfully, tried to uphold its end of the cultural bargain with America. Unlike hockey, it would not tolerate violence. Fighting was discouraged, however entertaining to fans; assaults, as when pitcher Juan Marichal took a bat to catcher John Roseboro, resulted in suspensions and fines. Neither fans nor players were permitted to intimidate umpires, in sharp contrast to the game's wild and wooly past. Unlike pro basketball and pro football, baseball would not welcome felons, thugs, wife-beaters and drug-users.

Once media scrutiny became pervasive enough that the unattractive foibles and habits of players emulating Ty Cobb, Babe Ruth, Mickey Mantle, Grover Cleveland Alexander or Billy Martin could not be disguised or hidden, players were given no choice: Baseball was about heroes, and players had better try to meet minimum standards of heroic conduct. In 2000, star Atlanta Braves reliever John Rocker gave a *Sports Illustrated* reporter his impressions of New York, saying,

> *Imagine having to take the 7 Train to the ballpark, looking like you're riding through Beirut next to some kid with purple hair, next to some queer with AIDS, right next to some dude who just got out of jail for the fourth time, right next to some 20-year-old mom with four kids…The biggest thing I don't like about New York are the foreigners. You can walk an entire block in Times Square and not hear anybody speaking English. Asians and Koreans and Vietnamese and Indians and Russians and Spanish people and everything up there. How the hell did they get in this country?*

Rocker was fined and suspended, and his career went into a permanent tailspin. Players got the message. Baseball was for good guys, and the national sport of an ethical culture.

Game Ethics

Ethically, that was the easy part. Americans, despite the vociferousness of their disagreements, are in concert about basic ethical values about 95 percent of the time, according to Michael Shermer, author of *The Science of Good and Evil*. But ethics in a competitive context, like baseball, politics, law and warfare, is always complicated. To the extent that a profession operates under sets of

rules, they supply the compliance aspect of ethics: Obeying the rules, be they the laws of a state or the Rules of Civil Procedure, is only the threshold of ethical conduct.

But ethics is the study of what conduct is right and wrong, and what is right and wrong in Major League Baseball must be examined on five levels:

- Conduct governed by society's laws
- Conduct governed by the rules of the game
- Conduct governed by the traditions and culture of the game
- Baseball etiquette, or "unwritten rules"
- Conduct governed by basic cultural ethical systems and values.

In a unique project, Prof. Willy Stern of Carleton College collected 133 examples of baseball conduct for his innovative class on baseball ethics, providing much of the source material for this article. Many other ethical issues in the sport did not make the list. They all fall into one or more of these categories, and by determining which conduct is ethical and which is not, the ethics of Major League Baseball begins to come into focus.

Conduct Governed by Society's Laws

That which is illegal in society is illegal and unethical if it occurs on the baseball field and in the clubhouse. It is wrong when baseball players break the law. One of the more fatuous of the defenses offered for the alleged steroid use by Barry Bonds, Mark McGwire and others was that the players began using steroids before the substances were specifically banned by Major League Baseball. This is nonsense. The substances involved were illegal, their use a felony under U.S. law, long before baseball enacted its redundant rules against them.

Baseball does not have to specifically prohibit all the conduct proscribed by United States criminal statutes. Baseball players are working in the country, and subject to the country's laws. Violating those laws is just as unethical whether the conduct is singled out by baseball for prohibition or not. If conduct is illegal, it is already prohibited to baseball players, and players who violate those laws to gain an advantage over law-abiding players are felons as well as cheats.

There have been other examples of illegal activity connected with baseball games. Gamblers' fixing of games in the 1919 World Series has already been mentioned. Less significant but clearly illegal have been player assaults on fans and umpires, which are well-represented on the Carleton College list: Many players, most famously Ty Cobb, have attacked obnoxious fans in the stands. Ted Williams once tried to hit foul balls into the stands at a particularly vocal fan's head and came extremely close to succeeding, which would have constituted assault.

The rule in place seems to be based on the concepts of trespass and self-defense: No matter how badly a fan behaves, a player is not justified in going into the stands to fight him (or to throw or hit a ball with the intent of injuring him). But if the fan enters a player's domain on the field or dugout, the player has a right to use reasonable force to repel him.

A core tenet of most ethical systems is that harming or seeking to harm another human being is inherently unethical unless special circumstances, like the consent of the harmed or self-preservation, are involved. Fights between players, while tightly controlled by baseball in recent years, do not cross into illegality or unethical conduct until the violence becomes extreme, potentially lethal, and beyond the inevitable flaring of tempers endemic to sports involving physical contact.

Juan Marichal's bat attack on catcher John Roseboro (Marichal, who was at the plate, was alarmed when he felt Roseboro's throw back to the mound whiz by his ear) was clearly over the line. Also unethical and potentially illegal are physical attacks of any kind by players on umpires, coaches and managers, unless they are arguably in self-defense, as when Pedro Martinez pushed the charging septuagenarian Yankee coach Don Zimmer to the ground in 2003.

Conduct Governed by the Rules of the Game

Attempting to win by violating the written rules of baseball is cheating, and therefore unethical. But distinguishing between violating the rules, which is an unethical act, and gamesmanship, which can encompass exploiting loopholes in the rules, breaking rules that are seldom enforced, or exploring the gray areas that the rules of every profession inevitably contain, can be difficult.

In the 19th century, clever players like Chicago White Sox player-manager Cap Anson and Boston's King Kelly looked for opportunities within the rules to gain an edge in games. Anson tried distracting tactics like jumping from the left side of the plate to the right side (he was a switch-hitter) while the pitcher was winding up, or running the bases in reverse order. Kelly's masterpiece occurred when he was in the Boston Beaneaters dugout as the other team's batter hit a high foul ball just in front of his seat. When Kelly realized that the Beaneater catcher could not reach the ball, Kelly quickly called out "Kelly now catching for Boston!" and snagged it for the out. Rules were quickly put in place to ban mid-play substitutions, mid-pitch batting changes and creative base-running.

Bill Veeck's signature stunt of putting a midget in the lineup so his miniscule strike zone all but guaranteed a base on balls resulted in a ban on midgets. ("Is Phil Rizzuto just a tall midget?" Veeck protested). Several enterprising outfielders found that they could knock down potential home runs and stop line drives in the gap by throwing their gloves at the ball, and catchers found they could do the same with wild pitches, throwing their gloves or masks: These practices were also stopped by rules.

Jackie Robinson made a habit of breaking up double plays by running into the ball. It worked…until baseball changed the rule. Throwing balls defaced or covered in spit or slippery elm, deceptive pickoff moves and many other on-field tactics began as innovations and ended as rules violations. None could reasonably be called unethical, until the rules changed.

Breaking the rules is cheating, and thus unethical, and the easiest way to identify cheating conduct is whether there is an effort to hide it. Sign-stealing constitutes the largest category in the Carleton College list, and the demarcation between the ethical and unethical is clear. It is acceptable under baseball's rules to steal the other team's signs if it occurs on the field and doesn't involve special equipment, signals or undercover personnel. But teams have employed surreptitious telescope-using spies in the scoreboard and in the stands for about a hundred years, most infamously the New York Giants in 1951.

Manager Leo Durocher installed a complex relay system involving a telescope, a buzzer and a towel signal from the bullpen catcher to intercept the opposing catchers' signals at the Polo Grounds. A 2001 *Wall Street Journal* story claimed the unethical system was responsible for the most celebrated home run in baseball history, Bobby Thomson's pennant-winning "shot heard round the world" in the playoff against the Brooklyn Dodgers. A later HBO documentary challenged the claim. (On film, Thomson confirmed that the Giants used the system but denied that it was used during that game and that he received any signs before his blast.)

But the incident underscores the danger of unethical conduct in baseball. The sense that a great event in the game's history may have been created by cheating rather than athletic prowess and skill injures the reputation of the game and challenges its integrity. A baseball hero's aura is dimmed, and the exuberance of the moment (Russ Hodges' immortal "The Giants win the pennant! The Giants win the pennant!") is now tempered with cynicism, just like Barry Bonds' 762 home runs and Mark McGwire's 70 in 1998.

Another famous case of alleged but unconfirmed unethical conduct and cheating occurred in the 1925 World Series, when Hall of Famer Sam Rice of the Washington Senators disappeared over the center field fence as he tried to catch a fly ball and take a potential home run away from Pirates catcher Earl Smith. Rice climbed back onto the field 10 seconds later with the ball in his glove. Smith was called out.

The game was in Pittsburgh, and Pirates fans who were in that section of the ballpark signed sworn statements that Rice had not caught the ball, but placed it in his glove after landing. Rice went to his grave swearing that the catch had been legal. The controversy is fun for baseball historians, but the specter of a World Series game being decided by a quick-thinking cheat is a scar on the game's integrity.

Illegal equipment, especially bats fortified with cork, nails or superballs, cannot be defended ethically. Obviously they are unfair, and also have the tell-tale stain of secrecy. Sammy Sosa's popularity with the Chicago Cubs began to unravel when he was caught with a corked bat. Amos Otis, a player greatly admired for his steadiness and professionalism during his career, forfeited much of his reputation when he announced after his retirement that he had used a corked bat virtually his whole career. If a player like Otis cheated, how many other players had enhanced their batting averages, hit extra home runs and won games for their teams using unfair bats?

Again, cynicism follows unethical conduct. Although Gaylord Perry managed to turn his periodic use of the long-banned spitball into both a trademark and a joke, his 314 career wins clearly were inflated by cheating, as were those of likely spitball-practitioners Jim Bunning, Vida Blue, Whitey Ford, Ferguson Jenkins, Tommy John, Phil Niekro and Don Drysdale, among others.

It is intriguing that the illicit use of the spitball never carried as much stigma as the corked bat, though it is equally unethical. Perhaps this is because the pitch was once legal. The fact that spitball specialists like Burleigh Grimes were permitted to continue using the pitch after it was banned lent the pitch a share of legitimacy as well as romance. Perhaps the spitball doesn't offend because, unlike the corked bat, it requires substantial skill to throw the pitch effectively, or because it appeals

to nostalgia. Whatever the reason, the day the Hall of Fame admitted Gaylord Perry, baseball made the unfortunate statement that cheaters could prosper and be celebrated for it, if they were winners. That statement eventually may be the ticket that gets baseball's steroid-users into Cooperstown.

Conduct Governed by the Traditions and Culture of the Game

As mathematician Kurt Gödel proved in 1931 with his Incompleteness Theorem, laws, rules and systems written by imperfect human beings never can be perfect, and always create anomalies. Baseball's preferred method of handling anomalies in the rules is to enforce them selectively in the interests of the game. Thus catchers are allowed to block the plate before they receive the ball, second basemen can avoid injury from sliding runners and still get credit for making the force-out in the "phantom double play," and pitchers are not called for every technical balk. Players taking advantage of these unenforced rules are not in any way cheating, any more than a pitcher who aims pitches four inches outside the strike zone knowing that the home plate umpire is calling such pitches strikes.

The culture of baseball allows the umpires to define reality, much as the culture of law allows the judge to decide what is admissible evidence and acceptable tactics. The lawyer's ethical rules (primarily based on the American Bar Association's Rules of Professional Conduct) could prohibit lawyers from offering hearsay testimony they believe is inadmissible, for example, hoping that opposing counsel will fail to object or that the judge will make a favorable but incorrect ruling. But it doesn't: Lawyers may ethically attempt to slip inadmissible evidence past inattentive opponents and mistaken judges.

The ethics and culture of baseball similarly do not condemn batters feigning being hit by pitches, catchers "framing" balls out of the strike zone to appear as strikes, first basemen smacking their gloves to make the umpire who is listening as he watches the foot of the baserunner approach the bag think that the throw hit the glove first, or outfielders who know they trapped a fly ball acting as if they caught it on the fly.

Various forms of deception and misdirection practiced by fielders to fool baserunners into errors and outs also have cultural approval, and must be judged ethical; they are as well within the gamesmanship of baseball as bluffing in poker and posturing in financial negotiations. The Carleton College list raises an implied eyebrow at infielders "deking" runners at second base or pretending to field a throw to force a slide when the ball is actually still rolling around in the outfield; at outfielders who mime catching an uncatchable hit so that baserunners will delay their advance, and at the "hidden ball trick." But they are clear examples of ethical deception that tradition, logic and entertainment value have rendered ethical in the culture of baseball. Baserunners are permitted their deception too: Players from King Kelly to Reggie Jackson to current-day practitioners have feigned injuries and limps only to steal second on the next pitch. That's not unethical. It's smart baseball.

There are, of course, limits. Players have caused opposing pitchers to balk by calling "Time!" out of earshot of the umpires and then denying it. This is considered a dirty trick that carries chicanery over the line into unethical conduct. In the same category, based on the violent reaction to it, was Yankees baserunner Alex Rodriguez causing a popup to fall between Tampa Bay fielders in a 2007 game because he yelled "Ha!" or "I got it!" (accounts differ) behind them. This trick was standard practice as recently as the 1970s, according to several ex-players, but somewhere it moved from acceptable to unethical. Ethical standards are always fluid, in baseball and everywhere else.

Psychological warfare is a legitimate part of all sports and games, from chess to baseball, but there are ethical limits, and they evolve over time. It was once completely acceptable for loud-mouthed "bench jockeys" to try to unsettle the opposing players with vicious insults to their race, nationality, religion, family, appearance and ability. As the fate of John Rocker showed, this is no longer tolerable. Perhaps the last remaining vestige of the tradition is catchers attempting to distract batters with chatter, jokes and other diversions. This has not yet passed into the category of unethical conduct, but seems to be losing favor, perhaps because it never was that effective in the first place.

Baseball culture also allows for teams to tailor a home park to their strengths, a time-honored practice that is ethical as long as it seems fair: Both teams must play under the same conditions. Thus leaving the grass long to aid infield hits, pounding the base paths hard to help the running game, and even tilting the ground on the foul lines so bunts will roll fair (or foul) is within ethical norms. So is wetting down the area around first base to foil a master base-stealer on the other team (as was done to slow Maury Wills and Lou Brock).

Unethical: actually tampering with the proscribed measurements of the field, as when the Atlanta Braves were caught in 2000 drawing the lines for the catcher's box wider than the rules allowed them to be, to help their catchers set up for outside pitches. Also unethical: Constantly changing the direction and force of the air conditioning in the Twins' Metrodome to help blow the home team's hits forward but to blow against opposition hits. Outrageously unethical (and dangerous): Team owner Bill Veeck's plan in the 1930s to get his fans to buy small hand-held mirrors to reflect the sun into the eyes of the opposing team's batters. All of these tricks raise issues of fairness that go beyond simply trying to maximize a home team advantage.

The most interesting tests of baseball ethics arise when the prime objective of winning comes close to conflict with the ethic of playing the game the right way. Sometimes playing to win (or avoid losing) defines playing the right way. There have been several instances when the game has degenerated into a farce in which the winning team, at bat, is trying to make outs and the losing team in the field is trying to avoid an official loss by delaying the end of the inning so the game can be rained out before the completion of the fifth inning.

Is this unethical, as the practice's presence on the Carleton list suggests? Not at all. The conduct is within the rules, is aimed at accomplishing legitimate goals (winning or avoiding a loss), and is even entertaining, if bizarre. It doesn't harm the integrity of the game, because it is rational within its context. But the practice of a home team's ground crew attempting to delay protecting the field when a downpour threatens to wash out a game in which the home team is well behind is absolutely unethical. Once the game starts, a stadium's staff and employees are obligated to do their jobs without favoritism or bias.

Baseball Etiquette: the Golden Rule in Baseball

The ethical principle of reciprocity, better known as the Golden Rule ("Do unto others as you would have others do unto you") comes into play in Major League Baseball primarily through the so-called "unwritten rules." Almost every profession has such unwritten rules, covering behavior that has come to be regarded as uncivilized within the culture of that profession, corrosive to the profession's image and its members' enjoyment of its practice, and generally to be avoided. "Unwritten rules" usually must be enforced informally by a profession's members, usually by social pressure. And the rules change: slowly, subtly, and often confusingly.

Many unwritten rules that still receive lip service today date from earlier eras of baseball when different conditions were in effect. The edict that a team winning in a rout should never try to run up the score by using one-run tactics like stealing bases and bunting, or engaging in aggressive offensive approaches like swinging on a 3-0 count, is such a rule. When runs were at a premium during the low-scoring "dead ball era," this rule made some sense: If the game was already won, running up the score was just gratuitously mean-spirited. But in the current era of frequent home runs and double-digit scores, it is erased by the higher value of doing what is necessary within the written rules to win the game.

Nonetheless, "Don't run up the score" still may apply in unusual circumstances. During the Aug. 21, 2007 historic blowout between the Orioles and Rangers that Texas eventually won 30-3, Rangers manager Ron Washington reportedly told his third base coach not to send runners home unless he was sure they could score without a slide. Washington's directive was profoundly ethical and the kind and fair thing to do (though it didn't do much to limit his team's scoring) because a 30-3 score was almost as hopeless in 2007 as it was in 1907.

When Washington chose to apply this almost-extinct unwritten rule, he was embracing the ethical impulse behind many such rules, which can be stated as, "Don't embarrass a fellow professional, and especially a teammate, unnecessarily." This strong baseball ethic frequently finds itself in conflict with the baseball prime directive of winning the game, for applying the Golden Rule in competitive professions is often difficult, and sometimes impossible.

Frank Robinson, managing the Washington Nationals in 2006, found himself in just such an ethical conflict in one game against the Houston Astros. With his team struggling and needing a win badly to bolster its sagging morale, and his catching staff riddled with injuries and inexperience, he started seldom-used, third-string catcher Matt LeCroy. Robinson thought that the Astros, then without speed or base-stealing threats, seemed unlikely to be able to exploit LeCroy's weak arm and general shakiness afield.

It looked like a good gamble when the Nationals leaped to a large lead in the game, but then the Astros decided to test LeCroy's skills. They stole seven bases and provoked the overwhelmed catcher to make a throwing error, bringing the Astros close to tying the score. When LeCroy made his second throwing error of the game in the seventh inning, allowing the Astros to put the go-ahead runs in scoring position, Robinson had to choose between a devastating loss for his team and a devastated player. He chose his team, and pulled his struggling catcher from the field mid-inning, violating the baseball taboo. (Pulling a player out of the game for failing to hustle, as Billy Martin did to Reggie Jackson in 1977, is a different matter entirely, for there the intention is to embarrass the player for unprofessional conduct on the field.)

With a new Nationals catcher, the Astros stopped running amok and the game was saved. Afterwards, Robinson faced reporters with his face streaming with tears. He felt that he had humiliated one of his players, and that violated all of his Golden Rule instincts. Robinson had been a player himself, and knew how such treatment would have felt. But Robinson was ethically correct: His first obligation was to win the game, not to preserve LeCroy's feelings. Unfortunately for LeCroy, the Golden Rule—and the unwritten rule—didn't apply.

The principle of not embarrassing a player frequently yields to game realities, as when an ineffective pitcher is left in a game to absorb a beating to preserve the bullpen for upcoming games. Sometimes, however, players and managers allow the principle to trump the need to win, especially when the player facing embarrassment is widely respected. This anomaly was on display in the 2004 ALCS and World Series, when no opposing batters forced Red Sox pitcher Curt Schilling to field a bunt even though the fact that his ankle tendon was severely injured was well-publicized.

The Red Sox were the recipients of this "unwritten rule" largesse again in 2008, when no Angels batters bunted on Sox third-baseman Mike Lowell, who was known to be playing on an injured hip that made fielding bunts painful, and perhaps impossible. In these instances and others like them, the adherence to an unwritten rule results in *un*ethical conduct that violates baseball's integrity. It is the duty of a player to exploit the weaknesses of the opposing team, whether it embarrasses opposing players or not. Here the ends justify the means, and utilitarianism, not reciprocity, should apply.

One of the greatest changes in the culture of baseball is the ascendance of another unwritten rule with a Golden Rule pedigree: "Don't jeopardize an opponent's career." In the 1970 All-Star game, Pete Rose electrified the crowd and won the game by bowling over catcher Ray Fosse at home to jar loose the ball and score the winning run. Fosse was injured and never the same player again. Since that famous play, almost universally praised at the time as good, hard, winning baseball, players have become increasingly reticent about causing other players pain, and, perhaps more to the point, robbing them and their families of million-dollar contracts.

Earlier players were not so concerned with their opponents' welfare. There were no long-term contracts, and the ethics of the ball field often resembled those of the battlefield. The tradition of trying to hurt opposing players began early in baseball's history.

In the 1890s, Tommy Tucker, first baseman for the Boston Beaneaters, was well known for trying to spike every base-runner who went by. Though Ty Cobb has become the symbol of this kind of conduct, he was just one of many, and probably far from the worst. Dick "Rowdy Richard" Bartell, a famously mean little shortstop whose 18-year career ended in 1941, had a reputation for trying to spike opposing players' hands at second base. Maury Wills, the man who broke Cobb's single-season stolen base record, admitted, "I spiked more guys than Ty Cobb. I did it in a way that appeared accidental. It wasn't."

Pitchers intentionally hitting batters is another once-accepted practice that has gradually gone from being considered part of the sport's enforcement mechanism to conduct largely regarded as unethical. Batters were "plunked" for such offenses as showing up the pitcher by admiring a home run too long, running the bases too slowly after hitting a homer, or just hitting the home run at all. A batter was asking for a beaning by sliding into a fielder too hard, or crowding the plate.

But while some pitchers, like the infamous Sal "the Barber" Maglie, claimed that they could hit a player with precision so as to deliver both maximum pain and the most cogent message with minimal injury, the fact was that batters often suffered concussions and broken bones. After young slugger Tony Conigliaro's horrible beaning by pitcher Jack Hamilton in 1967 (Conigliaro habitually crowded the plate), brush-back pitches started to decline. The advent of the designated hitter in the American League, removing the pitcher from any danger of retaliation himself, eventually led to "plunking" batters becoming less acceptable.

What has happened, over the years, is that combat ethics, essentially a utilitarian "the ends justify the means" approach to physical contact in baseball, has yielded to a reciprocity-based ethical system in which players respect the right of every individual to remain healthy enough to keep playing the game and earning seven- and eight-figure salaries. Undoubtedly, some of the intensity and competitiveness has been lost. Ethically, however, the game has moved in the right direction. Unlike NFL football, baseball does not need to be about hurting people.

A companion principle to the avoidance of embarrassing or hurting fellow players is the principle that players should not make a special effort to prevent another player from completing a historic or career-enhancing achievement. This Golden Rule-based impulse is rooted in collegial respect as well as appreciation for the entertainment value of the game. Seeing a pitcher pitch a no-hitter or a batter hit for the cycle excites fans and strengthens the sport, which in turn benefits all players. Thus breaking up a no-hitter with a bunt, or intentionally walking a batter who is three-fourths of the way to a cycle, is traditionally frowned-upon as "bush league."

But is it? In 2001, San Diego Padres player Ben Davis broke up a Curt Schilling (then with the Arizona Diamondbacks) attempt at a perfect game with an eighth-inning bunt single. (Schilling has a penchant for being at the center of ethical controversies.) Schilling's manager, Bob Brenly, and his teammates savaged Davis in the press. But Davis was on the right side of the ethical conflict. The score was only 2-0 at the time, and his job was to win the game, not to help Schilling get a no-no. One wonders if Davis would have bunted on Schilling three years later when he was wearing the bloody sock. Alas, we will never know.

On the other side of the line from Davis was pitcher Denny McLain, who admitted to "grooving" a pitch to Mickey Mantle in the slugger's last game. McLain's instincts to send a gift to a baseball legend was admirable, but his obligation, not just to the game and the fans, but to Mantle, was to do his best.

Baseball's unwritten rules are an odd mix, including common sense warnings ("Don't put the go-ahead run on base with an intentional walk") and silly superstitions ("Never mention a no-hitter when one is in progress"). Some are ethical traditions that protect an inherent flaw in the game. For example, a batter is never supposed to peek at the catcher's signals to the pitcher. While sign-stealing by the runner at second is completely within the boundaries of baseball culture, the batter doing so directly is regarded as "cheating." This is a classic example of an evolved cultural ethical norm that preserves order in the game. It has become accepted that having batters constantly trying to see catchers' signals and catchers trying to change signals they thought has been seen would slow the game unacceptably.

The most troubling unwritten rule is perhaps the most zealously enforced of all: "What happens in the clubhouse stays in the clubhouse." When 30 or so men live and travel together six months out of the year and have to make their living playing as a team, it is obviously crucial for these men to have each other's trust and respect, if not affection. But while adherence to the rule fairly and wisely protects players' privacy and personal secrets, it also has contributed to many of baseball's most damaging scandals.

Self-policing is a necessary component of any profession, and it is also the most detested and distained ethical obligation of all. Lawyers are required to report colleagues who have engaged in conduct that calls into question their fitness to practice, but few do. Doctors protect drug-addicted and mistake-prone physicians; police often erect a "blue wall" around corrupt or brutal officers.

Baseball players, now bolstered by their union, have observed drug abuse, steroid abuse, gambling and lesser misconduct by other players, and steadfastly refused to report any of it. Is the damage to the game that results from allowing serious misconduct and even law-breaking to persist unreported greater than the damage to baseball's team structure that would result if it became acceptable to be a "snitch"? Perhaps, but that is a pointless question. Although it is an ethical obligation on the part of any employee or organization member to report misconduct by others, the Golden Rule operates perversely here to guarantee an unethical result. No player would want someone else to report on his substance abuse, steroid use or gambling problems, so doing the right thing, in this case, feels wrong. And the unwritten rules of baseball are all about what feels *right*.

Conduct Governed by Basic Cultural Ethical Systems and Values

Though professions create their own ethical context, they also do not exist in a vacuum. The ethical standards of the rest of American society count, and baseball's players and culture cannot afford to ignore them. When

major league teams colluded to keep player salaries down in the 1980s, in violation of the spirit of the agreements signed with the players union, even public dislike of the rapidly inflating player salary levels couldn't overcome the fact that the collusion was unfair, dishonest, and unethical. Despite his overwhelming popularity in Boston, when outfielder Manny Ramirez this season begged out of games, faked injuries and appeared not to play hard on the field to force a change in his contract status, popular opinion there and elsewhere rejected his conduct as unethical—disloyal, a breach of responsibility and trust, dishonest and venal. Moreover, Boston's willingness in the past to tolerate insubordination and other misconduct from Ramirez that would have led to stiff sanctions against a lesser player was suddenly being questioned, raising a major ethical issue—unequal treatment of star performers—that faces all organizations in and out of sports.

Society's ethical standards govern other situations in baseball, such as substance abuse. Excessive drinking and alcoholism are no longer regarded as an ethical breach, but allowing either to affect on-field performance is. Similarly, a player hiding an injury to sign a long-term contract runs afoul of basic workplace ethics, regardless of how much sympathy such a player may have among other players. The public does not like liars, and liars cannot he heroes. While considerations of self-preservation may have led Pete Rose to lie about his gambling and Rafael Palmeiro to lie about his steroid use, their dishonesty alone was sufficient to change their status from heroes to outcasts.

For in the end, all of baseball ethics rely on the sympathy and tolerance of the public. If the sport appears fair and honest, played with integrity and courage by men who do not display values parents must condemn to their children, then Major League Baseball will thrive. It is fine and appropriate for the National Pastime to have its own system of ethics, but it also must be seen as ethical by those who watch and love the game. As Terrance Mann, the disaffected author played by James Earl Jones, intones in his memorable speech at the climax of "Field of Dreams," "baseball reminds us of all that once was good and that could be again."

In baseball, ethics matter.

The Business of Baseball

by Brian Borawski

Is a golden era over? Heading into the 2008 season, Major League Baseball seemed to be on an unprecedented elevator of success. In 2007, the sport set an attendance record for the fourth consecutive season and for the first time ever league revenue topped the $6 billion mark. MLB.com continued to set the standard for sports web sites and the league's Internet wing, Major League Baseball Advanced Media (MLBAM), was still making money hand over fist.

Still, sometimes you can do everything right, and circumstances outside your control can create bumps in the road. The United States economy began showing chinks in its armor in the second half of 2007, spiralling into one of the worst stock market crashes our country has seen in 2008. We'll take a closer look at the numbers later, but while baseball did manage its second best season in attendance, you wonder whether we're just hitting a bump in the road or whether we'll look back at 2007 as the multi-year peak.

Of course there are also the things you can control, and in December 2007, the Mitchell Report finally was released. In a lot of ways, the steroid story was put to rest, but for a few players, a new can of worms was opened. You had Barry Bonds, the recently crowned home run champion, all but blackballed from the majors since he had the unenviable task of standing trial for perjury and obstruction of justice. For Roger Clemens, the steroid saga was just beginning and he's currently embroiled in a defamation lawsuit with his accuser and former trainer, Brian McNamee.

Still, baseball didn't just survive. In a lot of ways, it thrived. Don't take my word for it though, because we'll count the ways.

Peaking Attendance

The 78,614,880 tickets MLB sold in 2008 look good in just about every light except for one: when you compare it to the record-setting season in 2007. The 2008 mark was the second best of all time and seven teams broke their franchise attendance records, but this was one short of last year's eight new records. Twenty-three teams topped the two million mark in 2008, also one fewer than in 2007, when 24 did. I don't want to take too much away from what was simply another fantastic season at the gate, but I'll discuss the downturn in a couple of paragraphs.

The positives to the 2008 season were many. The New York Yankees set an American League attendance record of 4,298,543, breaking the record that they set just the year before. The New York Mets became just the fourth team to top the four million mark with a record year in their last season at Shea Stadium; they led the way in what turned out to be a National League record average attendance of 34,201. Wrigley Field had the best attendance of any venue in the city of Chicago's history. The Boston Red Sox set their ninth consecutive attendance record and still have the longest-running consecutive sellout record with 469 games and counting.

Still, with all the positives, MLB has a couple of things working against it, and I foresee another drop in attendance in 2009.

The first reason just has to do with capacity. Successful teams like the Red Sox are selling as many tickets as they can and there are only so many new seats that can be put into a ballpark. In addition, both the Yankees and Mets will have new stadiums next year with lower capacities than their current venues. Even if everything were great, odds would be good that the majors would be set for at least a slight downturn in attendance.

Unfortunately, times are not good. A recessionary environment that began in the earlier parts of 2008 has developed into a full-fledged stock market crash. People are in full on panic mode and unemployment is at a multiyear high. In addition, it's hard to get any kind of loan and things aren't expected to turn until some time in late 2009. With teams pushing to get their season ticket renewals in order, many will be feeling the pain as businesses and individuals consider giving up their seats for more mundane things like making payroll and paying the mortgage.

My guess is baseball could get back down to around the 75 million mark. That sounds like a steep drop, but attendance in 2006 was just more than 76 million and times were still good then. Teams like the Yankees, Mets and Red Sox will continue to sell out, but teams like the Detroit Tigers, which set an attendance record for the second straight year, could see a steep decline because the Detroit area has been particularly hard hit by the downturn and the team had a pretty disappointing season. You're also going to see parity take a hit as the big market teams continue to make a lot of money, just not as much as before, while the smaller market teams could see their bottom lines shrink considerably.

The State of Minor League Baseball

While Major League Baseball failed to set a new attendance record in 2008, minor league baseball shined and set a record for the fifth consecutive season. The final number for 2008 was 43,263,740 tickets sold, topping the 2007 total of 42,812,812. The increase of nearly half a million was solid, but it fell short of the 1.1 million increase between 2006 and 2007. Still, those are some impressive numbers and my guess is that minor league baseball will continue to shine. It's more affordable than the big league product and most teams cater toward the family. With a tough economy, people are going to be looking for bargains. My guess is, while minor league baseball might fall short of setting a record in 2009, the slide should be a lot less steep than what you're going to see in MLB.

The success of the minor leagues doesn't mean change isn't on the way. As we see in a lot of even-numbered years, there's the potential for some big-time shuffling among minor league affiliates. In Triple-A alone, six major league teams will have a new minor league affiliate and two other cities will see their teams move. The Columbus Clippers kicked things off by announcing early in August that they'd be parting ways with the Washington Nationals. That allowed the Cleveland Indians to move in and have an affiliate just a couple of hours away. The New York Mets took advantage of this and switched their affiliate to the Buffalo Bisons, who were previously with the Cleveland Indians. The Florida Marlins moved into a former affiliate, the New Orleans Zephyrs. The Los Angeles Dodgers then set up shop with the Marlins' old affiliate, the Albuquerque Isotopes. That left the Las Vegas 51s and the Toronto Blue Jays as the odd teams out.

At the Double-A level, three teams will swap affiliates. The Carolina Mudcats will now be the Cincinnati Reds' affiliate, while their old affiliate, the Chattanooga Lookouts, will be the affiliate for the Los Angeles Dodgers. The Florida Marlins are the other team switching, but they'll now have the cross-state Jacksonville Suns as their farm club. Six Single-A affiliates will have new big league sponsors and one Single-A team, the Columbus Catfish, is relocating to Bowling Green, Ky.

The growing trend is to have your affiliates as close as possible. While at times it's impossible, some teams have done a nice job of setting up their systems. The Indians are a perfect example. Their new Triple-A affiliate is the cross-state Columbus Clippers, their Double-A affiliate is in Akron, Ohio and their Single-A affiliate is in Lake County, Ohio. The Cincinnati Reds also have two minor league affiliates within a two hour-drive. Travel costs aren't going down anytime soon, so if teams can cut costs by having their minor league teams close by, they're going to try to take advantage of it.

Building Ballparks

MLB had one new ballpark in 2008: Nationals Park in Washington, D.C. The construction of the park seemed anticlimactic after all of the troubles between the league and the city with the stadium deal, but it opened as advertised. Unfortunately, the Nationals struggled and while the team saw a nice bump in attendance, it was the lowest attendance total by a team with a new stadium since the "Camden Yards"-era of ballparks began back in 1992.

The New York Yankees and New York Mets will both be in their new ballparks when the season opens in 2009. There wasn't a lack of fanfare closing out the old ones. The Yankees closed out Yankee Stadium without making the playoffs for the first time since 1993, but the All-Star Game was played there. The Mets collapsed again down the stretch and failed to make the postseason despite the blockbuster trade for Johan Santana. Still, both teams topped the four million mark in attendance and at least a part of that was in anticipation of the new ballparks.

Next up in the new stadium chain are the Minnesota Twins; their ballpark is set to open for the 2010 season. The Twins already have sold the naming rights to Target, so Twins fans will get Target Field, which isn't too far away from the Target Center. Also in the works is Target Plaza, which will include a pedestrian bridge as well as a public gathering place that'll rest between the ballpark and downtown Minneapolis.

After that, things become less clear. The Florida Marlins finally got their stadium deal pushed through earlier in the year before things hit another snag. Local businessman Norman Braman sued to try to block the deal because he felt the tax dollars being used didn't serve a public purpose. In early September, Miami-Dade Circuit Court Judge Beth Cohen ruled in favor of the Marlins and with that, the team is moving ahead with its plans.

The Tampa Bay Rays announced their hopes for a new St. Petersburg waterfront ballpark on top of the Rays' spring training home, Al Lang Field. They proposed a plan that would involve selling their current home, Tropicana Field, to come up with the money for the new ballpark but the idea won't be a reality any time soon. While proponents got approval to get the St. Petersburg attorney to draft a stadium ballot proposal for this November's ballot, the referendum plan was shelved and the idea has been put on hold indefinitely.

The Oakland Athletics still have plans to open Cisco Field in Fremont, but as time passes, their hopes for a 2012 opening are in jeopardy. The whole plan is under scrutiny, including everything from parking and mass transit issues to just getting an environmental review finished.

Another major issue now, especially for deals without financing in place (such as the Rays'), is the current state of the credit crisis. Banks aren't lending, so any construction plans have to have an asterisk next to them; when it's time to dip into the money pot, there might not be anything there. That could cause a delay of a year or two.

Spring Training Wars

This was a good year for spring training baseball. For the third time in four years, the league set a spring training attendance record: 3.7 million fans came to spring training games in 2008, versus 3.4 million in 2007. For the first time, the average attendance at a spring training game topped 8,000.

What gets lost in the numbers is how Florida is losing team after team to Arizona. This past spring, 18 teams played in the Grapefruit League, 12 in the Cactus League. There will be a major shift in 2009 when the Los Angeles Dodgers and Cleveland Indians move to their new spring training homes in Arizona. The Indians will be opening a two-team facility in Goodyear, while the Dodgers will be moving from historic Dodgertown in Vero Beach, Fla. to Glendale, Ariz.

That shifts the number of teams between Florida and Arizona to 16 and 14 respectively in 2009. Beginning in 2010, the two states will have parity. The Cincinnati Reds were the latest team to announce their departure from Florida to the greener (money green) pastures of Arizona. When the Reds' current home in Sarasota dragged its feet on a stadium renovation bill, the Reds started to talk to Goodyear about sharing the two-team facility with the Indians. Around Opening Day, the Reds made their moving plans official.

The name of the game here is money. Arizona municipalities have been willing to put money into top-notch facilities while the Florida locations have decided to hold back. It's too bad, because for some

of these Florida towns, the month and half of spring training could make or break a lot of businesses. Towns like Tampa will be able to absorb the loss, but a smaller town like Vero Beach might be harder hit losing that big dollar push that comes with spring training season.

Instant Replay

Late in 2007, baseball general managers voted to institute instant replay, but as is usual in baseball, the implementation dragged on. In May 2008, MLB announced that it might begin experimenting with instant replay in the Arizona Fall League and then continue the trial in 2009 with the World Baseball Classic, but some controversial calls during the summer prompted baseball to accelerate its plans. In late August, the instant replay experiment began and for the first time, umpires are able to double-check the film on home run calls.

At first there was an outcry from both traditionalists and those who felt the game would be slowed down even more, but once the process was used and the delays were minimal, the controversy died. Umpires can check the replay to determine whether a fly ball went over the fence, whether it went fair or foul or whether there was fan interference. To review a play, the umpire actually has to leave the field to view the video. The crew chief makes the final decision. As time goes by, I'm sure replay will be used in more and more circumstances, but for now, I think this is a fairly painless start.

Baseball Teams for Sale

For the first year since I've been doing these *THT Annual* reviews, there were no ownership changes. That doesn't mean teams weren't moving in this direction, and while the quantity was down, the quality was as high as ever because one of the crown jewels of baseball, the Chicago Cubs, is on the block, although the sale will now drag on into another year.

Late in 2007, local real estate developer Sam Zell purchased the Tribune Company, which also owns Wrigley Field and the Chicago Cubs. Shortly after the purchase, Zell announced that he'd be selling the team for a couple of reasons. One was that Zell had an ownership interest in the crosstown Chicago White Sox. The second was that Zell used an inordinate amount of debt to purchase the company and by selling the team, he could relieve himself of at least a portion of it.

Initially, the plans were to break the Cubs up from their ballpark and sell them separately. A deal on the table would have sold Wrigley Field to the Illinois Sports Facilities Authority, a state agency that already owns and operates U.S. Cellular Field, where the White Sox play. That deal fell through and now Tribune is back to selling the Cubs and Wrigley Field as a package that has an estimated sales price of at least $1 billion.

Over the summer, the Cubs appeared to have their suitor list narrowed to five, but then Zell threw the league a curve ball when he announced he wanted to try to minimize his tax obligation as much as possible. Tribune bought the team for $20.5 million in 1981 and with a $1 billion sales price, you're talking about a lot of capital gains taxes in an outright sale. Zell is proposing setting up a leveraged partnership with a prospective buyer, having the partnership load up on debt, and then have the money come out to Tribune, which will retain a small stake in the partnership, as a tax free distribution.

What's good for the Tribune, though, is not viewed as good for the team and for the league. MLB has some pretty strict rules on how much debt a team can carry and this deal probably would push the Cubs beyond those limits. Still, there's some flexibility to the debt service rules when it comes to a sales transaction, so the deal may still get done. It'll just be a bumpy ride along the way.

The San Diego Padres aren't up for sale, but many feel a potential transaction is imminent. Owner John Moores is in the middle of a divorce with his wife, Becky, in California, a community property state. It's very unclear what will happen to the team when the dust settles. A rumor in early October that Moores had put 49 percent of the team up for sale was denied by the team and the league.

The End of a Golden Era

In last year's *Annual*, I wrote about baseball reaching a golden era in 2006. A new collective bargaining agreement was signed without so much as a peep about a work stoppage from either side and the league set another attendance record. This led into 2007 where the numbers looked even better and it looked like nothing could stop the MLB juggernaut.

The season just ended was still a good year, but it was a small step back, and the current credit crisis and the resulting stock market crash will cause problems not just for baseball, but just about every sport. Fans and businesses will be less likely to sign on for another season of tickets if times are tough, and the current lock-up in lending could cause problems with everything from the sale of the Cubs to some of the pending stadium deals. It'll also be interesting to see how baseball adjusts if there's a downturn in revenue. If the teams are hurting, they're less likely to dole out the amount of money they have the past couple of years.

In short, a lot of forces will be bearing down and some of those will be outside of baseball's control. How baseball reacts to a downturn in the world economy should determine how well the sport prospers over the next decade. Just about any sport with the tradition of baseball can thrive when things are good, but it's when things turn bad that you get to see the true mettle of baseball's leadership. My guess is that we'll be seeing whether the mettle is there sooner rather then later.

We Shall Not Be Saved

by Rich Lederer

Before 1969, a save was either something Jesus did or a hockey statistic used to measure the value of goaltenders. In fact, the two were mixed in a famous bumper sticker found on cars of Boston Bruins hockey fans of that era: "Jesus saves! And Esposito scores on the rebound!"

Phil Esposito, who led the NHL in scoring in five out of six seasons during the late 1960s and early 1970s, would plant himself in the slot near the net and score goals from all angles. The big center won the Hart Memorial Trophy as the MVP of the league twice and was inducted into the Hockey Hall of Fame in 1984.

Forty years ago, there was no mention of the word "save" in Major League Baseball's rules book. That's right, the save, which was the brainchild of sportswriter Jerome Holtzman, didn't become an official MLB statistic until 1969. It was the game's first new statistic since the 1920 introduction of the RBI.

The save, which has undergone a few changes in its definition over the years, started off slowly but has become so popular that managers have changed the usage patterns of their bullpens. In other words, managers now manage to the save rule itself.

What constitutes a save? Here is the definition, according to Major League Baseball's official rules: "A save is a statistic credited to a relief pitcher, as set forth in this Rule 10.19. The official scorer shall credit a pitcher with a save when such pitcher meets all four of the following conditions:

1. He is the finishing pitcher in a game won by his team;

2. He is not the winning pitcher;

3. He is credited with at least a third of an inning pitched; and

4. He satisfies one of the following conditions:

    - He enters the game with a lead of no more than three runs and pitches for at least one inning;

    - He enters the game, regardless of the count, with the potential tying run either on base, or at bat or on deck (that is, the potential tying run is either already on base or is one of the first two batters he faces); or

    - He pitches for at least three innings."

The save rule, which was first adopted for the 1969 season, was amended for the 1973 and 1975 seasons. The current rule has been in effect ever since. Using today's standards, researchers have retroactively calculated saves for all major league seasons prior to 1969.

Why are we talking about the save in 2008? Three reasons:

1. Francisco Rodriguez of the Los Angeles Angels set the single-season save mark with 62, breaking the Chicago White Sox's Bobby Thigpen's record of 57 in 1990.

2. Goose Gossage was elected to the Baseball Hall of Fame, becoming only the fifth relief pitcher to be enshrined in Cooperstown.

3. Jerome Holtzman, the creator of the save formula, died on July 19 at the age of 81.

Holtzman, a baseball beat writer and columnist for four decades, covered the Chicago Cubs and White Sox for the *Chicago Sun-Times* and *Tribune*. Nine years after being honored by the Baseball Writers Association of America with the J.G. Taylor Spink Award in 1989, Holtzman retired and was hired by Bud Selig as the first official historian for Major League Baseball.

The legendary writer, who began covering MLB in 1957, devised the idea for the save in 1960. In an article that appeared in *Baseball Digest* in May 2002, Holtzman wrote:

> *I invented the first formula for saves in 1960, in my fourth season as a baseball beat writer. At that time there were only two stats to measure the effectiveness of a reliever: earned run average and the win-loss record. Neither was an appropriate measure of a reliever's effectiveness.*
>
> *(...)For example, Elroy Face of the Pittsburgh Pirates was 18-1 in 1959, still the one-season record for the most victories by a reliever. Face was immediately acclaimed as the best bullpen artist in all baseball history.*
>
> *I knew better. He was much more effective the year before when he was 5-2.*
>
> *In 10 of his 18 victories, Face coughed up the tying or lead run but got the win because the Pirates had a strong hitting team and rallied for the victory while he was the pitcher of record.*

I was with the Cubs during that season. They had a righty-lefty bullpen tandem of Don Elston and Bill Henry, both of whom repeatedly protected leads but were comparatively obscure. They didn't have eye-catching stats.

And so one day, during the following season, while waiting on the team bus outside the Chase Hotel in St. Louis, I worked up the first save rule. I remember showing it to the Hall of Famer Lou Boudreau, then a Cubs broadcaster who was seated next to me.

Boudreau approved and so I brought it to the attention of The Sporting News. Mr. Spink also liked the idea and immediately decided to award annual Fireman Trophies to the top relievers in the National and American leagues.

To determine the winners, one point was given for a save and one point for a victory in relief. It was a mistake. Two points should have been given for a save. A save is twice as important. This was soon corrected.

(...)The Baseball Writers Association of America appointed me the chairman of a committee to approach the Official Scoring Rules Committee to make it an official rule and include it in the box scores.

I had kept the unofficial figures for nine years and during this period did a weekly story for The Sporting News along with a running list of the leaders. I bowed out in 1969 when the save was officially adopted and haven't been involved since.

It was baseball's first new major statistic since the run batted in was added in 1920. I knew it was a significant advance but never realized it would escalate to the current proportions. Also, it didn't occur to me that the managers would twist the rule and summon only their best reliever in save situations."

Holtzman's impact on relief pitchers—and closers to be more specific—cannot be overstated.

Former White Sox general manager Roland Hemond believes every relief pitcher in baseball is indebted to Holtzman because the save rule has substantially increased their market value.

"Pitchers owe him," Hemond said. "Jerome should have gotten a percentage from all the closers for creating the save. He helped a lot of relief pitchers become wealthy."

Steve Stone, the 1980 American League Cy Young Award winner and current color commentator for the

White Sox, said, "In the case of Jerome, every one of the closers over the last 30 years ... should take out their checkbooks and write a gigantic check to whatever foundation or charity the family directs. He's really the person responsible for being able to quantify what has become one of the most important positions on the field."

The commissioner weighed in after Holtzman's death last summer. "He created the save statistic which in turn increased the importance of the relief pitcher. He was a giant in his industry."

However, according to *Chicago Sun-Times* columnist Bill Gleason, Holtzman was "sorry he'd come up with the (save) concept" because "it wasn't necessary."

Relief Pitchers in the Hall of Fame
• Hoyt Wilhelm, 1985
• Rollie Fingers, 1992
• Dennis Eckersley, 2004
• Bruce Sutter, 2006
• Goose Gossage, 2008

While perhaps unnecessary, the save has become such an integral part of the contemporary game that a new role has emerged among relief pitchers. Star relievers, once known as "firemen" for entering a game with runners on base in the middle of an inning and putting out the fire, are now called "closers" because their job is to come in and close the game by shutting down the opposition in the last inning.

Closers almost never enter a game except in save situations and usually arrive on the scene at the beginning of the ninth inning. This practice is in stark contrast to earlier patterns of bullpen usage. Previously, a relief ace would be used in close contests, including tie games or even when his team was behind by one or two runs—and often for two or three innings at a time.

Gabriel Schecter, in "All Saves Are Not Created Equal" in *The Baseball Research Journal* (Number 35, pages 100-103), a publication of the Society for American Baseball Research, wrote: "It's as if the manager gears his game strategy toward providing his closer with the chance to accumulate a lot of saves, compared to the earlier generations when the manager identified his best reliever and sought to get as many innings as possible from him, with victories and saves the by-product of quality work."

As an example of the latter, Schecter cites the Los Angeles Dodgers Mike Marshall's Cy Young Award-winning season in 1974 when he set the record with 208.1 innings pitched in relief, "Ninety-three of those innings when he entered with his team losing or tied, and he became the winning pitcher in 15 of those appearances."

Another way to illustrate how the usage of top relievers has changed over the past four decades is to compare firemen of the past, such as Hall of Famers Rollie Fingers, Bruce Sutter, and Gossage, all of whom pitched predominantly in the 1970s and 1980s, with Trevor Hoffman, the all-time career saves leader who made his mark in the 1990s and the first decade of the current century.

MVP Relievers

- Jim Konstanty, Philadelphia Phillies, 1950
- Rollie Fingers, Milwaukee Brewers, 1981
- Willie Hernandez, Detroit Tigers, 1984
- Dennis Eckersley, Oakland A's, 1992

To wit, of Fingers' 341 career saves, 135 (or nearly 40 percent) entailed pitching two or more innings, including 36 of three or more innings. Sutter and Gossage recorded 130 and 125 saves (or 43 and 40 percent), respectively, of two or more innings. Hoffman, on the other hand, has earned just seven saves (or 1.2 percent) of two or more innings out of a total of 554. Only two of his saves have exceeded two innings and none have been as long as three innings.

Schecter reported that Sutter, in a matter of 39 days (from May 27 to July 4, 1984), had "more saves (nine) where he pitched at least two innings than Hoffman has in his whole career. Gossage did the same thing from Aug. 15, 1980, through the end of that season, and Fingers accomplished it in a 53-day stretch in 1979."

As Schecter pointed out, "The earlier pitchers acted as their own setup men. These firemen put out the fire and cleaned up after themselves."

Similarly, Fingers was credited with 101 of his saves (30 percent) when he entered the game with either the winning or tying run on base, while Hoffman has pulled off this feat in only 36 of his saves (less than 7 percent) and only once in the past seven years.

The biggest difference between yesteryear's firemen and the current crop of closers is the number of times they enter the game to start the ninth inning with no runners on base, "the easiest situation for a reliever to face," according to Schecter, "even with just a one-run lead." Thanks to Tom Ruane of Retrosheet, "if the home team starts the ninth inning with a one-run lead, it will win roughly 85 percent of the time ... Start the ninth inning with a two-run lead, and you'll win about 93 percent of the time; with a three-run lead, it jumps to a 97 percent win rate."

Hoffman has been used in the latter situation 142 times over the course of his career, while Fingers (11), Sutter (16) and Gossage (14) were rarely used in this manner.

Optimal Usage Patterns

Bill James, in "Valuing Relievers" in *The New Bill James Historical Baseball Abstract* (pages 232-239), tested relief aces from five different eras since the mid-1930s and boldly stated that the modern usage pattern of a relief ace is "clearly and absolutely not the optimal usage pattern."

The relief aces of the Hoyt Wilhelm era (1963-1978) were about 50 percent more valuable than modern relief aces, mostly because they pitched more innings, but also because the runs that they saved had more impact, one for one, than those saved by modern relief aces. "There are really two situations in which a run saved has a very high impact—when the game is tied, and when the reliever's team is one run ahead. In those two situations, a run saved has a huge impact on the team's won-lost record."

According to James, "each run saved in a tie game has more than eight times the impact of a run saved with a three-run lead. If you use your relief ace to save a three-run lead in the ninth inning, you'll win that game 99 percent of the time. If you don't use your ace in that situation, you'll win 98 percent of the time." James rhetorically asks, "Is that a smart thing to do, to use a precious asset in that situation?"

Based on his research, James believes the optimal usage pattern would be to go to the relief ace:

- two innings a game when the game is tied,
- two innings a game when you have a one-run lead, and
- one inning at a time in other games when the game is close at the end and the relief ace hasn't been used for a day or two.

In other words, as James wrote, "bring in your man when you're ahead by one after seven innings, when you're tied after seven innings, or when the game is close and the relief ace isn't tired."

James believes that managers in the late 1970s had one good idea, which was to define and limit the relief pitcher's role so that he wasn't overworked, and one bad idea, which was to use the reliever only in "save" situations.

Even Whitey Herzog, in *You're Missin' a Great Game* (page 129), opined, "it's better to have your closer go two innings every other day than one inning every day."

The huge dollar rewards of arbitration and free agency place undue pressure on managers to manage to the save rule itself. However, as James noted, "The salary-driven use of statistics takes precedence over the logical use of statistics only when you allow it to."

James argued that "when you're defining the most effective use of your closer, you should *start* with the tie games. That is when the impact of a run saved is the largest, when the game is tied." He believes a closer used in this manner "would not save 50 games—but he could win 20, and he might win 30" or perhaps "win 20 games and also save 20."

In conclusion, James claimed, "If the manager wants to win as many games as possible, he can get a lot bigger bang from his relief ace by pitching him in tie games than he can by pitching him with a three-run lead—eight times bigger. As percentage baseball goes, 800 percent is a big percentage."

A Better Way to Measure Relief Pitchers

If saves are not the answer, then how should we measure the effectiveness of relievers?

In addition to using stats that pitchers can control, such as strikeouts, walks and home runs allowed per batter faced, I would suggest that more attention be given to metrics like Win Probability Added (or WPA for short), available on Fangraphs (www.fangraphs.com). WPA is the difference in Win Expectancy (which is defined as the percent chance a particular team will win based on the score, inning, outs, runners on base and the run environment) between the start of the play and the end of the play. That difference is then credited/debited to the batter and the pitcher. Over the course of the season, each player's WPA for individual plays is added up to get his season total WPA.

The Leverage Index (LI) is a key component of Win Probability Added and Win Expectancy. LI measures how important a particular situation is in a baseball game depending on the inning, score, outs and number of players on base, as created by Tom Tango.

While Francisco Rodriguez had the highest Leverage Index (2.54) of any reliever in 2008, K-Rod finished sixth in WPA because he just wasn't quite as effective as Brad Lidge, Mariano Rivera, Joakim Soria, Carlos Marmol and Bobby Jenks. Sure, Frankie set the single-season high of 62 saves last season, but he also had seven blown saves (tops among the leaders in WPA). Lidge, who converted all 48 of his save opportunities during the regular season and postseason, led all relievers with a WPA of 5.37.

Top Relievers in 2008 WPA	
Pitcher	WPA
Brad Lidge	5.37
Mariano Rivera	4.47
Joakim Soria	4.08
Carlos Marmol	3.77
Bobby Jenks	3.47
Francisco Rodriguez	3.33
J.P. Howell	3.33
Joe Nathan	3.26
Brad Ziegler	3.20
Eddie Guardado	2.85

There are a lot of ways to measure a reliever's effectiveness. Grant Balfour had the highest K/G (12.65), Rivera produced the lowest BB/G (0.76), and Jim Johnson did not allow a single home run all year while tossing 68.2 IP. Hong-Chi Kuo may have had the best combination of stats (11.16 K/G, 1.95 BB/G, and 0.39 HR/G) en route to the lowest Fielding Independent Pitching (FIP) ERA of 1.99. Jonathan Papelbon (10.00 K/G, 1.04 BB/G, and 0.52 HR/G) and Rivera (9.81, 0.76, and 0.51) ranked second and third in FIP at 2.01 and 2.03, respectively.

Saves as a standalone statistic can be highly misleading. As with most baseball stats, saves need to be viewed in their proper context. How many opportunities did the pitcher have? Have many saves did he blow? How responsible was he for the saves and blown saves? How difficult or easy were the saves achieved?

When it comes to measuring relievers, there's a lot more to consider than just the raw number of saves recorded. Even Jerome Holtzman, save his soul, would agree with me on that point.

Many thanks to Dave Smith of Retrosheet for his expert analysis and feedback.

Underrated by Roto

by Brandon Isleib

It inevitably happens. You watch your team's scrappy second baseman and wonder what in the world he brings to the team besides a small strike zone. He never seems to do much; you certainly wouldn't come near him on your fantasy team. You get jealous of a team that doesn't have this problem at the position. Maybe you wish for a Chase Utley and forget temporarily that Phillies phans are as concerned about third base as you are about second. And yet, after the game, the other players are crediting this guy for all the "energy" or "spark" he brings to the team. Every team seems to love its David Eckstein, even when you're sitting there wondering why management doesn't get somebody who produces more.

As a whole, fantasy baseball hasn't helped our perception of these guys one bit. The reductionism that the sport-within-a-sport brings comes armed with loads of numbers, fulfilling our immediate craving for stats while encouraging us to view the world only through them. A pitcher who gives up a lot of walks but induces a lot of double plays frustrates us; couldn't he have gotten the outs without killing his WHIP? Not that we actually care about his WHIP; ours is far more important. As the French would say, c'est la fantasy baseball.

This article will compare overall rankings in Base Runs to overall rankings in Alex Patton's Standings Gain Points (SGP) to see who's been thriving or wilting under the fantasy spotlight. This isn't aimed at giving tips or sleepers for next year's fantasy team; it's aimed at helping you appreciate the guys you're having a hard time appreciating.

The Method

Base Runs is one of the best measures of true offensive value, putting linear weights for important offensive events into a team context and giving a balanced look at overall worth as a batsman. Similarly, SGP is one of the best measures of fantasy value, weighting categories in whatever fantasy environment the player finds himself to determine who brings the Yoohoo showers better than others. The beauty of both systems is that the results are based on other values—run expectancy for Base Runs, the quality of the league for SGP—so that the stats you get at the end are highly practical given all that goes into them.

There's one problem, though. In real life, hitters have an absolute offensive value. A player who has contributed a base run has done something positive no matter what else he does. Even Tony Pena contributed a few runs here and there; that's objectively better than if he hadn't. On the fantasy side, however, offensive contributions are entirely contextual. Any runs your team scores or stolen bases you thieve matter only insofar as they gain you points. A 12-team league's first place runs total typically will be less than a six-team league's due to talent dilution; this changes the value of a run, and so forth.

This is why I'm comparing overall rankings in both lists to determine who's undervalued and overvalued; it's inescapable that real baseball works on absolute values and fantasy baseball works on relative/marginal values. We can't make the numbers relate to each other, but we can compare rankings and see whose real-life rankings don't match their fantasy rankings or even close.

SGP requires numbers from a fantasy league to relativize player performance, so what I did for fairness is assume a 12-team mixed-league 5x5 Rotisserie format (measuring runs, RBIs, home runs, steals and batting average) with 14 players per team (two catchers, three corner infielders, three middle infielders, five outfielders, and one utility player). This would yield 168 active players at any given time, so I made a "Roto world" of players based on most plate appearances at each position—the top 24 catchers by plate appearance, the top 36 first/third basemen, the top 60 outfielders, and so on.

From that group of players, I took the 75th percentile for each stat at each position to give a league maximum and then a 25th percentile for league minimum in the various categories, e.g. seventh through ninth in first/third basemen for runs for one end and 27th through 29th on the other end, repeating the percentile for each stat and each position. After assigning replacement level as the 168th-best stats in the "Roto world" (which was Brian Schneider's 30 runs, Chone Figgins's 22 RBIs, several players with one home run, and no stolen bases) to subtract from SGP and deflate the numbers a bit, I sorted players by Base Runs and by SGP to measure the differences in rankings.

Some players stay the same in both systems. Albert Pujols is king of Base Runs and SGP, clocking in at 132 and 8.26 respectively. Among the 344 players with 200 or more plate appearances (which is who I'm measuring for the teams below), Tony Pena is last in Base Runs, with four, but it's his brother-in-performance Wily Mo who takes the SGP anticrown with -1.37 SGP.

One of the most interesting parts of the rankings is the stars who should be thought of as superstars and vice versa. Nick Markakis' fantasy value was 6.01 SGP—a very solid 36th place, just two spots behind Shane Victorino and two spots ahead of Jacoby Ellsbury. Base Runs, however, sees them very differently; Ellsbury is 97th, Victorino is 66th, and Markakis is a stunning 12th, two spots behind Jose Reyes and two spots ahead of fellow Oriole Aubrey Huff. A lot of Nick's production came from his 48 doubles, his 99 walks, and his fairly low 10 GIDP; that's a good recipe for covert success.

To The Lists

The Roto-underrated Hitters

Name	BR	Rank	SGP	Rank	Diff
C Jason Varitek	48	202	0.48	282	80
C Jason Kendall	56	171	1.03	247	76
1B Daric Barton	54	179	1.16	241	62
3B Jack Hannahan	49	198	0.72	267	69
CO Todd Helton	45	219	0.6	275	56
2B Akinori Iwamura	86	71	3.02	136	65
SS David Eckstein	39	251	0.18	295	44
MI Craig Counsell	30	288	-0.5	328	40
OF Brian Giles	95	47	3.75	108	61
OF Jack Cust	92	53	3.68	112	59
OF Gregor Blanco	56	170	1.33	227	57
OF Pat Burrell	99	36	4.11	92	56
OF Justin Upton	58	159	1.59	206	47
UT Kurt Suzuki	63	144	1.64	199	55

If you want to toss out below-median players by Base Runs, put Suzuki at catcher for Varitek, Lyle Overbay (+34) at first base, Scott Rolen (+31) at third base, Kevin Millar, Carlos Pena, or Troy Glaus (+33) at corner infield, Stephen Drew (+38) at shortstop, Orlando Hudson (+25) at middle infield, and Mark Teahen (+45) at utility for Suzuki.

The primary difference from reality to fantasy in this list is that hitters with low batting averages don't kill their team quite the way they kill their fantasy owners. Varitek only hit .220, but his walk rate was still good and his extra-base hits didn't change much in amount or type from the past two years. He just happened to have fewer singles, and that's trouble in Roto, especially because his average was only borderline acceptable in the first place.

The underrated team generally breaks down into three types: Varitek types with low averages but reasonable extra-base power and some walks (Varitek, Barton, Hannahan); lightweights with medium averages, no extra-base power and tons of walks (Eckstein, Counsell, and Blanco), and guys who look like the Varitek types except they have legitimate home run power and therefore are very useful (Cust, Burrell, Upton at least for now, and any Adam Dunn lookalike). It also breaks down into four A's and 10 other guys; I am in no way surprised that Billy Beane would stockpile this sort.

The ones that intrigue me the most, however, are Iwamura and Giles, as they fit none of the above molds. Iwamura's season is pedestrian prima facie—.274/.349/.380, 96 OPS+—but he has one of the most potpourri seasons imaginable, where everything adds just a bit of value here and there to give him as many Base Runs as Michael Young or Torii Hunter. He placed reasonably in all those minor components of the Base Runs formula—nine triples, eight steals, four HBPs, only grounding into two double plays—and he had decent doubles power and decent walk totals. Add it all together and you get 86 Base Runs almost out of nowhere. Eventually, I want to go through history with this method and identify who in each season has the season most like Iwamura's, the valuable season with no standout characteristic. Call it the Iwamura Sneakup Award or something like that.

Giles represents a different type of sneakup: the park-affected one. Being in a run-starved environment as he is, it may be that Giles's components don't add up to as many runs as they would elsewhere—adjusting for park gives him a whopping eight more Base Runs—but a .300 BA with a near-.400 OBP plays well anywhere. Add in some doubles and you've got a good season turned great. This is the sort of performance that looks right on any hitting "star" of the '60s Dodgers—pick a random season from Ron Fairly's career and you've nailed it—but looks less valuable in the modern game. Well, in Petco, and on the Padres, it's quite valuable, whether or not Roto cares as much.

Just for kicks, here's the SGP-overrated team:

The Roto-overrated Hitters

Name	BR	Rank	SGP	Rank	Diff
C Mike Napoli	49	194	2.36	166	-28
C Ryan Doumit	68	125	3.86	104	-21
1B Chris Davis	51	188	2.45	160	-28
3B Brian Buscher	28	299	0.87	257	-42
CO Greg Dobbs	34	268	1.25	233	-35
2B Alexei Ramirez	66	134	4.44	80	-54
SS Maicer Izturis	35	266	1.40	223	-43
MI Jeff Baker	44	225	2.08	180	-45
OF Willy Taveras	54	178	4.48	76	-102
OF Rajai Davis	24	316	1.41	222	-94
OF Juan Pierre	42	234	2.90	143	-91
OF Michael Bourn	45	222	2.68	150	-72
OF Joey Gathright	27	306	1.20	236	-70
UT Jacoby Ellsbury	78	97	5.91	39	-59

Ah, how the speed merchants dominate the marketplace of overrated as they fudge supply and demand for the precious fruit of the swiped bag. To be fair, at least Taveras has legitimate value outside his stolen bases; it's just that only in Roto are Willy Taveras and Alexei Ramirez approximate in value both to each other, to Derek Jeter, and to Russell Martin.

Ramirez is the odd case of a guy literally having only those offensive skills that Roto measures. Of course, we have almost nothing to go on as to whether he'll keep this up. Hopefully, we get a good read on him in 2009.

Doumit's case is puzzling—how can a guy with a .501 SLG be overrated, especially when his home runs were modest compared to his 34 doubles, which

normally helps underrate a player? The main answer is his batting average; .318 isn't insanely high, but he's one of only nine hitters in 2008 with at least 450 plate appearances who managed that figure. Nine is a pretty low amount for that threshold; the past two years have seen more than twice that, and the total usually fluctuates around 10-20. Good batting average was in such short supply that Doumit's .318 mattered more than it looks like it would, and it mattered far more than most years somebody bats .318.

As for Napoli, a .274/.374/.586 line is incredibly hard to overrate, but his line is a weird one. Two-thirds of his extra-base hits were home runs, so while that's incredibly valuable, there's not the typical assortment of other hits underneath it for Base Runs to "pull up" into his totals. Plus, he stole seven bases, which is a surefire way to get overrated and give envy to all Roto teams that aren't getting those bases from their second catchers.

Since the list above has so many bad players that it would be a new team if I threw out all the below-median players, here are the top five overrated above-median players by Base Runs that don't make the list: Carlos Gomez (-54), Carl Crawford (-53), Alfonso Soriano (-44), Brandon Phillips (-44), and Corey Hart (-36). Impatient hitters who can steal are the flip side of the doubles-walks guys on the other list, so there's not a lot of surprise here.

Conclusion

It's hard to separate different parts of fandom when you're looking at a player, but hopefully this article helps. When investigating an offseason pickup on your favorite team, don't think about how much of a Roto disaster he is, even when it's hard. At least make an effort to see if his value (even if low) is hidden.

This article would not exist without Derek "Rico" Carty.

Fantasy Baseball: Thinking Ahead

by Derek Carty

We had a busy year at The Hardball Times' Fantasy Focus. Early on, we discussed strategies for your fantasy baseball drafts, including whether catchers should be taken early (they should be), whether closers should be taken late (they should be in mixed leagues), and whether taking pitchers later because they are "risky" is a sound decision (it's not, at least not for this reason), among many others.

Throughout the regular season, we made use of MLB Advanced Media and Sportvision's fantastic new PITCHf/x system in player analysis and developed a number of cutting-edge new statistics. PITCHf/x allows us to see what pitches an individual throws, their speed and their movement. We also can look at how the pitcher uses the pitches in different situations, how he mixes them, how he locates them, how he hides them and a number of other incredibly useful and interesting things.

Perhaps the most intriguing of the new statistics developed at THT Fantasy Focus is True Home Runs (tHR). True Home Runs uses Greg Rybarczyk's revolutionary HitTracker system, which tracks every home run and measures things like speed-off-bat, launch angle and hit trajectory. The True Home Run stat then runs the data through each hitter's home park environment (assuming each park's average weather conditions) and through a league-average park environment (as a proxy for away games) and combines the two to arrive at the number of "true home runs" based on the distances each ball is hit in each environment. This gives us a clearer picture of each player's actual home run-hitting skills.

True Quality Starts looks at a pitcher's peripheral statistics to determine, on a start-by-start basis, how well he pitched. Those with wide variability are candidates for further analysis, as there may be some untapped talent there that the pitcher just can't harness consistently yet.

We introduced a stat that more accurately measures the combined contribution of a pitcher's strikeout and walk rates to his ERA (essentially measuring what K/BB fails to do, since one strikeout does not actually equal one walk), several plate discipline stats to measure a hitter's contact skills, and many other useful stats you won't find anywhere else.

For me, all of this culminated in my first expert league championship in as many attempts: I won the FOX Sports Expert Fantasy Baseball League by a 15-point margin.

Now, it's time to look at some players I believe will be either overrated or underrated going into the 2009 fantasy baseball season.

Keep in mind that the labels given to these players are not absolute. They are based on my general (and early) feel for a player's average market value. While I believe Carlos Quentin will be overvalued in 2009, if he falls to the 10th round, you can be sure I'll be taking him. And while I think Ricky Nolasco could be a good pitcher next year, if I end up needing to spend a fourth-round pick to get him, I'm going to have to pass.

Every player has a price. This should provide a pretty good picture of the price you'll need to pay in comparison to what you should be paying.

For simplicity's sake, all references to draft rounds assume a traditional, 12-team mixed league.

Likely to be Undervalued

Hitters

Robinson Cano | NYY | 2B Most people will tell you that Cano had a down year in 2008, but I don't believe this was the case. I believe it was an unlucky year. His True Home Run (tHR) numbers were right in line with previous years, meaning a power bounce-back should be expected in 2009. Combined with a steadily increasing fly ball rate and a career-high contact rate, the only thing to worry about is his BABIP. It's quite likely this was just unlucky in 2008, given his great BABIP history and his solid 2008 line drive rate. This makes Cano a huge bargain in the eighth or ninth round, especially if the Yanks allow him to hit second in the order next year.

Adam Lind | TOR | OF Lind was once a top prospect but never really has broken out in the majors. If he gets regular playing time in 2009, though, that breakout could finally happen. The tHR stat has seen him exceeding his actual HR/FB two years in a row, and a .280 batting average with 25 home runs in 550 at-bats seems like a distinct possibility. If he gets a spot in the heart of the batting order for RBIs and runs, Lind looks like a great end-game draft pick.

Ryan Spilborghs | COL | OF Spilborghs is probably the most obscure name on any of these lists, and he's a recommendation that is dependent on playing time. If Matt Holliday, Willy Taveras or Brad Hawpe is traded, Spilborghs could come into some regular playing time and would make a great sleeper pick with good upside and limited downside. He doesn't hit many fly balls (just 27 percent for his career), but he has very good raw power. He should pretty easily hit over .300 and could net double digit steals with 20 homers if given 600 at-bats at the top of the Rockies' order.

Kenji Johjima | SEA | C I doubt you'll hear many analysts predicting a bounceback for Johjima, but I'll go out on a limb and do that. His power should come back, tHR thinks, and he did manage to sustain his top-notch contact rate this year. If his .233 BABIP turns out to be simply a case of bad luck, Johjima could end up doing in 2009 exactly what most predicted for 2008: .285 with 15-plus homers and good RBI and run production for a catcher. This assumes, of course, his contract extension forces the M's to give him enough playing time at the start of the year (which could be difficult with Jeff Clement around). Operating under a new GM, this is far from guaranteed, but given his place outside the top 30 catchers on some early draft boards, the necessary investment will be at a bare minimum.

Pitchers

Jonathan Sanchez | SF | SP Sanchez looks a lot like Tim Lincecum did last offseason (though that isn't an implication that Sanchez will become the best pitcher in the NL next year) in that he posts big strikeout numbers with respectable ground ball rates. His walk rates are a bit on the high side (like Lincecum), but at age 26, if he manages to get that BB/9 to drop below four, he could become a serious fantasy force who would provide monster value to his owners. Improved control is largely what led to Lincecum's breakout this year. Further making Sanchez undervalued is his unlucky 5.01 ERA this past year compared to a 3.98 LIPS ERA. Early lists have him outside the top 75 starting pitchers, which is simply ridiculous.

Ricky Nolasco | FLA | SP The secret might be out on Nolasco by the time draft day rolls around, but for now, he's looking like a bargain. He posted an 8.1 K/9 and 1.8 BB/9 as a starter this year, and if you ignore his first five starts, he posted an 8.5 K/9 and 1.5 BB/9 from May 9 on. It'll be difficult to keep a walk rate that

low, but even with a rise to over 2.0 he'd still make a nice pick. He's got a great fastball, a good change-up and a splitter to complement it, plus what appears to be two different curveballs, and an okay slider (used mostly in hitter's counts as a "get me over" breaking ball). That's lots for hitters to think about. This was his first full season since 2006, but he had great results and the PITCHf/x data portray him quite favorably, so I'd call him a great pick anywhere after Round 12.

Aaron Harang | CIN | SP Harang had a rough 2008 campaign, marred by injury, bad luck, and an apparent (though relatively small) skill decline. A 7.5 K/9, 2.4 BB/9, and 34 percent ground ball rate, though, isn't anything to sneeze at. Sure, it's not great, and he'll be turning 31 in the middle of the year, but if Harang falls into the mid-teen rounds, he's exactly the kind of guy who's worth gambling on. If he stays healthy, you should at least have a solid pitcher to fill out your staff. If he regains his old form or even slightly improves on 2008 (sans the bad luck), you'll have a very good No. 2 fantasy starter.

Likely to be Overvalued

Hitters

Carlos Quentin | CWS | OF One of the biggest breakouts of the 2008 season, Quentin looks seriously overvalued going into 2009, even if we completely ignore natural regression. Positives are that he dramatically increased his contact rate and saw a rise in his fly ball rate, but the combination of just 21 tHR and no real stolen base value makes Quentin a huge stretch in the second or third round. Unless he further improves his contact rate or BABIP, look for a .265-.270 average with 25 home runs or so and a handful of steals. Good, but that doesn't bring him close to the elite outfielders.

Hanley Ramirez | FLA | SS A speedy, power hitting shortstop with a good batting average is every fantasy owner's dream. Many will use this logic to qualify the decision to take Hanley first overall this year. Don't make that mistake. While he does possess the skills mentioned above, he doesn't in the quantity necessary to make him the No. 1 pick. He saw a huge jump in HR/FB this year (from 14 percent to 21 percent), but tHR says he should have been closer to 13 percent and his fly ball rate actually dropped a few points. Also, despite reaching first base more often, he stole 16 fewer bases due to fewer attempts and a lower success rate. Furthermore, his contact rate (which greatly improved in 2007) regressed to its 2006 level of 80 percent. Hanley is a sure-fire first rounder, but as the first overall pick, there are better options. I'm not even sure he deserves to be the first shortstop off the board.

Ryan Ludwick | STL | OF Ludwick was a great story this year, but unfortunately, his "breakout" seems mostly to be smoke and mirrors. He strikes out a good deal, and his .349 BABIP was well above his career best. It was supported by 26 percent line drives, but that number will come down, dragging the BABIP with it. His increased HR/FB rate isn't supported by tHR, which suggests he should have hit 24 homers (as opposed to the 36 he actually hit). That's a decent amount, but it's something he has been capable of hitting for quite a while; it's just that he finally got 500 at-bats this year to do it. He'll post a similar line to Quentin (maybe .260 with 25 homers and a few steals), but in the first five or six rounds, this still isn't a line that should look very attractive.

Pitchers

Daisuke Matsuzaka | BOS | SP Dice-K had a very nice rookie year in 2007, but in 2008 he got incredibly lucky with his 2.90 ERA. His strikeout rate was good (but not great) at 8.3 strikeouts per nine innings pitched. His ground ball rate has been below average, and his walk rate jumped all the way to 5.1 per nine this year. Keeping his ERA down was a joint effort by his .267 BABIP, 81 percent left-on-base rate, and 6 percent HR/FB. All should regress next year. The control issues could have been injury-related, but there's no way I want any part of Matsuzaka next year if he's drafted inside the first 15 rounds, which he surely will be given that ERA.

David Price | TB | SP Price has gotten loads of hype this season as the best pitching prospect in baseball, and that figures to translate into a big pricetag on draft day. Early mock drafts have him going as early as Round 10. He posted good, but not great, numbers in the minors and pitched just 75 innings above Single-A (just 18 at Triple-A) before jumping to the majors. Even with all the praise he gets from scouts, the limited PITCHf/x data we have on him aren't overly impressive. He has been drafted in the top dozen rounds of early

mocks and ranked among the top 40 starters on early cheat sheets, which is simply too high for a guy we've seen so little.

Joe Saunders | LAA | SP Saunders had a great year on the surface with a 3.41 ERA, but his 4.61 LIPS ERA was more than a full run higher. He doesn't strike out many batters (just 4.7 per nine), induces ground balls at a slightly above league average rate (44 percent), and doesn't compensate with elite control (2.4 BB/9 is merely good). He was simply the beneficiary of some very good luck and figures to be overdrafted next year. Saunders, believe it or not, really isn't draftable at all in 2009 mixed leagues (unless they are exceptionally deep).

Francisco Rodriguez | LAA | RP I wanted to leave K-Rod off the list because there are so many starters to mention, but I couldn't resist. How is it that a guy who notches an all-time record 62 saves in 69 opportunities and will be signing with a new team this winter is being taken in the third round of early mocks? The man did nothing to receive all those opportunities! Do they honestly think he's going to surpass the previous saves record for the second year in a row on a different team? It makes zero sense. Oh, and all this is ignoring the early season injuries, a two-point drop in K/9, and the fact that his walk rate still remains at a dangerous 4.5 per nine. Take note of the owner who takes K-Rod this year and mark him as a sucker. You'll likely be able to work out some very nice trades with him throughout the season.

Closing Thoughts

While player evaluation is a very important part of preparation for the coming season, you shouldn't stop there. Concepts like economics, psychology and the ability to strategize and think creatively are essential for gaining a competitive edge over your opponents. We'll be discussing these topics, among many others, throughout the offseason at THT Fantasy Focus as we help guide you to fantasy baseball glory in 2009. If you're serious about winning your league next year, we hope you make it a priority to stop by.

GM in a Box: Pat Gillick

by Corey Seidman & Eric J. Seidman

Record and Background

Age: 71

Previous Organizations:

Colt .45's: Assistant Farm Director 1964-65

Astros: Director of Scouting 1974

Yankees: Scouting Director 1975-76

Blue Jays: General Manager 1978-94

Orioles: General Manager 1996-98

Mariners: General Manager 2000-03

Years of Service with the Phillies: Three. Retired after Phillies won World Series.

Cumulative Record: 2,276-1,993 (Toronto: 1,352-1,297, Baltimore: 265-221, Seattle: 393-255, Philadelphia: 266-220)

Playing Career: Gillick was a pitcher on the 1958 USC team that won the national title, and then spent five years in the Orioles farm system before joining the executive ranks in 1964.

Personnel and Philosophy

Any notable changes from the previous regime?

Pat Gillick has a very particular way of doing things and leaves little room for exception. Three weeks after arriving in Philadelphia, he traded Jim Thome for Aaron Rowand and the oft-traded Gio Gonzalez to clear up space for Ryan Howard. Soon after, he traded Vicente Padilla and Jason Michaels, two familiar faces in Philly. Michaels leaving was harder to understand than Padilla, because he had been the ideal fourth outfielder/right-handed bat off the bench. Gillick then made headlines by trading Bobby Abreu to the Yankees. The Phillies received next to nothing in return for Abreu, even having to throw in Cory Lidle to complete the deal, because the Yankees were the only team willing to eat the remaining $37 million on Abreu's contract.

Abreu had been the "leader" of the Phillies for the past eight seasons, so the move was questionable, but it eventually paid off, as the triumvirate of Jimmy Rollins, Chase Utley and Ryan Howard emerged as team leaders and gave the team a new edge. The trade also allowed Shane Victorino and Jayson Werth to receive more playing time. Werth was a better fourth outfielder than Michaels and the combination of him and Victorino, with fielding taken into account as well as offense, might even have been more productive than Abreu.

When Gillick takes over a team, he likes to make an immediate imprint, whether by bringing in players he knows or populating the team with savvy veterans. When he took over the Orioles prior to the 1996 season, he signed Randy Myers, Roger McDowell, B.J. Surhoff and Roberto Alomar; he brought back Mike Devereaux; and he traded for David Wells. In Seattle, prior to the 2000 season, Gillick brought in free agents John Olerud, Stan Javier, Mark McLemore, Arthur Rhodes, Aaron Sele and Joe Oliver, and signed Kaz Sasaki. He would later bring in Bret Boone and Ichiro Suzuki, doing what he could to ensure that the Mariners would win the most regular season games in major league baseball during his tenure.

He also does what he can to build a team that will buy stock in the collective whole mindset, avoiding superstars if possible. Whether publicly stating that his inaugural goals were to re-sign both Ken Griffey Jr. and Alex Rodriguez was an example of saying something for the sake of sounding positive or not, the fact remains that Griffey was traded to the Reds for Mike Cameron and Brett Tomko, among others, before the 2000 season got under way. Rodriguez left for the record deal with Texas following the 2000 season. The situation with Griffey in Seattle had deteriorated to the point beyond reconciliation prior to Gillick's arrival, so he was in a tight spot. Griffey wanted to be traded, so Pat began seeking suitors. Then Griffey would only go to the Reds, vastly limiting Gillick's leverage and what he could get in return. It's not as if he was terrible at evaluating talent, but his moves seemed to signify that he would rather have two versatile, slightly above average players who, together, equal the production of a superstar, rather than have the superstar.

What characterizes his relationship with ownership? What type of people does he hire? Is he more collaborative or authoritative?

When discussing Pat Gillick, it is important to remember that it is his way or the highway. He has a plan of action, a set mantra, and holds steadfastly to each. Because of his inability to truly adjust when his plan of action does not work out, his camp of fans is split: some love the win-now approach as it gives them the opportunity to experience the playoffs in more immediate fashion, while others dislike trading prospects due to the long-term ramifications.

He is definitely authoritative in every sense of the term, to the point that the adjective "arrogant" occasionally creeps into the discussion. He loves signing or acquiring veterans, attempts to avoid younger players at all costs, overvalues the bullpen, and despises in-season trades. In fact, Pat once hinted that he would outlaw such trades if given the opportunity or power. What in the world would baseball writers do for all of June and July if Gillick's wish were to come true? A general manager with a laundry list of beliefs that are stubbornly held cannot portend anything but authority. Due to this, the people he hires tend to be yes-men, ones who will not cross him and are sure to buy into his mindset.

What kinds of managers does he hire? How closely does he work with them?

When he arrived in Philadelphia, Larry Bowa and his fiery temper were on their way out. Previous GM Ed Wade had hired Charlie Manuel, his former special assistant, prior to the 2004 season. Charlie's laid-back, lighter approach to the game made him an attractive candidate for the Phillies, who ultimately hired him. After Wade's firing, much speculation arose that Gillick would want to bring in "his people" and that Manuel's job security was in question. Gillick opted to stay with "Uncle Charlie," and after leading the team to their first playoff berth in 14 years, Manuel was given a two-year extension through 2009.

In this case, he went with the definition of a "player's manager." Some teams are successful with Bowa or Jim Leyland-types, but others perform better in an easygoing atmosphere (see Manuel and Terry Francona). Similarly, Gillick hired Davey Johnson in Baltimore, whose easygoing managerial style cost him his job with the Mets in 1990. In Seattle, he hired former Diamondbacks bench coach Bob Melvin, another player's manager. After taking over the Toronto reins, Gillick proceeded to hire Bobby Mattick, Bobby Cox and Jimy Williams as skippers, all three of whom were known for being player's managers. Notice a trend emerging? After a slow start in 1989, Gillick fired Williams and hired Cito Gaston, who was initially reluctant to take the job. Having developed a reputation as a teacher and steady influence, the players all encouraged him to take the

position. Though Gaston had a public clash with David Wells, Cito was definitely known as a player's manager as well.

Not much is publicly stated about how closely he works with his managers, but based on his "my way or the highway" perception, and his unwillingness to deal with other Type-A personalities (he traded Lou Piniella for Randy Winn while with the Mariners), it can be assumed that Gillick has a huge impact on the style of play and everyday decisions with his team.

Player Development

How does he approach the amateur draft? Does he prefer major league-ready players or projects? Tools or performance? High schools or college? Pitchers or hitters?

Even though Gillick undervalues young players, he does have interesting ideas when it comes to the amateur draft. He does not really distinguish between hitters and pitchers but goes for major league-ready or toolsy players. With a love of experienced players like his, one would have to imagine that players taken who fail to meet his criteria are drafted primarily for future use as trading chips.

In Toronto, Gillick took over an expansion franchise and had to be creative to build his rosters since the amateur draft did not help too much. He launched a scouting blitz into Latin America that would become a characteristic of future Gillick-run teams. In Seattle, he hired Bob Engle to be his VP of International Scouting, who in turn established the Mariners as a force in Latin America. This ultimately brought Felix Hernandez to Seattle. Gillick allowed Engle to do whatever he desired—as long as it stayed within the budget—which sounds very collaborative and, well, unlike Pat. Even more surprisingly, Gillick handed off all draft duties to Frank Mattox. Though it would seem he collaborated with both Engle and Mattox, it was really a smokescreen: He hated the draft, felt it was a poor use of resources, and did not want any part of it.

Along similar lines, Dave Cameron of USS Mariner even recalled Gillick's acquisition of Raul Ibanez as occurring before the Royals offered him arbitration, just so that Gillick could punt their first-round pick the following year. All told, Gillick was very creative and resourceful when it came to the amateur and/or Rule 5 draft when he needed to be but preferred instances of such necessity to occur at a minimum.

Does he tend to rush players to the majors or let them marinate?

Gillick has an almost unhealthy love of veterans. If given the chance to let a young player garner experience or plug in a stopgap veteran, well, our tone probably gives away which type of player he will opt to go with. Not only will he never rush a player to the majors, he needs to be completely confident in the youngster, or up against the wall, to consider giving him a shot. Being in a tight spot led to a young Kyle Kendrick jumping from Double-A to the big leagues in 2007, but that was much more of an exception than a rule.

Based on tendencies, Gillick generally uses young players as trading chips to get veterans. His early years in Toronto taught him how to use certain assets to get different assets, which could then in turn be used to either fill gaps or serve as bait to earn the "right" player. As his experience as a general manager grew, this process soon developed with regard to young players as well as veterans.

At each stop, Gillick inherited or created a team chock full of experience, and relied on that experience to translate into success. Additionally, his farm systems were usually depleted of resources to the point that very few were even worth bringing to the majors, let alone worthy of an express ticket. Looking at the average ages of his teams, they are comfortably in the 29-31 years old range, if not older. The only rushing Gillick does is by quickly bringing in veterans to aid the current performance of his team.

Roster Construction

Is he especially fond of certain types of players? Does he like proven players or youngsters? Offensive players or glove men? Power pitchers or finesse guys?

Did we mention that Gillick loves veterans? Seriously, line up five of the most prized prospects of the future next to Stan Javier, Pat Borders, or Arthur Rhodes, and Gillick is very likely to go for the aged ones due to their ability to help the team win right now. In Philadelphia, his supposed final destination as a general manager, he brought in veteran role players like the aforementioned Rhodes, Alex Gonzalez, Abraham Nunez, Jose Hernandez, Randall Simon, Jeff Conine, Russell Branyan, Kyle Lohse, Joe Blanton, and Matt Stairs. As you can see, none of these guys are superstars, but rather experienced players that Gillick determined would enhance the Phillies' chance of winning now.

He rarely goes after young, unproven players unless he knows them. Two perfect examples would be Greg Dobbs and Jayson Werth. Gillick had Dobbs in Seattle, saw the potential in him, and signed him when the Mariners waived him. Dobbs is now a key part of the Phillies, and broke the team's single-season record for pinch hits in 2008.

Werth was drafted by Gillick's Baltimore Orioles in the first round of the 1997 draft. When Werth hit free agency after three years with the Dodgers, he was snatched up by Gillick and has received the most playing time of his career. This could technically be considered a "project" given that Werth never really played a productive full season and was recovering from significant lost time due to injuries, but many people forgot or never knew that Werth was a former first-round pick. To Gillick, the signing was a no-brainer.

Getting a bit more in-depth, Gillick seems to like versatility in both the offense and defense. He likes a guy who can play several positions and ably occupy numerous spots in the batting order without complaint, filling in whenever a need arises. He is not very fond of acquiring superstar talent, rather building teams with a 25-as-1 mindset. Gillick is definitely more interested in finesse pitchers, as evidenced by his acquisitions and rotations. In Toronto, his rotations were anchored by the likes of Jim Clancy, Jimmy Key, and Pat Hentgen. In Baltimore, guys like Mike Mussina, Scott Erickson, and again, Jimmy Key. Strike-throwers like Jamie Moyer, Ryan Franklin, Aaron Sele and John Halama, headlined his Mariners. With the Phillies, he has acquired or called up Moyer, Joe Blanton, and Kyle Kendrick to fill out the rotation. He has had power pitchers on his teams, but his tendencies definitely favor accuracy, control, and poise over heat.

Does he allocate resources primarily on impact players or role players? How does he flesh out his bullpen and bench? Does he often work the waiver wire, sign minor league free agents, or make Rule 5 picks?

Pat Gillick loves going after role players. Since joining the Phillies, the team has always been included in the rumor du jour but never seems to outbid other teams (see Alfonso Soriano, Manny Ramirez, CC Sabathia). The Soriano situation was a conflict on money, but the Ramirez and Sabathia ones were mostly due to a barren farm system.

But nothing stops Gillick from going after small upgrades or platoon players. When he needed a right-handed hitting first baseman to spell Ryan Howard in 2006, he traded for Jeff Conine. When he needed a lefty specialist that same year, he traded a young Jason Michaels for a semi-washed up Arthur Rhodes. When he needed a late-inning righty in 2007, he signed a completely washed up Antonio Alfonseca. And when he needed another major league-ready right hander to complete the bullpen several months later, he signed an utterly useless Jose Mesa.

Overvaluing the bullpen is another strong suit of Gillick's, as his Mariners relief corps routinely led the league in salary during his tenure there. While there is nothing wrong with assembling a great bullpen, as relief pitchers seem to plague every team and always seem to be the scapegoat for failure or underperformance, Pat loves himself a good relief pitcher, especially one with a proven track record, even if that record was from a track 10 to 12 years ago, with the train having long since departed.

Some of his best signings as Phillies GM have been of recently released players, such as Dobbs and J.C. Romero. He often picks up what other teams throw out quickly. In the case of Dobbs and Romero, he made their careers by bringing them to Philly. In the case of Branyan, Simon, and Mesa, he swung and missed. He loves the Rule 5 draft. He made three picks in the 2006 Rule 5, and two in 2007. None have panned out at the major league level yet, with Triple-A starting pitcher Travis Blackley being the closest. Tim Lahey, the first overall pick in the 2008 Rule 5 draft by the Tampa Bay Rays, was briefly on the Phillies' roster to start the season, but the right hander was released when Brad Lidge came off the DL.

In Toronto, the Rule 5 draft often proved more profitable than the amateur draft, as Gillick was able to acquire George Bell, Kelly Gruber, and middle infielder Manny Lee, three key pieces of the Blue Jays in the mid-to-late 1980s. As they began winning, however, his desire to acquire diminished and he was able to hone in on addressing specific needs as opposed to building an entire roster.

When will he release players? On whom has he given up? To whom has he given a shot? Does he cut bait early or late?

Gillick is not one to release players often, especially guys he takes chances on. Two current Phillies examples are Adam Eaton, who was given an absurd three-year, $21 million contract even though he had little success to that point, and Francisco Rosario, a hard-throw-ing righty Gillick signed during the first week of the 2007 season. Who released Rosario? The Blue Jays, of course, because Gillick only pays attention to his former teams.

Eaton hasn't lived up to 1 percent of his pay, hasn't performed out of the bullpen, and was somehow much worse in Single-A and Double-A when he was demoted in mid-2008. Yet, he still found himself back up for September call-ups instead of being cut. He is dead weight, but likely due to Gillick's unwillingness to admit how wrong he was in giving Eaton that contract, he won't be cut loose.

Rosario has pitched in 40 major-league games in two seasons, with poor results. A lot of walks, a lot of strike-outs, plenty of runs, and even more arm and shoulder problems have defined Rosario's major league career to date. Gillick must see something in Rosario that few see, future closer-type stuff, because there is no reason he should still have a job in the Phillies' system.

In his tenure with the Mariners, Gillick released Ruben Sierra and Carlos Baerga, a pair of underper-forming veterans he signed. Other than that, however, you would be hard-pressed to find anyone he released. In his final season with the Mariners, nobody was given the boot. Gillick could be described as someone who will hold onto the risks he takes, hoping one day they pay off and reward him. He is not one to make any surprising cuts, or any types of cuts at all, unless they are low-risk, low-paid, replaceable veterans.

Is he active or passive? An optimist or a problem solver? Does he want to win now or wait out the success cycle?

This is an interesting question to tackle given that Pat has held different mantras in his executive stops. He earned the nickname "Stand Pat," which might capture his passive sentiments, but is somewhat of a misnomer. Especially in his early days in Toronto, Gillick has been an active problem-solver. He does not like making moves in-season but is very quick to diagnose and address problems in the offseason.

In Toronto, he had to be very creative due to the onerous conditions placed on his expansion franchise. They had no national television money, were the last to pick in the amateur draft, and were forbidden to partici-pate in the free agent re-entry draft for three years. With all of these roadblocks, Pat launched a scouting blitz into Latin America, routinely worked the Rule 5 draft, and probed the minor league organizations of others for talent to either plug in or use as trading chip. His claim to fame during his stint with the Blue Jays was an ability to turn one acquired player into two or three "right" players.

One such example would be former batting champ Rico Carty: Gillick selected him in the expansion draft, then sent him to Cleveland for John Lowenstein and Rick Cerone. Cerone was then packaged with others for Damaso Garcia and Chris Chambliss. Carty would then find his way back to the Blue Jays, before being shipped to the Athletics for Willie Horton and Phil Huffman. Huffman would then be dealt to the Royals for Rance Mulliniks. As you can see, he was very active in acquiring players to serve as chips as a means of acquiring the players he felt were right for his team.

The problem many fans had with Gillick is that he got too satisfied with his creation and trusted in his assembled roster to ultimately pull through. Essentially, he was very active in diagnosing and fixing a problem, putting the right players in place, but once the "correct" roster was assembled, he became passive. Optimism reigned supreme for Gillick, as he completely trusted that his monster would make him look like a genius.

Someone who routinely gets rid of farmhands and does not care for the amateur draft definitely operates out of a win-now state. In Seattle, Gillick sought veterans and undervalued youngsters in an attempt to win it all each year. In Philadelphia, he went after CC Sabathia and Manny Ramirez, two superstar rentals with expiring contracts, and may have landed them both if not for the fact that other teams had better pieces.

Traders and Free Agents

Does he favor players acquired via trade, development, or free agency? Is he an active trader? Does he tend to move talent or horde it? With whom does he trade and when? Will he make deals with other teams during the season? How does he approach the trading deadline?

Gillick definitely favors players acquired via free agency out of these three options. He is not a fan of trades, unless the assets he surrenders are younger players who would not help his team win right now. Based on that, you can imagine his thoughts on players acquired via development. He routinely works the waiver wire and brings in many players via free agency. The only time Gillick will be an active trader is in the offseason following a disappointing year. In Toronto, we already covered the wheeling and dealing he had to do in order

to lift an expansion franchise off the ground. In his other stops, however, the teams were missing certain pieces and therefore more in need of a role player or a bullpen piece then of an entire roster assembly.

Mariners fans commented that the biggest trade he made during his tenure there was to bring, gasp, Ismael Valdez to the grunge capital of the world. When it comes to the trade deadline, Gillick doesn't get caught up in the hype. If his team has succeeded to that point and there are no glaring weaknesses or holes, he tends to trust in the group of veterans that produced the certain record. Along similar lines, if a team is underperforming, he might make a certain move to show that he is not merely sitting back and watching. But he is of the belief that the roster he has assembled will ultimately break through and perform to their capacity. This may come off as stubborn, but it is Pat Gillick in a nutshell.

In his last season in Philadelphia, he needed a starting pitcher to ensure Adam Eaton was not on the hill every fifth day. After falling short in the Sabathia sweepstakes and whiffing on Rich Harden, he ultimately settled on Joe Blanton. It could easily be said that he gave up too much for Blanton, because two of the three minor leaguers traded were top-five Phillies prospects, and Blanton's best qualities would not be utilized well at the bandbox that is Citizens Bank Park.

Are there teams or general managers with whom he trades frequently?

Given that he does not like trades as much as free agent signings, Gillick does not truly have a pattern as far as where he trades or with whom he likes to deal. The only real pattern is that he loves going after players he knows and previously employed. While he has a veteran's fetish, those veterans are all the more attractive if he already had them elsewhere. In Baltimore, he acquired players like Pat Borders, Jimmy Key, Roberto Alomar, and David Wells, all of whom he worked with in Toronto. In Seattle, he brought onboard the likes of Rickey Henderson, Arthur Rhodes, Eugene Kingsale, Pat Borders, and Ed Sprague from his previous two stops.

In Philadelphia, Gillick acquired Jamie Moyer, Greg Dobbs, Arthur Rhodes, Chris Snelling, Freddy Garcia, Ryan Franklin, and Jayson Werth, all of whom belonged to a team or two of his prior to joining Philadelphia's front office. He may not deal directly with certain teams on a consistent basis, but he definitely looks to deal for players he knows, who can help build that team mindset and produce right now.

Contracts

Does he prefer long-term deals or short? Does he backload his contracts very often? Does he lock up players early in their careers or is he more likely to practice brinksmanship? Does he like to avoid arbitration?

Gillick's philosophy is to give no more than three years to a pitcher or four years to a position player. Since everything isn't black and white, however, exceptions are made. He gave Chase Utley a long-term deal— seven years, $84 million to be exact—at the beginning of Utley's prime. The contract will end up being a steal financially, which is likely what led Gillick to make such a commitment. He was not willing, however, to pony up to the likes of Ken Griffey Jr. or Alex Rodriguez in Seattle, because both would have been enormous investments. Contracts like these would defy the mindset he likes to instill in his teams. He also dislikes Scott Boras, but so does anybody who doesn't give a percentage of their salary to the super-agent.

He made the right decision by letting Aaron Rowand walk after the 2007 season, because with Rowand's age and decreasing skills, offering more than three years made little sense. When it comes to Ryan Howard and Cole Hamels, Gillick has taken the year-to-year approach, letting Howard go to arbitration for a raise. He has been hesitant to give Howard a long-term contract, and given the fact 2008 was Gillick's last season in Philly, he won't have to make the hard decision of whether or not to keep him. Gillick definitely places a premium on the bullpen, so it came as no surprise that he broke from his general mold to sign Brad Lidge to a contract extension halfway through the 2008 season.

Gillick will only lock up a player early if it is a situation like Utley's, where the contract will not be absolutely ridiculous given the player's age, potential, and his financial responsibilities elsewhere on the team. He also needs to be completely sold on the player, which is one of the chief reasons Howard has not received a huge contract.

Anything unique about his negotiating tactics? Is he vocal? Does he prefer to work behind the scenes or through the media?

Gillick is not normally one to vent frustration through the media or call out players with reporters' microphones in his face. He picks his spots. On a Philadelphia television program in July, he mentioned that he would like Jayson Werth to play more. This wasn't necessarily a clear shot at Charlie Manuel's platoon usage of the wiry righty hitter, but rather his way of floating the idea that Werth should play more. He can be vocal but prefers to be so behind the scenes. In fact, in Philadelphia, he rarely makes announcements or speaks with the media. Instead, assistant general managers Ruben Amaro and Mike Arbuckle tend to shoulder most of that load.

In terms of negotiating, he does not like to go beyond three-year deals for pitchers or four-year deals for hitters, as longer and more lucrative deals are primarily designed for superstar players, whom Gillick tends to avoid, focusing more on the team-as-one mindset. He will bend the rules every now and then, but he is definitely stubborn in certain instances, usually deciding against bending them in order to either make a point or assert his authority.

The Toronto Blue Jays won two World Series with Gillick at the helm but haven't made the playoffs since he left after the 1994 season. The Baltimore Orioles made the playoffs in each of Gillick's first two seasons with the team but haven't had a winning record since. The Seattle Mariners won 91, 116, 93, and 93 games in Gillick's four seasons as GM but have failed to play baseball past September since his departure. And the Philadelphia Phillies made the playoffs for the first time in 14 years in Gillick's second-to-last year running the team but may have a different post-Gillick fate due to their core of young talent.

Gillick has had plenty of success as a GM, making the playoffs at every stop, but it could be argued with validity and ease that his win-now approach handcuffs the future success of a team more than it ensures success in the present.

We'd like to thank John Brattain, Dave Cameron, and Jeff Sullivan for their expert help and insight.

Pinstripes in the Mist

by Tim Marchman

From 1996 to 2007, housing prices in America's 20 largest cities more than doubled. Trillions of dollars were simply hallucinated into existence, as were tens of trillions more in fancy financial instruments, so that at the peak of the frenzy the economy was like a stack of pianos resting on a teacup balanced on a marble.

People everywhere, from the Inland Empire to the Research Triangle, were suddenly rich, at least in theory, and nowhere more so than in New York. As the boom began, the city was just a few years removed from race riots and wilding; by the time it ended, its psychic geography had been entirely remade. Whole neighborhoods were summoned out of the ether and set down in rows of desolate warehouses, industrial districts were turned into nightclubs, and working class families were pushed toward the farthest edges of the most distant regions of the outer boroughs, their places taken by shameless space pirates. It was a brighter, cleaner, quieter, safer and thoroughly decadent city, an open-air theme park so dependent on the financial industry that after the Wall Street crash Mayor Michael Bloomberg was, with the blessing of the city elders, able to simply ignore an incumbency law and run for a third term, claiming his fiscal savvy made him uniquely indispensable.

Through this whole period, the New York Yankees were, even more than Goldman Sachs or Jay-Z or the gaping crater downtown, the purest and most distilled essence of the city's baroque absurdity and relentless ambition. To chart their payroll from 1996 to 2007 alongside the Case-Shiller housing index from the same period is to wonder whether the team didn't after all have some mysterious psychic link with the hallucinated economy that radiated out across the country from Wall Street. Both rise steadily toward 1999; the Yankees break sharply upward and plateau, as if waiting for housing to catch them, and then both career insanely upward on parallel 45 degree angles, reaching toward a 2006 peak that looks suspiciously like the stock market circa 1929, tracing such increasingly hyperbolic underlying developments as the acquisition of every other declining ballplayer with an eight-figure salary or the development of a derivatives market several times larger than world GDP, helping turn the city into a bursting bottle of champagne.

As the Case-Shiller plunges toward the mean, each downward tick representing the destruction of hundreds of billions of dollars and bringing New York that much closer to insolvency, Yankees payrolls plateau and even reach a new peak in 2008, which is just to say that baseball is (thankfully) not finance. Still, the apparent symbiosis showed in various other ways: While it was nothing more than coincidence that Yankee Stadium saw its final game on Sept. 22, a week after Lehman Brothers went bankrupt and three days after the federal government was forced to propose a $700 billion financial bailout to prevent an incipient meltdown, it was an entirely fitting one.

In its way, the rise of a new Yankee Stadium in 2009 is equally fitting, both of its team and its city.

As the old one played out its last year, hosting the final end of the dynastic Yankees, there were thousands of sincere and moving tributes to what it had meant to millions of people, to whom it was less a ballpark with dubious sight lines and exorbitant prices than a living historical memory, a place where New York was, in one place, everything it had ever been for 80 years: a roaring port city, an immigrants' citadel, a dystopia of misguided public spending programs, a palace of great booms, a national landmark, a faded and majestic repository of the past, and above all, as home of the famous 26 world championships, a monument to unsurpassed success.

There was much less discussion of what the new Yankee Stadium meant, but it too means something specific. Financed for $1.6 billion in a murky deal that linked the public and private sectors in ways few understand and fewer believe will do anything other than benefit rich people at everyone else's expense, the new park is a sort of fantastic theme-park recreation of the old one, re-engineered to halve the number of bleacher seats and quadruple the number of luxury boxes. In its preposterous expense (the new yard is, according to *Forbes* magazine's estimate, worth more than the actual team) and vast scale, it's a monument to a time that's already passed, one in which money meant nothing because there would always be more of it and which a limitless city could be reimagined as a luxury product, its rougher contours and seamier bits presented as the colorful detritus of a safely distant past. In this reading, the park is a towering act of hubris, entirely suiting a team that spent more money on players this past year than the Boston Red Sox and Tampa Bay Rays combined.

If it isn't wholly unfair, though, to see the new stadium as the product of a time that reduced New Yorkers to the status of extras in a stage show being played out in their own city, and to view the dynastic Yankees' fall through that lens, it's no more unfair to say that the team, the park, and the city are also something much more than that, something that will, as time passes, come to seem less grasping and far greater than they might now.

Whatever their flaws were and no matter how bloated and self-parodic their roster at times came to be, for years the Yankees captured something about the city in a way few previous iterations had. Far from the living incarnation of excess, for most of the great run that lasted through the boom the Yankees stood in for hard work, fearlessness, and intelligence, the same virtues to which a city of strivers ascribed its renaissance.

No fielding metric is ever going to convince millions of people who saw his great play against Oakland in 2001 or the dive into the stands against Boston that Derek Jeter was anything other than a ferocious and brilliant defender. No one needs to be convinced that Mariano Rivera, as much as any player ever, was the embodiment of the easy grace under pressure to which everyone aspires. None of his misjudgments and flaws will ever make Joe Torre anything other than the model of a kind of steady and generous leadership that few can do anything but admire. In the end there were too many such men, too many indelible moments, and too many world championships to reduce the Yankees to anything less than a model of excellence.

Similarly, if right now their new park seems at worst like a gift given by a plutocracy to itself and at best like a cartoon expression of the franchise's famed self-regard, there's no warrant on its eventually seeming that way.

In its day, the much-mourned original was no less ludicrous. Built in a time when some parks were separated from the sidewalk by a wooden fence, and in which the largest parks fit about 30,000, the first Yankee Stadium had the walls of a high fortress and seated 60,000. Perhaps everything will collapse, and we'll all be reduced to hunting and gathering, and the new Yankee Stadium will seem like the high point of a decade of moral frivolity. More likely, as soon as this year those who can will scrape up the cash to get in and marvel at its technical ingenuity, at the brass of its creators, and at the raw power of capital, just as fans did at the old one and just as they likely will at a still newer one whenever this one gets hit by the wrecking ball.

And if they marvel at the park, so will people marvel at New York, at least so long as it's there. Its financial institutions, baseball teams, neighborhoods, politicians, press, and culture may all at times be ludicrously flamboyant, at times so much so as to seem grotesque, but they reflect little more than a vast, seething drive, the same thing that produced nuclear fission, the Internet, open-heart surgery, and the skyscraper, along with trillions of dollars in imaginary money and football. As its boom was just a more vivid version of the same one experienced everywhere else in the nation, so probably will be its bust, and as the city rediscovers its humility, so probably will the team that's tracked its fortune for so long. In their soaringly ambitious new ballpark, the Yankees will build their fortunes on a new generation of brilliantly talented young players, and if they fail they'll do so without the modern equivalents of Jose Canseco, Jeff Weaver, and Kevin Brown littering their roster. They'll still be a luxury product, but one suited for more modest times, and by May of this year the number on everyone's minds will most likely not be $1.6 billion, but rather 27.

Making a Baseball Fan

by Roel Torres

How do you learn to love baseball? How does it become an important part of your daily routine? How do you inject it into your bloodstream, get it racing through your veins, pumping life into your exhausted body when the humid summer days slow everything down to a crawl and the act of finding a morning box score is like unlocking the mysteries of a lost civilization? How does that happen?

In the Blood

If you've ever watched the movie Field of Dreams, the answer makes itself relatively obvious. It's the American game, passed down from fathers to sons, like a gift, like a mystical connection transmitted through the generations. The sentiment isn't even buried in the movie's subtext. It's explicit, clear for everyone to see, plain for everyone to understand. Great lengths were taken to make sure the message was not lost, diminished or misunderstood. According to the Internet Movie Database...

> The line, "Hey, Dad, you wanna have a catch," originally didn't include "Dad." Audiences were disappointed in the lack of acknowledgement of father and son, and the word "Dad" was looped in during post-production.

It makes perfect sense. I think it's a universally appealing message. The connection. That's how baseball works. A father teaches his son to root for his favorite team, the local nine, instructing him to cheer them on to victory and to follow their winding road to the World Series. A father buys his son his first glove and teaches him how to oil it down and how to wrap a baseball in the pocket to break it in so that he can snatch line drives with ease. A father takes his son to his first major league ballgame, buys him a hot dog and a coke and reminds him to be alert to any souvenir foul balls that might head in their direction. It's the American game, passed down from fathers to sons, which is great. Unless you're not an American. And it's a good system. Unless you don't have a father. Then, maybe it's not so great. Then, maybe it's not such a good system. In that case—maybe you're on your own.

Life Without Games

This is my story. I've told this story before, in other places, in other forms. I grew up in the Philippines in the 1970s. It was a Third World country with a dictator who had appointed himself president for life, and we operated under a national state of martial law. During this period, a psychologically imbalanced woman who was sleeping with my father and had strong ties to the government issued death threats against me and my family. So my mom, my brother and I moved to the United States. I was nine.

Twenty-seven years have passed since then. I can count the number of times I've seen my father in those 27 years with the fingers on one hand. He is not a part of my life, and I am not a part of his. And that's fine. My mom raised me, and I am eternally thankful for all the sacrifices she made in order to provide for my brother and me. I owe her everything. But my mom—for all her brilliance, all her warmth, and all her generosity—did not know how to throw a baseball. She did not know how to break in a glove. She never took me to a major league game. My mom was an illegal immigrant trained as a radiologist. She could look at x-rays and discover the invisible sickness. She could save lives in the balance. That was what she did. But she did not care for baseball.

Growing up in the Philippines, I was not exposed to the sport. I didn't play it. I didn't read about it. I didn't collect baseball cards. I never saw a game. When we immigrated to the United States, it stunned me that you could watch baseball games on TV. You couldn't do that in the Philippines. It was impossible. There were only two television channels for the entire country, and both of them were run by the state. They showed cartoons and inane American sitcoms like "Three's Company." They were not broadcasting Vin Scully calling Dodgers doubleheaders.

The Things You Borrow

I went to my first major league game when I was a teenager. Back in middle school, I had spent a couple of years unsuccessfully trying to date Sarah Lorge. (She claims we tried it, and it didn't take. I say she's completely and utterly delusional and that I would certainly remember if I ever had a girlfriend in middle school. That significant detail would not have escaped my attention. I mean, have you forgotten your first girlfriend? No, right? That's the kind of detail you carry with you for all your days. That's all I'm saying.) One day Sarah told me that her Uncle Barry wanted to take us to a Red Sox game. Sounded good to me. Game on.

We rode in together on the hour drive from Paxton to Boston. To put it kindly, I think I drove Uncle Barry bonkers that evening. The entire game, I never stopped talking. The entire ride going and coming back, I never shut up. I was manic. Completely manic. And unfortunately, there was absolutely nothing I could do about it. I just couldn't help myself. I kept making jokes and Sarah kept laughing. She was entertained. I was a teenage kid, trying to impress a girl. Good luck putting up with that.

I don't remember the visiting team. I don't remember the score. I don't remember who pitched or who won. I just remember thinking about how cool it was to be able to go to my first live major league ballgame, hanging out on a summer evening, sitting in Fenway Park, spending it in the company of a cute girl. It blew my mind. What could be better? Even now, I don't have a good answer to that one.

That was my first game. And even though I did a poor job of showing it, I was very thankful that Uncle Barry had gotten us tickets. Barry Lorge had no particular connection to me. He was Sarah's uncle, not mine. He wanted to take Sarah to the game. He wanted to spend time with her, to bond with her so that they could enjoy a family outing together. I was just along for the ride.

But when you grow up without a father, you learn not to be too proud to borrow father figures when and where you can find them. You learn that lesson pretty early on. Sometimes, it's all you've got.

Watch the Circle Turn

I'm not a sociologist. So I'm not going to write an extended treatise on the immigrant experience. But as the son of an illegal immigrant, I do think it's true that at some point, as the decades went by, I stopped thinking of myself as a Filipino transplanted to the States and more as an American who came from the Philippines. In the end, most immigrants want to assimilate. They want to fit in. They want to belong.

So it was a nice reversal of form when I found myself starting to take people to their first baseball games. I remember dating this gal Monica. She was bold and assertive, which she attributed in part to the fact that she was an African-American woman who grew up deep in the heart of Texas. She had a big laugh and was very charismatic. One day, I asked her if she had ever been to Fenway. She replied, no, in fact, she had never attended

a major league ballgame of any sort. No kidding? Well, lady, we've got ourselves a date.

Fenway is a great place to take a date. It's historic, and pretty, and a difficult ticket to score. You sit outside enjoying the weather, enjoying the company and enjoying the atmosphere. I love Fenway. I really do.

My brother Ry, my buddy Drew, Monica and I went to the game together. It was a gorgeous New England summer day, with a powerful sun turning everything beneath it bright and shiny with colors that looked like a kindergarten crayon drawing come to life. We were all in a good mood. The weather was great, the company was entertaining, and the 2003 Boston roster was fascinating. Johnny Damon, Nomar, Manny, Big Papi, Pedro. Bonding behind Kevin Millar's "Cowboy up!" rallying cry, the team would go deep into the postseason, only to come up heartbreakingly short. There would be a crushing, devastating end to the season.

But all that lay ahead. Those ghosts lay in wait, stretching out ahead of us in the treacherous and tragic future. We did not know about those events on that late June evening as the Florida Marlins rolled into town for their inter-league game.

It felt like any other game. And it started out like any other game. But then, gradually things started to shift and stir. Slowly, like some hazy, waking dream, it dawned on us that we were watching something strange—something special and different and beautiful. Do you ever get that feeling? It happens so rarely, but it's always surprising when it comes. June 27, 2003 was a historic day for me as a fan, it was a historic day for the Red Sox as a team, and it was a historic day for baseball as a sport. I'll be honest, I happened to be lucky enough to be in the ballpark that night, but I still have a hard time believing everything I saw.

There is No Mercy for the Weak in this Dojo

In the bottom of the first inning, the first batter, Johnny Damon, doubled. The second batter, Todd Walker, singled. Damon scored. 1-0 Sox, no outs. The third batter, Nomar, doubled. The fourth batter, Manny, homered. 4-0 Sox, no outs. The fifth batter, Big Papi doubled. The sixth batter, Millar singled, Papi scored. 5-0 Sox, no outs. Carl Pavano was taken out of the game, Michael Tejera came in. Pavano's final line for the start was six batters faced, six hits allowed, charged with six earned runs, retiring nobody, creating an infinite ERA for the game.

The seventh batter of the game for the Red Sox, Trot Nixon, singled. The eighth batter, Bill Mueller, walked.

(Bill Mueller would go on to win the batting title that year. He batted eighth in the order. It was a deep line-up.) The ninth batter, Jason Varitek, singled. Millar and Nixon scored. 7-0 Sox, no outs. The team had batted around. Nobody had been retired. Seven runs had crossed the plate.

Batting 10th, leadoff man Johnny Damon came up for the second time in the inning. He tripled. Mueller and Damon scored. 9-0 Sox, no outs. The 11th batter of the inning, Todd Walker, singled. Damon scored. 10-0 Sox, no outs. Tejera was taken out of the game, Allen Levrault came in. Tejera's final line for the game was five batters faced, five base runners allowed (four hits, one walk), five earned runs, nobody retired, creating an infinite ERA for the game.

The Sox had sent 11 men to the plate, picked up 10 hits, scored 10 runs, and had seen their third opposing pitcher of the game. Before making a single out.

That was major league history. No team had ever done that. We now have 30 teams in the league, each one of them plays 162 games a season, and Major League Baseball has been around for over 100 years; its existence traces back well into the late 1800s. That's thousands and thousands and thousands of first innings. And no team had ever done it.

And Monica, the young gal from Texas, saw it all while attending her very first major league game. "You're good luck," I told her. "Every time you come to a game, the Sox score 10 runs before making an out. There's a 100 percent, direct one-to-one correlation." She laughed. It was all so improbable and absurd. She had no idea how unusual the proceedings were. Welcome to Fenway, Monica!

We watched baseball history unfold. One run. Then another. Then another. Naturally, you start doing the calculations in your head. Ten runs for every out? They're on pace to score 270 runs for the game. No, scratch that. They won't need to bat in the bottom of the ninth. 240 runs, then. It was unreal. In the end, the pace slowed down and the Sox added another 15 runs to their total, winning by a score of 25-8. Good stuff.

But it didn't work out. It didn't take. My relationship with Monica stumbled getting out of the starting gates and never took hold. And Monica's affection for baseball and the Red Sox never grew. For her, it was a pleasant distraction, a nice diversion. But nothing beyond that. The moments and memories that seem so vivid to me have less meaning for her. Far less meaning.

You know, I wonder if Monica ever finds herself thinking back about that game. I tend to doubt it. That's OK. Life moves on.

For the Record

(First Post-Script: There was some bad blood after that game. Marlins manager Jack McKeon did not appreciate the way things played out. According to the AP wire report: "Jack McKeon accused the Red Sox of running up the score in one of their greatest offensive performances ever. 'I didn't realize your pitching was that bad over here at Boston that you would try to add on a 16-run lead in the seventh inning,' he said.")

(Second Post-Script: Behind Josh Beckett's dominating pitching performance in Game 6 against the Yankees, the Florida Marlins went on to win the World Series later that same year.)

(Third Post-Script: Monica and I didn't go out on another date ever again.)

The Magic Bullet

How do you learn to love baseball? How does it become an important part of your daily routine? How do you inject it into your bloodstream, get it racing through your veins, pumping life into your exhausted body when the humid summer days slow everything down to a crawl, and the act of finding a morning box score is like unlocking the mysteries of a lost civilization? How does that happen?

I'm not Field of Dreams. I don't think I have any answers. I've seen people immerse themselves in baseball. And I've seen others shrug it off with disinterest. It's just a bat and a ball. It's just a game.

You can introduce someone to the game. You can take her to the most picturesque park in the majors. You can hit the lottery and watch the home team score more runs before recording the first out than any other team in major league history. But that's not enough. A beautiful night, at a beautiful park, with an amazing game isn't enough. You can't force magic. You can't. You can't pluck it out of thin air and summon it on demand, when convenient. That's not how fans are created. That's not how love works. And Monica did not love baseball. Not before our date. Not after it.

How do you learn to love baseball? It doesn't come in a single day. It doesn't come in a single game. And it doesn't appear fully formed, complete and whole, even when history unfolds before your very eyes. It comes gradually, in small steps and steady doses. It takes time, it takes patience, it takes nurturing, and it takes chemistry. Like any other form of love, I suppose.

At least that's how it happened for me. Little by little, piece by piece. I can't identify a turning point. I don't have some critical moment that I can single out in my development as a fan. It was more subtle than that. Far more subtle. So subtle, in fact, that I can't re-create the steps, I can't trace the journey, and I simply can't figure it out.

As soon as I landed in this country, I began my quiet allegiance to the sport. We moved to New England, which was a region that loved its baseball and the Red Sox (dating back to the team's miraculous 1967 turn-around season, according to the consensus). The games were on TV all the time. The kids in my class collected baseball cards, and so did I. My brother and my friends liked the sport and we would talk about it. There were some addictive baseball video games that I played all the time. And I'm not sure how my mom knew that she should sign me up for Little League, but I thought that it was just about the coolest thing ever. I had a uniform! My mom bought me a glove! I had teammates! For a little brown boy from the Philippines, the son of an illegal immigrant who just wanted to fit in, you couldn't beat that. Even now—writing these sentences, thinking back to those days—it brings a smile to my face.

I was drawn to the game. Baseball agreed with me. And even though I had to wait until I was a teenager to see my first game with Sarah and her uncle, I was already hooked by then. I didn't need a father figure. And I guess that I didn't need some compelling, singular explanation to sum up the way I felt. There was no Unified Theory. Look, do we need reasons to fall in love? Or do we simply fall in love because it feels right, even if we can't explain it? I won't bother to answer that. You know how it goes.

Winding Down

I spend a lot of time thinking about this game and the way it consumes me. I think about how my life has revolved around scores and stats, wins and losses. I think about players, and games, and the friends with whom I've spent countless hours sharing these moments. Baseball fascinates me in a way that is hard to explain, to a degree that is almost beyond words. It was true when I was nine, stepping off a plane and into a new country, a new world, a new life. And it's true now at 36, in this familiar country, in this predictable world, in my static life.

How do you learn to love baseball? I'll be honest with you—I don't really know. I don't have any sure-fire formula. But I know for a fact that it does happen. Clearly, it does. Because I'm writing these words, I know it's happened in my life. And because you're reading these words, I'm pretty confident it's also happened in yours.

The Greatest Class of All?

by Joe Posnanski

The word "steroids" will not appear in the rest of this story. Nor will the letters "HGH" or the phrase "performance-enhancing drugs." There will be no clear and no cream, not in drug form anyway, no further mention of BALCO or former trainers in jail or former trainers testifying in Congress or, really, any former trainers at all. There will be no mention of injections, no statistics designed to cast suspicion based on odd aging patterns and no theories offered on where the blame should fall. Not here.

None of these things will be mentioned here because, I suspect, you may have read an article or two about all that. I suspect you already know that the out-of-whack power numbers of what we like to call the Meso-Selig Era (or simply the Age of Bud) may not have been entirely natural. I suspect that you may be tired of hearing about all that or, at the very least, could use a break. I sure could. That's why I'm writing this.

Trouble is, I also suspect that when you run across the names Barry Bonds and Roger Clemens in just a few paragraphs, you will be hit by a wave of emotion, something from the gut, something about them as people and as sportsmen and as wonders of chemistry. I suspect it will be weird to see their names and read a bit about their accomplishments and not get a single word about the charges and counter-charges and suspicions that have hounded them and branded them as athletes and men. It seems a bit like writing a story about Darth Vader and failing to mention the whole "he turned to the dark side" thing.

But, for a few minutes, I would ask you to forget all that. This is a story about what Hall of Fame Induction Day 2013 might have been, had it not been for all those things I promised not to mention. If everything was a little different, Induction Day 2013 might have been the most amazing crossroads in baseball history.

So here's the deal: I won't mention any of that stuff. But if you want to insert caveats and cautions and scientific research into the article, I certainly approve. I find that the margins are an excellent place for such observations, but please feel free to scribble directly on my words. I would also recommend using a red pen because red ink tends to stand out. Perhaps most of all, I would recommend you purchase this book beforehand.

The first Hall of Fame class was chosen in February 1936. Exactly 226 members of the Baseball Writers Association of America voted on the best baseball players of the 20th Century. The writers were told that every player who received at least 75 percent of the vote would be inducted into the Hall of Fame, and that up to 10 players would be inducted. As you probably know, five players received the necessary votes:

- Ty Cobb (222 votes, 98.6%)
- Babe Ruth (215 votes, 95.1%)
- Honus Wagner (215 votes, 95.1%)
- Christy Mathewson (205 votes, 90.7%)
- Walter Johnson (189 votes, 83.6%)

You could probably win a bar bet by naming the player who finished sixth in the voting,* but in the newspapers the next day there was a little bit of lament that Napoleon Lajoie, "the graceful, hard-hitting second baseman who spent 21 years in the majors," fell a few votes short. Lajoie was a great player, but the ballot featured two second basemen—Rogers Hornsby and Eddie Collins—who were probably even better. Of course, the Hall of Fame has always been shrouded in myth and mythmaking, and Lajoie was so good and beloved that the Cleveland team was named for him for a dozen years.

*Depending on if Bill James or Rob Neyer happened to be at that particular bar.

In any case, the newspapers of the time did seem to agree that the first five were no-brainers*. To pull out the punchiest description of each:

- Ty Cobb was a "fiery genius of the diamond," and he "shattered virtually all records known to baseball during his glorious era."
- Walter Johnson was the "fireball king of all-time."
- Christy Mathewson was "probably the most popular figure the game has ever known."
- Honus Wagner was both "the big daddy of shortstops," and the "best of all shortstops."
- Babe Ruth, as one press service ended its story, "needs no introdruction."

*Sorry, just have to say this: I really do not like the meaning of the phrase "no-brainer." It is defined to mean, "something that *requires or involves little or no mental effort." And I guess I can see the logic behind that—this decision is so easy you don't even need to use your brain to make it. What you use to make the decision, I don't know.*

But during the 2008 season, Kansas City Royals manager Trey Hillman took Gil Meche out of the game even though Meche's pitch count seemed manageable (103 pitches) and he had retired 17 consecutive batters. When questioned about it afterward, Hillman reacted a bit huffily and called the decision "a no-brainer." And I thought, "Yeah, you know, he's right, but those two words pushed together should have a very different meaning."

Obviously, the first class is the best and most famous Hall of Fame class ever. There have been other good ones—the 1947 class with Lefty Grove, Mickey Cochrane, Frankie Frisch and Carl Hubbell was awfully good. The 1966 class had Ted Williams and Casey Stengel. The 1972 class had Yogi Berra and Sandy Koufax and also Negro Leagues stars Buck Leonard and Josh Gibson; that could very well be the best class since the first.

In 1982, Hank Aaron and Frank Robinson were inducted together. In 1989 it was Johnny Bench and Carl Yastrzemski. In 1999 George Brett, Nolan Ryan, Robin Yount and Orlando Cepeda all went in on the same hot weekend.

None of those really push the first class. Let's face it: In 1936, you have perhaps the greatest hitter and most intense competitor (Cobb), perhaps the most overwhelming force (Ruth), perhaps the most complete player (Wagner), perhaps the greatest pitcher who ever lived (Walter Johnson) and—one more perhaps— perhaps the most respected gentleman to ever play the game (Mathewson). That seems an impossible group to beat.

But—close your eyes, imagine that some of the bad news of the past 10 years never happened—the Class of 2013 might be even more spectacular.

First Inductee: Barry Bonds

I know I promised not to mention anything about, well, you know. But I do wonder sometimes if Barry Bonds' story would have played out a little bit differently had he been a center fielder his whole career. You probably know that Bonds played center field his entire rookie season in Pittsburgh. His arm was a touch weak for the position, but he obviously had the speed and the instincts to be an outstanding center fielder. The next year, though, the Pirates traded Tony Pena to St. Louis for a package that included Andy Van Slyke. Bonds slid over to left so that Van Slyke could play center field.

And Bonds was, of course, an excellent defensive left fielder—he is probably acknowledged as the best defensive left fielder ever, for whatever that is worth. He won eight Gold Gloves as a left fielder, which is more or less like winning the Olympic 100-meter butterfly eight times against the current.*

*It's worth saying here that we have passed the point of absurdity when it comes to the Gold Gloves. I'm not talking here about the many flaws of the award itself—like the managers' and coaches' insistence on giving Derek Jeter three Gold Gloves, the obvious importance of offense in the Gold Glove voting and so on. No, I mean, specifically, that it is absurd the Gold Glove voters continue to treat all outfielders the same. Everyone in baseball knows that playing left field is wildly different from play center field, and playing center is night and day to playing right. And yet, when it comes to the Gold Glove voting, they throw all of them into the same pool.

If the Gold Glove rules had decided to give four Gold Gloves to the four best infielders instead of breaking them up by position, you would imagine that no first baseman would ever win an award. That's how it is with left fielders now. The Gold Glove voters will often pick three center fielders which is what they should do based on the current rules—but the current rules are ridiculous. Break 'em up.

What would have happened had Bonds stayed in center? I suspect that—even though his personality hardly made friends and influenced people—he would have received more respect during the early part of his career. Take a look at this comparison between two sons of excellent players, Ken Griffey and Barry Bonds, from 1990 to 1998.

- **Griffey**: .304/.384/.582 with 271 doubles, 27 triples, 334 homers, 957 RBIs, 879 runs, 127 stolen bases, nine gold gloves.
- **Bonds**: .305/.438/.600 with 279 doubles, 40 triples, 327 homers, 993 RBIs, 1,000 runs, 328 stolen bases, eight Gold Gloves.

It's pretty clear: Griffey was great, but Bonds was better in almost every way. He got on base a lot more and, as such, scored many more runs. He stole 200 more bases. He even had a better slugging percentage. The year-by-year Win Shares numbers—which take into account defense, of course—are even more stark:

- 1990: Bonds wins 37-24.
- 1991: Bonds wins 37-30.
- 1992: Bonds wins 41-25.
- 1993: Bonds wins 47-29.
- 1994: Bonds wins 25-20.

- 1995: Bonds wins 36-9
- 1996: Bonds wins 39-28
- 1997: Tied 36 win shares apiece
- 1998: Bonds wins 34-29.

This has been brought up many times—Bonds was pretty clearly the superior player, and yet Griffey was pretty commonly considered the best player in baseball at the time. The conventional reasoning for this is that Griffey was just so much easier to like—he played with a smile, he tilted with charisma, he did not seem to have disdain for his teammates. These are only perceptions, but they are powerful ones.

Personally, I think the center field thing is at play here. Griffey, of course, played center, and he fit the image we have of the great center fielder, the image of Mays and Mantle and DiMaggio and Snider and the rest. He could chase down fly balls, and he could hit the big home runs. He could make leaping catches at the wall, and he could steal (a few) bases.

The (awful) Fogerty song they play at ballparks everywhere is called "Centerfield." That's the place to be. Dale Murphy was a do-everything center fielder in the early-to-mid-1980s, and he won a couple of MVP awards. Fred Lynn showed off that all-around play in '75 and became the first rookie to win the MVP award. Eric Davis, Kirby Puckett, Amos Otis, Cesar Cedeno, this archetype of the fast and powerful center fielder is firmly in our minds. And Griffey represented.

Bonds, meanwhile, played left field, and to be honest there had never really been a left fielder quite like him. Left fielders are generally specialists. They are remarkable hitters like Ted Williams or base stealers like Rickey Henderson and Lou Brock or immense sluggers like Frank Howard and George Foster. Bonds, I think, did not quite fit the imagination playing left field. Something was just a little bit off. He may have been a better offensive player than Griffey, but Junior was a center fielder and that made him better.

I will not play amateur psychologist here, but the general thinking seems to be that it was a lack of respect that pushed Bonds to bulk up and after 1998 to put together the greatest flurry of offensive numbers in the history of baseball. If there was a lack of respect, I think a great deal of it came from Bonds playing left field. He put up Willie Mays numbers, but most people refused to see him like Willie Mays. The rest, of course, is in the record books.

Comparison to 1936: Bonds takes on the role of Ruth in this class, of course. The arguments will rage about Ruth vs. Bonds. Ruth played in an era without black or Latin players, with day games, with train travel and without relief specialists. Bonds played in an era with trainers and nutritionists, better equipment, tight strike zones and body armor. There's no way to compare them, really. All you can do is take one more glance at their most famous seasons and be in awe.

- **Bonds in 2001**: .328/.515/.863, 73 homers, 137 RBIs, 129 runs, 177 walks, 259 OPS+.
- **Ruth in 1927**: .356/.486/.772, 60 homers, 164 RBIs, 158 runs, 137 walks, 226 OPS+.

And both men had better seasons statistically. Ruth in 1920 had a 256 OPS+ and famously hit more home runs than any team in the league. Bonds in 2004 had a 263 OPS+ and an absurd .609 on-base percentage which is what happens when you are intentionally walked 120 times. Bonds was intentionally walked more times than anyone in the American League *actually* walked. With nods to Ted Williams, Willie Mays, Ty Cobb, Mickey Mantle and the rest, I think Ruth and Bonds are the two greatest offensive forces in the history of the game.

Second Inductee: Roger Clemens

When Dan Duquette made his now famous "twilight of his career" comment, Roger Clemens was 34 years old, and he had won 11 or fewer games for four straight years. Pitcher victories, of course, is a very flawed way of looking at how a pitcher is performing.*

During the 1994 strike year, for instance, Clemens' record was 9-7 but he had a 177 ERA+ and was averaging about a strike-out per inning. You could argue pretty convincingly that he was the best pitcher in the American League that year. David Cone won the Cy Young because of his 16-5 record, but Clemens had a better ERA, more strikeouts and pitched in a better hitter's park.

Still, it is pretty striking for a great pitcher—a guy who has a real argument as the greatest pitcher ever—to win only 40 games from age 30 to 33.

Here's an incomplete list of recent pitchers who won more than 40 games from age 30 to 33: Andy Ashby, Tom Browning, Mike Caldwell, Pat Dobson, Dock Ellis, Chuck Finley, Larry Gura, Bruce Hurst, Larry Jackson, Bob Knepper, Jim Lonborg, Doc Medich, Fred Norman, Bob Ojeda, Bob Purkey, Kirk Rueter, Bryn Smith, Kevin Tapani, Bob Veale, Woody Williams and Geoff Zahn and Tom Zachary. I could not find anyone whose last names begin with I, Q, U, X, or Y. That's why I gave you the extra Z.

The question here: how would we view Clemens now if he really *was* in the twilight of his career?

After the 1996 season, Clemens was 192-111 (a .634 winning percentage) with a 145 ERA+ and 2,590 strikeouts. That ERA+ is telling—it is, post-deadball, the second-best ERA+ for any pitcher his age. Only Lefty Grove, who has his own argument as the greatest pitcher in baseball history, had a higher ERA+ (152).

So I would say that even if Clemens had limped to the finish line, he's a first-ballot Hall of Famer. If he had just plugged along for four or five more years, he would have gone way over 3,000 strikeouts, he would have surely approached 250 wins, he already had three Cy Young Awards* and so on. As it turned out, he had a bit of renaissance after Duquette let him escape Boston. You may have heard about that.

*And he certainly should have won the award in 1990 when he went 21-6 with a 1.93 ERA and led the league in shutouts. He lost out to Bob Welch, who won 27 games that year despite an ERA that was a full run higher than Clemens. Welch's 1990 is amazing—from June 5 to August 2 he went 10-2 despite a 4.38 ERA. In both of his losses, he did not go five innings.

Comparison to 1936: Clemens fills the role of Walter Johnson, the Big Train, who was the most dominant pitcher of his time. It's hard to compare a pitcher from deadball to a pitcher from the Meso-Selig, but it is worth noting that Johnson had his last truly dominant season when he was 31, which not coincidentally was the last year of deadball. He was often very good after that—he went 23-7 with an excellent 149 ERA+ in 1924—but even then he wasn't the immortal Walter Johnson like in 1910 (1.36 ERA, 313 Ks), 1913 (36-7, 1.14 ERA) and 1919 (1.49 ERA, and, by the record books, no home runs allowed).

Bill James, in most moods, calls Walter Johnson the greatest pitcher who ever lived, but he says that Clemens certainly has a case.

Third Inductee: Mike Piazza

Here, in my opinion, are the five best players selected after the 40th round in the draft:

5. Marcus Giles. He was drafted by the Atlanta Braves in the 53rd round. He's been pretty dreadful the last two years, but he had a terrific year in 2003: .316/.390/.526 with 21 homers and 101 runs scored. Pretty good for a second baseman. I will say that as the brother of Brian Giles—who was just beginning to flash some talent in the big leagues when Marcus was drafted—I'm surprised he didn't go a few rounds higher.*

*Marcus also went to school with NASCAR titan Jimmie Johnson. Just a useless tidbit I had to share with someone.

4. Al Cowens. He was selected by the Kansas City Royals in—get this—the 75th round out of Compton High back in 1969. Of course, the Royals were an expansion team, and they were trying to fill out their system. Still, think about that: They went 75 rounds deep. And they didn't stop there. In the 76th round they took John Behrens, in the 77th they grabbed a catcher named Robert Proechel, in the 78th they took another catcher named Bill Akers. I was going to keep going, listing off every player the Royals took after Cowens but it turns out they went *90 rounds* in 1969, even though every other team stopped drafting after the 76th (only the expansion Montreal Expos even went that far with the Royals).

Anyway, Cowens finished second in the MVP voting in 1977, and he was outstanding that year: he hit .312/.361/.525 with 23 homers, 112 RBIs, 98 runs scored, 16 stolen bases, and he won a Gold Glove in right field. Cowens never came close to matching that season, though in 1982 he did bang 39 doubles and 20 homers for a terrible Seattle Mariners team. Anyway, he is undoubtedly the best 75th round draft pick in the history of any sport.

3. Jeff Conine. Another Royals pick, he was taken in the 58th round of the 1987 draft. Again the Royals kept drafting even after everyone else went home—they took the last four players of that draft, including a shortstop named Stewart Anthony in the 74th round.

My favorite Conine fact is that he was, apparently, a world-class racquetball player.* He was a good athlete who had a good career—he finished with 1,982 hits, more than 200 homers and more than 1,000 RBIs. I will say, though, that as a racquetball star I was always surprised he didn't walk more. I don't know why I connected those two things; I guess I just figured his hand-eye coordination had to be so good he would have a superior strike zone judgment. He did not. As it turned out he struck out about twice as often as he walked.

*Remember when ESPN would show racquetball matches? And they didn't just show them every so often; no, racquetball was on about as much as the World Series of Poker is on ESPN2 now. I think it's fair to say that the network has come a long way.

2. Keith Hernandez. He was a 42nd-round pick of the St. Louis Cardinals, and I think he has a pretty strong Hall of Fame case. I played this game on my blog not too long ago, but it's worth playing again:

- **First baseman No. 1**: .296/.384/.436, 2,182 hits, 426 doubles, 60 triples, 162 homers, 1,071 RBIs, 1,124 runs, 128 OPS+, one MVP award, one batting title, 11 Gold Gloves.

- **First baseman No. 2**: .307/.358/.471, 2,153 hits, 442 doubles, 20 triples, 222 homers, 1,099 RBIs, 1,007 runs, 127 OPS+, one MVP award, one batting title, nine Gold G)loves.

No. 1 is Hernandez. No. 2 is Don Mattingly. I suspect neither one will make it into the Hall of Fame. But if one does, I would choose Hernandez, even without his Seinfeld appearance. With it, he's a slam dunk.

1. Mike Piazza. The Dodgers famously took him in the 62nd round as a personal favor to Tommy Lasorda, who was a childhood friend of Mike's father Vince.

Piazza had more or less flopped as a first baseman at the University of Miami (a spot that Lasorda had apparently helped secure), and after transferring to Miami-Dade Community College he missed much of the season with an injury. It seems pretty unlikely that he would have been drafted had he not known Lasorda, and so the greatest hitting catcher in the history of baseball could easily have found himself in the cubicle next to you at work had his dad not palled around with Lasorda.

Mike promised Lasorda he would learn how to catch if he got drafted. And so he went to winter ball and worked hard to become a catcher. Piazza's defensive skills have often been mocked, and he certainly could not throw. In 1996, base runners stole 155 bases with him behind the plate, and he only managed to throw out 34 (82 percent success). That is more or less how it went for Piazza. He also committed a lot of errors, had numerous passed balls and so on. But he also has his defenders—including teammates—who say he handled pitchers pretty well and blocked the plate and so on.

Anyway, that's almost beside the point. Piazza could really swat. Piazza has the top three OPS+ seasons for catchers, including his remarkable 1997 season when he hit .362/.431/.638 with 40 homers, 124 RBIs and 201 hits. He's the best-hitting catcher in baseball history.

Comparison to 1936: He doesn't really have a good comp in the first class because, honestly, there really isn't a good comp in baseball history for Piazza.

Fourth Inductee: Craig Biggio

I'd say Biggio's 1997 season is one of my favorites of all time. It's a numbers and achievement smorgasbord. In 1997, Craig Biggio played in all 162 games. He won a Gold Glove at second base. He led the league in runs scored despite playing half his games in the dreadful-hitting Astrodome. He banged 37 doubles, eight triples and 22 home runs. He stole 47 bases. He walked 84 times. He got hit by 34 pitches, the third-highest total in

baseball history. He led the league in plate appearances, yet he did not hit into a single double play all year.

Of course, 1997 was a year for amazing performances. Piazza had the greatest-hitting season ever for a catcher. Larry Walker had a preposterous season with a .366 average, 49 homers, 46 doubles and a right field Gold Glove. Nomar Garciaparra had a fabulous rookie season with 44 doubles, 11 triples, 30 homers, 122 runs scored and 209 hits. Junior hit 56 homers and drove in 147 RBIs.

But Biggio's season stands out because he did so many of those quiet things that go unnoticed, like getting hit by pitches and avoiding the double play. Bill James has told me this is why Biggio became his favorite player; Bill enjoyed having a player he appreciated in a way that so few others appreciated.

In the end, everyone came to appreciate Biggio, though probably for less compelling reasons. He ended up with 3,000 hits, thanks to eight seasons at the end of his career when he was barely an average player. But I prefer to think of Biggio in 1997—baseball people often talk about those players who will do anything to help a team win. Normally they say that when the player's statistics simply don't look too good. I think Biggio fit that tag in measurable ways.

Comparison to 1936: Biggio is, of course, nowhere close to the player that Honus Wagner was. But I still think he's the Wagner stand-in for this class, the do-everything player who showed up every day. You probably have heard the Wagner quote: "I never have been sick. I don't even know what it means to be sick." Biggio was a catcher, a second baseman, a center fielder, and he played 150 or more games in 11 seasons and got hit by 285 pitches in his career. He didn't know what sick meant either.

Fifth Inductee: Sammy Sosa

No matter how many times I see this chart, it amazes me endlessly.

Most home runs in a single season:

1. Barry Bonds, 73
2. Mark McGwire, 70
3. Sammy Sosa, 66
4. Mark McGwire, 65
5. Sammy Sosa, 64
6. Sammy Sosa, 63
7. Roger Maris, 61
8. Babe Ruth, 60

It really is mind-boggling. Sammy Sosa hit more than 60 home runs in a season *three different times*. I don't really have much to add to that; it seems to tell a pretty good story. You can make an argument—in fact, it's more or less inarguable—that from 1998 to 2002, Sammy Sosa was the most prolific home run hitter in baseball history.

Most home runs over a five-year period.:

1. Sammy Sosa, 292 (1998-2002)
2. Mark McGwire, 284 (1995-1999)
3. Sammy Sosa, 279 (1997-2001)
4. Mark McGwire, 277 (1996-2000)
5. Barry Bonds, 258 (2000-2004)

The most home runs that Babe Ruth hit over a five-year period is 256.

This is not to say that Sosa was a truly great player; had he gotten as many plate appearances as Reggie Jackson, Sosa would have broken Reggie's career strike-out record. He was a great hitter for those magical five years, but before that his OPS+ was a fairly pedestrian 106, and afterward it was 109. His lifetime .273 average and .344 on-base percentage do not match up all that well with other corner outfielders in the Hall. And he often seemed a disinterested or slightly confused outfielder who was never quite sure what to do with his strong arm.

That said, Sosa was very good at one thing. He hit the ball out of the ballpark.

Comparison to 1936: Sosa, like Piazza, is such a unique player he probably does not compare all that well to any of the first class. He's more like a Ralph Kiner or Harmon Killebrew or Reggie.

Sixth Inductee: Curt Schilling

Schilling is talking about making a comeback in 2009. It could be tough. Even if he does come back, I can't imagine he would add much more to his career value. I think now we have to look at his career numbers and try and decide if they are Hall of Fame worthy.

Schilling has won 216 games, which does put him on the low end of the Hall of Fame. His argument would have to be the Don Drysdale argument—that he wasn't good for very long, but he was very good for as long as he pitched. I don't like comparing prospective Hall of Fame candidates to current Hall of Famers because situations are so different. Still …

- Schilling, like Drysdale, was a right-handed power pitcher.

- They both started about 450 games (Drysdale started 465, Schilling 436).

- Drysdale had the better ERA (2.95 to 3.46) but that seems to be entirely based on context. Drysdale pitched in a pitcher's era in perhaps the greatest pitcher's park ever. Because of this, Schilling has a substantial edge in ERA+ (127 to 121).

- Drysdale went 209-166 for mostly good teams.

- Schilling went 216-135 for a mishmash of good and bad teams.

- Schilling struck out 3,116 batters, 500 more than Drysdale.

- Schilling also walked fewer batters and gave up fewer hits. His WHIP is better.

- Drysdale threw 49 shutouts to Schilling's 20.

Drysdale also had some good postseason moments, including the shutout he threw against the Yankees in the 1963 World Series. But, of course, Schilling has been pretty close to legendary in the postseason. He's 11-2 with a 2.23 ERA in the postseason, he's even better in the World Series, and of course he started Game 7 against the Yankees in the remarkable 2001 World Series and pitched the bloody sock game.

All in all, Schilling seems like a better candidate for the Hall than Drysdale. But there are two other factors. First, you can make the same comparison I just made with a dozen pitchers who are *not* in the Hall of Fame, and Schilling will not come out as good. Second, it took 10 years for Drysdale to get elected into the Hall of Fame.

Personally, I think Schilling is a Hall of Famer. Now, I will admit that unlike many of my colleagues, I like Curt Schilling. Many of the sportswriters and baseball people I know think he's a loudmouth, a self-aggrandizer, a guy who will say anything. OK. I don't like him despite those things; I like him because of those things. To me, Schilling is generally fun and over the top and opinionated, he lets his emotions go, and he really has been great in the biggest moments. I don't agree with him much. But I like that he's out there.

Comparison to 1936: I suspect that even if Schilling gets in, he will not go first ballot. That's a guess. Still I see him as the Christy Mathewson of this class. He's nowhere close to Mathewson as a pitcher or as a statesman of the game. Mathewson remains one of the 10 best pitchers ever, and Schilling is probably closer to 25 or 30. I don't mean it like that. It's just that, like the Great Matty, he was awesome in the big moments. And the bloody sock, for whatever else, is about as big a part of baseball lore as Matty's three consecutive shutouts in the 1905 World Series.

Bonus Seventh Inductee: Pete Rose

So, 2013 will mark the 50-year anniversary of Pete Rose's first game in the major leagues. Pete will be 72 years old in April of that year. I think that would make for a great year to induct baseball's all-time hits leader into the Hall of Fame. Rose, obviously, would be the stand-in for Ty Cobb in that first class.

It won't happen because, as they say in elections, the math doesn't work for him. Even if someone could get Rose on the Baseball Writers ballot for the first time,* there is no way he would get 75 percent of the vote. Even if they could get his name on the ballot of the veteran's committee—which is now made up of all the living Hall of Famers—he would not get anywhere close to 75 percent of the vote. I think, based on the people with whom I've talked about this, Rose would get considerably less support among the Hall of Famers.

Here's a little known fact: Shoeless Joe Jackson got two votes in the first Hall of Fame ballot in 1936.

So when people ask: "Do you think Pete Rose will make it into the Hall of Fame?" my honest response has to be: "Not even the slightest chance."

But I need to put here—especially because this gives me a chance to get in a plug for my new book coming out about the 1975 Reds—that the Hall of Fame really is incomplete without Rose. You know, he is the all-time leader in:

- Games played.
- Hits.
- Plate appearances

- Singles
- Times on base.

Beyond that, though, Rose defined baseball for a generation. People hated him. People loved him. But he was inescapable in the way he ran to first base, the unrepentant way he upended second basemen and shortstops on double-play grounders, the way he slid head first, the way he memorized his own statistics, the way he fought for every dollar, the way he switched positions (sometimes midyear) to help the team, the way he treated his teammates (every single Reds player I've talked to has a story about Pete Rose being good to them), the way he would go for his fifth hit in a game like it was the most important thing on earth. He wasn't just a baseball player, he was *baseball*, for all the good and bad of his time.

I don't know how long you punish someone for breaking the gambling rule. It's baseball's cardinal rule, and Rose's refusal to admit it or apologize for it for a long time left a sour taste. Still, as far as I know, Pete Rose never threw a game. As far as I know, Pete Rose never adversely affected a game so that he could win a bet. As far as I know, Pete Rose played his guts out for a long time. Yes, he was a troubled guy who did a lot of lousy things, and he let a lot of people down, and it's at the discretion of the commissioner and the owners whether or not Pete Rose belongs in the game today.

But I wish that all these years later, they would allow Pete's name back on the Hall of Fame ballot. Maybe he would not get enough votes—in fact, as mentioned, I'm pretty sure he would not get enough votes. But I would vote for him. There was never another player like him.

History

The Aging of Honus Wagner

by Craig Wright

Early in my 21 years working full-time with major league teams, I saw the practical value in gaining a better understanding of how players age. That led to my developing aging profiles as part of my player evaluations, which in turn let me make useful recommendations such as tabbing Nolan Ryan at age 41 as a pitcher who had several effective seasons left in him.

Ryan had by far the best aging profile I had ever come across for a non-knuckleballer of such an advanced age. Over the next three years—ages 42, 43 and 44—Ryan surpassed even my high expectations. He went 41-25, threw two no-hitters, struck out 736 batters in 616 innings, and posted a 3.20 ERA (fourth best in the league).

These same aging profiles prompted me to alert the Los Angeles Dodgers to move Hubie Brooks—who had a poor aging profile—while he still had decent value after a season with 20 homers and 91 RBIs. That proved to be the last good year of his career, even though he was only 33. At the same time, I was able to distinguish a positive aging profile for Brett Butler, even though he was about the same age as Brooks. (For the next five seasons, at ages 34-38, Butler hit .303 with an on-base percentage of .397 that ranked third in the league.)

As part of the research behind my aging profiles, I did a historical study of position players in which one player stood out like a beacon. That player was the ever-remarkable Honus Wagner.

Speed

Speed is among the skills most vulnerable to the aging process, and yet the Flying Dutchman was still being mentioned as one of the fastest players in the league at an age when many players were retiring. He hit more triples after his 37th birthday than any other player in history, an incredible 76 three-baggers. Ty Cobb is the legendary base stealer of Wagner's era, but it was Wagner who held the record for most steals past his 30th birthday, and he held that record for 60 years until Lou Brock passed him in 1975. Along the way Wagner accomplished the following feats:

- **May 2, 1909**: Wagner stole second, third and home at age 35, the oldest player to steal his way around the bases.

- **July 31, 1912**: Wagner stole home, and at age 38 was believed to be the oldest player to do it. Ty Cobb would break that record in 1926, but this game had other features that are a fascinating testament to Wagner's unusual durability. In 1912, Wagner was the oldest non-pitcher in the National League. This steal of home took place in an intense game that went 19 innings, and Wagner's Pirates won by a single run, 7-6. Wagner played all 19 innings, all at shortstop, and drove in the winning run.

- **1915**: Wagner stole 22 bases at age 41. He remained the oldest to do this all through the 20th century. Rickey Henderson broke that record in the new millennium (2001).

- **1915**: The 41-year-old Wagner also hit 17 triples. The next oldest player to do this was—well, does the name Wagner sound familiar? Wagner had 20 triples in 1912 at age 38. (Jake Daubert also did it at age 38, but was a few months younger than Wagner.) The next year, 1916, Wagner hit nine triples, which remains the record for anyone 42 or older.

- **July 1, 1916**: Wagner raced around the bases for an inside-the-park home run that gave the Pirates a 2-1 victory. At age 42 years and four months, he was the oldest player to ever leg out an inside-the-park-homer. (To add further perspective to how old that is, only about 30 players ever have hit any home runs at that age.)

Defense

Shortstop was a young man's position in Wagner's era. Because runs were so scarce in that pitching-dominated era, a big premium was put on offensive speed to help pick up extra bases and to beat out bunts and infield hits. A lot was expected of the shortstop, who had to be quick and athletic and, far more than today, had to have a strong arm. He not only had to throw out runners who were selected more for speed than modern players, but he had to have the arm strength to recover from the fielding bobbles that were far more common in that era of poor glove design and scarred infields that were nowhere near the quality of modern playing surfaces.

Wagner's throwing arm was even more legendary than his quickness, and that allowed him to stay at short-stop long after the other top defensive shortstops were sliding over to other positions or retiring. Hall of Fame shortstop Bobby Wallace is from the same era, and he had a decent bat but never led the league in any offensive category except games played. He is in the Hall largely because of his outstanding defensive skills, and yet Wagner was able to play 65 percent more games at shortstop past the age of 32 than Wallace did. The other three great defensive shortstops of Wagner's era were Joe Tinker, George McBride and Mickey Doolan. Wagner played over 100 more games at shortstop past age 32 than those three combined.

Bill James' Defensive Win Shares estimate that if there had been a Gold Glove award in 1912, Wagner would have deserved it. He was 38 years old that year, and he is the oldest shortstop ever to lead in Defensive Win Shares.

When Wagner turned 40 in 1914, the most games a player in his 40s ever had played at shortstop in a season was 57 (Candy Nelson in 1890). That year, Wagner played 132 games at shortstop, and then played 131 more at age 41. As of 1916, no one ever had played more than five games at shortstop at age 42. Wagner played 92 (60 percent of the scheduled games).

On May 13, 1915, Wagner accomplished the unusual feat of fielding more than half his team's outs when he handled 14 chances cleanly in a nine-inning game (six putouts, eight assists). This is rare in any era, and Wagner did it at age 41. It is a pretty safe bet he is the oldest to do it. Only four others have played even 50 games at shortstop past their 41st birthday, and we know for sure that two of them (Omar Vizquel and Ozzie Smith) didn't match that feat.

Hitting

In studying the effects of aging on hitting, many years ago I put together lists of players who had a better OPS (relative to the position players in their league) at ages 31 to 37 than they had at ages 23 to 30. I discovered that, compared to the modern era, that was quite rare in the pitching-dominated Dead Ball era. When you think about it, that makes perfect sense.

1. Conditioning and rehabilitation of injuries were primitive in that era, making it tougher to age well.

2. It was an era in which walks and home runs were less of a factor, and those are two of the offensive categories that age best.

3. Speed played a bigger role in that era in getting hits and extra-base hits than it did in any other era, and speed tends not to age well.

This makes the hitting accomplishments of the "elderly" Wagner all the more remarkable.

In 1911, at 37, Wagner became the oldest batting champion to date, a record he held until Ted Williams passed him in 1958. More impressive than the batting title, Wagner also led in OPS (on-base percentage plus slugging percentage), and again he remained the oldest player to do this until Williams.

In 1912, at 38, Wagner was second in OPS and led the league in RBIs.

In 1915, at 41, Wagner banged out an incredible 55 extra-base hits (third most in the league). That's the most ever in a season by a player 41 or older. The second most is 50 by Dave Winfield in 1993—a point in history where the extra-base hit rate had escalated roughly 40 percent since 1916.

In 1916, at 42 and in his last full season, Wagner was eighth in the league in batting average, and he remains the oldest player to finish in the top 10. He was still playing shortstop, and among the other starting shortstops—from both leagues—he was still top dog in batting average, on-base percentage, and runs created per out.

Recently, doing research on another topic, I got a chance to look at the day-by-day logs of Wagner's 1915 and 1916 seasons: his last two full seasons, ages 41 and 42. It dawned on me that these data contained further evidence that Wagner's abilities had aged even better than is commonly perceived when looking at his seasonal numbers.

Wagner played in an era in which players were encouraged to play through minor injuries. Examples from Wagner's career show that he and the Pirates bought heavily into that philosophy, even to the point of having Wagner play through significant injuries if there was a chance it would help the team. Particularly well known is that in the first World Series in 1903, Wagner was playing with a fairly serious knee injury that was supposed to have ended his season. On Sept. 7, Wagner had injured his right knee in a collision on the base paths, and after an examination he was advised that he had damaged tendons around the knee and that he "probably wouldn't play another game that season."

It was even recommended that he have surgery on the knee.

In those days, knee surgery was a messy business, often involving uncertain diagnosis, and it usually did about as much harm as good. Wagner refused the operation and instead sought out John "Bone Setter" Reese of Youngstown, Pa. Reese had given some other players relief from joint injuries using a technique similar to that of a modern chiropractor. After missing only five games, Wagner was back in the lineup, but he clearly was not 100 percent. He would limp at times, had to take an occasional day off when the knee was too painful, and after the pennant was clinched, he sat out most of the last week of the season.

Further evidence that Wagner's knee still was not fully healed is that the Pirates temporarily hired "Bone Setter" to accompany the team during the World Series to work daily on the knee. The recent rest, plus the care from Reese, helped Wagner play well through the first four games. He was hitting .385, but then went hard into second base on a steal attempt, and the knee was a real problem the rest of the Series. In the remaining four games he was 2-for-14 and made a very uncharacteristic five errors. In the seventh game, Wagner was batting with a runner on third and one out. Rather than have him swing away to get the run in, the Pirates had the gimpy Wagner execute a suicide squeeze bunt.

Fortunately, an extended rest period in the offseason was enough to allow the knee to heal fully.

Five years later, in July of 1908, Wagner took a bad hop off a finger, and it was so "disjointed and inflamed" that manager Fred Clarke worried that the team needed to rest him for a few days to let it heal. But with the Pirates in first place by only half a game, Clarke was relieved when his shortstop agreed to play with the damaged finger.

On March 28 of 1913, a 39-year-old Wagner wrenched his left knee in a spring exhibition game so badly that he was unable to run, and he had to miss the first 19 games of the season. Reese diagnosed the injury as "floating cartilage." Almost a month after the injury, Wagner still was in pain and having trouble running hard. On April 25, he was examined by orthopedist Dr. David Silver, who recommended prolonged rest. But six days later Wagner tested the knee in an exhibition game and started his season the very next day.

He had his average up to .330 when, on June 23, he injured the knee again. (Some accounts say it was the other knee this time, the right knee that had gone out on him back in 1903). He was unable to play in the field for the next 24 games, but pinch-hit seven times, and then returned to the lineup even though it was obvious he was far from 100 percent. He had one horrendous week in which his average dropped 20 points, and he barely managed to maintain a .300 average for the season, but he played.

He was not a guy to pamper himself, and even in his 40s he was inclined to shrug off the lingering effects of an injury or the fatigue that can hit an older player late in the season. He was not someone who was going to volunteer: "Skip, I'm feeling a little sore today, how about a day off?"

In 1915, at age 41, Wagner played every one of his team's games (156) although he started the season with two injured fingers on his throwing hand. He started off pinch-hitting in four straight games—his only pinch-hit at-bats of the season—and then because it was still difficult for him to get a grip on the ball, the Pirates had him play second base through May 1 to make his throws easier. Even after he was able to return to shortstop, he was still having trouble swinging the bat and remained in a slump through the 41st game (27-for-129, .209). But after June 4, a healthier Honus started playing at an amazing level.

In the final 115 games of the 1915 season, Wagner hit .293 and slugged .455. By modern standards that hardly looks like the best player in the league, but in the context of 1915, that was a very strong performance. There were only five .300 hitters in the league, none higher than .320, and none of them hit with Wagner's power. His power percentage (isolated power) would trail only Cactus Gavvy Cravath, who had the advantage of playing in tiny Baker Bowl as his home field.

Now, add to this great offense the fact that Wagner was doing this while playing nearly every inning, and almost all of them at shortstop (107 of those 115 games), and it might be argued that he was the most valuable player in the league in those 115 games. How often could that be said about a 41-year-old player?

And Honus might have done even better with a judicious day off here and there. As durable as he was, Wagner was not invulnerable to fatigue in his 40s. In the last 19 games he hit .229 in 74 at-bats with just three extra-base hits. If Wagner was tired in those final three weeks, it is easy to sympathize. The Pirates had a lot of double headers back up on them, and at the end of August they had to play three consecutive twin bills.

1916

Wagner's incredible performance at an advanced age does not end in 1915. His next season (1916) does not seem that impressive on the surface, but it was severely marred by a serious injury that should have ended his season on Aug. 5. At that point Wagner was on his way to his third season of 150-plus games in his 40s; he was hitting the ball extremely well and had played all but six games at shortstop. He was hitting .323, slugging .425, and had a .387 OBP. Had he been able to sustain those marks, he would have finished second in batting average, eighth in slugging percentage, and first in on-base percentage. (Wagner again had a surprising year in triples, having banged out nine at that point with seven weeks left to go in the season.)

What happened on Aug. 5 is that after getting a hit in his first at-bat, Wagner was in the field when Hy Myers of Brooklyn hit a hard smash to short that took a bad hop and split open Wagner's right hand between two fingers. It took 10 stitches to close the wound. Wagner tried to come back just two weeks later, but he had to come out of the second game of a double header when the wound threatened to open up again.

He sat for another nine days and then made five pinch-hitting appearances. On Sept. 7, he returned to the lineup, but the hand was still so troublesome that he played mostly first base the rest of the year. In his attempt to come back from this serious injury, he was 19-for-105 (.181) and had only three extra-base hits, all doubles. That's why no one appreciates today what he did for most of that season.

But Wagner's 1916 season is actually worth celebrating for its part in what is likely the most astounding performance ever by a player in his 40s. From June 5, 1915 (when Wagner was 41 years, four months old) to Aug. 5, 1916 (when he was 42 years, seven months old), Wagner played 204 of his team's 208 games, and he played 93 percent of his games at shortstop. In those 204 games he hit .306 (49 points above the league) and surely was among the top sluggers in the league.

1915-16 NL leaders in Slugging Pct.

1) .477 Gavvy Cravath

⟶ .442 (Wagner during this streak)

2) .433 Bill Hinchman

3) .425 Cy Williams

Perhaps most incredible of all is that during this streak, this 42-year-old player had one of the best triples rates in the league.

1915-16 NL leaders in triples per game

1) .135 Tom Long

⟶ .112 (Wagner during streak)

2) .097 Bill Hinchman

3) .085 Zach Wheat

1917

Wagner retired after the 1916 season, but in midseason he decided to come back and made his debut on June 7. Wagner had gotten married in the offseason and the home cooking had added a few pounds, so the Pirates thought it was best to use him at first base, where the Pirates had been using a variety of players who were hitting abysmally. Wagner also played a couple of games at second base, 18 games at third base and, for old-time's sake, one inning at shortstop.

The 18 games at third base were notable in that practically nobody that age (43) still has the arm to make the long hard throw to first base. Wagner did, and to this day those 18 games remain the most games at third base by a player after his 43rd birthday.

I do not have Wagner's day-by-day logs for that final 1917 season, but his biography by Dennis and Jeanne DeValeria indicates Honus was leading the team in hitting at the end of June, and that he was still "well over .300" when on July 14 a young Casey Stengel spiked Wagner in his right foot. Honus had to miss several games and the foot bothered him the rest of the year. When he came back, he hit poorly, and by the end of the year his average slipped all the way down to .265, or right around the league average. As poorly as he played overall in his 74 games, he still hit far better than the ragtag crew that played first base when he wasn't available.

How did Wagner do it?

Part of Wagner's longevity was simply beginning with a level of physical talent that was in the outer stratosphere. This was particularly true for the extremely long life of Wagner's defensive value, which really is unprecedented in the history of the game. So much of aging well on defense is a matter of not falling below the physical skill thresholds needed to play the position. This is particularly a challenge at shortstop, which relies on two physical gifts–quickness and arm strength–that generally do not age well.

It's not rocket science to understand that the surest way to be quick and to run well in your late 30s and early 40s is to have had electrifying quickness when you were in your 20s and early 30s. And the same is true for arm strength.

Suppose we have a scale where 100 is the average arm of a shortstop, and if your arm falls below 90, you are going to have a tough time staying at shortstop. So, if you are an average shortstop and your arm strength declines 10 percent by the time you are 33, you still can play shortstop, but it is a bit of a strain. Lose another 5 percent in the next few years, and you can't play the position.

But say you are Honus Wagner, and you have an arm like no infielder has ever had. Consider the following:

- In the old days, baseball staged long-distance throwing contests, which were almost always won by outfielders. The only infielder to hold the record was a young Honus Wagner, who in October of 1898 unleashed a throw of 403 feet that broke a mark that had stood for 26 years. I suspect this may be the greatest long-distance throw under the contest rules used at that time.

- When Wagner's record was broken in 1910, it was done by such a huge distance that it seems almost certain that there had been a change in the contest guidelines, such as the number of steps you could take. Wagner had extended the record by only a few feet, and when Larry LeJeune challenged his record in 1907, he was close, but still three feet back of Wagner. Then, in a contest in 1910, LeJeune suddenly put the record into another universe with a throw of nearly 427 feet. These contests continued into the 1950s, when it is known that contestants were allowed a six-step running start.

  Wagner took the mound for 8.1 innings during his career and had a strikeout rate more than double the league rate.

- Tommy Leach never forgot the first time he saw Wagner play, and how Honus knocked down a ball at third base, scrambled after it 10 feet and made a bullet throw that made Leach's eyes pop out as it easily nailed the runner at first base.

Let's put Wagner's arm on our scale at 130 in his prime. No one is saying that his arm was invulnerable to the aging process, but he was starting at such a high level that he could lose 10 percent by age 33 and still have an exceptionally strong arm for a shortstop (117). He could lose another 5 percent and he'd still be around 110. There probably never was a day in Wagner's long career that he did not have an average arm for a shortstop. And through age 42, at least, he retained enough of his early quickness to man the position.

Having vastly superior talent to begin with is going to help you in all areas of the game as you age, but it is certainly not the only key to aging well. Babe Ruth was about as immense a talent as the game has ever seen, and he was toast by the time he celebrated his 40th birthday.

Conditioning, particularly the right kind of conditioning, was a big factor in Wagner's longevity. He valued staying in shape year-round, which we know today is easier on the body and the right way to go. Hall of Fame teammate Max Carey, one of the greatest base-stealers of all-time, remembers how the older Wagner emphasized to him the importance of keeping his legs in shape on a year-round basis.

And Wagner essentially followed a regime of cross training, which is now understood to be helpful in staying in shape while avoiding repetitive stress injuries. Wagner was a marvelous all-around athlete, and he loved a variety of sports that he would participate in year-round. In the winter he was ice skating and playing hockey, and oh, he loved the new-fangled sport of basketball probably more than any sport but baseball. He fooled around with weight lifting and throwing Indian clubs, and was pretty much game to try any sport.

Overall athleticism is another indicator for players who age well. For proprietary reasons I cannot go through some of the measures that I found were predictive in aging profiles, but I can say that a common theme in those measures is that they reflected to some degree an unusual degree of athleticism. Wagner scored extremely high in all of them, and certainly he was not considered just a great ballplayer, but an astounding athlete.

Intelligent hitting and the ability to adapt are key elements in aging well as a position player. There is such a mixture of things you can do to refine your hitting ability that you can literally spend a whole career searching for the approach that best suits your skill set. That's why we occasionally see some players have significant breakthroughs surprisingly late in their careers. And something every ballplayer has to go through is that his skill set is changing as he ages. Those who are best geared to adapt and adjust have the edge in aging gracefully.

The aging process of a ballplayer is not all negatives. There is one huge positive to draw on, and that is the experience you gained while you were doing all that aging. What did you learn about the game and yourself? How can you use that to adapt to the aging of your physical skills?

This tends to make it sound like it is all about intelligence, but it's not. There is also an emotional or personality aspect to the ability to adapt. Some very bright people have trouble learning things for a variety of reasons, while some of ordinary intelligence have a surprising ability to pick things up. Some folks are simply more open and comfortable with change than others, while others flat out resist change; they fear going outside their comfort zone, or they latch onto an identity of themselves as a hitter, and they fear that change will cost them their identity.

And then there is the hard truth that the ability to adapt as a hitter still requires a minimum physical skill set to make it happen. If it didn't, Pete Rose would still be playing today. Some players have better skill sets than others, and that gives them more options to adapt to the aging process and its effect on their hitting.

Consider Omar Moreno, whose contributions on both offense and defense were so exclusively built on speed. When his speed and quickness slid from spectacular to merely very good, nothing could have saved his career. He could have had the mind of Einstein and the open, calm, adaptive personality of Gandhi, and he still wasn't going to age well as a ballplayer. His physical skill set was too weak to give him any options to pull it off. The only thing that would have been different is that he would have been smart enough to retire three years earlier to work on the Theory of Relativity and win a Nobel Peace prize in his spare time.

Wagner's great raw talent provided a skill set with which he had more options than most to improve and fine-tune his hitting, and it seems likely that he had the intelligence and character to adapt and adjust better than most players.

Wagner had little formal education, but he was sharp, observant, and open to new ideas. When automobiles were still a novelty and some people didn't want anything to do with them, he was one of the early devotees. In fact, one of his friends was inventor, innovator and industrialist Henry Ford, and Ford was not the kind of guy who was going to hang out with a narrow-minded rube. Instead, picture them taking trips together with Wagner driving and Ford standing on the running board, experimenting with adjustments of the carburetor. (This is actually one of Wagner's recollections.)

Bill James once noted, "I don't think there was any sport you can't document Wagner playing," and isn't this also an indication that Honus had a willingness and interest to learn a lot of different and new sports? Basketball didn't even exist when Wagner was growing up, but he started playing it with a passion as an adult in his late 20s just 10 years after its invention. And Wagner's adaptability on defense in the early years of his career is unmatched in the history of the game. In one season in which his team had many injuries, he was used as a utility man who played every day, moving day to day to whichever position needed to be filled. (He never did catch a game, but maybe they never asked.)

Outfielder Fred Clarke was the playing manager of the Pirates for most of Wagner's career, and he was one of the brighter players of his day, an inventor in his own right and the holder of at least one U.S. patent. He thought enough of Wagner that as Honus gained experience, Clarke came to rely heavily on him to run the infield, which meant calling for pickoff plays, setting the defense in bunt situations, and checking with the pitcher to save Clarke the trip from the outfield. When Clarke was ejected by umpires, he often called on Wagner to manage the team in his absence, as did Clarke's successor, Nixey Callahan.

In the 1930s, years after Max Carey cited Honus Wagner as his greatest teacher, an interesting story unfolded in Pittsburgh. In 1933, after 16 years of retirement, Wagner returned to coach with the Pirates, and specifically to coach their young shortstop, Arky Vaughan. They worked together for nine of Vaughan's 14 seasons. In each of those nine seasons, they even roomed together on the road. That close association and education paid big dividends. Vaughan became the best offensive shortstop since Wagner himself, and joined

Honus in the Hall of Fame—voted in largely on the basis of the years he was coached by Wagner.

Arky Vaughan	BA	OBP	SLG
Coached by Wagner	.325	.419	.478
Other seasons	.298	.370	.391

We don't know the details of the adjustments Wagner was making as a hitter that allowed him to age so gracefully. But we do know that as he gained experience in his 20s, he began to walk more, and that his walk rate took a large and sustained leap forward at age 30. This indication of greater plate discipline, and perhaps more judicious swings, coincides with an improvement in Wagner's ability to hit for both better average and power. He was literally a better and more efficient hitter from age 30 to 38 than he had been in his 20s.

Honus Wagner	OPS	BA	Pow%	BB%
Age 23-29	.885	.341	.147	.071
LG position players	.704	.281	.082	.074
Ratio age 23-29	1.26	1.21	1.79	0.96
Ratio age 30-38	1.36	1.31	1.92	1.20
Age 30-38	.909	.341	.155	.100
LG position players	.668	.260	.081	.083

There are a few players who aged as hitters more gracefully than Wagner did, though they did it in eras that gave more options to a hitter to stave off the ravages of age. But when it comes to aging gracefully as an all-around player, Honus Wagner truly stands alone.

The Kids are Alright: Youth Culture and Baseball in 1968

by Anthony Giacalone

Bill James once argued that the baseball played in the 1960s was "the most God-awful boring brand of baseball ever conceived of." Moreover, while James did not note it directly, by extension the baseball season of 1968 was the most boring of the most boring. That year was the celebrated Year of the Pitcher. The year the game stood still.

"Baseball was so boring," continued James, "that people who should have been carrying banners saying, 'Hit It Here, Willie' and arguing about who was going to be the NL's Rookie of the Year got all wrapped up in politics instead, and started carrying peace signs and worrying about evil and social injustice and stuff. Attendance suffered. And the nation with it."

Bill James was, of course, wrong.

James' flaw was not in his assessment that baseball 40 years ago was boring. It surely was. His mistake was in the notion, shared by many of baseball's devotees, that the game performs a transcendent role in American life. Baseball's men of letters have argued for decades that the pastime "explains America," that if you understand baseball you can understand the United States. Similarly, James argues that the disenchanting baseball of the 1960s "explains" the problems of that tumultuous decade. Baseball is the catalyst for American history in this view.

The problem is that baseball hardly ever explains anything about America. With the possible exception of the Jackie Robinson saga, there is nary an example of how baseball is anything more than a supporting actor in history's drama. Far from being an engine of American development, baseball is a byproduct of it. One can understand America perfectly well without any knowledge of baseball, but baseball in its totality is incomprehensible without understanding its relationship to the nation as a whole.

The boring baseball of the 1960s did not have repercussions in the wider world. No one ever said, "If only Eddie Bressoud stole more bases, then I'd stop protesting this war." However, wide, powerful forces in American society fundamentally brought about both the boring baseball of the 1960s and then the much more exciting brand of ball, and the far-reaching changes to the game, that followed in the 1970s.

Baseball's most tedious season, 1968, was the turning point.

Profound demographic waves from 1930 to 1960 caused both baseball's lost generation in the 1960s and the youth culture that changed the game so dramatically in the 1970s. A dearth of prime-aged talent in the early 1960s caused those who ran baseball to look toward much younger players. In turn, the youth culture of these players, derived from the world around them, altered the game in unexpected ways.

Among the many developments furthered by these changes were a rush to further incorporate Latinos into the game, a greater sense of individualism by players, the rise of a strong, confident players' union and the subsequent sweeping restructuring of the game, a greater awareness of the prejudices of race, and the responsibilities of ball players to their society in a time of war. If in 1968 the "whole world was watching," then we have been watching 1968's influence on the game of baseball ever since.

Baseball's troubles in the 1960s began with the troubles of ordinary people during the Great Depression of 1929 to 1941. The hard times of the 1930s depressed not just the economy but also the nation's birth rate. From a high of between 2.9 million and 3 million births a year before 1929 the total number of births plummeted by over a half million births a year, to between 2.3 and 2.5 million from 1931 to 1940. Baseball teams suffered tremendously from 1952 to 1963 due to this loss of between 15 to 20 percent of their talent base. Major league baseball's expansion from 16 to 20 teams in 1961, at the peak of the demographic crisis, further exacerbated the game's dilemma.

Faced with a rapidly declining number of American-born players, baseball owners tapped hitherto underdeveloped sources of talent. The percentage of Latinos in the U.S. population has been growing steadily in the postwar years, increasing by 30 to 40 percent every decade. Increasingly, baseball turned to Latinos to fill the gap created by the low birth rates of the 1930s and early-1940s.

Baseball always had been ahead of the national curve in its inclusion of Latino ball players, but from the late 1950s into the early 1970s, (not coincidentally the exact

127

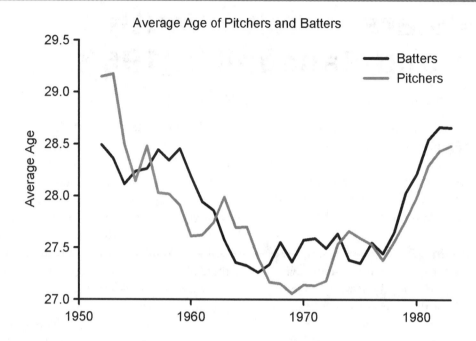

years that baseball needed more players), Latino partici-pation in professional baseball grew rapidly. The Latino population in the sport rose from approximately 7.5 percent in the late 1950s to 9.9 percent in 1960 to over 13 percent at mid-decade and then to a generational peak of almost 17 percent by 1971. One could argue that it was this 10 percentage point increase in the number of Hispanic ballplayers that allowed baseball to continue being played at a high level despite the dramatic reduc-tion in American-born talent.

The other way baseball compensated for the immense gap in talent was by turning to young players. A post-war baby boom meant a very rapidly increasing pool of young players. From 1946 to 1965 and peaking in the late 1950s, a massive surge in the number of babies born in the United States produced between 500,000 and a million new men coming of age every year beginning during the second half of the 1960s.

In increasing numbers, baseball hierarchy turned to these young men to fill the gap caused by the low birth rates of the 1930s. In 1960, the average age of a major league hitter was approximately 28.5 years old. For every one of the next 21 years, the average age of baseball's batters would be younger than that.

The age of pitchers plummeted even more dramati-cally. It was not until 1983, when the game had incorpo-rated nearly the entirety of the baby boom generation, that major league pitchers reached the same average age as were the pitchers of 1956.

From this evidence, one might conclude that major league executives, having been forced to turn to younger players out of demographic necessity in the early-1960s, learned to have faith in the abilities of young players to perform at the major league level. Therefore, even after more players were available to them after 1968, baseball's decision-makers continued to rely on much younger athletes than at any time in the modern history of the game. Not until nearly the totality of the baby boom generation was of major league age, and the older boomers were past their prime baseball-playing years, do we see this trend change.

In one sense then, the young ballplayers of 1968 and their culture, like young people all over the world that year, forced a revolutionary change upon the game of baseball and its culture. Youth culture came to domi-nate baseball much in the same way that it came to dominate all aspects of American life.

Youth culture in the 1960s was more than just a bunch of kids marching in the streets, more than just a political force; it was an increasingly important way of life. In addition to political activism, the new youth culture was typified by original styles of dress, groom-ing, speech and music, an enhanced level of frankness regarding matters formerly held to be private, like sexu-ality, and a greater acceptance of those formerly omit-ted from mainstream society.

What made these new social norms the dominant force in American society after the mid-1960s was the total number of young people in the country at the time due to the baby boom. Through sheer numbers and purchasing power, if nothing else, these baby boomers have dictated the democratization of American culture since the mid-1960s. This democratization in the 1960s meant passion for casual clothing, original music, passionate slang and even more passionate sexual freedom. It was all about the attitude. The suit-and-tie was out; the rock-'n'-roll was in.

This spilled out into all facets of American life, and baseball was no exception. After the mid-1960s, the game became much younger, much faster and more energetic. The players became more assertive, more individualistic and more ambitious. With the first baby boom-age players to reach the big leagues in the mid-1960s, the game rapidly changed, becoming nearly unrecognizable from the way that baseball was played, both on and off the field, just a few years before.

Even in 1968, conventional baseball wisdom said there were few bigger gambles than to use young pitchers in the major leagues. They exposed both field managers and general managers to criticism. Almost by definition, veteran pitchers were safer bets. In the early 1960s, though, the dramatic drop in talent due to the low birth rate of the 1930s and the addition of four new teams forced younger pitchers into big league jobs.

As these young players succeeded, baseball executives increasingly felt confident in the abilities of young pitchers and turned to them in increasing numbers. In 1963, there were only 13 starting pitchers under the age of 23 on the 20 major league teams, but that number grew steadily thereafter. In 1965, there were 17 young starters and then there were 27 in 1967. In 1968, 80 percent of National League teams featured at least one starting pitcher who was 23 or younger; four teams fielded two such pitchers and the Chicago Cubs had three.

The most fabled of these youngsters in 1968 was the New York Mets' phenom, 21-year old Nolan Ryan. Ryan struck out a batter an inning that season, despite battling blood blisters on his pitching hand for much of the season. With Ryan, 23-year-old Tom Seaver, three other starting pitchers and seven position players all of who were younger than 26, the Mets were the youngest team in baseball in 1968.

They exemplified the national obsession with youth. "Now, for the first time," said Ron Swoboda, the Mets 24-year-old veteran of four seasons, "we know when we go out to play that youth is taking over ... It isn't like other years when a lot of guys were just putting in their time and adding to their pension plans."

Pete Rose of the Cincinnati Reds most exemplified the youthful enthusiasm of 1968. A "hyperactive, all-round athlete," Rose was equal parts effort, confidence and ambition. In 1968, he was a whirlwind in wool and stirrups. He led the league in batting average, on-base percentage, hits, runs created and times on base that year and finished second in the balloting for the National League's Most Valuable Player award, while playing both infield and outfield positions. His effort was remarkable to casual observers, like a *Sports Illustrated* writer who proclaimed that he galloped "around the bases and the outfield ... making more quick starts and stops than a water bug on LSD."

Motivated by a nearly manic self-assurance and an overarching ambition, Rose also had a knack for self-promotion so common among the young generation, raised as it was on television. Eventually, in middle age, Rose's hubris and ambition would be his undoing, as it would for many baby boomers in the 1980s, but in 1968, he was "a great thing for baseball."

For the Generation of 1968, self-assurance manifested itself nearly as often off the field as it did on it. As young men, moving with the changing times, baseball players in 1968 increasingly added distinctive elements to their appearances and expanding wardrobes. "Hell, we are individuals," said Cardinals center fielder Curt Flood in 1968, "and we want to dress like individuals and be treated like individuals should be."

Detroit starting pitcher Earl Wilson, a 32-year old bachelor, took pride in his closet filled with 50 suits and three dozen pairs of shoes. "I'm not a swinger," Wilson contended, "but once the season is over I move out real good." Philadelphia's iconoclastic slugger Dick (nee Richie) Allen was known to wear a both a dashiki and spats, but not at the same time, fortunately. Despite the fact that pension and compensation issues still were being haggled over, one of the early complaints voiced by players to their union was that there "aren't enough outlets for hair dryers in the clubhouses."

Ken "Hawk" Harrelson, the Red Sox' homer-hitting outfielder, was as flamboyant a dresser as any player. Flashy in everything he did, Harrelson, a 27-year-old father of three, wore his hair long, his medallions swinging and his powder blue suits with a Nehru collar. Some considered Harrelson a "put-on," but, as with nearly everything in his life, there was a method to The Hawk's showy madness. "I wear my hair the way I do because of the size of my nose," Harrelson admitted in 1968. I have "my hair styled so my nose wouldn't be so prominent." These were the kinds of decisions that went uncontemplated by an older generation of ballplayers.

Faced with multiple crises in and around the game, many baseball managers chose to make an issue out of how their players dressed. A few club managers took philosophical views of player fashion (examples were the Cardinals' Red Schoendienst and the Red Sox' Dick Williams), but they tended to be a minority among baseball's supervisors. Many more were akin to Chicago White Sox manager Eddie Stanky, who would launch into a bratty tirade if he spotted one of his players wearing a fashionable turtleneck instead of a tie. Mets manager Gil Hodges had fined and benched Harrelson for wearing his hair too long and in 1968 dictated that none of his Metropolitans shall wear "love beads."

Perhaps the most infamous example of this attitude in baseball was a series of authoritarian memos that Bob Howsam issued while running the Cardinals: "Sit up straight in the bullpen. Don't run on the grass when you leave the plate. All socks cut the same way." A decade into the Space Age, baseball was still "frantically trying to figure out what its young men should be allowed to wear in order to keep the image of the game within the framework of the 1800s."

While major league executives worked themselves into a lather over the decisions players made about what went on their bodies, they worried hardly at all about what players put into their bodies. That fact that baseball players self-medicated during the 1960s is not a revelation. Many Americans, not just those in the youthful counter-culture movement, looked to pharmacology to help them with the problems of the modern world. "Better Living Through Chemistry" was more than just the corporate slogan of Dow Chemical, the maker of napalm—it was a national motto.

Baseball players generally opted for amphetamines, commonly "greenies," to help them function at high levels through a seemingly endless, 162-game schedule. While most players took greenies occasionally, they became habit-forming for many players. "Some of the guys have to take one just to get their hearts to start beating," said Jim Bouton. Greenies were illegal without a prescription and laws forbade team trainers from dispensing them, but ballplayers had no trouble securing a supply. According to veteran starting pitcher Milt Pappas, "if you knew your local druggist you could walk in and buy them from the guy ... Or there were guys who would find them for us without any problem."

Ballplayers ingested amphetamines in all shapes and sizes. Pappas told of one drug, called "The Sox" or "Red Juice," that he tried after seeing Reds teammates Pete Rose and Jim Maloney taking it. It came in both a liquid and pill form and "would immediately get into you, and you were just flying sky high," said Pappas.

The Braves' Pat Jarvis took a huge 25-milligram pill that he called "black beauty."

It was more than just uppers in baseball that was the problem with the times, it was a societal belief that one could and should take drugs on a daily basis to help perform any necessary task. A drug for every occasion.

In the game, Yankees outfielder Joe Pepitone best exemplified this attitude. By the time that he finished his career with the Cubs, the playboy Pepitone would spend his after hours sampling the nightlife, only to report for the next morning looking "like death warmed over." So, he would take a greenie to get himself up for the game. That night he would take a sedative to get to sleep after drinking, and so be in need of another greenie the next day. Better living through chemistry, indeed.

While the players' sartorial independence might have worried big league managers unnecessarily, the surging youth culture presented more dangers than just the possibility of a bad drug trip. Detroit's star pitcher Denny McLain sampled more than his share of those dangers. A stocky, six-foot tall right-hander from Chicago's South Side, McLain had a hot-tempered, eccentric and addictive personality that quickly led him into many forms of trouble.

Both a "Super Flake" and a "Mighty Mouth," McLain frequently found himself at odds with many of his teammates. He nurtured a long-standing, bitter feud with starter Mickey Lolich, frequently complained about Tigers icon Al Kaline; rankled his own fans with disparaging remarks, and nurtured a "mutual irritation" with Tigers general manager Jim Campbell. "Everyone felt this way about him," said California Angels manager Bill Rigney: "all the pitches you ever need but a bad attitude."

McLain's other problems were even more detrimental. He gambled on nearly everything and hustled people for money at golf and bowling. Quickly, his gambling addiction brought him trouble with bookies and their musclemen. *Sports Illustrated* reported that one such run-in with an organized crime figure over McLain's failure to pay a debt led to a broken bone in the pitcher's foot and caused him post an 8.27 ERA down the stretch in 1967. Detroit lost the 1967 pennant by a single game.

He became a silent partner in an illegal bookmaking business. Baseball suspended him for half of the 1970 season for that infraction, one of three suspensions for McLain that season.

Not surprisingly, he severely overextended himself financially early in career. "I always had this great urge to go spend money—on anything. I'd get an itch, and the money would be gone. Now I think I've bailed out about 90 percent," McLain claimed during the 1968 season. And then he bought his own jet after the season.

Baseball was just McLain's day job. Deep down McLain burned with "the incandescent flame of show biz." He was a professional organist and frequently talked of leaving baseball for the nightlife circuit that he toured during off-seasons. A licensed pilot, McLain loved to fly, an obsession that nearly cost him his life during the 1968 season. Appearances on "The Ed Sullivan Show," "The Smothers Brothers Special" and "The Tonight Show" during his whirlwind 1968 season, in which he won 31 games, the Cy Young Award and the Most Valuable Player Award, fed his delusions of grandeur. "We might gross a quarter of a million. Isn't that what it's all about?" he asks. "Money?"

Like many young people, McLain lived his life as if he were bulletproof. When his shoulder balked and then frayed after nearly 1,400 innings of sidearm fastballs and wicked sliders before his 26th birthday, McLain's youthful delusions evaporated. In his post-baseball career, his weight ballooned to 330 pounds. He was convicted of embezzlement, drug trafficking, and racketeering and spent years in jail. As both McLain and the young generation of 1968 learned the hard way, reality had a nasty way of conquering youthful dreams of glory.

The rising occurrence of liberated thoughts and actions by players led many in baseball's management to believe that there were sinister forces at play. This, too, was emblematic of the times. The revolutionary changes wrought by the new youth culture induced leaders of the older generation to look everywhere for Svengalis: "teachers, preachers and politicians" who lead the innocent children astray, as Republican Presidential candidate Richard Nixon said. Baseball's owners believed that a Svengali in their game, former steelworkers union negotiator Marvin Miller, had seduced their players into revolting against the sport's existing economic structure.

Like the young people in the streets, baseball players did not consider themselves anyone's dupes. Although they were very different from the marching students of 1968, baseball players shared several traits with them. Like students who clustered together on college campuses at a young age, baseball players generally shared a common and rather democratic minor league apprenticeship. These experiences taught both students and players to view cynically the motivations of those who controlled their destinies (governments, military officers, college administrators, baseball owners, team management). Further, the nature of baseball instilled in players a rough egalitarianism—a realization that the sport needed both its burly home run hitters and its wiry utility infielders. Marvin Miller labored to build upon this spirit of communalism.

Miller restructured the players association to make it responsive directly to the players, just as the student leaders of the 1960s sought to do with their movements. By seeing the players frequently, urging them toward participation and responding to their concerns, Miller created a kind of "participatory democracy" to which the leaders of the student movements could only aspire. "This is *your* office; this is *your* union," Miller repeatedly reminded them.

Miller's methods of leadership allowed the union to produce unanimous consent—"Anything less than 100 percent is unacceptable" was Miller's motto—even as the student organizations devolved into anarchy. While Miller treated the players like adults—"He was a master at never telling anybody how to do anything," one players' representative recalled. "He would just ask questions until you could see the answer for yourself"—the owners treated the players like children.

In their efforts to warn of Miller's malevolent influence, the owners alternately bullied and condescended to the players. In 1968, the owners' inability to treat the players as mature individuals squandered their best opportunity to create a cooperative accord and a moderate solution to their grievances. Why would the owners not negotiate with the players union during the 1968 season? That would "be harmful to the players," the owners said patronizingly, "and take their minds off the game."

Miller exploded at the affront to the players' maturity. The players could no more ignore this issue than they could the other tumultuous events of 1968. Do the owners also think that the players "should shut their eyes to the war in Vietnam, the demonstrations in Chicago and other current events and think only about the game?" demanded Miller. By treating the players like immature children, baseball's owners had forced the players "into the streets," figuratively. They would prove unable to pacify them until the union had won a fundamental restructuring of the sport.

If young white players had to fight a war against the forces of authority for equitable treatment, then young African-Americans had to fight a two-front war in 1968. While waging the same battles against ownership as the other players, African-American players also had to battle for equality against teammates and others in and around the game. The constant fight for minor gains engendered frustration in many young African-American players.

"The black players in particular were deeply affected by what went down in 1968," recalled the Cardinals' Bob Gibson years later. "We were angrier than usual, and I think it showed." It was this "anger," this black militancy, in the parlance of the times, that frightened many white Americans.

In 1968, the term "militant" quickly became a code word to characterize not just an "unreasonable" individual but any African-American who was outspoken in his or her pursuit of equality. For example, in his autobiography Pappas defended baseball's cliques unless they caused "dissension." What kinds of cliques caused dissension? "Occasionally," Pappas recalled disdainfully more than 30 years later, "the militant black players brought their politics to the park."

One particular incident stayed with Pappas. An African-American player he didn't name "actually" insisted that the Reds integrate their spring training locker room by placing the lockers of some black players next to the lockers of some white players, he related. "I don't know if he was with the NAACP or what," said Pappas. "We didn't have many guys like that, and I'm glad we didn't."

A militant was not just an activist though. He could be any African-American who bucked the club's authority. Further, the definition of a player's militancy could, and did, change based on the player's club. Outfielder Lou Johnson was a vital piece of the pennant-winning Los Angeles Dodgers teams of 1965 and 1966, but he became a "militant" with the more-parochial Chicago Cubs, necessitating that he be traded to Cleveland for a more moderate African-American player. Slugger Dick Allen was a "militant" with the Phillies, but a clubhouse cut-up with the Cardinals. Then he was a "militant" again in Los Angeles before becoming a veteran leader with the Chicago White Sox en route to being a "militant" once again in his return trip to Philadelphia.

Throughout 1968, the shade of Vietnam touched all aspects of youth culture. Without the war, young men and women would not have marched in Paris, Berlin, New York, Chicago, Berkeley and hundreds of other places. And the forces of "law and order" would not have beaten them. Without the war, thousands of young American service members and tens of thousands of young Vietnamese would not have died in 1968.

Even though ballplayers remained silent about the war in 1968, many of them harbored reservations that became known later. For example, Seaver, a graduate of the University of Southern California and a reservist in the Marines, was not a radical by any stretch of the imagination, but he opposed the war. After leading the young Mets over the veteran Baltimore Orioles in 1969—a victory for youth over the establishment—Seaver proclaimed, "If the Mets can win the World Series, then we can get out of Vietnam."

Seaver's teammate on the 1968 Mets, Ron Swoboda also grew increasingly disenchanted with the war. Years later, he lamented, "I don't think anything has changed us as a country more in terms of squandering our living capital and our living assets ... the money wasted that could have gone somewhere else. And look what we did to (Vietnam) ... we just decimated the culture."

The war was only a marginal threat to the well-being of most baseball players in 1968, however, because so many received coveted positions in National Guard and Reserve units. In many cities, sports executives peddled their influence and accommodating reserve boards bumped local ballplayers to the tops of waiting lists. The New York Mets had more than a dozen reservists on their 1968 roster, while the Chicago Cubs placed 15 men from their 38-man roster in National Guard or Reserve units. On other clubs, at least 40 percent of the talent was required to perform some form of military service during the 1968 season. That year, more than 140 draft-eligible baseball players found their way into Reserve units.

Some players, like the Cardinals' Mike Torrez, understood that the baseball players were fortunate in 1968. "I'm lucky to be in the reserves," he said. "For so many kids my age, the service is a part of our time and, although it confuses us, I think we understand that aspect of it."

Even with these preferences, "all of baseball," noted one informed observer, was "uneasy these days." Sports Illustrated observed that a "pall hovers over the careers of almost every one" of the 1968 rookies because of the war. Nearly every team had to scramble to cover anticipated war-related absences. The beneficiaries of all this uncertainty were baseball's marginal veteran players.

Baseball's situation with military reservists and with an expansion draft looming at season's end meant that a hoard of baseball's aging lesser-lights were invited to spring training camps in 1968. Former lesser-stars and those who once aspired to be lesser-stars or even major league regulars were suddenly in demand. "Hal Reniff and Phil Linz may be worth more to us (than prospects) now," Mets general manager Johnny Murphy argued, citing two mediocre, aging ex-Yankees as examples, "because they are "service-proof." It was a last shot at glory for many ballplayers who soon would be competing with an enormous glut of baby boom players.

"Anything that a ballplayer did on the field that summer seemed relatively insignificant," recalled St. Louis' great pitcher Gibson, who on baseball fields that summer did more than almost any player ever. Gibson was right. The game on the field in 1968 was more or less inconsequential when compared to the changes going on in the wider world, and even within the game itself.

Although it was not readily apparent at the time, young players and the culture that they moved in were changing the game in dramatic ways. After 1968, players earned their freedom from both the direct control of ownership and many societal conventions. Minorities within the game increasingly came to be seen as individuals and not as members of a defining group. The game became more vibrant both on and off the field. After 1968, the old game grew younger.

History's Greatest Fielders

by Sean Smith

For most of baseball history, measuring defense has been much harder than measuring offense. Branch Rickey, one of the first baseball executives to use statistical analysis, considered it unmeasurable. *The Hidden Game of Baseball* published Rickey's team efficiency formula, and quotes Rickey as saying "There is nothing on earth anyone can do with fielding."

The difficulty of working with fielding statistics is that the recorded stats, putouts and assists, aren't descriptive enough, and the problem is further complicated by the difficulty of measuring a player's opportunities. A shortstop gets an assist when he fields a ground ball and throws the runner out at first, but he also gets one on relay throws from the outfield. A shortstop also could field a ground ball and step on second base to force out the lead runner, but that is indistinguishable in the books from catching an easy pop-up.

Without accurate measurement of the value of a defensive player, you might hear an exaggeration— "player x saves 1-2 runs every game"—or a severe underestimate, where baseball decision-makers look primarily at offensive statistics and mostly ignore defense, using it maybe as a tie-breaker. This type of decision-making is how poor fielders like Carlos Lee wind up with nine-figure contracts.

The introduction of Zone Rating in 1987 was a huge step forward in defensive statistics. Play-by-play databases such as those maintained by STATS and Baseball Info Solutions are even better, though they are expensive to obtain. Retrosheet, the free source of play-by-play data, doesn't have the same detail of those proprietary databases, but it does have enough information to develop a zone-like system. That's what I've done; I call my system "TotalZone."

TotalZone and its Variations

The process to calculate a player's TotalZone rating differs depending on how much detail is available in the Retrosheet files. The basic system was described last spring in two articles on The Hardball Times website, which are listed at the end of this article. Retrosheet has enough detail in almost every game to tell you who fielded every out. By looking at where a batter hits his outs, and where outs are hit off each pitcher, we can estimate the ball distribution of hits and calculate a zone-type rating.

For the years 2003 to 2007, Retrosheet has more complete data, telling us whether hits are ground balls, fly balls, line drives, or pop-ups, and which fielder eventually fielded every hit. While this information is far from perfect in telling us what part of the field a hit goes to, it's an improvement, and we can better estimate to which fielder we should charge each hit.

For example, if we know that a ground ball hit is fielded by the left fielder, then we know that the first and second basemen had no chance to record an out (except for a rare and weird shift). The left fielder had no chance to record an out either, as we know it was a ground ball. That leaves the third baseman and shortstop. We don't know if this ball was closer to one position or the other, so we split the responsibility.

Originally, I had a 50/50 split on ground ball singles to left, though more detailed analysis of years with Project Scoresheet zones indicates it should be closer to 60/40 in favor of the third baseman. Ground ball singles to center are split 55/45 between the shortstop and second baseman, and those hit to right field are charged 56 percent to the first baseman, 44 percent to second.

For 1989 to 1999, Retrosheet actually has the Project Scoresheet hit location zones. This allows much more precise ratings, and the ratings for these years will be very close in precision to the best play-by-play systems out there today, such as Mitchel Lichtman's UZR (Ultimate Zone Rating), David Pinto's PMR (Probabilistic Model of Range) or John Dewan's plus/minus.

Finally, I have added data for years 1953 to 1955, as Retrosheet has added these seasons since I first published this system. My goal is to provide the best ratings possible given the data available for each year.

Leaders, 1953 to 2007

The leader lists have changed since I published the ratings for The Hardball Times website. Part of the change is methodology, as I've used the most detailed data available for the 1990s. I'm using arm or double play ratings combined with range to rank the leaders, and I've added a few seasons to the data. Willie Mays pulls ahead of Paul Blair in center field thanks

Leading Outfielders

Right field	Range	Arm	Total
Clemente, Roberto	119	85	204
Kaline, Al	100	56	155
Barfield, Jesse	89	60	149
Jordan, Brian	138	7	145
Sosa, Sammy	128	-18	110

Left field	Range	Arm	Total
Bonds, Barry	146	31	176
Yastrzemski, Carl	81	54	135
Wilson, Willie	74	2	76
Gonzalez, Luis	85	-12	74
Cruz, Jose	79	-12	67

Center field	Range	Arm	Total
Jones, Andruw	166	57	223
Mays, Willie	127	49	176
Blair, Paul	140	32	172
Piersall, Jim	106	22	128
White, Devon	128	-17	112

Leading Infielders

First base	Range	DP	Total
Hernandez, Keith	111	6	117
Olerud, John	87	6	93
Scott, George	85	4	89
Grace, Mark	84	-7	77
O'Brien, Pete	69	4	73

Second base	Range	DP	Total
Mazeroski, Bill	110	40	150
White, Frank	119	5	124
Randolph, Willie	75	37	112
Fox, Nellie	89	3	91
Whitaker, Lou	70	8	78

Shortstop	Range	DP	Total
Belanger, Mark	232	6	238
Smith, Ozzie	212	23	235
Ripken, Cal	136	38	174
Aparicio, Luis	143	2	145
Vizquel, Omar	120	2	122

Third base	Range	DP	Total
Robinson, Brooks	267	26	293
Bell, Buddy	165	3	168
Boyer, Clete	151	10	161
Ventura, Robin	146	8	154
Nettles, Graig	136	-2	134

to having data for his 1953-55 seasons, as well as his strong throwing arm. The data for Mays are still not complete; his 1951 rookie season is not yet part of the Retrosheet years.

The biggest changes in the outfield rankings are Jordan, Jones, White and Bonds. Using the hit location data available for the 1990s shows each player to be much better than estimated by the earlier ratings. Willie Wilson's rating in left field is especially impressive, considering he played center field for two-thirds of his career. Wilson played his early years in left due to Amos Otis playing center. He was fast for his whole career, but his peak defensive years were probably the years he played in left. At least when it comes to catching the ball, he may have been the best defensive left fielder of all time.

Among infielders, Ozzie Smith and Cal Ripken also benefit from the additional data detail. Brooks Robinson remains the top defensive player of this time period, at least relative to position. Omar Vizquel was (and still is) a fine shortstop, but a superficial comparison to Ozzie Smith should not be used to get him into the Hall of Fame. Vizquel's 11 Gold Gloves are the second

highest for a shortstop after Smith (13), and Omar has more career hits. The voters should look a bit deeper, though—according to Baseball Reference, Vizquel trails Smith by about 100 batting runs, and according to these numbers he trails by another 100 in the field. A much better candidate would be Alan Trammell, who misses the top five list with a +77 defensive figure, but who was worth about 300 runs more than Omar on offense. His teammate Lou Whitaker would be a good pick as well.

Outfield Arms

I'm not the first to rate outfield arms using Retrosheet data, and not even the first to do so in a Hardball Times article. John Walsh provided great information on this topic two years ago. I haven't done a comprehensive comparison of the results, and do not claim to have improved on his analysis. I started from scratch here because I wanted complete ratings for every outfielder from 1953 and on. For better or worse, my system looks at these situations and compares every outfielder to the league average in terms of allowing advancement, holding runners, or throwing them out, and then converts to runs saved/lost:

1. Single with runner on first, provided there was no runner on second who stops at third

2. Single with runner on second

3. Double with runner on first

4. Flyball out, less than two out, runner on third

5. Flyball out, less than two out, runner on second, third base open

6. Outfield errors of advancement—not always due to throwing, but these have to be measured and this seemed the best place to put them

7. Batter thrown out by outfielder trying to stretch a hit

These players rated as the best and worst in career outfield throwing at a given position, from 1953 to 2007:

Top Throwers	Position	Throwing Runs
Roberto Clemente	RF	85
Ken Griffey Jr.	CF	61
Jesse Barfield	RF	60
Andruw Jones	CF	57
Larry Walker	RF	56
Al Kaline	RF	56
Rick Monday	RF	55
Carl Yastrzemski	LF	54
Dwight Evans	RF	50
Willie Mays	CF	49

Worst Throwers	Position	Throwing Runs
Bernie Williams	CF	-38
Lou Brock	LF	-37
Juan Pierre	CF	-36
Johnny Damon	CF	-29
Claudell Washington	RF	-29
Frank Howard	LF	-29

I don't think anyone will disagree that the first list contains players well known for the quality of their throwing, and the second list has players who base runners loved to run on. Frank Howard is the only one who appears out of place, as he did have a cannon for an arm, but was so slow and took so long to get his throw off that base runners had no trouble taking extra bases on him.

Infield double plays

This was described in the second THT spring article. The information needed to look at double play opportunities through Retrosheet is available for every year we have data. The methodology, simplified, is this: If a ground ball is fielded by an infielder in a double play situation (runner on first, less than two out), how often is a double play completed?

Player Highlights

The original Killer Bs: Blair, Belanger, Brooks Robinson

Jeff Bagwell, Craig Biggio and Lance Berkman have been known as the Killer Bs in Houston, and put a lot of runs on the scoreboard for several Astros playoff and one World Series team. I don't know if anyone used that nickname for the Orioles of the late '60s and mid '70s, but Brooks Robinson, Mark Belanger and Paul Blair excelled in taking runs off the scoreboard. They each rank among the greatest defenders of the last 50-plus years at their respective positions and it's quite amazing to think that three players of that caliber played on the same team at the same time. The success of those teams, especially in team defensive stats, as well as their reputations makes me believe they are rated accurately. Their TotalZone ratings are listed on the next page.

Darin Erstad

Erstad was the top pick overall in the 1995 draft. It took him only 114 games to reach the majors to stay, joining the Angels about one year after he was drafted. While it was obvious that Erstad was a capable center fielder, I'm not sure the Angels realized just how good he was for a while. While he played mostly center field at the end of 1996 due to Jim Edmonds' injuries, the Angels opened 1997 with four quality outfielders and no first baseman. Erstad probably should have been

Darin Erstad Outfield Defense, 1998-2003

Year	Position	Range	Arm	Total
1998	LF	-1	1	0
1999	LF	19	3	22
2000	LF	19	3	22
2000	CF	6	1	7
2001	CF	10	4	14
2002	CF	35	4	39
2003	CF	14	1	15

Orioles defense, 1968-1975			Brooks		Belanger		Blair	
Year	Team DER	DER rank	3B Range	3b DP	SS Range	SS DP	CF Range	CF arm
1968	.739	1	31	2	27	0	13	4
1969	.742	1	22	1	12	0	22	4
1970	.722	3	5	0	8	1	21	5
1971	.728	2	19	2	14	-1	6	2
1972	.739	1	17	1	8	0	16	2
1973	.730	1	17	1	23	3	16	3
1974	.715	1	14	1	17	3	13	2
1975	.730	1	17	2	32	3	8	4

Total: 443 runs saved by trio over eight years

the last of that group to switch to first, but he was the selection mostly because he had the least big league experience and seemed to be the most willing to go to the infield. (A young player trying to establish himself in the majors rarely is going to refuse to learn a new position. Instead he'll say "Sure, Skip, I can play there. Please don't send me back to Vancouver.")

Erstad played mostly at first base, and played well there for the 1997-1998 seasons, but his flyball catching talents were wasted. He finally got a chance to play outfield in 1999 when Edmonds was hurt again. He went to left field, with Garret Anderson in center, and saved 19 runs over an average left fielder. He did it again in 2000, also getting a chance to play a little center.

In 2001, the Angels finally realized that between Erstad and Anderson, Erstad was the superior defender and switched the two between left and center. Erstad was good that year, but in 2002 he registered the greatest single season ever among the years TotalZone has calculated for center field (just ahead of Devon White's 1992). If the system is wrong about Erstad's year, it is in good company: UZR, a far more comprehensive system, lists him at +57 runs for that year. Erstad's bat wasn't very good in 2002, and he hasn't been an offensive force since. Still, when the Angels signed him to a four-year, $32 million extension, they would have gotten their money's worth on defense alone. Unfortunately, Erstad was injured the following year and never has been able to play regularly in center field since.

Ken Griffey Jr.

Even in his early years, I had my doubts about how good Griffey's defense was. He was fast, gave a great effort, and made spectacular catches, but did not have the blazing speed of guys like Gary Pettis or Devon White. I thought that if there was a good way to quantify it, we would understand that Griffey made spectacular catches on plays that White would make look easy.

Ken Griffey Jr. Career Defensive Ratings

Year	Team	Pos	Chances	Range	Arm	Tot
1989	SEA	CF	415	-6	9	3
1990	SEA	CF	481	0	2	2
1991	SEA	CF	536	0	7	7
1992	SEA	CF	482	-5	1	-3
1993	SEA	CF	417	5	3	8
1994	SEA	CF	325	7	4	12
1995	SEA	CF	244	13	1	14
1996	SEA	CF	486	27	5	32
1997	SEA	CF	531	7	8	14
1998	SEA	CF	630	-8	5	-3
1999	SEA	CF	605	-19	6	-13
2000	CIN	CF	547	8	3	11
2001	CIN	CF	307	-10	0	-10
2002	CIN	CF	153	-11	1	-10
2003	CIN	CF	157	0	1	1
2004	CIN	CF	297	-7	3	-4
2005	CIN	CF	529	-25	1	-23
2006	CIN	CF	414	-18	1	-18
2007	CIN	RF	522	-6	-10	-17

In the charts in this article, "Chances" refers to how many opportunities a player had, including plays made, errors and estimated hits allowed.

Overall, Griffey was an above average defender in center field during his Seattle career. His arm rating is the best in the last 50-plus years for a center fielder. The 1996 season stands out, but does not necessarily mean that a slightly-above-average center fielder played at an elite level for one season. There is enough uncertainty in these ratings that it could easily be a case of getting easier chances for one year. Ratings are more effective when you have more sample data. Any single season rating could easily be explained as a fluke; I have much more confidence in multi-year and career ratings for players.

Griffey's injuries started almost as soon as he went to Cincinnati. His legs no longer could handle the demands of center field and his ratings confirmed it. Still, every time he came back from the DL he went right back out to center field because his contract said he was a center fielder. He finally moved to right in 2007, but at this point wasn't very good anywhere in the field, and the Reds did not have a DH position. In my opinion, Griffey, the Reds, and all of baseball would have been better off had he moved to right early in his Reds career. It's possible that less running would have aided his health and allowed him to rank even higher on the all-time home run list, but we'll never know for sure.

Mazeroski and Clemente

The next two players played before my time, so I don't have anything to add beyond the statistical record. Mazeroski wasn't much of a hitter, but he's in the Hall of Fame because of his defense and a World Series-ending home run. The defensive record shows that he had good range and turned the double play better than anyone else. He's responsible for more runs above average (+150) than any other second baseman, but does not dominate the ratings the way Robinson and Belanger dominate third and short.

Everyone knows about Clemente's arm, and the defensive record agrees. He is estimated to have saved 85 runs over his career just with his arm, more than any other outfielder at any position. Clemente wasn't too bad at catching fly balls either, worth another 119 runs.

Bill Mazeroski Career Defensive Ratings

Tm	Year	Pos	Chances	Range	DPruns	TOT
PIT	1956	2B	191	1	1	2
PIT	1957	2B	504	6	2	8
PIT	1958	2B	600	21	2	23
PIT	1959	2B	490	-4	2	-2
PIT	1960	2B	544	2	3	5
PIT	1961	2B	623	5	3	8
PIT	1962	2B	614	4	3	7
PIT	1963	2B	638	17	6	23
PIT	1964	2B	701	11	2	13
PIT	1965	2B	495	15	3	18
PIT	1966	2B	617	3	6	9
PIT	1967	2B	619	8	0	8
PIT	1968	2B	546	12	3	15
PIT	1969	2B	250	3	0	3
PIT	1970	2B	413	7	3	10
PIT	1971	2B	168	0	-2	-2
PIT	1972	2B	56	-1	0	-1
Total				110	40	150

Roberto Clemente Career Defensive Ratings

Year	Tm	Pos	Chances	Range	Arm	Tot
1955	PIT	RF	179	-1	3	2
1956	PIT	RF	182	1	2	3
1957	PIT	RF	300	18	5	23
1958	PIT	RF	395	23	4	27
1959	PIT	RF	307	9	4	13
1960	PIT	RF	369	-4	7	3
1961	PIT	RF	391	-6	6	0
1962	PIT	RF	382	9	6	15
1963	PIT	RF	331	-3	4	1
1964	PIT	RF	397	4	4	8
1965	PIT	RF	345	13	4	17
1966	PIT	RF	417	10	7	17
1967	PIT	RF	361	1	3	4
1968	PIT	RF	370	18	6	24
1969	PIT	RF	342	3	8	11
1970	PIT	RF	272	2	2	4
1971	PIT	RF	367	12	8	20
1972	PIT	RF	269	10	1	11
Total				119	85	204

Richie Ashburn Centerfield Defense, 1953-1962

Year	Team	Pos	Chances	Range	Home	Home-PO	Road	Road-PO	Arm	Total
1953	PHI	CF	459	14	5	237	9	152	5	19
1954	PHI	CF	535	19	12	254	7	186	-1	19
1955	PHI	CF	503	7	11	219	-4	150	-1	6
1956	PHI	CF	702	16	6	254	10	245	0	16
1957	PHI	CF	698	18	7	257	11	242	2	20
1958	PHI	CF	705	5	3	266	2	227	-1	4
1959	PHI	CF	546	-9	-8	186	-1	173	-8	-17
1960	CHN	CF	317	-1	-1	107	0	101	-4	-5
1961	CHN	CF	167	-9	-4	41	-5	64	-4	-13
1962	NYN	CF	171	-5	-4	38	-1	72	-4	-9
Total				55	27	1859	28	1612	-15	40

Richie Ashburn

Richie Ashburn had "the best defensive statistics of any outfielder ever to play major league baseball," according to Bill James in the *Historical Baseball Abstract*, 1988 edition. Richie had four seasons of 500 or more putouts, and a few other seasons in the 490s. James explains that outside influences may have affected Ashburn's putout totals, referencing the work of Bruce H. Garland for the *Baseball Analyst*. Ashburn's advantages included:

1. The ballpark, Connie Mack Stadium, had the second-deepest center field in the league, and it was far deeper than you'll find in any modern stadium. According to ballparks.com, the distance from home plate to center field ranged from 440 to 468 feet during the years Ashburn played there. Too bad he didn't play in the early 1900s, when it was more than 500 feet!

2. The Phillies' pitchers during this time were below average in striking batters out and inducing double plays, indicating that flyball opportunities were plentiful. Robin Roberts, in particular, forced batters to put the ball in play, and often in the air, judging by his homers-allowed totals.

The chart at the top of the page shows that Ashburn, at least during his years with the Phillies, had quite a few more putouts at home than on the road. I can't be certain how meaningful this is, however, since Retrosheet likely has some missing plays in some of the years. His 1953-1955 splits do not match up with his official putout totals, though his 1956 and later seasons are very close. TotalZone applies a park factor to all data

based on every fielder, home and away, who played at a position over a multiyear period. While Ashburn has a huge advantage in putouts at home, once the adjustments work their magic, his multiyear rating is almost identical at home and on the road.

As Retrosheet adds more seasons from the past, we will have a better picture of Ashburn's defensive value. His top two putout totals were recorded in 1951 (538) and 1949 (514). His rating might increase considerably once we are able to evaluate those seasons. At this point, the defensive record supports Ashburn as one of the greatest defensive center fielders of all time, but not as someone head and shoulders above the other greats.

Defensive Flukes

To find the biggest defensive flukes, I looked for the players whose single-season ratings differed the most from their average career ratings. For offensive fluke seasons, I can think of a few off the top of my head: Norm Cash, Ken Caminiti's MVP season, Darin Erstad getting 240 hits, Brady Anderson or Luis Gonzalez topping the 50-homer level. In the other direction, you've got Jermaine Dye's injury filled 2003 season in which he hit like a pitcher. For defensive flukes, injuries also can be a cause, or in some cases you have players whose talent levels are very different at opposite ends of their careers.

Here are a few defensive fluke seasons:

Kirby Puckett, 1984 and 1993. Puckett's career rating was slightly below average for center field, about two runs per season. As a rookie, he caught everything in the Metrodome, and wound up with a +28 rating despite starting the season in the minors. Almost a decade later, Kirby's rating was –26 runs, so Kirby takes both top and bottom honors on the fluke list. He was moved to right after the 1993 season. In Kirby's case, the ratings can be fit to mathematical functions. His defensive ratings are inversely proportional to his home run totals and to his probable playing weight.

Ken Griffey Jr., 1996. Griffey was +27 runs that year compared to an average career rating of -3 per season. In 1996, it would not have appeared as such a great fluke, since as he was at least a very good center fielder. His later career dragged his rating down, and made the 1996 total stand out even more.

Rey Ordonez, 1999. Rey was a very good defender, though not the next Ozzie Smith as some of the hype around him suggested. In 1999 though, he had a +29 rating, compared to a +6 average career rating.

Lonnie Smith, 1989. No system is perfect and as to the ratings of Lonnie, I don't trust the results I'm getting. He was, by accounts of contemporaries, a terrible fielder, but I'm still getting a +3 rating per year for him. That's not too big a deal, but in his 1989 season, when he came out of nowhere to have his best season for the Braves, Lonnie's rating was +20.

Greg Gagne, 1986. Gagne was a good shortstop (+7 per year), but his first full season did not go well (-17). This could be a case of learning how to field on turf and cutting down on errors as he gained confidence in the big leagues.

Andruw Jones, 2007. Andruw always has been regarded as a great fielder, but his defensive ratings vary greatly depending on who is doing the evaluating. In recent years he has been rated very well by John Dewan's system, but not as well by the systems using STATS data, from the simple (Zone Rating) to the complex (UZR). Andruw's TotalZone ratings have been extremely good … until last season. His season average is +16, but last year he was only –7. Calling his 2008 season a disaster would be too kind.

What's Next for TotalZone?

Depending on the year we are looking at, TotalZone is at its best a poor man's play-by-play defensive system and at its worst an upgrade over systems using only traditional stats (putouts, assists, and errors). When batted ball type, player fielding the ball and hit location are recorded, Retrosheet provides almost every data element that STATS or Baseball Info Solutions provides, and provides it for free. Project Scoresheet zones are not as detailed as STATS zones, but they do add much more information than knowing just that a ball was hit to center field. It has been reassuring, a sign that the project is doing something right, that most players who rate highly are the players with strong defensive reputations, and who won multiple Gold Gloves.

When I started this project, Retrosheet had almost 50 years of data, 1957 to 2006, excluding 1999. Since then, it has added the 2007 season, 1999, 1954 to 1956, and 1953 for the National League. As Retrosheet adds more back seasons, this framework eventually can provide defensive ratings for every player in history. How did Phil Rizzuto's defense compare to Ozzie and Belanger? Ted Williams was a better hitter than Joe DiMaggio, but how much of the gap is closed by DiMaggio's superior defense?

When we can aggregate the data for players who played multiple positions, we can study if and how the defensive spectrum has changed over time. With Retrosheet, I can come up with additional questions to explore much faster than Microsoft Access can crunch the queries.

Sources:

First TotalZone article:

www.hardballtimes.com/main/article/measuring-defense-for-players-back-to-1956

Second TotalZone article:

www.hardballtimes.com/main/article/measuring-defense-for-players-back-to-1956-part-2

The information used here was obtained free of charge from and is copyrighted by Retrosheet. Interested parties may contact Retrosheet at 20 Sunset Road, Newark, Del. 19711.

Have Bat, Will Travel: The Free Agency of Pete Rose

by Craig Brown

Just two years into the free agency era, it was clear that allowing players to move to the highest bidder was reshaping the landscape of the game. Some teams, like the Kansas City Royals and Atlanta Braves, were aggressive, often submitting the highest bid, but had difficulty landing the big player they were so desperately seeking. Others, like the Detroit Tigers and Minnesota Twins, remained on the sidelines and weren't active participants.

Then there were teams like the New York Yankees and California Angels, who were landing the biggest names in the game with varying degrees of success. The Yankees hit paydirt with Reggie Jackson and Goose Gossage, but struck out on the oft-injured Don Gullett. Meanwhile, the Angels had rotten luck with injuries as high-priced acquisitions Joe Rudi and Bobby Grich both missed signifcant time in 1977 and underperformed on those rare occasions when they were in the lineup.

As free agency rolled into its third year in 1978, the jury was still out on the impact. Clearly, salaries were sliding upward, and some owners were more than happy to pander to their fan bases by throwing money at top players. However, the mixed results on the field scared many. Besides, most of the players who were becoming free agents were over 30 and on the downward side of their careers. For many, it was an expensive gamble.

One item not in dispute was that free agency was keeping the embers of the hot stove lit for most of the winter. In the first two years, baseball fans became transfixed with following the top players, tracking their movements and meetings, and trying to conjure where they would be playing the following spring. And with top names like Jackson, Grich and Don Baylor changing uniforms, there was plenty to follow.

As the 1978 free agent draft began to take shape, it was clear it lacked the star power of the previous classes. Jim Slaton, Mike Lum and Darrell Evans didn't excite many fans, or teams for that matter. But one name stood front and center. An 11-time All-Star with more than 3,000 career hits was looking for a new home and a big contract, and he was available for every major league team.

Pete Rose was on the move.

1976-1977

The groundwork for Rose to leave Cincinnati and the Reds was laid in the winter of 1976, when the first free agent draft was held at the Plaza Hotel in New York. With the reserve clause confined to the dustbin of history, the initial free agent class consisted of 24 players, including three future Hall of Famers (Jackson, Rollie Fingers and Willie McCovey) and several superstars of the day (Rudi, Grich, Baylor, Sal Bando and Gullet.)

Under the rules of the draft, each team could select as many players as it wished to negotiate with, although in an effort to prevent the big spenders from cornering the market, they were allowed to sign only two. (An exception was made for the Baltimore Orioles, California Angels and Oakland A's, who each had more than two players in the free agent pool.)

On the flip side, a player could be selected by no more than 12 teams, not including his current club. Once that player was selected by the maximum number of teams, his name was removed from the draft board. In other words, a player could talk with a maximum of 13 teams. If he wasn't selected at all, he was free to discuss a contract with all 26 clubs. Negotiations between the teams and the players would commence immediately following the draft.

Most of the top teams of the day, including the Yankees, Royals and Philadelphia Phillies, were active participants in the inaugural free agent draft, and several selected 10 or more players. However, one club was notable in selecting only a single player: The Cincinnati Reds' only choice was starting pitcher Gullett, their lone player to declare for free agency.

Gullet had battled injuries throughout the Reds' championship seasons of 1975 and 1976 and was losing some of his effectiveness, despite posting an ERA of 3.00 in '76. His walk rate inched from 3.2 BB/9 in '75 to 3.4 BB/9 while his strikeout rate slid from 5.5 K/9 to 4.6 K/9 in '76. While the Reds were leery of his injury history and declining performance, under the rules of the draft, if they wanted to continue to negotiate with Gullett, they needed to select him. By making Gullett their lone choice, the Reds were choosing to retain negotiating rights with their pitcher, and at the same time, they were able to express their displeasure with the new system. Other clubs may haved opened their wallets and waved big money to entice the best talent of the day, but the Reds were determined not to be one of those teams.

Most eyes were on Jackson, the star of Oakland's three consecutive World Championships and the 1973 American League MVP, as the marquee talent in the draft. Jackson, who hit .286/.375/.550 with 27 homers and 91 RBIs for the Baltimore Orioles in '76, was looking to double his $200,000 salary and was asking for a five-year package with salary and signing bonus worth a total of $3 million.

His salary demands, which owners thought exorbitant, and his desire to play in either California or New York, kept Jackson on the table longer than expected, but in the end he was selected by the full complement of teams. Jackson eventually tripled his 1976 salary, signing a five-year pact with the Yankees. Set to earn $400,000 a year over the next five seasons, he did in fact, double his annual pay. With a $900,000 signing bonus, the total value of the package Jackson received from the Yankees totaled $2.9 million. Jackson didn't hit his $3 million mark, but he came awfully close.

Pete Rose noticed.

In 1976, Rose was a 14-year veteran who was playing for his hometown team. As the Reds of the early 1970s steamrolled the National League and Rose continued to accumulate hit after hit, he began to see himself as the leader of the franchise. Cincinnati was known as the Big Red Machine, but the way Rose saw it, he was the spark plug, the engine and the gears of that machine. In his mind, without Pete Rose, the Big Red Machine would grind to a halt.

Rose had his best season since 1969 as he played out the final year of his contract in 1976, hitting .323/.404/.450, playing third base and batting leadoff as the Reds successfully defended their title. While Joe Morgan hit .320/.444/.576 with 60 stolen bases to win his second consecutive MVP award and George Foster slugged .530 with 29 home runs and a league leading 121 RBIs, Rose still saw himself as the best player on the best team in baseball. He was Charlie Hustle, who would do whatever it took to get on base. That meant he needed to be paid accordingly.

As the Reds prepared to open negotiations with their third baseman that winter, they budgeted to pay Rose $225,000 for each of the next two seasons. It would be a modest raise from his previous paycheck of $188,000

and one the Reds' front office, including new general manager Dick Wagner, felt was more than equitable.

While Rose had enjoyed his best season since 1969, the Reds' front office wondered how much longer he could continue to perform at such a high level. With his head-first slides and all-out hustle, Rose was known for playing with a kind of reckless abandon that takes a toll on a body. Combine that with the fact that he was turning 36 in April, and it's easy to understand the Reds' reluctance to give a big raise to a player who almost surely would see his production drop over the life of the contract.

Rose, mindful of the payday Jackson had signed earlier with the Yankees, entered negotiations by asking for $400,000 a year for two years, an increase of more than 100 percent. Reds management was stunned that it had completely underestimated Rose's salary demands. The team countered at $250,000 per year, which was flatly rejected by Rose and his agent, Reuven Katz, who insisted the $400,000 was non-negotiable.

Under the rules of the day, Rose could decide to play out the 1977 season under the reserve clause of his contract (which would net him $188,000, the same amount he earned the previous year) and then declare for free agency following the season. The negotiations presented a public relations nightmare for the Reds. Just a month earlier, Wagner had shipped one of his most popular players and true clubhouse leader, Tony Perez, to Montreal and the Reds' fan base was less than pleased. How would it look if the front office let Rose, not only a popular and productive player but a local boy as well, get away over a contract dispute? As spring training grew closer, Wagner and the Reds bumped their offer to $325,000 for the next two years. Again, the offer was rejected.

Rose reported to camp unsigned and mad as hell.

Never one to shy away from a microphone or camera, Rose stepped up his assault on Cincinnati management, taking his contract issues to the public. With the fans firmly in Rose's corner, Wagner's unpopularity seemed to grow by the minute. As the drama played out, the Reds decided to take out advertisements in Cincinnati newspapers explaining their position and telling their side of the story. While Rose would approach reporters willing to discuss his contract situation, Rose felt betrayed by Reds management's tactic. It was a stunning development in an already circus-like atmosphere.

The two sides finally reached an agreement the day before the Reds opened the 1977 season. Rose signed a two-year deal that would net him a total of $730,000.

It was less than Jackson's reported $400,000 per year but most importantly, the new contract failed to make him the highest paid player on the Big Red Machine, a distinction held by Morgan.

While Rose topped 200 hits for the ninth time in his career in 1977 (tying him with Ty Cobb for most seasons with 200 or more base hits), his overall production declined to .311/.377/.432 and the Reds finished in second place, 10 games behind the Dodgers. That winter, despite the acrimonious negotiations from the prior year, Rose approached Cincinnati management about a long-term contract that would ensure he would spend his entire career in a Reds uniform. Wagner demurred.

Rose later speculated in his book "My Prison Without Bars," that his off-field escapades were eclipsing his on-field performance. Despite being married at the time, Rose was openly flaunting his girlfriends in Cincinnati and on the road. He was also facing a paternity suit and his trips to the horse racing track were becoming more frequent. The Reds front office was aware of the turmoil in Rose's life and was not pleased.

Spurned in his approach to Reds management, Rose prepared for the 1978 season with a chip on his shoulder and something to prove. He set his sights on reaching the 3,000-hit plateau, needing just 34 hits to become the 13th player in major league history to reach the milestone that would cement his place in baseball immortality.

3,000 and 44

Rose did the math and predicted he would collect his 3,000th hit sometime in early May. On May 5, the Reds hosted the Montreal Expos at Riverfront Coliseum and when Rose lined a two-out single to left field off Steve Rogers, he punched his ticket to join the exclusive hit club.

It was quite an accomplishment for Rose, and one he had been looking forward to for years. But it was just a warmup for something bigger.

On June 14, Rose collected singles in the first and fifth inning against Dave Roberts in the final game of a three-game series against the Chicago Cubs. He singled in the next game and the next game and the next. When baseball took a break for the All-Star Game, Rose had hit in 25 consecutive games. (He collected a double in the seventh inning of the All-Star Game for good measure.)

As the second half of the season began, it became a hitting streak that took America by storm. Daily breakdowns of the pitchers Rose was due to face that evening were found in newspapers across the country and as his streak surged past 30 games, there were comparisons with the record holder, Joe DiMaggio, whose hitting streak of 56 games had stood since 1941.

All of baseball benefitted from the streak. On July 25 in New York, Rose passed modern-day National League record holder Tommy Holmes, who hit in 37 consecutive games for the Boston Braves in 1945. The attendance that night at Shea Stadium was 38,158, well above the Mets' average gate of 12,592. It was more of the same in Atlanta (where average attendance that year was 11,167) at the end of the month, when more than 45,000 fans turned out to see Rose tie Wee Willie Keeler for the all-time NL record of 44.

With Keeler tied, no one remained between Rose and the holy grail of hit streaks: DiMaggio's.

Unfortunately for Rose, his quest ended the following night in a 16-4 loss; Larry McWilliams and Gene Garber combined to hold him hitless in his five plate appearances. Following the game, Rose expressed his displeasure with the Braves' pitchers: "He (Garber) pitched to me like it was the seventh game of the World Series. It's easy to make pitches like that when you're winning 16-4."

Over the course of the streak, Rose totaled 70 hits in those 44 games and hit .385/.421/.462. However, as a team, Cincinnati didn't see a benefit. The Reds went 26-18 over the course of those 44 games, a .590 winning percentage, exactly matching their percentage over the first 61 games of the season and the start of the streak.

For nearly a month and a half, Rose was the toast of baseball, but when the streak ended and the spotlight dimmed, he struggled. By the end of August, it was so bad that Rose was either benched or rested, depending on your perspective. Regardless, what's not in dispute is that his production fell sharply after the hitting streak ended. For the month of August, he hit .236/.309/.373 while the Reds dropped 18 of 28 and went from a half game out of first place on Aug. 1 to seven games back at the end of the month.

The Reds rebounded with a fine September, winning 18 games, but still fell 2.5 games short of the division-winning Dodgers. Rose bounced back as well, hitting .315 over the last month of the season to push his final average to .302. It was the 13th time in 16 major league seasons he topped .300. Overall, Rose hit .302/.362/.421, finishing with 198 base hits.

As the Reds prepared for their second consecutive October without postseason baseball, Rose turned his attention to more pressing issues.

Free Agent Courtship

Immediately following the close of that 1978 season, Wagner met with Rose and Katz to offer a modest raise for the 1979 season. That offer was quickly rejected. A week later, Rose returned with a proposal of his own, which the Reds quickly shot down. With the Reds due to leave for a month-long trip to Japan at the end of October, time was of the essence. With that in mind, Wagner came to Rose with one final offer: $400,000 to play in 1979. The catch was that his proposal came with a deadline. The Reds wanted an answer before the team left for the tour.

Rose, not wanting to be pressured into signing a contract, stalled. On Oct. 12, the Reds decided they had waited long enough, pulled the offer and declared a stalemate. With negotiations seemingly over, Rose declared himself a free agent on Oct. 18. Almost immediately, speculation began: "Where will Pete go?" Rose himself had a grand time fanning the flames, providing reporters a list of teams he would consider, naming the Dodgers, Phillies, Padres, Royals and Angels as possible contenders for his services.

A week after the Yankees beat the Dodgers in six games to win their second consecutive World Series, the Reds, including Rose, embarked on a 17-game barnstorming tour of Japan. While the Reds were conquering Japan (they finished with a 14-2-1 record), Rose and Katz were awaiting the outcome of the free agent draft.

That year's free agent class was lean compared to the previous two, as teams were adjusting to the new market by signing their key players to long-term deals. For example, Don Sutton, who made $155,000 in 1976, subsequently was locked in to a four-year, $1 million deal by the Dodgers. While Rose would have been the marquee name no matter what year he entered the draft, Rose's star shone a little brighter in this one— big names among the other 41 available players included Tommy John, Darrell Evans, Larry Gura, Lee Lacy and Luis Tiant.

When the draft was held on Nov. 4, Rose was quickly off the board after being drafted by the full complement of 12 teams, including five in the first round. Under the rules of the draft, Cincinnati could continue to negotiate with its player, meaning Rose could play for any one of the 13 teams in 1979.

Teams selecting Rose in the 1978 free agent draft

- Atlanta Braves
- California Angels
- Cincinnati Reds
- Cleveland Indians
- Kansas City Royals
- Los Angeles Dodgers
- New York Mets
- New York Yankees
- Philadelphia Phillies
- Pittsburgh Pirates
- St. Louis Cardinals
- San Diego Padres
- Texas Rangers

Rose had named several of the teams as those he would consider. Others, like the Mets, Braves, Indians and Cardinals, were thought to be longshots since they were among the worst teams in the majors in 1978 and lagged in attendance.

While Rose was clearly the marquee player in the draft, there was plenty of interest in the pitchers who made themselves available. Gura was selected in the first round by six teams and was the first player removed from the draft board after being chosen by 12 teams.

Number of teams selecting each player in the first round, 1978

- Larry Gura - 6
- Pete Rose - 5
- Tommy John - 5
- Mike Marshall - 4
- Lee Lacy - 2
- Jim Slaton - 2
- Darrell Evans - 1
- Tom Paciorek - 1
- Elias Sosa - 1

Most clubs made five or more selections. Only the Detroit Tigers remained on the sidelines, refusing to make a pick. The Oakland A's made 17 picks, which was strange considering Charley Finley was in the business of selling, not buying, talent. They didn't sign a single free agent.

When Rose returned from the tour of Japan, he declared himself pleased with his options and maintained there were no front-runners for his services. Quickly though, teams began falling from contention. The Padres had Ray Kroc's money, but in their 10 years of existence had never been a contender, so they fell by the wayside. The Rangers contacted Rose later than other teams and never made a serious offer. The Yankees decided to use free agency to address pitching needs and appeared set at positions where Rose could help.

From the beginning, it was unlikely that Rose would move to the American League. While his lust for cash was becoming readily apparent, there was also his need to break records to cement his place in baseball immortality. And after reaching 3,000 hits faster than any player in history, Rose had his sights set on Stan Musial and his National League hit record of 3,630. For Rose to break that record, he would need 466 hits. At his normal pace, that would take two years and change. Set to turn 37 that April, he was seeking at least a three-year contract so he could reach what he called his "ultimate goal."

With the Musial record established as a factor, attention turned to teams in the NL that would have the means to satisfy Rose's demands for salary and championships.

The Dodgers had pipped Rose's Reds two years running for the Western Division championship and Rose would welcome the exposure playing in LA could provide. He had spent previous winters shooting commercials for products such as Aqua Velva and Atari and embraced the cash that came with such endorsements. But like the Yankees, the Dodgers were set at positions where Rose could play.

The Pittsburgh Pirates were an option. They'd finished second in '78, just a game and a half behind the Phillies, and featured the reigning league MVP in Dave Parker. Even better, they had a need that Rose could fill at third base. But Parker would be playing the final year of his contract in '79 and with his numbers (he hit .334/.394/.585 in '78) the Pirates knew they would have to come up with some cash to keep their slugger in the fold. Besides, at 28, Parker was 10 years Rose's junior.

Despite playing in the American League, the Kansas City Royals fancied themselves contenders. The Royals had come up short in the AL Championship Series three years running and desperately wanted to make a statement that they wouldn't rest until they won the pennant. They had the money and a plan to move Rose to first base while allowing him to DH occasionally. But their league was a stumbling block they could do nothing about.

Then there were the Phillies. Philadelphia, like the Royals, had come up short in the Championship Series three years in a row. The Phils also had a need at first base and lacked a true leadoff hitter. But they already had the highest payroll in the league.

As discussions began with eligible clubs and offers began to roll in, Rose began to whittle his list. After the early eliminations he was left with the Braves, Cardinals, Phillies, Pirates and Royals.

With the contenders decided upon, Rose leased a private jet and began a whirlwind tour that took him to each of the cities over a four-day period in late November.

Rose and Katz began the week in Atlanta meeting with Braves owner Ted Turner. Turner never had been shy about diving into the free agent market. He signed Andy Messersmith in 1975 and was fined $100,000 by the commissioner's office in 1976 for tampering after telling reporters he was going to go after Gary Matthews in that winter's inaugural free agent draft. Flush with cash from his cable superstation, Turner reportedly offered Rose $1 million per year for as long as he wanted to play.

Up next was a Tuesday morning meeting with Royals owner Ewing Kauffman in Kansas City. The traveling party toured Royals Stadium and then convened at Kauffman's pharmaceutical company, Marion Labs. In the meeting, Kauffman and his general manager, Joe Burke, acknowledged Rose's passion for breaking Musial's record and became the first team to dangle the big prize in front of Rose: Ty Cobb's all-time hit record. The Royals put together a package of four years and $2.4 million, plus two option years. The Royals also reportedly offered Rose stock in Kauffman's company.

From there, it was a cross-state journey to St. Louis for a meeting with Cardinals owner August Busch Jr. Instead of gathering at Busch Stadium, they met at a St. Louis hospital where Busch was to undergo surgery for a hernia the next day. Busch and Cardinal GM John Claiborne were a little more vague in their talks, telling Rose they would match his best offer with some additional money on top. They also offered a stake in a Budweiser beer distributorship if Rose would become a Cardinal.

"I'd probably have a hernia too, if I had to carry all that money he wanted to give me," Rose quipped after his stop in St. Louis.

The next day, Rose was in Columbus, Ohio to meet with Dan Galbreath, the owner of the Pirates. Galbreath owned racehorses, so the meeting seemed a natural fit since Rose was a self-declared "horse freak." At $400,000 a year for three years, their offer trailed those of other clubs interested. However, Galbreath threw in a quality broodmare valued at more than $800,000 with the potential of being worth "several times that amount."

Despite being left off the itinerary, the Mets made an unexpected strong play while Rose and Katz were on the road, offering two years at $500,000 per before adding another year to bring the total value to three years and $1.5 million. Rejected both times, the Mets sweetened the offer: Three years at a total of $1.8 million plus a front office job at the end of the contract. Rejected a third time, and since the Mets' board approved only $2 million for the acquisition of Rose, they dropped out of contention.

Finally, the road show landed in Philadelphia for a meeting with Phillies owner Ruly Carpenter. From the beginning of the process, Rose had the Phillies at the top of his list and the feeling was mutual. Often, Rose had spoken publicly about how the Phillies were a fit, saying, "All they lack is a team leader." He told *Sports Illustrated's* E.M. Swift. "Two of my three favorite baseball people are on the Phils—Larry Bowa and Greg Luzinski. And they need a leadoff hitter. They need me."

Rose and Katz expected the lunch meeting to be a mere formality; despite protests that there were no front-runners, Philadelphia was clearly their favorite. Then the Phillies presented their offer: Three years for a total of $1.8 million.

To Rose, who already had solid proposals in hand from three teams, it was a low offer both in terms of money and years. As he left for the airport, it seemed Philadelphia would have to be crossed off his list. But it was on that ride to the airport that Katz told Bill Giles, the executive vice president of the Phillies, that while the money was below what they were expecting, there was still some room for negotiations to continue.

Convinced that Philadelphia was Rose's first choice, the Phillies braintrust went back to work to structure a deal to the All-Star's liking. They came up with an extra $300,000 over the three-year life of the proposed contract, bringing his annual salary up to $700,000, still less money than other teams had offered. Katz rejected the deal, but told the Phillies they were still in the hunt.

The Phillies needed help. Early in the process, they estimated it would take $2.2 million to acquire Rose, but other teams in the derby had blown that budget out of the water. Giles took the quandary to the team's television broadcast partner, WPHL-TV.

The thinking was, by the mere presence of Rose, television ratings for Phillies games would increase, thus the station's advertising revenue would increase. Under the Phillies' new agreement with WPHL signed following the 1978 season, the station was paying the club roughly $1.4 million for the broadcast rights. On top of the up-front rights fee, the station had agreed to a down-the-middle split on advertising revenue, giving the Phillies 50 cents of every dollar of advertising sold after the station hit a certain amount of ad sales. With an expected ratings increase for Phillies games, with the ratings and subsequent ad increases in mind, Giles asked WPHL to guarantee that the split would give the Phillies at least $600,000 a year over the life of Rose's contract.

Station management was skeptical. Could one player make such a difference in television ratings and advertising revenues? After crunching the numbers, the brass at WPHL decided that yes, one player could and if Rose was a Phillie, he undoubtedly would.

In effect, WPHL guaranteed 75 percent of Rose's salary with the Phillies.

Left on the sidelines just days prior, the Phillies were able to return to Rose and Katz with the dollars they wanted, plus a fourth year. That brought the final total of the contract to $3.2 million.

At $800,000 per year, the 37-year-old Rose was now the highest paid baseball player in history.

Aftermath

Rose was introduced as a member of the Phillies before a press conference at the start of the annual winter meeting in Orlando. Although Rose maintained that his primary motivation wasn't about breaking the bank, he was nonetheless pleased with the result. "You could stack the money up, and a show dog couldn't jump over it," he boasted.

Perhaps it was true, The Pete Rose Road Show wasn't all about the money. Both Rose and Carpenter said that the Phillies' offer was the lowest of the final four. Philadelphia was the only team in the bidding not to throw in outside income—race horses, beer distributorships, stock options—so their total package was well under the other offers.

Rose, always the competitor, got in one last dig at his old employer. "Last May, the Cincinnati Reds could have signed me for a lot less," he said. "Maybe a little more than half this contract."

Rose wasn't the only player to cash in that winter. Teams weren't shy about throwing money to veteran players with skills on the decline. The Yankees continued to lead the way, signing two starting pitchers: 36-year-old Tommy John got a three-year deal valued at $1.2 million and 38-year-old Luis Tiant got two years and $900,000. The Twins, who were forced to trade Rod Carew to California that winter because they feared they would lose him to free agency the next year, spent some of their savings on 36-year-old relief pitcher Mike Marshall, signing him to a three year, $900,000 contract. The Royals lost out on John despite offering a reported $2 million, but they re-signed Gura to a five-year, $1.35 million deal.

Veteran players were excited about the contract Rose received and the salary bar that continued to drift higher. Eyes immediately turned to Parker and the Pirates. Parker, the 1978 NL MVP, was due to play out the final year of his contract at $225,000, an amount that suddenly became quite the bargain. Several baseball people expressed disbelief that the Pirates could be so active in the Rose sweepstakes when they already had a younger, more complete player already on their roster; and one who would see a considerable raise in his immediate future. The following season, The Cobra became the first ballplayer to break the $1 million average salary barrier when he re-signed with Pittsburgh for five years and $5 million.

Commissioner Bowie Kuhn was irate at the dollars that were being showered on the players. Rather than take aim at individual players such as Rose, Kuhn focused on teams, specifically the New York Yankees. Over the three-year period of free agency, the Yankees had handed out the top contract in '76 (to Reggie Jackson) and '77 (to Rich Gossage) and awarded the third highest in '78 to John (behind Rose and Gura).

"This trend fulfills a prophecy some of us made that the star free agents would tend to sign with the best teams," Kuhn protested in his opening remarks at baseball's winter meetings. "It's inevitable that this process will lead to a group of elite teams controlling the sport."

Another byproduct of free agency was the slowing of the trade market. Suddenly, contract length mattered; teams were no longer evaluating solely on talent. Teams were slow to acquiesce to a deal if they could lose a player after only a year of service.

On the other hand, many teams with star players with a year remaining on their contracts were actively shopping them. The Twins knew they weren't going to re-sign All-Star first baseman Rod Carew when he became eligible for free agency following the 1979 season, so they sought a deal at the winter meetings. They found a taker in the San Francisco Giants, but Carew invoked his rights as a veteran player with 10 years in the league and five with one team and vetoed the trade. Even after the Giants offered to extend his contract for an additional $4 million over the next five years, Carew turned them down. The market was at a standstill.

According to *The New York Times*, 53 players changed teams in 22 deals in the winter meetings of 1977, right at the average over the previous six meetings. However, at the winter meetings of '78, only 12 deals were consummated with just 31 players obtaining a new address.

Meanwhile, the Phillies made money before Rose ever stepped on the field. In addition to the guarantee of $600,000 from its television partner, Philadelphia sold close to 19,000 season tickets for the 1979 season, an increase of more than 4,000 from the previous year. As increasing television rights fees and growing attendance intersected with a free, open market for players, team budgets were radically altered. The average salary jumped from $51,501 in 1976 to $113,558 in 1979.

In 1979, the Phillies slumped to fourth place in the NL East, finishing just six wins over .500. Rose played first base and again reached the 200-hit plateau, finishing with 208, and his final numbers of .331/.418/.430 represented his best overall season since he won the MVP in 1973. Rose's performance dipped to .282/.352/.354 the following year, but he hit .400/.520/.400 in the Phillies' five-game triumph over the Houston Astros that sent Philadelphia to its first World Series since 1950. Squaring off against the Kansas City Royals, the Phillies won their first world championship in franchise history.

On Aug. 10, 1981, in the first game back from the player strike, Rose singled in the eighth inning off Cardinals reliever Mark Littell for his 3,631th career hit, passing Musial for the NL hit record.

By the end of his time in Philadelphia in 1983, Rose was clearly in decline at age 42. Philadelphia exercised its option year before the 1982 season, so over five years for the Phillies, he hit .291/.365/.361, collecting a total of 826 hits. Philadelphia advanced to the postseason three times, and to the World Series twice, including the title year of 1980.

To the Phillies, Rose was worth every penny.

Piazza, Hall of Fame Catcher

by Craig Wright

Mike Piazza's career has "Hall of Fame" written all over it. He is a no-doubter, a sure-fire bet to go in on his first ballot. The great Negro League slugger Josh Gibson is likely the greatest offensive catcher of all time, but fair or not, there will always be a question about how great Gibson really was because of the difficulty in assessing the quality of Negro League seasons compared to major league seasons. With Piazza, we can say with certainty that he is the greatest offensive catcher in the history of the major leagues. No one else is remotely close.

Piazza's raw numbers are so impressive that it is easy to overlook that *every* season of his career his home field was one that favored the pitcher. During his years in LA, he was performing in the toughest park in the league for hitters, especially in hitting for batting average. Yet one could just throw out the park factors, and his offensive numbers remain mind-boggling for a catcher.

There have been 18 seasons in which a major league catcher hit 35 or more homers and Piazza has a third of them (six). Johnny Bench is next with two, the only other catcher to do it more than once. If you prorate the strike seasons of 1994-95, Piazza would have a seventh such season and come close to an eighth. Piazza's .362 batting average in 1997 is the highest ever by a catcher qualifying for the batting title, and his relative career batting average is comfortably the highest of any catcher in history ("relative" means compared to other non-pitchers in his league).

As a catcher, minimum 5,000 PA	BA	Avg non-P in Lg	Relative BA
Mike Piazza	.313	.270	+42 points
Thurman Munson	.292	.259	+33 points
Ivan Rodriguez	.301	.270	+31 points
Ernie Lombardi	.306	.275	+31 points
Mickey Cochrane	.320	.290	+30 points

This combination of high average and power made Piazza unique among catchers. He holds the record for the highest slugging percentage by a catcher in a season (.638 in 1997), and he has three of the top five seasons, as well as eight of the top 18 seasons. To put it another way, Piazza's sixth-best season in slugging percentage (.570) is better than the best season of every Hall of Fame catcher except Gabby Hartnett, Roy Campanella and Bench. That's right: His sixth-best slugging season is higher than anything Cochrane, Bill Dickey, Lombardi, Gary Carter or Carlton Fisk ever posted. And Mike's eighth-best slugging season of "only" .561 tops the best of future Hall of Famer Pudge Rodriguez (.558)

Piazza's career slugging percentage as a catcher (.560) is more than 50 points higher than any other catcher in history. In relative slugging percentage as a catcher, the gap between Piazza and the No. 2 man, Bench, is larger than the gap between Bench and No. 10, Bill Dickey. (See chart.) And remember, none of these numbers has been park-adjusted. None of these other great offensive catchers played with home fields as tough as Piazza's.

Career slugging percentage as catchers compared to other non-pitchers in their league:

Rank	Diff	Player
1	+.131	Piazza
2	+.099	Bench
3	+.087	Campanella
4	+.086	Yogi Berra
5	+.082	Hartnett
6	+.077	Fisk
7	+.074	Javy Lopez
8	+.072	Walker Cooper
9	+.071	Lombardi
10	+.070	Dickey
11	+.062	Ted Simmons
12	+.061	Cochrane
13	+.054	Jorge Posada
14	+.052	G. Carter
15	+.048	I. Rodriguez

About the chart: Actual plate appearances as a catcher are not available before 1956, and for those seasons I simply use the overall numbers for the seasons in which a player's primary position was catcher. I usually use 5,000 plate appearances as the minimum for a chart like this, but because catchers miss so many games and Campanella was able to make the Hall of Fame with only 4,816 plate appearances, I made that the minimum.

In the very early days of baseball, catching equipment was so primitive that catchers routinely missed large chunks of the season and had short careers. None of those early catchers would come close to the minimum plate appearances for this chart. When the great Buck Ewing (first catcher in the Hall of Fame) finished his last season as a catcher in 1890, he had the third most plate appearances ever as a catcher but it was barely over 3,000. If we allowed him on the list, he would rank all the way up at No. 2 (+.103), and another catcher from the 1800s, Jack Clements, would be between Cochrane and Rodriguez.

During my 21 years working full-time with major league teams, I was asked to make evaluations or recommendations involving several future Hall of Famers. It was fun to see their careers fulfill their promise, but I rarely felt like I had done anything to help their careers along. Players with Hall of Fame talent are generally so obvious that they rarely need any help in getting their careers on track. Mike Piazza was a very different case, perhaps the most unusual in the history of great players.

Unlike most Hall of Famers, Piazza was far from a scout's dream. No one drafted him out of high school; no one considered signing him as an undrafted player. He didn't throw or run well, and he played first base, a position where you had to hit like Ted Williams to get noticed.

And there was always something about Piazza's stance and swing that bothered a lot of visual scouts. He was abnormally upright in his swing, with little bend in his knees, and his swing seemed a tad long. His hands were way down on the bottom of the bat, with the pinky over the knob, and he would stand a little far off the plate. While other hitters with that stance would dive into the plate to compensate on certain pitches, Piazza seemed to be just reaching out to cover the plate, almost flicking at the outer pitch, though with surprising pop.

It was different, and it was easy to be concerned that he might eventually hit a wall—that he would start to be overwhelmed by power pitchers, that against good pitchers he'd have a big hole low and away, and that he wouldn't be able generate power on quality pitches away.

I remember having two distinct thoughts the first time I saw Piazza hit. One was that he must be incredibly strong in his wrists and forearms to make that swing work, and, two, that this guy wasn't going to get hit by too many pitches. (He ended up never being hit more than three times in a season, and his overall hit-by-pitch rate during his career was less than half the normal rate.)

Piazza did get a chance to play with a top college team at the University of Miami, but that program didn't see his potential either, and rather than play as a reserve he transferred to a community college (Miami Dade) to get more playing time. Dodgers manager Tommy Lasorda was a friend of Mike's father, the godfather to Mike's brother Tom, and he had known Mike since he was a baby. Tommy asked the Dodgers to draft Mike—not to sign him, but simply to help pad his resume in hopes he could get a tryout with another Division I school.

Piazza is destined to be the Hall of Famer selected in the lowest round of the amateur draft. In 1988, he was selected in the 62nd round. No one is going to beat that because now there are just 50 rounds. Sometimes writers erroneously say Piazza was the last player taken in the 1988 draft. Not quite, though he was the last taken by the Dodgers, and 13 teams had stopped drafting players at that point. Piazza—the player who would prove to be the best of the entire 1988 draft—was the 1,389th player selected. To put it another way, it would take about four pages to list every player selected in front of him.

None of the big college programs were interested in Piazza, and two months after the draft the Dodgers brought him in for a tryout. They decided that if he were willing to convert to catching, they'd give him a token signing bonus and give him a shot on the lowest rung in the minors. His catching experience at that point was next to nothing. He had been primarily a first baseman, but apparently had caught a few games in his brief college career, as he was listed in the 1988 draft as "1B-C."

To start working immediately on his catching skills, Piazza went to the Dodgers' baseball academy in the Dominican League. The Academy was meant for local players; he was the first American ever sent there. He didn't speak Spanish and hardly anyone there spoke any English. His hard work in that difficult situation was our first sign of how dedicated he was to becoming a big leaguer.

When he made his pro debut in the Northwest League in 1989, he was not considered even good enough to be the club's No. 1 catcher (that honor went to a lad named Hector Ortiz, who can have fun telling folks that the great Mike Piazza was once his backup). Piazza did show surprising pop with the bat that first year. His home field in Salem was a huge park; his eight homers led the team, and he hit them in less than 200 at-bats.

I started to get excited about Piazza's big league prospects during his 1991 season in the California League. He made gigantic strides in his command of the strike zone and led the league in slugging percentage. When I park-adjusted his numbers, he really stood out as the best power hitter in the 10-team league—and he was doing this while playing the most physically demanding position on the field (fifth in the league in games caught).

When I expressed my excitement about Piazza that offseason to Dodgers general manager Fred Claire, I was surprised to hear that the assessments of Piazza by our scouts and player development people were very mixed, and the consensus was, at best, lukewarm about his prospect status. Some felt he would never be more than a "minor league hitter," and some also thought he would never make it as a catcher and would have to move back to first base.

(Reporter Ken Gurnick cites Lasorda as his source in a story that says that during Piazza's 1991 season in A-ball "some club officials pushed for Piazza's release." That surprised me; Fred Claire never mentioned anyone having that negative a view. The idea of someone "pushing" for a player's release in midseason suggests there may have been some side issues involved rather than just an assessment of the player's potential.)

Also working against Piazza was that the team had two good prospects ahead of him at both catcher and first base. Carlos Hernandez was a good defensive catcher hitting .345 at Triple-A. *Baseball America* ranked Hernandez as the second-best position player in the Dodgers' system, behind Raul Mondesi and even ahead of Eric Karros. And Karros had just had a big year at Triple-A and was slated to be given a solid shot as the Dodgers' starting first baseman in 1992. (Karros would end up as the league's Rookie of the Year.)

Claire indicated that he was encouraged by Piazza's 1991 season, but with so many conflicting views, and with the prospects the team had in front of Piazza, the Dodgers could not be making any plans around him. That disappointed me. I had nothing against Carlos Hernandez as a prospect, but our team had too many positions without power, and in my eyes, Piazza was our best power-hitting prospect, especially valuable because he could do it as a catcher.

I thought the concerns about Piazza's defense were way overblown. Piazza hadn't gotten in the way of

the Bakersfield team having the league's second best ERA. The team's pitchers had thrown strikes (lowest walk rate in the league) and stayed away from the long ball, allowing a paltry 43 homers in the 136-game season, and it wasn't the ballpark holding down the homer total. The Bakersfield Dodgers hit more than 100 homers that year.

This is a good spot to discuss my views of the scouting and developing of catchers. In a study of the amateur draft, I had shown that among position players, the ones most often misranked by the visual scouts were the catchers. Looking at more than 25 years of draft data I saw the problem as similar to why pitchers so often fool us. There is nothing like the workload of a professional pitcher in the amateur ranks. You are essentially flying blind when trying to estimate whether an amateur pitcher's arm will be able to handle a professional workload.

Catching is like that, too. You don't see amateur catchers going through a summer catching five games a week. A lot of catchers can look good working on a high school or college schedule, but then wilt on a professional schedule. With most position players, you expect progress in hitting ability simply with the gain in experience from playing nearly every day. But a lot of highly drafted catchers actually regress offensively because the defensive workload is so draining.

Sure, I love a catcher with the raw talents you can't teach, the great arm and the quick feet, but those gifts aren't worth much if you can't hit enough to play. Once a catcher has shown he has the minimal physical skills for the position, what I most want to know is whether he can take a lickin' and keep on tickin'. The ability to catch a lot without having your hitting skills go in the toilet is a huge advantage in a catching prospect. I would rather know that than how fast he gets out from behind the plate or how strong or quick his throws are.

And if you really stop to think about it, isn't there a lot to catching that isn't driven by raw physical talent? Is there another position where the combination of experience, memory, intelligence and personal interaction skills are worth more? Teaching can take you only so far in turning someone into a good defensive player, but you can "teach" catching far more than you can "teach" defense at any other position.

It's a small thing, but—as with pitchers—there is a long-term durability risk in acquiring catchers who have caught a lot of games at a young age. If you check, you will find many of our best, most durable catchers were converted from other positions, or for some other reason did not catch much in their formative years.

So, with my approach on finding and developing catchers—plus my belief that the concept "minor-league hitter" is largely a myth resulting from improper performance analysis—you can see why I tended to be well ahead of the curve in valuing Piazza and working to see that he got the opportunities he deserved. His arm was always going to be a liability, but on the positive side:

1. Mike certainly hadn't been abused as a young catcher. It did not become his primary position until he was 21 and he would be 23 before he ever caught 100 games in a season.

2. He was incredibly driven to learn how to catch. He understood this was his ticket into professional baseball, and he latched onto it like a junkyard dog onto a bone.

3. Most important was his ability to shrug off the pain and fatigue of catching and knock the snot out of the ball. He was born with a silver spoon in his mouth, the privileged son of a multi-millionaire, but he was tough as nails.

Shortly after the 1992 All-Star break, just a half-season further in Piazza's development, Claire asked me to recommend what we should do with the rest of our season. I wrote:

> I cannot see any reason to bring back [Mike] Sciosica [who would be a free agent at end of the year] at age 34.
>
> … we have been given a golden opportunity to gamble on a catcher with exactly what this team is crying for, power. I know when I have asked about Piazza, you have shown little interest in making him part of the mix, but I'd be doing you a grave disservice if I didn't fight and fight hard on this point.
>
> In 1991, he belted 29 homers which is amazing enough for a catcher, but it was also the most by any Dodger in the whole system. Here we are in 1992, and despite being jumped up 2 leagues, he continues to hit about 100 points higher than he did in A-ball, has cut his [relative] strikeout rate dramatically, and is again leading the organization in HR (21 in 338 AB). We are desperate for power, and he had no trouble adjusting to AA or AAA pitching for the first time this year.
>
> … You are looking for recommendations of what we should be doing with the remainder of the 1992

> season. My absolute No. 1 recommendation is that we promote Piazza and play him."

We weren't ready to do that—or at least it was explained to me that the field staff wasn't ready to do that. Tommy Lasorda genuinely loved Mike as a person and was plenty willing to help him along up to a point, but contrary to legend, Lasorda was far from fighting to pave the way for him to be a big league regular. Scioscia remained the No. 1 catcher, and Piazza was not brought up until September, when the minor league season was over and the major league roster expanded.

A month after my recommendation, the Pittsburgh Pirates sought to make a trade with us that would include Scioscia. As part of the deal, the Dodgers would get catcher Mike LaValliere, whose contract had gotten too expensive for the small-market Pirates. On the surface it was a very good deal, but when asked to analyze it I concluded:

> … [at this stage of their careers] I personally consider LaValliere a … better catcher than Scioscia. Yet I can see refusing to make this deal if we have to take on LaValliere.
>
> We don't need what LaValliere can offer us as a catcher; what we need is what Mike Piazza can offer us as a catcher. And if Piazza were a bust – which would surprise the hell out of me – Carlos Hernandez has a better chance of giving us what we need from our catcher.
>
> I've played with this in my mind for hour upon hour now. I am in favor of anything that will clear the deck for Piazza, and I find I can't endorse any move that will make it harder for him to establish himself in the majors. I cannot see a manager taking a veteran catcher making $2,000,000 a year and making it a fair competition with a couple kids where the veteran might come out as the No. 3 catcher."

Fred Claire was steadily becoming more enamored with Piazza as he continued to play well, and he declined the Pittsburgh deal. I ended up repeating my theme in my season review in September, which included my response to a recent conversation with Fred in which he indicated that he was leaning toward offering Scioscia a 1993 contract because the field staff was reluctant to be solely dependent on a couple of young catchers. They wanted a veteran presence among our catching corps.

That scared me. Lasorda was 66, and he already had shown signs of a common affliction that creeps up on older managers, a tendency to overplay veterans at the expense of young players. Scioscia was a Dodger institution and very popular with the field staff, who had demonstrated in 1992 that they were willing to play him as a No. 1 catcher even though he had nothing left. Lasorda had given him 389 plate appearances in 1992 even though his on-base average and slugging percentage were both under .287! I wrote:

The best thing we have going for us is Mike Piazza (boy, that sounds like a broken record). The chance to put this kind of bat in our lineup and to do it at the catching position is just a tremendous break …

… [This is] what I disagree the most with in the notes I took from our conversation. As far as I can see, we don't need a veteran catcher, and if we do, it better not be Mike Scioscia. … As sure as the Dodgers wearing blue, if Mike Scioscia is on the 1993 team, he will be taking playing time away from Piazza … [and putting] unnecessary pressure on Piazza.

If you really feel we need a veteran No. 3 catcher, make sure it is someone who won't – even in the best of light – be mistaken for a No. 1 catcher. Hey, we have 29-year-old Wakamatsu at AAA who has experience with the knuckleball. I'd rather have him than pay serious bucks to Sciosica just to take away playing time from the player we need most.

Claire found this logic persuasive, and he ultimately declined the recommendations to re-sign Scioscia. Instead he signed the veteran catcher Lance Parrish to a minor league contract. (Parrish was on the last legs of his distinguished career and would make close to the minimum salary.)

In retrospect this was obviously the right move, but I think it was remarkably courageous on the part of the Dodgers, and particularly by Fred Claire, who would bear the responsibility if things didn't work out. I think the norm for most GMs in the same situation would have been to bring back Scioscia for a year to help with the transition. And a lot of folks would have been tempted to say yes to the Pittsburgh deal, which would have given the Dodgers a clear catching upgrade with LaValliere, as well as protection if Piazza were not ready.

Remember, this is just a year removed from a time when Piazza was a questionable prospect and when the Dodgers were not willing to make any plans around him. Yes, Piazza did have a great minor league season, but it was his first season with a single plate appearance above A-ball and he had not hit well in his brief

September call-up: a .232 batting average with little power (.319 slugging percentage).

After that 1992 season, analyst Bill James wrote that he saw Piazza as a prospect but cautioned he did not like him as much as guys like Willie Greene, Melvin Nieves or Chipper Jones. (Greene and Nieves were decent prospects who had weak careers and were retired by age 28.)

And while *Baseball America* now included Piazza among its 100 top prospects, it still rated 37 minor leaguers ahead of him, and once you get past the top 30, the number of misses and so-so players far out-number the successes. Here are the players who were listed just ahead of Piazza: Tyler Green, Jim Pittsley, Calvin Murray, Mike Kelly, Kevin Young, John Roper and Nigel Wilson. That was hardly a grouping to encourage the absolute commitment the Dodgers were making.

The next spring Piazza was the talk of the spring camp. He led the team in batting average (.478) and tied for the team lead in homers and extra-base hits. The Dodgers broke camp with just two catchers, Piazza and Hernandez, and on May 7 Lance Parrish was released at Triple-A. I remember the date because it was my birthday, and I considered this final commitment to Piazza as a pretty nice birthday gift. (Parrish was immediately signed by Cleveland as a backup catcher.) That ended the "veteran" threat to Piazza's rookie season. The organization's No. 3 catcher was now John Wakamatsu, as I had recommended the preceding September.

With that kind of unfettered opportunity, Piazza would either blossom or leave us with egg on our faces. He blossomed, and you know what? The slugging catcher turned out to be a pretty decent defensive catcher.

It is pure speculation on my part, but I believe his obviously below-average throwing arm actually helped his development as a catcher. I've seen more than a few catchers with good throwing arms who put too much focus on the aspect of defense they are good at: stopping the running game. In steal situations, they'll tend to call a good pitch to throw on rather than a good pitch to get the batter out. Some will let the finer nuances of catching slide because they already are perceived as being good catchers simply because they throw well.

Piazza knew he didn't throw well and would always be limited in his ability to contain the running game. I believe that drove him to learn the skills of catching that have nothing to do with arm strength. It paid off. He knew what he was doing back there. Pitchers liked working with him; they were successful, and Piazza was a part of it.

Take a look at this table:

Dodgers	Team's No. 1 Catcher	Rank of Staff ERA
1992	Mike Scioscia	6th
1993	Mike Piazza	3rd
1994	Mike Piazza	9th
1995	Mike Piazza	2nd
1996	Mike Piazza	1st
1997	Mike Piazza	2nd
1998	Charles Johnson	5th
Mets		
1997	Todd Hundley	6th
1998	Mike Piazza	4th
1999	Mike Piazza	5th
2000	Mike Piazza	3rd
2001	Mike Piazza	5th
2002	Mike Piazza	5th
2003	Vance Wilson	10th
2004	Jason Phillips	7th
2005	Mike Piazza	3rd
Padres		
2005	Ramon Hernandez	7th
2006	Mike Piazza	1st
2007	Josh Bard	1st

1. Piazza was the No. 1 catcher for 11 pitching staffs and 10 of the 11 finished in the top five in ERA (average rank of 3.9).

2. When Piazza became the Dodgers' No. 1 catcher, the staff ERA improved from sixth to third.

3. When Piazza was traded away from the Dodgers, the staff ERA declined from second to fifth.

4. When Piazza became the No. 1 catcher for the Mets, their staff ERA improved from sixth to fourth.

5. When a groin injury to Piazza made Vance Wilson the No. 1 catcher in 2003, the staff ERA fell from fifth to tenth, and when Piazza came back, playing mostly first base in 2004, the staff ERA was seventh.

6. When Piazza again became the No. 1 catcher in 2005, the staff ERA improved from seventh to third.

7. When Piazza became the No. 1 catcher of the Padres (his last year as a catcher), their staff ERA improved from seventh to first.

In 2003, if you took the Mets' staff ERA just when they were pitching to Piazza (532.1 innings) that ERA would have ranked third in the league. In 2004, the staff ERA when pitching to Piazza (388.1 innings) would have ranked fourth in the league. In the context of the above chart, that's rather fascinating, isn't it?

In 1987 I began writing about my study of the impact of a catcher on the pitcher's effectiveness by comparing the results with the other catchers who worked with the same pitchers in the same season. There are a lot of influences you ideally would like to control, but the most important, and the easiest to manage, was to distribute evenly the quality of the pitchers being caught. I originally did that with matched innings, but that is not as practical today because in 2000 I lost access to the comprehensive database I used for matched-inning studies.

Fortunately, the wonderful folks at Baseball Reference, using the data from the even more wonderful folks at Project Retrosheet, have made it possible for anyone with Internet access, and the right combination of interest and work ethic, to control the "distribution of pitchers" factor by creating a set of matched "plate appearances" according to which catcher is catching them.

I'll quickly explain the process with an example. In 1997, knuckleballer Tom Candiotti and Mike Piazza were combined on defense for 467 plate appearances by opposing batters. The Dodgers' other catchers that year were behind the plate for 106 plate appearances with Candiotti on the mound. Whichever number of plate appearances is lower, that's the common number of plate appearances, or what I call the "matched plate appearances." You reduce the stat line from the other side of the ledger down to the rate of occurrence in the number of matched plate appearances. So, in this example, you are multiplying the things that happened in the Candiotti-Piazza plate appearances by .2270 (106/467).

A number of critics of this approach have worked with matched innings and matched plate appearances in a way that leads them to believe that it shows nothing, and they believe catchers have no impact on a pitcher

Performance in matched PA by pitchers	BA	SLG	OBP	OPS	SB	CS	SB%
Mike Piazza behind plate	.255	.401	.322	.723	649	184	77.9%
Other catchers	.262	.413	.335	.748	388	214	64.5%

beyond things like the catcher's ability to control the running game. This is not the place to debate that at length. It will be clear to the reader when examining just this single example, Mike Piazza, that a catcher can have a positive impact on a pitcher's effectiveness. You can even get a pretty clear view of how he was doing it, or at least what he was emphasizing that had the most significant impact.

Mike Piazza was behind the plate for almost 58,000 plate appearances during his career. Because he was a No. 1 catcher in most of those years, a lot of those plate appearances will need to be set aside to create the exact distribution of plate appearances by pitcher in each year with other catchers. But adding up those year-by-year matched plate appearances is still going to produce a massive sample of 26,255 matched plate appearances from Piazza's career.

What is going on in the first four columns of the above table is worth considerably more in preventing runs than what is reflected in the last three columns, which deal with Piazza's weakness in stopping the running game.

Some will say that these are such small differences in the first few columns that they might occur by chance. But keep in mind the sample size we are talking about. Consider even the smallest difference, the six points in batting average. Would you tell Pete Rose that hitting .303 in his career—which had almost 2,000 more plate appearances than any other player in the history of the game—was not enough to establish his ability as a .300 hitter? Heck no, and Rose's record-setting career plate appearances are still miles behind this huge sample of matched plate appearances with Piazza behind the plate. We are talking about a sample size that is almost two-thirds greater than the plate appearances in Rose's career.

And would you say a 25-point different in OPS in a huge sample can't tell us anything? Then you are going to have trouble separating the offensive efficiency of a Joe DiMaggio or a Willie Mays from that of someone like Lance Berkman, Chipper Jones or Vladimir Guerrero. They are all within 25 points of each other in their relative career OPS, and in far smaller samples to boot.

These differences in pitcher perfomance are not occurring by chance, and the key difference in these plate appearances is the catcher behind the plate.

As far as I know, Piazza never had any association with Earl Weaver, the Hall of Fame manager of the Orioles, but in working with pitchers, Piazza emphasized exactly what Weaver was always preaching to his pitchers and catchers: "You have to throw strikes early and stay ahead in the count." Having his pitcher throw strikes early to a batter meant more to Piazza than having the pitcher throw pitches that were tougher to hit. He didn't call for a lot of pitches off the plate or particularly hard inside to set up a hitter. (That's why the hit-by-pitch rate went down 20 percent with Piazza behind the plate.) When he wanted to work outside the strike zone, he wanted to do it when his pitcher was ahead in the count and the batter was more likely to swing.

It was a strategy that reduced walks, reduced hit-by-pitches. As Weaver often preached, giving in a little bit early in the at-bat so that you will be ahead in the count late in the at-bat is going to net you extra strikeouts and overall make you tougher to hit.

Reinforcing that these differences should be credited as part of Piazza's defensive impact is that the intentional walk rate barely changes in these matched data. Intentional walks are largely a decision by the manager, reflecting his strategic preferences. While matching plate appearances isn't intended to distribute the plate appearances evenly by field manager, it ends up doing pretty much exactly that. In this matched plate appearance sample you would expect the intentional walk rate to be essentially the same in the two sides of the split.

And that is exactly what you find when you separate out the intentional walks from the walk total. You see Piazza's impact in a 10 percent reduction in the unintentional walk rate, but the intentional walk rate stays largely the same and even swings in the other direction.

Performance in matched PA by P	Unintentional walk per PA	Intentional walk per PA
Mike Piazza behind plate	.074	.0097
Other catchers	.082	.0094

Net estimated impact, career defense as catcher	Base runners prevented	Outs gained on extra strike-outs and balls batted into play	Extra bases allowed on steals	Extra outs missed on caught stealing
Mike Piazza	758	584	574	65

Performance in matched PA by pitchers	Unintentional walks plus hits plus HBPs	Hitless at-bats plus sacrifices plus GDPs
Mike Piazza behind plate	8,104	18,345
Other catchers	8,448	18,080

It is reasonable to estimate from these matched plate appearances that Piazza's work with his pitchers prevented 344 base runners and helped pick up 265 more outs. And if we assume, quite reasonably, that his influence was approximately at that level for *all* the plate appearances in which Piazza was behind the plate, it becomes 758 base runners and 584 outs for his career. That's a lot of defensive value, and those positives are far, far more valuable than the negative of what was surrendered to the opposition's running game by his weak arm.

Mike Piazza was *not* a defensive liability who made up for it with his bat. The greatest offensive catcher in the history of Major League Baseball was a good defensive catcher as well.

Analysis

Hit Tracker 2008

by Greg Rybarczyk

Hit Tracker is a method and tool for detailed trajectory analysis of flying baseballs. It is best known for providing the most accurate home run distances available anywhere, but it also can be used to provide interesting additional details about the flight of the ball, such as the speed off the bat, the precise direction the ball was hit, and much more.

In this article, I will recap the 2008 season in home runs, and then detail a new home run projection system based on Hit Tracker, using three well-known MLB sluggers to illustrate the method, and reveal some interesting results.

2008 Home Run Demographics

MLB hitters knocked 4,878 home runs in 2,428 games, an average of 2.01 per game. This is a 1.5 percent drop from 2007, where there were 2.04 per game, and 9.4 percent fewer than 2006, where there were 2.22 per game. The Chicago White Sox led the way with 235 homers, with Philadelphia, Florida and Detroit also reaching or exceeding 200 homers. San Francisco mustered only 94 homers, and only 45 in 81 games at AT&T Park. In comparison, the White Sox hit 46 homers in 36 road games against their AL Central opponents.

This past season, 496 players went deep, from Ryan Howard's 48 home runs to the 86 players who hit exactly one. Twenty-eight players hit 30 or more homers, including three members of the Florida infield: Mike Jacobs, Dan Uggla and Hanley Ramirez. (Marlins third baseman Jorge Cantu just missed with 29.)

There were 11 inside-the-park homers in 2008, including two by Kansas City's Mark Teahen. There was a very clear relationship between the ballparks and the likelihood of those homers. Three each were hit at Coors Field and Kauffman Stadium, which are both very large fields; two each at Minute Maid Park and Miller Park, which both have lots of irregular fence features, and one at Dodger Stadium.

This past season, 584 pitchers allowed a home run. Brandon Backe gave up 36, one more than Aaron Harang and three more than Ted Lilly. Philadelphia starter Brett Myers surrendered 11 first-inning homers to lead the league, while Trevor Hoffman of the Padres, the all-time saves leader, coughed up eight homers in the ninth inning. Dan Wheeler and Pedro Feliciano each gave up three extra-inning home runs. Cubs pitcher Jon Lieber pitched 46.2 innings over 26 appearances against 14 teams, but somehow managed to give up eight of his ten home runs to the Reds, and the other two to Colorado.

The top four ballparks for home runs in 2008 were the "usual suspects": The White Sox's U.S. Cellular Field (a league-high 226), Cincinnati's Great American Ball Park, Rangers Ballpark in Arlington and Camden Yards in Baltimore, but the park with the fifth most homers is a surprise: Detroit's Comerica Park, where the Tigers and their opponents combined for 202 homers. Detroit third baseman Miguel Cabrera led all hitters there with 19: eight into the reachable right field seats, 10 over the reachable left field wall, and one over the all but out-of-reach center field fence, over which only 13 balls have been hit in the last three seasons.

With so many home runs being hit, there will always be some extreme splits. Some players enjoyed a great deal of home run success in their home park: Twins catcher Joe Mauer hit seven of his nine homers at the Metrodome, Nick Swisher hit 19 of his 24 at U.S. Cellular Field and Justin Upton hit 12 of his 15 homers at Arizona's Chase Field.

Other players showed much more power on the road. Casey Blake hit only one of his 11 home runs as an Indian at Progressive Field (but later regressed to a five-five home/road split with the Dodgers). Rickie Weeks hit only three of his 14 homers at Miller Park. Texas second baseman Ian Kinsler knocked 18 homers in 518 at-bats in 2008, but only four came in his home park, while fellow Rangers infielder Travis Metcalf belted five balls over the fence in Texas in only 41 at-bats.

2008 Home Run Distances

Adam Dunn hit the year's longest home run on Sept. 27, a 497-foot missile that struck the scoreboard above the center field fence at Chase Field some 67 feet above field level. He also hit the second longest of the year on July 10, a 485-foot blast that flew over the right field bleachers at Wrigley Field and the street beyond before striking the house at 3633 Sheffield Ave. Dunn led all players in 2008 with six home runs of more than 450 feet. MLB needs to find a way to get Dunn in the Home Run Derby in 2009.

Dunn had an outstanding overall year for long distance homers, claiming the 2008 Golden Sledgehammer Award with a 412.2 foot average standard distance on his 40 homers (standard distance is how far a homer would have flown if hit in 70 degree calm weather at sea level). The Sledgehammer winner of 2006, Alex Rodriguez, gave Dunn a close contest, averaging 411.1 feet on his 35 homers. Third place was a surprise, with new Angel Torii Hunter racking up an average of 410 feet on his 21 homers.

Dunn's Diamondbacks teammate Justin Upton earned an honorable mention with an astounding 425.5 foot average, but his 15 homers fell three short of the minimum 18 to be considered for the award. Upton hit 14 of his 15 homers more than 400 feet, and nine of his homers flew more than 430 feet, more than all but five other players in the league. On July 6, Upton smashed a pitch from San Diego's Josh Banks 481 feet, fourth-longest of the year.

Projecting Home Run Totals, and the Mystery of Dodger Stadium

For as long as baseball has been played on asymmetrical fields that were different in each city or borough, fans have speculated on how a player from one team might perform in another park, or as a member of another team. How many home runs might Ted Williams have hit if he played half his games in Yankee Stadium with its short right field fence? How many home runs might his contemporary Joe DiMaggio have hit if he didn't have to reach the distant left field seats in the Bronx, but instead could lift fly balls over the tall but close left field wall at Fenway Park?

We'll never know for sure, and there's probably no harm in having questions like the Williams-DiMaggio one remain unanswered, but there are certainly lots of folks who would like to know how modern-day sluggers will perform when they switch teams. Some of these interested parties are the ones who negotiate, or pay, or collect on multi-million dollar contracts to play major league baseball. Others are commentators paid for their inside knowledge of baseball and its players.

Finally, the most numerous contingent is the millions of fans who watch baseball, and perhaps manage fantasy baseball teams. Accurate projections represent extremely valuable information, and as you will see shortly, projections made with only crude park factors and the like can turn out to be very misleading.

Hit Tracker has the capability of accurately recreating the trajectory of batted balls and "projecting" them into other ballparks and weather, to see how far they would have flown and with what result. With accurate observations of the applicable hits and corresponding weather, and through the use of precise ballpark diagrams, we can make predictions to answer the same sort of "what-if" question that fans have been asking for decades: "I wonder if that would have been a homer in…"

Method

With the help of two of my outstanding volunteers, Brenton Blair and Felix Stetten, I analyzed three years (2006-08) worth of long fly balls hit by three high-profile sluggers: Jason Bay, Adam Dunn and Manny Ramirez. Every one of their fly balls that flew far enough to reasonably approach (or clear) the home run fence of any park was analyzed. There were 231 batted balls for Bay, 223 for Dunn and 248 for Ramirez over the three-year period.

The flight of each batted ball was observed, the weather conditions noted, and the data fed into Hit Tracker to determine the initial launch parameters of the hit: Speed Off Bat (SOB), Vertical Launch Angle (VLA) and Horizontal Launch Angle (HLA). Using these initial conditions, each batted ball was then projected into each of the 30 MLB ballparks (including the New Yankee Stadium and Citi Field), in the average weather conditions for each park as measured over a five-year period. Each batted ball in each park was then evaluated as either a home run or not a home run, and the results were tallied.

Examples

On May 27, 2008, Bay hit a 388-foot double to left-center field off Johnny Cueto at Great American Ball Park that landed on the warning track, just in front of the bullpen. In Dodger Stadium and Wrigley Field, in average weather for those two parks, this ball would have cleared the fence for a home run, while in the other 28 ballparks this ball would have stayed in the park. As the ball was in the air for just short of five seconds, depending on positioning some center fielders would have run it down, while others would have missed it for a double or triple.

On Aug. 30, 2008, Ramirez ripped a Dan Haren pitch for a line-drive 417-foot home run at Chase Field. In 29 ballparks, this hit would have left the yard, but in Fenway Park in Boston, it would have struck the 37-foot-high Green Monster about a foot short of the top (you decide if this would have turned out to be a single or a double).

Some of the analyzed balls didn't turn out to be homers in any park, and lots of balls ended up clearing the fence in all 30. All the outcomes were combined into the following table, showing how each hitter would do if he were to play 162 games in each park. A 3-2-1 scheme was used to weight the data for seasons 2008-2007-2006.

The top five home run parks for these three sluggers would be...

2009 HR per 162 Games

Park	Bay	Dunn	Ramirez
Dodger Stadium	46.7	57.7	52.8
Great American Ball Park	43.9	53.4	53.3
Citizens Bank Park	40.9	48.1	49.3
U.S. Cellular Field	37.2	51.0	47.4
New Yankee Stadium	37.0	46.5	52.1

Of all 30 MLB parks, Dodger Stadium ranked No. 1 overall. That popping sound you just heard was probably your brain exploding (sorry about that).

Dodger Stadium? The same Dodger Stadium that saw a major-league-low 120 homers in 2008? The same Dodger Stadium that had a 0.857 park factor (source: ESPN) for home runs, 24th in the league in 2008? These sluggers will hit more homers at Dodger Stadium than in Citizens Bank Park, or U.S. Cellular Field?

You must be thinking either (a) this analysis isn't worth the zeroes and ones its made of, or (b) we're about to learn something about ballparks and home runs that box score counting stats could never, ever tell us. (Hint: The answer is (b).)

Dodger Stadium: A Launching Pad in Waiting

The explanation for why Dodger Stadium is the premier home for long balls involves the layout of the field and the characteristic spread of home runs by major league hitters, particularly sluggers (who were in short supply in Chavez Ravine before Aug. 1). We'll start by looking at the hitters.

In 2008, the direction of home runs for all major league players broke down as follows (each field representing 30 degrees of the total 90 degrees of fair territory):

• Left field: 45.8 percent

• Center field: 20.4 percent

• Right field: 33.8 percent

However, this distribution of home run directions is not uniform across all home run hitters. It turns out that hitters who hit more home runs (the "sluggers") hit a larger proportion of their home runs to center field than do the "non-sluggers".

# HR by Hitter	% Hit to CF
1-10	14.9%
11-20	17.8%
21-30	23.9%
31-40	25.4%
40+	31.3%

The reason for this trend is fairly straightforward: For the sluggers, the center field fence is reachable with less-than perfect contact, and less than perfect aim. Non-sluggers must square up the ball better, and hit the ball at closer to the optimal launch angle, to reach the center field fence with their lesser maximum launch power, so a smaller proportion of their fly balls to center end up clearing the fence.

Another factor may be intentional behavior on the part of the hitter: Non-sluggers may shy away from hitting fly balls to center field, knowing that fly balls to left or right field stand a better chance of avoiding the fielders' gloves, while the sluggers confidently hit the ball to all fields, knowing they have the power to hit the ball out in any direction. There is no way to measure how important this factor is, but it certainly seems plausible.

If sluggers hit a lot of homers to center field, while non-sluggers do not, it follows that a ballpark with a short center field fence would further amplify this effect; this is because the sluggers also hit more "near-misses" (i.e., warning track flies) to center field than do the non-sluggers, and these near-misses are the ones that would make it out over a more shallow fence.

Dodger Stadium is a perfect example of a park with a shallow center field fence. In the diagram on the next pages, the layout of Dodger Stadium is shown, along with a gray dotted line approximating the league average fence location in MLB. (Fence height is a minor factor: Dodger Stadium's fence is eight feet high, while the league average fence is between 10 and 11 feet high, so this is one more factor that makes Dodger Stadium an even better home run environment.)

Dodger Stadium curves back sharply from the poles to create a segment of fence on each side of the field that is deeper than average, then the fence curves outward towards center field. This graceful curved section of the fence gradually gets deeper, but not as quickly as the average MLB fence, which means that relative to average, it

Dodger Stadium

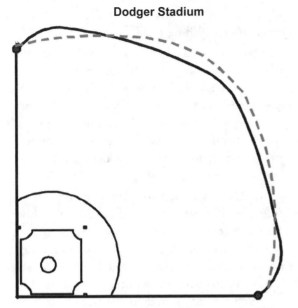

gets easier to hit homers as the hitter aims towards center field. In fact, Dodger Stadium has the easiest center field fence overall in the league for home runs.

The following chart shows the differences between Dodger Stadium and the league average even more clearly. Positive values indicate sections where the fence is farther from home than average, and negative values indicate sections that are closer than average.

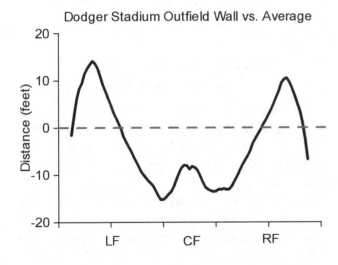

Dodger Stadium Outfield Wall vs. Average

Clearly sluggers are in a very favorable environment when they swing for the shallow center field fences at Dodger Stadium. However, in the opposite type of stadium, it is the non-sluggers who enjoy the benefits of the park layout.

The opposite type of stadium layout to Dodger Stadium is typified by Houston's Minute Maid Park. Minute Maid Park has a distant center field fence, but claustrophobically close left field and right field seats.

In this sort of park, non-sluggers gain a relative advantage, because although both sluggers and non-sluggers benefit from the short corners, only the sluggers are penalized by the extra-deep center field (the non-sluggers are a non-factor in that direction already). In such a park, you tend to see results like these from 2008, where a mid-level home run talent like Ty Wigginton managed to hit 15 homers at Minute Maid, rivaling a true slugger like Lance Berkman, who hit 16 homers there, even though Berkman hit his homers an average of 10 feet farther in 2008 than did Wigginton.

Beyond Ballparks: Bay, Dunn and Ramirez on Each MLB Team

Of course, even Cal Ripken Jr. played only 81 games per year in his home park (except in 1996, when he snuck an extra one in), so to project actual home run totals, we need to account for playing time and for each team's schedule. Playing time was weighted on a simple 3-2-1 basis without any additional regression or aging curves applied; the values used for games played for Bay, Dunn and Ramirez were 152, 156 and 143 games, respectively. The actual 2009 schedule was used: The unbalanced nature of the schedule makes a player's inter-division rival ballparks considerably more important than the rest of the league.

Here are the projections for how many home runs each player would hit as a member of the listed team (remember, based on the 3-2-1 games played projection above, and not including any factor for aging).

2009 Projected Homers

Team	Bay	Dunn	Ramirez
ARI	27.9	38.5	33.1
ATL	29.7	42.5	34.3
BAL	32.6	45.1	37.4
BOS	29.1	40.4	32.3
CHC	31.8	42.1	34.1
CIN	36.0	47.1	41.2
CLE	31.6	44.2	39.1
COL	31.3	43.2	36.2
CWS	32.3	45.3	38.9
DET	26.0	37.8	33.9
FLA	29.0	40.4	33.8
HOU	30.9	41.4	36.5
KC	25.4	38.2	31.0
LAA	29.2	42.1	33.6
LAD	37.5	49.3	41.1
MIL	33.5	44.6	39.0
MIN	31.8	43.7	38.7

2009 Projected Homers

Team	Bay	Dunn	Ramirez
NYM	24.9	35.9	29.3
NYY	32.0	43.1	40.3
OAK	28.2	41.4	32.8
PHI	34.2	44.1	39.1
PIT	29.9	43.2	35.4
SD	32.3	45.3	37.9
SEA	29.6	42.8	39.0
SF	34.3	45.0	36.0
STL	32.1	45.6	37.4
TB	31.7	41.4	38.1
TEX	31.3	44.6	39.9
TOR	28.1	40.5	34.7
WAS	31.4	44.4	35.7
Average	**30.9**	**42.8**	**36.3**

Looking at the home run table by team, the projection suggests that if Ramirez plays for the Dodgers in 2009, he will hit 41 home runs (and a closer look inside the data indicates 23 of these would come at home). However, as powerful as Ramirez would look in 2009 in his No. 99 L.A. uniform, Dunn would look even better in Dodger blue. Analysis of Dunn's long fly balls from the past three years suggests that in 2009 he would hit 49 homers as a Dodger, including 28 at home. Ramirez' "replacement" in Boston, Jason Bay, also would thrive in LA, where he projects to hit 38 homers as a Dodger in 2009, with 22 of those coming at home.

Other Notable Results

While some of the ballpark projection results are not surprising (Bay, Dunn and Ramirez will hit lots of homers in Cincinnati? Really?), here are a few more results from the team table that defy the standard park-factor-based analysis, highlighting the importance of individual analysis of hitters and their batted balls:

- Manny in Seattle: Safeco Field ranked as the 7th best park for Ramirez to hit homers, despite its 2008 home run park factor of 0.900, 20th in the league.

- Bay in San Francisco: AT&T Park was No. 4 for Bay, despite that park's not being known as a home run park for anyone not named Barry Bonds.

- Dunn in St. Louis: Busch Stadium is Dunn's fifth-ranked park, while for both Bay and Ramirez it ranks 13th.

Bay is under contract with the Red Sox for 2009 and is not likely to change teams until 2010. His Boston projection for 2009 is 29 home runs, with 14 coming at Fenway Park and 15 on the road. Among the 30 teams,

Bay's Boston projection ranks 23rd, while his Pittsburgh projection ranked 19th best.

Bay's home run totals have been less than he might have achieved in a more homer-friendly park. PNC Park has a deep left-center field fence, while Fenway Park has the closer but 37-foot high Green Monster in left field. Next year Bay will dent the Monster with several balls that would have flown out of another park, continuing in the tradition of Red Sox left-fielders Jim Rice and Ramirez before him.

More on Dunn's remarkable 2008 season: Despite recording his fifth straight season of 40-plus home runs, Dunn was extremely unlucky with respect to home runs in 2008. Dunn hit 16 balls more than 400 feet that were not home runs! In contrast, Red Sox second baseman Dustin Pedroia hit a total of 17 homers in 2008, none of which carried more than 394 feet.

Dunn's tough luck peaked during the final weekend of the 2008 season, when as a Diamondback, he hit two fly balls totaling 862 feet that both stayed in the park. Each struck Chase Field's 25-foot-high center field fence within two feet of the top, at a distance of roughly 410 feet from home plate.

However, Dunn's luck was not entirely bad. Earlier that same weekend, Dunn hit his 497-foot homer, the year's longest, which was described earlier. So at least he got one trip around the bases after hitting three balls an average of 453 feet each...

Citi Field: Abandon Hope All Ye Sluggers Who Enter

Citi Field, the new ballpark for the New York Mets, is poised to become MLB's new Grand Canyon. Citi Field is a vast, cool weather, sea-level stadium, and those factors will have a hugely negative impact on home runs.

Comparing the fence distances at Citi Field to the league average, the difference between the Mets' new park and Dodger Stadium is remarkable. While Dodger Stadium offers an invitingly short center field fence, offset by deep corners, in Citi Field, there is only a short fence segment in front of section 103 in the right field corner that is shorter than league average, while the rest of the park is deeper, and often much deeper than average.

Bay, Dunn and Ramirez collectively project to hit 39 percent fewer homers than average at Citi Field. Johan Santana and the rest of the Mets pitching staff will like the new park, but the Mets' front office should sign their power hitters now, before the word gets out. In spring 2009, baseball fans are going to get a live demon-

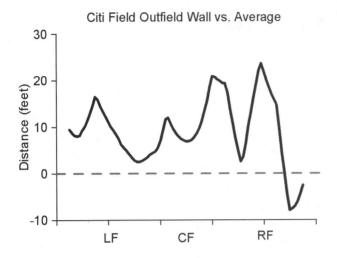

Citi Field Outfield Wall vs. Average

stration of what happens when a team sets out to design a pitcher's park, and overdoes it (although this isn't the first time this has happened; it wasn't that long ago that Comerica Park opened in Detroit).

On the other hand, the Phillies sure will be shocked when they make their first trip to Queens in 2009…

Acknowledgments

I'd like to extend my most sincere appreciation to my outstanding site volunteers Brenton Blair, Brian O'Malley, Norm Chouinard and Felix Stetten for their contributions this year. They are intelligent, meticulous and insightful baseball researchers, and I am fortunate to have had their help this season.

Thanks to the legion of baseball fans who contacted me throughout the year with questions, suggestions and comments, and to the many media representatives who have helped extend the reach of Hit Tracker over the past year, particularly Dave Studenmund of The Hardball Times, and Gordon Edes with Yahoo.

Thanks also to Sean Forman for providing us all with Baseball Reference, the sine qua non of any in-depth baseball research project.

Please direct questions or comments to grybar@ hittrackeronline.com. I am always delighted to hear from you.

163

The Cliff Lee Turnaround

by Mike Fast

Cliff Lee entered the 2008 season with a career ERA of 4.64. In spring training, he competed with Aaron Laffey and Jeremy Sowers for the fifth spot in the Cleveland Indians' starting rotation after a difficult 2007 season which included a strained abdominal muscle, a five-week demotion to the minor leagues, and a move to the bullpen upon his return in September.

If you paid attention to major league baseball in 2008, you probably know that Lee posted an outstanding season, greatly exceeding expectations with a 2.54 ERA in 223.1 innings. He also posted a stellar 22-3 won-loss record that may garner him the American League Cy Young Award. In addition to those gaudy numbers, Lee struck out 170 opposing batters, while walking only 34 and allowing 214 hits, of which only 12 were home runs.

How did he accomplish all this?

The simplest answers are pitching at its most basic: He added a new pitch, got his offerings to go where he wanted them to go, and induced a lot more ground balls. But we want to know much more than that ...

Pitch Repertoire

First, let's learn a little about his pitches. To do that, we turn to the PITCHf/x data set. PITCHf/x is a system of cameras and software that tracks every pitch thrown in the major leagues and records detailed information about its trajectory, including speed, movement and location. This system was deployed in most major league ballparks throughout the 2007 season, recording detailed data on about a third of all the pitches thrown in that season. In 2008, the PITCHf/x system was installed in all 30 parks and recorded data on almost every pitch thrown in major league games.

In 2007, Lee mainly relied on a four-seam fastball, supplemented by a change-up, curveball, cut fastball and occasional slider. The detailed pitch data from the 2007 PITCHf/x camera system is somewhat limited for Lee. The system tracked only 491 of his total 1,647 pitches for the season, but we have enough data to get a basic read on his repertoire.

We can identify his pitches by looking at their movement and speed. The graphs below show the deflection of a pitch from its original straight-line path due to

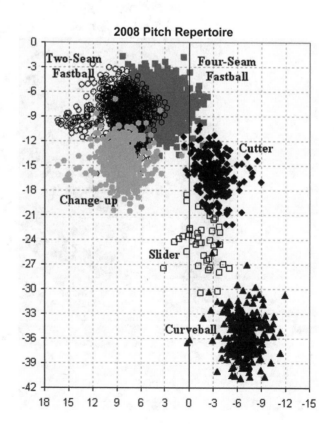

gravity and the spin put on the ball by the pitcher. For example, Lee's typical curveball drops about three feet below where the ball was headed out of his hand and moves about six to nine inches in on a right-handed hitter.

As you can see in the graphs, Cliff Lee added a two-seam fastball in 2008, and in fact, it became his main pitch to right-handed hitters.

A brief detour here to discuss fastball types: A four-seam fastball is the typical hard fastball, gripped with the index finger and middle finger across both seams. In physics terms, when the pitch is thrown, the spin of the ball creates an aerodynamic force that pushes the ball at a right angle to the direction the ball is traveling and to the axis around which the ball is spinning. In other words, the backspin imparted to the ball when the pitch is thrown causes the four-seamer to "hop," or fall less than it normally would due to gravity alone.

Since most pitchers don't throw right over the top but instead drop their arm down a little, not only does the fastball hop due to the spin force pushing the ball up, but it also tails because some of the spin force is now acting toward the side. In the case of a left-handed pitcher like Lee, the fastball tails away from a right-handed hitter, roughly four inches on average, as we can see from the preceding charts.

A popular variation on the four-seam fastball is a two-seamer. It usually is gripped with the index finger and middle finger each lying along a seam. When the two-seam fastball is released, the pitcher applies uneven pressure with his fingers to impart extra sidespin to the ball. This spin force to the side causes the pitch to hop less and tail more. Lee's two-seamer drops about four inches more than his four-seamer and also tails away about four inches more. Many pitchers have to trade a mile per hour or two of speed for the extra sidespin on the two-seamer, but a few pitchers like Lee are able to throw both fastballs at about the same speed.

The cut fastball can be a variation on either a fastball or a slider, depending on the pitcher. There are many ways to throw a cutter and many variations of the pitch, but a typical cutter is gripped similar to a two-seam or four-seam fastball but with the ball held off-center in the pitcher's hand. When the ball is released, the pitcher gives it extra sidespin by applying pressure with the middle finger. The sidespin is in the opposite direction from the sidespin on the two-seamer, so that the spin force causes the pitch to "cut" in toward a right-handed hitter.

In Lee's case, his cut fastball moves about three inches to the right. If the cutter is disguised well, the batter won't be able to detect the difference in spin between the cutter and the regular fastball and will be surprised by the break in the opposite direction after it is too late to adjust his swing. The cut fastball usually is thrown a few miles per hour slower than the four-seam fastball and a few mph faster than the slider.

(If you are interested in how the trajectories of Lee's pitches look, check the appendix at the end of this article. I've put several extra graphs there.)

Now that we've seen how Lee's pitches moved, let's look at how he used them.

2007 Pitch Repertoire

Type	To Lefties	To Righties	Total pitches	Avg. speed (mph)
Four-seamer	73%	72%	355	89.6
Change-up	2%	21%	81	82.6
Curveball	10%	3%	24	75.3
Cutter	7%	4%	22	85.5
Slider	8%	0%	9	78.8

In 2007, a 90 mph four-seam fastball was Lee's go-to pitch against both left-handed and right-handed hitters. Against right handers his secondary pitch was a change-up, and against left handers, he used a mix of curveball, cut fastball and slider.

2008 Pitch Repertoire

Type	To Lefties	To Righties	Total pitches	Avg. speed
Two-seamer	21%	45%	1237	90.7
Four-seamer	53%	23%	1052	90.5
Change-up	0%	18%	413	82.6
Curveball	11%	8%	290	74.5
Cutter	11%	5%	224	85.1
Slider	4%	0%	40	77.4

Let's take one more cut at this data. Let's directly compare Lee's pitching repertoire in 2007 and 2008, broken out by the handedness of the batter. And let's add in the difference in the speed of Lee's pitches between the two years. The table is on the following page.

Change in Pitch Mix from 2007 to 2008

Type	To Lefties	To Righties	Avg. speed
Two-seamer	+21%	+45%	---
Four-seamer	-20%	-49%	+0.9
Change-up	-2%	-3%	0
Curveball	+1%	+5%	-0.8
Cutter	+4%	+1%	-0.4
Slider	-4%	0%	-1.4

Results for Each Type of Pitch

Pitch Type	# of Pitches		Runs/pitch		Total run value	
	LHB	RHB	LHB	RHB	LHB	RHB
Two-seamer	209	1028	+.018	-.017	+3.7	-17.9
Four-seamer	518	534	-.019	-.019	-10.1	-10.0
Change-up	3	410	-.099	-.007	-0.3	-3.0
Curveball	112	178	+.027	-.038	+3.0	-6.8
Cutter	104	120	-.016	+.000	-1.6	+0.1
Slider	37	3	-.096	+.034	-3.5	+0.1
Total	983	2273	-.009	-.016	-8.8	-37.4

What a difference a year makes! In 2008, Lee added about 1 mph to his fastball, and he actually threw his two-seamer as hard or harder than his four-seam fastball. The addition of the two-seam fastball made a huge difference in his pitching approach, as we'll see in more detail later, but he also made some minor adjustments to his mix of off-speed pitches, using the curve more often against right handers, for example.

How does the ball-strike count affect which pitch Lee throws? Like most pitchers, when he falls behind in the count, he's very likely to go with a fastball. The type of fastball depends mainly on the handedness of the hitter, but his use of the four-seamer to right handers generally increases as he gets more strikes. The curveball and cutter are used early in the count, with no or one balls and one or two strikes on the hitter, the cutter more often on the one-strike counts and the curve more often on the two-strike counts. Lee also likes to throw the change-up to right-handed hitters early in the count, similar to the curve and cutter, except that he will also throw it with two balls or with no strikes.

Results by Pitch Type

Now that we know what pitches Lee throws and when, what kind of results does he get? We can calculate a run value for each pitch Lee threw in 2008 by applying linear weights batting runs to value the results of each plate appearance and adjusting for the differing run values of each particular ball-strike count.

In other words, we not only apply a linear weight value to each outcome when a ball is struck (for an out, single, home run, etc.) but we also apply a linear weight value to each pitch that changes the count (say, from 1-1 to 2-1). We do that by referencing standard tables that show the difference in eventual outcome of all major league batters at each ball and strike count. It sounds complicated, but the results are straightforward, as you can see.

Lee's best percentage pitch to right-handed hitters in 2008 was the curveball, but he also got outstanding results from his two-seam and four-seam fastballs. His change-up was a decent pitch to right handers, and his cutter was mediocre. Left-handed hitters had a much easier time with his two-seam fastball and curveball, but had more trouble with the cutter and occasional slider.

As we look through the results, we find a few other interesting facts. For example, Lee did an outstanding job of throwing his fastball for strikes, particularly to left-handed hitters. This, of course, is reflected in his amazing total of only 34 walks allowed in 223.1 innings. And he didn't allow a home run on a breaking ball all year while throwing 330 of them. (In 2007, he allowed three home runs on approximately half as many breaking pitches.)

But let's go through each of the pitch types in more detail and see how well Lee used each pitch against left-handed and right-handed hitters in 2008. You can consult the appendix to see charts showing the strike zone location of every pitch.

Lee threw his two-seam fastballs toward the inside half of the plate against left-handed hitters and toward the outside half of the plate against right-handed hitters. He threw the pitch 69 percent of the time for strikes and had decent but not great results when the ball was put in play. Right-handed hitters hit for a .323 batting average and a .455 slugging percentage on balls in play off of Lee's two-seamer, and left-handed hitters hit .370/.481.

By comparison the American League hit .330/.518 on balls in play against all pitch types, and the numbers against the fastball are slightly better than that. (All statistics quoted in this article regarding balls in play include home runs unless noted otherwise.) You can see from the opposing batting lines one reason he used the pitch more than twice as often against righties than against lefties. On the plus side, he allowed only three home runs off two-seamers all year, even though it was his most frequent pitch.

The four-seam fastball was located opposite of the two-seamer: outer half of the plate against left handers and inner half against right handers. He did an excellent job locating the four-seamer against left handers, throwing only 23 percent of the pitches for balls and getting 29 percent called strikes. Despite the pitch always being right around the strike zone, left handers fouled off twice as many four-seamers (27 percent) as they put in play (14 percent). When the left-handed hitters did put it in play, they got pretty good results: a .360 average and .480 slugging.

Lee didn't fare as well getting strikes against right handers, throwing the four-seamer for a ball 32 percent of the time, although that still displayed above-average control. Right-handed hitters put the four-seamer in play at a more typical frequency, 21 percent of the time, but they got fairly poor results: a .289 average and .412 slugging.

Lee hardly used the change-up to left-handed hitters. Against right-handed hitters, once again, he showed great control with the change, targeting the outer half of the plate and throwing 70 percent strikes. A high percentage of change-ups were put in play against Lee (31 percent), but that ended up as a positive for the pitcher, since the hitters managed to hit only .291/.433.

The typical trajectories of a change-up and a two-seam fastball from Lee look similar, except that the change-up drops a few inches more and arrives about 0.04 seconds later. Hitters swinging early and over the pitch usually were able to make contact with the baseball, but they often swung early and over the top of the pitch, grounding weakly to the left side of the infield. On the rare occasions they managed to get the change-up in the air, it was Lee's one Achilles heel. He allowed five home runs on change-ups, four of them on pitches that were right over the heart of the plate.

Lee spotted his curveball over the middle of the plate, as most pitchers do, to both left handers and right handers. It was the only pitch on which he did not display

better than league-average control. He had good luck getting right-handed hitters to chase the pitch down, but left-handed hitters laid off that pitch and let it go for a ball. The curve was a groundball machine; 42 of 66 curves put in play were hit on the ground. Righties had no success with the curve no matter where it was located, hitting .243/.297 on balls in play. Lefties had some success when Lee left the curve up over the plate, hitting .310/.517 on balls in play.

Lee tended to spot his cut fastball similarly to his four-seam fastball, outside to left handers and inside to right handers. He threw the pitch for strikes 71 percent of the time, which, as with his other pitches, is outstanding. However, when the ball was put in play, he had better results against the left-handed hitters (.269/.308) than he did against the right-handed hitters (.406/.500). This should come as no surprise when you realize that the cutting action of the pitch takes the ball away off the plate to left handers but tends to bring it back toward the middle of the plate against right handers.

Finally, the slider was his least-used pitch, mostly thrown against left-handed hitters down and away. He allowed only two infield singles on 14 sliders put in play.

Balls in Play

Now that we've looked closely at Lee's pitches, one other aspect of his game that made a dramatic change from 2007 to 2008 deserves some scrutiny.

Prior to 2008, his career groundball to flyball ratio was 0.74, and in no year had it ever been higher than 0.84. In 2008, his groundball to flyball ratio took a big jump to 1.30. What caused this change? Let's take a look at the type of balls put in play in 2008 broken out by pitch type.

LHB	Fly	Grnd	Line	Pop	Bunt	Total
Two-seamer	13	30	5	5	1	53
Four-seamer	20	32	14	8	1	74
Change-up	0	1	0	0	0	1
Curveball	4	17	7	1	0	29
Cutter	8	12	4	1	1	25
Slider	0	10	2	2	0	14
Unknown	0	2	0	0	0	2
Total	45	104	32	17	3	198

RHB	Fly	Grnd	Line	Pop	Bunt	Total
Two-seamer	60	61	35	9	2	165
Four-seamer	36	37	23	15	3	111
Change-up	36	65	16	9	1	126
Curveball	7	25	3	2	0	37
Cutter	2	18	9	3	0	32
Slider	0	0	0	0	0	0
Unknown	1	4	1	1	0	7
Total	142	210	87	39	6	478

We already observed that Lee added a two-seam fastball for 2008 and used it frequently. Were the extra sinking and tailing action on the two-seamer responsible for the increase in ground balls? Maybe to some degree, but it actually appears that the change-up, curveball, cutter and slider were responsible for more grounders than the two-seam fastball.

Lee threw his two-seamer away from right-handed hitters, so unsurprisingly, they tended to hit it to the opposite field, both in the air and on the ground. On the one hand, he may have gotten a bit lucky by allowing only two home runs on 60 outfield flies. On the other hand, opposite-field fly balls don't go out of the park at nearly the same rate as fly balls that are pulled, and right handers managed to pull only two two-seamers in the air to the outfield off of Lee.

He did get quite a few ground balls with the two-seamer against left-handed hitters, but a lot of them found their way through the infield. We can't tell from this data whether they were harder-hit ground balls or whether Lee just got a little unlucky.

Lee induced a fair amount of ground balls using the four-seam fastball, but there aren't any particular outstanding or unusual patterns in the data for that pitch. Left handers hit the outside four-seamer the opposite way, and right handers are able to pull the four-seamer that they see on the inside part of the plate.

However, if we look at the ball-in-play distribution against the change-up and curveball to right-handed hitters, we do see some interesting patterns. One of them we discussed previously. Those outside change-ups to right-handed hitters generated a lot of ground balls to the left side of the infield that were vacuumed up by his fielders. They also got pulled in the air fairly often and were the primary home-run pitch off Lee in 2008.

As also mentioned previously, the curveball to right-handed hitters generated a lot of weak ground balls, most of them toward the left side of the infield, and very few fly balls. Nobody could hit Lee's curveball with authority in 2008. Only two of 25 ground balls hit by right-handed hitters off the curveball made it through to the outfield.

I don't really have a good answer for why Lee became a groundball machine in 2008. The introduction of the two-seam fastball made some difference, but it was less of a factor than the new groundball tendencies on his off-speed stuff. There are some hints in the data that better location on his off-speed stuff may have played a role, but I don't feel confident in claiming that as the cause.

Improved Command

Now that we've taken a look at Lee's repertoire, how he located his pitches, and what types of balls were put in play against him, let's turn to another subject frequently offered as a reason for his improvement from 2007 to 2008—his command.

One of the few shortcomings of the PITCHf/x data is the inability to directly measure command, which I am using to mean the ability of the pitcher to put the pitch where he wants it. However, with a little extra work, I believe we can come close, at least qualitatively if not quantitatively, to assessing a pitcher's command of his pitches.

We begin by noting that you can infer a pitcher's arm angle from the strike zone location data when it is accurately classified by pitch type and separated by handedness of the batter. I'm not the first person to observe this fact. Harry Pavlidis of Cubsfx.com, and perhaps others, have noted that arm angle can be observed in the PITCHf/x data.

For example, look at Lee's curveball and two-seam fastball location to right-handed hitters on the next page. His arm angle is fairly obvious if you realize what you're seeing—Cliff Lee is a lefthander, and his arm path is going to determine where the ball can possibly end up. If you imagine his arm sweeping across the zone as he releases the pitch, you get a swath of final pitch locations much like that in the following curveball graph. The graph for the four-seam fastball displays a similar effect, but not quite as obvious. Between the two graphs, we can estimate that Lee's arm angle is somewhere between 23 to 28 degrees to the left of vertical. If you go to the appendix and look at the strike zone location charts for the other pitch types, you'll see a

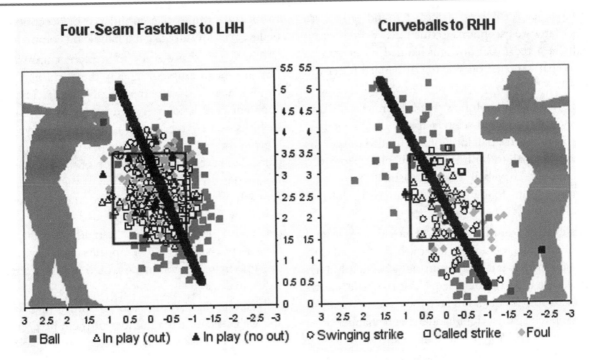

Four-Seam Fastballs to LHH   **Curveballs to RHH**

■ Ball   △ In play (out)   ▲ In play (no out)   ◇ Swinging strike   □ Called strike   ◆ Foul

similar pattern for most of them, if slightly more subtle in some cases.

You can see the effect of command in two dimensions. He has good command of his four-seamer in the dimension along the path of his arm; thus he is able to pound the strike zone with that pitch. On the other hand, his command of the curveball in that dimension is not as good. He releases some curves too early and others too late, resulting in pitches that stay too high or bounce in the dirt. In the side-to-side dimension, his command of the curveball is as good or better than his command of the four-seamer.

When measuring the effect of command, it's important to know where the pitcher was aiming. A good way to measure this is from the catcher's target for each pitch. Unfortunately, this information isn't yet captured by PITCHf/x, so we must consult game video if we want to record the location of the catcher's glove.

Doing that is complicated by several facts, however. The television camera angle generally is slightly offset from straight-up center field, and it may shift perspective between left-handed and right-handed batters. In addition, the camera lens has significant spherical distortion. Moreover, the catcher catches the ball a few feet behind home plate, and some pitches may drop more than half a foot from where they crossed the plate to the catcher's glove.

I watched Lee and another pitcher in several games and discovered some facts that simplify the process, at least for those two pitchers. (Someone with more experience with baseball may inform me that these facts are not generally applicable, but I believe they apply to Lee, at the minimum.) First, the catchers mainly moved their target left and right. Rarely did the catcher move the target vertically; typically, it was set near the bottom of the strike zone. Second, the catchers had roughly three distinct target positions, and keying off the movement of the catcher's feet was sufficient to indicate which position the catcher was in.

For curveballs, the catcher took a wide stance with his feet and set the target in the middle of the zone left and right. For all other pitch types (fastballs, change-ups, sliders, cutters), the catcher shifted one leg toward the direction the pitch was supposed to go and positioned the target near the low-outside corner or low-inside corner of the strike zone. On a 3-0 count, the catcher might set up down the middle for the fastball, and he might shade that way on 3-1, but otherwise all four of the catchers I watched seemed to have the same three basic target positions.

During this process, I noticed something that was already hinted at in the strike zone location charts we saw earlier. Lee threw each pitch type to only one location, almost without fail. Certainly, he made some small variations in where he aimed the ball, and his execution sometimes matched the plan better than other times, but the catcher's target was always near the same place for a given pitch type—in the middle for the curveball, to Lee's right for the four-seamer, the cutter and the slider, and to Lee's left for the two-seamer and the change-up.

In 201 pitches across two games, I found only three pitches that were exceptions to this rule: two two-seam fastballs targeted inside to right-handed hitters, and a 0-2 curveball targeted outside to left-handed hitter Jim Thome.

In 2007, Lee did not follow this pattern with his fastball. He didn't use a two-seam fastball with any regularity, so to vary his fastball location; he needed to spot his four-seam fastball to both sides of the plate. However, his change-up, curveball and cut fastball target locations appeared to follow the same pattern in 2007 as they did in 2008.

This change from 2007 to 2008 could have helped Lee in at least two ways. First, he now had a fastball with tailing action that ran away from right-handed hitters. He could use it on the outside part of the plate, allowing him to restrict his straighter four-seam fastball to an inside pitch against right handers. If he happened to miss and get a little too much of the plate on an outside fastball, the break on the two-seamer helped moved the ball out of the hitter's sweet spot more than on the four-seamer that he had to rely on in 2007. Second, always throwing a given pitch to the same area could have helped him gain consistency, and with the addition of the two-seamer he could now do this without ceding part of the plate to the hitter.

The Indians' pitching coach, Carl Willis, was quoted by Anthony Castrovince in a September article on MLB.com as saying about Lee, "It all comes off the same release point. He's repeating his delivery so well that it's basically just a turn of the grip. You do the same thing 100 times, and there it is. The fastball command is the beginning."

Perhaps throwing the same pitch to the same area has allowed Lee to improve the consistency of his delivery and command of his pitches. I don't know any way

to measure things like confidence or deception, but I believe we can start to get a handle on command.

There are many ways to explore command, and I'm just beginning to scratch the surface. One way to look at it is on a game-by-game basis. There is an apparent correlation between Lee's fastball command as measured by the spread of pitches thrown toward a given target location and his performance in a given game. However, my investigation of this avenue to date has involved video confirmation of the catcher's target for each pitch. If the catcher target tracking were automated by Sportvision and included in the PITCHf/x data or if a pitcher is unusually rigid in his target location by pitch type, as Lee appears to be, exploration of game-by-game command would not require tedious video analysis.

It's clear that Lee did a lot of things right in 2008, and we've examined a number of them here. It's obvious that Lee is a much different and much better pitcher than he was in 2007, having added an effective two-seam fastball, greatly improved his command, and significantly increased his ground ball rate.

I hope this analysis has piqued your interest in the possibilities for understanding pitchers using the PITCHf/x data, as it has mine. I feel as if the analysis I have presented only sets the stage for more serious analysis of Lee. How does he match up against certain hitters or types of hitters? When he misses his spot, why does he miss? The possibilities for investigating the pitcher-hitter matchup are endless.

I also believe the area of command is ripe for investigation through the lens of PITCHf/x, aided by careful pitch classification. There is a link here to a better understanding of a pitcher's mechanics and the art of pitching that has been unexplored before now. PITCHf/x can open that door.

The Cliff Lee Appendix

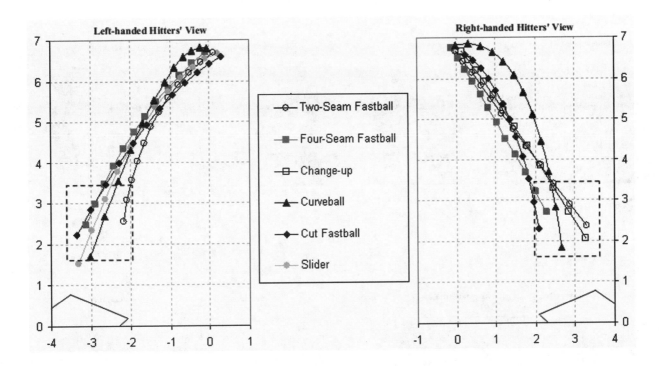

Outcomes by Type of Pitch, Broken out by Batter Type

LHB	#Pitches	Ball	Foul	CStrk	SwStrk	InPlay	Avg	BABIP	SLG	HR
Two-seam	209	29%	26%	15%	4%	26%	.370	.358	.481	1.9%
Four-seam	518	23%	27%	29%	8%	14%	.360	.351	.480	1.3%
Change-up	3	0%	33%	33%	0%	33%	.000	.000	.000	0.0%
Curveball	112	44%	18%	5%	7%	26%	.310	.310	.517	0.0%
Cutter	104	30%	17%	19%	9%	25%	.269	.269	.308	0.0%
Slider	37	35%	5%	8%	14%	38%	.143	.143	.143	0.0%
Total	983	27%	24%	21%	7%	20%	.327	.320	.437	1.0%

RHB	#Pitches	Ball	Foul	CStrk	SwStrk	InPlay	Avg	BABIP	SLG	HR
Two-seam	1028	32%	23%	22%	8%	16%	.323	.315	.455	1.2%
Four-seam	534	32%	22%	18%	7%	21%	.289	.270	.412	2.6%
Changeup	410	30%	14%	17%	9%	31%	.291	.262	.433	3.9%
Curveball	178	38%	18%	10%	13%	21%	.243	.243	.297	0.0%
Cutter	120	29%	19%	12%	13%	27%	.406	.406	.500	0.0%
Slider	3	100%	0%	0%	0%	0%				
Total	2273	32%	20%	19%	8%	21%	.306	.291	.430	2.1%

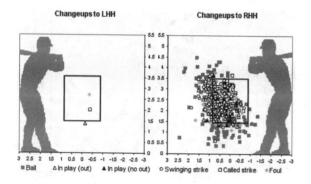

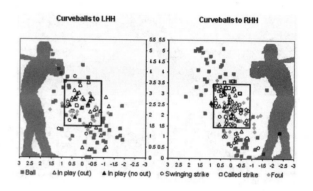

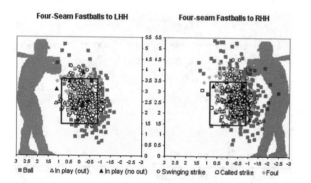

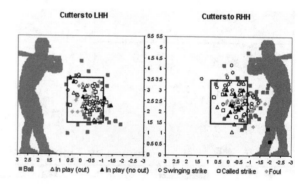

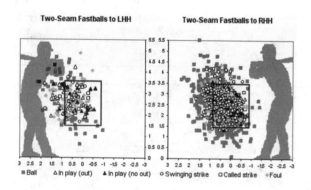

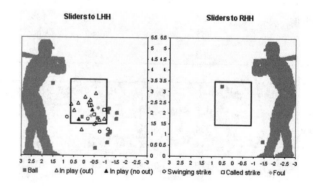

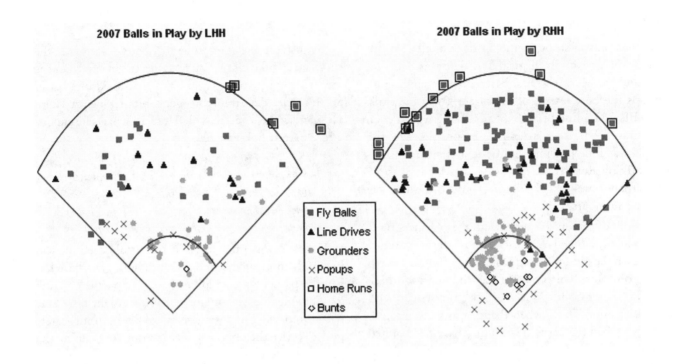

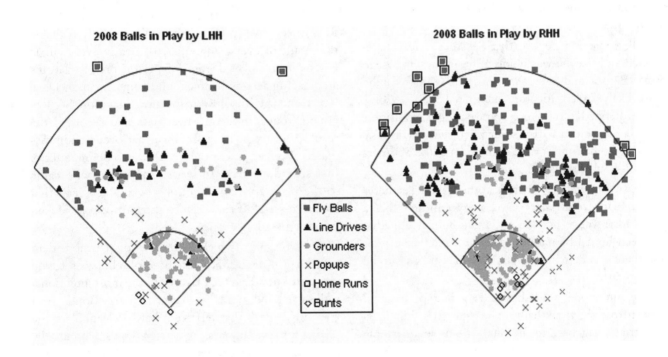

The Sweet Taste of Revenge

by John Walsh

Richie Sexson stood in the on-deck circle and spit on the ground in disgust. The date was Sept. 19, 2005 and the Mariners' first baseman was winding up perhaps the best season of his career: 39 home runs, 121 RBIs and a line of .263/.369/.541. He would even get a few MVP votes after the season. So, why the $!&@$ was Blue Jays pitcher Miguel Batista intentionally walking Raul Ibanez? To get to Richie Sexson? Sure, Ibanez was a good hitter, but he didn't have Sexson's numbers.

The top of the ninth started with the Mariners trailing 4-3 and the Blue Jays' closer, future Mariner Miguel Batista, on the mound. Greg Dobbs led off with a sharp single to center. Ichiro Suzuki then bunted for a base hit, and Ramon Santiago moved both runners up with a sacrifice bunt. That's when Ibanez was walked intentionally to load the bases. Sexson may have felt insulted by the walk to Ibanez, but he probably shouldn't have. The Blue Jays were clearly going for the platoon advantage and in a one-run game, Ibanez the base runner meant little.

Still, you gotta believe that Sexson *did* feel disrespected and that he was going to be trying his best to prove Batista and Jays manager John Gibbons (who most likely called for the intentional walk) wrong. Sexson stepped into the box and went right to business taking a huge cut at Batista's first pitch. The result was a towering home run, a grand slam, that put the Mariners ahead 7-4, which was the game's final score.

Ah, sweet revenge. There is nothing like it, is there? Research in evolutionary psychology indicates that a desire for revenge may be an innate human trait that has been honed by natural selection. Whether it is or not, there's no denying that a hit like Sexson's has to be deeply gratifying.

The intentional walk has been a part of baseball almost from the time that umpires started calling balls and strikes, way back in the 1860s. Many smart people have tried to determine when it makes sense to issue a freebie and when it doesn't. Sabermetrician Mitchel Lichtman wrote up his detailed analysis on the Hardball Times website this past summer. As far as I know, however, nobody ever has studied the psychology of the batter who comes to the plate after an intentional walk.

It must not feel good to be that batter—after all, the message is quite clear: You're easier to get out than the guy batting in front of you. Will that make the batter all the more determined to get a hit? Ex-player Keith Hernandez believes it will. Here is what Hernandez wrote in his book *Pure Baseball*:

> I've had a beef with the intentional walk for years. Why not opt instead for the quasi-intentional walk that's not such an obvious insult to the next batter? I've seen it happen too many times. The next batter accepts the challenge and makes the pitcher pay.

Hernandez is implying that the insulted batter will be highly motivated, more than usual, to get a base hit. But the psychology could be just the opposite, couldn't it? The angry batter might tense up, might not "stay within himself," might chase a bad pitch, in his eagerness to prove the opposing team wrong for walking the previous batter.

Well, this is something we can study with the data available at Retrosheet.org. The good folks at Retrosheet have compiled and made publicly available the result of every single play of nearly every single baseball game played from 1954 to the present day. It's an amazing accomplishment and I tip my cap to Dave Smith and the whole Retrosheet organization. So, I've gone through the Retrosheet data and recorded the result of every plate appearance that occurred immediately after an intentional walk. Let's define a term: Just so I don't have to write "the batter who came to the plate after an intentional walk," let's call that batter "dissed." If they walked the guy in front of you, you got dissed.

Can you guess which batter was dissed more than any other in the last 50 years or so? Well, let's see, you probably know that the player with the most intentional walks ever, and by a large margin, is Barry Bonds. And you might recall that Jeff Kent batted cleanup for the Giants for several years, right after Bonds, who usually batted third. Indeed, Jeff Kent has been dissed 175 times in his career, more than 50 times more often than runner-up Ron Santo (123 times). Now you can see already that getting dissed doesn't mean you aren't a good, or even great, player. Many believe Santo belongs in the Hall of Fame and Kent may be headed there himself.

Here is the top 10 list of most-dissed batters of all time ("all time" henceforth means from the mid-'50s through 2007):

Batter	PA
Jeff Kent	175
Ron Santo	123
Benito Santiago	122
Todd Zeile	120
Gary Carter	113
Ron Cey	111
Tino Martinez	111
Tony Perez	109
Johnny Bench	103
Deron Johnson	103

Let's see, I count three Hall of Famers (Carter, Bench, Perez) and two other borderline cases (the aforementioned Kent and Santo). And the other five on this list had careers of which they justly can be proud. No, getting dissed is more about who bats in front of you, as well as game context, especially getting the lefty-righty platoon advantage, as we saw above with Sexson.

I was curious to know who were the sluggers getting walked in front of our top 10—you might wonder if Kent ever got tired of Bonds getting walked in front of him, if the continual dissing might give rise to some animosity between the players themselves? Indeed, Kent was preceded by Bonds in the majority of his 175 PAs. Santo was most often dissed after a walk to Billy Williams. Santiago followed Bonds, Zeile came up after Mike Piazza, Carter was dissed mostly because Andre Dawson preceded him. Cey followed Steve Garvey, and pitchers often preferred to face Tino Martinez rather than Bernie Williams. Tony Perez probably got sick and tired of watching other teams walk Johnny Bench to get to him.

Sometimes baseball is a game of beautiful symmetries—the batter most walked ahead of Bench? Tony Perez. Deron Johnson, like all these players, should not be ashamed, since he was batting behind Hall of Famers Frank Robinson and Reggie Jackson for many of those PAs.

Here are some other pretty good hitters who were dissed at least 50 times in their career: Dave Winfield (98), Carlton Fisk (91), Orlando Cepeda (88), Manny Ramirez (72), Edgar Martinez (68), Willie McCovey (65), Jim Rice (64), Cal Ripken (64), Rafael Palmeiro (63), Eddie Murray (62), Willie Stargell (62), Harmon Killebrew (55), Ernie Banks (53), Dave Parker (52) and, if you can believe it, Hank Aaron (51).

I tried to find some guys who hardly got dissed at all and I came up with a few names: Willie Mays (19), Rickey Henderson (16), Derek Jeter (12), Mickey Mantle (2) and Ted Williams (1). Now there are some caveats here: The Retrosheet era covers only the end of Williams' career and it missed Mays' and Mantle's early years, when most Hall of Famers accrue most of their disses. Also, lead-off hitters like Henderson rarely get dissed, because number nine hitters rarely get free passes.

Okay, those are the guys that got dissed. How did they react to the affront: Did they tend to exact revenge on their adversaries or did they try *too* hard and tense up? To answer these questions, I tabulated the diss data for each player, coming up with his batting line in those situations. Then I compared that to their results for all situations, to see if they there is any difference in their diss PAs.

(A technical note, which you may feel free to skip: the "all situations" stats are calculated by summing up a player's yearly numbers after weighting by the number of diss PA in each year. This is necessary because a player's ability changes throughout his career and good hitters usually get dissed only when they are very young or well past their prime. The weighting by diss PA ensures an apples-to-apples comparison.)

So, here's how our most-dissed batters performed when given a chance for revenge.

Batter	PA	OPS	OPS_all	OPS_diff
Jeff Kent	175	.922	.877	.045
Ron Santo	123	.947	.831	.116
Benito Santiago	122	.621	.727	-.106
Todd Zeile	120	.808	.775	.033
Gary Carter	113	.865	.785	.080
Ron Cey	111	.860	.800	.060
Tino Martinez	111	.889	.822	.067
Tony Perez	109	.866	.812	.054
Johnny Bench	103	.669	.812	-.143
Deron Johnson	103	.749	.734	.015

OPS - in diss situations

OPS_all - in all situations (weighted as mentioned in text)

OPS_diff = OPS - OPS_all

Hey, look at that: Most of these guys hit better when being dissed. I don't plan to carefully evaluate if this is a statistically significant result, but I will say that I doubt that it is. Differences on the order of 100 points of OPS in 100 PAs can be attributed to "the bounce of the ball" and do not reflect an underlying difference in true talent. In other words, if I looked at random groups of 100 plate appearances by Jeff Kent, say, I would see his OPS bouncing around by 100-200 points.

Anyway, it is curious that eight of the 10 did show some improvement when being dissed.

Now I'd like to look at the batters who improved most in diss situations. The following list shows the 10 batters who most improved (in terms of OPS) in diss situations (minimum 50 plate appearances):

Batter	PA	OPS	OPS_all	OPS_diff
Richie Sexson	59	1.665	.853	.812
Dave Kingman	64	1.439	.796	.643
Tony Armas	57	1.234	.745	.489
Kurt Bevacqua	58	1.127	.655	.472
Hubie Brooks	83	1.173	.727	.446
BJ Surhoff	53	1.183	.740	.443
Sid Bream	51	1.176	.759	.417
Bob Aspromonte	64	1.022	.651	.371
Kevin McReynolds	87	1.116	.789	.327
Phil Garner	72	1.037	.718	.319

I don't know about you, but I don't see any deep meaningful pattern in this list. Looking at the OPS_diff values, though, you will notice that Richie Sexson and Dave Kingman stand well above the others—you might call them outliers. Let's have a look at their stat lines in diss situations. First, the man they called Kong:

Batter	PA	H	D	T	HR	BB	BA	OBP	SLG
Kingman	64	24	3	0	11	1	.407	.422	1.017

Wow, how about that? Kingman sure didn't let himself get pushed around, did he? Twenty-four hits after being dissed and 11 of them left the ballpark. Pitchers (managers, actually) dissed him mostly to avoid pitching to Bill Buckner, Willie McCovey and Rusty Staub. They obviously made the wrong choice there.

If anything, Richie Sexson's diss-line is even more impressive:

Batter	PA	H	D	T	HR	BB	BA	OBP	SLG
Sexson	59	26	5	2	8	3	.510	.508	1.157

He really made opposing pitchers pay for choosing to pitch to him rather than, usually, Raul Ibanez or Geoff Jenkins. He didn't match Kingman's homer total, but he batted over .500 after being dissed and his

1.665 OPS is sort of hard to grasp. Of course, this is a small sample and Sexson's performance doesn't mean anything. Except, of course, that he exacted the most and sweetest revenge in the last 50 years of major league baseball.

Kingman and Sexson were somewhat similar players. Both were tall (Sexson stands 6-foot-8, Kong is 6-6), strong right-handed power hitters with pronounced uppercut swings. Sexson has hit for a bit higher average and has walked more than Kong (who walked very seldom indeed), but they have similar stats including OPS+ of 120 (Sexson) and 119 (Kingman), through age 33. Oh, yeah, they also both made enemy pitchers and managers wince in pain and regret when they decided to intentionally walk the preceding batter.

Here, on the other hand, are the guys who performed worst after being dissed, the guys who made the opposing managers look smart:

Batter	PA	OPS	OPS_all	OPS_diff
Hank Aaron	51	.505	.901	-.396
Tim Salmon	54	.514	.893	-.379
Rick Dempsey	53	.297	.659	-.362
Jose Pagan	51	.320	.646	-.326
Mickey Stanley	53	.395	.683	-.288
Jim Spencer	53	.427	.712	-.285
Jay Buhner	98	.585	.855	-.270
Steve Finley	57	.506	.769	-.263
Tom Brunansky	77	.498	.751	-.253
Brooks Robinson	100	.461	.709	-.248

It's strange to see Hank Aaron's name on a "Worst of" list of any kind, even a meaningless ranking like this one. Come to think of it, it's surprising that Aaron was even dissed more than 50 times. I mean, really, you're going to put a man on base for the privilege of pitching to *Hank Aaron*? Well, the first thing to realize is that Hank Aaron came to the plate more than any player in major league history, so on a per-plate apppearance basis he wasn't dissed very often. And most of those disses came early in Aaron's career when he was batting behind the established slugger Eddie Mathews. In the 10-year period from 1963 to 1973, Aaron was dissed only four times.

In any case, Aaron really struggled in those diss situations, managing an OPS of only .505. Here is his full stat line for his diss situations:

Batter	PA	H	D	T	HR	BB	BA	OBP	SLG
Aaron	51	8	1	0	1	3	.190	.219	.286

Oy, that is a brutal line for anybody, much less for one of the titans of the game. I don't want to give you the impression that this *means* anything—it's only 50 plate appearances, after all. I just thought it was interesting that Hank Aaron happened to hit like Mario Mendoza when being dissed.

As for the others on the list above, they are actually a solid group of hitters. Aaron and Brooks Robinson are, of course, Hall of Famers, while Finley, Buhner and Brunansky were All-Stars. And Tim Salmon is widely regarded as the best player never to play in an All-Star game. In any case, each of these hitters was completely unable to get revenge on the other team when he was dissed.

Walk-off Revenge

If you know who Mickey Owen was, it's probably because you heard something about a dropped third strike in some World Series game way back when. It was Game 4 of the 1941 World Series, the first of seven Fall Classics between the Brooklyn Dodgers and the New York Yankees. The Dodgers led 4-2 in the ninth inning and were about to knot the Series at 2-2. Tommy Henrich struck out for the final out, but wait, the ball gets by catcher Mickey Owen and Henrich gains first base. Joe DiMaggio starts off the ensuing fireworks with a single and before the Dodgers could get off the field the Yanks had a 7-4 lead, the game and (the following day) the championship. It was a stunning turn of events and Owen suffered the ignominy of that misplay, I dare say, for the rest of his career.

Owen was a fine player—he was selected for four All-Star teams and once finished fourth in the MVP voting. However, after the 1945 season, he was among a group of players who jumped to the newly formed Mexican League. That was a no-no as far as Major League Baseball was concerned, and when the upstart league failed, Owen and his cohorts were not immediately allowed back into organized ball. Owen was re-admitted in 1949 after a three-year wait—he signed with the Cubs—but his career dropped off quickly, as the careers of catchers in their mid-30s often do. His last year would be filled as a part-time backstop for the Boston Red Sox in 1954.

On July 19 of that year Owen stood in the on-deck circle as the batter in front of him was intentionally walked. Nobody likes being dissed, but it's hard to complain when the batter in question is one Theodore Samuel Williams, sometimes known as Teddy Ballgame. Still, you have to think Owen stepped into the batter's box wanting to show Orioles manager Jimmy Dykes a thing or two. This was not a particularly meaningful game—the Red Sox would finish 42 games behind the pennant-winning Indians—but still, Owen's career was winding down rapidly and every at-bat was an opportunity to go out with a bang.

Perhaps these thoughts were passing through the old catcher's mind as he dug in against the immortal Mike Blyzka (that's his real name; I'm not making it up). Or maybe he was thinking about what he'd eat after the game, who knows? In any case, the walk to Williams filled the sacks, there were two outs in the bottom of the ninth and the Red Sox trailed the Orioles by a score of 7-5. This was a true shot at redemption, and Owen did not miss his chance as he drove in all three Boston runners and himself, too, with a home run off of Blyzka. That's a walkoff homer, after getting dissed by the opposing manager. That must have been some *sweet* revenge.

The wonderful thing about researching these diss situations is that you uncover cases where the most mediocre, undistinguished, forgettable players rise above their everyday mediocrity and unexpectedly, dramatically, gloriously make the enemy pitcher pay for intentionally walking the previous batter. Bob Zupcic was a first-round pick of the Boston Red Sox in the 1987 amateur draft. I think it's safe to say that Zupcic, who played four seasons in the big leagues, accruing some 800 at-bats as a fourth outfielder, did not fulfill the expectations that the Red Sox had for him, nor perhaps the expectations he had for himself.

Zupcic was out of the majors by 1994 and after a couple of years back in the minors, left the game for good. Of course, a career like Zupcic's, filled with so many disappointments, must also have had its high notes. I imagine that Bob Zupcic, now 42 years old, often thinks back to a day in 1992, a day when he was starting in center field and batting second for the Boston Red Sox against the Detroit Tigers. The Tigers scored five runs in the third inning and would still be leading, 5-4, when the Red Sox came to bat in the bottom of the ninth.

Tiger closer Mike Henneman came in to shut down the Sox, but Phil Plantier drew a one-out walk and Scott Cooper doubled, with Plantier stopping at third. Zupcic grabbed a bat, since now he was on deck with Jody Reed stepping to the plate. The Tigers elected to walk Reed and pitch to Zupcic. Reed was not a fearsome hitter by any means, but he was an established regular with a .290 average at the time, while Zupcic was just an unproven rookie. Walking Reed to load the bases also created a double play situation.

Of course, Zupcic did not ground into a double play, as you probably have figured out by now. Henneman threw three straight balls to Zupcic and now the pressure was really on the Tigers' reliever. Zupcic took the 3-0 pitch for a called strike. You might think a rookie would be taking the 3-1 pitch as well in this situation, but you'd be wrong. Zupcic swung and hit the ball over the Green Monster for his second of seven career home runs. The unlikely hero trotted home after Plantier, Cooper and Reed and you can imagine the scene as the 25-year-old Bob Zupcic touched home plate after his vengeful walkoff slam.

I found nine walkoff home runs after the previous batter was walked; nine instances of the sweetest revenge possible. It's a great and dramatic feat, so I want to list the protagonists: Ron Santo, Roger Repoz, Hal King, Dante Bichette, Sammy Sosa, Matt Stairs, Jason Kubel, Mickey Owen and Bob Zupcic.

The Psychology of Being Dissed

So far I've been discussing individual players for the most part: the top 10 best and worst and the most dramatic successes. But can we draw any general conclusions from the diss data? Are batters more motivated to perform well after being dissed? You would think so. Are they able to use that extra motivation to improve their performance? Well, we can try to answer that by looking at the data.

A few paragraphs ago, I showed you how some players fared in diss situations compared to how they did in all situations. There's no reason that we can't do that for all players and then look at their average improvement. I did that and I found that the average improvement in OPS is...

Wait, before I give you the result, let me put in a disclaimer: This is not a rigorous analysis of diss situations. I'm not taking into account several factors that should be considered. For example, the strength of the opposing pitcher may not be the same in diss situations as for all situations. Similarly, there are necessarily runners on base in diss situations and often the bases are loaded, and batters on average do not hit the same

with runners on base (especially when the bases are loaded) as they do generally.

I could take these and other factors into account, that would lead to a complicated analysis that I don't feel like doing and you wouldn't feel like reading. So I'm just going to give you the quick-and-dirty version. According to the Retrosheet data, batters in diss situations improve their OPS by .002 points over their average performance. That's in a sample of more than 60,000 plate appearances. So, keeping in mind the caveats I just gave, it certainly doesn't *appear* that batters hit better after they've been insulted.

To wrap up, I want to look at the diss stats for just one more batter:

Batter	PA	BA	OBP	SLG	OPS
Keith Hernandez	51	.395	.431	.581	1.013

Hey, Hernandez was a fabulous diss-hitter himself. You should compare these numbers to his expected line of .279/.369/.422 (OPS .797). So maybe that's why Keith was so worried that the insult of the intentional walk to the preceding batter would inspire the dissed hitter to get revenge—he was a pretty "vengeful" hitter himself.

Resources

1. *Pure Baseball* by Keith Hernandez and Mike Bryan is published by Harper Perennial.

2. Regarding the Retrosheet data: The information used here was obtained free of charge from and is copyrighted by Retrosheet. Interested parties may contact Retrosheet at www.retrosheet.org.

3. Mitchel Lichtman's articles on the tactical implications of the intentional walk can be found here:

http://www.hardballtimes.com/main/article/when-to-walk-part-1/

http://www.hardballtimes.com/main/article/when-to-walk-part-2/

4. Many thanks to Dan Walsh, for providing food for thought and interesting conversation on this topic.

How Do Players Age?

by Phil Birnbaum

It's conventional sabermetric wisdom that players improve up to the age of 27, then start a slow decline that weeds them out of the league sometime in their 30s. Can we quantify the effects of aging? Is there a way to try to figure out, for instance, exactly—or even approximately—how much we expect the average player to decline between the ages of 30 and 37?

The question appears to be pretty straightforward, but it's harder than it looks. I won't have an answer in this article, at least not a specific numerical one. But we can learn something by looking.

The Naive Method

One way of looking at the issue, which I'll call the "naive" method, is to just measure the skill of players at various ages. What's the average performance of a 21-year-old player, or a 26-year-old, or a 34-year-old?

Let's start with pitching. I took all pitching player-seasons from 1947 to 2007 and calculated the pitcher's Component ERA. (Component ERA, or CERA, is a measure of how many earned runs per nine innings the pitcher "should have" given up based on the composite batting line of the batters who faced him.) I then calculated the overall CERA by pitcher age.

Here's what the result looked like. (Keep in mind that the graph is denominated in CERA, so higher numbers are worse.)

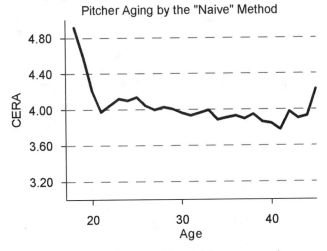

It's pretty flat after age 22, which suggests that you can't tell how good a pitcher is just by knowing his age.

For batters, I measured their proficiency in Runs Created per 27 outs (RC27), which is an estimate of how many runs a team would score if its batting line comprised nine copies of the same player. As it turns out, the equivalent curve for batting isn't quite what we expected. It shows a steady increase from ages 21 to 39. Here's the graph. (Higher is better, of course, for the batting curves.)

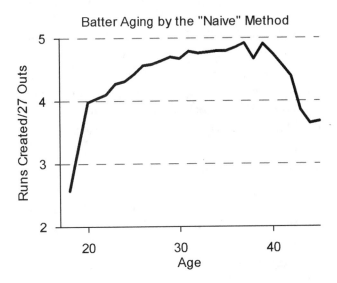

So just looking at these two curves, we might think that age doesn't matter a lot, at least between, say, 24 and 40. But that would be wrong.

On the graph, it looks like 35-year-olds do at least as well as 30-year-olds. However, what it's really telling us is that those 35-year-olds in the major leagues are as good as 30-year-olds in the major leagues. But that's not what we want to measure. We want to know how much players decline between 30 and 35, and to do that, we need to compare the same players at both ages.

The group of 35-year-olds in the above graph aren't the same players as the group of 30-year-olds. There are a lot more batters age 30 than batters age 35. Between 30 and 35, many batters decline so much that they're out of the league. So when you look at the 35-year-olds, you're seeing only the survivors, the players good enough to stick around into (baseball) old age.

For example, Damaso Garcia created 3.7 runs per game at age 30. Mike Schmidt created 8.9.

But, at age 35, Garcia was long out of baseball. Schmidt, of course, was still going strong, but not quite as strong as when he was 30—his RC27 was only 7.3.

Garcia declined, from 3.7 to out of baseball. Schmidt declined, from 8.9 to 7.3. But if you take the average at each age and ignore the fact that Garcia didn't last, you get:

- Average of two players at age 30: 6.3
- Average of one player at age 35: 7.3

So you wind up with your conclusion completely backwards: this analysis seems to say that players improve when they age, whereas in reality, they all declined! The naive analysis severely underestimates any decline.

You can construct more elaborate examples than the simple two-player model I've done here. Or you can take a look at Bill James' debunking of this naive method back in the 1982 Baseball Abstract.

And you can even do a real-life example. Pick an arbitrary year and find all the 30-year-old hitters. Go five years later and look for the same players. You'll find that:

- Many of the players are out of the league by 35.
- Of the players still around, most of them will have experienced significant declines.

but ...

- If you compare the average 30-year-old to the average surviving 35-year-old, there won't be that huge a difference.

So the naive analysis doesn't work. Let's try something else.

Paired-Seasons Analysis

Suppose we find all the 23-year-olds in the league last year and note how they did. Then let's check how they did this year at age 24. Conventional wisdom is that 23-year-olds are improving at that young age, so we should find, on average, that we see better performance at 24 than at 23.

The big question, though, is how much weight do you give to each player?

As a 23-year-old in 1979, Rance Mulliniks created 1.2 runs per game, but he had only only 65 at-bats. The next season, now with Kansas City, he created 3.8 runs per game, but again, in very little playing time: only 54 at-bats.

On the other hand, Steve Sax was already a regular in his early 20s. In 1983, his RC27 was 4.1 as a full-time player with 623 at-bats. In 1984, he dropped to 2.9 runs per game and lost a bit of playing time (but still had 569 at-bats).

Mullinks improved a lot in very few at-bats. Sax dropped significantly, but as a full-time hitter. We shouldn't weight them equally, should we?

Common sense says that since Sax had about 10 times as many plate appearances as Mulliniks, we should weight him 10 times as much.

But what happens if a player has significantly different numbers of at-bats in his two seasons? For instance, Jerry White had 278 at-bats in 1976 when he was 23. But he only had 21 at-bats in 1977. What do we do then?

Typically, in studies like this, analysts use the smaller of the two at-bat figures of the two seasons and use that as the weight. So you wind up with these weights:

- Rance Mulliniks: +2.6 in 54 at-bats
- Steve Sax: -1.2 in 569 at-bats
- Jerry White: -2.0 in 21 at-bats

That seems like a reasonable way to do it. And if you go ahead and take the average of these three guys, with these weights, you get a difference of −0.91, and you'd conclude that hitters decline by almost a whole run between the ages of 23 and 24.

Of course, this is only three arbitrarily selected players. I reran this study, but using all hitters from 1947 to 2007 (I also weighted seasons by outs instead of at-bats). And it turns out that the results confirm the conventional wisdom: from age 23 to 24, hitters improve from 4.54 to 4.68. That's about a 1.7 percent increase in performance, as measured by RC27.

We can repeat this analysis for every pair of ages. Then we'd be able to compare any two different ages just by multiplying the percentages together. I did that, and here's what I got:

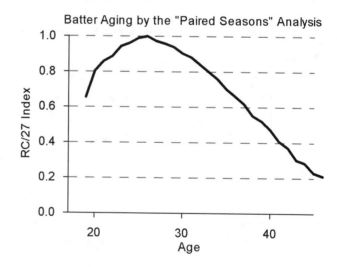

The graph shows performance "relative to peak;" it turns out the peak is at 26, a bit short of what conventional wisdom (and various studies, including that Bill James chapter from 1982) holds.

Here's the same study repeated for pitching:

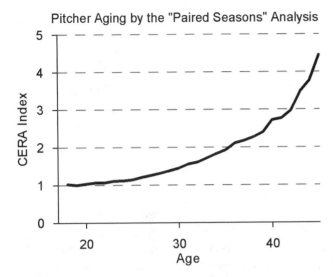

It's a whole other story for pitching. Instead of seeing young pitchers improve, as we did for young hitters, we see the peak is at age 20 and that pitchers decline immediately and continuously from there.

Other than that, the results don't look too unreasonable. Sometimes they look a bit exaggerated—a pitcher with an ERA of 3.30 at age 27 projects to over 5.00 by age 34—but you have to keep in mind that we included players who are well out of the league by then. It could be that half the 27-year-olds are still around at 34 and have an overall ERA of 4.00. But the other half are out of baseball, and if you made them come back and pitch, they'd be over 6.00. Half at 4.00 and half at 6.00 does indeed work out to 5.00. So the results aren't necessarily unreasonable.

Paired Seasons Analysis: The Flaw

But this analysis suffers from a problem: the same kind of selective sampling we saw in the naive method.

There's a fair bit of luck in individual player statistics. A pitcher with a talent level that would typically produce a 4.00 ERA could easily get lucky and have a good year with an ERA of 3.00. Or he might get unlucky and wind up at 5.00.

Those occurrences tend to even out—there'll be about as many 3.00s as 5.00s in the long run. And the luck usually won't repeat itself next year; both the lucky pitchers and unlucky pitchers will wind up back at their normal levels in subsequent seasons.

However, it's likely that the pitcher with the 5.00 ERA won't get as much playing time next year as the pitcher who went 3.00. So while both pitchers may wind up at 4.00, they'll do it in different numbers of innings.

Suppose the lucky pitcher gets 200 innings of work, but the unlucky one gets only 100 innings. The two lines then look like:

- Pitcher L: 3.00 ERA in 200 innings last year; 4.00 ERA in 200 IP this year
- Pitcher U: 5.00 ERA in 200 innings last year; 4.00 ERA in 100 IP this year

Remember that for each pitcher, we weight by the lower of their two innings pitched. Which means:

- Pitcher L: declines 1.00 ERA in 200 innings
- Pitcher U: improves 1.00 ERA in 100 innings

If you average those out, giving pitcher L twice the weight of pitcher U, you get an overall decline of 0.33 ERA.

See what's happened? By our assumptions, there was actually zero decline over the two seasons. But because the pitcher more likely to decline was given more innings, we wind up with a selective sampling problem, and then we observe an overall decline where we shouldn't have.

The problem is even more acute when some players retire. If pitcher U was released after his unlucky season, we'd be left only with pitcher L. He'd decline by a whole run, there would be nobody to offset him, and we'd wind up estimating a 1.00 decline—much worse than 0.33 and much farther from the real-life value of zero.

This method, then, will always cause us to overestimate declines, and underestimate improvements. The graphs are almost certainly overly pessimistic, for both batters and pitchers, because of this selective sampling issue. Players probably don't decline anywhere near as quickly as what the curves seem to tell us.

Correcting the Selective Sampling Problem

So is there a way to fix this problem? Maybe. The problem was caused, mostly, by players getting lucky or unlucky in the first of the two years. Perhaps if we correct for that, we might be able to get better results.

In general, a player's talent is closer to average than his performance indicates. A pitcher with an ERA of 2.00 is probably not that good; a pitcher with an ERA of 6.00 is probably not that bad. Same for hitters—a batter who hits .340 is probably performing a bit over his head. And a guy who hits .220 is probably just having a bad year.

(To see why this is true, consider a guy who goes 3-for-4. He's certainly not a .750 hitter; he's probably a .290 hitter or something who just had a good day. The same is true, to a lesser extent, for a week, month or season. That means that batters who hit .340 for the season are probably, on average, just (as a guess) .310 hitters who had a good year.)

Suppose that we have three players this year, each of whom gets 500 at-bats. One of them hits .300, one of them hits .270, and the third hits .240.

- Player A: .300 in 500 AB
- Player B: .270 in 500 AB
- Player C: .240 in 500 AB

In reality, player A is a .285 hitter who got lucky. Player B is a .270 hitter who did about what was expected. Player C is a .255 hitter who got unlucky. (And again, let's assume no age-related changes.)

Because of their performance, they won't all get 500 at-bats again next year. Player A will, because he hit .300. But player B might get only 400 at-bats, and Player C might get released.

So next year, only players A and B survive and hit exactly according to their abilities:

- Player A hits .285, for a decline of .015 in 500 at-bats
- Player B hits .270, for a decline of .000 in 400 at-bats
- Player C is gone

Overall, we find a decline of .0083. This contradicts our omniscient knowledge that the real change is zero.

That is, the paired-seasons method is overly pessimistic; it will show a steeper age-related decline than actually exists.

But suppose that instead of measuring the actual decline, we measured the decline based on expected talent. Then, instead of saying that player A declined from .300 to .285, we say that he stayed level, from a talent level of .285 to an actual performance of .285. If we do that, we get exactly the right answer.

Of course, that leads us to another difficult problem: without being God, how do we know player A's actual talent? We don't. But even a decent guess at his talent will give us a better estimate. To get there, we adjust the numbers by "regressing to the mean."

We know that a player who hits .300 is probably less than a .300 hitter. Suppose we bring him down to .290 (instead of .285). And suppose we don't regress the .270 hitter at all, because he's right at the league average. Then,

- Player A declines .005 in 500 at-bats
- Player B declines .000 in 400 at-bats

And we get a decline of .0027 points—still not the exact figure of .0000, but much closer than the unregressed estimate of .0083.

If we regressed perfectly and brought player A all the way down to .285 where he belongs, we'd get exactly the correct answer of .000.

So if you're able to take the players in Year 1 and regress them to the mean by the exact amount so that the regressed estimate matches their talent, you'll eliminate the effects of selective sampling and get the correct results.

Regressing

What I'll do now is try to find the appropriate average level of regressing to the mean and apply that level to all the players. But again, that requires an answer to a hard question: how much regression is appropriate? I don't know. For now, the best I can do is to try a couple of different amounts and see what comes out.

For a first attempt, let's try this: we'll regress enough so that a pitcher with 200 innings pitched winds up 10 percent closer to the mean. To do that, we add 22.2 innings of average pitching to his record. (That gives him 222.2 innings; 10 percent of that is the 22.2 we added.)

Tom Tango has pointed out that if you've chosen the correct number of innings to add for one pitcher, it's the same number for all pitchers. So we'll add 22.2 innings of average ERA to every pitcher in the sample. Those with 200 innings will regress 10 percent, and those with only 22 innings will regress 50 percent (which is appropriate, since a pitcher with a 2.00 ERA in 22 innings is much more likely to be average than a pitcher with a 2.00 ERA and 200 innings).

If we do that, and rerun the matched pairs calculations, we get an aging curve that's less steep. Here it is for pitching:

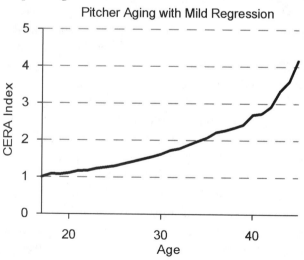

Pitcher Aging with Mild Regression

Now, instead of 40-year-old pitchers having three times the ERA of the young guys, it's only about two-and-a-half times.

We can regress even more. Here's another pitching graph, adding 84 average innings (about a 30 percent regression for a pitcher with 200 innings):

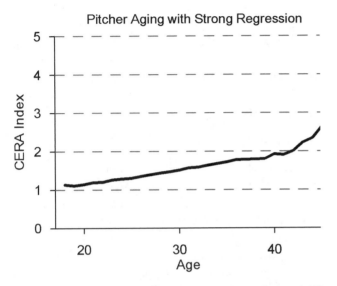

It's really flat now, perhaps too flat. A pitcher at 4.50 at age 30 now rises to only 5.40 by age 40. Intuitively, it seems like maybe we regressed too much.

For hitters, let's start by adding 66 league-average outs, which moves a player with 400 outs about 14 percent closer to the mean:

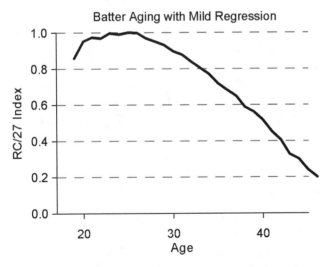

The curve flattens a bit. Without regression, there was an obvious increase from 19 to 26. Here, once the hitter reaches age 20, it's pretty flat to age 28.

We can regress even more—I've added 257 league-average outs to each batter (regressing 39 percent for a batter with 400 outs) to the following graph:

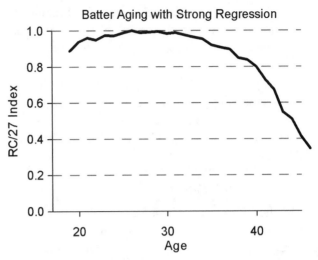

Again, this is probably a bit too flat.

So which curve is right? The honest answer is, I don't know. It depends on what the correct level of regression is. That's a question for further research.

However, there is one piece of objective evidence we can use right now to help us decide. In his 1982 study, Bill James gave us the total of "approximate values" for hitters at every age. The grand totals aren't all that useful for our purpose here, because "approximate value" includes playing time, and we want to look at rate statistics, not playing-time-dependent statistics.

We're lucky, however, in that Bill broke down the hitters by talent level. One of his categories is "superstar." We can probably assume that superstar hitters should all be full-time players regardless of the ups and downs of their performance, which means that we don't have to worry about varying playing time.

Here are those superstars by age. (I've included only ages 23-32, out of fear that outside that range, playing time variations might become significant even for superstars.)

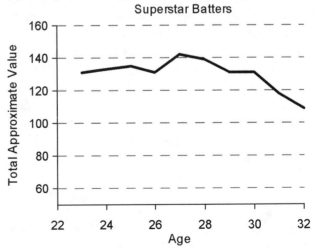

At these ages, the curve seems pretty flat, nothing like the graceful rise we saw for young players in the non-regressed case. Actually, I think this curve is closest to the "14 percent" curve for hitters, so I'd bet that curve is reasonably accurate, at least for superstar-caliber hitters.

But comparing curves by eye is pretty weak, and Bill James is measuring something different than we are, so I'd say any conclusions here should remain tentative for now.

A Puzzle: Why Don't Pitchers Appear to Improve?

In the hitting curves, we see that hitters improve up to approximately age 27, then start to decline. But the pitching curves show that pitchers seem to decline almost immediately! They start out great at age 20, then get worse and worse and worse until they're out of the league.

At first, it seems this must be wrong. There are a lot more 25-year-old pitchers in the major leagues than 21-year-old pitchers. But if younger pitchers are better, it should be the other way around. Indeed, if there are more MLB pitchers at 25 than at 21, you'd expect to see the same kind of curve we saw in the first graph.

So something must be going on. What could it be? A few possibilities:

Injuries

It could be that healthy pitchers don't decline as much as the graph suggests. The overall population is a combination of healthy young pitchers who might stay in the league and improve, and unhealthy young pitchers, who decline badly and may no longer stay in baseball. That effect might be stronger for pitchers than hitters; it does seem like batters don't have anywhere near as many career-ending injuries as pitchers do.

(However, if that's the case, then it's still true that the average pitcher declines. He declines because of injury, but that's still something a general manager or rotisserie player has to keep in mind when projecting his future.)

To check, I looked for "collapses," which I defined as a young pitcher going from above average to below replacement level (league ERA + 1) the next season. There were indeed more of those pitcher collapses than hitter collapses. So maybe this is part of the answer.

Maturity

In a blog conversation, someone suggested that perhaps pitchers have to learn to master a few different pitches before making the major leagues. That happens suddenly, in their early 20s. At that point, the pitcher would get called up but not necessarily progress any further.

In that case, you'd have a combination of two things:

- Most young pitchers don't yet have the mastery to pitch in the major leagues.
- Young pitchers' arms start to decline at a very young age.

That would explain why young pitchers get worse and worse, and also why there aren't many 21-year-olds despite the fact that their arms are stronger.

This hypothesis explains the data, but I'm not sure how plausible it is.

Statistical Illusion

Remember how the selective-sampling issue made declines look worse than they actually were by giving lucky players (who are set for a decline) more innings than unlucky players (who are set for an improvement)? That effect could be larger for pitchers than for hitters.

Suppose you have two hitters with .315 talent, but one hits .300 and the other hits .330. They'll both get full-time jobs with equal numbers of plate appearances, and so forth.

Next year, both return to .315. One declines, the other improves, but because they have the same playing time, the effects cancel out to zero.

Now suppose you have two star pitchers, both expected to have an ERA of 2.75. But, as the season plays out, one winds up with an ERA of 2.50, the other with an ERA of 3.00. They probably didn't get equal playing time. They might both be full-time starters, and each might have gotten 30 starts. But the 3.00 pitcher will have pitched fewer innings than the 2.50 guy, simply because he'll have had more bad games, where he'll have been taken out earlier. (For the sake of this example, let's suppose that you lose 25 innings for every 0.25 increase in ERA.)

Next year, when both pitchers revert to 2.75, the situation looks like this:

- Pitcher A: Last year, 2.50 in 250 innings. Next year, 2.75 in 225 innings
- Pitcher B: Last year, 3.00 in 200 innings. Next year, 2.75 in 225 innings

Again remembering that we use the lesser of the two innings, we get:

- Pitcher A: decline of .25 in 225 innings
- Pitcher B: improvement of .25 in 200 innings

Because of the differences in playing time, these average out to a decline of .015—not zero, as it did for the hitters.

So the playing time effect is worse for pitchers than for hitters. Is the extra effect enough to make the young pitchers appear to decline when they're actually improving? I'm not sure, but it's something to look at anyway.

Conclusions

If you're a general manager thinking of signing a 33-year-old slugger, and you want to know the future expectations for players of his age—well, other than being pretty sure that there's going to be a decline, there's not much we can tell you. What looks like a simple problem really isn't.

How can we get a better answer to the question? The most direct way would be to force teams to give their players the exact same amount of playing time from year to year, at least until they turn 40. Since that's not likely to happen, we'll have to hope someone comes up with better, more ingenious ways to measure the effects of aging.

Many of the ideas in this paper grew out of discussions with Tom Tango and Mitchel Lichtman, on our respective blogs. Thanks to Tom and Mitchel and the commenters.

In Search of the Anomalous Superstar

by Don Malcolm

In Every Travesty There is a Grain of Truth

In 1971, at the tender age of 18, with absolutely no intention of doing so, I created the most singular superstar in the history of baseball.

Some 30-odd years later, I realized that this frivolous, off-the-cuff construction had brought me face-to-face with the very definition of a superstar and what his statistics are "supposed to look like." My youthful fervor had inadvertently located a missing shape in hitting statistics—a collection of batting skills that has never found a mode of manifestation in any flesh-and-blood, bat-swinging human being.

Who was that exists-only-in-fiction superstar?

Why, it was me—of course.

Thanks to Brock Hanke's formidable affinity for applied mathematics, it was a relatively trivial matter for the two of us to construct our own baseball simulation game using a simple deck of playing cards—which is exactly what we did one spring evening in 1971.

We created a team that we thought would rival the 1962 Mets for laugh-inducing ineptitude—a team, so our addled creation myth went, forced into existence due to a stunning personality clash at the highest levels of baseball that prompted that most imperial of commissioners, Bowie Kuhn, to toss an entire franchise out of baseball.

That team, according to our rickety lore, was the Houston Astros.

Our replacement franchise, in keeping with the spirit of absurdity, was built from old chewing gum and table scraps, then moved west a hundred or so miles to the unwitting metropolis of San Antonio, where we appropriated the most sacred site in Texas (the Alamo) and transmogrified it into a jackleg, ramshackle ballpark.

To populate this travesty, of course, we began with ourselves. With Hanke's skill at probability theory, it was no trouble to make up all kinds of theoretically apt falsehoods about our abilities to hit major league pitching. Two individuals were beneficiaries of the biggest lies (at least those available to us in 1971): Charlie Finley's Mule, sent to us in a "waiver" deal, who became the team's center fielder, and yours truly.

How a Mule can play center field—or, for that matter, swing a bat—is something that should be left entirely to one's own imagination (if one wishes to visit that slippery slope). But once he worked out the math, Hanke could tailor factors to anything, and these were applied to that ubiquitous deck of cards, with a couple of extras—jokers, of course—thrown in for "unexpected events" (errors, base running, acts of God, etc.)

The factors for "Don Malcolm" were derived from a dim characterization of the type of hitter I'd been in high school: high batting average, high walks, low-to-moderate power.

We thought we would lose 130 games and have a rip-roaring time creating the most improbable set of team statistics ever to be assembled in any *Baseball Encyclopedia*. (Big Mac, as it has come to be called, was only 3 years old at the time, and I'd brought my copy with me to college, knowing instinctively that it would be far more entertaining than my academic textbooks.)

In the midst of all this, of course, ol' Charlie O. the Mule was imperceptibly but inevitably transformed into a four-legged analogue of Babe Ruth (just imagine how far the horsehide could travel if a 500-lb. member of the equine "extended family" was able to *really* lean into it.).

And yours truly, "Dandy" Don Malcolm, became the Superstar Who Never Was.

So What's So Unique, Anyway?

As our 1971 season played out, of course, the San Antonio Trotters became both intricate and bizarre in their boundless contradictions. At the time, neither of us (and no one else, either) had any inkling about the concept of park effects—but it was soon clear that our home park was not anything like the pitcher's paradise that the Astrodome had been. And, as we kept the kind of detailed stats that would take another decade to see the light of day elsewhere, it became clear that the 18-year-old *wunderkind* (Malcolm) and the 5-year-old, four-legged dynamo (known from then on only as "the Mule") were reaping massive benefits from the cozy, crazy-angled confines housing the rag-tag Trotters.

True to our original impetus, the team started out by losing 16 of its first 20. At that point, however, the team

186

Our Hero's 1971 Batting Line

Player	G	AB	R	H	D	T	HR	RBI	SB	CS	BB	SO	BA	OBP	SLG
Malcolm	162	561	122	204	42	9	14	109	18	9	126	55	.364	.480	.545

started to win a lot of games at home, and by the All-Star break was over .500. The team cratered in August, however (6-24). The month of September was a capsule of the team's Jekyll-and-Hyde plight: 10-1 at home, 3-12 on the road (the final splits: 51-30 in the Alamo, 26-55 elsewhere).

At season's close, the Mule had led the NL in slugging average (nosing out Hank Aaron, who demanded a recount), and that obnoxious kid Malcolm had edged out Joe Torre for the batting title, .364 to .363.

The Mule's absurd stats (.334, 38 homers, 130 RBIs) at least made conventional sense. After all, he weighed in at roughly a quarter-ton.

Malcolm's numbers, though, were something else again.

First, there was the idea of the insanely precocious prodigy (inherited directly from Tony Conigliaro, but with the statistical shape modified). Without consulting your favorite reference source, you will already know that no 18-year-old has ever:

- Led the league in batting average;
- Amassed 200+ hits;
- Drawn more than 100 walks.

And as a result of the above:

- Produced an on-base percentage of .480.

In fact, no 18-year-old has come within several solar systems of such a performance.

The next wrinkle, though, was (and is) somewhat subtler. Working it out (with adjustments fully made to alter the 1971 NL stats for the presence of the Trotters and their "Alamo" ball park, where run scoring was enhanced by around 13 percent as opposed to the 25 percent suppression of the Astrodome), Malcolm's adjusted on-base plus slugging (OPS+) works out to 190.

While Malcolm had a reasonable number of extra-base hits (65) and his 42 doubles led the league, his 14 homers was the lowest total since the introduction of the live ball in 1920 for any player with an OPS+ of 190 or higher. (Harry Heilmann had 18 homers en route to a 194 OPS+ in 1923; he hit .403 that year. Arky Vaughan clubbed 19 homers in 1935, when his OPS+ was 190; he hit .385.)

This combination of high batting average, low-moderate power, and a very high walking percentage (a bit over 18 percent) produced a superstar totally at odds with the evolving shape of hitting excellence in baseball.

Since 1971, there has been only one player season remotely in this uncharted territory—Rod Carew in 1977, who hit .388 with 14 home runs, but whose walk total was only about half of Malcolm's fictional 1971 season. His OPS+ was 178.

The conclusion is both stark and startling: The class of players who can be said to have had "superstar seasons" (years where their OPS+ is 160 or higher) literally has no place in it for someone with the statistical shape embodied by Malcolm's numbers.

The Changing Shape of Excellence

Let's shift gears now, and take a stab at defining what a "superstar hitting season" might be, and how the definition of that offensive excellence can be seen as a shifting statistical shape.

First, some context. From 1920 through the 2007 season, there have been 61 seasons where batters who qualified for the batting title have had an OPS+ of 190 or higher. There have been 111 seasons at 180 or higher; 231 seasons at 170 or higher; and a grand total of 423 seasons where their OPS+ was 160 or higher.

Let's look at that in chart form, with all 88 years displayed (the decades are listed on the left, the individual years are listed across the top):

Dec	0	1	2	3	4	5	6	7	8	9	Tot	Avg
20s	5	4	7	6	5	5	1	6	5	7	51	3.19
30s	6	4	6	5	4	4	4	6	4	5	48	3.00
40s	4	6	5	3	8	2	4	3	4	3	42	2.63
50s	1	3	3	4	6	5	2	6	4	2	36	2.25
60s	4	7	4	4	8	2	6	8	5	13	61	3.14
70s	5	4	9	2	4	3	1	4	2	3	37	1.50
80s	3	3	2	0	0	2	1	5	4	5	25	0.96
90s	3	4	6	6	8	6	10	8	6	5	62	2.15
00s	11	13	7	7	6	6	6	5			61	2.54
Sum	42	48	49	37	49	35	35	51	34	43	423	2.26

As you can see from the rightmost column (average players a year per the total number of teams in each decade), it became much more difficult for hitters to excel relative to their league in the 1970s and 80s; by the 80s, only about one player per year was putting up an OPS+ value of 160 or higher. Things have reversed themselves in the past two decades.

One side question that comes up here is why it became harder for players to have dominant seasons in the 70s and 80s. It is a mysterious phenomenon, to be sure. Brock Hanke has a few theories that might apply here. The first is that there was a lingering effort to tone down home runs after Roger Maris broke the Babe's record in 1961. The second is that the advent of the cookie-cutter ballparks took away most of the remaining possible "park advantages" that had come into being as the game become more dependent on the home run in the 50s.

But that is a topic for another essay: We were speaking of the "evolving shape" of hitting excellence. How can we show that as it has morphed over time? The chart at the bottom of the page shows the average stats for OPS+ seasons above 160 by decades.

The average OPS+ over the full 423-player sample is 176, so what you see here reflects what the aggregate shape and value of the stats would look like for a player at that level of performance in each decade. Note the values for isolated power (ISO) and walking percentage (BBP); we will return to these numbers further below.

Our next table examines extra-base hitting by itself. Bill James recently introduced a "shape" construct for extra-base hit distribution that has some bearing on the issue. His "hitter family" formulation creates a shorthand for percentages of doubles, triples, and homers. For example, the elite hitters from the 1920s had an extra-base hit distribution as follows: 50 percent doubles, 15 percent triples, 35 percent homers. This has mutated over time, and the elite hitter distribution in this decade looks like this: 45 percent doubles, 3 percent triples, 52 percent homers. James' shorthand for these percentages (5-1-4 for the 20s, 5-0-5 for the 00s) tends to blur the details and understate the historical shift, so we'll show the decade-by-decade changes as percentages in the next column.

Decade	D%	T%	HR%
20's	50%	15%	35%
30's	43%	12%	45%
40's	48%	13%	39%
50's	41%	9%	50%
60's	39%	7%	54%
70's	46%	6%	48%
80's	47%	7%	47%
90's	45%	3%	51%
00's	45%	3%	52%

Looking at the data in this way, we can see that the home run is institutionalized as the primary weapon of the elite hitter in the 50s, and reaches its zenith in the 60s. While some retrenchment occurs in the 70s and 80s, it returns with a move back over the 50 percent mark in the 90s, and has continued to climb in the present decade.

Remember, these are the average percentages for hitters who post a 160 OPS+ or higher, and aren't representative of the entire batter population. Note that the continuing extinction of the triple makes it virtually

Average Batting Line of all Players with an OPS+ of at least 160 in a Year, Grouped by Decade

Dec	AB	R	H	D	T	HR	RBI	BB	SO	BA	OBP	SLG	BBP	ISO	LgISO	ISOr
20s	532	120	198	38	11	27	121	84	43	.372	.450	.638	.132	.266	.113	2.35
30s	543	122	188	34	9	36	134	93	57	.346	.441	.640	.144	.294	.121	2.43
40s	539	109	178	34	9	28	112	91	48	.331	.429	.583	.143	.252	.109	2.31
50s	540	110	177	30	7	37	111	96	64	.328	.428	.612	.149	.284	.134	2.12
60s	536	102	163	27	5	37	106	83	91	.305	.399	.580	.132	.275	.124	2.22
70s	527	95	165	30	4	32	107	85	85	.313	.408	.565	.137	.252	.120	2.10
80s	523	101	163	32	5	31	99	85	93	.312	.407	.571	.138	.259	.130	2.00
90s	515	106	166	34	2	38	113	96	90	.323	.430	.618	.155	.295	.147	2.01
00s	533	112	173	36	2	42	121	103	101	.325	.437	.639	.159	.315	.160	1.97
AVG	532	109	175	33	6	35	115	91	76	.329	.427	.609	.144	.280	.130	2.15

impossible for a moderately powerful hitter to amass the requisite slugging average without resorting to the long ball.

As you might suspect, when we apply this formulation to that fictional 1971 Don Malcolm season, the percentages simply don't fit at all into this continuum. Malcolm's extra-base hit distribution is as follows: 64 percent doubles, 14 percent triples, 21 percent homers.

Malcolm's distribution is out of whack with the aggregate of elite hitters in each and every decade since the introduction of the live ball.

So you can see that, in order to be in that hitter elite today, it is almost mandatory to be able to hit 30-plus homers, as the next table demonstrates:

Dec	<30HR	30+HR	<30%	30+%
20s	41	20	67%	33%
30s	14	34	29%	71%
40s	21	21	50%	50%
50s	9	27	25%	75%
60s	12	49	20%	80%
70s	17	20	46%	54%
80s	10	15	40%	60%
90s	13	49	21%	79%
00s	4	57	7%	93%
TOT	141	292	33%	67%

This chart makes it clear that Malcolm's anomalous achievement is primarily due to the fact that his season occurred in the 1970s, when he still had almost a 50-50 chance of being an elite hitter with less than 30 homers. His total of 14 still made for an uphill struggle, however: only two players (the aforementioned Rod Carew, and Joe Morgan, in 1975) hit fewer than 20 homers en route to a 160+ OPS+ season.

An Absolute Anomaly

Please recall our brief discussion of isolated power above, for it is key to the "Malcolm anomaly." Isolated power has gone through the roof since 1993, as the following comparison shows:

When	AL	NL
1901-92	.113	.111
1971	.117	.114
1993-	.159	.153

While isolated power spiked in the 1950s, it receded back toward 1901-92 historical levels in the 1970s and 1980s, which left a wider range of possibility for offensive excellence. There was about a one-in-five chance of a 160+ OPS+ season being turned in by someone hitting fewer than 20 homers in 1971.

Today, however, those odds are more like one-in-50. When we bring the fictional 1971 Don Malcolm season into the present offensive context, without adjusting it for the rise in isolated power, we find that its league-relative value has dropped. This will be unsurprising to those of you well-versed in era and league adjustments, but you might still be surprised to see how much of this value has degraded due to the change in both offensive levels and statistical shapes.

The 190 OPS+ that the underfed young Malcolm posted in 1971 would translate, with similar adjustments for the hitter-friendly Alamo, to a present-day value of 156.

In other words, Malcolm would no longer have an OPS+ that ranked him in the top 100 of all such "seasons of hitting excellence." He'd be somewhere down in the high 400s.

Given an OPS+ of "only" 156, it's likely that in this day and age, even an estimable publication such as this one might express some reservations about the young kid because he simply didn't have enough power: "Sure, he hit .364, but that's a fluke, right? Nobody hits that high over a career anymore, now, do they? Yeah, he was only 18, but he's probably lying about his age—after all, this *is* the age of cheating, isn't it?"

In order for the 1971 Malcolm to retain that 190 OPS+ in the present day with the exact same power and walk stats, he'd have to add 42 more singles to his hit total. That would mean that instead of hitting .364, he'd have to hit .439. Conversely, if we were going to fix his batting average at the 1971 level, he'd need to hit three times as many homers (a total of 42) to keep his OPS+ at 190.

In other words, he'd have to either shatter the modern-day batting average record (and give Hugh Duffy's corpse a reason to consider turning over in his grave) or start swingin' from the heels.

It should be clear by now that the run scoring environment in baseball can produce profound alterations in the mode of what constitutes hitting excellence due to the fluctuations of shape that orbit around isolated power. Those more flexible offensive eras—the 1920s, the late 1940s, the 1970s—allowed for greater contrasts and wider ranges of possibility than what became the

The Two Seasons That Come Closest to Malcolm's Batting Line

Player	Year	OPS+	H	D	T	HR	BB	BA	OBP	SLG	BBP	ISO	LgISO	ISOr
Arky Vaughan	1935	190	192	34	10	19	97	.385	.491	.607	.162	.222	.114	1.93
John Olerud	1993	186	200	54	2	24	114	.363	.473	.599	.171	.236	.141	1.67
(Don Malcolm)	1971	190	204	42	9	14	126	.364	.480	.545	.179	.181	.114	1.59

norm in the 1950s and that has, for lack of a less damning phrase, metastasized over the last fifteen years.

Yet even within those more flexible environments, there has never been a season with the precise combination of shape and value as the one that played out via a dozen decks of cards, on a succession of tables in dorm rooms, greasy spoons, and assorted kitchens in anonymous, long-forgotten apartments over those green months of 1971. There are only two seasons that really come close to it, listed above.

But both of these great hitters (each with an early peak: Vaughan was 23 and Olerud 24 in their Top 100 single-season performances) had a bit too much power. High-average hitters, even in days of yore, tended to have more power relative to their league, or else they drew fewer walks. When we look at hitters with an OBP of higher than .450 and who hit more than .340 (see table below), there is a massive gap in isolated power between those few deadball-era stars with big walk seasons (Ty Cobb and Eddie Collins) and Wade Boggs in 1986 and 1988 (but not the homer-spike year in between) and Vaughan's 1935 season.

How massive is that gap? Quite massive: nearly a hundred points of isolated power. There are, of course, a lot of high-average hitters in that gap who don't have extremely high walk totals (a walking percentage lower than 15 percent), but they are all deadball-era hitters (Cobb, Collins, Tris Speaker, Joe Jackson). But high-average, high-walk hitters are simply absent in the ISO range between .129 (Boggs' 1986 season) and .222 (Vaughan).

And where is that Don Malcolm season with respect to this? Why, smack dab in the middle of that gap: an ISO of .181.

There is no one else there.

Odds are that there never will be.

And though I'm obviously biased beyond any possible hope of redemption, I cannot help but think that baseball is somehow the poorer for it.

In the midst of this mourning, however, I remain buoyed by one more unalterable confirmation of my moth-to-flame penchant for the unique, the unclassifiable—and the plain-and-simply non-existent. It was, in retrospect, a remarkable portent of things to come.

All things considered, being the Superstar Who Never Was is better than nothing at all.

Locating "the Gap": ISO for Batters with OBP above .450 and BA above .340

Player	Year	H	2B	3B	HR	BB	BBP	BA	OBP	SLG	ISO	OPS+	ISOr
Eddie Collins	1914	181	23	14	2	97	.156	.344	.452	.452	**.108**	176	1.44
Ty Cobb	1915	208	31	13	3	118	.173	.369	.486	.487	**.118**	185	1.51
Wade Boggs	1988	214	45	6	5	125	.176	.366	.476	.490	**.124**	166	0.85
Wade Boggs	1986	207	47	2	8	105	.153	.357	.453	.486	**.129**	156	0.98
Arky Vaughan	1935	192	34	10	19	97	.163	.385	.491	.607	**.222**	190	1.93
Wade Boggs	1987	200	40	6	24	105	.160	.363	.461	.588	**.225**	173	1.41
Tris Speaker	1922	161	48	8	11	77	.153	.378	.474	.606	**.228**	179	2.02
John Olerud	1993	200	54	2	24	114	.171	.363	.473	.599	**.236**	186	1.67

Catcher 911

by Tom M. Tango

Helping a Catcher Today

Help me if you can, I'm feeling down.
And I do appreciate you being 'round.

On Friday, June 8, 2007, in the top of the 10th inning, slick-fielding third baseman Pedro Feliz found himself behind home plate as catcher for the San Francisco Giants. Bengie Molina had started the game as catcher, and was replaced by backup catcher Eliezer Alfonzo in the fifth inning, following a double-switch with the pitcher. Alfonzo was injured in a play at the plate later in the game, paving the way for Feliz's emergency stint as catcher. Feliz's opposing manager that day, the A's Bob Geren said, "I thought Feliz did a great job. It almost looks like he's done it before."

What are emergency catchers, and how well do they perform? I went through every single player who played at least one game as catcher between 1956 and 2007. For each season, I determined whether his primary position was catcher. If he was a catcher in at least 50 percent of his games, I considered him primarily a catcher at some point in his career.

Dale Murphy, who started his career as a catcher, and Johnny Bench, who ended his career as something other than catcher (but did play some catcher in those twilight years), were pooled into the "Primarily catcher, at some point in their careers" group. All the other players were pooled into the "Never primarily catcher" group.

No better friend does the baseball analyst have than Retrosheet. It is a wonder. Virtually every play over the last 50-plus years has been recorded and made publicly available at no charge. We know when every player played catcher, and what happened when he was behind the plate. What we need to do now is gather the data, and try to make some sense of them.

In last year's *Annual*, I introduced a method to analyze all baserunning events and attribute their impact to the catcher. For each catcher, I looked to see who was on the mound, and compared that catcher to all others who ever caught that particular pitcher at some point in their careers. So, a Carter/Gooden combination would require me to look at all Mets and Yankees catchers who ever caught Doc. If the Gooden/Carter combination was involved in fewer passed balls and wild pitches than a Gooden/non-Carter combo, then we know that Carter had a positive impact on Gooden.

I repeated that step for every pitcher Carter caught. And I did that for every catcher. In this way, I controlled for the pitcher, and end up comparing each catcher to several dozen, even hundreds of, catchers, under similar conditions.

The leaderboard (and trailer) from last year's *Annual* is reprinted below, including catchers with at least seven full seasons.

The Best (and Worst) Catchers at Controlling the Running Game
(from last year's *Annual*)

CATCHER	LWTS	Seasons	SB	CS	PK	BK	WP	PB
Ivan Rodriguez	10.4	13.1	-46	-1	0	-1	8	-2
Rick Dempsey	10.0	10.4	-17	3	3	0	-9	-3
Jim Sundberg	9.8	13.5	-14	5	4	-1	-4	-4
Steve Yeager	9.2	7.9	-13	1	4	-2	-9	-3
Gary Carter	8.9	14.5	-4	10	-1	0	-8	-5
Johnny Bench	8.2	12.2	-22	-3	4	0	-7	-1
Bob Boone	7.8	15.6	-17	4	2	1	-1	-3
Brad Ausmus	7.1	11.0	-15	0	0	-1	-8	-6
Lance Parrish	6.8	12.9	-24	2	0	0	-4	4
Dan Wilson	6.8	8.1	-19	-3	-1	-3	-8	-6
Mike Piazza	-9.6	10.5	36	-6	1	1	-6	-1

To read the (first) line: Ivan Rodriguez has been behind the plate for effectively 13.1 seasons of 5,000 batters (a total of 65,566). Per 5,000 batters, he allowed 46 fewer stolen bases than his baseline group. That is, by far, the best total of all catchers. His arm is legendary, and deservedly so. His caught-stealing rate is close to the average in his group (one less than average). If no one is stealing, it's hard to throw anyone out, and still, Rodriguez managed to throw out his fair share. Why runners tried to steal on him, who knows.

In the rest of the categories, Rodriguez and his pitchers picked off runners at the average rate. His pitchers allowed one fewer balk. Rodriguez had problems with wild pitches, allowing eight more than his peer group, but allowed two fewer passed balls. The LWTS column is the linear weights run value, which essentially is figured this way: Every positive event for Rodriguez (caught stealing, pickoffs) is worth 0.50 runs, and every negative event (stolen base, balk, wild pitch, passed ball) is worth -0.25 runs. (Think of a run being worth four bases, meaning each base is worth 0.25 runs. An out would be worth an additional 0.25 runs.)

As Bill James once said, if a metric always surprises, it's probably wrong. A metric that never surprises is probably useless. If a metric confirms 80 to 90 percent of what you know, then it's probably solid overall. You might be surprised that Rick Dempsey has such a strong showing, or that Tony Pena is nowhere to be found. Otherwise, the rest of the names are fairly comforting. If those give us comfort, then it's easy for us to accept the metric in general, even if we don't necessarily understand its nuances.

Anyway, I simply took the results of all the catchers, broken down by the two pools of catcher career paths: the "Primarily catcher, at some point in their careers" group and the "Never primarily catcher" group. Here are their totals:

Catcher	LWTS	Seasons	SB	CS	PK	PB
Primarily catcher	0.8	1,443	-2	0	0	0
Never primarily catcher	-9.2	23	20	-1	0	7

That is quite a difference: -9 runs per season for the non-catchers, and +1 for the real catchers. Of course, we expected players who were never primarily catchers

to be in the negative, and now we have a quantification of that performance. That is the power of the numbers. It may not be a shock that Mike Piazza is the worst-fielding catcher (with respect to baserunners) in the last 50 years. But, we really didn't know the extent to which he was bad: -9.6 runs bad. The "Never primarily catcher" group is as bad as Piazza.

What if we split our two groups into subgroups? Let's start with the "Primarily catcher, at some point in their careers" group. What I'm going to do is split it up into two groups. Consider the following:

- Dale Murphy played exclusively catcher in his first two seasons (total of 37 games); he spotted some games as catcher in the next two seasons, while playing primarily first base.
- In Gary Carter's 1975 rookie season, he played 92 games in right field, and 66 as catcher. That was the only season in his career in which catcher was not his primary position. Johnny Bench, in his final three seasons, was primarily a corner infielder, with some spot games as catcher.
- Bob Boone was primarily a catcher in each of his 19 MLB seasons.

I'm going to take each season from this main group, and split them into: "Primarily catcher in this season" group and "Primarily catcher in some other season, but not this one" group. So, Murphy's first two years go in the former group, while his next two years go in the latter group. Carter's rookie season and Bench's last three seasons go in the latter group. The rest of Carter's and Bench's careers, along with Boone's career in its entirety, go in the former group. You know, those group names are starting to get long. I'm going to shorthand their names as "Primo catcher" and "Ex-catcher" groups.

Let's also split the "Never primarily catcher" group based on these illustrations:

- Craig Wilson was primarily an outfielder-first baseman in every season of his seven-season career, with a handful of games as catcher in each of his first four seasons. He totaled 40 games as catcher, including 20 starts.
- Bob Watson, in a 19-year career, played a total of 10 games as catcher in three different seasons.
- Veteran Pedro Feliz played one game at catcher.

I'm going to draw a line at 10 games, so that anyone with more than 10 games will be considered a "Never primarily catcher but spots a lot as catcher." Craig

Fielding Performance by Type of Catcher

Type	LWTS	Seasons	SB	CS	PK	BK	WP	PB
Primo catcher	0.8	1442.7	-2	0	0	0	-1	0
Ex-catcher	-8.5	20.6	19	-2	0	1	5	5
Optional catcher	-3.9	1.6	5	9	2	1	13	19
Emergency catcher	-49.6	0.6	68	-13	4	5	60	48

Wilson belongs to this group. Any player who played at most 10 games as catcher will be considered as "Never considered a catcher and rarely spots there." Similarly to the other groups, I'll give shorthand names here as well: "Optional catcher" group (that's for guys like Craig Wilson) and "Emergency catcher" group (which is where you will find Pedro Feliz and Bob Watson).

To recap, we have four buckets of catchers in which to put each catcher's season:

- Primo catcher: played at least half of his games in that season as catcher
- Ex-catcher: at some point in his career was considered primarily a catcher, but in this particular season was not primarily a catcher
- Optional catcher: was never primarily a catcher in any of his seasons, but played more than 10 games at catcher in his career
- Emergency catcher: was never primarily a catcher in any of his seasons, and played 10 or fewer games at catcher in his career

Now, I simply took the results of all the catchers, broken down by the four buckets of catcher career paths and listed them above.

Among the primo catchers, the total run value was +1 runs per season compared to all catchers (including themselves). No surprise here. With the ex-catchers, there were 21 full seasons with a run value of -9 runs per season. Basically, what we see here is that players who once were (or about to become) catchers, when they were not primarily catchers, were nine runs below average. We expected them to be in the negative, and now we have a quantification of that performance. They look a lot like Mike Piazza. The optional catchers (those guys who never were catchers to begin with), had a pretty decent performance at -4 runs per season, but based on only 1.6 full seasons.

But, what about the category that most interests us: the true emergency catcher, like Pedro Feliz? Well, among that group, of which there was a total of only 0.6 seasons, they were worth -50 runs per season! It is a shockingly poor performance. They allowed 68 more stolen bases than the average catcher, caught 13 fewer runners, allowed 60 more wild pitches and 48 more passed balls. It is an across-the-board collapse. It is based on a very small sample size, but the degree to which they were terrible and our prior expectation that they would be terrible make the results fairly relevant.

Our expectations, therefore, should be that a player with no prior catching experience should be some 50 runs worse than average. Well, perhaps not that bad. If we use the sample size line for the optional catcher (they should be worse than their performance indicates), then we should do the same for the emergency catcher (they can't be as bad as their performance indicates). This is called regression toward the mean. Let's say the emergency catcher is probably -40 runs.

A catcher on the downside of his career, who perhaps has done some spot catching, would be around 10 runs worse than average, based only on the baserunning game. It would seem that a decent hitter, with some practice behind the plate, could be a serviceable player. Indeed, Mike Piazza, who became a catcher by experience and not innate talent, was revealed in last year's Annual to be worth 10 runs worse than average (as noted in the earlier chart). This is in line with the above numbers.

(This doesn't really fit anywhere, but I thought I'd throw it in anyway: Since 1955, there have been 236 games in which a true emergency catcher entered the game. The big use of emergency catchers started in 1970, when eight different emergency catchers played a total of 23 games. It ended in 1989, with seven playing 10 games. Since then, no season has seen more than four emergency catchers or seven emergency games.)

Helping a Catcher Tomorrow

When I was younger, so much younger, than today.
I never needed anybody's help in any way.

Another spot where catchers need help is when they play too many consecutive games. Most often, you'll hear about catchers playing a Sunday day game following a Saturday night game, or more generally a day game after a night game. The idea is that when you sit the catcher on Sunday, and with a likely Monday off, he is well-rested for Tuesday. This would imply that the catcher will probably hit better on Tuesday than he otherwise would. Is it true?

Here's what I'm going to do, and I'll use Gary Carter to illustrate the process. I selected every game for every catcher in the last 50 years. I separated all his catcher games between under the age of 30 and 30-plus years old. I simply used the season in question minus the player's year of birth to determine age. It doesn't matter how you calculate the age, as long as you are consistent among all the players. Carter had 4,508 plate appearances as catcher in his 20s, and 3,664 as catcher in his 30s.

Then I ask, for each game as catcher, "When did he last play (catcher or otherwise)?" Focusing on Carter in his 20s, he had 33 plate appearances when he didn't play at all prior to the game in question (i.e., his first game of the season), 163 where he played on the same day (i.e., doubleheaders), 3,528 when he played the day before, 601 when he had a day of rest (e.g., played Sunday then Tuesday), 115 when he had two days of rest, and 68 when he had at least three days of rest (most likely due to some injury).

If we count all the games in which he had at least one day of rest (601 plus 115 plus 68 plate appearances), then Carter had 16.1 percent of his 4,508 plate appearances while rested. Among catchers in their 20s with at least 2,000 plate appearances, Carter had the fourth-lowest rate of rested PA. On the right, you will find a list of the 20 least-rested catchers from the Retrosheet era.

These are basically the catchers who have been worked the hardest in their 20s. Now, we need a way to evaluate their overall hitting. A fairly simple way is to use wOBA (weighted On Base Average). This metric is analogous to OBP (On Base Percentage), except instead of weighting each of the safe events in the numerator as 1, it weights each event more appropriately. While it makes sense in the OBP context to weight a walk and

The Least Rested Catchers

Catcher	PA	Rested rate
Piazza, Mike	2,794	.170
Simmons, Ted	4,910	.173
Bench, Johnny	5,092	.173
Carter, Gary	4,508	.174
Hundley, Randy	2,667	.181
Sundberg, Jim	3,740	.183
Fisk, Carlton	2,144	.189
Rodriguez, Ivan	4,395	.190
Davis, Jody	2,313	.195
Pena, Tony	3,070	.198
Kendall, Jason	4,149	.201
Santiago, Benito	3,910	.210
Martinez, Victor	2,425	.215
Torre, Joe	2,975	.221
McCarver, Tim	3,786	.221
Freehan, Bill	3,875	.223
Munson, Thurman	3,879	.226
Parrish, Lance	3,875	.229
Rodgers, Bob	2,943	.230
Kennedy, Terry	2,974	.232

a home run identically, this doesn't serve our purposes for an overall hitting measure. The weights I use are 0.7 (for walks, hit batters), 0.9 (singles, reaching base on error), 1.3 (doubles, triples), 2.0 (home runs). The justification for these weights has been described on my site (see footnote). If you are having a bit of trouble grasping this metric, think "OBP" every time you see "wOBA".

If we look at these 20 hard-working catchers in their 20s, let's see how they performed when they played with no rest compared to when they played with one or two days of rest...

Catcher wOBA with No Rest vs. 1/2 Days Rest

Player	PA	Rested Rate	wOBA 1	PA 1	wOBA 23	PA 23
Piazza, Mike	2,794	.170	.438	2,293	.387	430
Martinez, Victor	2,425	.215	.386	1,874	.360	490
Bench, Johnny	5,092	.173	.373	3,997	.373	817
Torre, Joe	2,975	.221	.369	2,103	.373	549
Simmons, Ted	4,910	.173	.367	3,849	.386	781
Fisk, Carlton	2,144	.189	.366	1,693	.381	350
Kendall, Jason	4,149	.201	.366	3,262	.389	788
Carter, Gary	4,508	.174	.363	3,528	.351	716
Munson, Thurman	3,879	.226	.356	2,843	.359	797
Rodriguez, Ivan	4,395	.190	.352	3,498	.372	751
Freehan, Bill	3,875	.223	.347	2,718	.347	791
Parrish, Lance	3,875	.229	.343	2,873	.363	763
Pena, Tony	3,070	.198	.337	2,391	.354	551
McCarver, Tim	3,786	.221	.335	2,742	.326	734
Davis, Jody	2,313	.195	.330	1,820	.334	409
Kennedy, Terry	2,974	.232	.325	2,205	.336	572
Sundberg, Jim	3,740	.183	.320	2,931	.331	634
Santiago, Benito	3,910	.210	.316	3,036	.308	759
Hundley, Randy	2,667	.181	.301	1,928	.339	434
Rodgers, Bob	2,943	.230	.292	2,012	.265	615

The first line says that Mike Piazza has 2,794 plate appearances in his 20s, of which 17 percent were rested. The wOBA was .438 when he played the one day before (i.e., zero days of rest); he has 2,293 such PA. When he last played two or three days earlier (i.e., one or two days of rest), his wOBA was .387, on 430 PA. As you go through the list (which is sorted by wOBA_1), you will see that some performed better and some performed worse. Now, with only several hundred plate appearances, it's too hard to ascertain whether each individual was actually affected by the extra rest. Here are the simple averages for those 20 catchers:

Player	PA	Rested Rate	WOBA_1	PA_1	WOBA_23	PA_23
Simple Average	3,521	.202	.349	2,680	.352	637

The overall average is a .349 wOBA with no rest (i.e., played the day before) and a .352 wOBA with a short-term rest (last played two or three days earlier). I'm not sure what we should have expected. There seems to be mild short-term improvement. However, with almost 12,000 total PA in our sample, one standard deviation is actually 5.0 points in wOBA. The actual difference here

is 3.0 points. So, we are less than one standard deviation from the mean, which is statistically insignificant.

Even if we want to argue that the 3.0 point difference is real, it is barely noticeable. That hardly seems like what we expected. Even if we believe that resting is a kind of preventative medicine (the rest doesn't improve you, but it at least doesn't make you worse), the performance with no rest should, eventually, take its toll. We should have seen some larger degradation in the numbers, and we don't see it. Perhaps the degradation does exist—as it really should, since catchers are human beings—but its effect is rather muted.

What if we looked at all catchers, and not just our workhorses? We'll weight the wOBA of each of our catchers by the lower of their plate appearances with no rest and with one or two days of rest. In this way, if someone has 2,000 plate appearances with no rest and 100 with short-term rest, and someone else has 1,000 plate appearances with no rest and 300 with short-term rest, we will weight their performances with and without rest at 100 plate appearances and 300 plate appearances, respectively. The key is that both samples, for the same catcher, must be the same for the two pools. The overall results show that both groups had a wOBA of .323. No difference.

If we can't see the difference in the numbers, and we did a good job in controlling for variables in our study, then whatever reality exists is simply obscured by other things that have much more impact. I would listen to my catcher, if he says he's tired or needs rest. But I shouldn't really expect to see much difference once he comes back from his rest.

Helping a Catcher Next Year and Beyond

And now my life has changed, in oh so many ways.

My independence seems to vanish in the haze.

How do catchers age? Catchers collapse much faster than players at other positions, don't they? We know that the greats like Johnny Bench and Gary Carter didn't survive into their late 30s or early 40s. Then again, Carlton Fisk did, albeit at a position other than catcher.

Of players born since the year Ruth was born, there have been a little over 10 million plate appearances by non-pitchers. A little over 5 million of those occurred by the age of 28. We can say, therefore, that the average player, through the age of 28, is at the midpoint of his career. What about catchers? What happens to catchers starting at age 29? How well do they perform? When are they moved off catcher? What happens to catchers as they age?

The first thing I will do is go through every single non-pitcher since the Ruth time period, add up their games played through age 28, and mark them as catcher, infielder, outfielder, or first baseman. Then I will add up their hitting stats to get:

Pos	#	PA	Runs per 650 PA
C	959	553,854	-9.7
IF	2,047	2,045,750	-8.2
OF	2,158	2,016,346	4.4
1B	602	545,041	9.8

This table shows that, of players born since the year Ruth was born, nearly 1,000 players were considered primarily catchers, and through their age 28 seasons, they have accumulated more than half a million plate appearances. Their hitting production level is 10 runs per 650 plate appearances lower than average, compared to all non-pitchers.

Now, let's ask some questions. What happens to those 959 catchers, and what happens to those 602 first basemen, and what happens to all those infielders and outfielders after the age of 28?

And before we answer those questions, I must point something out that will likely be apparent once we see some of the results. (As I write these words, I have yet to look at the data.) Whatever one thinks of Bill James, there can be no denying that he knows how to frame the debate and ask the right questions most of the time. He introduced something that prima facie seems benign and obvious. And yet, within his defensive spectrum lies the truth of the baseball talent distribution. His spectrum goes something like this:

C-SS-2B-CF-3B-RF-LF-1B

(He might have presented it in reverse order, but that's really irrelevant.) We can quibble a bit about the ordering, especially if you want to get era-specific. But there is great knowledge in such a seemingly simple presentation. As he once said, if you want to know how good a fielder was regarded, and yet you knew nothing about him, consider the defensive spectrum. Movement of players goes from the left side to the right side. And

any movement going the other way is fairly uncommon and indicative of good fielding talent.

Let's suppose you've never seen Tim Raines play, but you know how many games he played at each position. In the minor leagues, he was a second baseman. He started his career in MLB as a second baseman, but was quickly moved to left field. (That's a shift to the right side.) In his second full year in MLB, he played some second base. (That's a bit of shift back to the left side.) In his fourth year he was the team's regular center fielder. (A big shift to the left side.) He went back the following season to being a left fielder, with a spot inning here or there in center field. And in his 30s, played some DH.

So, what can we infer about Raines? He was probably a decent fielder to have started his career as a second baseman, but something was lacking. He moved to left field, where he showed enough talent to move to center field for a full year. But, he wasn't good enough to stay there, so he had a long career at left field, even into his late 30s. He was probably hurt enough that he could only DH, and he missed a lot of games in his 30s. That's a pretty good picture for a guy you've never seen. You can do this for every player, and you'll probably get a decent picture most of the time.

Anyway, I'm going to apply the spectrum a bit more loosely as follows:

P – C – IF – OF - 1B

It is easier to consider the second basemen, shortstops and third basemen as one big pool of players. There is a lot of movement within those three positions for any given player, over a player's career. The same can be said even more forcefully for the three outfield positions. Movement of fielders goes from the left side to the right side. For example, it will be fairly rare that a player will start his career as an outfielder and become an infielder. I'll call this the Fielding Pool Spectrum (FPS).

Now that we've got that settled, let's get back to the data. Let's start with the easy one: first basemen. What do you think happens to players who are primarily first basemen through the age of 28? According to the FPS, they've got nowhere to go. So, we should expect almost all of these players to remain first basemen. What actually happened? Actually, 95 percent remained first basemen. The remaining few became primarily infielders or outfielders, while one became a catcher.

Adam Melhuse started his MLB career at the age of 28, playing four games in the field, three at first base and one at catcher. For the purposes of this study, he was a first baseman. In his career from the age of 29, he played 202 of his 223 games as catcher. It's clear that he was always a catcher, and it's just the wrinkle of him having so few games that makes it look otherwise. Since we are really looking for generalities more than anything, we're not going to start investigating each of these kinds of anomalies. So, we got pretty much the results we expected.

Remember also that I said that, on average, the number of plate appearances from all players through the age of 28 is almost identical to the number from the age of 29 onward? This is true. But, once you remove players who were pitchers and became non-pitchers (e.g., Rick Ankiel), and you remove players who started playing only from the age of 29 onward, when you compare the non-pitchers through age 28 to the number of plate appearances those same players had afterward, there is actually a seven percent drop in the number of plate appearances. Players who were primarily first basemen through age 28 had 545,041 plate appearances, and from the age of 29 they had 520,853 or a drop of four percent. They had some decent staying power. Not a lot, but a bit. The DH probably helped.

Outfielders remained outfielders 89 percent of the time. Of the remaining times they were no longer outfielders, they moved into the first base pool 84 percent of the time. The remaining few times they became infielders or catchers. They had six percent fewer plate appearances from age 29 onward, than through age 28.

Infielders remained infielders 87 percent of the time. When they were no longer infielders, they became outfielders 51 percent of the time, and first basemen 45 percent of the time. A tiny few became catchers. They had 14 percent fewer plate appearances from age 29 onward compared to otherwise. This is a substantial drop, which shows that life as an infielder is somewhat limiting. Their fielding talents may not translate to the outfield or first base, and/or they don't have the bat to sustain themselves elsewhere.

Finally, catchers. Catchers remained catchers 91 percent of the time. The rate of remaining in the same position pool is roughly 90 percent among catchers, infielders and outfielders. When players were no longer catchers, they become outfielders roughly half the time, infielders 30 percent of the time, and first basemen 20 percent of the time. But the most surprising number is that players as catchers through age 28 totaled 553,854 plate appearances, while from age 29 onward that number increased to 620,089. It seems that being a catcher gives you a certain amount of life afterward!

This phenomenon may be due to the Fielding Pool Spectrum. With so many more opportunities to expose themselves (infielder, outfielder, first base), it seems like catchers can continue to fill some role on a team.

Even though first basemen generated 20 more runs than catchers per season with the bat, and even though the number of plate appearances by first basemen and catchers was virtually identical through age 28 (2 percent higher for catchers), the number of plate appearances for these players from age 29 onwards was 19 percent higher for catchers.

Now that we know where all these players went, let's find out how well they continued to hit. First basemen were +10 runs per 650 PA through age 28, and those players produced +13 runs from age 29 onwards. Outfielders and infielders showed a similar three-run improvement with the bat. Catchers, however, showed only a 1.5-run improvement.

(It must be pointed out that while the pool of players is identical in the two age groups, each player will not have the same number of plate appearances in each group. There is a case of survivorship bias. It is possible that the catchers most likely to show improvement in hitting simply weren't given the chance. Nonetheless, the numbers are not so strikingly different that we have to worry too much.)

Another interesting finding is that the players who were considered catchers but were moved to another position later were really good hitters. Those 91 percent who remained at catcher were -9 runs per 650 plate appearances through age 28, and -10 from age 29 onward. The other 9 percent were zero runs through age 28 (i.e. average) and +10 runs from age 29 onward. It is possible that these players, freed from their catching shackles, went on to be the good hitters they always were.

There was also a large group of catchers who simply never played beyond age 28. They were -23 runs per 650 plate appearances as young hitters. Clearly, whatever fielding value they had couldn't overcome their dismal hitting.

Sum Of the Parts – The Catcher's Help

But every now and then I feel so insecure,
I know that I just need you like I've never done
before.

It seems that there is a great burden being placed on a catcher, as evidenced by how often he is rested (see Part 2). Let's tie in the Mike Piazza finding from Part 1, and the shackles finding we just found in Part 3. If you take an average player, and put him at catcher full time, two things will happen:

- As a fielder, he will be worth minus 10 runs in stopping the running game
- As a hitter, he will be worth minus 10 runs in diminished hitting production

So, just by becoming a catcher, an average player will lose 20 runs of production. However, someone has to be the catcher. If a player can stand the grind of catching, has a good bat, and can't really field anywhere, I think catching might be a beneficial career choice. An in-depth exploration of Piazza's career—including his years before joining the Dodgers—is offered elsewhere in these pages, by Craig Wright; it points to just such an experiment and with obviously great success. When you compare a catcher to a non-catcher, make sure to account for the penalty due to his tools of ignorance.

References:

http://sports.yahoo.com/mlb/recap?gid=270608126
http://www.InsideTheBook.com/woba.shtml
Help!—The Beatles

What are Those Other Prospects Worth?

by Victor Wang

Near the trade deadline and during the offseason, we often see blockbuster trades of established major league stars for unproven minor league prospects. Fans like to debate the merits of those trades, especially the ones for players no one has heard of. Fans and analysts tend to make immediate judgments, and often the team receiving the prospects will be criticized for not receiving enough "star" talent in return. These types of trades are often hard for the GM, given the difficulties of evaluating prospects and the win-now attitudes fans and media may have.

Remember the Johan Santana rumors in the 2007 offseason? The Yankees and Red Sox decided to keep their prospects while the Mets traded a few of theirs. How do we know if these teams made the right decision? If we want to analyze these trades objectively, how do we evaluate them?

Here's another example: When the Pirates traded Jason Bay at the trade deadline, how could we put a value on the players the Pirates received? It is easy to see that the Pirates traded away a valuable commodity in Bay. While he might not have the fan appeal of a Manny Ramirez, Bay is a very good hitter who is signed to a below-market deal. Obviously, this sort of player must have a lot of trade value. But what about those prospects the Pirates received? Are Andy Laroche, Bryan Morris, Craig Hansen and Brandon Moss enough return for Bay?

To properly evaluate this deal, we need to know the "trade value" of the prospects the Pirates received. This can be a tricky process. Prospects are harder to project than major league players for a couple of reasons. Most notably, they are farther away from the majors and they still have time to improve or regress. Even if we can project how a prospect will perform, how exactly do we transform that into his trade value?

Those are the questions I like to tackle. First, let me define trade value as the "surplus value" of a player, which is what he would make on the free agent market subtracted by what he is actually paid.

In a sense, trades are exchanges of surplus value, and the easiest way to evaluate a trade is to see who got more value. Obviously we need to consider other factors, like a team's playoff chances, draft picks that may be award-ed in compensation and a team's risk preference. We won't look at those in this article, though.

Trade value is easy enough to figure for major league players with lots of major league playing time, like Bay. We simply use one of the many projection systems available to see how good a player Bay is. Then we calculate how much a player of his caliber typically makes as a free agent and compare that to his actual salary.

As you can imagine, the process for estimating surplus value for prospects is a little trickier but here are the basic steps:

- Divide prospects into talent pools. These pools can be figured out using prospect rankings.
- Find what the average player in a talent pool produces in his first six years in the major leagues. Why only the first six years? That is how long a team has control of a player until he reaches free agency. If we go back to our definition of surplus value, we see that a player has no value if he is being paid what he would get on the free agent market.
- Next, estimate what a player would make on the free agent market versus what he actually would be paid.
- Finally, subtract the free agent estimate by the actual estimate to get a player's surplus value.

I have done this sort of analysis in the past. I calculated the trade value for Top 100 hitting and pitching prospects. Specifically, I broke down hitting and pitching prospects into talent pools rated from 1-10, 11-25, 26-50, 51-75 and 76-100. Prospect rankings were taken from *Baseball America's* top 100 prospect lists from 1990-1999. Here is the average surplus trade value of each type of prospect, in millions:

Rating	Hitters	Pitchers
1 to 10	$36.5	$15.2
11 to 25	25.1	15.9
26 to 50	23.4	15.9
51 to 75	14.2	12.1
76 to 100	12.5	9.8

A few notes about my original findings:

- Hitting prospects have a lot more value than pitching prospects of the same talent pool, largely because pitching prospects are a lot riskier than hitting prospects.

- Pitchers are very hard to project. I found that pitchers rated from 11-25 and 26-50 actually had more value than top 10 pitchers. Part of this could be due to the small sample size (only 26 pitchers) of the top 10 group.

- Elite prospects are valuable enough that usually it is not worth it to trade one for a two-month rental at the trade deadline.

- Top 10 hitting prospects are among the most valuable commodities in baseball.

Applying these results to the Pirates, we find that one of the players they received falls into the elite prospect category. Andy Laroche has been a highly touted prospect for the past few years and *Baseball America* rated Laroche as the No. 31 prospect in baseball at the beginning of the season. Other rankings also rated him highly. This is a very good start for the Pirates. Most trades, though, involve just one or two top 100 prospects. If we want to get a full picture of a trade, we need to know the value of the lower-rated prospects, too. This article will attempt to find the value of these types of prospects.

Methodology

Here is the process I used to find the value of lower rated prospects:

- Using John Sickels' prospect rankings from 1997 and 1999, divide prospects into talent groups. Sickels rates prospects using letter grades. Comparing his prospect grades to those of *Baseball America's* top 100 prospects, almost all the top 100 prospects had A, A- or B+ grades while a few had B grades. Since we are looking at the value of lower-ranked prospects, I removed those Sickels gave A, A- or B+ grades. Then, I grouped hitting and pitching prospects into two groups: B prospects (including B-) and C prospects (including C+ and C-). I had enough of a sample size within the C prospect group to break down that group of prospects even further into C prospects 22 or younger and C prospects 23 or older.

- Find the WSAB (Win Shares Above Bench) of each prospect in his first six major league years. WSAB, introduced by Dave Studenmund, takes a player's Win Shares, created by Bill James, and compares

that to the production of an average bench player. Win Shares is essentially an estimate of how many wins a player contributed to his team.

- Estimate what each player would make on the free agent market at that level of production. This is very easy to do since Dave has found that there is a direct relationship between WSAB and a player's salary.

- Estimate what each player would actually make in his first six years. Salary rules in the major leagues make this easy enough if we know the WSAB of a player.

- Take the difference between the third and fourth steps to find the savings.

Results

First let's look at the results for B hitters and pitchers:

B Hitters

WSAB Rank	Number	Percent
Bust	82	59%
Contributor	50	36%
Everyday	6	4%
All-Star	0	0%
Superstar	0	0%
Total	138	100%

Average Surplus Value: $5.5 million

B Pitchers

WSAB Rank	Number	Percent
Bust	58	52%
Contributor	37	33%
Everyday	9	8%
All-Star	5	5%
Superstar	2	2%
Total	111	100%

Average Surplus Value: $7.3 million

I broke down prospects' major league performance into these groups to give readers a better understanding of the distribution of outcomes for the prospects. The headings should be pretty self-explanatory; a "contributor" is equivalent to a good bench player or middle reliever.

The first thing that jumps out is that the pitching prospects have more value than the hitting prospects. This didn't happen among any of the top 100 prospect ranking groups. Also, the B hitting prospects did not produce any all-star or superstar caliber players. While this does not mean that B hitting prospects can never become an all-star or superstar, it does suggest that the odds may be low.

B prospects also have huge rates of attrition. In fact, more than half were busts. While it is not shown in the data, B pitching prospects who turn out to be successful tend to become major league relievers. Included were such pitchers as Keith Foulke, Joe Nathan, Octavio Dotel and, to a lesser extent, Billy Koch and Danny Graves. I'm not sure if this trend will continue, but it could prove meaningful in the future.

We also see that there is not much of a difference between a B pitching prospect and a pitching prospect in the lower half of the top 100. The dropoff is a bit larger for B hitting prospects. This suggests that a GM, when trading, would be wise to ask for one or two elite hitting prospects while stocking up on lower-rated pitching prospects.

Now let's look at the value of the C prospects:

C hitters 22 or younger

WSAB Rank	Number	Percent
Bust	128	83%
Contributor	22	14%
Everyday	3	2%
All-Star	1	1%
Superstar	0	0%
Total	154	100%

Average Surplus Value: $0.7 million

C hitters 23 or older

WSAB Rank	Number	Percent
Bust	236	84%
Contributor	41	15%
Everyday	4	1%
All-Star	1	0%
Superstar	0	0%
Total	282	100%

Average Surplus Value: $0.5 million

C pitchers 22 or younger

WSAB Rank	Number	Percent
Bust	117	73%
Contributor	36	23%
Everyday	3	2%
All-Star	4	3%
Superstar	0	0%
Total	160	100%

Average Surplus Value: $2.1 million

C pitchers 23 or older

WSAB Rank	Number	Percent
Bust	192	78%
Contributor	46	19%
Everyday	7	3%
All-Star	1	0%
Superstar	1	0%
Total	247	100%

Average Surplus Value: $1.5 million

From this we see again that lower-rated pitching prospects have higher value than hitting prospects of the same age and ranking. And while C hitting prospects may not be worthless, they don't provide much value. The dropoff in value from B prospects to C prospects is about the same for both hitters and pitchers.

While rare, it is possible to have a C prospect turn into an All-Star. Notable former C prospects include Jimmy Rollins, Tim Hudson, Eric Gagne and Magglio Ordonez. Just as for B prospects, the rate of attrition is huge for C prospects. This time more than 70 percent of all prospects became busts. It is also interesting to note that age does not seem to affect the bust rate much for C prospects.

Given all this, it seems that if one were to choose between quality or quantity, the best decision would be to go for quality. It will take a few C prospects to match the value of one B prospect and even more to match the value of a top 100 prospect. Even if offered, say, four C pitching prospects for one B pitching prospect, I'm not sure a team would accept that. While you're getting more overall value, there is still an opportunity cost that occurs when developing talent in the minors and then seeing if that talent is good enough to perform in the majors. Taking this to an extreme example, I doubt a team would want 50 C prospects for a single top 10 hitting prospect.

The data suggest that the best trading strategy would be to go for elite hitting prospects while asking for lower-rated pitching prospects to fill the rest of the spots. Hitting prospects in the 51-75 group have almost the same value as any pitching group in the top 50. The high costs of acquiring pitching on the free agent market make it appealing to acquire pitching prospects, but the tremendous value of elite hitting prospects makes it foolish to ask for an elite pitching prospect instead. If a team wants to acquire young pitchers, it would be best to do so by acquiring lower-rated prospects in bulk. Given how reluctant teams seem to be to trade pitching prospects, the price for an elite one likely will be too high.

It's also important to note the surplus value of C pitching prospects 23 or older. That $1.5 million figure is equal to the signing bonus the No. 17 pick in the most recent draft received. I am sure that most GMs would gladly trade a C pitching prospect for the No. 17 pick in the draft. This suggests that draft picks are underpaid.

Overall, C prospects are throw-ins for a reason. They don't provide much additional value in the trade, especially so for hitters.

Conclusion

So what can we gather from this study?

- Unlike the findings from the top 100 prospects, pitchers have more value than hitters of the same group. This likely occurs because pitching prospects are harder to project than hitting prospects, so lower-rated pitching prospects may have more upside than hitters of the same group. This can be seen clearly at the C prospect level, where roughly three C hitting prospects equal one C pitching prospect of the same age level.

- Low-rated prospects have huge rates of attrition. I found that in each group, more than half did not give even average bench production in the majors.

- Draft picks are underpaid. For example, the surplus value of a C pitching prospect 23 or older is exactly equal to the signing bonus of the No. 17 pick in the 2008 draft. Teams would almost certainly give up that kind of prospect for that pick.

- A good trading strategy appears to go for one or two elite hitting prospects while filling the rest of the trade with pitching prospects.

I hope this research provides a solid base on which we can objectively evaluate future trades involving major leaguers and prospects.

So, then, how did those Pirates do? It turns out they did pretty well. Trading Bay didn't hurt their nonexistent playoff chances for 2008 and probably won't for 2009, so we don't have to worry about that. At the time of the trade, Bay had about $10 million in trade value. If you want to knock Laroche's prospect ranking down because of his struggles in the majors so far, then the Pirates came out with about $18.3 million in value. If you trust *Baseball America's* judgment, then Pittsburgh came out with about $27.5 million in value. Either way, this looks like a nice trade for the Pirates.

Sources

1. *Baseball America's* All Time Top 100 Prospects, http://www.baseballamerica.com/today/prospects/rankings/top-100-prospects/all-time/

2. 2007 Net Win Shares Value, Dave Studenmund, http://www.hardballtimes.com/main/article/2007-net-win-shares-value/

3. A previous article on my prospect valuation research can be found here: http://www.philbirnbaum.com/btn2007-11.pdf

4. CBS Sports Salary Data, http://www.sportsline.com/mlb/salaries/avgsalaries

5. STATS *1997 and 1999 Minor League Scouting Notebooks*

6. How are free agent deals determined, Vince Gennaro, http://sports.yahoo.com/mlb/news;_ylt=Atey BrOmgwgJ8hFNqBGc0PwRvLYF?slug=ys-gennaroanalysis042408&prov=yhoo&type=lgns#send

7. This study could not have been done without the help of Dave Studenmund, who was kind enough to give me all the Win Shares information I needed.

Sizing Up the Players

by David Gassko

Once in awhile, I get an e-mail question from someone in the media. Sometimes, the questions are straightforward, and I don't spend more than a few minutes thinking about them, but sometimes I get a question so interesting and original that I end up spending hours, or even days, researching the answer. The following e-mail falls into the latter category:

> I'm writing an article for a magazine about the influence of size on performance in baseball. I have a theory that with the decline of the steroids-fueled HR era, shorter players are closing the value gap on larger players, and thanks to defense, may be surpassing larger players in overall value ... (Do) you know of any study out there that has compared the declining HR rates of big players vs. smaller players over the last few years?

If he is right, the author has stumbled onto a potentially huge change in the makeup and demographics of the major leagues, and indeed the way the game is played—a shift in strategy that would reject reliance on the three-run homer and bring back a focus on running and moving runners over.

Certainly, his theory sounds reasonable. After all, we know that home run hitters tend to be bigger guys, and with home runs down significantly across baseball, you might think the bigger players have suffered the most. A team can deal with a low batting average and bad defense when its slugging first baseman is hitting 40 home runs a year, but if he's hitting only 30, that takes a huge chunk out of his overall value.

Things might go the other way, too. If every player has lost the same number of home runs over the past few years, tall players would be no less valuable today than they were a few years back. And moreover, what image from the steroids era is more memorable: The giant slugger hitting 60+ home runs, or the tiny shortstop suddenly cranking 30? The sluggers might have gotten more press, but there were a lot more of the shortstop types, and their collective impact may have been much greater. In that case, it might be that small players have suffered a lot more from this league-wide downturn in power numbers than the big guys.

It's a fascinating question, but I want to lend some context to it first. To do that, we'll first explore how the role of player size has changed throughout the existence of professional baseball, starting with 1871.

That year, the average player was 5-foot-8.6, and the tallest player in baseball was Fort Wayne Kekiongas outfielder Bob Armstrong, who stood at an imposing 6-foot-2. By comparison, the average player in 2007 was 6-foot-1.6-inches tall, led by pitcher Jon Rauch of the Washington Nationals, who is 6-foot-11. Here is a graph of the changes in average player height between 1871 and 2007:

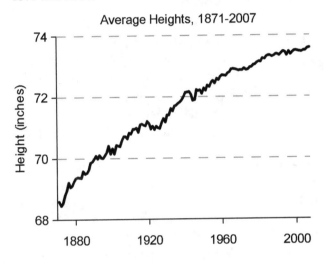

We observe a constantly rising pattern, though growth certainly has slowed in recent years. Overall, the average player today is five inches taller than the average player in 1871, implying a growth rate of one inch every 27 years. Over the past 40 years, however, the height of the average major leaguer has increased by just .7 inches, meaning a growth rate of one inch every 57 years, less than half that of the historical average.

And though this historical rise has been extraordinarily consistent, there are a few visible kinks in the graph. The most prominent is in 1944 and '45, when many major league stars were fighting the war abroad, and lesser, smaller players replaced them. The average height dropped two-tenths of an inch between 1943 and '44, and then jumped a third of an inch in 1946.

But of course, if we are to answer the query that originated this piece, we cannot look just at the average size of major league baseball players. (To be clear, we will use "size" and "height" interchangeably in this piece. Height correlates very closely with weight among major league baseball players, but weight information is much less reliable and can change drastically over a player's career. For those reasons, I've decided to limit my definition of player size to height.) Instead, we need to be looking at the biggest and smallest major leaguers, and seeing how their performances compare.

So how do we define a "tall" or "short" player? A fair definition would be to find the top 10 percent at each extreme in a given year. Throughout much of baseball history, that has meant that "short" players are three inches (or more) shorter than average, while tall players are three inches (or more) taller than average. For example, in 1871 a player had to be 5-feet-5.8-inches to be classified as short, but by 2007, that threshold had grown to 5-feet-10.6 inches.

That's not much less than the threshold for tall players in 1871, which was 5-feet-11.4 , but which has since risen to 6-feet-4.5 inches today. Someday, though it may be another half century, a "short" player will be tall enough to have qualified as a "tall" player in 1871.

Now that we have defined what we mean by "short" and "tall" (or "big" and "small"), let's look at how those two groups of players have performed over the years. My statistic of choice here is OPS+, which is on-base percentage plus slugging average normalized to the league average (usually, OPS+ is also adjusted for park effects, but I have not done so here). An OPS+ of 100 is average, an OPS+ of 120 means that the hitter was 20 percent better than average, and an OPS+ of 80 means he was 20 percent worse. Here is how short and tall hitters have performed in OPS+ since 1871:

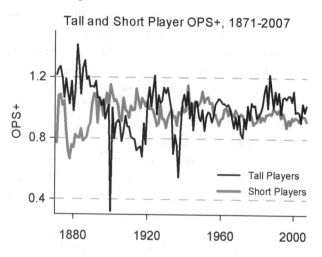

Tall and Short Player OPS+, 1871-2007

The first thing we see is a lot of variation, especially among taller hitters. At their worst, in 1900, tall hitters

had a collective OPS+ of 32, which is Mario Mendoza territory (actually, significantly worse), though at its best, their OPS+ reached 141, in 1882. Short hitters have a lot less variation, though at their worst, they have hit 66 (1888), and at their best, they have gone up as high as 115 (1900).

Overall, though, short players have been pretty clearly a bit below average (especially in the past 50 years), while taller players have bounced around, though in total, it turns out, they have been almost exactly average.

Our original research, however, was not sparked by an interest in how big or small hitters perform versus the league average hitter, but rather how their performances compare to one another. Let's therefore look at another graph, this one comparing tall players' OPS+ in a given year to that of the short hitters, with a ratio above one favoring the taller guys, and a ratio below one favoring the short players:

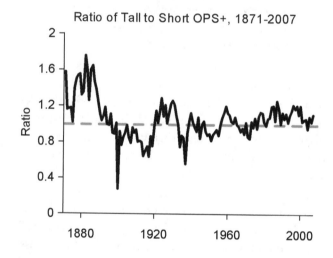

Ratio of Tall to Short OPS+, 1871-2007

Again, there is quite a bit of variation in this graph, though the swings have lessened considerably in modern times. Tall players were as much as 76 percent better (1882) and 72 percent worse (1900). Overall, bigger players have had a slight advantage over their smaller counterparts, on the order of about 5.2 percent since 1871, though that advantage has been around 6.6 percent in this century.

There are some notable points in all this variation: From 1921 through 1932, tall players sported a 15 percent advantage. Immediately thereafter, between 1934 and '38, the ratio swung the other way, as the bigger hitters performed 22 percent *worse* than the small guys. In fact, we can try to group every year in major league history into a few eras, based on whether big or small players were dominating at the time.

This is an imperfect exercise, but I come up with six fairly distinct eras:

- **1871-1896,** which is dominated by tall players, with an average ratio of tall-to-short-hitter OPS+ of 132 (meaning that tall players were about 32 percent better at creating runs than their shorter counterparts).
- **1897-1920,** an era dominated by short hitters, with an average ratio of 82.
- **1921-1932,** a tall player era, sporting an average ratio of 115.
- **1933-1956,** years which were favorable to short hitters, with an average ratio of 92.
- **1957-1965,** a tall player era, where the average ratio was 108.
- **1966-1976,** the last short hitter era, with an average ratio of 95.
- **1977-2007,** where the average ratio has been 110.

You can see, first of all, that many of these eras correspond roughly to other commonly accepted eras in Major League Baseball history. The first two eras we defined, for example, closely correspond to the generally established 19th century and deadball eras. The last era starts at the same time as modern free agency. The time periods in between do not comport quite as well, but still, there is something going on here. In fact, I have a theory about what it is; take a look at this table of the runs per game scored in each era:

Era	Label	R/G	Change
1871-1896	Tall	5.90	--
1897-1920	Short	4.10	-1.80
1921-1932	Tall	4.92	0.82
1933-1956	Short	4.53	-0.39
1957-1965	Tall	4.24	-0.29
1966-1976	Short	3.99	-0.25
1977-2007	Tall	4.56	0.58

In all but one case, runs per game go down when we go from a tall player era to a short player era, and they go up when we go back. The one exception is when we go from a short hitter era in 1933-1956 to a tall player era in 1957-1965, when runs per game nonetheless declined from 4.53 to 4.24. Home runs per game, however, rose from 0.62 to 0.88 between these two periods, so there does to be some evidence even there that eras that favor smaller hitters tend to be lower scoring and less powerful while those that favor bigger hitters involve more scoring and power. In that case, the evidence would

suggest that our reporter's theory—that short hitters will benefit from the end of the steroid-fueled past decade—looks correct.

(Statistically speaking, the correlation between runs per game and the ratio is 0.42, which is fairly strong. Note that the correlation is the same for the period of 1901-2007 as it is for 1871-2007. If we correct for auto-correlation—the problem being that the "ratio" and run scoring have both trended upward over the years—we still find a highly significant correlation of 0.25. So yes, when run scoring goes up, bigger players benefit, and when it declines, it's the smaller hitters who win.)

But does that general conclusion apply to the past few years?

This is really at the heart of the question that began this essay. Major league baseball experienced an offensive boom in the 1990s, a trend that has reversed itself only in the past few years, likely thanks to a changed steroid policy. We know that run scoring is down, but we don't know yet how that will affect the game.

If steroid testing changes the demographics of the game, favoring smaller players over taller ones, then we might be about to see a shift in the way the game is played, placing a greater emphasis on small ball and defense, while eschewing home runs to a greater degree. But the question remains: Is that actually what has happened? Let's start by looking at what has changed since the peak of this recent offensive boom, 2000. This is the percentage change that occurred in all major offensive categories between 2000 and 2007, with 2000 numbers set as the baseline:

Runs	-7%
Singles	1%
Doubles	3%
Triples	-1%
Home Runs	-13%
Walks	-12%
HBP	12%

We see that runs have declined significantly since 2000, by 7 percent, and the difference is largely accounted for by three offensive categories: home runs, walks and hit-by-pitch (which have actually increased 12 percent). Let's look at how those statistics have changed among short and tall players specifically—have tall players, as we might expect, seen more of a decline than their smaller counterparts?

Changes in selected offensive categories between 2000 and 2007, by height class

Height	HR	BB	HBP
Short	-24.6%	-21.3%	-10.3%
Medium	-10.4%	-9.3%	16.5%
Tall	-20.7%	-13.8%	16.4%

This is an interesting result, and the one that sparked my interest in this issue in the first place. Short and tall players seem to have experienced a similar percentage decline in home runs since the peak of the juiced era, but that decline is much greater for both than it is for the rest of baseball. Walk rates declined least among medium-sized players, a bit more among tall players, and still more among short players. Hit-by-pitch rose equally for tall and medium-sized players, but paradoxically dropped a lot for shorter hitters.

Let's step back for a moment, and see how numbers in these three categories changed going into the juiced era. Here is the same table, but looking at the change between 1992 and 2000, instead:

Changes in selected offensive categories between 1992 and 2000, by height class

Height	HR	BB	HBP
Short	82.1%	5.8%	54.0%
Medium	54.9%	14.1%	31.3%
Tall	50.0%	8.5%	68.5%

Short players saw a much greater percentage increase in their home run rate during the juiced era than did the other two categories of players, suggesting, perhaps, that they had some kind of advantage that medium and tall players did not.

By the way, the larger increase in home run rate for small players does not imply that they drove the increase in scoring that occurred in the 1990s. First of all, home runs are just one category—as we'll shortly see, shorter players saw a much smaller increase in walks and hit-by-pitch in those years than did medium and tall players. Secondly, a 50 percent increase in home runs for a tall player could well be greater in absolute terms than an 80 percent increase for a short hitter—a hitter who starts

with 20 home runs a year and jumps to 30 (a 50 percent increase) sees a greater absolute increase in his home run totals than a hitter who starts at 10, and sees an 80 percent increase to 18. This is why we see an increase in the ratio of tall-to-short players' OPS between 1992 and 2000, even though short hitters see a greater increase in home run rate. But I digress.

There are two possibilities in play here, as far as I can tell. The first is that the juiced ball and more hitter-friendly ballparks benefited shorter hitters more than they did everyone else, because a lot more of their fly ball outs turned into home runs (at least on a percentage basis). The second is that the short players radically changed in terms of their ability to hit for power during the juiced era … in other words, they were more likely to use steroids.

How do we test that theory? We'll get to that in a moment. For now, let's look at one more table, this one combining the results of the last two, to show how each height class changed between the beginning of the juiced era, 1992, and the end, 2007.

Changes in selected offensive categories between 1992 and 2007, by height class

Height	HR	BB	HBP
Short	37.4%	-16.7%	38.1%
Medium	38.8%	3.5%	52.9%
Tall	19.0%	-6.4%	96.1%

The ultimate winners, when all is said and done, appear to be medium-sized players, who saw their home run rates, walk rates, and hit-by-pitch rates all go up over the last 15 years. Tall players saw their hit-by-pitch rates almost double, suggesting that they have taken much more advantage of the body armor now available, and spend a lot more time hanging over the plate, but their walk rates have fallen some since 1992, and their home run rates have seen only half the increase of the other 90 percent of major league baseball players. Short players, meanwhile, saw a huge increase in home run rate, but a relatively smaller increase in hit-by-pitch and a very large drop in walks.

These are all cool data, but let's get to the point. There are two theories we want to test out here:

1. The question with which this article began, asking if smaller players have benefited from the reduction in offense over the past few years, and

2. Does our evidence point toward pervasive steroid use among smaller hitters during the juiced era.

The problem with the numbers we have run thus far is that we have looked at groups of players as a whole, instead of individual players. Here's the issue: Short (tall) hitters who played in 2000 are not the same short (tall) hitters who played in 2007. Therefore, we cannot really compare their statistics. Instead, we need to look at short (tall) players from 2000, and see how they performed in 2007.

This isn't so difficult. All you have to do is weight each player's statistics from each season by his lesser number of plate appearances in those two years, so if a hitter had fewer plate appearances in 2000 than in 2007, we weight his statistics in both years by that number, and vice-versa. Once we've done that, we derive the following table:

Changes in selected offensive categories between 2000 and 2007, by height class, weighted by lesser number of plate appearances

Short/Tall	Change(HR)	Change(BB)	Change(HBP)
Short	-32.3%	-23.4%	-12.7%
Medium	-18.7%	-5.7%	-6.6%
Tall	-23.9%	-11.4%	63.1%

We see here some continuation of the trends we saw in the first table, though with a couple of big differences. The first is that while short hitters still see a huge decline in their home run rate, tall players did not differ much from medium-sized hitters. The second is that short-and-medium-sized players now see a similar decline in hit-by-pitch rate, while tall hitters see an even more ridiculous explosion.

So we can immediately reject our reporter's theory, that short players somehow benefited from the current decline in run scoring. Though small players generally do better relative to large hitters when offense declines, the ratio of short-to-tall player OPS+ has not declined in this current period, and the home run rate has actually dropped more for shorter players. This drop is not quite statistically significant, as there is a 17.7 percent chance that it could have occurred due to random chance alone, but that still means that there is an 82.3 percent chance that it *is* meaningful, which I don't think should be fully ignored, especially in light of the following evidence.

Let's also look at how these statistics changed between 1992 and 2000 to get a full picture of what's happened over the juiced era, and since.

Changes in selected offensive categories between 1992 and 2000, by height class, weighted by lesser number of plate appearances

Short/Tall	Change(HR)	Change(BB)	Change(HBP)
Short	68.4%	10.6%	-1.8%
Medium	55.2%	23.0%	9.6%
Tall	40.1%	10.8%	34.1%

While short players have seen the greatest decline in home run rates since the juiced era ended, they also saw the greatest increase during the boom years of the '90s. The 68.4 percent increase is significantly different from the 40.1 percent increase among tall hitters, as there is just a 0.3 percent chance that we would see such a disparity due to random chance alone. In other words, something definitely changed in the power numbers of small hitters during the juiced years in a way that was much more drastic than the increased home run totals among big players.

We might explain this away by saying that short hitters had, on a percentage basis, many more deep fly balls that suddenly became home runs as parks got smaller and the ball got bouncier. However, in conjunction with the stark decline in home run rates among short hitters since 2000 (which by the way, when compared to the decline in home run rates among the rest of major league baseball as opposed to just tall hitters, is significantly different, with just a 3.3 percent chance of getting such a result by random chance alone), I think there is fairly strong evidence that smaller hitters were more likely to juice, and have been hurt the most by baseball's tough new steroid policy.

When you think about it, that conclusion is not unreasonable. As we have seen, smaller hitters these days are below-average hitters, meaning that major league teams likely view them as more expendable. The salary difference between bouncing around in the minor leagues and having a guaranteed spot on a major league roster—if only as a utility player—is huge, and so players in that position would have the most incentive to cheat.

Who were those players? Naturally, guys not known for their hitting, for whom a few extra home runs was a big deal—in other words, generally speaking, smaller players. In fact, author Nate Silver came to a similar conclusion in the book *Baseball Between the Numbers*: "The typical steroid user might not be the prima donna slugger who endorses Budweiser between innings," he wrote, "but the 'hardworking late bloomer' who is struggling to maintain his spot in the lineup or is trying to leverage a good season into a big free-agent contract." Based on the evidence we've uncovered here, I tend to concur.

Overall, then, we see that while smaller hitters tend to benefit from lower-scoring eras, this particular one is shaping up differently. Because the juiced era bene-fited smaller players to a greater degree, its end also has been the hardest on that same class. Therefore, I wouldn't advise you to expect the end of the burly home run hitting slugger. Instead, the one player that Major League Baseball's steroid policy might indeed eradicate is the 5-foot-9 middle infielder who drives the ball 450 feet. Dustin Pedroia excluded, of course.

I would like to extend a big thank you to Russell Carleton, who provided me with a ton of help in writing an article that originally was supposed to go in this space. The article didn't make it, but given how much Russell aided me, the thank you still should.

BOSS JR. CAM.

The Best Run Estimator

by Colin Wyers

(Editor's Note: This article is a reprint of the first two of Colin Wyers' Run Estimator posts at the Statistically Speaking blog. Before Colin's posts, articles that measured the effectiveness of run estimators relied on team scoring by season or by game. Colin's is the first analysis we've seen that relies on scoring by inning. We feel this is a major step forward in run estimator analysis, and Colin has given us permission to reprint his work for you.)

To study runs is to study baseball. We want to know which hitters produce the most runs and which pitchers allow the fewest. We want to know the best ways for teams to score runs. And we want to know which teams will win the most baseball games next year, and the easiest way to do that is to figure out how many runs they'll score and how many they'll allow.

It helps to establish models of run scoring—both concretely, to answer questions we may have, and abstractly, to inform what questions we want to ask. The basic principles of run estimation are simple: Every event contributes to or detracts from run scoring in the following ways:

- **Provide a baserunner.** Except with a home run, no event is capable of scoring runs without baserunners ahead to drive in. Every baserunner provides run scoring potential, sort of like the kinetic energy potential in a pile of kindling and tinder.
- **Advance the baserunner.** Once you have your baserunners—your potential energy—you drive them in by advancing them. This is your set of flint and steel, to provide a spark and create potential energy into actual energy.
- **Avoid making outs.** Once you reach three outs in the inning, the run potential drops to zero, no matter how many baserunners you have. Outs are like oxygen. Fire won't burn without oxygen and runs won't score without outs remaining in the inning.

All a run estimator does is, well, estimate the value of an event in light of these three aspects.

Different Types of Run Estimators

There are three types of run estimators: linear, dynamic and simulation.

Linear Estimators

Linear estimators are based upon the average value of an event in a certain context. There are many different implementations of linear weights formulas, but they all follow the same basic principles and really differ only in the offensive categories they consider (some include more esoteric events like bases reached on error or grounding into double plays) and the weights they assign each event. We'll look at the reduced version of Extrapolated Runs (XR), Jim Furtado's version of a linear weights formula.

Why Extrapolated Runs? Because it's a popular linear weights implementation, it's solid and it meets the needs of the study very well. It is not necessarily the linear weights formula I would use for other purposes.

Here's the formula:

$$(.50 * 1B) + (.72 * 2B) + (1.04 * 3B) + (1.44 * HR) + (.33 * (HP+TBB)) + (.18 * SB) + (-.32 * CS) + ((-.098 * (AB - H))$$

Essentially, every event is multiplied by its average run value, based on a certain run context. (In the case of XR it's team seasons from 1995 to 1997, but you could use any context you wanted. You could put together a linear weights formula for, say, Greg Maddux' career if you wanted to.)

This begs the question of how to determine the run value of an event. Looking simply at Runs Batted In won't help—a single with the bases empty provides value. So what do we do? Here's where a concept called run expectancy comes in handy. Every base/out state has a certain run expectancy, which essentially is how many runs on average a team scores from that point of the inning going forward. On the next page, you'll find a table of the average run expectancy of each base/out situation based upon Retrosheet play-by-play data from 1956 to 2007.

Bases:	No outs	1 Out	2 Outs
Empty	0.486	0.259	0.098
1B only	0.859	0.512	0.220
2B only	1.106	0.674	0.327
3B only	1.334	0.936	0.374
1B & 2B	1.480	0.905	0.435
1B & 3B	1.743	1.156	0.494
2B & 3B	1.972	1.371	0.591
Loaded	2.324	1.542	0.752

There's one case not strictly defined on the table: Three outs means a run expectancy of zero.

The linear weights value of an event is the average change in run expectancy by an event. Let's say you have runners on first and second, no outs; that's a run expectancy of 1.480. A player hits a double, scoring the two runners in front of him.

The double scored two runs and leaves the game with an run expectancy of 1.189, for a total run expectancy of 3.106. Subtract 1.480, and you get 1.626, the run contribution of that particular double. Take the average run expectancy change of every double available in your dataset, and there's your linear weights value of a double.

(You can generate linear weights in other fashions—you can use a linear regression or you can use a dynamic run estimator or a model to generate linear weights. The empiric method is "correct" in that it measures the actual run value of each event in that context, with the caveat that if you do not have enough events in your sample it can introduce inaccuracies and clearly unrealistic weights for some events, especially triples and other rare events.)

Pros:

- Linear weights estimators are very simple to use. The only math involved is subtraction and multiplication.

- You can apply them directly to individual players and get very reasonable results.

- They're very flexible; you can come up with custom linear weights for almost anything imaginable. Want linear weights by pitch location? No problem!

Cons:

- They don't work very well at the extremes; linear weights measure the average run contribution in the average run environment for the sample.

- Events in a linear weights model don't interact with each other. If a team takes more walks and hits more home runs, the value of the home runs doesn't increase to reflect the increased likelihood of baserunners being on when the homers are hit; the value of the walk doesn't increase to reflect the increased likelihood of scoring on a home run.

- Unlike a dynamic run estimator, you have to build a custom linear weights model for different environments—or at least you do if you want your results to be close to accurate.

Dynamic Run Estimators

Dynamic run estimators attempt to describe the interaction of different events. On a team with a .500 on-base percentage, a home run is worth more runs than for a team with a .200 on-base percentage. The two main dynamic run estimators are Bill James' Runs Created and David Smyth's Base Runs.

The original **Runs Created** (RC) formula is probably the simplest run estimator possible: OBP * SLG * AB.

This is fantastically useful if you ever have to estimate run scoring from nothing but crumpled up issues of The Sporting News, or from the full screen graphics on ESPN during SportsCenter. (And if you've never had to do that, you've never written 4,000-plus words on the accuracy of various run estimators. Not because you need to do one to do the other, but because you need to be that kind of person.)

Unfortunately it didn't end there. It was only beginning.

I should back up a moment and explain that the above is really shorthand for the actual Runs Created Basic formula. (Not a shortcut, though—it's algebraically identical.) The full formula is:

$$(H+W)*TB/(AB+W)$$

Generally represented as:

$$A * B / C$$

Where A is baserunners, B is advancement and C is opportunities. (Opportunities in this case means plate appearances.) Since then, it's been a succession of more complex and yet more complex formulas still, all following the basic A*B/C construct. (There are also "theoretical team" versions designed to correct flaws in applying RC to individual batters.)

I won't give you an in-depth explanation of the differences between Tech-1 RC and Tech-7 RC and so forth; I do want to look a bit more closely at the basic framework behind RC, though. You could rewrite RC as this:

Runners * % of runners that score
with B/C being your estimated scoring rate

Pros

- Basic versions of RC are very easy to use; Basic Runs Created is the perfect run estimator for when you're on vacation or otherwise need a quick-and-dirty run estimator that's also easy to remember.

- You can find Runs Created at pretty much any baseball web site—even ESPN's. It's like the McDonald's of run estimation—fast, hot and available on every street corner.

Cons

- There's a reason that James bothered to come up with even more complex versions of Runs Created—the simpler versions of RC leave something to be desired in the accuracy department. They of course sacrifice most of the simplicity of Basic RC.

- Using B/C as your scoring rate estimator leaves you with the problem that you can, in fact, end up with more runs scoring than there ever were baserunners, because you can get B values in excess of C. This is not in fact possible in baseball.

- On that note … well, consider a player with a solo home run in his first PA. His AVG/OBP/SLG would be 1.000/1.000/4.000. Well, according to Runs Created: $1.000 * 4.000 * 1 = 4$. So, a solo home run is expected to score four runs. This is not in fact possible in baseball. And this is only an extreme example of how Runs Created handles the home run, not the breaking point. (The more sophisticated versions of Runs Created handle the home run better, but are still flawed in that regard.)

- Application to individual hitters leads to distorted numbers, hence the creation of "theoretical team" versions.

Base Runs (BR) was created by David Smyth to address the aforementioned problems in RC, and it follows a similar construction, with a few key differences. The basic framework for BsR is:

$$A * B/(B+C) + D$$

The D factor is equal to home runs. A home run guarantees at least one run scoring, so BsR conforms to that reality. That means a reduced weight for the home run in the A and B values, which just as in RC stand for baserunners and advancement. (C is still opportunity as well, but BsR uses outs instead of plate appearances.)

The other key difference is that BsR includes B in both the numerator and denominator of the scoring percentage estimator. By doing this, BsR caps the numbers of runs that can score at the number of baserunners in the inning, plus home runs.

Pros

- BsR is the best simulation (as of right now) of actual baseball scoring in the form of a single equation. That's not just useful for accuracy, but if we want to use our run estimator as a model to solve a larger problem.

- Many BsR equations come with a "tuning factor" in the B factor to allow you to tweak the equation to fit a particular run scoring environment.

Cons

- More complicated than Basic RC (although, in my opinion, no more complicated than any of the further refinements of RC).

- Like RC, it's problematic to apply to individual hitters, hence the need for "theoretical team" versions.

A Brief Word about Simulators

A simulator goes one step further, and actually details the workings of a baseball lineup, generally through matrix math and Markov chains. Such models are infeasible as a single equation, and are normally implemented as computer programs. Studying a full Markov model is beyond the scope here; I just wanted to mention them for completeness' sake.

How Accurate are Run Estimators?

As you move from one type of estimator to the next, you generally end up with more accuracy in exchange for more complexity. (Another benefit of linear run estimators is that they work very well for individual hitters; the other methods require additional steps in order to accurately portray a hitter's contribution to a team context.)

Most studies of run estimator accuracy have concerned themselves with accuracy at the team level, using seasonal totals. This makes sense for a lot of reasons—run scoring is a team process, and team level run scoring data are readily available for entire seasons. Here's the rub, though—estimating runs at the seasonal team level isn't that hard. Here's a look at the distribution of team runs per game, 1954-2007:

R/G	Seasons
2-3	7
3-4	305
4-5	805
5-6	197
6-7	4

Notice how everything bunches up in the center? That's because there isn't a vast difference in run scoring totals between teams over the course of an entire season. But we're not interested in studying only things that fall in the limited range of team run scoring totals. Take pitchers, for instance. What does a similar table of qualified starters look like?

RA/G	Seasons
1-2	10
2-3	276
3-4	1,517
4-5	1,557
5-6	475
6-7	57
7-8	4

That's a bit more diverse, isn't it? And we're selectively sampling only those pitchers who were starters good enough to pitch for a whole season. Ace relievers and guys who get shelled in their first start and are banished back to the minors are an even more diverse group.

When you get down to brass tacks, run scoring happens on the inning level. Once you record the third out in the inning, you've closed the book on everything that happened before. A home run in the third inning won't drive in a guy who takes a walk in the fourth inning. The inning is the smallest fundamental unit of the team run scoring process. So to study run estimation at its fundamental unit, you need to look at innings.

A warning to those who pass through here...

As I just hinted, it is dangerous to apply a dynamic run estimator to an individual player—okay, not in a "It's going to explode!" sort of sense, but it's not advisable. The reason is because a hitter is (assuming a full-time starter) only one-ninth of his run environment. While a player's individual batting stats might look like the distribution of a pitcher's runs allowed, his environment looks more like the team distribution.

Or put another way—a player's three aspects of run generation do not interact with each other, but with his team as a whole. He will provide a base runner for the hitters behind him, and drive in the players who bat ahead of him. When he avoids making an out, he more directly secures more plate appearances for his teammates in that inning; only indirectly does he provide more plate appearances for himself.

For this reason, most dynamic run estimators come in a "theoretical team" version, where a player plays in a lineup consisting of eight average players in addition to himself.

Linear weights provide a theoretical team construction as well, although it's slightly different from the construct provided by a dynamic run estimator. A linear run estimator will generally play a player on a team that is average on the whole. That means that a very good hitter will be viewed in the context of being on a team of eight slightly below-average players, and a very poor hitter will be viewed in the context of being on team of eight slightly above average players.

In practice, the difference between theoretical team and linear run estimators in setting that baseline is minimal and rarely shows up in practice. Rarely is not the same as never, though.

Burying a Lie

You will often hear people debate linear weights versus Runs Created by arguing about whether a certain measure values players above average, or above replacement, or above absolute runs.

This is completely irrelevant to our purposes. Any run estimation framework can be tweaked to produce runs above any baseline you desire. So long as you are aware of the context in which a player generated those runs (in short, how many plate appearances or outs he used) the answers are all the same. It's entirely a matter of presentation, not of accuracy.

In our case, since we are attempting to validate against absolute runs, we will be tweaking our run estimators used to produce those values. This doesn't mean that this is "correct" or desirable. The question you are trying to answer determines the correct baseline you should use, and nothing else.

A Statement of Principles

There is a real danger in doing a study like this. If you've ever read a run estimation study, you'll generally find that the author's pet run estimator comes out on top. (This is an exaggeration, but many of the people who publish run estimation studies do so in concert with a run estimator of their own, and I've never seen one that said that the author's own run estimator is merely middle-of-the-pack.)

There are generally two reasons for this. The first is publishing bias—generally when you review your run estimator and find it isn't best of breed, you go back to the drawing board and try to improve your run estimator.

The other concern is that you can generate a lot of pointless accuracy by writing to your benchmark. If all you're concerned about is generating the smallest RMSE or the highest R-squared against your test data set, guess what? You'll probably end up with the metric with the smallest RMSE or the highest R squared.

The problem, of course, is that you're eking out a slightly higher bit of accuracy against your sample data by sabotaging the overall construction of your model. You end up with things like the situational hitting adjustment and the reconciliation factor in sacrifice flies are considered more valuable than doubles.

It should not be true that "A sufficiently advanced run estimator is indistinguishable from the teams table in the Baseball Databank." If you really just want to know how many runs the Yankees scored in 1987, then look it up. The idea behind validating run estimators is to test their theoretical validity against a set of data where we know the answer to the question we're asking, not as some sort of exercise in mathematical self-indulgence but so that we can take those run estimators and apply them to more interesting things.

Designing a run estimator with an R-squared fetish makes it less, not more, suitable for those purposes. I'm less interested in validating that sort of construct, and more interested in validating the framework behind the various types of run estimators.

The Problem of Negative Runs, and Other Concerns

One issue with most run estimators is that they will, in extreme low-scoring environments, estimate negative runs. In the case of a linear weights formula, there's nothing you can do about it, and so I left XR untouched in this regard.

In the case of RC and BsR, however, you don't need to include negative coefficients in the B factor. So … I removed them. I also included all known outs on the bases (caught stealing and double play) in the A factor for both RC and BsR.

I also counted reach on error as a single and an intentional base on balls as a walk. The two main reasons I've

heard for excluding them is because of lack of data or to avoid giving a player credit for events he deserves no credit for. I question the second response, but neither is really relevant here.

Two play categories that are situation-dependant are sacrifices and double plays. Sacrifices (sac flies and sac hits) vary widely year-to-year in run scoring value, because they can occur only in a limited number of plate appearances and so a handful of plays can greatly skew the value. Some years they have a positive value according to run expectancy charts, other years a negative value. And I view them as a mostly arbitrary scoring category—you don't change anything fundamental about the game if you no longer award sacrifices. I decided to exclude them from the test, counting them only as outs.

You could make a case for excluding double plays for similar reasons, but I didn't for two reasons. One, double plays are much less volatile in their value year to year. Two, baseball without double plays is markedly different—if you no longer awarded double plays, game strategy would change.

And for all cases where an equation called for the number of outs, I simply used three. In the "real world" of team seasonal totals, many outs are unaccounted for. (For instance, if a runner is awarded a single but thrown out trying to stretch it into a double, it doesn't show up as an out anywhere in the official statistics.)

And in the event of partial innings (either due to the home team scoring in the ninth or later, or a stop in play for other reasons), I am simply considering the difference between outs recorded and three outs to be implied outs; once the inning is over you have a drastic change in run expectancy that you need to account for if you want your model to work at all on partial innings.

The Test

The formulas used for the test, starting with linear weights (derived from XR):

$$(.50 * (1B+E)) + (.72 * 2B) + (1.04 * 3B) + (1.44 * HR) + (.33 * (BB+IBB+HBP)) + (.18 * SB) + (-.32 * (CS + DP)) + (-.098 * Outs)$$

Runs Created, based upon the formula published in the Bill James Handbook:

$$A: (1B + 2B + 3B + HR + BB + IBB + HBP + E - CS - DP)$$

B: (1.125*(1B+E) + 1.69*2B + 3.02*3B + 3.73*HR + .29*(BB + IBB + HBP) + .492*SB)

And Base Runs, based on Smyth's Base Runs Primer version:

A: (1B + E + 2B + 3B + BB + HBP + IBB - CS - DP)

B: (.88*(1B+E) + 2.42*2B + 3.96*3B + 2.2*HR + .11*(BB + HBP) + .99*SB)

C: 3

D: HR

I tested the accuracy of each estimator in three ways:

- Correlation, measured in R. R ranges from –1 to 1, with 0 meaning that there is no relationship between the two datasets, 1 meaning that there is a perfect positive relation between the two datasets, and –1 meaning there is a perfect negative relationship between the two datasets. Higher is better.

- Average Absolute Error (also called Mean Average Error). It's a measure of the average distance from the estimated value to the actual value. Distance is figured by taking the absolute value (in other words, making negative values positive) of the difference between estimated runs and actual runs. Lower is better.

- Root Mean Square Error. Similar to AAE, except instead of taking absolute value, you take the square of the difference between estimated runs and actual runs, find the average, and then find the square root. The key difference between AAE and RMSE is that RMSE especially penalizes larger errors in estimation. Lower is better.

Each estimator was tested against the innings from Retrosheet's play-by-play data. All data are from 1956-2007, with the exception of the 1954 NL dataset. I generated line scores for each inning using a MySQL database based upon Tango's RetroSQL schema.

And now, the results of that trial:

Estimator	R	AAE	RMSE
RC	0.899	0.334	0.583
BsR	0.916	0.259	0.425
XR	0.871	0.374	0.495

BsR is the clear winner in all three tests; RC is second in R and AAE, while XR is second in RMSE. Rather than try to explain what's going on here, I'll show you.

I've got some scatterplots of our three estimators against the actual runs scored per inning coming up. Now, due to the fact that you can only have integer values for actual run scoring, and frequently have fractional estimates, you'll notice an odd striping pattern. Also, since we can't fit roughly 1.9 million innings into a relatively small space (there are only about 66 thousand here, selected randomly from the big sample), these graphs may miss some of the graphic nuance in the data. You can find graphs with all the data points on the Internet.

Here's the graph for Runs Created. You may not quite notice it in this graph, but at higher levels of run scoring, estimates start to outstrip actual run scoring—real runs in an inning tops out at 16 in the Retrosheet era, while RC tops out over 20 estimated runs.

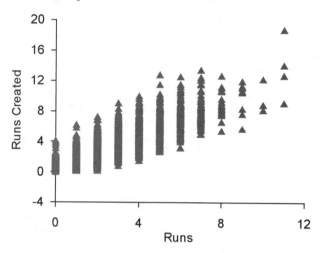

RC also has very tall bars. Those tell us that RC has a lot of variance in its estimates. For instance, compare the RC graph to this graph of Extrapolated Runs vs. actual runs scored per inning:

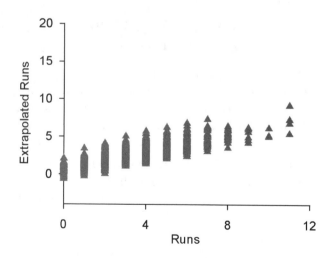

XR has a few things going against it. Unlike RC, which tops out too high, XR tops out too low, at about 10 runs. It also (as mentioned previously) has a problem with negative run estimates, even at actual run scoring of one run in an inning. All our models suffer from missing information (like balks, catcher's interference or wild pitches) that can contribute to run scoring. (There are other reasons you can get negative estimates and positive runs, I should add.)

If RC was too hot, then XR is too cold.

Here is the scatterplot of Base Runs compared to actual runs scored per inning:

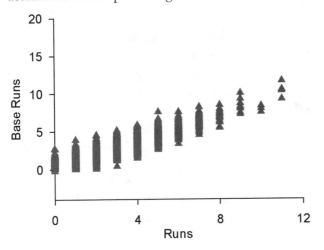

Base Runs, if it isn't just right, is at least closer to functioning at the high end of run scoring than XR or RC. It also seems to have the smallest bars of any run estimator for almost all sets of values. It does seem to have a tendency to trend a little low for its run scoring estimates.

But it's the only graph where the size of the x-axis and the y-axis can be the same; Base Runs seems to fit a lot better at the high end of run scoring than the other models, while not performing any worse down at the lower end of run scoring.

This isn't the final word on run estimator accuracy. I haven't tested every variant of every run estimator imaginable out there. I'm more interested in validating the model of each estimator than the actual implementation; if you want to know how, say, Equivalent Average works as a run estimator, it should work an awful lot like Extrapolated Runs, since they're both linear models of run scoring. One may be more accurate than the other, but what you'll find is that when comparing run estimators of a similar vein, each of them is more accurate when used against the data set they were tuned against, and less accurate when used on some other data set.

What I hope you take away from this is the idea that (beyond some very basic applications) you should be using Base Runs instead of Runs Created when you need a dynamic run estimator. Linear weights, despite not performing as well in the tests as our other estimators, have a lot of applications that a dynamic estimator is not well-suited for. Runs Created, on the other hand, brings nothing to the table that Base Runs does not except inaccuracy.

You can find Colin's original articles at:

http://statspeak.net/2008/08/what-run-estimator-would-batman-use-part-i.html

http://statspeak.net/2008/09/what-run-estimator-would-batman-use-part-ii.html

The information used here was obtained free of charge from and is copyrighted by Retrosheet. Interested parties may contact Retrosheet at 20 Sunset Road, Newark, Del. 19711 or at www. retrosheet.org.

The Manager of the Year

by Mitchel Lichtman

In preparation for this article, I began by researching the historical list of the Manager of the Year awards. A disturbing pattern (at least to me) caught my eye. Out of 51 total winners, 37 led their teams to a division title. As some of my poker playing buddies like to say, "What are the odds?"

What do I mean by that?

Let's say that we concede that some managers are better than others in somehow coaxing extra wins out of the personnel the GM and owners hand them on Opening Day and throughout the season. What is that skill reasonably worth? Four games? Five? Six or seven if we strain the boundaries of credulity?

Now, what is the average difference in talent between the best and worst teams in baseball, regardless of the manager? Is it 25 wins? 30? In light of those numbers, it seems to me that a team's won-loss record at the close of the season is vastly more a function of player talent than managerial acumen.

So how is it that the best managers in baseball just happen to be at the helm of the best teams, more than 72 percent of the time? You could argue that great managers don't manage bad teams, by definition, but I'm afraid that argument wouldn't hold much water. We can find plenty of examples of otherwise great managers (we think) leading teams with bad talent to bad records (and vice versa). Bobby Cox, the leader of 14 division champions in 15 years, led his team to 72 victories this year. Did he suddenly lose his moxie? Probably not. What he lost were the great Atlanta pitchers of the '90s (as well as some healthy players and a bit of luck). What about the great Earl Weaver, considered one of the best managers of all time? His team won only 73 games in 1986.

And this year's greats? As I write this, Joe Maddon appears to be a lock to win the best-manager award in the American League, and Lou Piniella will probably capture the NL prize. This is the same Maddon who won 66 games last year and 61 the year before. Where was his mojo back then? And let's see, Piniella won 63, 70 and 67 games from 2003-2005, while managing the same crummy Tampa team that eventually was dumped on Maddon.

Let me sum up my point in one sentence: A team's won-loss record is primarily a function of the talent that is foisted upon the manager rather than the skills of the manager himself. A team with great talent and a lousy manager probably will win lots of games, and a team with poor talent but a great manager will likely lose a lot of games.

So how is that most of the managers who are anointed "the best" by the baseball writers happen to be at the helm of first place teams? The answer is probably two-fold: One, figuring out who the best managers are is indeed a "tough nut to crack." Two, as with most of the end-of-season awards, the voters generally prefer a "story" rather than cogent analysis.

So here's what I'll do to fix this problem. I am going to evaluate the talent of each team going into the season, based on some rough estimates of personnel and playing time (I used Baseball Prospectus' preseason depth charts). Then I'm going to evaluate each team by using the actual playing time of each player instead of projected playing time. In both cases, I'll calculate each team's runs scored and runs allowed using my preseason projections for each player. Based on that, and their schedule, I'll project each team's wins and losses.

By comparing the two, we can at least begin to separate the manager from his players. After all, according to MLB, the Manager of the Year award is supposed to be given to:

> … *The Major League manager who takes the talent given to him by the team owner and accomplishes more than expected…*

I'll also show you how well each team performed in the various areas: pitching, hitting, base running and defense (the "big four"), as compared to their preseason projections. This will let you see the strengths and weaknesses of your favorite team going into the season, as well as how they actually performed in each of the areas during the season. And finally, I will provide you with updated projections for each team, given the same players and identical playing time (as in 2008), so that you really will be an expert on your team's chances in 2009.

Keep in mind a few things as you ponder these charts. All the numbers you see under each heading are indicative of each team's estimated true talent in the various components that make up "total team talent." They are adjusted for context so that a league-average

Philly team and a league-average San Diego team (or Oakland or Texas) will both have a total run value of zero. Also note that "plus" runs are always good and "minus" ones are bad.

The way the individual pitcher projections get translated into a "total team pitching" number is this: Starters and "swingmen" are assumed to pitch in situations where the leverage is exactly 1.0. However, it is assumed that closers, on the average, pitch in double (2.0) leverage situations, set-up men, 1.5, and middle and long relievers, .9. The amount of leverage in which each pitcher pitches is the amount that I weight his expected pitching performance. For example, if a closer is expected to pitch 65 innings, he actually gets "credit" for 130 innings, as compared to a starter or swingman.

Also, remember that each team's actual schedule is used to produce the projected won-loss totals.

So let's compare each team's preseason projected won-loss records to projected won-loss records that are based on each player's actual playing time during the year. The difference reflects injuries, trades, players getting more or less playing time, and player movement to and from the minor leagues.

Those teams whose "updated" expected won-loss records are substantially better than their preseason ones either gained lots of quality plate appearances and innings pitched, or made astute personnel decisions, or both. (Or perhaps Baseball Prospectus' preseason depth charts were not very good—at least for those teams.) The top teams in that department (better player talent than we expected) are:

Team	Difference
Phillies	+7 wins
White Sox	+7 wins
Cubs	+4 wins
Baltimore	+3 wins
Giants	+2 wins
Royals	+2 wins

Maybe the managers (and/or the GMs) of these teams deserve some credit right off the bat for creating lineups and rosters that were better than we anticipated before the season started, especially the Phillies and White Sox.

For the Phillies, pitching was key. Adam Eaton was expected to be the Phillies' No. 5 starter, with a near replacement level projection. He pitched in only 21 games, 19 as a starter, and was replaced by a very good pitcher in Joe Blanton (he was average in the AL, but very good in the NL). They also put together and maintained a very good bullpen.

Weak hitters on the White Sox, like Pablo Ozuna and Jose Uribe, got less playing time than expected. The ChiSox also managed to keep four of their five starting pitchers healthy all year long and managed their bullpen personnel better than projected.

Okay, let's now look at each team's updated preseason projection (given that we know who played for what team, and how often) and compare that to its 2008 Pythagorean record, based on the number of runs actually scored and allowed this year. This differential represents how much each team over or underperformed (in runs scored and allowed) its "true expectancy," at least based on our preseason player projections. The table is on the next page.

As you can see, in the AL, the Twins produced a whopping 12 wins or around 120 runs better than expected, based on their runs scored and runs allowed. Somehow their manager, Ron Gardenhire, was able to take a team with mediocre talent and turn it into an outstanding, 90-win (at least according to Pythagoras) pennant contender. Toronto was close behind, outdoing our expectation by 11 wins. We hesitate to give their dual skippers, Cito Gaston and John Gibbons, too much credit however. As you'll see, they managed to win only 86 games, despite a Pythagorean win total of 94.

The likely actual winner of the "real" Manager of the Year award is Maddon of the Tampa Bay Rays. Despite the media's story that the Rays shocked the world by going from last to first in 2008, they really over-performed by only six wins, compared to the estimated true talent of their players. Three other AL teams (managers) did better than that, and two others were right behind them at five wins above what we expected.

In the NL, three teams over-performed by eight wins: Houston, Philadelphia, and St. Louis. In addition, the Astros and their manager, Cecil Cooper, managed to exceed their Pythagorean win total by another nine wins! (Of course the bad news for Astros fans is, don't expect much from them in 2009 unless they make some major changes in the offseason—or get really lucky again.)

Updated preseason projected won-loss records compared to actual Pythagorean won-loss records

Team	Expected record, based on updated preseason player projections	Pythagorean record, based on actual runs scored and allowed	Diff
ARI	86-76	83-79	-3
ATL	86-76	78-84	-8
CHC	93-69	100-61	7
CIN	77-85	71-91	-6
COL	81-81	73-89	-8
FLO	75-87	81-80	6
HOU	69-93	77-84	8
LAD	84-78	87-75	3
MIL	85-77	88-74	3
NYM	93-69	90-72	-3
PHI	86-76	94-68	8
PIT	73-89	66-96	-7
SDP	83-79	66-96	-17
STL	79-83	87-75	8
SFG	71-91	67-95	-4
WAS	69-93	61-100	-8
LAA	81-81	89-73	8
BAL	73-89	72-89	-1
BOS	92-70	97-65	5
CWS	85-77	90-73	5
CLE	88-75	86-76	-2
DET	82-80	78-84	-4
KCR	71-91	71-91	0
MIN	78-84	90-73	12
NYY	90-72	88-74	-2
OAK	79-83	75-86	-4
SEA	73-89	66-96	-7
TBR	86-76	92-70	6
TEX	78-84	75-87	-3
TOR	83-79	94-68	11

The likely actual Manager of the Year winner in the senior circuit, Lou Piniella, did very well in that his players outperformed their expected talent by seven wins. Charlie Manuel, also likely to receive some votes, gets some props from us as well. So does our old friend

Tony LaRussa, who was the third skipper in that three-way tie.

How about the teams that came up short of their expectations?

In the NL, I am afraid that there is no competition. Bud Black, in his second year at the helm of the Padres, took a team that had 83-win talent and somehow managed to coax (or de-coax) it into only 66 Pythagorean wins (and 63 actual wins, to add insult to injury)! In the AL, no team was nearly as bad as the Padres. However, Seattle easily led the field with a -7 win differential.

Next, to strip away even more "luck" (remember, that is why thus far we have been using team Pythag records rather than actual records—it better represents a team's actual talent and/or production), we will look at how each team performed in the various offensive and defensive categories and then compare them to how we expected them to perform in each of those categories. The results are on the next page.

Keep in mind that all the numbers in the tables (other than the last column, "actual run differential") are theoretical runs, not actual ones. The offensive runs are linear weights based on each player's component batting stats, the defensive numbers are Ultimate Zone Rating (UZR) runs, the pitching runs are based on component ERAs (ERC), and base running linear weights are computed from how often all the runners on a team take the extra base on hits and outs, or get thrown out trying (they do not include stolen base attempts). All the numbers are context-neutral; that is, the parks and opponents are accounted for in the computations (and the defense is "factored out" of the pitching numbers).

Looking at the last three columns, we can see how many runs each team was supposed to score and allow based on our linear weights player projections (column 10), its estimated runs scored and allowed based on its linear weights underlying performance (column 11), and finally, how many runs it actually scored and allowed (column 12). The difference between 10 and 11 is how much better or worse the team performed, statistically, than expected, and the difference between 11 and 12 is a measure of timely or clutch performance and generally has little or no predictive value.

Let's look at which teams were particularly good or bad at the second of these "differentials" (getting the most or least out of their offensive and defensive performance, in terms of their actual runs scored and allowed).

National League projected linear weights runs versus actual linear weights runs.

Team	Batting Projected	Actual	Fielding Projected	Actual	Baserunning Projected	Actual	Pitching Projected	Actual	Total linear weights runs Projected	Actual	Actual run differential
ARI	-23	-63	4	-42	1	-6	70	101	52	-10	14
ATL	49	57	6	-5	-3	3	-7	2	45	57	-25
CHC	34	69	19	1	-3	5	45	67	95	142	184
CIN	-6	-48	-33	-92	-4	3	13	-53	-30	-190	-96
COL	1	0	6	-12	4	2	-2	32	9	22	-75
FLO	16	43	-39	0	1	-3	-17	12	-39	52	3
HOU	-32	-16	-14	18	-8	5	-42	-31	-96	-24	-31
LAD	-4	-33	-2	14	5	-1	37	94	36	74	52
MIL	42	51	-20	15	6	1	11	-17	39	50	61
NYM	30	69	25	7	8	6	43	17	106	99	84
PHI	13	20	27	42	-4	2	14	40	50	104	119
PIT	-11	1	-6	-45	1	-7	-49	-119	-65	-170	-149
SDP	0	-9	12	70	-4	3	14	8	22	72	-127
STL	17	74	19	58	2	-9	-63	-80	-25	43	54
SFG	-86	-79	11	23	-1	-2	8	-9	-68	-67	-119
WAS	-38	-62	-15	-43	4	2	-40	-28	-89	-143	-184

American League projected linear weights runs versus actual linear weights runs

Team	Batting Projected	Actual	Fielding Projected	Actual	Baserunning Projected	Actual	Pitching Projected	Actual	Total linear weights runs Projected	Actual	Actual run differential
LAA	-32	-69	0	16	4	9	21	50	-7	-39	68
BAL	10	52	-9	-34	-2	-2	-75	-122	-76	-59	-87
BOS	56	112	-14	-2	-8	-5	69	98	103	203	151
CWS	-1	37	6	24	-8	-13	31	69	28	117	82
CLE	21	4	16	32	0	1	12	18	49	55	44
DET	50	70	3	5	-1	0	-48	-86	4	-11	-36
KCR	-74	-133	6	34	1	-3	-21	6	-88	-96	-90
MIN	-28	-25	10	-12	-2	12	-11	-54	-31	-79	84
NYY	52	42	-14	-30	6	-7	34	28	72	33	62
OAK	-32	-103	17	4	0	10	-12	-20	-27	-109	-44
SEA	-46	-83	-3	-58	2	1	-35	-101	-82	-241	-140
TBR	22	19	-6	14	4	-8	31	77	51	102	103
TEX	29	72	-24	-55	7	8	-59	-123	-47	-98	-66
TOR	-25	-23	12	42	-4	-6	38	105	21	118	104

Los Angeles Angels of Anaheim

As you can see, the Angels performed a little better in pitching, defense and baserunning, and a lot worse in hitting, than we expected. Combined, they were a little worse (32 runs) than our player projections suggested. Yet somehow their run differential was 117 runs better than their underlying performance! One reason for this was that they batted a little better with runners in scoring position than overall, and their actual ERA was less than their DIPS or component ERA. Yet neither of these differences was extreme.

Somehow, Mike Scioscia was able to almost miraculously coax an extra 11 Pythagorean wins out of a team that should have won only about 77 games. Maybe, like the apparitions in "Angels in the Outfield," Lady Luck was on his side.

Minnesota Twins

Even better than the Angels, while the Twins performed 48 runs worse than expected in linear weights offense, defense, base running and pitching, they somehow produced a run differential that was 163 runs better than their underlying performance. That is amazing! No doubt the fact that they were only 11th in overall OPS in the AL but second with runners in scoring position didn't hurt their cause. And like the Angels, their regular ERA was better than both their DIPS and component ERA.

Oakland A's

The Athletics underlying performance was also decidedly worse than what we expected based on our preseason player projections. Most of that was on offense. Almost every regular other than Jack Cust and Frank Thomas had awful batting statistics. Kurt Suzuki, Mark Ellis, Jack Hannahan, Daric Barton and Bobby Crosby all posted OPS figures less than .700. Surprisingly, unlike Seattle and Minnesota, their hitting (OPS) with runners in scoring position was not much higher than overall, nor was their component ERA substantially different from their regular ERA. Yet, somehow they were able to post a run differential 65 runs better than their underlying performance suggested.

Because they under-performed, based on their underlying context-adjusted statistics, but over-performed based on their run differential, their Pythagorean win percentage was right around what we expected based on our player projections.

Atlanta Braves

The Braves had an utterly disappointing season after being touted as a preseason pennant contender. Interestingly, their offensive, defensive and pitching projections were pretty much right on the money as far as what their players actually produced. Unfortunately for the team and their fans, their run differential was 72 runs worse than their underlying performance would have predicted. (To add insult to injury, they were 11-30 this year in one-run games, such that their actual record was another six wins worse than their Pythagorean record.) Much of that 72-run differential was due to the fact that the Braves pitchers' regular ERA was a lot worse than their DIPS or component ERA.

So the Braves seemed to have a double dose of bad luck. The good news for Braves fans is that if they can replace Mark Teixeira and John Smoltz with reasonably similar talent, they should bounce back nicely next year, given average luck.

Colorado Rockies

The Rockies, like the Braves, also performed about as expected, to the tune of +22 runs (total actual linear weights), yet somehow they managed to post a run differential of -75 runs, a 97-run swing! Also, like Atlanta, most of that was bad pitching when it "counted." Since overall their pitching was good, and their total projections and underlying performance were also good, I expect them to bounce back next year, unless they lose premier players like Matt Holiday or one of their three good starting pitchers.

San Diego Padres

Like Seattle (and Cleveland) in the American League, their season was a disappointment on many fronts. (The difference between Seattle and San Diego was that I expected the former to be bad and the latter to be good.) The Padres, however, were really in a class by themselves; Towers and DePodesta, and others in ownership and the front office, really have to be scratching their heads.

They actually outperformed their player projections by 50 runs. All of that was on defense. Literally, the only player with more than a few games in the field who was negative in UZR was Jim Edmonds. After accounting for all their injuries, the players performed overall about as well as expected. In fact, given their underlying performance, they "should have" won—are you sitting down?—88 games! Yet their Pythagorean win total was

66 and their actual games won was 63. What the heck went wrong? I have no idea.

Not surprisingly, their ERA was worse than their DIPS and component ERA. However, while they were dead last in overall team OPS, their OPS with runners in scoring position was only 12th in the league. All I can say is that in baseball, as in life, stuff happens. The good news for San Diego fans is that the Padres are overwhelmingly likely to improve next year, by a lot, even with no major personnel moves.

Washington Nationals

The Nats as they are affectionately called (although I don't know why anyone would want to be affectionate toward such a bad organization) were bad, bad and worse this year. They not only fell short of their player projections, but their run differential was even worse than their underlying performance. Again, that is not a good recipe for success.

Most of their under-performing was on offense and defense (they actually pitched a little better than expected, despite pitching poorly). Ronnie Belliard was awful with the glove other than at first base, rookie Emilio Bonifacio was bad, Elijah Dukes was not very good in the outfield, Felipe Lopez was a poor defender at second base, and Lastings Milledge was terrible in center field. Only Austin Kearns, Cristian Guzman, and Willie Harris in the outfield were any good, and even then, no one broke the bank on defense.

Offensively, while there were some pleasant surprises, like, Belliard, Guzman, Dukes, Harris and Dmitri Young, there were more than enough total disasters to cancel out the overachievers—and then some. Among players with at least 100 at-bats, Wily Mo Pena, Paul Lo Duca, Kory Casto, Kearns, Bonifacio and Wil Nieves were utterly anemic at the plate. If you want to impress your friends and family with your baseball acumen, ask them, "Who was allowed to amass 195 at-bats while posting an OPS of .509?" Wily Mo Pena.

Boston Red Sox

Believe it or not, the only team in the AL to substantially under-perform, in runs scored and allowed, as compared to their actual linear weights runs, were the Red Sox. However, to offset a 52-run difference between their context-adjusted stats and their run differential, they managed to outdo their player projections by 100 runs. How did they do that? Basically they did better than I expected across the board, but mostly in the hitting department.

The list of players who outdid their projections is long: Sean Casey, Coco Crisp, Alex Cora, J.D. Drew, Mike Lowell, Brandon Moss, Dustin Pedroia, Manny Ramirez and Kevin Youkilis. The only players who fell short of their projections were Jason Varitek, David Ortiz, Jacoby Ellsbury, and Julio Lugo, and only Varitek and Ortiz were by more than 10 runs. Boston really did have a great team. Probably the best team in baseball.

(By the way, there is a bias in the numbers: AL teams will tend to over-perform and NL teams will tend to under-perform, both in their Pythagorean and actual records. The projected totals are league-based, as I explained at the outset, such that a total linear weights of zero in the NL team represents an average National League team, and a zero linear weights in the AL represents an average American League team. However, because the AL is substantially better than the NL, inter-league games will cause AL teams to improve their run differentials and actual won-loss records, while NL teams will appear to under-achieve.)

Think about this. Here are the teams that significantly under-performed with respect to our pitching projections: Cincinnati, Pittsburgh, Baltimore, Minnesota, Seattle and Texas. None of those teams made the postseason.

Only three teams did a whole lot better than we expected in the pitching department: Los Angeles Dodgers, Tampa Bay and Toronto. Two of the three played in October.

On defense, Arizona, Cincinnati, Pittsburgh, Washington, Baltimore, Seattle and Texas were a lot worse than we expected. And of course none of those teams, save Arizona, made much (pennant) noise during the season.

On the plus side, Florida, Houston, the Dodgers, Milwaukee, San Diego, St. Louis, Kansas City and Toronto played a lot better on defense than our UZR projections suggested. Five or six of these teams were in the hunt for a postseason berth at one time or another during the season.

Maybe pitching and defense really do win championships!

Now that we've gotten most of the numbers out of the way, let's get back to the original question: How can we figure out who the best managers in baseball are? Last year, I invented a "toy" we can use to answer this question. Keep in mind that a "toy" in baseball is not meant as a rigorous metric by any means. It is merely a manipulation or look at the numbers through which we might reach some tenuous, and hopefully interesting, conclusion.

Before I describe the toy, I want to introduce one more data point we can use to evaluate our managers: team stolen base and caught-stealing totals. If you have ever read a *THT Annual* or any other sabermetric tome or article, you probably know that unless a team can boast a stolen base success percentage in the neighborhood of 70 to 75 percent, it probably is costing itself runs and wins.

I took each team's stolen base and caught-stealing totals and converted them into net runs by assigning a run value of -.46 for a caught stealing and .18 for a stolen base. In the Manager of the Year toy, as you will see, if a team had negative net stolen base runs, it was penalized, and if it was plus in SB/CS net runs, it received some credit.

You'll find each team's net stolen base record in the table appendix.

Okay, here's the toy:

- Take half of the difference between a team's "updated" preseason projected wins (based on player projections and their actual playing time), and its expected wins based on its actual underlying performance (linear weights runs).
- Add that to half of the difference between a team's projected wins based on actual underlying performance, and its Pythagorean wins (based on runs scored and allowed).
- Add to that 25 percent of the difference between its Pythagorean wins and its actual wins.
- Finally, add that total to half the number of wins a team generated from its stolen base and caught-stealing numbers (net runs divided by 10), if they were above average, and 100 percent of the number of (negative) wins if they were below average. (The theory is that if a team accumulates lots of positive stolen base runs, it probably has very good base stealers, and the manager may not be wholly responsible for those runs. However, if a team is "minus" in the stolen base net runs department, the manager probably should have halted many of those stolen base attempts, or at least those with a negative win expectancy.)
- The result is each manager's Manager of the Year score.

THT's Manager of the Year Results

Manager	Team	2008 MOY score	2007 score
Cooper	HOU	5.2	-1.8
LaRussa	STL	4.1	-4.25
Piniella	CHC	3.7	2.8
C. Manuel	PHI	3.4	3.1
Gonzalez	FLO	2.9	-3.7
Yost/Sveum	MIL	1.7	-1.1 (Yost)
Torre	LAD	-.8	-4.1
Randolph/J. Manuel	NYM	-1.2	2.5 (Randolph)
Bochy	SFG	-1.6	-1.4
Melvin	ARI	-2.1	2.2
Baker	CIN	-3.1	-
Hurdle	COL	-3.5	.3
Russell	PIT	-3.9	-
Cox	ATL	-5.2	-.4
Acta	WAS	-5.8	-1.9
Black	SDP	-8.1	.2
Sciosca	LAA	6.1	5.0
Gardenhire	MIN	5.1	-1.3
Maddon	TBR	4.0	-7.5
Francona	BOS	2.3	3.2
Gibbons/Gaston	TOR	2.1	1.4 (Gibbons)
Guillen	CWS	1.8	-4.3
Hillman	KCR	.6	-
Washington	TEX	.2	.9
Girardi	NYY	-.1	-
Geren	OAK	-.6	-2.95
Wedge	CLE	-1.4	1.1
Trembley	BAL	-1.5	-1.25
Leyland	DET	-3.3	4.8
McLaren/Riggleman	SEA	-4.1	.4 (McLaren)

Looking at column three on the right, the National League THT Manager of the Year award goes to the Houston skipper, Cecil Cooper, with runners up LaRussa, Piniella and Charlie Manuel.

The American League award winner is once again Mike Sciosca, the Angels' manager, with Gardenhire and Maddon not too far behind.

If we could award a W(worst)MOY award, it would go to Seattle's dual managers, Messrs. John McLaren and Jim Riggleman in the AL, with some competition by Jim Leyland. In the NL, it is San Diego's Bud Black.

All of these picks seem reasonable to me, which is a good thing for a "toy."

Finally, what can we expect from each team, assuming that their players and playing time are exactly the same next year as they were in 2008? (Realistically, that won't be the case, of course.)

I'll update the player projections to include this year's performances, and do the same thing I did before the 2008 season started—put everything (all the player projections) into a computer that combines the individual player projections into team "expected true talent" and then simulates an entire season 10,000 times. You can see the results below.

Remember, that these are not necessarily realistic projections for the 2009 season. I am not trying to estimate each team's personnel and playing time for next year. I simply took every player's current updated projection going into next year and prorated it for his actual playing time in 2008. Those are the numbers that are combined to generate a "true talent" for each team.

In other words, for each team, I assumed that every player who played in 2008 will play again in 2009 in an identical role and with same number of plate appearances, innings pitched and games played in the field.

If you really want to get an idea as to how your favorite team is slated to do next year, take these numbers and apply your own personnel adjustments.

Even without those adjustments, if you eyeball the above chart, several things might jump out at you.

In the Senior Circuit:

The Mets and Cubs appear to be poised to make another run at the postseason. While the Mets certainly have enough money to upgrade their team, don't be fooled by talk radio or the mainstream media into thinking that they need "wholesale changes." They don't—unless you believe that "chemistry and character" win championships, and that the Metropolitans lack either or both in their current configuration.

The Pirates, Nationals and Giants, barring a major miracle or two, are headed for another disappointing season, to say the least. The Astros, Cardinals and Marlins are likely in for a rude awakening, and whoever

2009 Team Projections, based on the exact same personnel and playing time as in 2008

American League

Team	Batting	Fielding	Baserunning	Pitching	Run Diff	Win/Loss
LAA	-47	2	4	30	-11	81-81
BAL	-3	-6	-4	-68	-81	73-89
BOS	41	-13	-8	77	97	91-71
CWS	-15	7	-10	33	15	83-79
CLE	6	26	0	14	46	86-76
DET	37	3	2	-47	-5	81-81
KCR	-82	8	-2	-18	-94	72-90
MIN	-36	12	-1	-8	-33	79-83
NYY	38	-13	1	37	63	88-74
OAK	-50	10	1	-4	-43	78-84
SEA	-61	-8	3	-33	-99	70-92
TBR	8	-6	0	35	37	84-78
TEX	11	-30	4	-52	-67	75-87
TOR	-39	20	-8	48	21	82-80

National League

Team	Batting	Fielding	Baserunning	Pitching	Run Diff	Win/Loss
ARI	-42	-3	-1	48	2	82-80
ATL	31	2	-2	-29	2	81-81
CHC	11	12	-2	24	45	87-75
CIN	-28	-40	-4	-15	-87	73-89
COL	-19	2	2	-27	-42	77-85
FLO	-1	-25	-1	-41	-68	74-88
HOU	-50	-6	-3	-67	-126	70-92
LAD	-18	-1	3	17	1	82-80
MIL	23	-12	2	-15	-2	80-82
NYM	11	13	6	18	48	87-75
PHI	-5	31	-4	-12	10	82-80
PIT	-31	-14	-3	-77	-125	68-94
SDP	-23	17	-6	-9	-21	80-82
STL	-1	23	-1	-90	-69	73-89
SFG	-109	9	1	-15	-114	71-91
WAS	-57	-18	1	-64	-138	67-95

said that the Reds might be the next Tampa Bay Rays next year, well…

The rest of the teams could go either way, depending on what happens during the offseason and which way the wind blows in 2009.

In the American League:

The same thing I said about the Reds applies to the Royals. They will likely have another terrible campaign in 2009. Those who keep waiting for their "young talent" to take off, or their new GM to "right the ship," well—they'll likely have to keep waiting I'm afraid.

Boston should remain a powerhouse, of course, and the Yankees' dynasty is definitely not over, especially if they end up acquiring an impact free agent or two. Cleveland should bounce back, while Baltimore, Oakland, Seattle and Texas—let's just say that they have a lot of work to do.

Minnesota, Anaheim and the White Sox don't look so good on paper (the White Sox a little better than the other two), but for some reason those teams usually end up making me look like a foolish forecaster when the dust settles.

Stolen base/caught stealing numbers.

Team	Stolen bases	Caught stealing	Total net runs
ARI	58	23	0
ATL	58	27	-2
CHC	87	34	0
CIN	85	47	-6
COL	141	37	8
FLO	76	28	1
HOU	114	52	-3
LAD	126	43	3
MIL	108	38	2
NYM	138	36	8
PHI	136	25	13
PIT	57	19	2
SDP	36	17	-1
STL	73	32	-2
SFG	108	46	-2
WAS	81	43	-5
LAA	129	48	1
BAL	81	37	-2
BOS	120	35	6
CWS	67	34	-4
CLE	77	29	3
DET	63	31	-3
KCR	79	38	-3
MIN	102	42	-1
NYY	118	39	3
OAK	88	21	6
SEA	90	32	1
TBR	142	50	3
TEX	81	25	3
TOR	80	27	2

Statistics

We've Got Your Numbers

And now for something completely numeric. It's the *Hardball Times Baseball Annual* statistics section, an important part of the *Annual* since we began publishing five years ago. I'm going to explain what's in the pages ahead, but first I'd like to tell you about our unique take on baseball statistics: the Batted Ball stats.

Batted Ball Stats

For every team, every batter with at least 100 plate appearances and every pitcher who faced at least 100 batters, you'll find a row of stats like the one for Dustin Pedroia at the bottom of this page.

Specifically, you'll find…

- The percentage of plate appearances that resulted in a strikeout or walk (the latter includes intentional walks and HBPs).

- The proportion of all batted balls, not including bunts, that were ground balls, line drives and fly balls.

- Two breakdown stats: the percentage of fly balls that were infield flies (caught in the infield) and the percentage of outfield flies that were home runs.

- The percentage of ground balls and outfield flies that were outs (home runs not included in the outfield fly category).

- The average run value of each type of batted ball. This is calculated by assigning linear weights to each batted ball outcome (such as singles, doubles, home runs and double plays) and averaging them over the total number of each batted ball type.

- The "bottom line": a comparison of how many runs each player contributed, relative to the major league average, over the entire season. This is a function of both batted ball frequency and run value. The denominator is the number of outs made by each batter or pitcher.

The numbers don't just tell you how many somethings a batter hit or a pitcher gave up, but the way he hit and pitched. Did he hit the ball in the air a lot, or was he a groundball pitcher? Were his flyballs more likely to be pop-ups or home runs? When he hit a line drive, was it for power?

Those are just some of the "scouting" questions our batted ball stats answer for you. You gain a deeper appreciation for the ballplayer, his strengths and his weaknesses by reviewing these stats. You also discover some interesting things about your favorite teams.

For instance, here is the number of runs (above/below the major league average) that the New York Mets' batters produced for each type of batted ball last year. "Balls Not in Play" are strikeouts, walks and HBP.

- Balls Not In Play (NIP): +27
- Groundballs (GB): -9
- Line Drives (LD): +52
- Flyballs (FB): -38

The Mets were an elite line-drive team, with the third-highest run total in the majors (+52). They also struck out less than most teams. That +27 figure on balls not in play was also the third-highest figure in the bigs.

But they didn't hit for fly ball power: -38 runs on fly balls was in the bottom 25 percent in the majors. That's a bit of a surprise, don't you think? Although it mirrors their pattern from 2007 (but more extremely), they were more of a fly ball-hitting team three years ago.

The simple reason, as you'll find in our pages, is that only 31 percent of their batted balls were fly balls; the major league average was 36 percent. They were more likely to hit ground balls (2 percentage points more often than the major league average) and line drives (3 percentage points more often).

I was particularly taken by the different styles of the Mets' Big Four. Here is the number of runs each player produced above (or below) average for each batted ball type:

Player	NIP	GB	LD	FB	Tot
Wright D	12	3	23	11	48
Beltran C	12	1	15	4	32
Reyes J	4	16	10	-7	24
Delgado C	5	-12	16	14	24

Batted Ball Batting Stats

Player	% of PA		% of Batted Balls			IF/F	HR/OF	Out %		Runs Per Event				Total Runs vs. Avg.				
	K%	BB%	GB%	LD%	FB%			GB	OF	NIP	GB	LD	OF	NIP	GB	LD	FB	Tot
Pedroia D	7	8	43	21	36	.10	.09	70	83	.13	.07	.41	.16	5	9	15	3	32
MLB Average	18	10	44	20	36	.10	.11	74	84	.05	.04	.39	.18	--	--	--	--	--

Every one of the Big Four was more of a line drive hitter than a fly ball hitter, even Carlos Delgado. Yet they also had complementary strengths and weaknesses. Delgado clearly wasn't beating out any ground balls, but Jose Reyes sure was. In fact, Reyes had the fifth-highest groundball run total in the majors last year.

David Wright and Carlos Beltran exhibited more plate discipline than the other two. They both struck out less often and walked more often than average. Reyes struck out much less than average, too, but also walked a bit less than average.

How do we arrive at these figures? It's not terribly difficult. Baseball Info Solutions (BIS) does the hard work by providing us with batted ball information for every major league player, laid out exactly the same way for batters and pitchers. The data include the number of times they hit (or allowed) a ground ball, fly ball or line drive.

We also have the outcome of each type of batted ball for each player, so we know how often each ground ball was converted into an out or a double play, for example. We can see how many fly balls never left the infield, or fell for a single, double or triple. Or cleared the fence for a home run.

To convert these baseline stats into runs above and below average, we multiply the number of outcomes by simple "linear weights" for each type of outcome (.48 for a single, .8 for a double, etc.). The linear weights we use add up to the total number of runs scored in the majors, when multiplied by the number of respective events.

Finally, to get our ranking, we divide the total runs for each type of batted ball by the number of outs the batter or pitcher made, and then compare them to the major league average.

Here's an example. The average outfield fly ball yielded .17 runs. The average ground ball, .05 runs. But players sometimes verge from these averages dramatically. Ryan Howard averaged .48 runs for each of his outfield flies (more than any other player) and -.01 runs for his ground balls (not the worst – about the same as Delgado).

Said differently, the Phillies scored a run for every two fly balls that Howard hit. They scored no runs when he hit ground balls, no matter how often he hit them.

Anyway, when you multiply those rates by the total number of ground balls and fly balls Howard mashed, you discover that he was 48 runs above average on fly balls (most in the majors) and 11 runs below average on ground balls (third lowest in the majors).

You're probably not surprised by Howard's results. But my guess is that you will find a number of surprises in these pages, lots of "scouting" information you didn't know. Let me give you some more examples.

The White Sox were the most extreme fly ball hitting team in the majors last year. They were 73 runs above average on fly balls, tied for the highest in the majors with the Rangers. But, unlike the Rangers, they were below average in all other categories combined:

- NIP: +10
- LD: -11
- GB: -26
- Tot: -27

The White Sox truly did have a one-dimensional offense. No above-average offensive team relied more on one weapon than the Sox relied on their flies. Here are the lines for their Big Three:

Player	NIP	GB	LD	FB	Tot
Quentin C	14	0	-2	29	41
Dye J	-3	1	13	15	26
Thome J	8	-13	-3	27	20

Carlos Quentin showed plate discipline, and Jermaine Dye threw in some line drive hitting, but these three hitters were 71 runs above average on just their fly balls.

For a little perspective, the following batters were the top 10 flyball run producers in the majors last year:

Player	Fly
Howard R	44
Rodriguez A	33
Ludwick R	32
Youkilis K	31
Guerrero V	30
Sizemore G	29
Quentin C	29
Uggla D	28
Thome J	27
Pena C	27

Want to see groundball hitters? Sure. Here are all the players who were at least 14 runs above average on ground balls:

Player	GB
Suzuki I	25
Victorino S	18
Gomez C	18
Weeks R	16
Reyes J	16
Guzman C	15
Iwamura A	14
Holliday M	14
Lopez J	14

There are all sorts of different types of hitters in that table, from the superb (Matt Holliday) to the pathetic (Carlos Gomez). The major league average groundball out rate was 74 percent last year; every one of these batters were thrown out less often. Obviously, speed is a huge factor in groundball hitting as well as the general ability to hit lots of them (57 percent of Ichiro's batted balls were ground balls, his highest total since 2004, but not out of line with recent years. The major league average is 44 percent.)

Holliday sure did it all last year. I was curious to see which other batters posted such an "even" profile. Here's my list, in descending order of total runs above average, of the best all-around hitters in baseball last year:

Player	NIP	GB	LD	Fly	Tot
Pujols A	25	9	20	24	77
Jones C	19	4	18	15	56
Berkman L	17	2	6	27	52
Ramirez H	13	11	9	19	51
Wright D	12	3	23	11	48
Holliday M	9	14	12	11	46
Bradley M	12	7	9	17	46
Markakis N	14	7	12	8	42
Utley C	11	-2	16	16	41
Ramirez M	7	3	15	13	37
Ramirez Ar	11	1	9	10	31

Very few surprises here. Well, you might be surprised to see Nick Markakis, but you shouldn't be. He's one of the best young hitters in baseball. Well, okay, I was

surprised to see Aramis Ramirez on this list. Prior to 2008, he was more of a fly ball hitter (+23 in 2007). This year, he wasn't nearly as strong on the fly, but his plate discipline was much better. I don't know if that's a good trend for him or not.

That "Ramirez M" line is Manny's performance in just Los Angeles. I'll get back to that in a minute.

Pitching

One of the things I love about these stats is that we can present them exactly the same way for pitchers as we do for batters. All the same metrics, all calculated and presented exactly the same way. The only difference is that negative numbers are good for pitchers, positive numbers are good for batters.

To give you a feel for the pitching stats, let's look at the Diamondbacks' top three starters:

Player	NIP	GB	LD	FB	Tot
Haren D	-20	0	-4	-7	-31
Webb B	-7	2	-12	-13	-30
Johnson R	-13	13	-7	1	-6

Dan Haren and Brandon Webb were 12th and 14th in runs below average allowed; the Big Unit was much lower on the list. However, their profiles were pretty different.

Haren and Johnson are classic "control the plate" pitchers. They don't let batters hit the ball (Haren struck out 23 percent of batters he faced, Johnson 22 percent; the MLB average is 18 percent) and they don't walk batters (5 percent and 6 percent for Haren/Johnson; the MLB average is 10 percent).

Webb also has fine control but only a slightly above-average strikeout rate. Really, Webb is the archetypal groundball pitcher; 64 percent of his batted balls were ground balls, which leads to a slightly counter-intuitive result on his batted ball profile: Ground balls were the only category in which he gave up more runs than the average pitcher.

Bottom line, Webb gave up two more runs than average on ground balls because he allowed so many of them. The real power of the groundball pitcher is that he doesn't give up line drives and fly balls (-12 and -13 for Webb, respectively).

On the other hand, Randy Johnson gave up lots of runs on ground balls! The only other "good" major league pitcher who compares is Tampa's Andy Sonnanstine, who gave up 11 runs more than average on ground balls.

Why? Well, in Johnson's case, his infield simply didn't back him up. Only 64 percent of his ground balls were fielded for outs—the major league average is 74 percent. If his infield had done an average job (and, to be fair, maybe they were hard-hit, "seeing eye" grounders), the Big Unit would have give up 13 fewer runs, lowering his ERA from 3.91 to 3.28.

Here are a couple of NL East Beasts:

Player	NIP	GB	LD	Fly	Tot
Hamels C	-17	-12	-7	0	-36
Santana J	-14	0	4	-25	-35

Cole Hamels and Johan Santana both have outstanding changeups, but their profiles differ markedly. Both are outstanding at controlling the plate and their proportion of batted balls allowed are similar. But their fielders seemed to have different impacts on their results.

Hamels didn't give up many runs on his ground balls, because his infielders converted 80 percent of them for outs. On the other hand, Met outfielders caught 94 percent of Santana's fly balls. Combine that with a low home run rate (9 percent) and high infield fly rate (14 percent), and you've got a pitcher with the lowest number of runs allowed on fly balls in the majors.

According to our scouting reports, the best three pitchers in the majors were…

Player	NIP	GB	LD	Fly	Tot
Halladay R	-20	-8	-9	-11	-48
Lincecum T	-12	-4	-8	-22	-46
Lee C	-19	3	-6	-19	-41

Roy Halladay was phenomenal. He was a groundball pitcher who gave up eight fewer runs than average on ground balls! Kudos to that Toronto infield. Tim Lincecum struck out an amazing 29 percent of batters who faced him. Combined with a 10 percent walk rate, that means that only 60 percent of the batters who faced him hit a fair ball. No wonder he gave up less than average on every kind of batted ball.

Cliff Lee? You can read all about Lee's season in Mike Fast's article in the very book you're holding. And you probably noticed that CC Sabathia doesn't appear on the list of top pitchers. That's because our stats are split by team. If we merge his split stats, we find that CC had the best batted ball profile of any major league pitcher last year:

Player	NIP	GB	LD	Fly	Tot
Sabathia, CC	-20	-6	-9	-14	-50

Finally, here are a few pitching and hitting fun facts, examples of data points you can find yourself in these pages:

- 85 percent of Justin Masterson's ground balls were fielded for outs last year. Don't expect that to continue in 2009.

- Only 10 percent of Carlos Marmol's batted balls were line drives. Marmol gave up 16 less runs than average on line drives, the lowest rate in the majors. I'd expect some bounce back there, too.

- On the other hand, Bronson Arroyo was 16 runs above average on line drives. Last year, he was seven runs above average. From a batted ball perspective, that was the only real difference between 2007 Arroyo and 2008 Arroyo.

- 23 percent of Kelly Shoppach's fly balls were home runs and (this is amazing) only 68 percent of his non-homer fly balls were caught for outs. He must have thought he was still playing in Fenway.

Now let's compare Manny and Manny:

Team	NIP	GB	LD	FB	Tot
Boston	6	2	-1	19	26
Dodgers	7	3	15	13	37

Manny's LA record is more impressive when you consider that he was 37 runs above average in only 229 plate appearances; he had 425 plate appearances in Boston.

Here's a further breakdown of Boston and LA Manny.

Stat	Boston	Dodgers
K%	20	17
BB%	14	17
GB Rate	41	32
LD Rate	19	32
HR/OF	.20	.29
GB Outs	69%	59%
OF Outs	78%	89%

Once Manny hit the West Coast, he struck out less, walked more, hit less ground balls and more line drives and hit more outfield flies for home runs. To add insult to injury, only 59 percent of Manny's Dodger ground balls were fielded for outs (an astoundingly low total). The only chink in his Dodger Blue armor was the out rate on his non-HR outfield flies, 89 percent.

And that's the overview. I hope get hours of pleasure reading the Batted Ball stats of your favorite players. Next, let me explain how the stats section is laid out.

League Statistics

In the beginning of our stats section, there is a relatively short statistical review of each league, consisting of:

- Graphs that pick apart the offense, defense and overall performance of each team. We think our graphs provide an intuitive visual feel.

- Summary offense, defense and overall performance stats, located under each related graph. That way, you can compare and contrast the pictures with the numbers.

- Miscellaneous stats for each team, such as base-running, home/away and righty/lefty splits, fielding stats and win stats (WPA and Win Shares).

- Our "patented" (not really) Batted Ball stats.

For example, the first graph is a display of how many runs each team scored and allowed, graphed in a way that relates to the number of games each team won. Below the graph is a table that gives more detail regarding how each team scored runs, gave up runs and turned its run differential into victories.

In the far right column of that table, PWINS stands for "Projected Wins" or "Pythagorean Wins" depending on how technical you want to get. VAR stands for variance, the difference between each team's actual wins and its projected wins. You can read more about Pythagorean Wins in the Glossary.

That's the opening page. The offense and defense graphs and stats are easy to interpret, as are most of the miscellaneous stats.

Player Statistics

The bulk of the statistical section consists of player statistics broken out by team. These include...

- A graphical recap of the team's season.

- A month-by-month overview of the team's performance, broken out into key offensive and defensive stats.

- Common batting stats, plus Base Runs (BR) and Gross Production Average (GPA), which are both described in our Glossary.

- Common pitching stats, plus Pitching Runs Created (PRC). Again, in the Glossary.

- Fielding stats, including Revised Zone Rating, courtesy of BIS.

To save space, we listed only players who produced at least one Base Run or one Pitching Run Created for each team.

A Couple of Special Cases

There are two special types of statistics that need a little more explanation: Split Stats and Fielding Stats.

Split Stats

There are two types of splits embedded in each table of "traditional" stats:

- Home/Away splits (labeled "H-A"), and

- Lefty/Righty splits (labeled "L^R" for batters and "R^L" for pitchers)

Both statistics are simply computed as the difference in Gross Production Average (GPA—it's in the Glossary) for each split. The Home/Away splits are simply computed as each player's home GPA minus his GPA on the road.

The lefty/right splits are a little more difficult to present in a simple table, but we were determined to make it work. Here's how we did it:

- We put a "handedness" label next to each batter and pitcher in the table. Each left-handed batter or pitcher has an asterisk (*) next to his name, while switch hitters have a plus sign (+) next to theirs. Right-handed players have no label.

- We vary the lefty/righty calculation according to the player's handedness. For righty batters, the calculation is L-R (average versus lefthanded pitchers minus average versus righthanded pitchers). For lefty batters, the calculation is R-L. For switch hitters, we stuck to the more conventional L-R.

- For pitchers, we switched the calculations—for right-handed pitchers, it's R-L, for southpaws, it's L-R.

This is why we use the label "L^R." The exact calculation depends on the player's natural handedness and whether he was a pitcher or batter.

Why do we do this? To make the tables easier to read. Remember this rule: Natural splits for batters are positive, and natural splits for pitchers are negative (said another way: more offense is good for batters, and less offense is good for pitchers).

Use these guidelines for judging splits: On average, batters batted .013 points (in GPA) better at home last year. Obviously, pitchers were -.013 points better at home. Righty batters were .019 points better against lefty pitchers, and lefty batters were .028 points better against righthanders. Switch hitters were slightly better against right-handed pitchers.

Our splits may take a little getting used to, but this approach allows us to pack a lot of information into a little space.

Fielding Stats

The Annual contains a few different descriptions of team fielding statistics, which might be a bit confusing. Please be aware of the differences between each statistic when we refer to it.

Defense Efficiency Ratio, or DER, is the number of batted balls successfully fielded for outs (not including home runs). It is listed for every team and every pitcher, and its batting equivalent, Batting Average on Balls in Play (or BABIP) is listed for every team.

Plus/Minus is the system developed by John Dewan of Baseball Info Solutions. It is based on the type of ball hit, where it was hit and how hard it was hit. This statistic is described in John's article, "Fielding Breeds Winning" and included in the pitching/fielding team graphs. It is the best metric in this book for judging fielding.

Additionally, our player fielding statistics include BIS's Revised Zone Rating (RZR), as well as plays made out of zone. Revised Zone Ratings were first introduced by John Dewan in the *Fielding Bible*, and THT is the only place you will find them on a daily, updated basis.

Average RZR differs by position, so here is a handy reference table for you. BIZ stands for "Balls in Zone," and OOZ stands for balls fielded that were "Out Of Zone."

POS	BIZ	Plays	ZR	OOZ
1B	6,570	4,858	.739	1,312
2B	12,794	10,516	.822	1,128
3B	10,624	7,400	.697	1,662
SS	12,745	10,558	.828	1,632
LF	8,262	7,294	.883	1,927
CF	10,471	9,651	.922	2,919
RF	8,761	7,877	.899	2,100

We've added a grade for every player who played the equivalent of at least 80 games at a position or caught 700 innings. These grades will help you interpret the Revised Zone Ratings a little more easily. But please remember that these grades (which are distributed evenly from A to F) are interpretations of 2008 fielding stats, not true player rankings. For those, we highly recommend you purchase John Dewan's *Fielding Bible— Volume II*, to be published early next year.

Constellations and Downloads

After all the stats, you'll find one other unique offering: 30 unique contributed by John Burnson of *HEATER Magazine*. These are called "Playing Time Constellations," and they are graphical representations of who played which position for each team throughout the year. They're terrific companions to our fielding stats.

We have created a special web page for purchasers of the *THT Annual 2009*. The URL is http://www.hardballtimes.com/THT2009Annual/ (make sure you use capitals where appropriate). The page is password-protected; the username is "tht09" and the password is "garza".

We'll post additions and corrections to this page. More importantly, you'll be able to download two valuable Excel spreadsheets from us:

1. Batted Ball Stats for every major league player, exactly as you see them in the Annual.
2. Win Statistics: WPA and Win Shares for every major leaguer.

Be sure to download these "bonus statistics."

That's all the explanation that's fit to print. We hope you enjoy the next 140 pages of numbers.

American League Team Stats

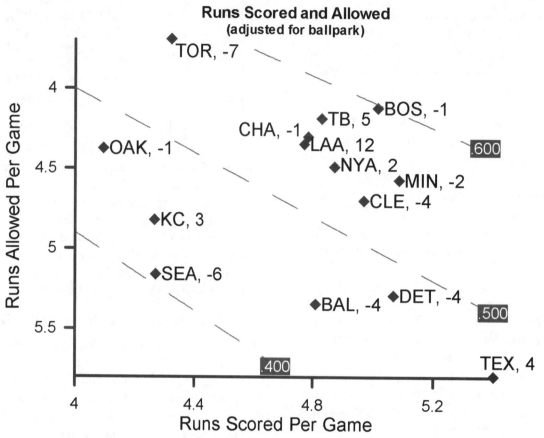

Runs Scored and Allowed
(adjusted for ballpark)

Notes: The dotted lines represent winning percentage based on run differential. The number after each team name represents the difference between the team's actual record and its run differential record.

	Team Record					Scoring Runs			Preventing Runs				Projection	
Team	W	L	RS	RA	RS-RA	AB/RSP	BA/RSP	HR	ERA	HRA	K	DER	PWINS	VAR
BAL	68	93	782	869	-87	1,343	.287	172	5.13	184	922	.691	72	-4
BOS	95	67	845	694	151	1,499	.280	173	4.01	147	1,185	.700	96	-1
CHA	89	74	811	729	82	1,300	.277	235	4.06	156	1,147	.688	90	-1
CLE	81	81	805	761	44	1,447	.272	171	4.45	170	986	.686	85	-4
DET	74	88	821	857	-36	1,414	.268	200	4.90	172	991	.686	78	-4
KC	75	87	691	781	-90	1,380	.286	120	4.48	159	1,085	.691	72	3
LAA	100	62	765	697	68	1,353	.279	159	3.99	160	1,106	.693	88	12
MIN	88	75	829	745	84	1,491	.305	111	4.16	183	995	.690	90	-2
NYA	89	73	789	727	62	1,470	.261	180	4.28	143	1,141	.684	87	2
OAK	75	86	646	690	-44	1,303	.259	125	4.01	135	1,061	.701	76	-1
SEA	61	101	671	811	-140	1,346	.257	124	4.73	161	1,016	.683	67	-6
TB	97	65	774	671	103	1,421	.246	180	3.82	166	1,143	.712	92	5
TEX	79	83	901	967	-66	1,538	.287	194	5.37	176	963	.673	75	4
TOR	86	76	714	610	104	1,409	.260	126	3.49	134	1,184	.706	93	-7
Average	83	79	775	758	17	1,408	.273	162	4.35	160	1,066	.691	81	2

Scoring Runs:
OBP and Power

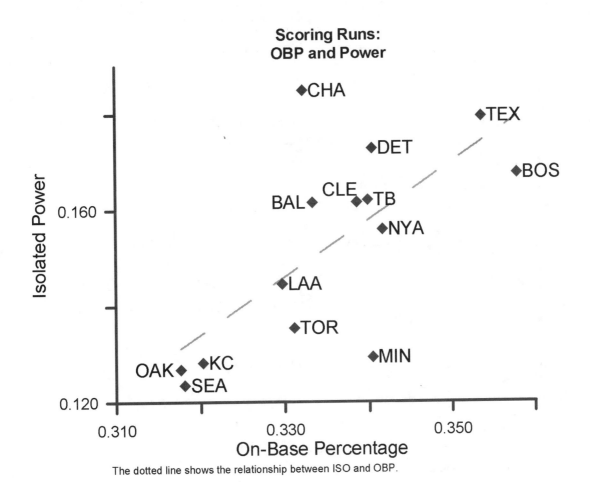

The dotted line shows the relationship between ISO and OBP.

Team	Runs	PA	H	1B	2B	3B	HR	TB	SO	BB	HBP	SH	SF	BA	OBP	SLG	GPA	ISO
BAL	782	6,211	1,486	962	322	30	172	2,384	990	533	42	27	48	.267	.333	.429	.257	.162
BOS	845	6,402	1,565	1,006	353	33	173	2,503	1,068	646	70	28	62	.280	.358	.447	.273	.168
CHA	811	6,231	1,458	914	296	13	235	2,485	1,016	540	63	28	47	.263	.332	.448	.261	.185
CLE	805	6,299	1,455	923	339	22	171	2,351	1,213	560	103	43	49	.262	.339	.424	.258	.162
DET	821	6,331	1,529	995	293	41	200	2,504	1,076	572	44	30	44	.271	.340	.444	.264	.173
KC	691	6,118	1,507	1,056	303	28	120	2,226	1,005	392	50	32	36	.269	.320	.397	.243	.128
LAA	765	6,155	1,486	1,028	274	25	159	2,287	987	481	52	32	50	.268	.330	.413	.252	.145
MIN	829	6,331	1,572	1,114	298	49	111	2,301	979	529	36	52	72	.279	.340	.408	.255	.129
NYA	789	6,257	1,512	1,023	289	20	180	2,381	1,015	535	80	31	39	.271	.342	.427	.261	.156
OAK	646	6,138	1,318	900	270	23	125	2,009	1,226	574	48	30	35	.242	.318	.369	.235	.127
SEA	671	6,176	1,498	1,069	285	20	124	2,195	890	417	38	36	42	.265	.318	.389	.240	.124
TB	774	6,312	1,443	942	284	37	180	2,341	1,224	626	68	23	52	.260	.340	.422	.259	.162
TEX	901	6,478	1,619	1,014	376	35	194	2,647	1,207	595	63	37	54	.283	.354	.462	.275	.179
TOR	714	6,191	1,453	992	303	32	126	2,198	938	521	59	48	56	.264	.331	.399	.249	.135
Average	775	6,259	1,493	996	306	29	162	2,344	1,060	537	58	34	49	.268	.338	.420	.257	.152

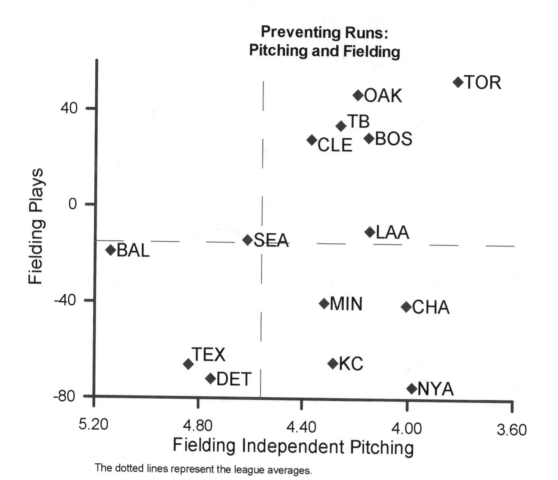

Preventing Runs:
Pitching and Fielding

The dotted lines represent the league averages.

Team	RA	IP	BFP	H	HRA	TBA	K	BB	ShO	Sv	Op	%Save	Holds	ERA	FIP	UERA	DER
BAL	869	1422.0	6,414	1,538	184	2,415	922	687	4	35	59	59%	56	5.13	5.14	0.37	.691
BOS	694	1446.0	6,180	1,369	147	2,137	1,185	548	16	47	69	68%	66	4.01	4.16	0.30	.700
CHA	729	1457.0	6,218	1,471	156	2,315	1,147	460	10	34	52	65%	74	4.06	4.01	0.44	.688
CLE	761	1437.0	6,164	1,530	170	2,372	986	444	13	31	51	61%	51	4.45	4.37	0.31	.686
DET	857	1445.0	6,411	1,541	172	2,457	991	644	2	34	62	55%	60	4.90	4.75	0.44	.686
KC	781	1445.0	6,214	1,473	159	2,314	1,085	515	8	44	60	73%	59	4.48	4.28	0.38	.691
LAA	697	1451.0	6,161	1,455	160	2,263	1,106	457	10	66	89	74%	74	3.99	4.15	0.33	.693
MIN	745	1459.0	6,221	1,568	183	2,466	995	406	10	42	65	65%	75	4.16	4.32	0.43	.690
NYA	727	1441.0	6,175	1,478	143	2,245	1,141	489	11	42	51	82%	79	4.28	3.98	0.26	.684
OAK	690	1435.0	6,112	1,364	135	2,115	1,061	576	7	33	52	63%	68	4.01	4.20	0.31	.701
SEA	811	1435.0	6,368	1,544	161	2,418	1,016	626	4	36	67	54%	57	4.73	4.61	0.36	.683
TB	671	1457.0	6,145	1,349	166	2,200	1,143	526	12	52	68	76%	80	3.82	4.26	0.33	.712
TEX	967	1442.0	6,506	1,647	176	2,602	963	625	8	36	64	56%	73	5.37	4.84	0.67	.673
TOR	610	1446.0	6,067	1,330	134	2,075	1,184	467	13	44	56	79%	72	3.49	3.82	0.30	.706
Average	758	1,444.0	6,240	1,476	160	2,314	1,066	534	9	41	62	67%	67	4.35	4.35	0.37	.691

Running and Miscellaneous Batting Stats

Team	SB	CS	SB%	GDP	P/PA	BABIP	H-A	L-R
BAL	81	37	69%	111	3.79	.296	.014	-.005
BOS	120	35	77%	148	3.87	.315	.023	.018
CHA	67	34	66%	158	3.77	.281	.029	.003
CLE	77	29	73%	123	3.95	.305	.022	.007
DET	63	31	67%	144	3.85	.301	.027	.018
KC	79	38	68%	144	3.67	.307	.005	.027
LAA	129	48	73%	140	3.65	.299	.003	.005
MIN	102	42	71%	144	3.76	.316	.017	-.009
NYA	118	39	75%	150	3.86	.302	.013	-.013
OAK	88	21	81%	126	3.89	.289	.002	-.018
SEA	90	32	74%	137	3.69	.294	.008	.018
TB	142	50	74%	111	3.86	.302	.025	-.016
TEX	81	25	76%	117	3.86	.325	.033	-.009
TOR	80	27	75%	150	3.77	.295	.008	-.014
Average	94	35	73%	136	3.80	.302	.016	.016

Win Probability Added / Win Shares

Team	Bat	Starters	Bullpen	LI	Bat	Pitch	Field	WSAge	CWS
BAL	-3.3	-4.5	-4.7	1.01	115	58	31	28.3	1,308
BOS	6.0	5.5	2.6	1.05	131	104	50	28.3	2,694
CHA	-2.3	4.6	5.2	1.02	119	105	43	28.6	2,455
CLE	-0.9	6.0	-5.1	0.98	122	81	40	26.6	1,492
DET	-1.2	-1.5	-4.4	1.06	124	65	33	28.7	2,800
KC	-6.7	-3.9	4.5	0.91	97	86	42	26.4	1,147
LAA	6.3	6.0	6.7	1.24	132	115	52	27.4	1,892
MIN	4.6	-0.3	2.2	1.02	145	81	39	25.5	1,218
NYA	0.6	-0.9	8.3	0.94	127	99	41	31.2	3,782
OAK	-6.9	-2.7	4.0	1.10	89	92	44	25.8	1,477
SEA	-8.1	-6.3	-5.6	1.05	90	62	31	28.4	1,746
TB	5.3	1.4	9.3	1.14	130	109	52	25.8	1,332
TEX	0.6	-4.8	2.2	1.06	161	50	27	27.0	1,235
TOR	-2.9	4.6	3.3	1.23	96	114	48	28.8	2,442
Average	-0.6	0.2	2.0	1.06	120	87	41	27.6	1,930

Leverage Index (LI) for bullpen only.

Fielding and Miscellaneous Pitching Stats

Team	DER	Fld %	UER	SBA	CS	%CS	PO	E	TE	FE	DP	GIDP	H-A	R-L
BAL	.691	.983	59	163	33	20%	7	100	52	46	163	142	.002	.004
BOS	.700	.986	49	128	32	25%	11	85	41	44	149	119	.007	-.005
CHA	.688	.983	71	169	30	18%	20	108	47	57	155	136	-.027	-.016
CLE	.686	.985	50	94	27	29%	5	94	34	60	183	161	-.018	-.017
DET	.686	.981	71	105	36	34%	8	113	39	71	172	153	-.007	-.006
KC	.691	.984	61	104	26	25%	11	96	46	49	160	133	-.013	-.016
LAA	.693	.985	53	140	31	22%	10	91	47	44	160	141	-.007	-.002
MIN	.690	.982	70	103	34	33%	14	108	61	47	168	143	-.038	-.009
NYA	.684	.986	42	169	56	33%	11	83	41	41	141	111	-.017	.001
OAK	.701	.984	50	111	41	37%	35	98	52	40	169	142	-.026	.013
SEA	.683	.984	57	129	37	29%	18	99	43	54	160	139	-.017	-.032
TB	.712	.985	53	107	31	29%	7	90	44	45	153	134	-.029	.000
TEX	.673	.978	107	151	37	25%	7	132	64	66	191	160	.003	-.014
TOR	.706	.986	49	123	37	30%	12	84	36	46	137	111	-.015	-.027
Average	.691	.984	60	128	35	27%	13	99	46	51	162	138	-.014	-.009

Batted Ball Batting Stats

Team	% of PA		% of Batted Balls					Out %		Runs Per Event				Total Runs vs. Avg.				
	K%	BB%	GB%	LD%	FB%	IF/F	HR/OF	GB	OF	NIP	GB	LD	OF	NIP	GB	LD	FB	Tot
BAL	16	9	43	19	38	.11	.10	73	85	.06	.05	.40	.17	4	17	10	3	34
BOS	17	11	41	20	39	.09	.11	73	82	.07	.05	.38	.19	44	19	3	61	127
CHA	16	10	40	19	41	.13	.14	75	86	.06	.03	.38	.21	10	-26	-11	73	46
CLE	19	11	40	20	40	.10	.11	73	83	.05	.05	.37	.19	9	-4	-17	43	31
DET	17	10	43	19	38	.10	.12	72	84	.05	.06	.40	.19	7	20	-4	44	67
KC	16	7	46	20	34	.10	.09	74	82	.03	.05	.36	.16	-44	12	-13	-27	-72
LAA	16	9	46	18	36	.11	.11	73	84	.05	.05	.38	.17	-10	28	-28	-1	-10
MIN	15	9	46	20	34	.10	.08	74	81	.05	.04	.38	.16	1	27	4	-31	1
NYA	16	10	46	20	35	.09	.12	73	84	.06	.05	.37	.19	16	6	-11	35	46
OAK	20	10	41	19	40	.13	.08	76	84	.04	.03	.39	.14	-8	-28	-38	-51	-125
SEA	14	7	46	20	34	.13	.09	72	86	.04	.06	.36	.13	-27	34	-13	-71	-78
TB	19	11	44	19	36	.09	.12	73	85	.05	.05	.39	.19	18	21	-19	28	49
TEX	19	10	42	22	36	.08	.13	73	83	.05	.05	.40	.21	7	15	54	73	148
TOR	15	9	44	20	36	.10	.08	75	84	.06	.04	.38	.14	12	-15	5	-41	-39
MLB Average	18	10	44	20	36	.10	.11	74	84	.05	.04	.39	.18	--	--	--	--	--

Batted Ball Pitching Stats

Team	% of PA		% of Batted Balls					Out %		Runs Per Event				Total Runs vs. Avg.				
	K%	BB%	GB%	LD%	FB%	IF/F	HR/OF	GB	OF	NIP	GB	LD	OF	NIP	GB	LD	FB	Tot
BAL	14	12	45	18	37	.10	.12	72	85	.10	.06	.36	.18	79	39	-29	33	122
BOS	19	10	43	19	37	.12	.10	76	83	.04	.04	.37	.18	-5	-21	-38	-6	-70
CHA	18	8	46	20	35	.11	.11	75	83	.03	.04	.40	.18	-39	-4	2	-1	-42
CLE	16	8	45	20	35	.10	.11	74	85	.04	.05	.38	.17	-23	15	11	2	5
DET	15	11	42	19	39	.10	.10	74	83	.08	.04	.40	.18	51	-1	14	40	104
KC	17	9	42	20	38	.11	.10	74	86	.04	.04	.41	.16	-14	-1	14	-13	-14
LAA	18	8	44	19	36	.11	.11	75	82	.03	.04	.37	.19	-29	-13	-27	18	-51
MIN	16	7	42	20	38	.10	.11	73	84	.03	.05	.36	.18	-46	11	-7	34	-8
NYA	18	9	46	19	35	.10	.10	72	83	.03	.06	.37	.17	-25	34	-30	-13	-34
OAK	17	10	41	20	39	.10	.09	75	86	.06	.04	.38	.13	16	-15	-9	-41	-50
SEA	16	11	45	19	36	.10	.10	73	84	.07	.05	.39	.17	37	27	8	9	81
TB	19	9	41	18	41	.13	.10	73	85	.04	.05	.36	.17	-16	-6	-62	2	-82
TEX	15	11	43	21	36	.09	.11	72	83	.08	.06	.39	.19	49	31	36	46	162
TOR	20	9	47	19	34	.09	.10	78	83	.03	.03	.38	.17	-33	-36	-35	-26	-130
MLB Average	18	10	44	20	36	.10	.11	74	84	.05	.04	.39	.18	--	--	--	--	--

National League Team Stats

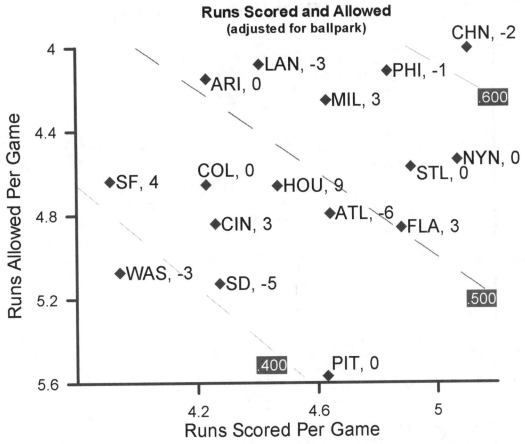

Runs Scored and Allowed
(adjusted for ballpark)

Notes: The dotted lines represent winning percentage based on run differential. The number after each team name represents the difference between the team's actual record and its run differential record.

Team	Team Record					Scoring Runs			Preventing Runs				Projection	
	W	L	RS	RA	RS-RA	AB/RSP	BA/RSP	HR	ERA	HRA	K	DER	PWINS	VAR
ARI	82	80	720	706	14	1,378	.257	159	3.99	147	1,229	.687	82	0
ATL	72	90	753	778	-25	1,492	.272	130	4.46	156	1,076	.695	78	-6
CHN	97	64	855	671	184	1,529	.277	184	3.87	160	1,264	.706	99	-2
CIN	74	88	704	800	-96	1,267	.240	187	4.55	201	1,227	.674	71	3
COL	74	88	747	822	-75	1,490	.256	160	4.77	148	1,041	.679	74	0
FLA	84	77	770	767	3	1,334	.265	208	4.43	161	1,127	.694	81	3
HOU	86	75	712	743	-31	1,326	.262	167	4.36	197	1,095	.699	77	9
LAN	84	78	700	648	52	1,387	.253	137	3.68	123	1,205	.693	87	-3
MIL	90	72	750	689	61	1,412	.245	198	3.85	175	1,110	.700	87	3
WAS	59	102	641	825	-184	1,349	.249	117	4.66	190	1,063	.690	62	-3
NYN	89	73	799	715	84	1,469	.253	172	4.07	163	1,181	.699	89	0
PHI	92	70	799	680	119	1,351	.263	214	3.88	160	1,081	.696	93	-1
PIT	67	95	735	884	-149	1,336	.275	153	5.08	176	963	.676	67	0
STL	86	76	779	725	54	1,456	.276	174	4.19	163	957	.697	86	0
SD	63	99	637	764	-127	1,257	.250	154	4.41	165	1,100	.697	68	-5
SF	72	90	640	759	-119	1,442	.260	94	4.38	147	1,240	.686	68	4
Average	79	82	734	749	-15	1,392	.260	163	4.29	165	1,122	.692	81	-2

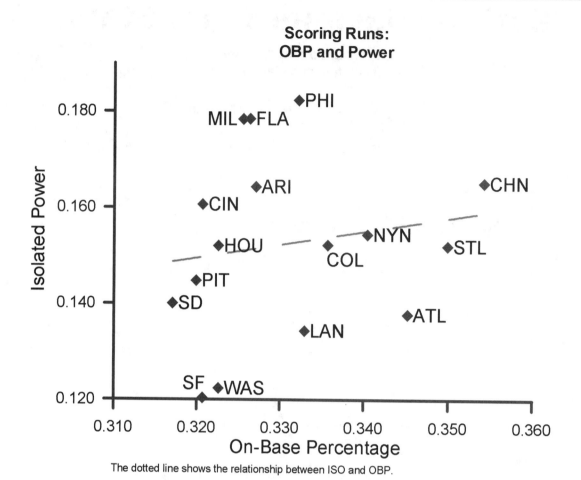

Scoring Runs: OBP and Power

The dotted line shows the relationship between ISO and OBP.

Team	Runs	PA	H	1B	2B	3B	HR	TB	SO	BB	HBP	SH	SF	BA	OBP	SLG	GPA	ISO
ARI	720	6,156	1,355	831	318	47	159	2,244	1,287	587	49	68	43	.251	.327	.415	.251	.164
ATL	753	6,368	1,514	1,035	316	33	130	2,286	1,023	618	42	69	34	.270	.345	.408	.257	.138
CHN	855	6,384	1,552	1,018	329	21	184	2,475	1,186	636	50	65	45	.278	.354	.443	.270	.165
CIN	704	6,188	1,351	871	269	24	187	2,229	1,125	560	50	72	41	.247	.321	.408	.246	.161
COL	747	6,312	1,462	964	310	28	160	2,308	1,209	570	57	90	38	.263	.336	.415	.255	.152
FLA	770	6,206	1,397	859	302	28	208	2,379	1,371	543	69	49	46	.254	.326	.433	.255	.179
HOU	712	6,051	1,432	959	284	22	167	2,261	1,051	449	52	57	41	.263	.323	.415	.249	.152
LAN	700	6,194	1,455	1,018	271	29	137	2,195	1,032	543	43	64	38	.264	.333	.399	.249	.134
MIL	750	6,252	1,398	841	324	35	198	2,386	1,203	550	69	54	43	.253	.325	.431	.254	.179
WAS	641	6,192	1,376	964	269	26	117	2,048	1,095	534	67	64	36	.251	.323	.373	.238	.122
NYN	799	6,388	1,491	1,007	274	38	172	2,357	1,024	619	39	73	49	.266	.340	.420	.258	.154
PHI	799	6,273	1,407	866	291	36	214	2,412	1,117	586	67	71	40	.255	.332	.438	.259	.182
PIT	735	6,278	1,454	966	314	21	153	2,269	1,039	474	59	66	51	.258	.320	.403	.245	.145
STL	779	6,370	1,585	1,102	283	26	174	2,442	985	577	42	71	44	.281	.350	.433	.266	.152
SD	637	6,244	1,390	945	264	27	154	2,170	1,259	518	53	59	46	.250	.317	.390	.240	.140
SF	640	6,145	1,452	1,010	311	37	94	2,119	1,044	452	48	57	44	.262	.321	.382	.240	.120
Average	734	6,250	1,442	954	296	30	163	2,286	1,128	551	54	66	42	.260	.331	.413	.252	.153

Preventing Runs:
Pitching and Fielding

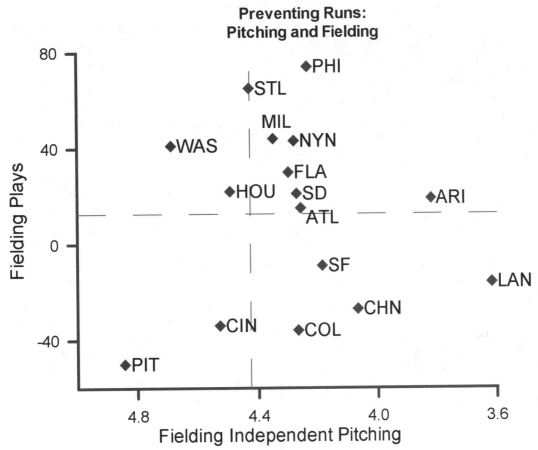

The dotted lines represent the league averages.

Team	RA	IP	BFP	H	HR	TBA	K	BB	ShO	Sv	Op	%Save	Holds	ERA	FIP	UERA	DER
ARI	706	1434.0	6,119	1,403	147	2,180	1,229	451	9	39	62	63%	68	3.99	3.82	0.45	.687
ATL	778	1440.0	6,244	1,439	156	2,316	1,076	586	7	26	44	59%	76	4.46	4.26	0.40	.695
CHN	671	1450.0	6,194	1,329	160	2,170	1,264	548	8	44	68	65%	74	3.87	4.07	0.29	.706
CIN	800	1442.0	6,352	1,542	201	2,525	1,227	557	6	34	55	62%	58	4.55	4.53	0.44	.674
COL	822	1446.0	6,338	1,547	148	2,418	1,041	562	8	36	59	61%	59	4.77	4.27	0.35	.679
FLA	767	1435.0	6,271	1,421	161	2,239	1,127	586	8	36	60	60%	87	4.43	4.30	0.38	.694
HOU	743	1425.0	6,125	1,453	197	2,419	1,095	492	13	48	65	74%	80	4.36	4.49	0.33	.699
LAN	648	1447.0	6,127	1,381	123	2,065	1,205	480	11	35	55	64%	61	3.68	3.62	0.35	.693
MIL	689	1455.0	6,209	1,415	175	2,245	1,110	528	10	45	71	63%	68	3.85	4.35	0.41	.700
WAS	825	1434.0	6,310	1,496	190	2,415	1,063	588	8	28	56	50%	66	4.66	4.69	0.52	.690
NYN	715	1464.0	6,338	1,415	163	2,212	1,181	590	12	43	72	60%	99	4.07	4.28	0.33	.699
PHI	680	1449.0	6,229	1,444	160	2,280	1,081	533	11	47	62	76%	80	3.88	4.23	0.34	.696
PIT	884	1455.0	6,528	1,631	176	2,586	963	657	7	34	56	61%	65	5.08	4.84	0.38	.676
STL	725	1454.0	6,264	1,517	163	2,426	957	496	7	42	73	58%	106	4.19	4.43	0.30	.697
SD	764	1458.0	6,286	1,466	165	2,280	1,100	561	6	30	56	54%	55	4.41	4.27	0.31	.697
SF	759	1442.0	6,341	1,416	147	2,222	1,240	652	12	41	60	68%	56	4.38	4.19	0.36	.686
Average	749	1445.6	6,267	1,457	165	2,312	1,122	554	9	38	61	62%	72	4.29	4.29	0.37	.692

Running and Miscellaneous Batting Stats

Team	SB	CS	SB%	GDP	P/PA	BABIP	H-A	L-R
ARI	58	23	72%	105	3.90	.299	.031	.017
ATL	58	27	68%	143	3.71	.309	.012	-.017
CHN	87	34	72%	134	3.88	.321	.026	.007
CIN	85	47	64%	101	3.76	.278	.019	.015
COL	141	37	79%	119	3.86	.308	.032	.021
FLA	76	28	73%	98	3.96	.300	-.008	-.023
HOU	114	52	69%	116	3.78	.296	.023	.008
LAN	126	43	75%	153	3.82	.301	-.000	.018
MIL	108	38	74%	98	3.86	.287	.001	.024
WAS	81	43	65%	153	3.74	.292	.003	.011
NYN	138	36	79%	129	3.85	.296	.013	.012
PHI	136	25	84%	108	3.85	.283	.012	.012
PIT	57	19	75%	111	3.81	.290	.004	-.002
STL	73	32	70%	151	3.68	.312	-.001	-.013
SD	36	17	68%	129	3.81	.294	-.013	-.015
SF	108	46	70%	139	3.67	.305	.007	-.004
Average	93	34	73%	124	3.81	.298	.010	.004

Win Probability Added   Win Shares

Team	Bat	Starters	Bullpen	LI	Bat	Pitch	Field	WSAge	CWS
ARI	-1.0	3.2	-1.2	1.01	97	105	44	26.7	1,688
ATL	-6.4	-1.0	-1.6	0.92	111	72	33	27.0	2,092
CHN	7.7	6.9	1.9	1.13	136	107	48	28.7	1,805
CIN	-2.7	-4.7	0.4	0.97	98	84	41	27.6	1,673
COL	-3.8	-3.7	0.5	1.00	103	83	36	26.7	1,380
FLA	6.9	-4.0	0.7	1.13	135	80	38	26.5	1,257
HOU	2.6	-2.7	5.5	0.97	121	91	46	30.4	2,208
LAN	2.0	-0.8	1.8	1.03	105	106	41	27.4	2,900
MIL	6.5	1.8	0.7	1.20	123	98	49	27.7	2,081
NYN	6.7	3.9	-2.6	1.16	138	87	42	28.5	2,768
PHI	3.5	-0.8	8.3	1.18	127	103	45	29.1	2,044
PIT	-2.8	-11.9	0.7	1.00	123	50	28	27.3	1,057
SD	-9.6	-4.2	-4.3	1.04	96	62	32	28.6	1,981
SF	-5.9	-1.2	-2.0	1.05	86	87	43	27.8	1,314
STL	5.0	1.9	-1.9	1.21	132	85	41	28.0	1,807
WAS	-11.9	-7.3	-2.3	1.03	79	63	35	26.5	1,246
Average	-0.2	-1.5	0.3	1.06	113	85	40	27.8	1,831

Leverage Index (LI) for bullpen only.

Fielding and Miscellaneous Pitching Stats

Team	DER	Fld %	UER	SBA	CS	%CS	PO	E	TE	FE	DP	GIDP	H-A	R-L
ARI	.687	.981	71	118	31	26%	5	113	48	64	137	115	-.001	.002
ATL	.695	.983	64	148	35	24%	9	107	56	50	149	129	.002	.004
CHN	.706	.983	47	123	36	29%	13	99	38	59	118	97	-.007	-.022
CIN	.674	.981	71	135	40	30%	4	114	63	50	156	130	-.002	.003
COL	.679	.985	56	116	30	26%	15	96	37	59	176	142	-.001	-.012
FLA	.694	.980	60	142	32	23%	7	117	59	57	122	100	-.005	-.009
HOU	.699	.989	52	68	21	31%	7	67	28	39	142	120	-.005	-.008
LAN	.693	.984	57	108	26	24%	7	101	50	50	138	124	-.046	-.025
MIL	.700	.984	66	116	45	39%	10	101	48	53	160	131	-.012	-.011
WAS	.690	.980	83	156	38	24%	11	123	57	66	143	119	-.004	-.000
NYN	.699	.986	53	94	28	30%	11	83	35	48	126	112	-.031	-.023
PHI	.696	.985	55	143	34	24%	12	90	33	56	142	127	-.012	-.019
PIT	.676	.983	62	150	46	31%	14	107	47	60	180	157	-.015	-.005
STL	.697	.986	48	75	26	35%	8	85	44	40	156	134	-.013	-.007
SD	.697	.986	50	206	38	18%	5	85	48	36	149	123	-.040	-.008
SF	.686	.983	58	140	41	29%	5	96	32	64	129	105	.004	.013
Average	.692	.984	60	127	34	27%	9	99	45	53	145	123	-.012	-.008

Batted Ball Batting Stats

Team	% of PA		% of Batted Balls			IF/F	HR/OF	Out %		Runs Per Event				Total Runs vs. Avg.				
	K%	BB%	GB%	LD%	FB%	IF/F	HR/OF	GB	OF	NIP	GB	LD	OF	NIP	GB	LD	FB	Tot
ARI	21	10	40	21	40	.11	.11	76	83	.04	.04	.41	.18	-9	-35	5	8	-32
ATL	16	10	45	22	33	.09	.09	74	86	.07	.04	.41	.13	29	-4	60	-66	20
CHN	19	11	43	21	36	.07	.11	74	84	.06	.05	.42	.19	20	-3	47	32	96
CIN	18	10	45	20	36	.11	.13	76	85	.05	.04	.37	.19	-1	-10	-42	6	-47
COL	19	10	44	21	35	.09	.11	74	83	.04	.04	.38	.19	-4	-5	3	12	5
FLA	22	10	42	20	39	.11	.13	73	84	.03	.05	.42	.21	-27	1	-10	51	14
HOU	17	8	46	19	35	.12	.12	75	85	.04	.04	.39	.19	-28	2	-12	0	-37
LAN	17	9	46	21	32	.09	.10	75	85	.05	.04	.37	.16	3	-11	7	-36	-38
MIL	19	10	42	18	39	.12	.13	72	86	.04	.06	.40	.19	-6	28	-26	28	23
NYN	16	10	46	23	31	.11	.11	76	85	.07	.04	.38	.17	27	-9	52	-38	32
PHI	18	10	42	21	36	.12	.14	77	86	.06	.03	.39	.21	16	-35	12	46	38
PIT	17	8	42	20	37	.10	.09	76	84	.04	.04	.37	.16	-19	-24	-6	-12	-61
SD	20	9	43	20	37	.09	.10	75	85	.03	.04	.38	.16	-31	-21	-34	-18	-104
SF	17	8	48	19	33	.10	.07	75	81	.04	.04	.40	.15	-29	-5	-8	-51	-93
STL	15	10	44	21	34	.10	.11	72	85	.06	.05	.38	.17	19	17	32	-7	62
WAS	18	10	48	21	31	.11	.08	74	86	.05	.04	.38	.13	0	-9	-0	-94	-103
MLB Average	18	10	44	20	36	.10	.11	74	84	.05	.04	.39	.18	--	--	--	--	--

Batted Ball Pitching Stats

Team	% of PA		% of Batted Balls			IF/F	HR/OF	Out %		Runs Per Event				Total Runs vs. Avg.				
	K%	BB%	GB%	LD%	FB%	IF/F	HR/OF	GB	OF	NIP	GB	LD	OF	NIP	GB	LD	FB	Tot
ARI	20	8	45	20	35	.09	.10	73	84	.02	.05	.40	.17	-43	9	-10	-26	-70
ATL	17	10	48	21	31	.09	.11	76	82	.06	.04	.39	.20	12	-11	11	-2	10
CHN	20	10	42	20	39	.11	.10	75	85	.04	.04	.39	.16	-16	-16	-27	-19	-78
CIN	19	10	43	21	36	.11	.13	73	83	.04	.05	.41	.21	-6	10	36	53	92
COL	16	10	47	21	33	.10	.11	76	80	.06	.04	.40	.20	12	-11	29	24	55
FLA	18	10	42	21	38	.12	.10	73	84	.05	.05	.38	.16	11	15	-10	-21	-4
HOU	18	9	43	20	37	.09	.13	76	84	.04	.04	.40	.20	-19	-18	4	49	16
LAN	20	9	50	19	31	.09	.10	76	84	.03	.04	.40	.16	-38	-12	-19	-57	-125
MIL	18	9	45	20	34	.10	.12	75	85	.04	.04	.36	.19	-13	-6	-23	1	-40
NYN	19	10	43	22	35	.11	.09	73	88	.05	.05	.41	.12	10	6	37	-92	-39
PHI	17	9	45	22	33	.12	.11	76	86	.05	.03	.39	.18	-2	-21	25	-22	-20
PIT	15	11	44	21	35	.08	.11	75	83	.08	.04	.40	.19	52	0	60	41	153
SD	17	10	42	21	37	.12	.11	73	86	.05	.05	.37	.17	-2	-5	-7	-16	-29
SF	20	11	39	22	39	.10	.09	72	84	.06	.06	.37	.15	26	12	-9	-19	11
STL	15	9	45	21	34	.10	.11	77	83	.05	.03	.39	.19	-3	-26	27	14	11
WAS	17	10	42	21	36	.10	.12	73	86	.06	.05	.39	.18	18	14	28	7	66
MLB Average	18	10	44	20	36	.10	.11	74	84	.05	.04	.39	.18	--	--	--	--	--

Arizona Diamondbacks

Stat Facts:

- No D-back with as many as 200 PAs had a GPA as high as .270
- Chris Young had a ZR of .947 and made 92 OOZ plays
- Justin Upton's H-A of .143 was highest in the majors among 150+ PA players
- Mark Reynolds, setting the record with 204 Ks, struck out in one-third of his PAs
- Reynolds led the majors with 18 fielding errors, and with 16 throwing errors
- Chris Snyder committed zero errors
- Adam Dunn led the majors in BB%
- Juan Cruz struck out one-third of the batters he faced
- Brandon Webb's GB rate was highest, his FB rate lowest, and his LD rate tied for lowest in the majors among 162+ IP pitchers
- 64% of the ground balls allowed by Randy Johnson resulted in outs, the lowest rate in the majors among 162+ IP pitchers

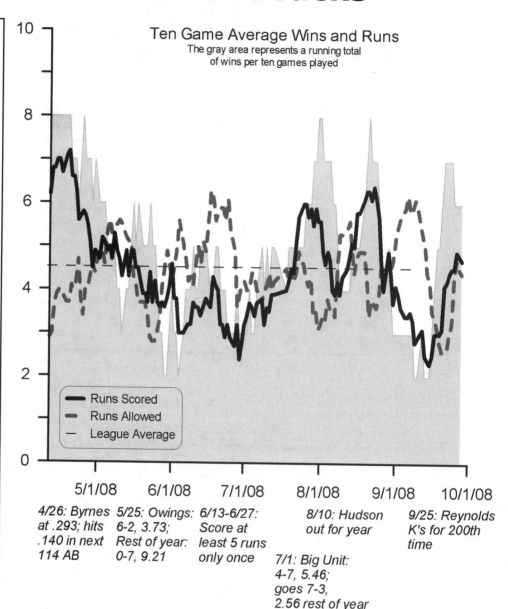

Ten Game Average Wins and Runs
The gray area represents a running total of wins per ten games played

- Runs Scored
- Runs Allowed
- League Average

4/26: Byrnes at .293; hits .140 in next 114 AB

5/25: Owings: 6-2, 3.73; Rest of year: 0-7, 9.21

6/13-6/27: Score at least 5 runs only once

7/1: Big Unit: 4-7, 5.46; goes 7-3, 2.56 rest of year

8/10: Hudson out for year

9/25: Reynolds K's for 200th time

Team Batting and Pitching/Fielding Stats by Month

	April	May	June	July	Aug	Sept/Oct
Wins	20	11	11	14	13	13
Losses	8	17	16	11	15	13
RS/G	5.9	4.2	3.3	4.8	4.8	3.7
RA/G	3.9	4.5	4.7	4.0	4.7	4.3
OBP	.345	.328	.291	.335	.326	.334
SLG	.468	.402	.361	.421	.408	.426
FIP	3.77	3.65	4.04	4.02	3.57	3.89
DER	.728	.675	.684	.713	.653	.670

Batting Stats

Player	BR	Runs	RBI	PA	Outs	H	2B	3B	HR	TB	K	BB	IBB	HBP	SH	SF	SB	CS	GDP	H-A	L^R	BA	OBP	SLG	GPA
Drew S *	91	91	67	663	441	178	44	11	21	307	109	41	6	1	3	7	3	3	5	.052	.041	.291	.333	.502	.262
Young C	84	85	85	699	485	155	42	7	22	277	165	62	2	1	6	5	14	5	10	.026	.056	.248	.315	.443	.240
Reynolds M	84	87	97	613	422	129	28	3	28	247	204	64	0	3	1	6	11	2	10	.013	.086	.239	.320	.458	.246
Jackson C	80	87	75	612	394	162	31	6	12	241	61	59	3	9	1	3	10	2	14	.001	.058	.300	.376	.446	.268
Hudson O +	61	54	41	455	302	124	29	3	8	183	62	40	2	2	3	3	4	1	18	.068	-.045	.305	.367	.450	.264
Snyder C	52	47	64	404	262	79	22	1	16	151	101	56	5	4	5	5	0	0	7	.003	.031	.237	.348	.452	.257
Upton J	46	52	42	417	274	89	19	6	15	165	121	54	6	4	0	3	1	4	3	.143	.018	.250	.353	.463	.261
Tracy C *	30	25	39	292	205	73	16	0	8	113	49	16	2	1	0	2	0	0	5	.035	-.019	.267	.308	.414	.231
Dunn A *	26	21	26	187	112	35	9	0	8	68	44	42	7	1	0	0	1	0	3	.010	.080	.243	.417	.472	.291
Ojeda A +	24	27	17	272	181	56	9	2	0	69	24	26	2	10	4	1	0	0	6	.064	.009	.242	.343	.299	.218
Montero M *	21	24	18	207	138	47	16	1	5	80	49	19	3	2	1	1	0	0	1	-.016	-.022	.255	.330	.435	.245
Byrnes E	20	28	23	224	172	43	13	1	6	76	36	16	0	2	0	0	4	4	5	.043	.081	.209	.272	.369	.205
Salazar J *	17	17	12	152	105	27	5	3	2	44	41	21	1	2	1	0	0	2	2	.026	.027	.211	.331	.344	.224
Burke C	13	20	12	199	135	32	5	1	2	45	33	27	8	2	2	3	5	0	2	-.029	.034	.194	.310	.273	.198
Romero A *	11	13	12	142	107	31	8	2	1	46	20	3	0	1	2	1	4	0	3	-.001	.091	.230	.250	.341	.188
Clark T +	7	7	13	77	56	13	2	0	2	21	23	12	1	1	0	1	0	0	6	-.007	.123	.206	.338	.333	.224
Owings M	5	7	3	58	39	15	2	0	1	20	21	5	0	0	1	0	0	0	2	.130	-.169	.288	.351	.385	.242
Eckstein D	5	5	4	73	51	14	3	0	1	20	5	7	0	1	0	1	0	0	1	.247	-.028	.219	.301	.313	.204
Webb B	4	2	11	81	57	10	4	0	0	14	30	1	0	0	13	0	0	0	0	.064	.188	.149	.162	.209	.119
Haren D	4	8	6	85	61	16	7	0	0	23	15	3	0	0	5	1	0	0	1	-.195	.009	.211	.238	.303	.174
Hammock R	3	4	2	48	34	8	1	0	0	9	9	5	1	1	0	0	0	0	0	.022	-.045	.190	.292	.214	.176
Johnson R	3	2	5	60	43	7	1	0	0	8	26	4	0	0	6	0	0	0	0	-.027	-.000	.140	.204	.160	.125
Whitesell J	2	1	1	9	5	2	0	0	1	5	2	1	0	1	0	0	0	0	0	-.698	--	.286	.444	.714	.361
Bonifacio E	1	3	2	12	10	2	1	0	0	3	5	0	0	0	0	0	1	0	0	-.275	-.165	.167	.167	.250	.131
D'Antona J	1	2	1	19	14	3	0	0	0	3	4	2	0	0	0	0	0	0	0	-.024	.025	.176	.263	.176	.155
Davis D	1	0	3	50	39	4	0	0	0	4	13	0	0	0	8	0	0	0	1	-.006	.082	.095	.095	.095	.063

Italicized stats have been adjusted for home park.

Batted Ball Batting Stats

Player	% of PA		% of Batted Balls					Out %		Runs Per Event				Total Runs vs. Avg.				
	K%	BB%	GB%	LD%	FB%	IF/F	HR/OF	GB	OF	NIP	GB	LD	OF	NIP	GB	LD	FB	Tot
Jackson C	10	11	40	22	38	.11	.07	71	82	.13	.07	.38	.14	9	5	8	-1	21
Drew S	16	6	35	23	43	.07	.11	75	82	.01	.05	.45	.19	-7	-1	15	12	19
Upton J	29	14	37	21	42	.10	.17	66	81	.04	.11	.37	.29	1	5	-4	9	11
Dunn A	24	23	33	19	48	.06	.16	79	84	.11	.01	.46	.25	8	-2	-0	5	10
Hudson O	14	9	48	23	29	.06	.08	77	79	.07	.02	.44	.17	2	-4	11	-1	8
Snyder C	25	15	38	18	44	.15	.18	74	85	.06	.05	.39	.28	4	-2	-5	8	5
Reynolds M	33	11	36	19	45	.11	.20	68	85	.00	.07	.49	.29	-8	0	-3	15	4
Montero M	24	10	36	22	41	.09	.10	78	83	.02	.03	.47	.19	-1	-2	3	1	1
Young C	24	9	38	19	43	.17	.13	74	80	.01	.05	.42	.24	-7	-2	-3	9	-2
Salazar J	27	15	37	16	47	.15	.06	72	82	.05	.09	.39	.12	1	1	-3	-2	-3
Tracy C	17	6	29	24	47	.08	.08	77	89	.01	.02	.39	.10	-4	-3	4	-3	-5
Romero A	14	3	47	19	34	.05	.03	75	89	-.04	.04	.39	.04	-3	-0	-0	-5	-8
Byrnes E	16	8	39	19	42	.24	.09	83	86	.04	-.01	.42	.14	-1	-4	-0	-3	-9
Ojeda A	9	13	50	20	31	.11	.00	87	82	.16	-.03	.40	.04	6	-7	1	-9	-9
Burke C	17	15	38	18	44	.19	.04	78	91	.10	.02	.33	.03	4	-2	-4	-8	-9
Webb B	37	1	60	17	23	.00	.00	86	75	-.10	-.01	.49	.13	-4	-3	-3	-3	-14
MLB Average	18	10	44	20	36	.10	.11	74	84	.05	.04	.39	.18	--	--	--	--	--

Pitching Stats

Player	PRC	IP	BFP	G	GS	K	BB	IBB	HBP	H	HR	DP	DER	SB	CS	PO	W	L	Sv	Op	Hld	H-A	R^L	RA	ERA	FIP
Haren D	112	216.0	881	33	33	206	40	4	6	204	19	16	.690	9	2	0	16	8	0	0	0	-.008	.017	3.58	3.33	3.02
Webb B	108	226.7	944	34	34	183	65	5	12	206	13	30	.687	24	10	1	22	7	0	0	0	.021	-.045	3.77	3.30	3.29
Johnson R *	77	184.0	778	30	30	173	44	6	6	184	24	13	.676	21	3	2	11	10	0	0	0	.010	-.063	4.50	3.91	3.73
Davis D *	56	146.0	650	26	26	112	64	4	4	160	13	16	.663	8	3	2	6	8	0	0	0	-.009	.020	4.68	4.32	4.14
Qualls C	39	73.7	300	77	0	71	18	2	3	61	4	13	.701	3	0	0	4	8	9	17	22	-.089	.023	3.54	2.81	2.75
Cruz J	34	51.7	215	57	0	71	31	0	3	34	5	2	.724	5	5	0	4	0	0	2	8	-.012	.058	2.96	2.61	3.69
Owings M	30	104.7	466	22	18	87	41	0	12	104	14	4	.705	3	2	0	6	9	0	0	1	.024	-.017	6.28	5.93	4.80
Scherzer M	28	56.0	237	16	7	66	21	1	5	48	5	7	.664	0	1	0	0	4	0	0	0	-.066	-.104	3.86	3.05	3.34
Pena T	27	72.7	313	72	0	52	17	5	3	80	5	7	.674	2	0	0	3	2	3	8	23	-.018	-.031	4.71	4.33	3.28
Petit Y	22	56.3	229	19	8	42	14	2	1	45	12	1	.788	2	1	0	3	5	0	0	0	-.052	.024	4.63	4.31	5.17
Lyon B	21	59.3	265	61	0	44	13	1	0	75	7	4	.642	1	1	0	3	5	26	31	3	.087	.056	5.16	4.70	3.86
Gonzalez E	13	48.0	221	17	6	32	21	2	3	58	8	5	.675	2	1	0	1	3	0	0	0	.062	.036	6.38	6.00	5.41
Rosales L	11	30.0	136	27	0	18	15	3	1	32	2	3	.680	2	0	0	1	1	0	1	1	.116	-.038	4.50	4.20	4.17
Slaten D *	10	32.3	147	45	0	20	14	1	4	33	4	5	.686	0	0	0	0	3	0	0	4	-.004	-.055	5.57	4.73	5.15
Buckner B	8	14.0	59	10	0	11	4	1	1	16	3	4	.675	0	0	0	1	0	0	0	0	.008	.116	3.21	3.21	5.27
Medders B	6	19.7	88	18	0	8	11	2	2	17	2	1	.754	5	1	0	1	0	0	1	0	-.039	-.086	5.03	4.58	5.39
Rauch J	6	23.3	103	26	0	22	9	1	0	27	6	3	.667	0	1	0	0	6	1	2	6	-.085	-.005	6.94	6.56	5.69
Peguero J	3	9.3	38	7	0	5	4	0	1	9	0	3	.679	0	0	0	0	0	0	0	0	-.132	-.170	5.79	4.82	3.74
Robertson C	2	7.0	32	6	0	2	2	1	1	8	1	0	.731	0	0	0	0	1	0	0	0	-.324	.014	5.14	5.14	5.34

Italicized stats have been adjusted for home park.

Batted Ball Pitching Stats

Player	% of PA		% of Batted Balls			IF/F	HR/OF	Out %		Runs Per Event				Total Runs vs. Avg.				
	K%	BB%	GB%	LD%	FB%			GB	OF	NIP	GB	LD	OF	NIP	GB	LD	FB	Tot
Haren D	23	5	44	21	35	.08	.09	74	84	-.03	.05	.38	.15	-20	0	-4	-7	-31
Webb B	19	8	64	15	20	.07	.10	75	80	.02	.03	.41	.20	-7	2	-12	-13	-30
Qualls C	24	7	58	19	23	.04	.09	77	83	-.01	.01	.36	.18	-5	-3	-4	-5	-17
Cruz J	33	16	27	16	57	.06	.09	83	79	.04	-.01	.38	.19	1	-4	-6	2	-6
Scherzer M	28	11	42	28	30	.05	.13	74	91	.02	.03	.38	.14	-2	-2	1	-4	-6
Petit Y	18	7	33	17	50	.10	.11	84	87	.01	-.01	.50	.15	-3	-4	-0	1	-6
Johnson R	22	6	40	18	42	.09	.11	64	87	-.01	.11	.39	.17	-13	13	-7	1	-6
Pena A	17	6	47	20	32	.07	.07	71	82	.01	.07	.38	.14	-3	4	0	-2	-2
Owings M	19	11	34	23	43	.12	.11	74	87	.06	.06	.36	.15	2	-0	1	-1	2
Rosales L	13	12	45	18	37	.14	.06	71	87	.10	.07	.44	.11	2	2	1	-2	2
Slaten D	14	12	39	19	43	.04	.09	79	78	.10	.01	.36	.21	2	-1	-1	4	4
Lyon B	17	5	40	22	38	.10	.09	66	86	-.01	.10	.42	.16	-4	4	5	0	5
Davis D	17	10	47	22	31	.12	.10	74	81	.06	.04	.41	.19	2	0	6	-2	7
Gonzalez E	14	11	38	20	43	.07	.10	77	82	.08	.03	.55	.16	2	-1	6	2	9
MLB Average	18	10	44	20	36	.10	.11	74	84	.05	.04	.39	.18	--	--	--	--	--

Fielding Stats

Name	Inn	SBA/G	CS%	ERA	WP+PB/G	PO	A	TE	FE	Grade
Catcher										
Snyder C	922.7	0.67	29%	3.83	0.361	777	69	0	0	A
Montero M	404.7	0.73	18%	4.58	0.578	352	23	2	2	--
Hammock	107.3	1.01	8%	3.10	0.252	92	3	0	0	--

Name	Inn	PO	A	TE	FE	FPct	DPS	DPT	ZR	OOZ	Grade
First Base											
Jackson C	571.7	533	30	2	2	.993	1	1	.674	15	--
Tracy C	523.0	528	26	0	4	.993	5	0	.691	16	--
Clark T	133.0	148	14	0	1	.988	2	0	.786	4	--
Dunn A	128.0	123	7	0	3	.977	0	0	.667	0	--
Burke C	63.0	67	4	0	0	1.000	0	0	.818	2	--
D'Antona J	7.0	7	2	0	0	1.000	0	0	.500	1	--
Whitesell J	7.0	7	0	0	0	1.000	0	0	.000	0	--
Reynolds M	2.0	1	0	0	1	.500	0	0	.000	0	--
Second Base											
Hudson O	904.7	200	284	2	7	.982	26	34	.784	27	F
Ojeda A	286.0	70	92	0	0	1.000	9	15	.829	7	--
Eckstein D	152.0	30	65	0	0	1.000	13	3	.857	6	--
Burke C	92.0	21	34	0	0	1.000	1	6	.963	2	--
Shortstop											
Drew S	1294.0	190	378	6	8	.976	38	37	.788	52	F
Ojeda A	126.7	17	39	1	2	.949	3	1	.906	9	--
Burke C	13.7	2	4	0	1	.857	0	3	1.000	1	--
Third Base											
Reynolds M	1288.0	82	240	18	16	.904	22	1	.669	35	F-
Ojeda A	110.3	6	32	0	0	1.000	2	0	.765	5	--
Burke C	20.0	2	5	0	0	1.000	0	0	.500	1	--
Tracy C	16.0	2	2	0	0	1.000	0	0	1.000	0	--

Name	Inn	PO	A	TE	FE	FPct	DPS	DPT	ZR	OOZ	Grade
Left Field											
Jackson C	656.0	146	5	2	1	.981	6	0	.929	28	C
Byrnes E	419.7	76	1	1	0	.987	0	0	.928	12	--
Salazar J	133.3	17	2	0	0	1.000	0	0	.867	4	--
Burke C	116.3	43	1	0	0	1.000	0	0	1.000	7	--
Dunn A	65.0	19	0	0	0	1.000	0	0	1.000	6	F-
Romero A	42.3	5	0	0	0	1.000	0	0	.800	1	--
Bonifacio E	2.0	0	0	0	0	.000	0	0	--	--	--
Center Field											
Young C	1390.0	393	5	0	3	.993	4	0	.947	92	B
Salazar J	27.7	3	1	0	0	1.000	0	0	1.000	0	--
Romero A	13.7	4	0	0	0	1.000	0	0	1.000	1	--
Byrnes E	3.3	2	0	0	0	1.000	0	0	1.000	0	--
Right Field											
Upton J	860.3	175	6	3	8	.943	4	0	.854	46	C
Romero A	221.0	39	1	0	1	.976	0	0	.939	8	--
Dunn A	182.7	29	0	0	1	.967	0	0	.794	2	--
Salazar J	92.0	16	0	0	0	1.000	0	0	.941	0	--
Burke C	62.7	9	0	0	0	1.000	0	0	.857	3	--
Bonifacio E	16.0	1	0	0	0	1.000	0	0	.000	1	--

Atlanta Braves

Stat Facts:

- Jair Jurrjens allowed 28 stolen bases in 31 attempts
- No other Braves pitcher allowed as many as 10
- Chipper Jones had the second-highest GPA in the majors
- Jeff Francoeur had more than twice as many outs as total bases
- Yunel Escobar hit a ground ball on 58% of his balls in play, tied for highest in the majors
- 24 of Escobar's grounders were double plays
- Chuck James allowed 10 homers in 30 innings
- Kelly Johnson committed just 1 throwing error, but 13 fielding errors
- Jeff Bennett induced a ground ball on 64% of his batted balls
- Only 21% of the balls hit off Bennett were fly balls
- Tim Hudson's ERA (3.17) was much better than his FIP (3.79)
- 9 different Braves' pitchers made at least 5 starts

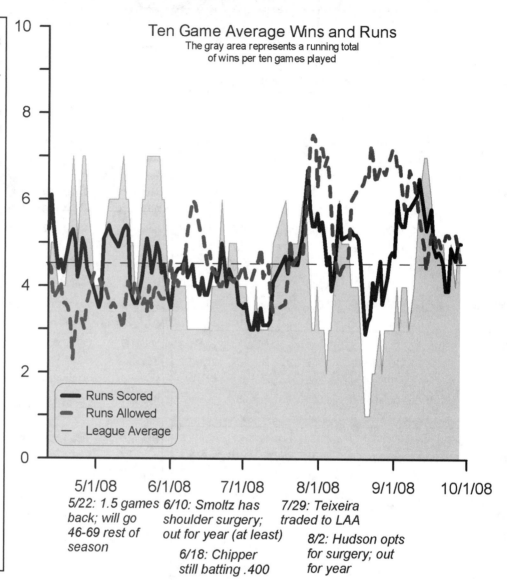

Ten Game Average Wins and Runs
The gray area represents a running total of wins per ten games played

Legend:
— Runs Scored
-- Runs Allowed
- League Average

5/22: 1.5 games back; will go 46-69 rest of season

6/10: Smoltz has shoulder surgery; out for year (at least)

6/18: Chipper still batting .400

7/29: Teixeira traded to LAA

8/2: Hudson opts for surgery; out for year

Team Batting and Pitching/Fielding Stats by Month

	April	May	June	July	Aug	Sept/Oct
Wins	12	17	11	10	9	13
Losses	15	12	16	15	20	12
RS/G	4.8	4.7	4.0	4.8	4.4	5.3
RA/G	4.0	3.6	4.5	5.6	6.1	5.1
OBP	.341	.362	.334	.332	.342	.359
SLG	.437	.414	.407	.393	.382	.414
FIP	3.84	4.03	4.27	4.36	4.27	4.81
DER	.716	.716	.697	.703	.655	.691

Batting Stats

Player	BR	Runs	RBI	PA	Outs	H	2B	3B	HR	TB	K	BB	IBB	HBP	SH	SF	SB	CS	GDP	H-A	L^R	BA	OBP	SLG	GPA
Jones C +	93	82	75	534	292	160	24	1	22	252	61	90	16	1	0	4	4	0	13	.056	.001	.364	.470	.574	.354
Johnson K *	88	86	69	614	399	157	39	6	12	244	113	52	2	2	9	4	11	6	3	.026	-.006	.287	.349	.446	.268
McCann B *	87	68	87	573	373	153	42	1	23	266	64	57	4	4	0	3	5	0	17	-.002	.028	.301	.373	.523	.298
Teixeira M +	72	63	78	451	286	108	27	0	20	195	70	65	9	3	0	2	0	0	13	.038	-.010	.283	.390	.512	.303
Escobar Y	69	71	60	587	395	148	24	2	10	206	62	59	4	5	7	2	2	5	24	.032	-.043	.288	.366	.401	.264
Blanco G *	59	52	38	519	330	108	14	4	1	133	99	74	2	6	6	3	13	5	3	-.014	-.004	.251	.366	.309	.242
Francoeur J	51	70	71	653	475	143	33	3	11	215	111	39	5	10	0	4	0	1	18	.033	-.032	.239	.294	.359	.222
Infante O	45	45	40	348	229	93	24	3	3	132	44	22	2	2	2	5	0	1	4	-.003	.036	.293	.338	.416	.256
Prado M	38	36	33	254	159	73	18	4	2	105	29	21	0	1	2	2	3	1	3	-.029	-.012	.320	.377	.461	.284
Kotsay M *	37	39	37	345	242	92	17	3	6	133	34	25	2	0	1	1	2	3	13	.026	.065	.289	.340	.418	.257
Norton G +	27	27	31	202	136	42	10	0	7	73	40	31	4	0	0	0	0	0	7	-.002	-.064	.246	.361	.427	.269
Anderson J *	19	21	12	146	98	40	7	1	3	58	33	8	2	1	1	0	10	1	1	-.044	.145	.294	.338	.426	.258
Kotchman C *	17	18	20	175	120	36	4	1	2	48	16	18	2	4	0	1	0	0	4	-.087	.031	.237	.331	.316	.228
Jones B *	16	16	17	128	88	31	10	1	1	46	28	7	2	1	3	1	1	0	3	-.120	-.022	.267	.312	.397	.239
Diaz M	10	9	14	140	108	33	2	0	2	41	32	3	0	1	0	1	4	2	4	.124	.131	.244	.264	.304	.195
Gotay R +	10	10	8	117	83	24	5	0	2	35	32	13	0	0	2	0	1	1	4	.023	-.083	.235	.322	.343	.230
Lillibridge	7	9	8	85	64	16	6	1	1	27	23	3	0	1	1	0	2	0	0	-.015	-.057	.200	.238	.338	.191
Hampton M	3	3	4	29	19	5	2	0	0	7	11	2	0	0	3	0	0	0	0	.120	-.055	.208	.269	.292	.194
Campillo J	2	4	2	51	37	8	1	0	0	9	16	1	0	0	5	0	0	0	0	.033	-.015	.178	.196	.200	.138
Bennett J	2	0	1	12	7	2	1	0	0	3	2	2	0	0	1	0	0	0	0	-.105	-.118	.222	.364	.333	.247
Sammons C	2	2	4	59	48	8	0	0	1	11	12	5	0	0	0	0	0	0	2	.094	.069	.148	.220	.204	.150
Glavine T *	2	2	1	25	17	2	0	0	0	2	5	3	0	0	3	0	0	0	0	.188	-.201	.105	.227	.105	.128
Miller C	1	4	5	67	57	5	0	0	1	8	15	5	0	0	1	1	0	0	2	-.103	.020	.083	.152	.133	.101
Carlyle B *	1	1	0	10	7	2	0	0	0	2	1	1	0	0	0	0	0	0	0	-.063	-.050	.222	.300	.222	.190
Parr J	1	1	0	10	6	2	1	0	0	3	4	2	0	0	0	0	0	0	0	.060	-.350	.250	.400	.375	.273

Italicized stats have been adjusted for home park.

Batted Ball Batting Stats

Player	% of PA		% of Batted Balls			IF/F	HR/OF	Out %		Runs Per Event				Total Runs vs. Avg.				
	K%	BB%	GB%	LD%	FB%			GB	OF	NIP	GB	LD	OF	NIP	GB	LD	FB	Tot
Jones C	11	17	43	24	33	.05	.18	70	84	.16	.06	.45	.27	19	4	18	15	56
McCann B	11	11	37	20	43	.12	.12	74	84	.11	.04	.45	.20	7	-1	12	12	29
Teixeira M	16	15	43	20	37	.08	.16	72	85	.11	.05	.42	.24	10	1	4	9	25
Prado M	11	9	42	23	35	.08	.03	71	78	.08	.06	.45	.15	1	2	8	-0	10
Johnson K	18	9	39	25	36	.08	.07	76	84	.04	.05	.46	.12	-2	1	16	-7	8
Escobar Y	11	11	58	17	25	.04	.09	70	90	.12	.06	.40	.12	8	7	0	-9	7
Norton G	20	15	45	24	31	.08	.19	71	87	.09	.05	.26	.28	4	0	-2	3	5
Infante O	13	7	33	30	37	.11	.02	70	89	.05	.08	.39	.03	-1	2	13	-11	2
Kotsay M	10	7	43	22	35	.05	.04	75	88	.08	.03	.46	.05	0	-2	10	-7	1
Anderson J	23	6	52	22	26	.19	.14	62	78	-.01	.12	.33	.26	-3	4	-1	-1	0
Jones B	22	6	44	24	33	.07	.04	79	77	-.01	.00	.51	.15	-2	-2	3	-1	-2
Blanco G	19	15	50	24	26	.15	.01	75	93	.09	.05	.40	-.02	10	7	2	-20	-2
Gotay R	27	11	42	23	35	.13	.10	69	95	.02	.06	.40	.09	-1	-0	-0	-3	-4
Kotchman C	9	13	55	22	23	.09	.07	81	89	.15	-.00	.26	.10	3	-3	-2	-4	-5
Diaz M	23	3	52	25	24	.04	.09	72	95	-.06	.06	.31	.06	-4	1	-1	-5	-9
Francoeur J	17	8	45	21	34	.12	.07	78	86	.03	.02	.40	.09	-5	-6	3	-14	-22
MLB Average	18	10	44	20	36	.10	.11	74	84	.05	.04	.39	.18	--	--	--	--	--

Pitching Stats

Player	PRC	IP	BFP	G	GS	K	BB	IBB	HBP	H	HR	DP	DER	SB	CS	PO	W	L	Sv	Op	Hld	H-A	R^L	RA	ERA	FIP
Jurrjens J	77	188.3	813	31	31	139	70	9	4	188	11	19	.683	28	3	0	13	10	0	0	0	.050	-.015	4.16	3.68	3.52
Hudson T	67	142.0	573	23	22	85	40	5	2	125	11	17	.731	6	4	0	11	7	0	0	0	-.008	-.057	3.36	3.17	3.79
Campillo J	63	158.7	655	39	25	107	38	2	1	158	18	15	.713	8	2	0	8	7	0	0	4	-.003	.019	4.20	3.91	4.03
Bennett J	40	97.3	419	72	4	68	47	6	7	86	5	16	.719	7	3	0	3	7	3	4	15	-.069	-.043	4.07	3.70	3.95
Reyes J *	30	113.0	512	23	22	78	52	4	3	134	18	15	.668	9	4	1	3	11	0	0	0	.047	-.062	6.13	5.81	5.25
Carlyle B	30	62.7	259	45	0	59	26	6	1	52	5	6	.720	5	1	0	2	0	0	0	0	-.048	-.039	3.73	3.59	3.36
Ohman W *	25	58.7	248	83	0	53	22	4	1	51	3	3	.704	1	2	1	4	1	1	4	23	-.016	-.049	4.14	3.68	3.03
Hampton M *	23	78.0	331	13	13	38	28	6	1	83	10	14	.689	4	4	2	3	4	0	0	0	.016	.041	5.19	4.85	4.78
Julio J	21	12.3	54	12	0	19	8	1	1	9	0	1	.654	3	0	0	3	0	0	1	0	-.164	.006	0.73	0.73	2.07
Acosta M	20	53.0	226	46	0	31	26	5	1	48	7	9	.727	7	0	0	3	5	3	5	4	-.025	-.020	4.25	3.57	4.99
Boyer B	20	72.0	313	76	0	67	25	4	2	73	10	3	.689	8	2	0	2	6	1	5	14	-.012	-.018	6.38	5.88	4.10
Smoltz J	19	28.0	117	6	5	36	8	1	0	25	2	1	.676	1	0	0	3	2	0	1	0	-.074	-.032	2.57	2.57	2.31
Glavine T *	18	63.3	281	13	13	37	37	4	1	67	11	8	.703	1	4	3	2	4	0	0	0	.075	-.033	5.68	5.54	5.90
Morton C	17	74.7	345	16	15	48	41	2	2	80	9	2	.694	7	2	1	4	8	0	0	0	.046	-.059	6.75	6.15	5.13
Nunez V	14	32.7	146	23	0	24	19	5	1	32	0	4	.667	2	2	0	1	2	0	0	0	.043	.051	3.86	3.86	3.11
Tavarez J	12	34.7	162	36	0	35	14	4	2	42	5	2	.623	2	0	0	1	3	0	0	6	-.074	.008	5.19	3.89	4.10
Gonzalez M *	11	33.7	142	36	0	44	14	3	1	26	6	2	.727	1	0	0	0	3	14	16	0	.142	.106	5.61	4.28	3.97
Soriano R	8	14.0	57	14	0	16	9	2	1	7	1	1	.800	1	1	0	0	1	3	4	0	.062	-.160	3.21	2.57	3.56
Parr J	7	22.3	102	5	5	14	9	0	0	29	4	2	.653	0	1	1	1	0	0	0	0	-.079	.085	5.24	4.84	5.49
Resop C	5	18.3	82	16	0	13	10	2	2	16	2	2	.727	1	0	0	0	1	0	0	2	-.039	.112	5.89	5.89	4.84
Moylan P	5	5.7	25	7	0	5	1	0	1	5	1	0	.706	1	0	0	0	1	1	2	4	-.025	-.010	1.59	1.59	4.79
James C *	5	29.7	146	7	7	22	20	2	3	36	10	2	.703	5	0	0	2	5	0	0	0	.026	-.150	9.10	9.10	8.22
Ridgway J *	4	9.7	38	10	0	8	1	0	1	7	3	0	.840	0	0	0	1	0	0	1	0	-.277	-.194	3.72	3.72	6.20
Ring R *	3	22.3	113	42	0	16	10	3	2	32	2	3	.578	3	0	0	2	1	0	0	4	-.015	-.129	10.07	8.46	4.14

Italicized stats have been adjusted for home park.

Batted Ball Pitching Stats

Player	% of PA		% of Batted Balls			IF/F	HR/OF	Out %		Runs Per Event				Total Runs vs. Avg.				
	K%	BB%	GB%	LD%	FB%			GB	OF	NIP	GB	LD	OF	NIP	GB	LD	FB	Tot
Hudson T	15	7	59	19	22	.06	.10	78	81	.04	.02	.32	.19	-3	-4	-8	-7	-21
Bennett J	16	13	64	15	21	.07	.09	77	83	.09	.03	.35	.17	5	-2	-8	-7	-11
Campillo J	16	6	38	23	39	.09	.09	79	89	.01	.02	.42	.12	-8	-4	9	-7	-11
Carlyle E	23	10	44	19	37	.13	.09	80	78	.03	.01	.32	.20	-1	-4	-5	0	-9
Jurrjens J	17	9	52	22	27	.11	.08	73	83	.05	.05	.37	.15	-1	2	2	-12	-9
Ohman W	21	9	36	28	35	.15	.06	77	89	.03	.02	.34	.08	-1	-3	2	-7	-8
Smoltz J	31	7	49	14	38	.15	.09	80	62	-.03	.02	.46	.32	-3	-1	-2	2	-5
Gonzalez M	31	11	31	25	44	.19	.17	88	79	.00	-.05	.46	.26	-2	-4	1	1	-3
Acosta M	14	12	53	19	28	.13	.15	77	88	.10	.02	.36	.23	3	-1	-1	-0	0
Nunez V	16	14	39	31	29	.07	.00	83	71	.10	-.01	.32	.12	2	-3	2	-2	0
Boyer B	21	9	46	16	38	.06	.12	68	86	.02	.10	.44	.17	-3	6	-2	1	1
Tavarez J	22	10	49	28	23	.08	.09	74	81	.03	.06	.56	.16	-0	1	8	-2	7
Hampton M	11	9	53	22	26	.09	.15	76	76	.09	.03	.37	.29	1	-1	3	5	8
Morton C	14	12	50	18	31	.08	.13	80	77	.10	.02	.43	.27	5	-2	1	6	10
Glavine T	13	14	47	21	31	.07	.18	78	87	.12	.03	.46	.25	5	-2	4	4	11
James C	15	16	31	17	52	.16	.19	60	76	.12	.15	.35	.35	4	2	-2	9	13
Reyes J	15	11	49	19	32	.06	.15	71	84	.08	.06	.45	.24	4	3	6	7	19
MLB Average	18	10	44	20	36	.10	.11	74	84	.05	.04	.39	.18	--	--	--	--	--

Fielding Stats

Name	Inn	SBA/G	CS%	ERA	WP+PB/G	PO	A	TE	FE	Grade
Catcher										
McCann B	1143.3	0.90	18%	4.25	0.315	879	70	8	1	D
Miller C	164.3	0.82	40%	3.83	0.329	129	18	3	0	--
Sammons C	133.0	0.74	0%	7.11	0.677	106	3	0	0	--

Name	Inn	PO	A	TE	FE	FPct	DPS	DPT	ZR	OOZ	Grade
First Base											
Teixeira M	898.7	963	65	0	2	.998	8	0	.834	35	A+
Kotchman C	353.3	367	23	0	0	1.000	4	0	.731	9	A+
Prado M	124.3	123	11	1	0	.993	0	0	.706	3	--
Norton G	64.3	73	2	1	1	.974	2	0	.444	2	--
Second Base											
Johnson K	1198.0	262	425	1	13	.980	40	53	.826	28	D
Prado M	142.0	33	55	1	2	.967	5	3	.738	5	--
Infante O	74.0	14	19	0	0	1.000	4	2	.824	2	--
Gotay R	26.0	3	10	0	0	1.000	1	1	1.000	3	--
Shortstop											
Escobar Y	1105.0	193	396	10	6	.974	41	32	.843	61	A
Lillibridge B	182.0	39	61	4	2	.943	9	5	.750	10	--
Infante O	138.0	27	45	1	4	.935	4	8	.775	6	--
Prado M	15.0	2	2	1	0	.800	1	0	.500	1	--
Third Base											
Jones C	987.3	64	235	6	6	.958	18	4	.695	59	A+
Infante O	228.7	13	55	3	1	.944	6	0	.700	12	--
Prado M	158.7	9	46	0	1	.982	3	0	.787	7	--
Gotay R	64.0	2	13	0	2	.882	0	0	.615	4	--
Lillibridge B	2.0	0	1	0	0	1.000	0	0	--	--	--

Name	Inn	PO	A	TE	FE	FPct	DPS	DPT	ZR	OOZ	Grade
Left Field											
Blanco G	512.7	86	3	0	2	.978	0	0	.900	23	--
Diaz M	288.7	59	2	0	1	.984	2	0	.879	8	--
Infante O	225.0	44	0	0	1	.978	0	0	.914	12	--
Jones B	219.7	45	2	0	0	1.000	0	0	.914	13	--
Norton G	137.7	29	0	0	0	1.000	0	0	.862	4	--
Anderson J	33.7	9	0	0	0	1.000	0	0	.875	2	--
Prado M	23.0	7	0	0	0	1.000	0	0	1.000	4	--
Resop C	0.3	0	0	0	0	.000	0	0	--	--	--
Center Field											
Kotsay M	696.0	173	3	0	0	1.000	2	0	.887	39	--
Blanco G	494.3	128	4	0	0	1.000	0	0	.918	27	--
Anderson J	236.0	55	1	1	1	.966	0	0	1.000	18	--
Infante O	14.3	4	0	0	0	1.000	0	0	1.000	1	--
Right Field											
Francoeur J		282	14	3	1	.987	4	0	.909	64	B
Perry J	41.0	13	0	0	0	1.000	0	0	.917	2	--
Jones B	34.7	8	0	0	0	1.000	0	0	.875	1	--
Blanco G	34.0	8	0	0	0	1.000	0	0	1.000	0	--
Norton G	2.0	0	0	0	0	.000	0	0	--	--	--
Anderson J	0.3	0	0	0	0	.000	0	0	--	--	--

Baltimore Orioles

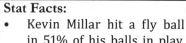

Stat Facts:

- Kevin Millar hit a fly ball in 51% of his balls in play, highest among ML regulars
- Only 33% of the balls hit by Nick Markakis were fly balls
- Daniel Cabrera's K:BB ratio was worst in the majors among 162+ IP pitchers
- He hit 18 batters with a pitch, most in the majors
- Brian Roberts turned 63 double plays
- Brian Burres's .093 H-A was highest in the majors among 50+ IP pitchers
- Dennis Sarfate walked 19% of the batters he faced
- Jim Johnson allowed zero home runs in 69 innings
- Adam Jones was almost five times more likely to strike out than to walk
- 69% of the batted balls off Chad Bradford were grounders
- Jeremy Guthrie's FIP (4.60) was nearly a run higher than his ERA (3.63)
- Melvin Mora stole 3 bases in 10 attempts

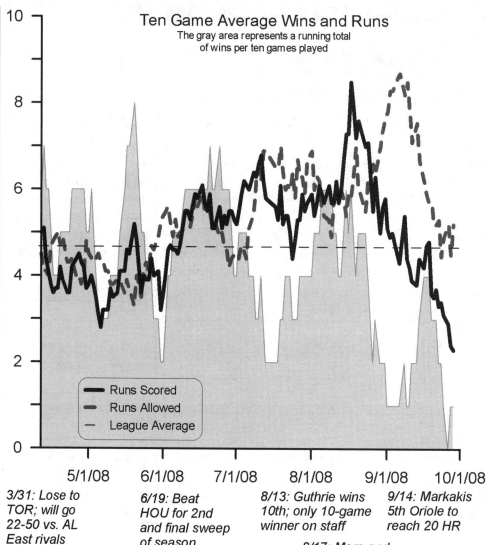

Ten Game Average Wins and Runs
The gray area represents a running total of wins per ten games played

- Runs Scored
- Runs Allowed
- League Average

3/31: Lose to TOR; will go 22-50 vs. AL East rivals

6/19: Beat HOU for 2nd and final sweep of season

8/13: Guthrie wins 10th; only 10-game winner on staff

8/17: Mora and Scott both reach 20 HR in 16-8 win over DET

9/14: Markakis 5th Oriole to reach 20 HR

Team Batting and Pitching/Fielding Stats by Month

	April	May	June	July	Aug	Sept/Oct
Wins	15	11	15	10	12	5
Losses	12	16	12	16	17	20
RS/G	4.25	3.85	5.41	5.81	6.36	3.36
RA/G	4.46	4.22	4.96	6.46	6.32	6.04
OBP	.326	.306	.345	.341	.370	.304
SLG	.403	.380	.472	.474	.471	.359
FIP	5.21	4.37	5.41	5.20	5.42	5.05
DER	.731	.700	.708	.666	.664	.679

Batting Stats

Player	BR	Runs	RBI	PA	Outs	H	2B	3B	HR	TB	K	BB	IBB	HBP	SH	SF	SB	CS	GDP	H-A	L^R	BA	OBP	SLG	GPA
Markakis N *	114	106	87	697	430	182	48	1	20	292	113	99	7	2	0	1	10	7	10	-.046	.027	.306	.406	.491	.302
Huff A *	113	96	108	661	425	182	48	2	32	330	89	53	7	3	0	7	4	0	9	.012	.073	.304	.360	.552	.297
Roberts B +	102	107	57	704	448	181	51	8	9	275	104	82	3	2	3	6	40	10	8	.013	.011	.296	.378	.450	.280
Mora M	90	77	104	570	388	146	29	2	23	248	70	37	3	11	3	6	3	7	14	.044	.064	.285	.342	.483	.272
Scott L *	70	67	65	536	362	122	29	2	23	224	102	53	10	5	0	3	2	2	7	.039	.043	.257	.336	.472	.266
Millar K	69	73	72	610	416	124	25	0	20	209	93	71	3	2	0	6	0	1	8	.031	.012	.234	.323	.394	.241
Hernandez R	60	49	65	507	353	119	22	1	15	188	62	32	3	5	1	6	0	0	9	.028	-.007	.257	.308	.406	.238
Jones A	57	61	57	514	363	129	21	7	9	191	108	23	0	7	2	5	10	3	12	.006	-.014	.270	.311	.400	.237
Payton J	37	41	41	364	264	82	10	2	7	117	53	22	1	1	2	0	8	1	7	-.021	.042	.243	.291	.346	.215
Montanez L	17	18	14	117	79	33	6	1	3	50	20	4	0	0	0	1	0	0	0	.053	-.058	.295	.316	.446	.251
Salazar O	14	13	15	94	60	23	3	0	5	41	13	12	0	0	0	1	0	1	1	-.038	-.148	.284	.372	.506	.291
Cintron A +	14	12	10	144	102	38	5	1	1	48	15	7	0	0	4	0	0	2	5	.051	-.025	.286	.321	.361	.233
Quiroz G	11	12	14	149	112	25	5	0	2	36	34	12	0	1	1	0	0	0	3	.034	.068	.187	.259	.269	.182
Fahey B *	10	8	12	113	85	24	9	2	0	37	25	3	0	1	2	1	0	0	3	.051	.011	.226	.252	.349	.199
Castro J	8	15	16	166	129	31	6	0	2	43	26	10	0	1	2	2	0	0	9	-.011	.029	.205	.256	.285	.185
Hernandez L	6	9	3	91	62	19	1	0	0	20	11	7	0	0	3	2	2	0	2	.054	-.035	.241	.295	.253	.194
Bynum F *	4	13	8	121	97	20	3	1	0	25	31	5	0	1	3	0	2	3	2	-.062	.085	.179	.220	.223	.153
Moore S *	1	1	1	9	7	1	0	0	1	4	3	1	0	0	0	0	0	0	0	-.295	--	.125	.222	.500	.223

Italicized stats have been adjusted for home park.

Batted Ball Batting Stats

Player	% of PA		% of Batted Balls			IF/F	HR/OF	Out %		Runs Per Event				Total Runs vs. Avg.				
	K%	BB%	GB%	LD%	FB%			GB	OF	NIP	GB	LD	OF	NIP	GB	LD	FB	Tot
Markakis N	16	14	46	21	33	.06	.12	71	81	.10	.07	.46	.22	14	7	12	8	42
Huff A	13	8	41	17	42	.12	.15	72	80	.06	.06	.46	.27	1	4	6	24	35
Roberts B	15	12	40	24	36	.07	.05	67	86	.09	.10	.42	.10	9	11	15	-8	25
Scott L	19	11	39	17	44	.13	.15	75	87	.05	.04	.52	.22	1	-1	4	10	14
Mora M	12	8	42	21	37	.15	.16	79	85	.08	.01	.35	.25	1	-3	2	13	13
Montanez L	17	3	47	14	39	.06	.09	55	90	-.04	.17	.47	.11	-2	6	-0	-1	2
Cintron A	10	5	49	22	29	.09	.03	72	90	.03	.05	.38	.02	-1	0	2	-5	-5
Millar K	15	12	30	19	51	.12	.10	79	89	.09	.02	.34	.13	6	-6	-6	0	-6
Hernandez R	12	7	47	20	33	.09	.11	77	87	.06	.03	.36	.15	-1	-3	-0	-2	-7
Jones A	21	6	47	18	35	.15	.07	66	83	-.01	.09	.43	.14	-9	9	-1	-6	-7
Fahey B	22	4	45	20	35	.04	.00	83	81	-.05	-.01	.49	.08	-3	-3	1	-3	-8
Quiroz G	23	9	50	15	35	.23	.07	82	88	.01	-.00	.37	.10	-2	-3	-4	-4	-12
Castro J	16	7	50	14	36	.20	.06	75	88	.02	.03	.26	.07	-2	-1	-6	-5	-14
Bynum F	26	5	42	17	41	.06	.00	82	83	-.04	.00	.20	.03	-3	-1	-5	-5	-14
Payton J	15	6	45	19	36	.17	.07	72	90	.03	.05	.32	.08	-3	2	-4	-9	-15
MLB Average	18	10	44	20	36	.10	.11	74	84	.05	.04	.39	.18	--	--	--	--	--

Pitching Stats

Player	PRC	IP	BFP	G	GS	K	BB	IBB	HBP	H	HR	DP	DER	SB	CS	PO	W	L	Sv	Op	Hld	H-A	R^L	RA	ERA	FIP
Guthrie J	86	190.7	796	30	30	120	58	2	7	176	24	18	.731	13	4	0	10	12	0	0	0	.032	-.008	3.87	3.63	4.60
Cabrera D	56	180.0	821	30	30	95	90	5	18	199	24	27	.694	27	4	0	8	10	0	0	0	.057	-.051	5.45	5.25	5.62
Johnson J	45	68.7	281	54	0	38	28	3	3	54	0	14	.726	3	2	0	2	4	1	1	19	-.046	-.024	2.36	2.23	3.35
Burres B *	34	129.7	596	31	22	63	50	2	6	165	17	11	.676	11	2	1	7	10	0	1	0	.093	.001	6.25	6.04	5.21
Olson G *	33	132.7	621	26	26	83	62	1	8	168	17	14	.654	20	2	1	9	10	0	0	0	-.008	-.019	6.78	6.65	5.20
Sarfate D	30	79.7	359	57	4	86	62	2	7	62	8	13	.714	6	2	1	4	3	0	2	3	-.034	.008	5.31	4.74	4.90
Cormier L	28	71.7	319	45	1	46	34	3	1	78	4	8	.679	6	2	0	3	3	1	3	0	-.037	.024	4.52	4.02	4.01
Sherrill G *	23	53.3	239	57	0	58	33	6	1	47	6	4	.695	3	0	0	3	5	31	37	0	-.029	-.085	4.73	4.73	4.09
Albers M	21	49.0	208	28	3	26	22	1	2	43	4	9	.734	3	1	0	3	3	0	2	6	-.105	.112	3.86	3.49	4.64
Waters C *	21	64.7	291	11	11	33	29	0	3	70	9	6	.710	3	0	0	3	5	0	0	0	.076	.056	5.29	5.01	5.50
Liz R	20	84.3	393	17	17	57	51	3	3	99	16	9	.680	12	2	1	6	6	0	0	0	-.052	-.052	7.15	6.72	6.16
Bradford C	16	40.3	160	47	0	13	7	3	1	41	2	10	.693	0	3	1	3	3	0	1	16	.048	-.040	3.79	2.45	3.60
Castillo A *	13	26.0	121	28	0	23	10	0	7	27	3	1	.679	2	0	0	1	0	0	1	0	-.148	.011	3.81	3.81	4.92
Bierd R	13	36.7	178	29	0	25	19	2	3	48	3	2	.648	0	0	0	0	2	0	0	0	.087	.007	5.15	4.91	4.57
Cabrera F	10	28.3	132	22	0	31	17	2	0	32	9	2	.680	4	2	0	2	1	0	1	0	-.041	-.044	5.72	5.40	6.76
Walker J *	9	38.0	178	59	0	24	11	3	1	53	12	2	.677	2	1	1	1	3	0	4	9	-.136	-.056	7.34	6.87	6.78
Bass B	7	21.0	85	5	4	13	9	1	2	14	1	3	.783	0	0	0	1	0	0	0	0	-.146	.063	5.57	4.71	4.04
Trachsel S	6	39.7	194	10	8	16	27	0	1	53	10	5	.679	6	3	0	2	5	0	0	0	-.080	.121	9.30	8.39	7.82
Loewen A *	4	21.3	102	7	4	14	18	0	0	25	5	1	.692	3	2	1	0	2	0	0	1	-.049	-.077	8.02	8.02	7.50
Miller J	4	7.7	39	8	0	8	5	2	1	9	0	0	.560	2	0	0	0	2	1	2	0	-.095	-.093	3.52	1.17	2.71
Cherry R	4	17.0	85	18	0	15	16	3	1	15	3	2	.680	1	1	0	0	3	1	3	2	-.022	.022	7.94	6.35	6.23
Simon A	3	13.0	59	4	1	8	2	0	2	16	4	1	.721	1	0	0	0	0	0	0	0	--	.188	6.92	6.23	6.92
Mickolio K	3	7.7	36	9	0	8	4	0	0	8	0	0	.625	1	0	0	0	1	0	1	0	-.247	.131	5.87	5.87	2.71
Bukvich R	1	5.3	30	4	0	5	6	0	0	9	2	1	.588	0	0	0	0	0	0	0	0	.036	-.477	6.75	6.75	9.61
Aquino G	1	9.3	54	9	0	9	9	0	2	17	1	0	.515	1	0	0	0	0	0	0	0	.149	.137	12.54	12.54	6.23

Italicized stats have been adjusted for home park.

Batted Ball Pitching Stats

Player	% of PA		% of Batted Balls					Out %		Runs Per Event				Total Runs vs. Avg.				
	K%	BB%	GB%	LD%	FB%	IF/F	HR/OF	GB	OF	NIP	GB	LD	OF	NIP	GB	LD	FB	Tot
Johnson J	14	11	59	14	27	.07	.00	76	87	.09	.02	.33	-.01	3	-2	-6	-12	-18
Guthrie J	15	8	44	18	38	.10	.11	79	85	.05	.01	.35	.17	-2	-8	-7	2	-16
Albers M	13	12	53	12	34	.09	.06	73	89	.11	.04	.38	.06	3	1	-4	-5	-6
Bradford C	8	5	69	16	15	.10	.11	75	88	.06	.02	.33	.15	-1	0	-2	-4	-6
Sherrill G	24	14	34	13	53	.10	.09	60	84	.06	.12	.38	.14	2	2	-6	-0	-2
Sarfate D	24	19	41	17	42	.07	.10	67	93	.09	.08	.33	.11	10	2	-8	-5	-2
Cormier L	14	11	57	21	22	.10	.09	72	79	.09	.05	.29	.18	3	3	-3	-4	-1
Castillo A	19	14	44	16	39	.10	.11	74	76	.08	.05	.35	.21	2	1	-2	1	2
Waters C	11	11	48	17	36	.09	.13	78	84	.11	.03	.42	.21	4	-0	-0	4	6
Bierd R	14	12	43	22	36	.17	.08	62	89	.10	.13	.44	.10	3	4	3	-3	7
Cabrera F	23	13	24	24	52	.09	.23	75	84	.05	.04	.34	.34	1	-1	-0	9	8
Walker J	13	7	36	16	49	.12	.20	60	83	.04	.14	.30	.30	-1	5	-3	11	13
Trachsel S	8	14	42	15	43	.03	.16	74	73	.18	.04	.36	.33	6	0	-1	14	18
Liz R	14	14	34	20	46	.15	.15	71	82	.11	.06	.33	.25	8	1	-1	12	19
Burres B	11	9	36	24	40	.07	.10	73	87	.10	.06	.38	.13	5	3	12	0	20
Cabrera D	12	13	48	20	32	.09	.13	73	85	.13	.05	.35	.20	16	3	-0	5	24
Olson G	13	11	42	19	39	.13	.11	65	86	.10	.11	.39	.17	7	14	2	3	26
MLB Average	18	10	44	20	36	.10	.11	74	84	.05	.04	.39	.18	--	--	--	--	--

Fielding Stats

Name	Inn	SBA/G	CS%	ERA	WP+PB/G	PO	A	TE	FE	Grade
Catcher										
Hernandez R	1039.3	1.04	18%	5.01	0.485	714	45	7	1	F
Quiroz G	354.3	0.94	19%	5.59	0.737	229	17	0	1	--
Santos O	28.3	0.32	0%	4.76	0.635	19	0	0	0	--

Name	Inn	PO	A	TE	FE	FPct	DPS	DPT	ZR	OOZ	Grade
First Base											
Millar K	1131.0	1099	110	1	5	.995	16	0	.704	45	C
Huff A	194.3	177	16	0	0	1.000	2	0	.680	6	--
Salazar O	83.3	79	5	0	0	1.000	1	0	.900	4	--
Hernandez R	10.0	11	0	0	0	1.000	0	0	.600	0	--
Cintron A	3.0	3	1	0	0	1.000	0	0	1.000	0	--
Second Base											
Roberts B	1320.0	289	441	2	6	.989	43	63	.829	42	A
Fahey B	48.0	10	11	0	0	1.000	2	6	.625	0	--
Hernandez L	21.0	3	9	0	0	1.000	3	0	.875	1	--
Cintron A	17.0	4	4	0	0	1.000	0	1	.600	0	--
Torres E	6.0	1	2	0	0	1.000	0	0	1.000	1	--
Moore S	6.0	2	2	0	0	1.000	0	0	.500	1	--
Bynum F	4.0	0	0	0	0	.000	0	0	--	--	--
Shortstop											
Castro J	390.7	72	136	2	3	.977	7	11	.782	16	--
Bynum F	283.3	56	81	2	3	.965	16	11	.873	8	--
Cintron A	257.0	50	92	3	4	.953	11	9	.723	13	--
Fahey B	248.0	43	87	2	3	.963	11	9	.775	6	--
Hernandez L	223.0	52	75	2	1	.977	7	12	.786	5	--
Torres E	18.0	2	5	1	2	.700	1	0	.833	0	--
Mora M	1.0	0	0	0	0	.000	0	0	--	--	--
Salazar O	1.0	0	0	0	0	.000	0	0	--	--	--

Name	Inn	PO	A	TE	FE	FPct	DPS	DPT	ZR	OOZ	Grade
Third Base											
Mora M	1059.0	85	252	9	5	.960	27	1	.666	26	F-
Huff A	275.0	23	64	1	2	.967	3	1	.692	14	--
Salazar O	51.0	3	10	0	0	1.000	3	0	.556	4	--
Cintron A	21.3	1	6	1	0	.875	0	0	.750	0	--
Moore S	9.0	0	2	0	0	1.000	0	0	1.000	0	--
Castro J	6.0	1	0	0	0	1.000	0	0	.000	0	--
Left Field											
Scott L	840.3	200	3	0	2	.990	2	0	.867	37	D
Payton J	407.3	132	2	0	0	1.000	2	0	.934	19	--
Montanez L	174.3	30	1	1	1	.939	0	0	.893	5	--
Center Field											
Jones A	1102.0	336	4	1	2	.991	2	0	.953	72	B
Payton J	301.0	99	6	0	0	1.000	0	0	.894	23	--
Montanez L	19.0	4	0	0	0	1.000	0	0	1.000	2	--
Right Field											
Markakis N	1367.0	327	17	1	2	.991	6	0	.925	56	C
Payton J	32.0	8	0	0	0	1.000	0	0	.857	2	--
Montanez L	23.0	1	0	0	0	1.000	0	0	.000	1	--

Boston Red Sox

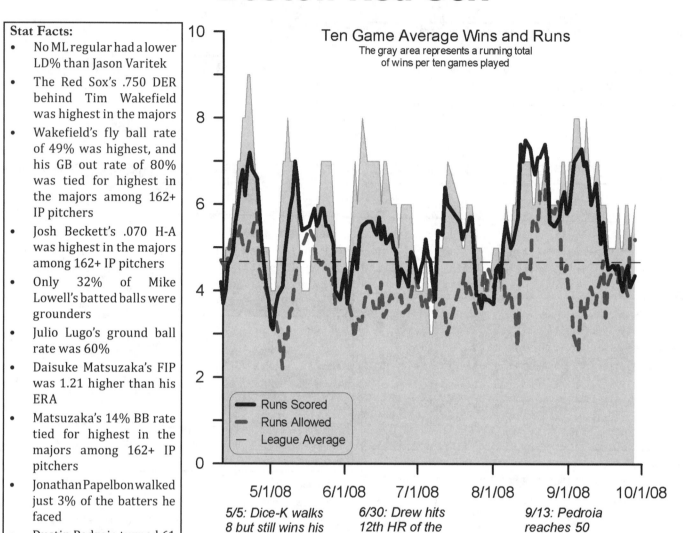

Ten Game Average Wins and Runs

The gray area represents a running total of wins per ten games played

Runs Scored

Runs Allowed

League Average

5/5: Dice-K walks 8 but still wins his 5th game

5/19: Lester hurls no-hitter vs. KC

6/30: Drew hits 12th HR of the month, finishes with 19

7/29: The Manny Era ends in Boston

9/13: Pedroia reaches 50 doubles and 200 hits

9/26: Ellsbury swipes 50th base; only 3rd BOS player ever to reach mark

Team Batting and Pitching/Fielding Stats by Month

	April	May	June	July	Aug	Sept/Oct
Wins	17	17	16	11	18	16
Losses	12	12	11	13	9	10
RS/G	4.7	5.3	5.1	4.6	6.3	5.3
RA/G	4.5	4.2	3.9	4.2	4.4	4.6
OBP	.353	.352	.358	.350	.382	.350
SLG	.422	.459	.473	.406	.472	.446
FIP	4.48	4.06	4.07	3.91	4.25	3.93
DER	.710	.698	.705	.692	.699	.694

Batting Stats

Player	BR	Runs	RBI	PA	Outs	H	2B	3B	HR	TB	K	BB	IBB	HBP	SH	SF	SB	CS	GDP	H-A	L^R	BA	OBP	SLG	GPA
Youkilis K	120	91	115	621	386	168	43	4	29	306	108	62	7	12	0	9	3	5	11	.036	.019	.312	.390	.569	.305
Pedroia D	104	118	83	726	458	213	54	2	17	322	52	50	1	7	7	9	20	1	17	.028	.012	.326	.376	.493	.281
Ortiz D *	84	74	89	491	317	110	30	1	23	211	74	70	12	1	1	3	1	0	11	.063	.061	.264	.369	.507	.282
Drew J *	72	79	64	456	277	103	23	4	19	191	80	79	5	4	0	5	4	1	11	.001	-.004	.280	.408	.519	.301
Ellsbury J *	71	98	47	609	420	155	22	7	9	218	80	41	2	7	4	3	50	11	10	.039	-.003	.280	.336	.394	.240
Ramirez M	68	66	68	425	268	109	22	1	20	193	86	52	8	8	0	0	1	0	12	-.004	-.070	.299	.398	.529	.299
Lowell M	60	58	73	468	320	115	27	0	17	193	61	38	2	5	0	6	2	2	14	-.015	.069	.274	.338	.461	.257
Crisp C +	49	55	41	409	272	102	18	3	7	147	59	35	0	1	8	4	20	7	6	.008	.006	.283	.344	.407	.247
Varitek J +	38	37	43	483	344	93	20	0	13	152	122	52	3	6	0	2	0	1	13	-.008	.079	.220	.313	.359	.222
Lowrie J +	36	34	46	306	201	67	25	3	2	104	68	35	0	1	2	8	1	0	8	.023	.090	.258	.339	.400	.243
Bay J	32	39	37	211	134	54	12	2	9	97	51	22	2	2	0	3	3	0	4	-.002	.122	.293	.370	.527	.287
Casey S *	25	14	17	218	141	64	14	0	0	78	25	17	3	2	0	0	1	0	6	.084	-.009	.322	.381	.392	.259
Lugo J	20	27	22	307	208	70	13	0	1	86	51	34	0	4	3	5	12	4	13	.056	.029	.268	.355	.330	.233
Cora A *	17	14	9	179	115	41	8	2	0	53	13	16	1	9	1	1	1	1	3	.040	.040	.270	.371	.349	.244
Kotsay M *	12	6	12	91	67	19	8	1	0	29	11	7	1	0	0	0	0	1	1	.120	-.016	.226	.286	.345	.207
Cash K	11	11	15	162	116	32	7	0	3	48	50	18	1	0	0	2	0	0	6	-.012	.117	.225	.309	.338	.215
Moss B *	11	7	11	86	56	23	5	1	2	36	25	6	0	0	0	2	1	1	0	-.043	.042	.295	.337	.462	.257
Bailey J	8	10	6	59	38	14	1	1	2	23	17	9	1	0	0	0	0	0	2	.091	.002	.280	.390	.460	.279
Van Every J	3	0	5	18	13	4	0	1	0	6	6	1	0	0	0	0	0	0	0	.050	-.024	.235	.278	.353	.205
Carter C *	2	5	3	20	12	6	0	0	0	6	5	2	0	0	0	0	0	0	0	.278	-.488	.333	.400	.333	.253
Velazquez G	1	0	1	8	7	1	0	0	0	1	0	0	0	0	0	0	0	0	0	--	-.100	.125	.125	.125	.084

Italicized stats have been adjusted for home park.

Batted Ball Batting Stats

Player	% of PA		% of Batted Balls					Out %		Runs Per Event				Total Runs vs. Avg.				
	K%	BB%	GB%	LD%	FB%	IF/F	HR/OF	GB	OF	NIP	GB	LD	OF	NIP	GB	LD	FB	Tot
Youkilis K	17	12	34	22	44	.03	.15	71	80	.07	.06	.39	.28	6	1	6	31	44
Pedroia D	7	8	43	21	36	.10	.09	70	83	.13	.07	.41	.16	5	9	15	3	32
Drew D	18	18	42	18	40	.03	.16	69	89	.12	.07	.43	.23	14	3	1	10	27
Ramirez M	20	14	41	19	40	.11	.20	69	78	.08	.07	.39	.35	6	2	-1	19	26
Ortiz D	15	14	37	19	45	.09	.16	78	87	.11	.01	.41	.24	10	-5	0	15	20
Bay J	24	11	38	14	48	.06	.15	63	71	.03	.10	.43	.34	-0	3	-3	13	13
Lowell M	13	9	32	21	47	.12	.11	74	84	.08	.04	.32	.18	2	-2	-2	9	8
Casey S	11	9	38	28	34	.07	.00	77	75	.09	.02	.37	.08	1	-1	6	-4	2
Cora A	7	14	42	25	33	.18	.00	81	84	.19	.00	.36	.04	5	-2	3	-6	0
Crisp C	14	9	41	20	39	.09	.07	77	77	.06	.03	.31	.18	0	2	-5	2	-0
Ellsbury J	13	8	52	20	28	.19	.09	72	86	.06	.06	.35	.14	-1	10	-0	-11	-2
Lowrie J	22	12	32	25	43	.03	.02	76	88	.05	.02	.47	.05	1	-3	6	-8	-3
Lugo J	17	12	60	18	23	.04	.02	75	84	.08	.03	.37	.07	3	2	-3	-8	-6
Cash K	31	11	50	18	32	.10	.11	77	75	.01	.02	.35	.25	-2	-2	-3	-0	-7
Varitek J	25	12	42	14	45	.14	.10	75	81	.03	.03	.38	.20	-0	-3	-12	2	-14
MLB Average	18	10	44	20	36	.10	.11	74	84	.05	.04	.39	.18	--	--	--	--	--

Pitching Stats

Player	PRC	IP	BFP	G	GS	K	BB	IBB	HBP	H	HR	DP	DER	SB	CS	PO	W	L	Sv	Op	Hld	H-A	R^L	RA	ERA	FIP
Lester J *	114	210.3	874	33	33	152	66	1	10	202	14	33	.695	8	5	3	16	6	0	0	0	-.021	-.056	3.34	3.21	3.72
Matsuzaka D	101	167.7	716	29	29	154	94	1	7	128	12	15	.733	15	5	0	18	3	0	0	0	.049	-.053	3.11	2.90	4.11
Beckett J	84	174.3	725	27	27	172	34	1	9	173	18	14	.679	7	5	1	12	10	0	0	0	.070	-.003	4.13	4.03	3.32
Wakefield T	75	181.0	754	30	30	117	60	0	13	154	25	14	.750	27	10	1	10	11	0	0	0	-.037	.008	4.43	4.13	4.94
Masterson J	51	88.3	365	36	9	68	40	3	8	68	10	17	.749	9	1	0	6	5	0	1	3	.006	-.072	3.16	3.16	4.69
Papelbon J	44	69.3	273	67	0	77	8	0	0	58	4	4	.674	2	0	1	5	4	41	46	0	-.022	-.033	3.12	2.34	2.11
Okajima H *	43	62.0	258	64	0	60	23	1	1	49	6	2	.738	0	1	0	3	2	1	9	23	.072	-.045	2.61	2.61	3.67
Delcarmen M	42	74.3	307	73	0	72	28	1	3	55	5	4	.734	7	0	0	1	2	2	5	18	-.049	.032	3.39	3.27	3.38
Lopez J *	37	59.3	247	70	0	38	27	0	2	53	4	13	.699	1	3	1	2	0	0	1	10	-.031	-.066	2.73	2.43	4.29
Buchholz C	19	76.0	357	16	15	72	41	1	2	93	11	8	.623	3	2	1	2	9	0	0	0	-.062	-.011	7.46	6.75	4.87
Byrd P	18	49.0	208	8	8	26	10	0	2	58	8	5	.691	2	0	2	4	2	0	0	0	.104	-.014	4.78	4.78	5.03
Aardsma D	16	48.7	228	47	0	49	35	2	5	49	4	4	.659	2	0	0	4	2	0	1	4	.138	.015	5.92	5.55	4.63
Timlin M	15	49.3	227	47	0	32	20	4	1	60	9	4	.679	6	0	0	4	4	1	1	0	-.006	-.080	5.84	5.66	5.34
Colon B	14	39.0	173	7	7	27	10	0	2	44	5	3	.682	0	0	0	4	2	0	0	0	-.041	-.119	5.31	3.92	4.44
Hansen C	8	30.7	146	32	0	25	23	1	1	29	2	2	.684	2	0	0	1	3	2	4	7	.030	-.071	6.75	5.58	4.70
Smith C	4	18.3	78	12	0	13	7	0	0	18	6	1	.769	0	0	1	1	0	0	0	0	-.197	.207	7.85	7.85	7.21
Bowden M	2	5.0	22	1	1	3	1	0	0	7	0	1	.611	0	0	0	1	0	0	0	0	--	.212	3.60	3.60	2.63
Tavarez J	2	12.7	64	9	0	6	9	0	1	18	3	0	.625	3	0	0	0	1	0	0	0	.115	-.135	8.53	6.39	4.65
Hansack D	2	6.7	26	4	0	5	1	0	0	6	0	1	.700	0	0	0	1	0	0	0	0	-.248	-.022	6.75	4.05	2.18
Pauley D	1	12.3	67	6	2	11	5	0	1	23	2	0	.542	2	0	0	0	1	0	0	0	-.044	-.087	12.41	11.68	5.01
Corey B	1	6.0	31	7	0	4	3	1	0	11	1	1	.565	0	0	0	0	0	0	0	1	.377	.247	10.50	10.50	5.06

Italicized stats have been adjusted for home park.

Batted Ball Pitching Stats

Player	% of PA		% of Batted Balls					Out %		Runs Per Event				Total Runs vs. Avg.				
	K%	BB%	GB%	LD%	FB%	IF/F	HR/OF	GB	OF	NIP	GB	LD	OF	NIP	GB	LD	FB	Tot
Matsuzaka D	22	14	39	18	43	.14	.07	78	83	.07	.02	.31	.13	8	-5	-15	-9	-21
Lester J	17	9	47	21	32	.14	.08	78	83	.04	.02	.39	.14	-3	-7	2	-12	-20
Papelbon J	28	3	49	20	31	.16	.06	72	80	-.07	.06	.40	.14	-10	1	-2	-5	-17
Beckett J	24	6	41	25	34	.10	.12	72	85	-.02	.06	.33	.18	-15	2	-0	-2	-16
Wakefield T	16	10	36	16	49	.10	.10	80	86	.06	.01	.40	.14	2	-9	-9	2	-15
Delcarmen M	23	10	52	13	35	.10	.08	72	88	.03	.06	.38	.12	-2	1	-8	-6	-15
Okajima H	23	9	32	20	48	.20	.09	80	85	.02	.02	.32	.15	-2	-3	-4	-3	-12
Masterson J	19	13	54	18	27	.01	.15	85	82	.08	-.04	.32	.25	4	-10	-6	2	-10
Lopez J	15	12	60	19	22	.08	.11	77	84	.09	.02	.38	.20	2	-2	-1	-2	-3
Colon B	16	7	40	21	39	.16	.12	67	87	.03	.09	.34	.17	-1	2	-1	-0	0
Hansen C	17	16	57	8	35	.26	.08	65	87	.11	.10	.56	.11	4	4	-3	-3	1
Byrd P	13	6	33	24	43	.15	.13	75	83	.03	.03	.38	.22	-2	-1	4	5	5
Aardsma D	21	18	44	18	38	.14	.09	75	75	.09	.05	.44	.22	6	0	-1	2	7
Timlin M	14	9	44	18	38	.11	.16	76	77	.07	.03	.42	.31	1	-1	1	9	10
Buchholz C	20	12	48	21	31	.11	.16	68	80	.06	.08	.38	.28	2	6	1	6	16
MLB Average	18	10	44	20	36	.10	.11	74	84	.05	.04	.39	.18	--	--	--	--	--

Fielding Stats

Name	Inn	SBA/G	CS%	ERA	WP+PB/G	PO	A	TE	FE	Grade
Catcher										
Varitek J	1041.3	0.60	19%	3.66	0.233	903	42	4	0	C
Cash K	372.0	1.26	27%	4.81	0.823	280	26	4	0	--
Ross D	25.0	0.72	0%	5.40	0.000	23	0	0	0	--
Kottaras G	8.0	0.00	0%	7.88	0.000	5	0	0	0	--

Name	Inn	PO	A	TE	FE	FPct	DPS	DPT	ZR	OOZ	Grade
First Base											
Youkilis K	984.7	923	87	0	4	.996	14	0	.712	28	C
Casey S	342.7	331	13	1	2	.991	4	0	.755	5	--
Bailey J	67.0	77	3	0	0	1.000	0	0	.778	0	--
Kotsay M	39.0	35	3	1	0	.974	2	0	.800	1	--
Moss B	13.0	10	0	0	0	1.000	0	0	1.000	0	--
Second Base											
Pedroia D	1376.0	279	448	0	6	.992	37	61	.826	37	B
Cora A	35.0	6	14	0	0	1.000	1	2	.923	0	--
Velazquez G	19.0	5	9	0	0	1.000	0	2	.700	0	--
Lowrie J	16.0	2	4	0	0	1.000	0	0	.800	0	--
Shortstop											
Lugo J	671.3	100	176	9	7	.945	23	9	.786	23	--
Cora A	386.0	74	136	2	4	.972	16	22	.795	16	--
Lowrie J	386.0	46	109	0	0	1.000	13	8	.862	14	--
Velazquez G	3.0	0	1	0	0	1.000	0	0	1.000	0	--
Third Base											
Lowell M	935.7	80	217	4	6	.967	17	0	.759	28	B
Youkilis K	252.0	23	70	0	3	.969	4	1	.729	15	--
Lowrie J	243.7	16	59	0	2	.974	8	0	.746	9	--
Cash K	15.0	1	1	0	0	1.000	0	0	1.000	0	--

Name	Inn	PO	A	TE	FE	FPct	DPS	DPT	ZR	OOZ	Grade
Left Field											
Ramirez M	537.7	99	6	0	1	.991	4	0	.817	14	--
Bay J	423.3	76	5	0	1	.988	0	0	.821	12	F
Ellsbury J	346.3	89	1	0	0	1.000	2	0	.932	21	--
Moss B	78.0	17	0	0	0	1.000	0	0	1.000	0	--
Bailey J	23.0	3	0	0	0	1.000	0	0	.500	1	--
Thurston J	19.0	5	0	0	0	1.000	0	0	1.000	1	--
Carter C	17.0	3	0	0	0	1.000	0	0	1.000	0	--
Lugo J	1.0	0	0	0	0	0.000	0	0	--	--	--
Van Every J	1.0	0	0	0	0	0.000	0	0	--	--	--
Center Field											
Crisp C	886.0	234	4	0	2	.992	2	0	.927	43	F-
Ellsbury J	546.7	171	3	0	0	1.000	2	0	.939	32	--
Van Every J	8.0	1	0	0	0	1.000	0	0	1.000	0	--
Drew J	5.7	0	0	0	0	0.000	0	0	--	--	--
Right Field											
Drew J	886.0	184	6	2	2	.979	2	0	.935	39	A+
Ellsbury J	281.0	72	0	0	0	1.000	0	0	.951	14	--
Kotsay M	151.7	32	0	0	0	1.000	0	0	.931	5	--
Moss B	86.0	19	2	0	0	1.000	0	0	.929	6	--
Van Every J	32.0	15	0	0	0	1.000	0	0	.900	6	--
Youkilis K	8.7	3	0	0	0	1.000	0	0	1.000	0	--
Bailey J	1.0	0	0	0	0	0.000	0	0	--	--	--

Chicago Cubs

Stat Facts:

- Derrek Lee had the most PAs in the majors (698) without a HBP
- Ryan Dempster led the majors with 19 sacrifice hits
- Ted Lilly induced just 9 double plays in 205 innings
- Lilly's .085 R^L was highest in the majors among 162+ IP pitchers
- Both Lilly and Dempster had a H-A of exactly .000
- More than one-quarter of Alfonso Soriano's walks were intentional
- Soriano started 10 double plays in left field
- The Cubs' DER behind Carlos Marmol was .814
- Marmol's LD rate of 10% was among the lowest in the majors
- Marmol struck out one-third of the batters he faced
- Kosuke Fukudome made 68 OOZ plays
- Ryan Theriot hit a grounder on 57% of his balls in play

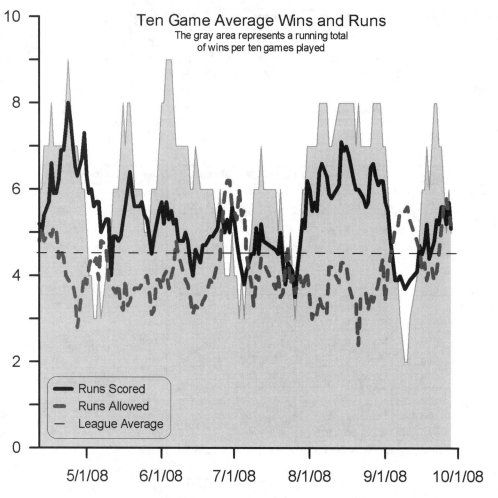

Ten Game Average Wins and Runs

The gray area represents a running total of wins per ten games played

- Runs Scored
- Runs Allowed
- League Average

5/15: Dempster: 12K, 1 BB, 0 R

6/12: Second trip to DL for Soriano

7/8: Harden obtained from OAK

8/1: Ramirez: .965 OPS rest of season

9/14: Zambrano tosses no-hitter

Team Batting and Pitching/Fielding Stats by Month

	April	May	June	July	Aug	Sept/Oct
Wins	17	18	15	15	20	12
Losses	10	11	12	11	8	12
RS/G	6.3	5.1	4.9	4.9	5.8	4.7
RA/G	4.4	3.8	4.5	3.8	3.7	4.9
OBP	.375	.359	.352	.336	.369	.329
SLG	.452	.449	.433	.445	.462	.413
FIP	4.22	4.09	4.31	4.20	3.77	3.79
DER	.719	.704	.685	.727	.713	.690

Batting Stats

Player	BR	Runs	RBI	PA	Outs	H	2B	3B	HR	TB	K	BB	IBB	HBP	SH	SF	SB	CS	GDP	H-A	L^R	BA	OBP	SLG	GPA
Ramirez A	104	97	111	645	409	160	44	1	27	287	94	74	7	11	0	6	2	2	13	.097	-.070	.289	.380	.518	.289
DeRosa M	91	103	87	593	370	144	30	3	21	243	106	69	0	9	2	8	6	0	9	.042	.019	.285	.376	.481	.278
Lee D	90	93	90	698	471	181	41	3	20	288	119	71	3	0	0	4	8	2	27	.003	.054	.291	.361	.462	.267
Soto G	78	66	86	563	365	141	35	2	23	249	121	62	6	2	0	5	0	1	11	.010	.022	.285	.364	.504	.279
Soriano A	76	76	75	503	338	127	27	0	29	241	103	43	11	3	0	4	19	3	9	.029	.101	.280	.344	.532	.277
Fukudome K *	72	79	58	590	383	129	25	3	10	190	104	81	9	1	2	5	12	4	7	.057	.001	.257	.359	.379	.246
Theriot R	69	85	38	661	434	178	19	4	1	208	58	73	1	3	4	1	22	13	19	-.013	.017	.307	.387	.359	.253
Johnson R	52	52	50	374	241	101	21	0	6	140	68	19	1	12	5	5	5	6	3	-.023	.047	.303	.358	.420	.256
Fontenot M *	46	42	40	284	170	74	22	1	9	125	51	34	2	3	3	1	2	0	1	-.046	-.000	.305	.395	.514	.295
Edmonds J *	44	47	49	298	194	64	17	2	19	142	58	45	2	1	0	2	0	1	7	.010	.156	.256	.369	.568	.296
Cedeno R	21	36	28	236	165	58	12	0	2	76	41	18	2	1	1	0	4	1	6	.087	-.033	.269	.328	.352	.226
Zambrano C +	14	9	14	85	59	28	4	1	4	46	24	0	0	0	2	0	0	0	4	.016	.090	.337	.337	.554	.279
Hoffpauir M	13	14	8	80	48	25	8	0	2	39	24	6	0	1	0	0	1	0	0	.019	.063	.342	.400	.534	.302
Ward D *	10	8	17	119	84	22	7	0	4	41	24	16	3	0	0	1	0	0	4	.052	.079	.216	.319	.402	.235
Blanco H	10	15	12	128	89	35	3	0	3	47	22	6	1	0	2	0	0	0	4	.056	.035	.292	.325	.392	.235
Pie F *	8	9	10	93	66	20	2	1	1	27	29	7	0	2	0	1	3	0	3	-.004	.081	.241	.312	.325	.213
Patterson E	5	5	7	44	31	9	1	0	1	13	12	5	0	0	0	1	2	1	1	.123	-.127	.237	.318	.342	.220
Marquis J *	3	8	10	66	47	12	3	0	2	21	17	3	0	0	4	0	0	0	0	.071	-.089	.203	.242	.356	.190
Lilly T *	2	2	5	75	51	11	2	0	0	13	29	1	0	0	12	0	1	0	0	-.019	.158	.177	.190	.210	.133
Murton M	2	2	6	42	32	10	2	0	0	12	5	1	0	1	0	0	0	0	2	-.016	-.097	.250	.286	.300	.196
Marshall S *	1	0	1	15	11	5	0	0	0	5	7	0	0	0	0	0	0	0	1	.194	.080	.333	.333	.333	.224
Dempster R	1	4	2	82	52	10	2	0	0	12	19	2	0	0	19	0	0	0	1	.060	.059	.164	.190	.197	.130

Italicized stats have been adjusted for home park.

Batted Ball Batting Stats

Player	% of PA		% of Batted Balls					Out %		Runs Per Event				Total Runs vs. Avg.				
	K%	BB%	GB%	LD%	FB%	IF/F	HR/OF	GB	OF	NIP	GB	LD	OF	NIP	GB	LD	FB	Tot
Ramirez A	15	13	31	20	48	.10	.12	72	88	.11	.06	.45	.17	11	1	9	10	31
DeRosa M	18	13	40	22	38	.07	.13	77	83	.08	.03	.46	.22	8	-3	11	10	25
Soto G	21	11	38	21	41	.06	.16	74	83	.05	.05	.44	.26	1	-1	5	17	22
Soriano A	20	9	29	23	48	.05	.16	81	84	.03	-.00	.45	.24	-2	-7	9	18	18
Fontenot M	18	13	38	24	38	.07	.12	75	80	.08	.05	.52	.23	4	-1	10	5	18
Edmonds J	19	15	40	17	44	.04	.21	84	86	.09	-.02	.53	.32	6	-6	1	15	16
Lee D	17	10	45	21	34	.03	.11	75	84	.06	.03	.43	.19	2	-3	10	6	15
Johnson R	18	8	41	24	35	.08	.07	67	81	.03	.10	.34	.15	-2	6	1	-2	4
Theriot R	9	11	57	23	20	.04	.01	74	83	.15	.05	.34	.03	11	6	7	-20	4
Fukudome K	18	14	51	19	30	.04	.08	71	89	.09	.07	.35	.11	9	8	-5	-10	2
Ward D	20	13	37	19	44	.11	.13	83	81	.07	-.03	.37	.22	1	-3	-1	2	-0
Cedeno R	17	8	52	18	30	.12	.04	70	72	.03	.08	.37	.15	-1	3	-2	-3	-3
Blanco H	17	5	42	17	42	.08	.08	60	88	-.01	.11	.36	.11	-2	2	-2	-1	-3
Dempster R	23	2	51	15	34	.21	.00	86	64	-.07	-.01	.19	.17	-3	-4	-5	-2	-14
MLB Average	18	10	44	20	36	.10	.11	74	84	.05	.04	.39	.18	--	--	--	--	--

Pitching Stats

Player	PRC	IP	BFP	G	GS	K	BB	IBB	HBP	H	HR	DP	DER	SB	CS	PO	W	L	Sv	Op	Hld	H-A	R^L	RA	ERA	FIP
Dempster R	113	206.7	856	33	33	187	76	1	7	174	14	20	.712	11	4	0	17	6	0	0	0	-.000	-.028	3.27	2.96	3.46
Lilly T *	89	204.7	861	34	34	184	64	2	7	187	32	9	.718	12	8	6	17	9	0	0	0	.000	.085	4.22	4.09	4.45
Zambrano C	81	188.7	796	30	30	130	72	1	6	172	18	24	.712	10	9	3	14	6	0	0	0	.015	-.002	4.05	3.91	4.29
Marquis J	59	167.0	738	29	28	91	70	6	8	172	15	21	.706	11	1	0	11	9	0	0	1	.037	.018	4.69	4.53	4.57
Harden R	57	71.0	284	12	12	89	30	1	2	39	6	1	.783	3	2	0	5	1	0	0	0	.016	-.025	2.15	1.77	3.10
Marmol C	54	87.3	348	82	0	114	41	3	6	40	10	5	.814	3	1	0	2	4	7	9	30	-.062	-.096	3.09	2.68	3.59
Wood K	39	66.3	276	65	0	84	18	4	7	54	3	2	.683	1	0	0	5	4	34	40	0	-.048	.009	3.26	3.26	2.21
Marshall S *	31	65.3	279	34	7	58	23	4	4	60	9	4	.719	5	2	0	3	5	1	2	3	-.029	.037	3.86	3.86	4.27
Howry B	23	70.7	311	72	0	59	13	5	2	90	13	6	.652	5	0	0	7	5	1	5	15	.014	-.018	5.60	5.35	4.35
Gallagher S	22	58.7	256	12	10	49	22	1	4	58	6	4	.680	4	4	0	3	4	0	0	0	-.050	.014	4.76	4.45	4.14
Lieber J	17	46.7	204	26	1	27	6	4	2	59	10	6	.673	0	0	0	2	3	0	1	3	-.008	-.122	4.63	4.05	5.09
Wuertz M	17	44.7	189	45	0	30	20	2	0	44	4	7	.681	4	3	0	1	1	0	3	3	-.015	-.001	4.63	3.63	4.23
Cotts N *	16	35.7	160	50	0	43	13	2	1	38	7	2	.646	3	0	0	0	2	0	2	9	.082	.038	4.54	4.29	4.35
Samardzija J	13	27.7	124	26	0	25	15	2	1	24	0	0	.687	5	1	1	1	0	1	4	3	-.074	.067	3.90	2.28	2.91
Hill R *	8	19.7	89	5	5	15	18	0	1	13	2	1	.792	2	1	1	1	0	0	0	0	-.061	.024	4.12	4.12	5.90
Gaudin C	7	27.3	119	24	0	27	10	2	0	29	5	1	.688	0	0	1	4	2	0	1	2	.102	.005	6.91	6.26	4.48
Hart K	6	27.7	142	21	0	23	18	3	3	39	2	4	.594	4	0	0	2	2	0	0	1	-.022	-.112	7.81	6.51	4.43
Guzman A	3	9.7	44	6	1	10	4	0	1	10	1	0	.679	0	0	0	0	0	0	0	0	.250	-.000	5.59	5.59	4.03
Eyre S *	3	11.3	53	19	0	14	4	1	1	15	1	1	.576	3	0	0	2	0	0	1	4	-.107	-.103	7.15	7.15	2.94
Ascanio J	1	5.7	30	6	0	3	4	1	1	8	1	0	.667	0	0	0	0	0	0	0	0	-.279	-.023	7.94	7.94	6.55
Fox C	1	3.3	14	3	0	1	3	0	0	2	1	0	.889	1	0	1	0	1	0	0	0	-.165	-.165	5.40	5.40	9.20

Italicized stats have been adjusted for home park.

Batted Ball Pitching Stats

Player	% of PA		% of Batted Balls					Out %		Runs Per Event				Total Runs vs. Avg.				
	K%	BB%	GB%	LD%	FB%	IF/F	HR/OF	GB	OF	NIP	GB	LD	OF	NIP	GB	LD	FB	Tot
Dempster R	22	10	48	20	32	.07	.08	76	89	.03	.03	.37	.11	-4	-4	-6	-16	-31
Marmol C	33	14	35	10	55	.15	.12	73	95	.02	.06	.33	.11	-2	-2	-16	-7	-26
Harden R	31	11	29	23	48	.14	.08	81	93	.01	.02	.35	.06	-3	-4	-5	-9	-21
Zambrano C	16	10	47	18	35	.12	.10	77	80	.06	.02	.35	.19	1	-5	-9	0	-13
Wood K	30	9	39	20	41	.06	.05	76	84	-.01	.05	.52	.09	-5	-1	0	-6	-12
Lilly T	21	8	34	22	44	.13	.13	76	88	.01	.03	.40	.19	-8	-6	2	6	-6
Samardzija J	20	13	46	22	32	.12	.00	70	87	.07	.08	.34	-.01	1	1	-1	-5	-4
Marshall S	21	10	41	17	42	.19	.14	79	76	.03	.02	.36	.28	-1	-2	-5	5	-2
Marquis J	12	11	48	20	33	.09	.09	74	89	.10	.04	.38	.13	7	-1	1	-8	-1
Wuertz M	16	11	46	25	29	.08	.08	84	82	.07	-.02	.47	.13	1	-3	6	-3	1
Gallagher S	19	10	44	18	39	.07	.09	71	83	.05	.08	.38	.16	0	2	-2	1	1
Gaudin C	23	8	34	24	43	.03	.12	78	83	.01	.02	.46	.21	-1	-1	2	2	2
Cotts N	27	9	37	21	42	.12	.17	58	87	-.00	.13	.41	.23	-2	3	-0	2	2
Lieber J	13	4	40	21	39	.18	.15	68	87	-.01	.08	.46	.24	-3	2	5	4	8
Hart K	16	15	57	20	23	.05	.10	69	63	.11	.10	.33	.36	3	5	-0	3	10
Howry B	19	5	35	18	47	.13	.12	66	79	-.02	.10	.43	.25	-6	4	1	12	11
MLB Average	18	10	44	20	36	.10	.11	74	84	.05	.04	.39	.18	--	--	--	--	--

Fielding Stats

Name	Inn	SBA/G	CS%	ERA	WP+PB/G	PO	A	TE	FE	Grade
Catcher										
Soto G	1150.3	0.68	21%	3.80	0.352	1011	55	3	1	C
Blanco H	257.7	0.73	43%	3.91	0.349	235	15	0	1	--
Hill K	42.7	1.48	14%	5.48	0.211	40	1	0	1	--

Name	Inn	PO	A	TE	FE	FPct	DPS	DPT	ZR	OOZ	Grade
First Base											
Lee D	1339.0	1193	110	1	8	.993	15	1	.735	43	C
Ward D	60.0	54	4	0	0	1.000	0	0	.727	2	--
Hoffpauir M	47.7	37	1	0	1	.974	0	0	.600	0	--
DeRosa M	2.0	2	0	0	0	1.000	0	0	1.000	0	--
Blanco H	1.7	3	0	0	0	1.000	0	0	--	--	--
Second Base											
DeRosa M	670.0	143	185	1	7	.976	11	19	.806	13	--
Fontenot M	498.7	101	143	0	1	.996	13	16	.868	17	--
Cedeno R	273.0	60	75	1	1	.985	7	11	.838	6	--
Patterson E	8.0	3	0	0	0	1.000	0	0	--	--	--
Soriano A	1.0	0	2	0	0	1.000	0	0	1.000	0	--
Shortstop											
Theriot R	1266.0	207	341	7	7	.975	32	32	.823	36	F
Cedeno R	182.7	41	50	3	0	.968	4	4	.830	5	--
DeRosa M	1.0	0	1	0	0	1.000	0	0	1.000	0	--
Fontenot M	1.0	0	0	0	0	0.000	0	0	--	--	--
Third Base											
Ramirez A	1282.0	83	225	5	13	.945	18	0	.659	51	B
DeRosa M	114.3	6	28	1	1	.944	2	0	.759	6	--
McGehee C	41.7	3	13	0	0	1.000	3	0	.818	4	--
Cedeno R	12.0	1	1	0	0	1.000	0	0	.500	1	--

Name	Inn	PO	A	TE	FE	FPct	DPS	DPT	ZR	OOZ	Grade
Left Field											
Soriano A	937.3	186	10	1	4	.975	10	0	.882	36	F
DeRosa M	185.0	39	0	0	1	.975	0	0	.886	8	--
Johnson R	124.7	35	1	0	0	1.000	0	0	.935	6	--
Patterson E	68.0	13	1	0	3	.824	0	0	1.000	2	--
Murton M	62.0	13	0	0	0	1.000	0	0	.917	2	--
Hoffpauir M	38.0	6	0	0	1	.857	0	0	1.000	2	--
Ward D	25.0	7	0	0	0	1.000	0	0	1.000	1	--
Pie F	8.7	3	0	0	0	1.000	0	0	.500	2	--
Cedeno R	2.0	0	0	0	0	0.000	0	0	--	--	--
Center Field											
Edmonds J	627.7	179	0	2	3	.973	0	0	.931	45	--
Johnson R	563.7	144	2	0	1	.993	2	0	.925	33	--
Pie F	197.3	58	1	0	0	1.000	0	0	.875	16	--
Fukudome K	59.0	10	0	0	0	1.000	0	0	1.000	4	--
Patterson E	2.0	0	0	0	0	0.000	0	0	--	--	--
Cedeno R	1.0	0	0	0	0	0.000	0	0	--	--	--
Right Field											
Fukudome K	1103.0	245	6	4	1	.980	0	0	.932	68	A+
DeRosa M	266.7	72	0	0	0	1.000	0	0	.918	16	--
Hoffpauir M	36.0	6	0	0	0	1.000	0	0	.857	0	--
Johnson R	23.3	4	0	0	0	1.000	0	0	1.000	2	--
Ward D	17.0	4	0	0	0	1.000	0	0	1.000	1	--
Murton M	4.0	1	0	0	0	1.000	0	0	1.000	0	--

Chicago White Sox

Stat Facts:

- Paul Konerko's H-A of .110 tied for the lead among ML regulars
- Joe Crede's L^R of -.168 was lowest in the majors among 75+ PA players
- Orlando Cabrera led the AL in Outs
- 85% of Jim Thome's ground balls were outs, highest among ML regulars
- Mark Buerhle allowed 240 hits, most in the majors
- He induced 39 double plays, also the most in the majors
- Buerhle allowed just 5 stolen bases in 12 attempts, and picked off 6 runners
- Gavin Floyd allowed 37 stolen bases, by far the most in the majors
- In 67 innings, Octavio Dotel allowed 16 stolen bases in 17 attempts
- Javier Vazquez's FIP was 0.86 lower than his ERA
- Nick Swisher made 4 fielding errors in 535 innings in center field
- Carlos Quentin was hit by 20 pitches

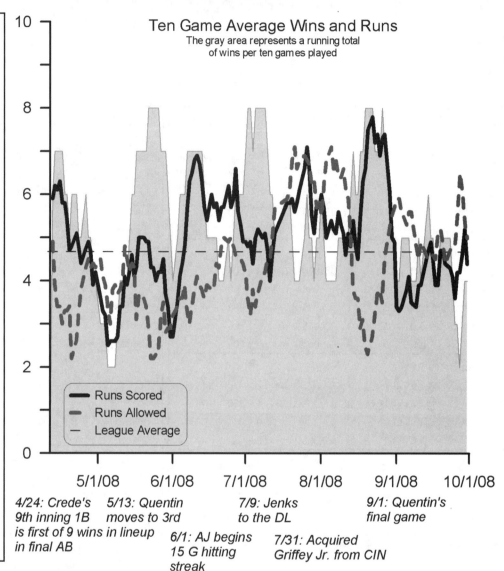

Ten Game Average Wins and Runs
The gray area represents a running total of wins per ten games played

Runs Scored
Runs Allowed
League Average

4/24: Crede's 9th inning 1B is first of 9 wins in final AB

5/13: Quentin moves to 3rd in lineup

6/1: AJ begins 15 G hitting streak

7/9: Jenks to the DL

7/31: Acquired Griffey Jr. from CIN

9/1: Quentin's final game

Team Batting and Pitching/Fielding Stats by Month

	April	May	June	July	Aug	Sept/Oct
Wins	14	16	17	13	17	12
Losses	12	13	10	12	12	15
RS/G	5.0	3.7	6.1	5.4	5.5	4.4
RA/G	4.0	3.3	4.2	5.8	4.8	4.9
OBP	.335	.317	.362	.339	.340	.301
SLG	.415	.390	.522	.458	.493	.407
FIP	3.67	3.43	4.33	4.32	3.87	4.31
DER	.697	.711	.699	.661	.675	.685

Batting Stats

Player	BR	Runs	RBI	PA	Outs	H	2B	3B	HR	TB	K	BB	IBB	HBP	SH	SF	SB	CS	GDP	H-A	L^R	BA	OBP	SLG	GPA
Quentin C	102	96	100	569	361	138	26	1	36	274	80	66	0	20	0	3	7	3	16	.009	-.015	.288	.394	.571	.308
Thome J *	96	93	90	602	398	123	28	0	34	253	147	91	9	4	0	4	1	0	18	-.025	.009	.245	.362	.503	.278
Dye J	89	96	96	645	438	172	41	2	34	319	104	44	3	6	0	5	3	2	18	.071	.014	.292	.344	.541	.279
Cabrera O	75	93	57	730	497	186	33	1	8	245	71	56	1	1	3	9	19	6	16	.001	.022	.281	.334	.371	.234
Ramirez A	75	65	77	509	364	139	22	2	21	228	61	18	3	3	4	4	13	9	14	-.006	.034	.290	.317	.475	.251
Swisher N +	70	86	69	588	405	109	21	1	24	204	135	82	6	4	1	4	3	3	14	.082	.009	.219	.332	.410	.242
Konerko P	59	59	62	514	350	105	19	1	22	192	80	65	4	7	0	4	2	0	17	.110	.018	.240	.344	.438	.254
Pierzynski A	59	66	60	570	398	150	31	1	13	222	71	19	5	8	3	6	1	0	14	.015	-.012	.281	.312	.416	.235
Crede J	45	41	55	373	265	83	18	1	17	154	45	30	0	4	0	4	0	3	10	.059	-.168	.248	.314	.460	.246
Uribe J	42	38	40	353	252	80	22	1	7	125	64	22	0	1	5	1	1	3	5	.014	.042	.247	.296	.386	.221
Anderson B	22	24	26	193	142	42	13	0	8	79	45	10	0	0	2	0	5	1	2	.051	.048	.232	.272	.436	.223
Griffey Jr.	19	16	18	150	103	34	10	0	3	53	25	17	1	1	0	1	0	0	6	-.021	.129	.260	.347	.405	.247
Wise D *	15	20	18	143	102	32	4	2	6	58	32	8	0	1	3	2	9	0	5	-.059	.161	.248	.293	.450	.235
Hall T	13	7	7	136	94	33	3	0	2	42	19	6	1	2	1	0	0	0	0	-.069	.159	.260	.304	.331	.211
Ozuna P	5	5	6	69	50	18	3	0	0	21	3	2	0	1	2	0	0	2	2	.140	.148	.281	.313	.328	.214
Fields J	1	3	2	35	27	5	1	0	0	6	17	3	0	0	0	0	0	0	0	-.182	.139	.156	.229	.188	.144
Getz C *	1	2	1	7	6	2	0	0	0	2	1	0	0	0	0	0	1	1	0	.233	-.210	.286	.286	.286	.192

Italicized stats have been adjusted for home park.

Batted Ball Batting Stats

Player	% of PA		% of Batted Balls					Out %		Runs Per Event				Total Runs vs. Avg.				
	K%	BB%	GB%	LD%	FB%	IF/F	HR/OF	GB	OF	NIP	GB	LD	OF	NIP	GB	LD	FB	Tot
Quentin C	14	15	41	15	43	.10	.22	73	89	.13	.05	.43	.31	14	0	-2	29	41
Dye J	16	8	35	22	43	.13	.17	70	91	.04	.06	.44	.23	-3	1	13	15	26
Thome J	24	16	40	18	42	.08	.24	85	84	.07	-.04	.44	.36	8	-13	-3	27	20
Ramirez A	12	4	47	17	37	.14	.15	72	84	.00	.05	.41	.24	-7	4	-1	9	6
Konerko P	16	14	41	22	38	.14	.17	79	87	.10	.00	.30	.24	9	-7	-4	7	5
Crede J	12	9	32	14	54	.15	.12	69	89	.08	.06	.34	.17	2	1	-7	5	0
Griffey Jr. K	17	12	35	25	40	.09	.08	81	83	.08	-.02	.36	.14	1	-3	2	-1	-1
Swisher N	23	15	35	21	45	.11	.16	82	90	.07	-.01	.37	.21	7	-10	-5	6	-2
Wise D	22	6	35	23	42	.15	.18	76	93	-.01	.01	.37	.21	-3	-1	-0	1	-3
Anderson B	23	5	45	17	38	.12	.15	74	90	-.03	.06	.47	.20	-4	1	-1	1	-4
Hall T	14	6	28	28	44	.21	.05	77	83	.02	.05	.28	.08	-1	-1	1	-3	-5
Uribe J	18	7	34	20	45	.21	.06	69	80	.01	.09	.34	.15	-4	3	-2	-3	-6
Pierzynski A	12	5	44	18	38	.11	.08	75	83	.01	.03	.40	.15	-7	-2	1	-1	-9
Cabrera O	10	8	46	21	33	.14	.05	74	84	.09	.05	.34	.09	2	2	2	-16	-9
MLB Average	18	10	44	20	36	.10	.11	74	84	.05	.04	.39	.18	--	--	--	--	--

Pitching Stats

Player	PRC	IP	BFP	G	GS	K	BB	IBB	HBP	H	HR	DP	DER	SB	CS	PO	W	L	Sv	Op	Hld	H-A	R^L	RA	ERA	FIP
Danks J *	106	195.0	804	33	33	159	57	1	4	182	15	21	.699	23	8	6	12	9	0	0	0	-.011	.008	3.42	3.32	3.52
Buehrle M *	91	218.7	918	34	34	140	52	4	5	240	22	39	.668	5	7	6	15	12	0	0	0	-.060	.014	4.36	3.79	3.98
Vazquez J	85	208.3	890	33	33	200	61	2	6	214	25	15	.679	9	3	1	12	16	0	0	0	-.052	-.018	4.88	4.67	3.81
Floyd G	82	206.3	878	33	33	145	70	6	9	190	30	20	.724	37	5	1	17	8	0	0	0	-.038	-.054	4.67	3.84	4.78
Thornton M *	48	67.3	268	74	0	77	19	2	2	48	5	5	.721	3	0	0	5	3	1	6	20	.012	-.031	2.67	2.67	2.75
Contreras J	45	121.0	522	20	20	70	35	0	3	130	12	11	.699	16	1	1	7	6	0	0	0	-.043	-.056	4.76	4.54	4.30
Jenks B	39	61.7	243	57	0	38	17	4	1	51	3	10	.734	5	0	2	3	1	30	34	0	.028	.015	2.63	2.63	3.31
Dotel O	32	67.0	288	72	0	92	29	3	5	52	12	2	.707	16	1	0	4	4	1	5	21	-.039	-.042	4.57	3.76	4.20
Linebrink S	23	46.3	186	50	0	40	9	1	0	41	8	4	.729	2	0	0	2	2	1	4	19	.011	.028	3.88	3.69	4.27
Carrasco D	18	38.7	158	31	0	30	14	1	5	30	2	6	.729	3	2	0	1	0	0	1	7	-.008	.110	3.96	3.96	3.75
Masset N	16	44.7	203	32	1	32	21	4	2	55	4	9	.639	2	0	1	1	0	1	1	1	.148	-.035	5.24	4.63	4.24
MacDougal M	13	17.0	78	16	0	12	12	2	2	16	0	3	.673	1	0	0	0	0	0	0	0	-.001	-.080	2.12	2.12	3.94
Logan B *	13	42.3	197	55	0	42	14	1	3	57	7	2	.617	4	1	1	2	3	0	1	3	.005	-.056	6.59	5.95	4.25
Richard C *	12	47.7	215	13	8	29	13	2	0	61	5	5	.643	6	0	0	2	5	0	0	0	-.021	-.071	6.99	6.04	4.07
Russell A	10	26.0	118	22	0	22	10	1	2	30	1	2	.639	0	0	0	4	0	0	0	0	-.087	-.039	5.19	5.19	3.31
Wassermann E	3	19.7	101	24	0	9	14	4	1	27	0	0	.623	5	1	0	1	2	0	0	2	.091	-.029	8.69	7.78	3.99
Broadway L	3	14.0	66	7	1	7	5	1	0	20	4	1	.660	0	1	1	1	0	0	0	0	-.175	.053	7.07	7.07	6.80
Ramirez H *	2	13.0	72	17	0	2	8	1	0	24	0	0	.597	2	0	0	0	3	0	0	1	-.108	.144	7.62	7.62	4.54
Loaiza E	1	3.0	13	3	0	1	0	0	0	3	1	0	.727	0	0	0	0	0	0	0	0	.064	-.475	6.00	3.00	6.90

Italicized stats have been adjusted for home park.

Batted Ball Pitching Stats

Player	% of PA		% of Batted Balls					Out %		Runs Per Event				Total Runs vs. Avg.				
	K%	BB%	GB%	LD%	FB%	IF/F	HR/OF	GB	OF	NIP	GB	LD	OF	NIP	GB	LD	FB	Tot
Danks J	20	8	43	22	35	.09	.08	77	86	.01	.03	.38	.12	-8	-4	1	-11	-22
Thornton M	29	8	53	20	27	.13	.13	74	94	-.01	.05	.31	.12	-5	0	-6	-7	-19
Jenks R	16	7	58	14	28	.13	.07	78	79	.03	.02	.36	.15	-2	-2	-5	-4	-13
Linebrink S	22	5	39	18	43	.19	.17	74	90	-.03	.04	.34	.22	-4	-1	-3	2	-7
Carrasco D	19	12	51	21	28	.17	.08	82	91	.07	-.00	.37	.08	1	-2	-1	-5	-7
Dotel O	32	12	38	16	46	.18	.19	67	83	.01	.09	.35	.29	-3	1	-8	5	-5
Contreras J	13	7	51	19	30	.11	.10	75	86	.05	.05	.38	.16	-2	2	0	-5	-4
Vazquez J	22	8	38	20	42	.13	.10	76	83	.00	.04	.48	.18	-12	-3	8	3	-4
Floyd G	17	9	41	19	40	.10	.13	77	87	.05	.03	.38	.19	-1	-5	-4	8	-2
Buehrle M	15	6	50	19	31	.10	.11	76	80	.02	.02	.41	.21	-8	-1	5	5	0
Russell A	19	10	45	13	41	.03	.03	57	81	.05	.15	.38	.08	0	4	-2	-2	0
Masset N	16	11	54	22	24	.03	.12	74	83	.08	.04	.50	.20	2	-1	5	-1	6
Richard C	13	6	50	23	27	.09	.12	76	70	.03	.04	.38	.27	-2	0	4	3	6
Logan B	21	8	43	23	34	.11	.15	66	77	.01	.10	.42	.30	-2	4	3	5	9
MLB Average	18	10	44	20	36	.10	.11	74	84	.05	.04	.39	.18	--	--	--	--	--

Fielding Stats

Name	Inn	SBA/G	CS%	ERA	WP+PB/G	PO	A	TE	FE	Grade
Catcher										
Pierzynski A	1134.3	0.84	9%	4.23	0.341	913	54	7	1	F-
Hall T	315.3	1.31	7%	3.68	0.485	231	15	0	0	--
Phillips P	8.0	0.00	0%	3.38	0.000	7	0	0	0	--

Name	Inn	PO	A	TE	FE	FPct	DPS	DPT	ZR	OOZ	Grade
First Base											
Konerko P	995.7	1010	75	1	6	.994	6	1	.758	27	C
Swisher N	462.0	447	32	1	1	.996	9	1	.759	3	--
Second Base											
Ramirez A	1017.0	237	327	1	10	.981	24	47	.790	16	F-
Uribe J	362.3	104	124	1	0	.996	9	24	.841	7	--
Ozuna P	52.0	10	11	0	1	.955	0	0	.769	0	--
Getz C	23.0	6	9	0	0	1.000	0	1	1.000	0	--
Bourgeois J	3.0	0	0	0	0	.000	0	0	.000	0	--
Shortstop											
Cabrera O	1389.0	242	472	6	10	.978	53	41	.834	57	A
Ramirez A	53.0	8	15	1	0	.958	3	1	.750	2	--
Uribe J	15.0	2	2	0	0	1.000	0	0	1.000	0	--
Third Base											
Crede J	834.7	57	207	8	12	.930	21	1	.729	39	A
Uribe J	460.3	41	125	4	2	.960	13	0	.699	19	--
Ozuna P	100.0	8	29	2	2	.902	5	0	.750	4	--
Fields J	61.7	6	16	1	1	.917	2	1	.714	0	--
Ramirez A	1.0	0	1	0	0	1.000	0	0	1.000	0	--

Name	Inn	PO	A	TE	FE	FPct	DPS	DPT	ZR	OOZ	Grade
Left Field											
Quentin C	1147.0	228	5	4	3	.971	4	0	.846	41	F
Swisher N	137.0	31	1	0	0	1.000	0	0	.926	6	--
Wise D	132.7	28	2	0	2	.938	0	0	.857	4	--
Owens J	25.0	3	0	0	0	1.000	0	0	1.000	1	--
Anderson B	16.0	3	0	0	0	1.000	0	0	1.000	0	--
Center Field											
Swisher N	535.3	138	2	0	4	.972	0	0	.904	34	--
Anderson B	447.3	102	0	0	0	1.000	0	0	.934	31	--
Griffey Jr. K	250.0	62	1	0	0	1.000	2	0	.915	19	--
Wise D	144.0	40	0	0	0	1.000	0	0	.917	7	--
Ramirez A	63.0	16	1	1	0	.944	0	0	.917	5	--
Owens J	18.0	4	0	0	0	1.000	0	0	1.000	1	--
Right Field											
Dye J	1312.0	266	5	0	1	.996	0	0	.887	55	C
Swisher N	118.0	25	0	0	1	.962	0	0	.913	4	--
Wise D	13.0	4	0	0	0	1.000	0	0	1.000	1	--
Griffey Jr. K	8.0	1	0	0	0	1.000	0	0	1.000	0	F-
Anderson B	6.0	0	0	0	0	.000	0	0	--	--	--

Cincinnati Reds

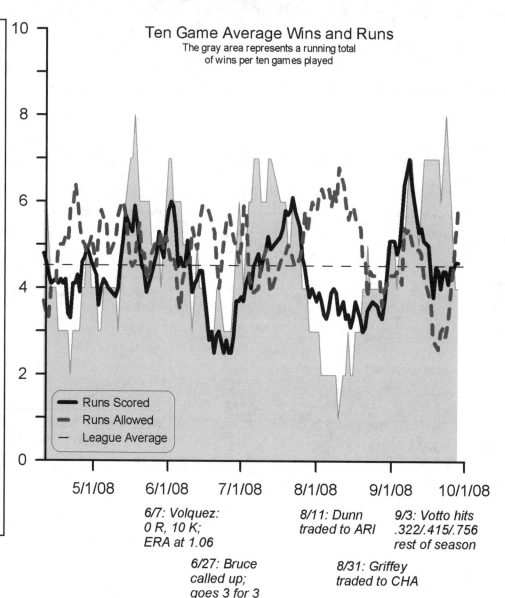

Ten Game Average Wins and Runs
The gray area represents a running total of wins per ten games played

6/7: Volquez: 0 R, 10 K; ERA at 1.06
6/27: Bruce called up; goes 3 for 3
8/11: Dunn traded to ARI
8/31: Griffey traded to CHA
9/3: Votto hits .322/.415/.756 rest of season

Team Batting and Pitching/Fielding Stats by Month

	April	May	June	July	Aug	Sept/Oct
Wins	12	15	12	12	10	13
Losses	17	12	16	13	18	12
RS/G	4.3	4.9	3.6	4.8	3.9	4.7
RA/G	4.8	5.1	4.9	5.1	5.0	4.7
OBP	.328	.339	.304	.327	.297	.329
SLG	.421	.417	.362	.433	.396	.421
FIP	4.25	4.38	5.03	4.32	4.63	4.54
DER	.693	.659	.690	.662	.660	.680

Batting Stats

Player	BR	Runs	RBI	PA	Outs	H	2B	3B	HR	TB	K	BB	IBB	HBP	SH	SF	SB	CS	GDP	H-A	L^R	BA	OBP	SLG	GPA
Votto J *	87	69	84	589	382	156	32	3	24	266	102	59	9	2	0	2	7	5	7	-.001	.006	.297	.368	.506	.286
Dunn A *	75	58	74	464	291	87	14	0	32	197	120	80	6	6	0	5	1	1	4	-.035	.045	.233	.373	.528	.294
Phillips B	73	80	78	609	436	146	24	7	21	247	93	39	6	5	0	6	23	10	13	.033	.080	.261	.312	.442	.246
Encarnacion	73	75	68	582	392	127	29	1	26	236	102	61	1	10	0	5	1	0	13	.031	.053	.251	.340	.466	.264
Griffey Jr.	58	51	53	425	279	88	20	1	15	155	64	61	13	2	0	3	0	1	7	.019	.040	.245	.355	.432	.263
Bruce J *	50	63	52	452	322	105	17	1	21	187	110	33	1	4	0	2	4	6	8	.086	.092	.254	.314	.453	.250
Hairston J	49	47	36	297	179	85	20	2	6	127	36	23	0	3	8	2	15	3	0	.122	.046	.326	.384	.487	.289
Keppinger J	47	45	43	502	352	122	24	2	3	159	24	30	3	2	6	5	3	1	14	-.044	.117	.266	.310	.346	.222
Bako P *	28	30	35	338	245	65	11	2	6	98	90	34	5	1	3	1	0	2	9	-.024	.007	.217	.299	.328	.212
Patterson C	24	46	34	392	303	75	17	2	10	126	57	16	0	1	5	4	14	9	3	.012	.035	.205	.238	.344	.189
Dickerson C	22	20	15	122	74	31	9	2	6	62	35	17	0	2	1	0	5	3	0	.091	.051	.304	.413	.608	.331
Ross D	18	17	13	173	107	31	9	0	3	49	36	32	4	1	5	1	0	1	3	.076	-.048	.231	.381	.366	.258
Freel R	18	17	10	143	99	39	8	0	0	47	18	8	0	1	2	1	6	4	3	-.125	.077	.298	.340	.359	.238
Valentin J +	15	10	18	144	98	33	8	0	4	53	27	14	0	0	0	1	0	0	2	-.020	-.069	.256	.326	.411	.245
Cabrera J	14	17	12	126	89	29	6	1	3	46	29	8	1	2	0	1	2	0	3	.082	.011	.252	.310	.400	.235
Hanigan R	11	9	9	98	64	23	2	0	2	31	9	10	1	3	0	0	0	0	2	.049	-.068	.271	.367	.365	.251
Phillips A	5	11	10	80	59	17	3	0	3	29	14	6	0	1	0	0	0	0	3	.041	.016	.233	.300	.397	.230
Janish P	5	5	6	89	67	15	2	0	1	20	18	7	0	2	0	0	0	0	2	-.005	.153	.188	.270	.250	.180
Arroyo B	4	4	6	74	50	12	3	0	1	18	21	4	0	0	9	0	1	0	1	.060	.055	.197	.246	.295	.181
Hatteberg S	4	3	7	61	44	9	3	0	0	12	7	7	0	0	0	2	0	1	0	-.134	.094	.173	.262	.231	.172
Hopper N	3	3	1	58	40	10	0	0	0	10	6	5	0	1	2	0	1	0	0	.058	.068	.200	.286	.200	.175
Castillo W +	3	6	1	34	23	9	1	0	0	10	5	1	0	0	1	0	0	0	0	-.150	-.029	.281	.303	.313	.210
Rosales A	2	0	2	30	23	6	1	0	0	7	4	1	0	0	0	0	1	0	0	.178	.041	.207	.233	.241	.162
Owings M	1	0	3	4	2	2	1	0	0	3	0	0	0	0	0	0	0	0	0	-.125	.383	.500	.500	.750	.404
Richar D *	1	4	3	37	29	8	2	0	0	10	9	0	0	0	1	0	1	0	1	-.003	.174	.222	.222	.278	.166

Italicized stats have been adjusted for home park.

Batted Ball Batting Stats

Player	% of PA		% of Batted Balls					Out %		Runs Per Event				Total Runs vs. Avg.				
	K%	BB%	GB%	LD%	FB%	IF/F	HR/OF	GB	OF	NIP	GB	LD	OF	NIP	GB	LD	FB	Tot
Votto J	17	10	44	25	31	.04	.18	74	81	.06	.05	.35	.30	2	2	6	16	26
Dunn A	26	19	37	17	45	.05	.25	74	88	.08	.05	.38	.35	10	-2	-7	22	23
Encarnacion E	18	12	34	16	50	.22	.16	71	84	.08	.06	.42	.23	5	1	-4	11	13
Dickerson C	29	16	37	18	45	.03	.21	58	77	.05	.21	.47	.39	1	3	-0	7	10
Hairston J	12	9	32	27	41	.18	.08	67	93	.08	.12	.42	.07	1	6	10	-7	10
Griffey Jr. K	15	15	39	19	43	.09	.11	80	85	.11	.01	.40	.17	9	-4	-1	3	7
Phillips B	15	7	50	16	34	.09	.14	73	84	.03	.05	.37	.22	-4	4	-6	7	1
Bruce J	24	8	45	21	34	.13	.23	76	87	.00	.03	.38	.33	-6	-2	-2	11	1
Ross D	21	19	38	25	37	.08	.03	78	84	.11	.03	.42	.08	5	-1	1	-4	1
Valentin J	19	10	41	16	44	.04	.09	74	79	.04	.06	.31	.18	-0	0	-3	2	-1
Cabrera J	23	8	47	21	32	.15	.13	73	70	.00	.05	.28	.32	-2	0	-2	2	-1
Freel R	13	6	56	20	24	.08	.00	74	75	.04	.05	.39	.09	-1	1	1	-3	-2
Bako P	27	10	56	18	26	.02	.08	78	79	.02	.01	.40	.17	-3	-2	-5	-5	-15
Keppinger J	5	6	51	21	28	.10	.03	76	89	.15	.03	.32	.02	1	-1	1	-18	-18
Patterson C	15	4	46	15	38	.08	.10	85	91	-.01	-.00	.38	.10	-7	-3	-7	-6	-23
MLB Average	18	10	44	20	36	.10	.11	74	84	.05	.04	.39	.18	--	--	--	--	--

Pitching Stats

Player	PRC	IP	BFP	G	GS	K	BB	IBB	HBP	H	HR	DP	DER	SB	CS	PO	W	L	Sv	Op	Hld	H-A	R^L	RA	ERA	FIP
Volquez E	97	196.0	838	33	32	206	93	5	14	167	14	20	.687	21	12	0	17	6	0	0	0	.032	-.012	3.77	3.21	3.59
Arroyo B	68	200.0	871	34	34	163	68	2	6	219	29	22	.676	5	2	2	15	11	0	0	0	-.051	-.060	5.22	4.77	4.54
Harang A	65	184.3	793	30	29	153	50	5	2	205	35	15	.687	17	4	0	6	17	0	0	0	-.018	-.022	5.08	4.78	4.78
Cueto J	60	174.0	769	31	31	158	68	1	14	178	29	14	.690	7	6	1	9	14	0	0	0	-.020	-.004	5.22	4.81	4.95
Cordero F	37	70.3	307	72	0	78	38	3	3	61	6	6	.676	7	3	1	5	4	34	40	0	.082	.055	3.58	3.33	3.71
Affeldt J *	35	78.3	335	74	0	80	25	0	3	78	9	7	.674	7	1	0	1	1	0	1	5	.087	-.009	4.14	3.33	3.73
Weathers D	33	69.3	311	72	0	46	30	8	3	76	6	12	.659	3	0	0	4	6	0	4	19	.031	.065	3.50	3.25	4.08
Burton J	29	58.7	257	54	0	58	25	3	2	56	6	4	.687	4	1	0	5	1	0	2	11	-.016	-.018	3.68	3.22	3.78
Lincoln M	26	70.3	297	64	0	57	24	1	3	66	10	8	.719	1	1	0	2	5	0	1	10	-.070	.033	4.73	4.48	4.54
Bray B *	24	47.0	215	63	0	54	24	5	1	50	4	6	.621	4	0	0	2	2	0	4	9	-.108	-.023	3.64	2.87	3.29
Ramirez R	17	27.0	105	5	4	21	11	0	1	17	3	3	.783	2	3	0	1	1	0	0	0	.021	-.199	2.67	2.67	4.42
Fogg J	15	78.3	362	22	14	45	27	1	6	97	17	9	.670	3	2	0	2	7	0	0	1	.055	.038	7.93	7.58	6.10
Majewski G	9	40.0	192	37	0	27	15	0	3	61	6	7	.603	1	0	0	1	0	0	1	2	-.039	.054	6.98	6.53	5.15
Masset N	9	17.3	68	10	0	11	5	0	0	16	3	4	.714	0	1	0	1	0	0	2	1	.049	.015	3.12	2.08	5.05
Mercker K *	6	13.7	58	15	0	6	8	1	0	13	1	4	.721	0	0	0	1	0	0	0	0	-.180	.088	3.29	3.29	4.81
Bailey H	6	36.3	180	8	8	18	17	1	0	59	8	5	.606	8	1	0	0	6	0	0	0	.133	.045	8.92	7.93	6.39
Belisle M	5	29.7	142	6	6	14	6	0	0	47	4	3	.610	3	1	0	1	4	0	0	0	.185	.064	8.19	7.28	4.62
Coffey T	5	19.3	87	17	0	8	6	0	1	25	4	3	.676	1	1	0	0	0	0	0	0	-.129	.096	6.05	6.05	6.15
Thompson D	3	14.3	69	3	3	6	7	0	1	20	3	2	.673	0	2	0	0	0	0	0	0	.104	-.009	6.91	6.91	6.76
Adkins J	2	3.7	15	4	0	3	3	1	0	4	1	2	.625	1	1	0	1	0	0	0	0	-.063	.170	2.45	2.45	6.75
Herrera D *	1	7.3	37	7	0	8	3	2	2	10	1	0	.609	0	0	0	0	0	0	0	0	.014	-.326	8.59	7.36	4.02
Roenicke J	1	3.0	18	5	0	6	2	0	1	6	0	0	.333	0	0	0	0	0	0	0	0	-.012	-.238	9.00	9.00	2.20

Italicized stats have been adjusted for home park.

Batted Ball Pitching Stats

Player	% of PA		% of Batted Balls					Out %		Runs Per Event				Total Runs vs. Avg.				
	K%	BB%	GB%	LD%	FB%	IF/F	HR/OF	GB	OF	NIP	GB	LD	OF	NIP	GB	LD	FB	Tot
Volquez E	25	13	46	20	34	.10	.08	74	77	.04	.05	.32	.20	3	-1	-14	-2	-14
Ramirez R	20	11	43	19	39	.19	.14	87	89	.05	-.04	.22	.16	0	-3	-3	-1	-6
Lincoln M	19	9	52	18	30	.11	.16	76	89	.03	.04	.39	.21	-1	-1	-3	-1	-5
Affeldt J	24	8	54	18	28	.03	.12	75	73	.01	.04	.44	.28	-4	-1	-2	3	-4
Cordero F	25	13	41	22	37	.13	.10	69	85	.05	.07	.33	.16	1	1	-3	-3	-4
Burton L	23	11	51	14	36	.10	.11	76	73	.03	.04	.43	.24	-1	0	-5	3	-3
Bray B	25	12	35	27	37	.08	.07	74	79	.03	.05	.44	.17	-0	-0	5	-0	4
Weathers D	15	11	44	24	32	.10	.09	72	90	.08	.04	.43	.12	2	0	7	-4	6
Belisle M	10	4	51	26	23	.00	.14	75	75	.02	.04	.45	.29	-1	0	7	3	9
Arroyo B	19	8	41	23	36	.18	.15	74	87	.03	.04	.45	.22	-4	-2	16	3	12
Cueto J	21	11	39	21	41	.11	.15	74	86	.04	.05	.42	.22	0	-1	3	11	13
Majewski G	14	9	50	19	30	.07	.15	64	86	.07	.10	.49	.23	1	5	4	3	13
Harang A	19	7	34	22	44	.09	.14	71	86	.00	.07	.41	.22	-10	2	6	17	15
Bailey D	10	9	43	25	31	.09	.18	57	81	.11	.15	.36	.29	2	6	4	5	17
Fogg J	12	9	38	19	43	.13	.14	66	85	.08	.09	.46	.22	2	5	6	8	21
MLB Average	18	10	44	20	36	.10	.11	74	84	.05	.04	.39	.18	--	--	--	--	--

Fielding Stats

Name	Inn	SBA/G	CS%	ERA	WP+PB/G	PO	A	TE	FE	Grade
Catchers										
Bako P	770.7	0.88	27%	4.36	0.420	679	39	5	0	B
Ross D	374.7	0.79	27%	5.09	0.408	323	29	1	2	--
Hanigan R	229.3	0.90	35%	4.16	0.353	186	19	1	0	--
Valentin J	67.7	0.13	0%	5.05	0.931	67	5	0	0	--

Name	Inn	PO	A	TE	FE	FPct	DPS	DPT	ZR	OOZ	Grade
First Base											
Votto J	1223.0	1050	136	5	6	.991	18	1	.750	57	A+
Hatteberg S	87.7	69	6	1	0	.987	0	0	.875	1	--
Valentin J	81.7	75	4	0	0	1.000	1	0	.667	3	--
Phillips A	30.7	35	0	1	0	.972	0	0	.667	1	--
Keppinger J	18.7	15	1	0	0	1.000	0	0	.500	1	--
Second Base											
Phillips B	1237.0	298	401	4	3	.990	31	53	.860	35	A
Richar D	55.7	12	16	1	0	.966	2	2	.867	1	--
Hairston J	46.0	11	17	0	0	1.000	3	1	.818	5	--
Keppinger J	23.0	5	5	0	0	1.000	0	1	.667	0	--
Phillips A	19.0	5	8	0	0	1.000	1	2	1.000	2	--
Castillo W	16.0	5	2	0	0	1.000	1	1	1.000	0	--
Rosales A	16.0	6	6	0	0	1.000	1	2	1.000	0	--
Cabrera J	15.0	4	6	0	0	1.000	1	2	.667	0	--
Freel R	12.0	4	5	0	0	1.000	0	0	1.000	0	--
Castro J	2.0	1	2	0	0	1.000	0	0	1.000	0	--
Shortstop											
Keppinger J	880.7	145	246	3	5	.980	36	28	.797	27	F-
Hairston J	271.0	61	68	2	2	.970	7	10	.776	10	--
Janish P	204.3	31	78	2	1	.973	6	7	.849	4	--
Cabrera J	60.3	7	14	0	0	1.000	4	1	.909	4	--
Castro J	18.0	1	4	0	0	1.000	0	0	1.000	2	--
Richar D	8.0	1	1	0	0	1.000	0	0	1.000	0	--

Name	Inn	PO	A	TE	FE	FPct	DPS	DPT	ZR	OOZ	Grade
Third Base											
Encarnacion	1237.0	91	216	16	6	.930	20	0	.628	34	F-
Keppinger J	71.3	3	18	0	0	1.000	2	0	.700	4	--
Phillips A	49.0	1	10	1	0	.917	2	0	.636	3	--
Freel R	33.0	4	4	1	0	.889	0	0	.571	0	--
Rosales A	29.0	2	1	0	0	1.000	1	0	.333	0	--
Valentin J	9.7	0	0	0	0	0.000	0	0	--	--	--
Cabrera J	9.3	1	2	0	0	1.000	0	0	.333	1	--
Hairston J	2.0	0	0	0	0	0.000	0	0	--	--	--
Castro J	2.0	0	4	0	0	1.000	0	0	.750	1	--
Left Field											
Dunn A	915.7	191	5	2	5	.966	2	0	.899	30	F-
Dickerson C	182.7	38	0	0	0	1.000	0	0	.903	10	--
Cabrera J	124.0	21	2	0	1	.958	0	0	.944	4	--
Hairston J	63.3	10	0	0	0	1.000	0	0	1.000	1	--
Freel R	46.3	6	0	0	0	1.000	0	0	.857	0	--
Bruce J	41.0	3	0	0	0	1.000	0	0	.667	1	--
Castillo W	38.0	6	0	0	0	1.000	0	0	1.000	2	--
Hopper N	31.3	5	0	0	0	1.000	0	0	1.000	0	--
Center Field											
Patterson C	798.0	242	3	1	2	.988	2	0	.935	55	C
Bruce J	285.0	77	3	1	1	.976	2	0	.951	19	--
Freel R	151.7	45	1	0	0	1.000	0	0	.946	10	--
Hairston J	116.7	27	1	0	1	.966	0	0	.875	6	--
Hopper N	46.0	12	0	0	0	1.000	0	0	1.000	1	--
Dickerson C	45.0	10	0	0	0	1.000	0	0	1.000	6	--
Right Field											
Griffey Jr. K	755.0	156	7	1	4	.970	0	0	.826	28	F-
Bruce J	590.0	143	5	3	6	.943	6	0	.884	36	--
Hairston J	47.0	17	0	0	0	1.000	0	0	.867	4	--
Hopper N	23.0	6	0	0	0	1.000	0	0	.800	2	--
Cabrera J	17.0	1	0	0	0	1.000	0	0	.500	0	--
Freel R	10.3	4	0	0	0	1.000	0	0	1.000	1	--

Cleveland Indians

- Grady Sizemore's H-A of .110 tied for the lead among ML regulars
- Sizemore led the AL with 122 Base Runs
- Sizemore stole 38 bases in 43 attempts
- Sizemore made 94 OOZ plays
- David Dellucci's L^R of .225 was highest in the majors among 200+ PA players
- Kelly Shoppach struck out in one-third of his PAs
- Just 3 stolen bases were attempted against Cliff Lee
- Lee's BB rate of 4% was lowest in the majors among 162+ IP pitchers
- Aaron Laffey's -.132 H-A was lowest in the majors among 40+ IP pitchers
- Ben Francisco hit a fly ball on 48% of his batted balls
- Fausto Carmona walked 14% of the batters he faced, and struck out only 11%

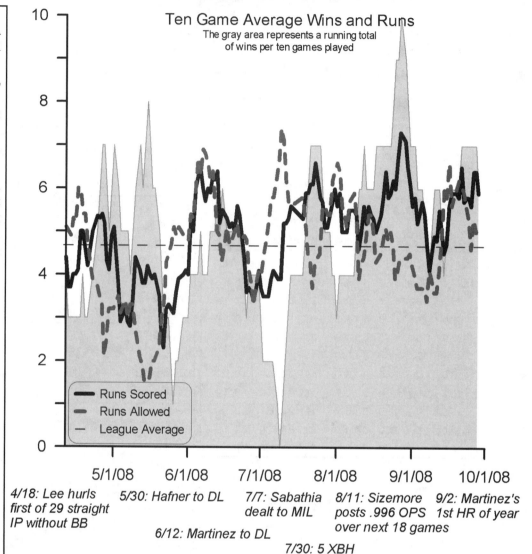

Ten Game Average Wins and Runs
The gray area represents a running total of wins per ten games played

— Runs Scored
-- Runs Allowed
- League Average

4/18: Lee hurls first of 29 straight IP without BB

5/30: Hafner to DL

6/12: Martinez to DL

7/7: Sabathia dealt to MIL

7/30: 5 XBH for Shoppach: 3 2B, 2 HR

8/11: Sizemore posts .996 OPS over next 18 games

9/2: Martinez's 1st HR of year

Team Batting and Pitching/Fielding Stats by Month

	April	May	June	July	Aug	Sept/Oct
Wins	13	12	12	10	18	16
Losses	15	15	16	14	10	11
RS/G	4.5	3.6	5.1	5.6	5.4	5.6
RA/G	4.3	3.3	5.3	5.8	4.6	5.0
OBP	.332	.297	.341	.335	.361	.362
SLG	.375	.366	.429	.483	.462	.429
FIP	4.60	3.75	4.79	4.33	4.20	4.37
DER	.699	.692	.679	.672	.698	.675

Batting Stats

Player	BR	Runs	RBI	PA	Outs	H	2B	3B	HR	TB	K	BB	IBB	HBP	SH	SF	SB	CS	GDP	H-A	L^R	BA	OBP	SLG	GPA
Sizemore G *	122	101	90	745	474	170	39	5	33	318	130	98	14	11	0	2	38	5	5	.110	.057	.268	.374	.502	.294
Peralta J	86	104	89	664	465	167	42	4	23	286	126	48	2	4	2	5	3	1	26	-.046	-.020	.276	.331	.473	.267
Garko R	78	61	90	563	370	135	21	1	14	200	86	45	1	15	0	8	0	0	10	.026	.047	.273	.346	.404	.257
Choo S *	72	68	66	370	227	98	28	3	14	174	78	44	4	5	0	4	4	3	5	.078	.061	.309	.397	.549	.316
Blake C	63	46	58	368	234	94	24	0	11	151	68	33	6	7	1	2	2	0	3	-.084	.035	.289	.365	.465	.280
Shoppach K	60	67	55	403	267	92	27	0	21	182	133	36	3	11	3	1	0	0	7	.010	.035	.261	.348	.517	.286
Francisco B	58	65	54	499	341	119	32	0	15	196	86	40	0	6	2	4	4	3	10	.034	.012	.266	.332	.438	.259
Cabrera A +	46	48	47	418	273	91	20	0	6	129	77	46	2	4	11	5	4	4	8	.039	.101	.259	.346	.366	.248
Carroll J	44	60	36	402	256	96	13	4	1	120	65	34	0	9	10	2	7	3	2	.091	-.032	.277	.355	.346	.246
Dellucci D *	43	41	47	375	270	80	19	2	11	136	76	24	1	11	0	4	3	2	12	-.056	.225	.238	.307	.405	.239
Gutierrez F	38	54	41	440	313	99	26	2	8	153	87	27	1	8	4	2	9	3	10	.029	.026	.248	.307	.383	.234
Martinez V +	35	30	35	294	204	74	17	0	2	97	32	24	4	1	0	3	0	0	12	.073	.095	.278	.337	.365	.243
Hafner T *	21	21	24	234	164	39	10	0	5	64	55	27	6	5	0	3	1	1	4	.030	.004	.197	.305	.323	.218
Marte A	17	21	17	257	190	52	11	1	3	74	52	14	0	1	7	0	1	2	5	-.024	.112	.221	.268	.315	.199
Fasano S	6	5	6	54	35	12	4	0	0	16	17	3	0	3	1	1	0	0	1	.039	-.017	.261	.340	.348	.240
Michaels J	5	3	9	67	47	12	4	0	0	16	13	4	0	1	1	3	1	1	0	.051	-.052	.207	.258	.276	.185
Gonzalez A	3	3	2	30	21	5	0	0	1	8	5	6	0	0	0	0	0	1	1	.075	.201	.208	.367	.333	.248
Aubrey M *	1	2	3	50	38	9	0	0	2	15	5	5	0	0	0	0	0	0	2	-.128	.218	.200	.280	.333	.209
Velandia J	1	1	0	9	5	3	1	0	0	4	2	1	0	0	0	0	0	0	0	-.750	-.500	.375	.444	.500	.325
Sabathia C *	1	1	1	3	2	1	0	0	1	4	2	0	0	0	0	0	0	0	0	-.483	.725	.333	.333	1.333	.483

Italicized stats have been adjusted for home park.

Batted Ball Batting Stats

Player	% of PA		% of Batted Balls			IF/F	HR/OF	Out %		Runs Per Event				Total Runs vs. Avg.				
	K%	BB%	GB%	LD%	FB%			GB	OF	NIP	GB	LD	OF	NIP	GB	LD	FB	Tot
Sizemore G	17	15	35	19	46	.11	.16	77	81	.10	.04	.34	.28	14	-2	-6	29	34
Choo S	21	13	41	23	36	.09	.16	68	79	.06	.09	.43	.31	4	5	5	11	25
Shoppach K	33	12	38	19	43	.09	.23	76	68	.01	.03	.47	.46	-4	-4	-3	23	13
Blake C	18	11	39	24	37	.07	.12	69	82	.06	.08	.34	.22	1	3	2	5	11
Peralta J	19	8	44	20	36	.06	.14	74	80	.02	.03	.39	.26	-5	-4	1	16	9
Garko R	15	11	39	20	41	.13	.09	75	81	.08	.04	.35	.17	4	-2	-1	2	3
Francisco B	17	9	34	18	48	.15	.10	67	85	.05	.08	.37	.17	-0	3	-3	4	3
Carroll J	16	11	45	27	27	.03	.01	70	84	.07	.08	.31	.06	2	4	2	-11	-2
Cabrera A	18	12	46	21	34	.12	.06	73	92	.07	.05	.46	.06	3	1	3	-12	-4
Martinez V	11	9	45	22	33	.13	.03	76	87	.09	.02	.40	.05	1	-2	5	-8	-5
Dellucci D	20	9	41	17	42	.07	.10	75	85	.03	.04	.36	.17	-2	-2	-6	1	-8
Gutierrez F	20	8	42	17	41	.12	.07	67	84	.02	.09	.38	.14	-4	5	-6	-4	-8
Hafner T	24	14	42	25	33	.08	.11	87	92	.06	-.03	.36	.12	2	-6	-1	-4	-9
Marte A	20	6	34	16	49	.12	.04	71	84	-.01	.05	.34	.08	-4	-1	-5	-5	-16
MLB Average	18	10	44	20	36	.10	.11	74	84	.05	.04	.39	.18	--	--	--	--	--

Pitching Stats

Player	PRC	IP	BFP	G	GS	K	BB	IBB	HBP	H	HR	DP	DER	SB	CS	PO	W	L	Sv	Op	Hld	H-A	R^L	RA	ERA	FIP
Lee C *	139	223.3	891	31	31	170	34	1	5	214	12	32	.690	3	0	0	22	3	0	0	0	.009	.017	2.74	2.54	2.92
Sabathia C *	59	122.3	507	18	18	123	34	1	3	117	13	13	.683	7	2	2	6	8	0	0	0	-.011	-.029	3.97	3.83	3.48
Byrd P	44	131.0	553	22	22	56	24	0	5	146	23	11	.719	3	5	1	7		0	0	0	-.051	-.081	4.81	4.53	5.32
Perez R *	40	76.3	313	73	0	86	23	3	2	67	8	11	.670	2	3	0	4	4	2	7	25	-.024	-.023	3.77	3.54	3.20
Carmona F	33	120.7	549	22	22	58	70	0	9	126	7	26	.677	6	1	0	8	7	0	0	0	-.012	-.047	5.97	5.44	4.99
Sowers J *	32	121.0	533	22	22	64	39	1	3	141	18	12	.682	9	6	1	4	9	0	0	0	-.032	.002	6.25	5.58	5.12
Laffey A *	31	93.7	409	16	16	43	31	1	9	103	10	18	.690	2	2	0	5	7	0	0	0	-.132	-.030	5.00	4.23	4.95
Lewis J	30	66.0	292	51	0	52	27	3	5	68	8	4	.690	1	1	0	0	4	13	14	4	-.022	-.003	3.95	3.82	4.55
Betancourt R	26	71.0	309	69	0	64	25	5	0	76	11	5	.684	10	1	0	3	4	4	8	12	-.024	.007	5.20	5.07	4.29
Reyes A	25	34.3	142	6	6	15	12	0	1	31	2	5	.732	2	1	0	2	1	0	0	0	.074	.009	1.83	1.83	4.25
Kobayashi M	20	55.7	244	57	0	35	14	2	1	65	8	5	.677	2	0	0	4	5	6	9	2	-.065	-.028	4.85	4.53	4.54
Westbrook J	17	34.7	139	5	5	19	7	0	1	33	5	6	.720	0	2	1	1	2	0	0	0	.018	.046	3.38	3.12	4.70
Jackson Z *	15	54.7	238	9	9	30	14	0	3	64	7	9	.674	1	0	0	2	3	0	0	0	.027	.069	5.93	5.60	4.73
Lewis S *	12	24.0	97	4	4	15	6	0	0	20	4	3	.750	0	1	0	4	0	0	0	0	.064	-.130	3.38	2.63	4.90
Mujica E	10	38.7	168	33	0	27	10	3	1	46	5	5	.672	0	1	0	3	2	0	2	1	.032	-.023	6.75	6.75	4.14
Rincon J	8	27.3	121	23	0	19	8	0	1	34	3	4	.656	2	0	0	1	1	0	0	2	-.110	-.063	5.93	5.60	4.25
Elarton S	7	15.3	70	8	0	15	9	2	0	16	0	0	.652	1	0	0	0	1	0	0	0	.050	-.097	4.11	3.52	2.64
Ginter M	7	21.0	87	4	4	12	3	1	0	25	3	4	.681	1	0	0	1	3	0	0	0	.030	.036	5.14	5.14	4.23
Julio J	6	17.7	78	15	0	15	11	1	0	18	3	4	.694	0	0	0	0	0	0	0	0	.198	-.096	5.60	5.60	5.44
Bullington B	5	14.7	60	3	2	12	2	0	1	15	4	2	.707	2	0	0	0	2	0	0	0	.246	-.104	5.52	4.91	5.75
Rundles R *	5	5.0	22	8	0	6	3	0	0	5	0	1	.615	1	0	0	0	0	0	0	1	.050	-.144	1.80	1.80	2.63
Breslow C *	5	8.3	40	7	0	7	5	0	0	10	1	0	.667	2	0	0	0	0	0	0	0	-.045	.154	3.24	3.24	4.91
Borowski J	3	16.7	82	18	0	9	8	2	0	24	4	0	.656	6	0	0	1	3	6	10	0	-.012	.058	7.56	7.56	6.35
Mastny T	3	20.0	100	14	1	19	11	2	0	28	6	0	.641	1	0	0	2	2	0	1	0	-.133	-.037	10.80	10.80	6.58
Donnelly B	2	13.7	69	15	0	8	10	0	0	20	2	1	.633	1	1	0	1	0	0	0	4	-.170	.064	8.56	8.56	6.16

Italicized stats have been adjusted for home park.

Batted Ball Pitching Stats

Player	% of PA		% of Batted Balls					Out %		Runs Per Event				Total Runs vs. Avg.				
	K%	BB%	GB%	LD%	FB%	IF/F	HR/OF	GB	OF	NIP	GB	LD	OF	NIP	GB	LD	FB	Tot
Lee C	19	4	46	19	35	.11	.05	73	84	-.03	.05	.37	.09	-19	3	-6	-19	-41
Sabathia C	24	7	43	21	36	.08	.11	74	80	-.01	.05	.34	.20	-8	1	-5	1	-12
Perez R	27	8	57	19	24	.10	.19	75	69	-.01	.03	.27	.38	-5	-0	-8	4	-10
Reyes A	11	9	46	21	34	.08	.06	76	88	.10	.03	.26	.08	1	-0	-2	-3	-5
Westbrook J	14	6	55	17	28	.13	.19	80	81	.02	.01	.29	.30	-1	-0	-3	2	-3
Rincon J	16	7	44	29	27	.12	.09	68	80	.03	.08	.28	.17	-1	2	1	-1	1
Kobayashi M	14	6	50	21	28	.05	.15	74	91	.02	.05	.36	.19	-2	2	1	0	1
Betancourt R	21	8	29	21	50	.12	.12	66	87	.02	.09	.39	.17	-3	1	0	3	1
Lewis J	18	11	35	25	40	.12	.08	67	92	.06	.09	.43	.08	1	2	6	-6	3
Byrd P	10	5	37	22	41	.09	.13	79	91	.04	.02	.38	.16	-4	-4	7	4	3
Laffey A	11	10	51	19	30	.10	.10	74	87	.11	.03	.41	.15	4	-0	3	-3	3
Jackson Z	13	7	51	15	34	.11	.13	69	78	.05	.06	.36	.25	-1	3	-3	5	4
Mujica E	16	7	30	23	46	.10	.09	74	88	.02	.04	.48	.14	-1	-1	5	0	4
Carmona F	11	14	63	15	22	.09	.06	75	73	.15	.03	.46	.20	14	1	0	-4	11
Sowers J	12	8	42	24	34	.08	.13	77	88	.07	.04	.40	.19	0	1	10	4	15
MLB Average	18	10	44	20	36	.10	.11	74	84	.05	.04	.39	.18	--	--	--	--	--

Fielding Stats

Name	Inn	SBA/G	CS%	ERA	WP+PB/G	PO	A	TE	FE	Grade
Catchers										
Shoppach K	872.7	0.48	21%	4.37	0.392	586	34	6	1	C
Martinez V	447.3	0.64	31%	4.31	0.241	328	16	1	2	--
Fasano S	117.0	0.85	27%	5.69	0.538	102	9	1	1	--

Name	Inn	PO	A	TE	FE	FPct	DPS	DPT	ZR	OOZ	Grade
First Base											
Garko R	1058.0	1039	80	0	4	.996	9	1	.710	29	D
Blake C	160.0	171	10	0	1	.995	1	0	.783	7	--
Aubrey M	94.3	99	6	0	0	1.000	0	0	.667	4	--
Martinez V	82.0	82	4	0	1	.989	0	0	.778	2	--
Gonzalez A	38.0	39	0	1	1	.951	0	0	.625	0	--
Fasano S	3.0	0	0	0	0	.000	0	0	--	--	--
Marte A	1.0	2	1	0	0	1.000	1	0	1.000	0	--
Second Base											
Cabrera A	776.7	202	281	0	3	.994	40	44	.815	28	B
Carroll J	580.3	105	192	1	2	.990	22	24	.831	11	--
Barfield J	71.0	26	24	0	0	1.000	3	6	.800	0	--
Velandia J	9.0	3	4	0	0	1.000	0	1	1.000	0	--
Shortstop											
Peralta J	1271.0	217	427	5	9	.979	47	54	.813	41	D
Cabrera A	154.7	38	59	2	3	.951	9	9	.745	10	--
Velandia J	9.0	1	4	0	0	1.000	1	1	1.000	1	--
Blake C	2.0	0	1	0	0	1.000	0	0	.500	0	--
Third Base											
Blake C	635.0	39	141	5	7	.938	12	1	.688	11	F-
Marte A	581.3	43	155	2	4	.971	18	2	.746	23	B
Carroll J	199.7	12	55	2	4	.918	5	0	.694	10	--
Gonzalez A	12.0	1	1	0	1	.667	1	0	.250	0	--
Peralta J	9.0	1	2	0	0	1.000	1	0	1.000	0	--

Name	Inn	PO	A	TE	FE	FPct	DPS	DPT	ZR	OOZ	Grade
Left Field											
Francisco B	643.0	150	7	0	2	.987	4	0	.897	28	--
Dellucci D	383.0	75	1	0	0	1.000	0	0	.875	19	--
Choo S	223.0	40	3	1	0	.977	0	0	.906	11	--
Michaels J	97.0	23	2	0	0	1.000	0	0	.889	7	--
Gutierrez F	78.0	14	0	0	0	1.000	0	0	.800	6	--
Tyner J	10.0	0	0	0	0	.000	0	0	.000	0	--
Carroll J	3.0	0	0	0	0	.000	0	0	--	--	--
Center Field											
Sizemore G	1338.0	382	2	0	2	.995	2	0	.932	94	A
Gutierrez F	97.0	30	1	0	1	.969	0	0	1.000	6	--
Francisco B	2.0	0	0	0	0	0.000	0	0	--	--	--
Right Field											
Gutierrez F	763.7	224	4	0	2	.991	0	0	.955	55	A+
Choo S	398.3	88	1	0	1	.989	0	0	.897	19	--
Francisco B	230.0	46	5	1	1	.962	2	0	.844	8	--
Michaels J	45.0	15	1	0	1	.941	0	0	1.000	1	--

Colorado Rockies

- Willy Taveras' GPA of .195 was lowest of any regular in the majors
- Taveras had 15 sacrifice hits, most in the majors by a non-pitcher
- Taveras stole 68 bases in 75 attempts
- Matt Holliday stole 28 bases in 30 attempts
- Aaron Cook led the NL with 236 hits allowed, and 36 double plays
- Cook allowed only 5 stolen bases in 13 attempts
- Ian Stewart struck out in 31% of his PAs
- Jason Grilli allowed just 1 home run in 61 innings
- Greg Reynolds allowed 14 in 62 innings
- Chris Ianetta committed zero errors
- Jorge de la Rosa's FIP (4.06) was much better than his ERA (4.92)
- Garrett Atkins had 10 sacrifice flies

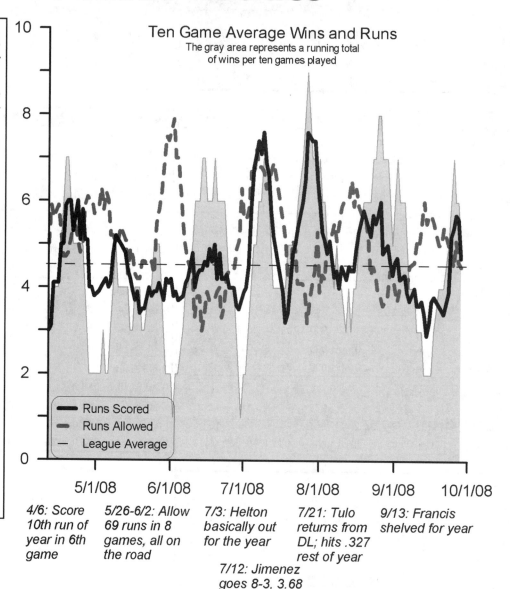

Ten Game Average Wins and Runs
The gray area represents a running total of wins per ten games played

— Runs Scored
-- Runs Allowed
- League Average

4/6: Score 10th run of year in 6th game

5/26-6/2: Allow 69 runs in 8 games, all on the road

7/3: Helton basically out for the year

7/12: Jimenez goes 8-3, 3.68 rest of year

7/21: Tulo returns from DL; hits .327 rest of year

9/13: Francis shelved for year

Team Batting and Pitching/Fielding Stats by Month

	April	May	June	July	Aug	Sept/Oct
Wins	11	9	12	17	15	10
Losses	17	19	15	10	13	14
RS/G	4.1	4.4	4.1	6.0	4.8	4.2
RA/G	5.1	5.9	4.6	5.1	4.8	5.0
OBP	.324	.330	.338	.371	.345	.303
SLG	.381	.408	.426	.496	.397	.384
FIP	4.54	4.61	4.31	4.05	3.84	4.22
DER	.708	.664	.689	.679	.670	.662

Batting Stats

Player	BR	Runs	RBI	PA	Outs	H	2B	3B	HR	TB	K	BB	IBB	HBP	SH	SF	SB	CS	GDP	H-A	L^R	BA	OBP	SLG	GPA
Holliday M	95	107	88	623	377	173	38	2	25	290	104	74	6	8	0	2	28	2	9	.028	-.017	.321	.409	.538	.292
Hawpe B *	80	69	85	569	359	138	24	3	25	243	134	76	6	3	0	2	2	2	7	.005	.026	.283	.381	.498	.272
Atkins G	70	86	99	664	457	175	32	3	21	276	100	40	0	3	0	10	1	1	20	.081	.099	.286	.328	.452	.239
Iannetta C	63	50	65	407	251	88	22	2	18	168	92	56	0	14	2	2	0	0	6	-.005	.020	.264	.390	.505	.277
Barmes C	51	47	44	417	292	114	25	6	11	184	69	17	0	2	4	1	13	4	9	.088	.059	.290	.322	.468	.240
Taveras W	45	64	26	538	370	120	15	2	1	142	79	36	0	5	15	3	68	7	4	-.010	.014	.251	.308	.296	.195
Stewart I *	42	33	41	304	201	69	18	2	10	121	94	30	4	7	0	1	1	1	3	.013	-.126	.259	.349	.455	.248
Helton T *	41	39	29	361	229	79	16	0	7	116	50	61	8	1	0	0	0	0	9	.024	.033	.264	.391	.388	.250
Tulowitzki T	40	48	46	421	300	99	24	2	8	151	56	38	5	2	2	2	1	6	16	-.016	.091	.263	.332	.401	.229
Spilborghs R	39	38	36	275	172	73	14	2	6	109	41	38	0	1	0	3	7	4	8	.028	.014	.313	.407	.468	.275
Baker J	38	55	48	333	224	80	22	1	12	140	85	26	2	1	1	6	4	0	5	.083	.055	.268	.322	.468	.240
Torrealba Y	22	19	31	261	192	58	17	0	6	93	44	12	0	5	5	3	0	4	10	.030	.023	.246	.293	.394	.211
Podsednik S	18	22	15	181	128	41	8	1	1	54	28	16	0	1	1	1	12	4	3	-.026	.125	.253	.322	.333	.209
Quintanilla	17	28	15	234	163	50	17	0	2	73	46	15	3	0	8	1	0	0	3	.105	.051	.238	.288	.348	.198
Smith S *	17	13	15	123	80	28	7	0	4	47	23	15	0	0	0	0	1	0	0	-.040	.254	.259	.350	.435	.244
Cook A	6	1	4	78	46	14	1	0	0	15	21	2	0	0	16	0	0	0	0	.145	.047	.233	.258	.250	.164
Koshansky J	5	5	8	40	32	8	3	0	3	20	17	1	0	1	0	0	0	0	2	.163	-.070	.211	.250	.526	.224
Herrera J +	5	5	3	66	48	14	1	1	0	17	10	4	0	0	1	0	1	1	0	-.050	-.010	.230	.277	.279	.178
Sullivan C *	2	3	4	24	18	5	0	1	0	7	5	0	0	1	0	0	1	0	0	.091	.016	.217	.250	.304	.173
Hernandez L	2	1	1	19	13	4	0	0	0	4	1	0	0	0	2	0	0	0	0	-.255	-.200	.235	.235	.235	.151
Reynolds G	1	1	0	17	12	3	2	0	0	5	5	1	0	0	1	0	0	0	0	.319	.039	.200	.250	.333	.180
Melhuse A +	1	2	1	10	9	1	1	0	0	2	4	0	0	0	0	0	0	0	0	-.190	--	.100	.100	.200	.087

Italicized stats have been adjusted for home park.

Batted Ball Batting Stats

Player	% of PA		% of Batted Balls			IF/F	HR/OF	Out %		Runs Per Event				Total Runs vs. Avg.				
	K%	BB%	GB%	LD%	FB%			GB	OF	NIP	GB	LD	OF	NIP	GB	LD	FB	Tot
Holliday M	17	13	46	22	33	.09	.16	65	83	.09	.11	.44	.26	9	14	12	11	46
Hawpe B	24	14	38	23	39	.03	.18	73	80	.06	.05	.42	.29	5	-1	5	20	28
Iannetta C	23	17	38	21	41	.10	.19	71	88	.09	.06	.48	.27	9	-0	4	9	22
Spilborghs R	15	14	55	21	24	.07	.14	72	73	.11	.05	.40	.31	6	2	3	4	14
Helton T	14	17	38	23	38	.07	.08	82	86	.14	-.01	.40	.12	11	-5	5	-3	8
Stewart I	31	12	31	25	44	.11	.15	74	81	.02	.04	.45	.26	-2	-2	3	5	5
Atkins G	15	6	37	22	41	.10	.10	74	82	.02	.04	.36	.18	-5	-3	4	8	4
Barmes C	17	5	29	22	49	.11	.08	70	77	-.01	.07	.36	.18	-7	0	3	8	4
Smith G	19	12	45	21	34	.00	.14	63	88	.07	.12	.25	.20	1	3	-2	1	3
Baker J	26	8	43	24	33	.00	.17	73	85	-.00	.05	.37	.26	-5	1	1	6	2
Tulowitzki T	13	10	42	20	37	.13	.08	79	79	.08	-.00	.38	.16	2	-7	2	-1	-3
Podsednik S	15	9	51	24	24	.03	.03	80	84	.06	.02	.34	.07	0	-1	1	-5	-4
Torrealba Y	17	7	50	17	33	.08	.10	73	91	.02	.05	.41	.13	-3	0	-2	-3	-7
Quintanilla O	20	6	52	20	28	.11	.05	71	89	-.00	.08	.39	.06	-3	2	-1	-8	-10
Taveras W	15	8	52	20	28	.14	.01	72	84	.04	.06	.27	.04	-2	12	-11	-19	-21
MLB Average	18	10	44	20	36	.10	.11	74	84	.05	.04	.39	.18	--	--	--	--	--

Pitching Stats

Player	PRC	IP	BFP	G	GS	K	BB	IBB	HBP	H	HR	DP	DER	SB	CS	PO	W	L	Sv	Op	Hld	H-A	R^L	RA	ERA	FIP
Jimenez U	87	198.7	868	34	34	172	103	4	10	182	11	20	.691	19	3	3	12	0	0	0	0	-.035	-.023	4.39	3.99	3.84
Cook A	80	211.3	886	32	32	96	48	2	4	236	13	36	.676	5	8	4	16	9	0	0	0	-.020	-.017	4.34	3.96	3.80
Francis J *	49	143.7	636	24	24	94	49	4	3	164	21	12	.689	9	2	1	4	0	0	0	0	.015	-.024	5.26	5.01	4.80
de la Rosa J	48	130.0	571	28	23	128	62	3	7	128	13	14	.665	13	5	3	10	8	0	0	0	-.003	.017	5.33	4.92	4.06
Fuentes B *	40	62.7	256	67	0	82	22	1	1	47	3	1	.696	4	1	2	1	5	30	34	6	.075	-.044	3.16	2.73	2.26
Buchholz T	39	66.3	263	63	0	56	18	2	2	45	5	6	.753	6	2	0	6	6	1	3	21	.013	-.010	3.12	2.17	3.31
Grilli J	36	61.3	264	51	0	59	31	6	1	55	1	10	.669	4	2	0	3	2	1	1	4	-.029	-.042	3.23	2.93	2.76
Corpas M	31	79.7	346	76	0	50	23	4	2	93	7	13	.663	2	0	0	3	4	4	13	19	-.012	.019	4.63	4.52	3.88
Rusch G *	24	64.0	275	23	9	43	14	3	0	72	8	4	.686	2	0	0	4	3	0	1	1	-.031	-.083	4.92	4.78	4.00
Speier R	22	51.0	217	43	0	33	18	2	4	52	3	9	.686	6	2	0	2	1	0	1	3	.048	-.039	4.06	4.06	3.85
Herges M	21	64.3	294	58	0	46	24	5	5	79	5	7	.640	1	2	0	3	4	0	5	4	.024	.048	5.60	5.04	3.90
Vizcaino L	17	46.0	203	43	0	49	19	1	1	48	10	5	.685	2	0	0	1	2	0	1	1	-.022	-.198	5.48	5.28	5.14
Reynolds G	11	62.0	294	14	13	22	26	3	4	83	14	8	.689	3	0	0	2	8	0	0	0	.010	-.040	8.42	8.13	6.73
Redman M *	9	45.3	211	10	9	20	16	2	1	61	7	7	.659	2	0	0	2	5	0	0	0	-.021	-.039	7.94	7.54	5.32
Wells K	8	27.3	126	15	2	22	19	2	1	29	3	6	.667	1	2	1	1	2	0	0	0	.121	.026	6.26	5.27	4.99
Arias A	7	13.7	56	12	0	5	4	0	1	12	1	2	.756	1	0	0	0	0	0	0	0	.239	-.093	2.63	2.63	4.52
Hernandez L	7	40.3	184	8	8	13	14	1	1	58	7	8	.651	0	1	1	3	3	0	0	0	-.033	.015	8.03	8.03	5.85
Morales F *	6	25.3	120	5	5	9	17	2	1	28	2	2	.714	5	0	0	1	2	0	0	0	-.102	-.125	6.39	6.39	5.41
de los Santo	3	8.0	40	2	2	10	11	0	0	6	1	1	.722	0	0	0	0	1	0	0	0	--	.259	5.63	5.63	6.45
Register S	2	10.0	49	10	0	8	6	1	0	13	4	0	.710	0	0	0	0	0	0	0	0	-.001	-.215	9.00	9.00	8.30
Newman J *	1	8.7	49	8	0	6	6	1	2	15	3	1	.625	1	0	0	0	0	0	0	0	.054	.131	9.35	9.35	8.74
Bowie M *	1	8.0	38	10	0	5	3	0	1	11	1	2	.607	0	0	0	0	1	0	0	0	.212	-.010	9.00	9.00	5.08
Hirsh J	1	8.7	46	4	1	6	4	0	0	15	3	0	.606	0	0	0	0	0	0	0	0	.057	-.081	10.38	8.31	7.70
Capellan J	1	2.0	9	1	0	2	0	0	0	3	0	0	.571	0	0	0	0	0	0	0	0	--	.083	4.50	4.50	1.20
Bowers C *	1	6.7	33	5	0	5	5	0	1	11	2	2	.550	0	0	0	0	0	0	0	0	.024	-.016	13.50	13.50	8.30

Italicized stats have been adjusted for home park.

Batted Ball Pitching Stats

Player	% of PA		% of Batted Balls					Out %		Runs Per Event				Total Runs vs. Avg.				
	K%	BB%	GB%	LD%	FB%	IF/F	HR/OF	GB	OF	NIP	GB	LD	OF	NIP	GB	LD	FB	Tot
Buchholz T	21	8	36	21	43	.14	.08	82	92	.01	-.01	.38	.07	-3	-5	-2	-7	-16
Fuentes B	32	9	33	22	46	.09	.05	79	81	-.01	.03	.38	.11	-5	-3	-4	-5	-16
Jimenez U	20	13	54	18	28	.08	.07	77	79	.07	.03	.40	.16	8	-2	-8	-11	-12
Grilli J	22	12	43	25	32	.05	.02	75	86	.05	.03	.42	.03	1	-2	4	-9	-6
Speier R	15	10	53	18	29	.06	.07	75	83	.07	.03	.39	.12	1	-0	-1	-3	-3
Cook A	11	6	56	20	24	.14	.09	78	73	.05	.02	.39	.24	-5	-6	9	-1	-3
Rusch G	16	5	40	23	37	.15	.12	76	84	-.00	.04	.42	.20	-4	-1	5	1	1
Corpas M	14	7	50	23	28	.08	.10	75	83	.04	.04	.41	.18	-2	-0	6	-2	2
Wells K	17	16	57	17	26	.05	.15	72	76	.11	.05	.36	.29	3	0	-1	1	3
de la Rosa J	22	12	46	20	34	.11	.12	72	78	.05	.06	.39	.22	2	2	-3	2	4
Morales F	8	15	40	20	40	.06	.06	89	75	.19	-.04	.41	.19	4	-3	1	2	4
Vizcaino L	24	10	33	18	50	.17	.19	67	77	.02	.08	.30	.34	-1	1	-4	9	4
Herges M	16	10	40	26	34	.08	.07	73	79	.06	.04	.41	.17	1	-1	8	0	9
Redman M	9	8	47	25	28	.02	.13	76	79	.10	.03	.43	.25	1	-1	7	4	11
Hernandez L	7	8	47	21	32	.08	.13	68	75	.13	.08	.35	.28	1	4	2	6	13
Francis J	15	8	44	20	36	.09	.11	76	81	.05	.05	.43	.20	-1	3	6	6	14
Reynolds G	7	10	45	22	33	.09	.19	71	88	.15	.07	.33	.29	4	4	2	10	20
MLB Average	18	10	44	20	36	.10	.11	74	84	.05	.04	.39	.18	--	--	--	--	--

Fielding Stats

Name	Inn	SBA/G	CS%	ERA	WP+PB/G	PO	A	TE	FE	Grade
Catchers										
Iannetta C	837.0	0.53	16%	4.61	0.462	606	51	0	0	D
Torrealba Y	581.0	0.88	21%	5.13	0.434	433	26	1	1	--
Melhuse A	22.0	0.82	0%	0.82	0.000	17	5	0	0	--
Bellorin E	6.0	0.00	0%	6.00	0.000	4	0	0	0	--

Name	Inn	PO	A	TE	FE	FPct	DPS	DPT	ZR	OOZ	Grade
First Base											
Helton T	715.3	830	57	1	2	.997	14	0	.819	30	--
Atkins G	527.7	551	23	3	3	.990	3	0	.681	9	--
Baker J	128.7	143	5	0	0	1.000	0	0	.783	4	--
Koshansky J	74.3	71	6	0	1	.987	2	0	.889	3	--
Second Base											
Barmes C	486.0	91	178	1	5	.978	13	21	.891	12	--
Baker J	369.7	71	131	1	3	.981	12	17	.823	11	--
Quintanilla O	212.7	40	72	0	1	.991	12	11	.848	5	--
Nix J	143.3	27	61	0	0	1.000	4	5	.889	6	--
Herrera J	122.0	34	48	0	2	.976	4	9	.791	5	--
Stewart I	93.0	16	38	0	1	.982	1	3	.861	3	--
Bernier D	11.0	5	2	0	0	1.000	0	0	1.000	1	--
Atkins G	8.3	3	5	0	0	1.000	2	0	1.000	0	--
Shortstop											
Tulowitzki T	863.3	190	311	4	4	.984	34	35	.884	18	D
Quintanilla O	288.7	42	100	2	1	.979	12	9	.854	11	--
Barmes C	285.0	57	113	1	2	.983	16	14	.822	11	--
Herrera J	9.0	2	4	0	0	1.000	0	0	1.000	0	--
Third Base											
Atkins G	797.0	47	197	5	4	.964	21	1	.699	27	D
Stewart I	531.3	40	127	4	6	.944	13	0	.718	14	--
Baker J	61.0	5	17	0	0	1.000	4	0	.632	2	--
Barmes C	48.3	1	10	0	1	.917	3	0	.727	1	--
Iannetta C	8.3	1	1	0	0	1.000	0	0	.500	0	--

Name	Inn	PO	A	TE	FE	FPct	DPS	DPT	ZR	OOZ	Grade
Left Field											
Holliday M	1229.0	240	9	0	3	.988	6	0	.905	50	C
Spilborghs R	166.7	30	0	0	0	1.000	0	0	.957	8	--
Podsednik S	30.0	7	0	0	0	1.000	0	0	.875	0	--
Smith S	17.7	5	0	0	0	1.000	0	0	.667	3	--
Sullivan C	2.3	0	0	0	0	.000	0	0	.000	0	--
Center Field											
Taveras W	993.0	282	6	2	5	.976	4	0	.908	74	B
Podsednik S	201.3	55	1	0	2	.966	0	0	.915	12	--
Spilborghs R	130.7	34	0	0	0	1.000	0	0	.969	3	--
Fowler D	49.7	12	1	0	0	1.000	2	0	1.000	2	--
Smith S	46.3	19	0	0	1	.950	0	0	.938	4	--
Sullivan C	25.0	3	0	0	0	1.000	0	0	.667	1	--
Right Field											
Hawpe B	1172.0	186	9	2	7	.956	0	0	.861	27	F-
Spilborghs R	146.0	37	0	1	1	.949	0	0	.886	6	--
Smith S	86.0	18	1	0	0	1.000	0	0	.941	2	--
Baker J	21.0	2	0	0	1	.667	0	0	.500	1	--
Sullivan C	11.0	1	0	0	0	1.000	0	0	1.000	0	--
Barmes C	6.0	2	0	0	0	1.000	0	0	1.000	0	--
Podsednik S	3.0	1	0	0	0	1.000	0	0	--	--	--
Fowler D	1.0	0	0	0	0	.000	0	0	--	--	--

Detroit Tigers

Stat Facts:

- Nate Robertson's 43 Pitching Runs Created was last in the majors among 162+ IP pitchers
- Base stealers went just 8-for-17 against Justin Verlander
- Kenny Rogers allowed only 1 stolen base in 3 attempts
- Rogers' 10% K rate tied for lowest among 162+ IP pitchers
- 51% of the batted balls by Marcus Thames were fly balls
- Of his outfield flies, 26% were home runs
- Armando Galarraga's FIP was 1.22 higher than his ERA
- Curtis Granderson made 86 OOZ plays
- Placido Polanco turned 61 double plays
- Mike Hessman put the ball in play 18 times, and hit 5 home runs
- Magglio Ordonez stole 1 base in 6 attempts, and grounded into 27 DPs
- Edgar Renteria's L^R was .135

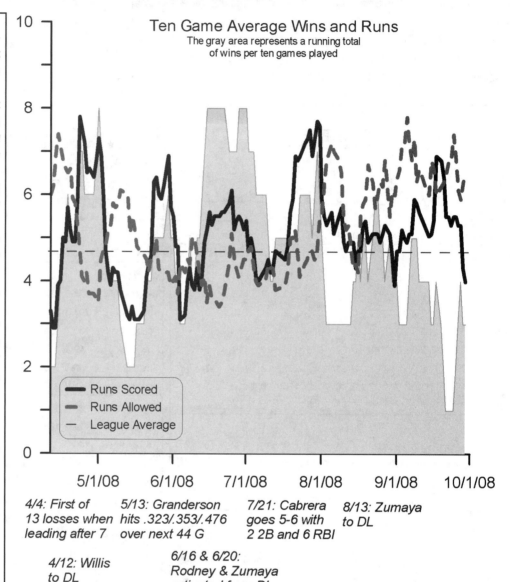

Ten Game Average Wins and Runs
The gray area represents a running total of wins per ten games played

Legend:
— Runs Scored
-- Runs Allowed
— League Average

4/4: First of 13 losses when leading after 7

4/12: Willis to DL

5/13: Granderson hits .323/.353/.476 over next 44 G

6/16 & 6/20: Rodney & Zumaya activated from DL

7/21: Cabrera goes 5-6 with 2 2B and 6 RBI

8/13: Zumaya to DL

Team Batting and Pitching/Fielding Stats by Month

	April	May	June	July	Aug	Sept/Oct
Wins	13	10	19	13	11	8
Losses	15	17	8	13	17	18
RS/G	5.1	4.4	5.1	5.8	4.7	5.3
RA/G	5.3	4.9	4.2	5.0	5.8	6.6
OBP	.355	.310	.360	.348	.333	.334
SLG	.436	.402	.466	.465	.434	.460
FIP	4.74	4.73	4.35	4.63	5.21	4.65
DER	.716	.688	.693	.696	.667	.652

Batting Stats

Player	BR	Runs	RBI	PA	Outs	H	2B	3B	HR	TB	K	BB	IBB	HBP	SH	SF	SB	CS	GDP	H-A	L^R	BA	OBP	SLG	GPA
Cabrera M	109	85	127	684	452	180	36	2	37	331	126	56	6	3	0	9	1	0	16	.002	.025	.292	.349	.537	.292
Granderson C	98	112	66	629	409	155	26	13	22	273	111	71	1	3	1	1	12	4	7	-.003	.055	.280	.365	.494	.288
Ordonez M	89	72	103	623	415	178	32	2	21	277	76	53	2	3	0	6	1	5	27	.059	.007	.317	.376	.494	.292
Polanco P	75	90	58	629	417	178	34	3	8	242	43	35	2	6	4	4	7	1	14	-.029	.030	.307	.350	.417	.262
Guillen C +	63	68	54	489	314	120	29	2	10	183	67	60	3	3	2	4	9	3	11	.036	.001	.286	.376	.436	.278
Renteria E	59	69	55	547	389	136	22	2	10	192	64	37	1	0	2	5	6	3	19	.080	.135	.270	.317	.382	.238
Sheffield G	53	52	57	482	345	94	16	0	19	167	83	58	3	5	0	1	9	2	19	.014	.007	.225	.326	.400	.246
Thames M	46	50	56	342	249	76	12	0	25	163	95	24	0	0	0	2	0	3	6	.003	.030	.241	.292	.516	.261
Inge B	45	41	51	407	283	71	16	4	11	128	94	43	2	8	5	4	4	3	4	.063	.010	.205	.303	.369	.229
Joyce M *	37	40	33	277	186	61	16	3	12	119	65	31	0	2	0	2	0	2	3	-.024	.021	.252	.339	.492	.276
Rodriguez I	34	33	32	328	223	89	16	3	5	126	52	19	1	2	3	2	6	1	9	.054	-.005	.295	.338	.417	.257
Santiago R +	25	30	18	156	90	35	6	2	4	57	17	22	0	5	5	0	1	0	1	.076	.046	.282	.411	.460	.300
Raburn R	20	26	20	199	142	43	10	1	4	67	49	16	1	0	1	0	3	1	2	-.016	.009	.236	.298	.368	.226
Thomas C *	16	7	9	133	84	33	9	1	1	47	26	14	1	1	2	0	2	0	1	.125	-.054	.284	.366	.405	.266
Larish J *	14	12	16	111	81	27	6	0	2	39	34	7	0	0	0	0	2	2	2	-.031	.059	.260	.306	.375	.232
Ryan D	8	6	7	50	30	14	2	0	2	22	13	5	0	0	0	1	0	0	0	.015	.285	.318	.380	.500	.296
Hessman M	8	6	7	31	19	8	1	0	5	24	9	2	0	2	0	0	0	0	0	.334	-.181	.296	.387	.889	.396
Sardinha D	3	2	3	49	38	7	0	1	0	9	11	4	0	0	1	0	0	0	1	.139	-.021	.159	.229	.205	.154
Jones J *	2	10	5	90	69	13	2	1	1	20	18	8	0	1	0	2	0	1	2	.135	.182	.165	.244	.253	.173
Hollimon M +	2	4	2	25	17	6	2	1	1	13	6	1	0	0	0	1	0	0	0	.045	-.279	.261	.280	.565	.267
Clevlen B	1	4	1	28	19	5	0	0	0	5	8	3	0	0	1	0	0	0	0	.193	-.037	.208	.296	.208	.185
Galarraga A	1	2	0	6	2	0	0	0	0	0	1	3	0	0	1	0	0	0	0	-.270	.300	.000	.600	.000	.270

Italicized stats have been adjusted for home park.

Batted Ball Batting Stats

Player	% of PA		% of Batted Balls					Out %		Runs Per Event				Total Runs vs. Avg.				
	K%	BB%	GB%	LD%	FB%	IF/F	HR/OF	GB	OF	NIP	GB	LD	OF	NIP	GB	LD	FB	Tot
Cabrera M	18	9	41	20	39	.11	.19	71	84	.03	.06	.40	.30	-3	3	2	26	28
Granderson C	18	12	40	19	41	.06	.11	68	84	.07	.09	.41	.20	5	8	1	11	25
Ordonez M	12	9	44	20	36	.07	.12	74	79	.08	.03	.38	.22	3	-2	6	13	20
Guillen C	14	13	45	20	35	.13	.08	68	91	.11	.08	.46	.10	8	6	8	-8	14
Joyce M	23	12	35	17	47	.12	.16	75	86	.04	.06	.49	.24	0	-0	0	8	8
Santiago R	11	17	44	23	33	.03	.12	71	86	.17	.07	.37	.18	6	1	1	0	8
Thames M	28	7	32	17	51	.19	.26	71	87	-.02	.06	.42	.37	-7	-1	-4	18	6
Polanco P	7	7	47	19	35	.08	.04	73	83	.11	.05	.40	.08	1	5	6	-11	1
Thomas C	20	11	40	19	41	.08	.03	75	73	.05	.04	.45	.17	1	-1	1	0	1
Rodriguez I	16	6	54	22	24	.03	.09	76	81	.02	.04	.39	.17	-3	0	4	-3	-2
Larish J	31	6	44	19	37	.12	.09	61	81	-.03	.13	.40	.16	-3	2	-1	-1	-3
Raburn R	25	8	47	14	39	.16	.10	70	78	-.00	.08	.41	.20	-3	3	-4	-0	-4
Sheffield G	17	13	43	14	43	.17	.13	73	91	.08	.04	.43	.15	6	-1	-7	-4	-5
Renteria E	12	7	46	22	32	.09	.08	74	83	.05	.04	.32	.13	-2	0	1	-6	-7
Inge B	23	13	37	16	46	.10	.10	77	88	.05	.03	.37	.15	1	-4	-8	-1	-12
MLB Average	18	10	44	20	36	.10	.11	74	84	.05	.04	.39	.18	--	--	--	--	--

Pitching Stats

Player	PRC	IP	BFP	G	GS	K	BB	IBB	HBP	H	HR	DP	DER	SB	CS	PO	W	L	Sv	Op	Hld	H-A	R^L	RA	ERA	FIP
Galarraga A	76	178.7	746	30	28	126	61	2	6	152	28	17	.745	7	1	0	13	7	0	1	0	.056	-.088	4.18	3.73	4.95
Verlander J	70	201.0	880	33	33	163	87	8	14	195	18	15	.696	8	9	2	11	17	0	0	0	-.015	-.009	5.33	4.84	4.16
Rogers K *	46	173.7	782	30	30	82	71	3	9	212	22	32	.674	1	2	3	9	13	0	0	0	.002	-.008	6.12	5.70	5.26
Miner Z	43	118.0	509	45	13	62	46	3	6	118	10	11	.717	8	4	0	8	5	0	3	6	.022	-.027	4.58	4.27	4.53
Robertson N	43	168.7	761	32	28	108	62	7	2	218	26	25	.648	7	4	1	7	11	0	0	0	-.065	-.016	6.62	6.35	4.97
Lopez A	38	78.7	344	48	0	61	22	4	2	86	9	6	.672	4	1	0	4	1	0	1	4	-.067	-.044	3.78	3.55	3.93
Bonderman J	25	71.3	319	12	12	44	36	2	3	75	9	9	.692	2	5	0	3	4	0	0	0	.044	-.020	4.92	4.29	5.19
Seay B *	25	56.3	246	60	0	58	25	7	2	59	4	5	.637	2	1	0	1	2	0	1	13	.037	.020	4.47	4.47	3.16
Dolsi F	21	47.7	218	42	0	29	28	5	3	50	3	4	.677	10	2	0	1	5	2	3	7	-.064	-.142	3.97	3.97	4.47
Rodney F	17	40.3	188	38	0	49	30	5	2	34	3	1	.680	4	0	0	6	13	19	5		-.109	.009	4.91	4.91	3.85
Fossum C *	13	41.3	179	31	0	28	18	1	3	44	4	7	.675	0	1	0	3	1	0	1	6	-.075	-.082	5.66	5.66	4.58
Jones T	9	41.7	193	45	0	14	18	3	4	50	5	6	.691	2	0	0	4	1	18	21	0	.034	-.006	6.48	4.97	5.49
Bautista D	9	19.0	83	16	0	10	14	0	2	15	1	3	.750	1	0	0	0	1	0	0	3	-.031	.090	3.32	3.32	5.39
Zumaya J	9	23.3	114	21	0	22	22	4	0	24	3	2	.672	1	0	0	0	2	1	5	5	-.009	.063	5.01	3.47	5.33
Rapada C *	8	21.3	94	25	0	15	14	1	1	19	0	2	.688	0	1	2	3	0	0	0	2	-.022	-.012	4.64	4.22	3.79
Glover G	8	20.3	86	18	0	15	4	0	1	22	4	2	.677	0	1	0	1	1	0	1	3	-.123	.052	4.87	4.43	4.90
Grilli J	7	13.7	59	9	0	10	7	1	1	12	1	2	.725	0	0	0	0	1	0	1	0	.063	-.077	3.29	3.29	4.25
Bonine E	6	26.7	117	5	5	9	5	0	2	36	3	8	.633	2	1	0	2	1	0	0	0	-.055	-.041	6.41	5.40	4.81
Garcia F	6	15.0	61	3	3	12	6	0	1	11	3	1	.795	1	1	0	1	1	0	0	0	.297	.074	4.80	4.20	5.63
Beltran F	5	13.0	56	11	0	9	6	1	0	13	3	2	.737	0	0	0	1	0	0	0	2	.070	.060	4.85	4.85	6.00
Lambert C	4	20.7	102	8	3	15	7	1	2	31	3	1	.600	7	0	0	1	2	0	0	0	.086	-.054	7.84	5.66	4.83
Willis D *	4	24.0	122	8	7	18	35	1	1	18	4	4	.781	0	0	0	0	2	0	0	0	.023	-.152	9.38	9.38	8.27
Farnsworth K	4	16.0	76	16	0	18	5	1	0	27	4	4	.510	1	1	0	1	1	0	3	3	-.145	.109	7.88	6.75	4.98
Cruceta F	4	11.7	56	13	0	11	10	1	0	13	2	2	.667	1	0	0	0	3	0	2	1	.085	-.066	6.17	5.40	5.89

Italicized stats have been adjusted for home park.

Batted Ball Pitching Stats

Player	% of PA		% of Batted Balls					Out %		Runs Per Event				Total Runs vs. Avg.				
	K%	BB%	GB%	LD%	FB%	IF/F	HR/OF	GB	OF	NIP	GB	LD	OF	NIP	GB	LD	FB	Tot
Galarraga A	17	9	44	17	40	.11	.14	79	87	.05	.01	.37	.21	-2	-8	-9	8	-11
Verlander J	19	11	40	18	42	.10	.08	71	90	.06	.07	.42	.10	5	5	-4	-13	-7
Miner Z	12	10	45	20	35	.07	.07	76	79	.10	.04	.30	.17	4	-2	-5	1	-2
Seay B	24	11	38	21	40	.11	.07	63	83	.03	.11	.39	.13	-0	3	-0	-2	0
Rodney F	26	18	40	26	33	.15	.10	80	81	.07	.02	.41	.19	3	-1	1	-2	2
Dolsi F	13	14	51	22	27	.07	.08	81	72	.12	-.00	.34	.20	5	-3	1	-0	2
Lopez A	18	7	29	22	49	.11	.07	69	86	.02	.07	.45	.11	-3	1	7	-1	3
Fossum C	16	12	45	19	37	.21	.11	72	70	.08	.04	.35	.27	2	0	-1	2	3
Bonderman J	14	12	47	16	37	.10	.12	67	88	.10	.08	.34	.16	4	5	-5	-0	5
Bonine E	8	6	46	20	34	.09	.10	76	74	.09	.01	.47	.24	-0	-1	3	3	5
Jones T	7	11	43	24	33	.08	.11	82	86	.17	-.01	.43	.16	4	-4	6	0	6
Rogers K	10	10	41	21	38	.11	.10	76	82	.11	.03	.44	.19	9	-3	15	9	29
Robertson N	14	8	44	19	37	.10	.13	73	75	.06	.05	.43	.28	0	5	6	23	35
MLB Average	18	10	44	20	36	.10	.11	74	84	.05	.04	.39	.18	--	--	--	--	--

Fielding Stats

Name	Inn	SBA/G	CS%	ERA	WP+PB/G	PO	A	TE	FE	Grade
Catchers										
Rodriguez I	706.3	0.62	35%	4.24	0.420	447	44	3	0	A+
Inge B	493.7	0.66	28%	5.62	0.565	370	33	0	0	--
Sardinha D	122.7	0.37	20%	4.70	0.147	109	8	1	0	--
Ryan D	122.3	0.81	36%	6.11	1.104	99	5	0	0	--

Name	Inn	PO	A	TE	FE	FPct	DPS	DPT	ZR	OOZ	Grade
First Base											
Cabrera M	1204.0	1117	73	0	8	.992	8	0	.757	25	D
Guillen C	162.0	142	11	0	2	.987	1	0	.714	7	--
Thames M	41.0	34	1	0	0	1.000	1	0	.500	0	--
Larish J	38.0	41	3	0	0	1.000	0	0	.750	1	--
Second Base											
Polanco P	1201.0	323	374	5	3	.989	33	61	.858	39	A+
Raburn R	118.0	27	34	2	3	.924	4	8	.767	3	--
Santiago R	117.7	30	36	0	0	1.000	4	9	.742	4	--
Hollimon M	8.0	3	2	0	0	1.000	0	0		0	--
Shortstop											
Renteria E	1173.0	197	365	5	11	.972	57	32	.800	42	D
Santiago R	227.7	45	70	1	2	.975	4	10	.791	4	--
Hollimon M	44.0	1	12	1	0	.929	2	0	.909	2	--
Third Base											
Guillen C	749.7	68	195	5	9	.949	14	1	.700	32	C
Inge B	324.3	38	80	0	1	.992	15	0	.750	13	--
Cabrera M	116.0	15	30	4	1	.900	2	2	.600	2	--
Larish J	83.0	10	17	1	1	.931	1	0	.542	2	--
Raburn R	79.0	8	14	0	3	.880	1	0	.700	1	--
Hessman M	70.0	7	20	1	0	.964	2	0	.750	6	--
Santiago R	21.0	2	3	1	1	.714	0	0	.250	1	--
Hollimon M	2.0	1	0	0	0	1.000	0	0	--	--	--

Name	Inn	PO	A	TE	FE	FPct	DPS	DPT	ZR	OOZ	Grade
Left Field											
Thames M	488.0	120	3	0	5	.961	2	0	.812	25	--
Joyce M	409.3	94	2	1	2	.970	0	0	.904	19	--
Jones J	172.0	38	1	0	1	.975	0	0	.857	8	--
Thomas C	139.0	40	4	0	2	.957	2	0	.848	12	--
Raburn R	127.7	29	2	0	0	.969	0	0	.952	9	--
Sheffield G	47.0	13	0	0	0	1.000	0	0	.909	3	--
Clevlen B	39.0	16	1	0	0	1.000	0	0	.933	2	--
Guillen C	17.0	6	0	0	0	1.000	0	0	.833	1	--
Inge B	6.0	0	0	0	0	0.000	0	0	--	--	--
Center Field											
Granderson	1188.0	366	5	0	4	.989	2	0	.921	86	C
Thomas C	112.0	40	0	0	2	.952	0	0	.943	7	--
Inge B	94.0	26	2	0	0	1.000	0	0	.947	8	--
Raburn R	30.0	12	0	0	0	1.000	0	0	.778	5	--
Clevlen B	21.0	6	0	0	0	1.000	0	0	.800	2	--
Right Field											
Ordonez M	1144.0	220	8	1	4	.979	0	0	.858	38	F-
Joyce M	161.0	42	0	0	1	.977	0	0	.865	10	--
Raburn R	84.0	22	0	0	1	.957	0	0	.905	3	--
Thames M	25.0	8	0	0	0	1.000	0	0		2	--
Thomas C	22.0	8	0	0	0	1.000	0	0	.875	1	--
Clevlen B	9.0	1	0	0	0	1.000	0	0	.500	0	--

Florida Marlins

Stat Facts:
- Jeremy Hermida's H-A of -.085 was lowest among ML regulars
- Hermida's L^R was exactly .000
- Dan Uggla's L^R of -.095 was lowest among ML regulars
- 20% of Uggla's outfield flies were home runs
- Scott Olsen intentionally walked 13 batters, most in the majors
- Olsen picked off 4 runners
- Andrew Miller's FIP was 1.91 lower than his ERA, furthest under in the majors among 60+ IP pitchers
- Matt Lindstrom allowed 1 home run in 57 innings
- Taylor Tankersley allowed 6 in 18 innings
- Hanley Ramirez grounded into 5 DPs in 693 PAs
- Ramirez tied for fourth in the NL with 120 Base Runs
- Ramirez committed 14 throwing errors

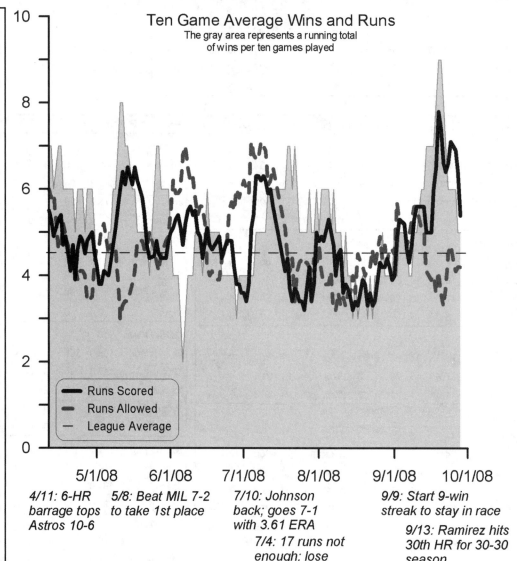

Ten Game Average Wins and Runs
The gray area represents a running total of wins per ten games played

— Runs Scored
- - Runs Allowed
- League Average

4/11: 6-HR barrage tops Astros 10-6

5/8: Beat MIL 7-2 to take 1st place

7/10: Johnson back; goes 7-1 with 3.61 ERA

7/4: 17 runs not enough; lose 18-17 to COL

9/9: Start 9-win streak to stay in race

9/13: Ramirez hits 30th HR for 30-30 season

Team Batting and Pitching/Fielding Stats by Month

	April	May	June	July	Aug	Sept/Oct
Wins	15	16	12	15	11	15
Losses	12	11	16	12	17	9
RS/G	4.5	5.3	4.5	5.0	3.7	5.9
RA/G	5.1	4.4	5.4	5.1	4.1	4.4
OBP	.323	.325	.307	.332	.321	.352
SLG	.450	.452	.421	.431	.383	.460
FIP	4.50	4.41	4.59	4.49	3.90	3.82
DER	.684	.721	.676	.697	.684	.708

Batting Stats

Player	BR	Runs	RBI	PA	Outs	H	2B	3B	HR	TB	K	BB	IBB	HBP	SH	SF	SB	CS	GDP	H-A	L^R	BA	OBP	SLG	GPA
Ramirez H	120	125	67	693	429	177	34	4	33	318	122	92	9	8	0	4	35	12	5	.015	-.051	.301	.400	.540	.321
Uggla D	101	97	92	619	408	138	37	1	32	273	171	77	6	8	0	3	5	5	10	-.054	-.095	.260	.360	.514	.297
Cantu J	94	92	95	685	471	174	41	0	29	302	111	40	6	10	0	7	6	2	15	.071	.029	.277	.327	.481	.273
Jacobs M *	76	67	93	519	366	118	27	2	32	245	119	36	10	1	0	5	1	0	7	-.039	.058	.247	.299	.514	.268
Ross C	74	59	73	506	347	120	29	5	22	225	116	33	2	7	0	5	6	1	5	-.035	.046	.260	.316	.488	.270
Hermida J *	69	74	61	559	390	125	22	3	17	204	138	48	5	7	1	1	6	1	12	-.085	-.000	.249	.323	.406	.252
Willingham J	59	54	51	416	271	89	21	5	15	165	82	48	2	14	1	2	3	2	7	-.008	-.002	.254	.364	.470	.287
Gonzalez L *	51	30	47	387	264	89	26	1	8	141	43	41	1	0	0	5	1	2	10	.010	.025	.261	.336	.413	.260
Amezaga A +	37	41	32	337	237	82	13	5	3	114	47	19	1	3	4	0	8	2	6	.058	-.028	.264	.312	.367	.237
Baker J *	37	32	32	233	144	59	14	0	5	88	48	30	4	2	1	3	0	0	6	.059	.087	.299	.392	.447	.294
Helms W	30	28	31	278	196	61	11	0	5	87	65	17	0	5	0	5	0	0	6	-.006	.047	.243	.299	.347	.226
Treanor M	25	18	23	234	159	49	7	0	2	62	53	18	1	3	5	2	1	0	2	-.012	-.036	.238	.306	.301	.217
Rabelo M +	8	9	10	122	89	22	1	0	3	32	25	8	0	1	1	3	0	1	1	-.108	.071	.202	.256	.294	.193
Andino R	8	7	9	68	51	13	2	0	2	21	23	4	0	0	1	0	0	0	1	.014	.009	.206	.254	.333	.202
Maybin C	7	9	2	36	16	16	2	0	0	18	8	3	0	0	1	0	4	0	0	-.090	-.080	.500	.543	.563	.393
Lo Duca P	5	3	3	40	25	10	2	0	0	12	2	6	0	0	0	0	0	0	1	.107	-.011	.294	.400	.353	.274
Nolasco R	3	1	5	75	55	9	2	0	0	11	35	2	0	0	10	0	0	0	1	-.100	-.093	.143	.169	.175	.122
Hendrickson	2	4	1	37	26	9	2	1	0	13	21	1	0	0	1	0	0	0	0	-.148	.171	.257	.278	.371	.222
Sanchez G	2	0	1	8	5	3	2	0	0	5	2	0	0	0	0	0	0	0	0	-.520	-.371	.375	.375	.625	.332
McPherson D	2	3	0	15	9	2	2	0	0	4	5	4	1	0	0	0	0	0	0	-.191	.350	.182	.400	.364	.276
Johnson J *	1	1	2	34	26	4	2	0	0	6	18	1	0	0	3	0	0	0	0	.014	.166	.133	.161	.200	.125
Olsen S *	1	1	3	73	54	8	0	0	0	8	28	3	0	0	8	0	0	0	0	.093	-.072	.129	.169	.129	.111
Jones J *	1	5	2	44	34	4	0	0	0	4	8	6	1	0	0	1	0	0	1	-.064	.128	.108	.227	.108	.132

Italicized stats have been adjusted for home park.

Batted Ball Batting Stats

Player	% of PA		% of Batted Balls					Out %		Runs Per Event				Total Runs vs. Avg.				
	K%	BB%	GB%	LD%	FB%	IF/F	HR/OF	GB	OF	NIP	GB	LD	OF	NIP	GB	LD	FB	Tot
Ramirez H	18	14	46	17	37	.10	.19	68	85	.09	.09	.52	.28	13	11	9	19	51
Uggla D	28	14	36	16	48	.08	.20	64	82	.04	.11	.43	.32	2	6	-8	28	28
Willingham J	20	15	39	19	42	.11	.12	70	85	.09	.08	.49	.19	7	2	3	3	16
Cantu J	16	7	34	21	45	.13	.14	68	89	.03	.09	.36	.19	-4	6	1	10	12
Baker J	21	14	49	25	26	.08	.11	74	78	.07	.04	.48	.20	3	1	6	-1	8
Ross C	23	8	36	21	43	.09	.13	78	81	.00	.02	.47	.25	-6	-5	6	14	8
Jacobs M	23	7	35	18	47	.10	.19	80	85	-.00	.01	.42	.30	-8	-6	-3	23	5
Gonzalez L	11	11	41	19	40	.13	.07	79	83	.11	.01	.42	.13	4	-4	2	-3	-1
Hermida J	25	10	46	18	36	.13	.14	71	84	.02	.06	.43	.22	-4	2	-4	2	-4
Rabelo M	20	7	49	20	31	.07	.08	72	87	.01	.06	.23	.11	-1	1	-3	-3	-7
Amezaga A	14	7	46	19	34	.13	.03	79	79	.03	.02	.41	.11	-2	-1	1	-6	-9
Helms W	23	8	42	20	38	.06	.07	74	79	.00	.04	.32	.14	-4	-1	-3	-2	-10
Treanor M	23	9	55	20	25	.26	.07	74	81	.02	.05	.38	.11	-2	1	-2	-7	-10
MLB Average	18	10	44	20	36	.10	.11	74	84	.05	.04	.39	.18	--	--	--	--	--

Pitching Stats

Player	PRC	IP	BFP	G	GS	K	BB	IBB	HBP	H	HR	DP	DER	SB	CS	PO	W	L	Sv	Op	Hld	H-A	R^L	RA	ERA	FIP
Nolasco R	98	212.3	868	34	32	186	42	6	6	192	28	12	.713	7	5	0	15	8	0	0	0	.017	-.018	3.73	3.52	3.76
Olsen S *	67	201.7	855	33	33	113	69	13	3	195	30	17	.725	8	7	4	8	11	0	0	0	-.054	-.079	4.73	4.20	4.89
Volstad C	41	84.3	365	15	14	52	36	4	5	76	3	6	.717	12	2	0	6	4	0	0	0	.018	.006	3.20	2.88	3.75
Johnson J	40	87.3	365	14	14	77	27	1	1	91	7	14	.660	5	2	0	7	1	0	0	0	.014	-.012	3.71	3.61	3.41
Hendrickson	36	133.7	590	36	19	81	48	7	5	148	17	11	.688	16	3	1	7	8	0	0	3	.045	-.026	5.86	5.45	4.68
Nelson J	35	54.0	230	59	0	60	22	4	2	42	5	4	.716	4	0	0	3	1	1	5	11	.008	.001	2.67	2.00	3.29
Gregg K	30	68.7	296	72	0	58	37	4	4	51	3	5	.727	6	2	0	7	8	29	38	4	.003	-.019	3.93	3.41	3.70
Lindstrom M	28	57.3	245	66	0	43	26	4	1	57	1	10	.672	1	1	0	3	3	5	6	14	-.017	-.077	3.30	3.14	3.13
Miller A *	27	107.3	492	29	20	89	56	4	4	120	7	12	.652	13	3	1	6	10	0	0	2	-.021	-.016	6.54	5.87	3.96
Waechter D	25	63.3	275	48	0	46	21	3	2	63	7	3	.704	6	1	0	4	2	0	1	9	-.039	-.076	4.12	3.69	4.13
Pinto R *	24	64.7	284	67	0	56	39	2	1	52	9	9	.727	1	1	0	2	5	0	2	17	.026	.083	4.59	4.45	5.18
Kensing L	23	55.3	254	48	0	55	33	5	4	50	7	5	.697	11	0	0	3	1	0	3	5	.024	.043	4.23	4.23	4.59
Rhodes A *	21	13.3	54	25	0	14	3	2	0	11	0	1	.676	0	0	0	2	0	1	1	11	-.174	-.208	0.68	0.68	1.33
Miller J	16	46.7	202	46	0	43	20	3	3	46	4	4	.674	4	1	0	4	2	0	1	7	.050	-.076	5.01	4.24	3.76
Sanchez A	15	51.7	241	10	10	50	27	2	6	54	7	2	.669	7	0	1	2	5	0	0	0	-.058	-.138	6.10	5.57	4.83
Badenhop B	12	47.3	218	13	8	35	21	1	3	55	7	2	.664	4	3	0	2	3	0	0	0	-.025	-.065	6.46	6.08	5.10
Tucker R	7	37.0	178	13	6	28	23	1	2	46	8	3	.667	2	1	0	2	3	0	1	0	-.004	-.046	8.27	8.27	6.45
Tankersley T	3	17.7	84	25	0	13	8	0	1	22	6	1	.696	0	0	0	0	1	0	2	4	-.155	-.006	8.15	8.15	7.67
VandenHurk	3	14.0	74	4	4	20	10	0	2	20	1	0	.537	0	0	0	1	1	0	0	0	-.154	.033	7.71	7.71	3.84
Gardner L	1	6.7	38	7	0	4	4	0	0	14	2	0	.571	0	0	0	0	0	0	0	0	.129	-.017	10.80	10.80	7.70

Italicized stats have been adjusted for home park.

Batted Ball Pitching Stats

Player	% of PA		% of Batted Balls					Out %		Runs Per Event				Total Runs vs. Avg.				
	K%	BB%	GB%	LD%	FB%	IF/F	HR/OF	GB	OF	NIP	GB	LD	OF	NIP	GB	LD	FB	Tot
Nolasco R	21	6	39	19	42	.12	.11	71	88	-.02	.07	.39	.16	-17	3	-6	-2	-21
Gregg K	20	14	45	20	35	.09	.03	79	82	.08	.01	.31	.07	4	-3	-5	-7	-12
Volstad C	14	11	53	18	29	.13	.03	79	77	.09	.02	.35	.11	3	-2	-4	-8	-10
Nelson J	26	10	40	23	38	.21	.12	82	86	.02	.00	.41	.17	-2	-4	-0	-3	-9
Johnson J	21	8	48	21	31	.09	.07	77	73	.01	.02	.39	.21	-4	-2	1	0	-6
Lindstrom M	18	11	46	23	30	.12	.02	73	86	.06	.05	.35	.05	1	1	0	-7	-5
Waechter D	17	8	32	23	44	.13	.09	71	87	.04	.08	.30	.13	-1	2	-2	-2	-2
Pinto R	20	15	46	17	37	.16	.13	75	89	.09	.04	.40	.15	5	0	-3	-3	-2
Miller J	21	11	32	24	44	.08	.07	65	86	.05	.10	.36	.13	0	2	1	-1	1
Kensing L	22	15	34	18	48	.23	.12	67	81	.07	.08	.34	.20	4	1	-4	1	2
Olsen S	13	8	37	20	42	.10	.11	74	89	.07	.05	.36	.15	0	1	-1	1	2
Sanchez A	21	13	40	27	32	.14	.12	68	95	.07	.09	.42	.11	2	2	5	-5	5
Badenhop B	16	11	54	20	26	.03	.18	72	75	.07	.06	.30	.33	2	2	-2	5	7
Hendrickson M	14	9	44	20	35	.12	.10	69	81	.07	.08	.33	.18	1	8	-3	2	8
Miller A	18	12	46	22	33	.09	.07	70	80	.07	.07	.44	.15	4	3	5	-4	8
Tucker R	16	14	44	18	39	.08	.16	67	89	.10	.09	.51	.20	3	2	2	3	11
MLB Average	18	10	44	20	36	.10	.11	74	84	.05	.04	.39	.18	--	--	--	--	--

Fielding Stats

Name	Inn	SBA/G	CS%	ERA	WP+PB/G	PO	A	TE	FE	Grade
Catchers										
Treanor M	524.7	0.96	21%	4.61	0.395	453	29	8	0	--
Baker J	496.0	0.83	13%	4.23	0.327	402	22	3	0	--
Rabelo M	262.7	0.72	24%	4.15	0.548	179	11	1	0	--
Hoover P	104.3	0.69	38%	5.95	0.949	84	8	0	0	--
Lo Duca P	47.7	0.94	0%	3.02	0.189	49	1	1	1	--

Name	Inn	PO	A	TE	FE	FPct	DPS	DPT	ZR	OOZ	Grade
First Base											
Jacobs M	927.3	825	62	5	6	.988	9	1	.624	15	F-
Cantu J	286.7	260	14	0	2	.993	4	0	.764	7	--
Helms W	209.3	185	13	1	1	.990	0	0	.750	6	--
Sanchez G	11.0	13	1	0	0	1.000	0	0	1.000	0	--
Lo Duca P	1.0	1	0	0	0	1.000	0	0	--	--	--
Second Base											
Uggla D	1272.0	297	390	5	8	.981	38	49	.812	45	B
Andino R	89.7	30	31	1	1	.968	2	5	.923	2	--
Amezaga A	73.0	19	18	0	1	.974	1	1	.929	2	--
Shortstop											
Ramirez H	1302.0	236	401	8	14	.967	47	34	.840	49	C
Amezaga A	125.3	22	31	0	0	1.000	2	2	.926	3	--
Andino R	8.0	0	2	0	0	1.000	0	0	1.000	0	--
Third Base											
Cantu J	1066.0	83	214	11	9	.937	24	0	.662	29	F-
Helms W	325.0	31	63	1	0	.989	3	0	.734	13	--
Amezaga A	25.7	2	5	0	0	1.000	0	0	1.000	1	--
McPherson D	17.0	0	1	0	0	1.000	0	0	.500	0	--
Andino R	1.0	0	0	0	0	.000	0	0	--	--	--

Name	Inn	PO	A	TE	FE	FPct	DPS	DPT	ZR	OOZ	Grade
Left Field											
Willingham J	855.3	166	7	0	0	1.000	0	0	.903	35	C
Gonzalez L	503.7	105	0	0	4	.963	0	0	.869	12	--
Ross C	45.0	10	1	0	0	1.000	0	0	.889	2	--
Jones J	20.3	4	0	0	0	1.000	0	0	1.000	2	--
Carroll B	10.0	4	0	0	0	1.000	0	0	.750	1	--
Helms W	1.0	0	0	0	0	.000	0	0	--	--	--
Center Field											
Ross C	866.0	254	7	0	0	1.000	4	0	.952	57	B
Amezaga A	457.3	144	6	0	1	.993	2	0	.942	33	--
Maybin C	63.0	23	0	0	0	1.000	0	0	.933	9	--
Jones J	41.0	13	0	0	0	1.000	0	0	.900	4	--
Andino R	6.0	2	0	0	0	1.000	0	0	1.000	0	--
Miller J	2.0	0	0	0	0	.000	0	0	--	--	--
Right Field											
Hermida J	1092.0	266	4	1	4	.982	0	0	.890	47	F-
Ross C	153.7	37	0	0	1	.974	0	0	.889	13	--
Gonzalez L	147.3	30	1	0	0	1.000	0	0	.857	6	--
Carroll B	28.3	9	2	0	0	1.000	0	0	1.000	3	--
Jones J	13.7	3	0	0	0	1.000	0	0	.750	0	--

Houston Astros

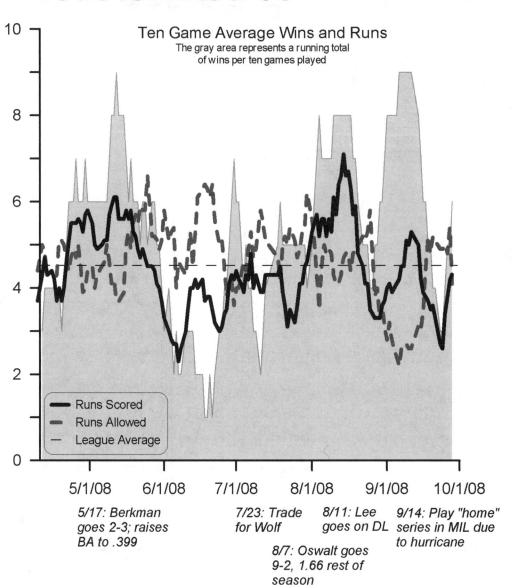

Stat Facts:

- Miguel Tejada led the majors with 32 GDP
- Lance Berkman stole a career-high 18 bases in 22 attempts
- Hunter Pence's LD% was lowest among NL regulars
- Pence had 16 assists, including 8 double plays
- Brandon Backe allowed 36 home runs, most in the majors, in just 167 innings
- 17% of the fly balls off Backe were homers, tied for the highest rate in the majors among 162+ IP pitchers
- Backe hit 2 homers himself, and had a .264 GPA
- The Astros turned zero double plays behind Jose Valverde
- Roy Oswalt allowed just 1 stolen base in 2 attempts
- 27% of Mark Loretta's batted balls were line drives
- Michael Bourn's GPA was .207
- Bourn made 82 OOZ plays

Ten Game Average Wins and Runs
The gray area represents a running total of wins per ten games played

- Runs Scored
- Runs Allowed
- League Average

5/17: Berkman goes 2-3; raises BA to .399

7/23: Trade for Wolf

8/11: Lee goes on DL

9/14: Play "home" series in MIL due to hurricane

8/7: Oswalt goes 9-2, 1.66 rest of season

Team Batting and Pitching/Fielding Stats by Month

	April	May	June	July	Aug	Sept/Oct
Wins	13	17	10	10	21	15
Losses	16	11	16	14	9	9
RS/G	4.5	4.8	3.8	4.3	4.9	4.2
RA/G	4.6	4.9	4.9	5.3	4.1	4.0
OBP	.300	.345	.318	.328	.323	.321
SLG	.405	.431	.417	.384	.470	.369
FIP	4.63	5.03	4.95	4.72	3.80	3.82
DER	.681	.705	.700	.691	.709	.711

Batting Stats

Player	BR	Runs	RBI	PA	Outs	H	2B	3B	HR	TB	K	BB	IBB	HBP	SH	SF	SB	CS	GDP	H-A	L^R	BA	OBP	SLG	GPA
Berkman L +	128	114	106	665	398	173	46	4	29	314	108	99	18	7	0	5	18	4	13	.032	-.081	.312	.420	.567	.334
Pence H	85	78	83	642	459	160	34	4	25	277	124	40	2	4	0	3	11	10	14	-.009	-.027	.269	.318	.466	.262
Lee C	84	61	100	481	308	137	27	0	28	248	49	37	7	3	0	5	4	1	8	.010	.009	.314	.368	.569	.311
Tejada M	61	92	66	666	492	179	38	3	13	262	72	24	4	6	1	3	7	7	32	.017	.008	.283	.314	.415	.248
Wigginton T	58	50	58	429	291	110	22	1	23	203	69	32	1	8	0	3	4	6	9	.111	.082	.285	.350	.526	.292
Matsui K +	51	58	33	422	273	110	26	3	6	160	53	37	0	0	7	3	20	5	3	.021	-.012	.293	.354	.427	.269
Bourn M *	43	57	29	514	373	107	10	4	5	140	111	37	0	2	7	1	41	10	3	.033	.035	.229	.288	.300	.207
Blum G +	43	36	53	356	254	78	14	1	14	136	54	21	2	3	0	7	1	2	5	.005	-.018	.240	.287	.418	.236
Erstad D *	37	49	31	342	239	89	16	0	4	117	68	14	3	2	2	2	2	3	3	-.035	.033	.276	.309	.363	.232
Loretta M	36	27	38	297	197	73	15	0	4	100	30	29	1	2	0	5	0	0	9	.021	.091	.280	.350	.383	.256
Ausmus B	24	15	24	250	175	47	8	0	3	64	41	25	3	2	6	1	0	2	4	.016	.082	.218	.303	.296	.213
Towles J	12	10	16	171	129	20	5	0	4	37	40	16	1	6	3	0	0	0	3	.075	.088	.137	.250	.253	.178
Newhan D *	11	11	12	111	80	27	5	2	2	42	28	6	0	0	0	1	1	0	3	.014	-.001	.260	.297	.404	.237
Quintero H	10	16	12	183	135	38	6	0	2	50	34	6	0	4	5	0	0	0	5	-.005	.025	.226	.270	.298	.198
Abercrombie	10	10	5	60	40	17	5	0	2	28	23	1	0	2	1	1	5	2	0	.077	.037	.309	.339	.509	.283
Backe B	4	8	3	56	34	13	2	0	2	21	18	3	0	1	5	0	0	0	0	.149	.302	.277	.333	.447	.264
Cruz J +	3	6	1	60	43	6	1	0	0	7	9	11	0	0	0	0	0	0	0	.121	.052	.122	.283	.143	.165
Castillo J	3	4	2	35	23	9	1	0	0	10	10	2	0	0	0	1	0	0	0	.004	.054	.281	.314	.313	.222
Oswalt R	2	3	5	75	55	15	0	0	0	15	18	0	0	0	5	0	0	0	0	.189	-.080	.214	.214	.214	.152
Saccomanno	2	1	2	11	8	2	1	0	1	6	3	0	0	0	0	0	0	0	0	.343	-.343	.200	.200	.600	.242
Chacon S	1	1	0	28	21	3	0	0	0	3	10	2	0	0	2	0	0	0	0	-.019	.223	.125	.192	.125	.119
Sampson C	1	0	0	26	19	3	0	0	0	3	9	1	0	0	3	0	0	0	0	-.038	.215	.136	.174	.136	.113
Hernandez R	1	0	1	6	3	1	0	0	0	1	2	1	0	0	1	0	0	0	0	-.200	.200	.250	.400	.250	.245
Cassel J	1	0	1	9	7	2	0	0	0	2	4	0	0	0	0	0	0	0	0	-.200	-.200	.222	.222	.222	.157

Italicized stats have been adjusted for home park.

Batted Ball Batting Stats

Player	% of PA		% of Batted Balls					Out %		Runs Per Event				Total Runs vs. Avg.				
	K%	BB%	GB%	LD%	FB%	IF/F	HR/OF	GB	OF	NIP	GB	LD	OF	NIP	GB	LD	FB	Tot
Berkman L	16	16	43	18	39	.07	.17	72	79	.11	.05	.46	.31	17	2	6	27	52
Lee C	10	8	35	21	44	.09	.16	73	90	.09	.05	.45	.21	2	1	12	14	29
Wigginton T	16	9	45	16	39	.12	.19	72	85	.06	.05	.45	.29	0	1	0	14	16
Pence H	19	7	52	14	34	.13	.17	67	85	.01	.09	.43	.27	-7	12	-8	12	8
Matsui K	13	9	46	21	34	.15	.07	76	82	.08	.04	.47	.14	1	0	8	-4	4
Loretta M	10	10	37	27	36	.06	.05	83	82	.12	-.02	.30	.12	3	-6	3	-2	-1
Newhan D	25	5	51	18	30	.26	.12	82	67	-.03	-.00	.49	.32	-3	-1	0	0	-3
Blum G	15	7	36	20	44	.18	.14	71	93	.03	.07	.28	.16	-3	2	-5	0	-6
Erstad D	20	5	51	25	24	.08	.04	76	77	-.03	.04	.40	.11	-7	1	6	-8	-8
Tejada M	11	5	48	23	29	.12	.09	79	84	.02	.00	.37	.15	-7	-8	10	-6	-11
Quintero H	19	5	59	12	29	.13	.06	72	81	-.01	.06	.25	.13	-3	2	-7	-4	-12
Ausmus B	16	11	45	18	36	.11	.05	79	78	.07	.02	.23	.12	1	-2	-7	-4	-12
Towles J	23	13	41	11	48	.18	.07	86	89	.05	-.03	.52	.09	1	-5	-4	-4	-13
Bourn M	22	8	54	17	29	.08	.04	71	91	.01	.07	.34	.05	-6	9	-12	-17	-26
MLB Average	18	10	44	20	36	.10	.11	74	84	.05	.04	.39	.18	--	--	--	--	--

Pitching Stats

Player	PRC	IP	BFP	G	GS	K	BB	IBB	HBP	H	HR	DP	DER	SB	CS	PO	W	L	Sv	Op	Hld	H-A	R^L	RA	ERA	FIP
Oswalt R	92	208.7	862	32	32	165	47	2	10	199	23	21	.710	1	1	0	17	10	0	0	0	.029	.001	3.84	3.54	3.84
Rodriguez W	57	137.3	587	25	25	131	44	3	5	136	14	13	.682	4	3	1	9	7	0	0	0	-.042	.032	4.26	3.54	3.62
Moehler B	50	150.0	650	31	26	82	36	1	4	166	20	8	.703	9	0	0	11	8	0	0	0	-.018	-.065	4.74	4.56	4.62
Backe B	45	166.7	756	31	31	127	77	2	4	202	36	21	.668	4	6	1	9	14	0	0	0	-.017	-.005	6.16	6.05	5.91
Sampson C	40	117.3	478	54	11	61	23	5	3	118	8	19	.697	2	2	0	6	4	0	2	11	.091	-.030	4.60	4.22	3.59
Geary G	39	64.0	262	55	0	45	28	5	2	45	3	6	.761	0	0	0	2	3	0	2	12	.045	-.044	2.53	2.53	3.58
Valverde J	38	72.0	303	74	0	83	23	6	2	62	10	0	.719	8	0	0	6	3	44	51	0	-.021	.018	3.50	3.38	3.49
Brocail D	31	68.7	286	72	0	64	21	5	3	63	8	6	.705	3	1	0	7	5	2	5	22	-.052	-.095	3.93	3.93	3.68
Wolf R *	31	70.7	301	12	12	57	24	4	4	68	7	5	.699	1	2	1	6	2	0	0	0	-.018	-.030	3.95	3.57	3.90
Chacon S	25	85.7	374	15	15	53	41	5	2	88	16	10	.718	2	3	2	2	3	0	0	0	.001	.012	5.46	5.04	5.72
Byrdak T *	24	55.3	237	59	0	47	29	2	2	45	10	4	.758	4	1	2	2	1	0	0	8	-.017	-.175	3.90	3.90	5.42
Hawkins L	23	21.0	79	24	0	25	5	1	0	11	0	0	.755	1	0	1	2	0	1	1	12	.051	-.068	1.29	0.43	1.39
Wright W *	18	55.7	250	71	0	57	34	4	4	45	8	4	.741	5	0	0	4	3	1	1	13	-.032	-.075	5.50	5.01	4.85
Villarreal O	10	37.7	168	35	0	21	17	0	2	42	12	6	.733	2	1	0	1	3	0	1	2	.001	.065	5.97	5.02	7.74
Borkowski D	7	36.0	173	26	0	24	14	5	1	54	9	4	.632	0	0	0	0	2	0	1	0	-.022	.014	7.50	7.50	5.95
Cassel J	7	30.3	132	9	3	14	8	2	1	38	5	5	.673	0	1	0	1	1	0	0	0	.011	-.009	6.23	5.64	5.11
Paronto C	3	10.3	41	6	0	4	2	0	0	11	2	3	.697	0	0	0	0	1	0	0	0	.082	.185	4.35	4.35	5.52
Hernandez R	3	19.3	98	4	4	15	11	1	0	32	4	3	.588	1	0	0	0	3	0	0	0	-.210	-.104	8.84	8.38	5.89
Nieve F	2	10.7	49	11	0	12	2	0	0	17	2	2	.545	0	0	0	0	1	0	1	0	.091	-.201	8.44	8.44	3.95
Arias A	2	8.0	39	3	2	8	6	0	1	11	0	2	.542	0	0	0	1	1	0	0	0	-.094	-.107	6.75	6.75	3.83

Italicized stats have been adjusted for home park.

Batted Ball Pitching Stats

Player	% of PA		% of Batted Balls			IF/F	HR/OF	Out %		Runs Per Event				Total Runs vs. Avg.				
	K%	BB%	GB%	LD%	FB%			GB	OF	NIP	GB	LD	OF	NIP	GB	LD	FB	Tot
Oswalt R	19	7	50	20	29	.07	.14	79	83	.01	.02	.36	.21	-11	-8	-5	0	-24
Geary G	17	11	44	15	41	.08	.04	76	92	.07	.03	.37	.03	2	-2	-5	-9	-15
Sampson C	13	5	56	15	29	.05	.07	75	82	.02	.04	.44	.14	-5	1	-1	-5	-10
Valverde J	27	8	39	20	41	.16	.13	71	90	-.01	.07	.38	.19	-5	1	-4	-1	-8
Rodriguez W	22	8	40	23	36	.11	.11	76	86	.01	.03	.39	.17	-6	-3	3	-3	-8
Brocail D	22	8	41	17	42	.10	.11	76	83	.01	.03	.40	.18	-3	-2	-3	1	-8
Wolf R	19	9	38	21	42	.11	.08	72	86	.04	.06	.40	.12	-1	1	0	-3	-3
Wright D	23	15	39	21	39	.08	.15	78	91	.07	.03	.37	.19	3	-2	-2	0	-1
Byrdak T	20	13	43	19	39	.12	.17	83	82	.07	.00	.34	.30	2	-3	-4	6	1
Moehler B	13	6	44	21	35	.07	.10	76	85	.04	.04	.38	.17	-4	0	5	2	3
Cassel J	11	7	45	19	36	.05	.14	74	81	.07	.05	.42	.24	-0	1	1	3	5
Villarreal O	13	11	41	17	43	.09	.24	79	84	.11	.00	.31	.38	2	-2	-2	12	10
Chacon S	14	11	37	18	45	.08	.14	75	84	.09	.03	.34	.24	4	-2	-3	12	10
Borkowski D	14	9	39	20	41	.11	.19	69	82	.06	.08	.54	.29	0	1	5	7	14
Backe B	17	11	38	21	41	.10	.17	73	82	.07	.06	.43	.27	4	1	10	26	41
MLB Average	*18*	*10*	*44*	*20*	*36*	*.10*	*.11*	*74*	*84*	*.05*	*.04*	*.39*	*.18*	--	--	--	--	--

Fielding Stats

Name	Inn	SBA/G	CS%	ERA	WP+PB/G	PO	A	TE	FE	Grade
Catchers										
Ausmus B	569.7	0.36	17%	3.71	0.205	428	33	2	0	--
Quintero H	447.0	0.44	32%	4.89	0.121	373	26	1	0	--
Towles J	408.7	0.40	28%	4.78	0.242	312	13	1	1	--

Name	Inn	PO	A	TE	FE	FPct	DPS	DPT	ZR	OOZ	Grade
First Base											
Berkman L	1307.0		132	0	5	.996	17	0	.821	53	A+
Erstad D	66.3	71	2	0	0	1.000	0	0	.667	1	--
Blum G	24.7	17	1	0	0	1.000	0	0	.333	2	--
Loretta M	17.0	14	0	0	0	1.000	0	0	1.000	1	--
Saccomanno	6.0	6	0	0	0	1.000	0	0	--	--	--
Ausmus B	4.0	5	0	0	0	1.000	0	0	--	--	--
Second Base											
Matsui K	806.0	190	219	5	7	.971	25	31	.799	14	F-
Loretta M	368.0	85	119	0	1	.995	7	19	.864	1	--
Newhan D	177.7	33	39	0	1	.986	2	9	.771	2	--
Blum G	40.7	9	17	0	0	1.000	0	2	.882	0	--
Perez T	15.0	2	2	0	0	1.000	1	1	.250	0	--
Castillo J	13.0	5	4	0	0	1.000	1	0	.800	0	--
Maysonet E	4.0	2	0	0	0	1.000	0	0	.000	0	--
Ausmus B	1.0	0	0	0	0	.000	0	0	--	--	--
Shortstop											
Tejada M	1354.0	187	443	4	7	.983	51	41	.879	43	B
Loretta M	36.0	3	18	1	1	.913	0	3	.875	1	--
Blum G	26.0	2	7	0	0	1.000	0	0	1.000	0	--
Maysonet E	9.0	0	6	1	0	.857	0	0	.667	2	--

Name	Inn	PO	A	TE	FE	FPct	DPS	DPT	ZR	OOZ	Grade
Third Base											
Wigginton T	652.0	46	144	3	3	.969	10	0	.732	25	--
Blum G	599.7	43	144	2	2	.979	8	0	.715	29	--
Loretta M	110.7	7	31	1	0	.974	1	0	.690	9	--
Castillo J	60.0	6	11	0	0	1.000	0	0	.833	0	F
Perez T	2.0	0	0	0	0	.000	0	0	--	--	--
Ausmus B	1.0	0	0	0	1	.000	0	0	.000	0	--
Left Field											
Lee C	915.3	187	4	0	1	.995	0	0	.845	45	D
Wigginton T	247.0	46	2	0	0	1.000	0	0	.969	15	--
Erstad D	205.0	37	1	0	0	1.000	2	0	.967	8	--
Abercrombie	32.0	7	0	0	0	1.000	0	0	.875	0	--
Cruz J	24.0	5	0	0	0	1.000	0	0	1.000	1	--
Newhan D	2.0	0	0	0	0	.000	0	0	--	--	--
Center Field											
Bourn M	1009.0	291	9	1	4	.984	4	0	.913	82	A+
Erstad D	304.0	97	1	0	0	1.000	0	0	.962	23	--
Abercrombie	77.3	29	2	0	0	1.000	2	0	1.000	5	--
Cruz J	35.0	9	0	0	0	1.000	0	0	.833	4	--
Right Field											
Pence H	1366.0	340	16	0	1	.997	8	0	.906	71	C
Erstad D	48.0	12	0	0	0	1.000	0	0	.889	4	--
Cruz J	11.0	4	0	0	0	1.000	0	0	.750	1	--

Kansas City Royals

Stat Facts:

- Tony Pena's GPA of .137 was lowest in the majors among 85+ PA players
- Joey Gathright hit a ground ball on 68% of his balls in play, highest in the majors
- Zack Greinke allowed just 2 stolen bases in 6 attempts
- Miguel Olivo walked 3% of the time, and struck out 26% of the time
- Joel Peralta allowed 15 homers in 53 innings
- Ramon Ramirez allowed 2 homers in 72 innings
- Horacio Ramirez faced 96 batters, and walked just 1 of them
- Ryan Shealy hit 7 home runs in 79 PAs
- No other Royal had a SLG higher than .480
- Mark Grudzielanek made just 8 OOZ plays
- David DeJesus had 3 assists in over 1,100 innings in the outfield
- Alex Gordon led the team in intentional walks, with 5

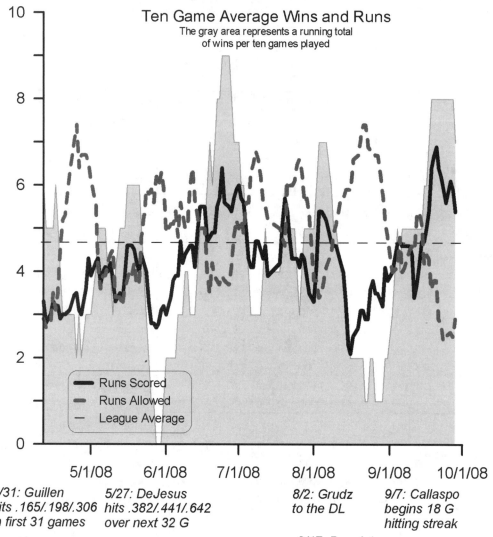

Ten Game Average Wins and Runs
The gray area represents a running total of wins per ten games played

Runs Scored
Runs Allowed
League Average

3/31: Guillen hits .165/.198/.306 in first 31 games

5/27: DeJesus hits .382/.441/.642 over next 32 G

6/6: Aviles replaces Pena as starting SS

8/2: Grudz to the DL

8/17: Bannister: 1 IP, 10 H, 10 ER

9/7: Callaspo begins 18 G hitting streak

Team Batting and Pitching/Fielding Stats by Month

	April	May	June	July	Aug	Sept/Oct
Wins	12	10	16	12	7	18
Losses	15	19	11	14	20	8
RS/G	3.7	3.5	5.2	4.3	3.8	5.2
RA/G	4.8	4.5	4.7	5.4	5.8	3.7
OBP	.316	.309	.331	.301	.320	.344
SLG	.364	.358	.446	.385	.380	.451
FIP	4.06	4.37	4.51	4.04	4.96	3.53
DER	.677	.705	.698	.678	.671	.719

Batting Stats

Player	BR	Runs	RBI	PA	Outs	H	2B	3B	HR	TB	K	BB	IBB	HBP	SH	SF	SB	CS	GDP	H-A	L^R	BA	OBP	SLG	GPA
DeJesus D *	92	70	73	577	377	159	25	7	12	234	71	46	3	5	4	4	11	8	10	-.002	.046	.307	.366	.452	.278
Gordon A *	74	72	59	571	375	128	35	1	16	213	120	66	5	6	1	5	9	2	8	.025	.069	.260	.351	.432	.266
Guillen J	72	66	97	633	464	158	42	1	20	262	106	23	3	9	0	3	2	1	23	-.007	.088	.264	.300	.438	.245
Teahen M *	67	66	59	623	435	146	31	4	15	230	131	46	4	3	0	2	4	3	6	-.002	-.005	.255	.313	.402	.241
Aviles M	61	68	51	441	298	136	27	4	10	201	58	18	4	2	0	2	8	3	12	-.045	.062	.325	.354	.480	.279
Butler B	57	44	55	478	345	122	22	0	11	177	57	33	0	0	0	2	0	1	23	-.006	.118	.275	.324	.400	.246
Buck J	45	48	48	418	302	83	23	1	9	135	96	38	2	6	0	4	0	3	12	.011	.050	.224	.304	.365	.228
Grudzielanek	40	36	24	360	241	99	24	0	3	132	41	19	1	5	3	2	2	1	8	.064	.113	.299	.345	.399	.255
Gload R *	39	46	37	418	298	106	18	1	3	135	39	23	4	3	1	3	3	4	12	.075	.034	.273	.317	.348	.229
Olivo M	38	29	41	317	234	78	22	0	12	136	82	7	2	3	0	1	7	0	6	-.065	.047	.255	.278	.444	.236
Gathright J	29	41	22	315	215	71	3	1	0	76	40	20	0	4	10	2	21	4	3	.009	-.011	.254	.311	.272	.208
German E	27	30	22	242	171	53	14	3	0	73	42	18	1	1	4	3	7	3	5	.038	.008	.245	.303	.338	.221
Callaspo A +	23	21	16	234	155	65	8	3	0	79	14	19	0	0	1	1	2	1	6	-.047	.014	.305	.361	.371	.255
Shealy R	15	12	20	79	53	22	1	0	7	44	19	5	0	1	0	0	0	0	2	-.138	-.044	.301	.354	.603	.310
Pena T	6	22	14	235	192	38	4	1	1	47	49	6	2	0	2	2	3	1	4	.009	.092	.169	.189	.209	.137
Maier M *	6	9	9	97	70	26	1	1	0	29	18	2	0	2	2	0	0	2	3	-.042	.007	.286	.316	.319	.222
Kaaihue K *	3	4	1	24	15	6	0	0	1	9	2	3	0	0	0	0	0	0	0	.022	-.081	.286	.375	.429	.276
Greinke Z	1	0	0	8	6	2	1	0	0	3	1	0	0	0	1	0	0	0	1	-.236	-.330	.286	.286	.429	.236
Smith J *	1	6	1	28	23	6	2	0	0	8	12	0	0	0	0	0	0	1	0	.113	.065	.214	.214	.286	.168

Italicized stats have been adjusted for home park.

Batted Ball Batting Stats

Player	% of PA		% of Batted Balls					Out %		Runs Per Event				Total Runs vs. Avg.				
	K%	BB%	GB%	LD%	FB%	IF/F	HR/OF	GB	OF	NIP	GB	LD	OF	NIP	GB	LD	FB	Tot
DeJesus D	12	9	46	25	29	.07	.08	73	86	.08	.06	.38	.14	2	4	12	-5	13
Aviles M	13	5	46	20	33	.13	.10	66	78	.00	.09	.38	.20	-5	9	4	4	12
Gordon A	21	13	31	21	48	.09	.10	70	80	.06	.07	.35	.19	4	0	-3	8	9
Grudzielanek M	11	7	46	24	30	.10	.04	77	78	.06	.03	.41	.11	-1	-1	10	-6	2
Callaspo A	6	8	47	26	28	.11	.00	78	82	.15	.03	.39	.03	2	-1	8	-8	2
Guillen J	17	5	47	18	35	.11	.13	74	82	-.01	.04	.37	.23	-10	-1	-3	8	-6
Olivo M	26	3	38	17	44	.21	.15	73	79	-.06	.05	.47	.27	-10	-1	-1	6	-6
Butler B	12	7	49	17	35	.10	.09	74	84	.05	.03	.36	.16	-2	-1	-4	-0	-7
German E	17	8	53	21	25	.02	.00	74	84	.03	.05	.35	.06	-1	1	-1	-7	-8
Teahen M	21	8	49	21	31	.07	.12	77	82	.01	.04	.35	.22	-7	-1	-4	2	-9
Gload R	9	6	46	22	32	.11	.03	75	84	.07	.04	.31	.06	-1	0	1	-11	-11
Buck J	23	11	43	16	41	.11	.09	75	87	.03	.04	.41	.14	-1	-2	-6	-4	-13
Gathright J	13	8	68	13	19	.05	.00	72	83	.06	.07	.24	.02	-1	7	-12	-12	-17
Pena T	21	3	55	16	29	.08	.02	82	84	-.06	.00	.18	.05	-7	-2	-11	-9	-29
MLB Average	18	10	44	20	36	.10	.11	74	84	.05	.04	.39	.18	--	--	--	--	--

Pitching Stats

Player	PRC	IP	BFP	G	GS	K	BB	IBB	HBP	H	HR	DP	DER	SB	CS	PO	W	L	Sv	Op	Hld	H-A	R^L	RA	ERA	FIP
Greinke Z	98	202.3	851	32	32	183	56	1	4	202	21	18	.680	2	4	3	13	10	0	0	0	-.034	-.061	3.87	3.47	3.65
Meche G	94	210.3	886	34	34	183	73	2	0	204	19	22	.689	12	2	0	14	11	0	0	0	.035	.027	4.19	3.98	3.68
Soria J	62	67.3	260	63	0	66	19	1	6	39	5	5	.787	2	1	2	2	3	42	45	0	-.083	-.023	1.74	1.60	3.30
Bannister B	50	182.7	811	32	32	113	58	1	7	215	29	22	.677	6	3	0	9	16	0	0	0	-.069	-.033	6.26	5.76	5.11
Ramirez R	45	71.7	295	71	0	70	31	6	0	57	2	7	.708	3	1	1	3	2	1	5	21	-.026	-.098	2.89	2.64	2.69
Davies K	43	113.0	487	21	21	71	43	0	2	121	10	16	.690	8	1	0	9	7	0	0	0	-.018	.015	4.54	4.06	4.32
Hochevar L	37	129.0	566	22	22	72	47	1	5	143	12	18	.679	14	4	0	6	12	0	0	0	-.027	-.055	5.86	5.51	4.51
Mahay R *	31	64.7	278	57	0	49	29	0	1	61	6	6	.699	2	2	0	5	0	0	1	21	-.011	.011	3.76	3.48	4.31
Nunez L	23	48.3	205	45	0	26	15	2	4	45	2	6	.709	1	1	1	4	1	0	3	7	.056	-.064	3.54	2.98	3.75
Tejeda R	20	39.3	157	25	1	41	19	0	1	22	3	2	.785	4	1	2	2	2	0	0	1	.101	-.044	3.89	3.20	3.66
Peralta J	15	52.7	224	40	0	38	14	0	2	56	15	6	.729	3	1	0	1	2	0	1	1	-.002	-.030	6.32	5.98	6.40
Tomko B	14	60.7	271	16	10	40	13	0	0	80	11	5	.647	3	0	0	2	7	0	2	0	.007	.002	7.27	6.97	4.91
Duckworth B	13	38.0	167	7	7	20	19	0	3	38	2	6	.707	3	3	1	3	3	0	0	0	.020	-.051	4.74	4.50	4.60
Yabuta Y	13	37.7	168	31	0	25	17	0	0	41	6	5	.692	4	0	0	1	3	0	0	1	.049	.096	5.02	4.78	5.33
Ramirez H *	12	24.3	96	15	0	11	1	0	2	21	1	2	.728	3	0	0	1	1	0	0	1	-.054	-.005	3.33	2.59	3.23
Bale J *	10	26.7	110	13	3	14	6	0	0	29	1	5	.674	3	1	1	0	3	0	0	2	-.056	-.007	4.39	4.39	3.34
Gobble J *	6	31.7	159	39	0	27	23	1	2	39	5	2	.657	2	0	0	0	2	1	2	4	.102	-.205	8.81	8.81	5.85
Fulchino J	2	14.0	72	12	0	12	8	0	1	21	2	1	.592	1	0	0	0	1	0	0	0	.110	-.051	9.64	9.00	5.30
Rosa C	2	3.3	12	2	0	3	0	0	0	3	0	0	.667	0	1	0	0	0	0	0	0	.289	-.200	2.70	2.70	1.43
Wells K	2	10.3	50	10	0	9	11	0	1	10	1	3	.679	0	0	0	0	1	0	0	1	-.087	.001	8.71	8.71	6.23
Lowery D	1	4.3	21	5	0	6	2	0	0	6	2	0	.636	1	0	0	0	0	0	0	0	-.119	-.225	10.38	10.38	7.85
Newman J *	1	7.0	35	4	0	2	6	0	0	10	1	2	.615	0	0	0	0	0	0	0	0	--	-.130	11.57	7.71	7.09

Italicized stats have been adjusted for home park.

Batted Ball Pitching Stats

Player	% of PA		% of Batted Balls					Out %		Runs Per Event				Total Runs vs. Avg.				
	K%	BB%	GB%	LD%	FB%	IF/F	HR/OF	GB	OF	NIP	GB	LD	OF	NIP	GB	LD	FB	Tot
Soria J	25	10	45	14	41	.10	.07	78	91	.01	.01	.33	.06	-3	-4	-8	-8	-23
Ramirez R	24	11	46	19	35	.20	.04	79	86	.03	.01	.43	.05	-1	-3	-2	-10	-16
Meche G	21	8	39	22	39	.08	.08	71	90	.02	.06	.39	.10	-8	3	2	-14	-16
Greinke Z	22	7	43	19	38	.09	.10	73	83	.00	.05	.41	.18	-12	1	-2	2	-11
Tejeda R	26	13	34	18	48	.22	.08	79	100	.04	.01	.40	.03	0	-2	-3	-6	-10
Ramirez H	11	3	60	20	21	.12	.00	78	87	-.01	.03	.38	.04	-2	-0	0	-4	-5
Nunez L	13	9	39	18	43	.24	.04	69	90	.08	.06	.45	.03	1	1	1	-8	-5
Mahay R	18	11	40	19	41	.14	.09	73	86	.06	.04	.37	.13	1	-1	-2	-2	-4
Bale J	13	5	51	21	28	.13	.05	81	85	.02	-.01	.54	.07	-1	-2	3	-3	-2
Davies K	15	9	39	22	40	.08	.08	73	86	.06	.04	.40	.12	1	-2	5	-3	0
Duckworth B	12	13	45	23	32	.08	.05	75	89	.13	.06	.30	.07	3	1	-0	-4	0
Yabuta Y	15	10	50	15	35	.18	.17	71	90	.07	.06	.51	.22	1	1	1	1	4
Hochevar L	13	9	52	17	32	.07	.09	74	84	.08	.04	.46	.15	2	2	2	-2	5
Peralta J	17	7	35	17	48	.06	.19	75	90	.02	.04	.39	.25	-2	-0	-1	10	6
Gobble J	17	15	28	19	53	.16	.06	53	80	.10	.18	.46	.16	3	3	1	1	10
Tomko B	15	5	45	20	35	.11	.16	75	86	-.00	.05	.52	.25	-4	1	8	6	12
Bannister B	14	8	37	22	41	.11	.13	76	81	.05	.03	.37	.23	-1	-4	7	20	22
MLB Average	18	10	44	20	36	.10	.11	74	84	.05	.04	.39	.18	--	--	--	--	--

Fielding Stats

Name	Inn	SBA/G	CS%	ERA	WP+PB/G	PO	A	TE	FE	Grade
Catchers										
Buck J	950.3	0.63	11%	4.55	0.436	751	24	6	2	F
Olivo M	494.3	0.56	39%	4.42	0.546	378	32	2	2	--
Tupman M	1.0	0.00	0%	0.00	0.000	0	0	0	0	--

Name	Inn	PO	A	TE	FE	FPct	DPS	DPT	ZR	OOZ	Grade
First Base											
Gload R	878.3	837	43	1	3	.995	13	0	.709	16	F-
Butler B	260.0	233	9	1	1	.992	0	1	.706	5	--
Shealy R	169.0	155	12	1	1	.988	1	0	.762	7	--
Teahen M	121.3	130	10	0	1	.993	1	0	.800	1	--
Kaaihue K	15.0	12	1	0	0	1.000	0	0	.667	1	--
Smith J	2.0	2	0	0	0	1.000	0	0	1.000	0	--
Second Base											
Grudzielanek	710.7	135	257	2	2	.990	24	35	.831	8	F
Callaspo A	365.7	74	119	0	0	1.000	14	19	.798	3	--
German E	214.0	41	77	0	3	.975	9	10	.778	1	--
Aviles M	114.3	26	33	0	0	1.000	2	3	.897	1	--
Smith J	41.0	5	16	0	0	1.000	1	1	1.000	0	--
Shortstop											
Aviles M	747.7	141	238	8	2	.974	37	27	.856	31	--
Pena T	592.0	74	180	2	7	.966	19	15	.821	28	--
Callaspo A	84.0	18	30	0	2	.960	4	5	.815	2	--
German E	22.0	2	4	0	1	.857	0	0	.600	1	--
Third Base											
Gordon A	1180.0	112	230	6	10	.955	21	1	.692	23	F-
Teahen M	166.0	18	24	3	0	.933	3	1	.636	1	--
German E	43.0	2	5	0	0	1.000	1	0	.714	0	--
Aviles M	29.7	3	3	0	0	1.000	0	0	.000	3	--
Smith J	19.0	5	1	0	0	1.000	0	0	--	--	--
Callaspo A	8.0	1	5	0	0	1.000	1	0	.833	0	--

Name	Inn	PO	A	TE	FE	FPct	DPS	DPT	ZR	OOZ	Grade
Left Field											
DeJesus D	482.7	136	1	0	0	1.000	0	0	.921	31	--
Guillen J	373.0	83	3	0	1	.989	2	0	.869	10	--
Teahen M	267.0	75	3	0	0	1.000	2	0	.841	17	--
German E	235.0	54	0	0	2	.964	0	0	.872	13	--
Gload R	64.0	18	0	0	0	1.000	0	0	.824	4	--
Callaspo A	14.0	0	0	0	0	0.000	0	0	--	--	--
Gathright J	9.0	2	0	0	0	1.000	0	0	1.000	1	--
Smith J	1.0	0	0	0	0	0.000	0	0	--	--	--
Center Field											
Gathright J	720.0	197	5	1	0	.995	0	0	.890	43	F-
DeJesus D	507.0	151	2	1	0	.994	2	0	.934	23	--
Maier M	217.7	69	0	0	1	.986	0	0	.983	10	--
Teahen M	1.0	0	0	0	0	0.000	0	0	--	--	--
Right Field											
Teahen M	756.3	185	4	0	2	.990	3	0	.922	32	C
Guillen J	539.3	121	7	1	2	.977	2	0	.858	12	--
DeJesus D	123.0	23	0	0	0	1.000	0	0	.944	6	--
Maier M	14.0	2	0	0	0	1.000	0	0	1.000	0	--
Gload R	13.0	3	0	0	0	1.000	0	0	1.000	0	--

Los Angeles Angels of Anaheim

Stat Facts:

- Jon Garland allowed just 3 stolen bases in 6 attempts
- Garland's 10% K rate tied for lowest in the majors among 162+ IP pitchers
- Joe Saunders' FIP was more than a run higher than his ERA
- Saunders' LD rate of 15% tied for lowest in the majors among 162+ IP pitchers
- One-quarter of Mike Napoli's outfield flies were home runs
- Casey Kotchman put the ball in play 88% of the time
- Howie Kendrick had just 1 infield pop-up
- Torii Hunter made 93 OOZ plays
- Chone Figgins made 49 OOZ plays at third base, and just 6 errors
- Jeff Mathis made 12 throwing errors
- Ervin Santana induced only 10 double plays
- Mark Teixeira's GPA was .364

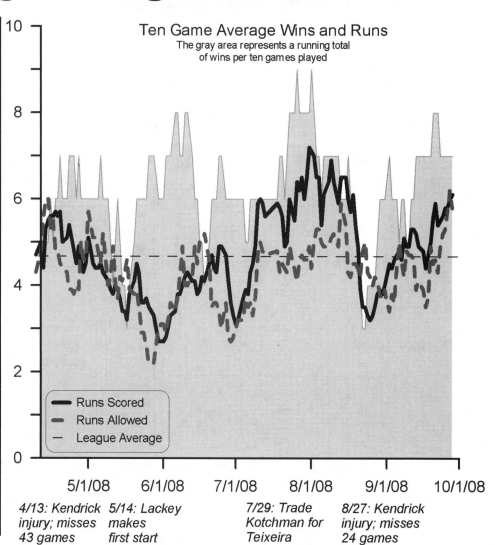

Ten Game Average Wins and Runs

The gray area represents a running total of wins per ten games played

Legend:
— Runs Scored
-- Runs Allowed
- League Average

4/13: Kendrick injury; misses 43 games

5/14: Lackey makes first start

7/29: Trade Kotchman for Teixeira

8/27: Kendrick injury; misses 24 games

9/13: K-Rod breaks Thigpen's save record

Team Batting and Pitching/Fielding Stats by Month

	April	May	June	July	Aug	Sept/Oct
Wins	18	15	16	19	15	17
Losses	11	13	10	6	13	9
RS/G	4.8	3.6	3.8	6.4	4.5	5.3
RA/G	4.4	3.9	3.7	4.4	4.4	4.9
OBP	.339	.300	.305	.355	.335	.346
SLG	.427	.346	.362	.491	.394	.460
FIP	4.46	4.05	3.85	4.38	4.10	3.85
DER	.699	.704	.721	.698	.683	.655

Batting Stats

Player	BR	Runs	RBI	PA	Outs	H	2B	3B	HR	TB	K	BB	IBB	HBP	SH	SF	SB	CS	GDP	H-A	L^R	BA	OBP	SLG	GPA
Guerrero V	96	85	91	600	407	164	31	3	27	282	77	51	16	4	0	4	5	3	27	-.039	-.023	.303	.365	.521	.298
Anderson G *	83	66	84	593	409	163	27	3	15	241	77	29	6	1	0	6	7	4	11	.025	.015	.293	.325	.433	.257
Hunter T	81	85	78	608	418	153	37	2	21	257	108	50	6	6	0	1	19	5	15	.024	.027	.278	.344	.466	.274
Figgins C +	56	72	22	520	348	125	14	1	1	144	80	62	3	3	2	0	34	13	7	.008	-.024	.276	.367	.318	.247
Kotchman C *	52	47	54	398	281	107	24	0	12	167	23	18	3	5	0	2	2	1	14	-.021	-.077	.287	.327	.448	.262
Kendrick H	49	43	37	361	248	104	26	2	3	143	58	12	3	4	1	4	11	4	8	-.014	-.004	.306	.333	.421	.258
Teixeira M +	48	39	43	234	128	69	14	0	13	122	23	32	4	4	0	5	2	0	4	.050	-.039	.358	.449	.632	.364
Matthews Jr.	48	53	46	477	338	103	19	3	8	152	95	45	2	4	0	2	8	3	12	-.008	.047	.242	.319	.357	.235
Napoli M	47	39	49	274	171	62	9	1	20	133	70	35	5	5	1	6	7	3	3	-.040	.015	.273	.374	.586	.318
Aybar E +	47	53	39	375	254	96	18	5	3	133	45	14	0	5	9	1	7	2	2	-.043	-.002	.277	.314	.384	.240
Izturis M +	38	44	37	321	223	78	14	2	3	105	27	26	0	1	2	2	11	2	9	.010	-.024	.269	.329	.362	.241
Mathis J	34	35	42	328	231	55	8	0	9	90	90	30	4	3	8	4	2	2	1	-.003	.067	.194	.275	.318	.205
Rivera J	29	31	45	280	204	63	13	0	12	112	33	16	0	0	0	8	1	1	10	.036	-.002	.246	.282	.438	.239
Quinlan R	16	15	11	181	128	43	1	2	1	51	28	14	0	2	0	1	4	2	5	.048	.007	.262	.326	.311	.227
Rodriguez S	13	18	10	187	137	34	8	1	3	53	55	14	0	3	2	1	3	1	3	.060	-.051	.204	.276	.317	.205
Willits R +	10	21	7	136	89	21	4	0	0	25	26	21	0	0	5	2	2	1	1	.009	.040	.194	.321	.231	.204
Wood B	8	12	13	157	123	30	4	0	5	49	43	4	0	1	1	1	4	0	3	.035	-.095	.200	.224	.327	.184
Morales K +	3	7	8	66	52	13	2	0	3	24	7	4	0	1	0	0	0	1	3	-.010	.058	.213	.273	.393	.223

Italicized stats have been adjusted for home park.

Batted Ball Batting Stats

Player	% of PA		% of Batted Balls					Out %		Runs Per Event				Total Runs vs. Avg.				
	K%	BB%	GB%	LD%	FB%	IF/F	HR/OF	GB	OF	NIP	GB	LD	OF	NIP	GB	LD	FB	Tot
Teixeira M	10	15	43	21	36	.08	.19	63	85	.17	.12	.44	.27	7	7	6	8	27
Guerrero V	13	9	47	17	36	.07	.17	75	73	.08	.02	.34	.34	3	-3	-5	30	25
Napoli M	25	15	31	17	52	.11	.25	60	91	.06	.13	.50	.33	3	3	-0	15	20
Hunter T	18	9	46	19	35	.10	.15	68	89	.04	.08	.39	.22	-1	9	-0	7	15
Anderson G	13	5	42	21	36	.13	.10	71	90	.02	.06	.42	.12	-6	5	10	-6	3
Kotchman C	6	6	52	16	32	.14	.13	77	86	.12	.03	.41	.18	0	0	1	1	3
Kendrick H	16	4	54	20	26	.01	.04	73	74	-.01	.06	.41	.17	-6	3	3	-2	-1
Izturis M	8	8	49	23	29	.11	.03	76	82	.12	.03	.32	.10	2	-1	1	-6	-5
Figgins C	15	13	46	24	30	.07	.01	74	83	.09	.04	.34	.03	7	2	2	-16	-5
Quinlan R	15	9	48	18	34	.04	.02	64	91	.05	.10	.29	.00	-0	4	-3	-7	-6
Rivera J	12	6	37	14	48	.15	.13	79	86	.04	.01	.30	.19	-2	-4	-7	6	-6
Aybar E	12	5	52	18	30	.09	.04	75	80	.02	.06	.40	.11	-4	5	-2	-7	-7
Willits R	19	15	44	16	40	.13	.00	69	86	.09	.10	.17	-.00	2	1	-6	-6	-8
Wood R	27	3	36	14	50	.26	.13	64	94	-.07	.09	.41	.13	-6	1	-4	-3	-11
Matthews Jr. G	20	10	59	14	27	.07	.10	77	82	.04	.02	.46	.18	-0	-2	-5	-4	-11
Rodriguez S	29	9	41	12	47	.08	.06	76	80	-.00	.03	.44	.16	-3	-2	-6	-1	-11
Mathis J	27	10	36	11	53	.21	.11	69	93	.01	.10	.47	.11	-4	1	-10	-7	-19
MLB Average	18	10	44	20	36	.10	.11	74	84	.05	.04	.39	.18	--	--	--	--	--

Pitching Stats

Player	PRC	IP	BFP	G	GS	K	BB	IBB	HBP	H	HR	DP	DER	SB	CS	PO	W	L	Sv	Op	Hld	H-A	R^L	RA	ERA	FIP
Santana E	113	219.0	897	32	32	214	47	2	8	198	23	10	.698	16	4	0	16	7	0	0	0	.016	-.032	3.66	3.49	3.37
Saunders J *	87	198.0	807	31	31	103	53	2	6	187	21	32	.716	18	7	3	17	7	0	0	0	.027	-.016	3.73	3.41	4.43
Lackey J	76	163.3	675	24	24	130	40	1	10	161	26	27	.706	11	3	1	12	5	0	0	0	.009	.062	3.91	3.75	4.61
Weaver J	73	176.7	745	30	30	152	54	4	6	173	20	11	.692	20	5	2	11	10	0	0	0	-.038	-.004	4.48	4.33	3.93
Garland J	59	196.7	864	32	32	90	59	4	8	237	23	28	.675	3	3	1	14	8	0	0	0	-.038	-.001	5.31	4.90	4.80
Arredondo J	46	61.0	244	52	0	55	22	0	1	42	3	6	.742	3	2	0	10	2	0	7	16	-.010	.082	2.21	1.62	3.20
Rodriguez F	46	68.3	288	76	0	77	34	4	2	54	4	6	.696	8	0	0	2	3	62	69	0	.004	-.042	2.77	2.24	3.14
Oliver D *	40	72.0	291	54	0	48	16	2	4	67	5	9	.711	5	2	1	7	1	0	2	12	-.088	-.021	3.00	2.88	3.55
Shields S	29	63.3	270	64	0	64	29	2	2	56	6	11	.692	8	1	0	6	4	4	9	31	.000	.053	4.12	2.70	3.81
Speier J	23	68.0	305	62	0	56	27	5	6	69	15	4	.716	7	1	0	2	8	0	2	10	.003	-.089	5.43	5.03	5.69
O'Day D	15	43.3	194	30	0	29	14	6	4	49	2	4	.676	2	1	0	0	1	0	0	1	-.035	-.022	4.98	4.57	3.32
Moseley D	13	50.3	237	12	10	37	20	0	2	70	6	3	.622	4	2	2	2	4	0	0	0	.004	-.038	6.79	6.79	4.62
Loux S	6	16.0	66	7	0	4	2	0	2	16	1	4	.719	0	0	0	0	0	0	0	0	-.026	-.231	3.38	2.81	4.29
Bulger J	4	16.0	73	14	0	20	9	0	2	15	3	1	.692	1	0	0	0	0	0	0	0	-.145	.087	7.31	7.31	5.23
Jepsen K	3	8.3	36	9	0	7	4	0	0	8	0	1	.680	1	0	0	0	1	0	0	3	-.192	.043	5.40	4.32	2.99
Bootcheck C	2	16.0	90	10	0	14	12	0	0	30	2	0	.548	1	0	0	0	1	0	0	1	.001	-.004	10.13	10.13	5.36
Adenhart N	2	12.0	63	3	3	4	13	0	0	18	0	3	.609	0	0	0	1	0	0	0	0	-.020	-.029	9.00	9.00	5.81

Italicized stats have been adjusted for home park.

Batted Ball Pitching Stats

Player	% of PA		% of Batted Balls			IF/F	HR/OF	Out %		Runs Per Event				Total Runs vs. Avg.				
	K%	BB%	GB%	LD%	FB%	IF/F	HR/OF	GB	OF	NIP	GB	LD	OF	NIP	GB	LD	FB	Tot
Santana E	24	6	39	20	42	.15	.11	72	85	-.02	.06	.37	.16	-18	1	-8	-6	-31
Arredondo J	23	9	51	17	31	.10	.06	78	89	.02	.02	.31	.09	-2	-2	-6	-6	-17
Saunders J	13	7	47	15	38	.09	.10	75	82	.05	.03	.34	.17	-2	-3	-13	3	-16
Rodriguez F	27	13	42	20	38	.09	.07	74	85	.03	.05	.36	.11	-0	-0	-4	-5	-10
Oliver D	16	7	47	16	37	.13	.06	74	80	.02	.05	.36	.13	-3	1	-5	-3	-9
Shields S	24	11	54	16	31	.09	.13	72	83	.04	.04	.31	.20	-0	1	-7	-1	-7
Lackey J	19	7	45	20	35	.04	.15	76	85	.01	.02	.33	.24	-7	-4	-6	12	-6
Weaver J	20	8	33	22	46	.14	.09	77	82	.02	.03	.40	.17	-7	-5	3	3	-5
O'Day D	15	9	55	17	28	.15	.06	75	79	.06	.04	.38	.17	0	1	-2	-2	-2
Speier J	18	11	35	15	50	.13	.15	76	78	.06	.03	.43	.28	1	-3	-4	13	8
Moseley D	16	9	48	21	31	.09	.12	69	77	.06	.08	.43	.24	1	4	4	3	11
Garland J	10	8	50	22	28	.08	.12	76	80	.08	.03	.39	.21	2	-3	15	5	19
MLB Average	*18*	*10*	*44*	*20*	*36*	*.10*	*.11*	*74*	*84*	*.05*	*.04*	*.39*	*.18*	--	--	--	--	--

Fielding Stats

Name	Inn	SBA/G	CS%	ERA	WP+PB/G	PO	A	TE	FE	Grade
Catchers										
Mathis J	793.3	0.83	22%	3.66	0.272	624	57	12	1	C
Napoli M	625.0	0.88	15%	4.45	0.490	469	21	2	1	--
Budde R	17.0	0.00	0%	3.71	1.059	13	2	0	0	--
Wilson R	16.0	0.00	0%	3.38	0.000	15	1	0	0	--

Name	Inn	PO	A	TE	FE	FPct	DPS	DPT	ZR	OOZ	Grade
First Base											
Kotchman C	857.0	838	73	0	2	.998	13	0	.820	32	A+
Teixeira M	436.3	431	34	1	2	.994	4	2	.765	15	A+
Quinlan R	114.0	105	11	0	0	1.000	1	0	.800	4	--
Morales K	41.0	30	3	0	0	1.000	1	0	.667	1	--
Rivera J	2.0	5	0	0	0	1.000	0	0	1.000	0	--
Sandoval F	1.0	0	0	0	0	.000	0	0	--	--	--
Second Base											
Kendrick H	776.0	155	287	1	3	.991	31	36	.819	22	C
Rodriguez S	423.7	97	127	1	1	.991	19	17	.821	9	--
Izturis M	183.7	49	61	1	1	.982	4	9	.808	7	--
Figgins C	63.0	10	19	0	0	1.000	3	1	.842	1	--
Aybar E	2.0	0	1	0	0	1.000	0	0	1.000	0	--
Brown M	2.0	1	1	0	0	1.000	0	0	1.000	0	--
Rivera J	1.0	0	0	0	0	.000	0	0	--	--	--
Shortstop											
Aybar E	784.7	140	276	11	7	.959	28	36	.852	30	A
Izturis M	448.0	69	147	0	2	.991	12	20	.847	21	--
Wood B	198.7	42	50	0	2	.979	8	10	.765	2	--
Rodriguez S	20.0	5	12	0	0	1.000	1	1	1.000	1	--
Third Base											
Figgins C	914.3	84	185	2	4	.978	13	0	.705	49	A+
Quinlan R	258.7	22	48	2	2	.946	7	2	.639	8	--
Wood B	188.0	18	40	2	0	.967	3	0	.744	6	--
Brown M	46.0	3	8	1	1	.846	2	0	.571	0	--
Izturis M	34.3	1	7	0	0	1.000	0	0	.667	1	--
Sandoval F	9.0	0	3	0	0	1.000	0	0	.667	0	--
Rodriguez S	1.0	0	0	0	0	.000	0	0	--	--	--

Name	Inn	PO	A	TE	FE	FPct	DPS	DPT	ZR	OOZ	Grade
Left Field											
Anderson G	689.3	144	9	0	0	1.000	4	0	.837	31	--
Matthews G	313.3	57	1	0	2	.967	0	0	.786	13	--
Rivera J	307.0	59	3	0	2	.969	2	0	.847	9	--
Willits R	134.3	24	0	0	0	1.000	0	0	.905	5	--
Quinlan R	7.3	1	0	0	0	1.000	0	0	--	--	--
Center Field											
Hunter T	1193.0	350	4	0	0	1.000	0	0	.889	93	B
Matthews G	221.0	66	3	1	3	.945	0	0	.964	13	--
Willits R	34.0	10	0	0	0	1.000	0	0	1.000	1	--
Rivera J	3.0	3	0	0	0	1.000	0	0	1.000	1	--
Right Field											
Guerrero V	839.0	180	8	0	4	.979	3	0	.889	36	C
Matthews G	344.0	77	2	1	1	.975	0	0	.885	8	--
Rivera J	115.0	19	1	0	1	.952	0	0	.783	1	--
Willits R	88.0	12	0	0	0	1.000	0	0	.786	1	--
Morales K	60.0	19	0	0	0	1.000	0	0	.895	2	--
Quinlan R	5.3	1	0	0	0	1.000	0	0	1.000	0	--

Los Angeles Dodgers

Stat Facts:

- Manny's L.A. GPA was .414; no one else in the majors with as many as 40 PAs matched it
- Manny in the NL hit a line drive 32% of the time; with the Red Sox it had been 19%
- Overall, Andre Ethier led the majors with 27% line drives
- Matt Kemp hit just 2 infield pop-ups
- Jonathan Broxton struck out 31% of the batters he faced
- Greg Maddux struck out 11%
- Broxton, Joe Beimel, and Takashi Saito combined to allow 3 HRs in 165 IP
- Only 17% of the batted balls of Derek Lowe were line drives
- James Loney made 58 OOZ plays
- Juan Pierre had zero assists in 622 innings in left field
- Andruw Jones' GPA was .181
- Jones hit a line drive on 13% of his batted balls, and struck out 32% of the time

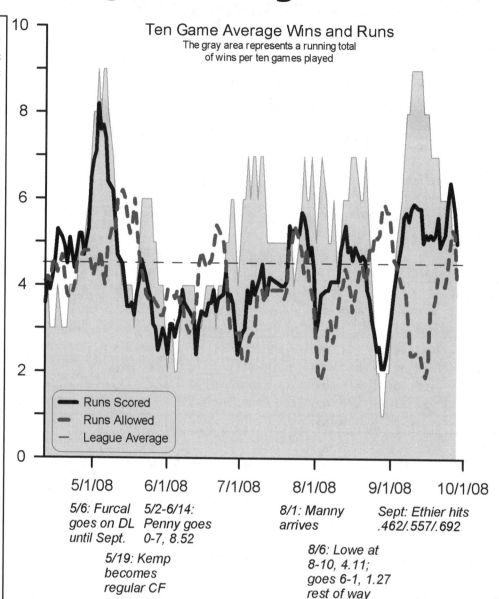

Ten Game Average Wins and Runs
The gray area represents a running total of wins per ten games played

— Runs Scored
- - Runs Allowed
— League Average

5/1/08   6/1/08   7/1/08   8/1/08   9/1/08   10/1/08

5/6: Furcal goes on DL until Sept.

5/2-6/14: Penny goes 0-7, 8.52

8/1: Manny arrives

Sept: Ethier hits .462/.557/.692

5/19: Kemp becomes regular CF

8/6: Lowe at 8-10, 4.11; goes 6-1, 1.27 rest of way

Team Batting and Pitching/Fielding Stats by Month

	April	May	June	July	Aug	Sept/Oct
Wins	14	13	11	16	13	17
Losses	13	15	16	10	16	8
RS/G	5.1	4.0	3.1	4.5	4.0	5.4
RA/G	4.0	4.6	3.6	3.8	4.5	3.4
OBP	.360	.312	.290	.320	.340	.372
SLG	.409	.356	.354	.385	.442	.443
FIP	3.79	3.84	3.56	3.14	4.18	3.09
DER	.687	.694	.687	.699	.694	.695

Batting Stats

Player	BR	Runs	RBI	PA	Outs	H	2B	3B	HR	TB	K	BB	IBB	HBP	SH	SF	SB	CS	GDP	H-A	L^R	BA	OBP	SLG	GPA
Ethier A *	98	90	77	596	374	160	38	5	20	268	88	59	0	4	1	7	6	3	6	.008	.079	.305	.375	.510	.302
Kemp M	88	93	76	657	452	176	38	5	18	278	153	46	6	1	1	3	35	11	11	.011	.088	.290	.340	.459	.273
Martin R	87	87	69	650	420	155	25	0	13	219	83	90	8	5	0	2	18	6	16	-.002	-.010	.280	.385	.396	.278
Loney J *	77	66	90	651	452	172	35	6	13	258	85	45	6	3	1	7	7	4	25	-.017	.048	.289	.338	.434	.266
Ramirez M	61	36	53	229	118	74	14	0	17	139	38	35	16	3	0	4	2	0	5	.057	-.082	.396	.489	.743	.414
Dewitt B *	49	45	52	421	277	97	13	2	9	141	68	45	9	3	0	5	3	0	6	.043	-.057	.264	.344	.383	.256
Kent J	48	42	59	474	331	123	23	1	12	184	52	25	1	7	0	2	0	1	13	-.014	.016	.280	.327	.418	.257
Pierre J *	46	44	28	406	284	106	10	2	1	123	24	22	1	3	5	1	40	12	3	-.020	-.058	.283	.327	.328	.234
Furcal R +	32	34	16	164	98	51	12	2	5	82	17	20	0	1	0	0	8	3	3	-.036	.018	.357	.439	.573	.348
Blake C	22	25	23	233	167	53	12	1	10	97	52	16	5	4	0	2	1	0	9	.021	-.014	.251	.313	.460	.261
Garciaparra	21	24	28	181	133	43	9	0	8	76	11	15	2	1	0	2	1	1	12	.013	.137	.264	.326	.466	.269
Berroa A	14	26	16	256	187	52	13	1	1	70	41	20	4	4	6	0	0	0	13	-.073	.024	.230	.304	.310	.219
Young D +	11	10	7	143	97	31	9	0	1	43	34	14	0	0	3	0	0	0	2	.025	.033	.246	.321	.341	.235
Jones A	7	21	14	238	182	33	8	1	3	52	76	27	1	0	1	0	1	0	5	.010	.063	.158	.256	.249	.181
Maza L	6	7	4	88	66	18	1	0	1	22	11	5	0	1	3	0	0	0	5	.059	.059	.228	.282	.278	.201
Hu C	4	16	9	129	100	21	2	2	0	27	23	11	4	0	2	0	2	0	5	.116	.038	.181	.252	.233	.175
Sweeney M *	4	2	5	108	80	12	3	0	0	15	28	15	0	0	0	1	0	0	0	-.023	.067	.130	.250	.163	.156
Ardoin D	4	3	4	54	41	12	1	0	1	16	10	2	0	1	0	0	1	0	2	-.150	.141	.235	.278	.314	.208
LaRoche A	3	6	6	69	52	12	1	0	2	19	7	10	0	0	0	0	0	0	5	-.103	-.055	.203	.319	.322	.229
Ozuna P	3	6	3	33	27	7	0	1	0	12	5	1	0	0	0	0	1	1	1	.198	.204	.219	.242	.375	.207
Bennett G	3	1	4	23	18	4	1	0	1	8	0	2	0	0	0	0	0	0	1	.024	-.048	.190	.261	.381	.217
Lowe D	1	4	5	75	56	9	0	0	0	9	20	3	0	0	7	0	0	0	0	-.021	.220	.138	.176	.138	.116
Penny B	1	2	2	32	21	5	0	0	0	5	7	0	0	0	6	0	0	0	0	-.058	.208	.192	.192	.192	.137
Loaiza E	1	1	1	9	5	2	0	0	0	2	1	0	0	0	3	0	0	0	1	.000	.350	.333	.333	.333	.238
Kuroda H	1	2	2	65	47	8	1	0	0	9	16	5	0	0	6	0	0	0	1	.027	.004	.148	.220	.167	.144
Tiffee T +	1	0	0	5	3	1	0	0	0	1	0	0	0	1	0	0	0	0	0	.700	-.425	.250	.400	.250	.247
Repko J	1	0	0	20	15	3	1	0	0	4	9	2	0	0	0	0	1	0	0	.521	.221	.167	.250	.222	.171

Italicized stats have been adjusted for home park.

Batted Ball Batting Stats

Player	% of PA		% of Batted Balls					Out %		Runs Per Event				Total Runs vs. Avg.				
	K%	BB%	GB%	LD%	FB%	IF/F	HR/OF	GB	OF	NIP	GB	LD	OF	NIP	GB	LD	FB	Tot
Ramirez M	17	17	32	32	36	.11	.29	59	89	.12	.12	.49	.39	7	3	15	13	37
Ethier A	15	11	41	27	32	.04	.15	74	86	.08	.06	.35	.22	4	3	11	9	27
Furcal R	10	13	49	19	32	.11	.15	69	69	.14	.08	.38	.34	3	5	1	6	15
Martin R	13	15	51	19	30	.14	.10	71	89	.13	.06	.36	.13	15	7	-1	-9	12
Kemp M	23	7	45	23	32	.01	.13	65	84	-.01	.10	.38	.21	-10	12	4	6	12
Loney J	13	7	44	22	34	.09	.08	74	82	.05	.03	.38	.15	-2	-2	8	-2	2
Dewitt B	16	11	47	19	34	.11	.09	77	85	.08	.03	.43	.14	3	-1	2	-4	0
Garciaparra N	6	9	40	18	43	.18	.15	89	80	.16	-.07	.36	.26	2	-7	-1	6	0
Kent J	11	7	40	23	37	.07	.08	76	89	.06	.02	.39	.11	-1	-3	9	-4	0
Blake C	22	9	35	19	45	.07	.15	77	88	.01	.01	.43	.20	-2	-3	0	4	-1
Young D	24	10	50	17	33	.13	.04	80	76	.02	.01	.53	.16	-1	-2	0	-2	-5
Hu C	18	9	61	12	27	.20	.00	79	75	.04	.01	.36	.09	-1	-1	-4	-4	-10
Pierre J	6	6	53	24	23	.04	.01	75	89	.12	.05	.27	.01	0	6	-1	-15	-10
Sweeney M	26	14	46	20	34	.05	.00	87	95	.05	-.02	.31	-.06	0	-2	-3	-6	-10
Berroa A	16	9	44	22	34	.13	.02	83	77	.06	-.03	.34	.11	0	-7	-1	-5	-13
Jones A	32	12	48	13	39	.08	.06	84	82	.01	-.02	.46	.13	-2	-5	-6	-4	-18
MLB Average	18	10	44	20	36	.10	.11	74	84	.05	.04	.39	.18	--	--	--	--	--

Pitching Stats

Player	PRC	IP	BFP	G	GS	K	BB	IBB	HBP	H	HR	DP	DER	SB	CS	PO	W	L	Sv	Op	Hld	H-A	R^L	RA	ERA	FIP
Billingsley	103	200.7	859	35	32	201	80	6	8	188	14	19	.665	8	4	0	16	10	0	0	1	-.032	-.057	3.41	3.14	3.33
Lowe D	96	211.0	851	34	34	147	45	7	1	194	14	21	.705	14	3	0	14	11	0	0	0	-.070	-.002	3.58	3.24	3.23
Kuroda H	71	183.3	776	31	31	116	42	8	7	181	13	12	.707	7	2	2	9	10	0	0	0	-.029	-.026	4.17	3.73	3.53
Kuo H *	57	80.0	323	42	3	96	21	2	3	60	4	4	.709	2	0	0	5	3	1	3	12	-.042	-.016	2.36	2.14	2.28
Kershaw C *	44	107.7	470	22	21	100	52	3	1	109	11	15	.670	5	2	2	5	5	0	0	1	-.032	.015	4.26	4.26	4.07
Wade C	40	71.3	275	55	0	51	15	3	4	51	7	10	.768	2	0	0	2	1	0	1	9	-.084	.020	2.78	2.27	3.72
Park C	40	95.3	412	54	5	79	36	7	4	97	12	12	.683	5	1	0	4	4	2	5	5	-.062	-.069	4.06	3.40	4.22
Beimel J *	34	49.0	214	71	0	32	21	4	3	50	0	4	.677	5	3	2	5	1	0	0	12	-.025	-.006	2.02	2.02	3.12
Broxton J	34	69.0	285	70	0	88	27	5	3	54	2	6	.673	10	3	0	3	5	14	22	13	-.071	-.130	3.78	3.13	2.12
Saito T	31	47.0	197	45	0	60	16	3	2	40	1	2	.669	1	1	1	4	4	18	22	0	.010	-.010	2.68	2.49	1.88
Penny B	22	94.7	426	19	17	51	42	0	3	112	13	14	.678	8	3	0	6	9	0	0	0	-.039	-.028	6.46	6.27	5.34
Stults E *	16	38.7	167	7	7	30	13	2	1	38	6	1	.709	2	1	0	2	3	0	0	0	-.092	.040	4.19	3.49	4.60
Troncoso R	15	38.0	160	32	0	38	12	1	3	37	2	8	.657	5	0	0	1	1	0	0	2	.004	.018	4.50	4.26	2.99
Maddux G	11	40.7	166	7	7	18	4	1	1	43	5	3	.717	3	2	0	2	4	0	0	0	.050	-.070	5.53	5.09	4.21
Proctor S	10	38.7	184	41	0	46	24	1	0	41	7	0	.664	1	1	0	2	0	0	1	2	-.079	-.011	6.98	6.05	4.96
Johnson J	8	29.3	130	16	2	20	12	3	2	32	5	4	.692	1	0	0	1	2	0	0	1	-.117	-.030	5.83	5.22	5.18
Loaiza E	6	24.0	103	7	3	9	5	1	1	24	3	0	.741	0	0	0	1	2	0	0	0	-.125	-.064	5.63	5.63	4.70
Falkenborg B	3	11.7	49	16	0	9	4	1	0	11	2	1	.735	1	0	0	2	2	0	1	1	-.289	.071	6.17	6.17	4.66
Brazoban Y	1	3.0	16	2	0	3	5	0	0	4	0	1	.600	0	0	0	0	0	0	0	0	.040	-.052	6.00	6.00	4.20
Elbert S *	1	6.0	31	10	0	8	4	0	1	9	2	1	.563	2	0	0	0	1	0	0	2	-.101	-.014	12.00	12.00	7.37

Italicized stats have been adjusted for home park.

Batted Ball Pitching Stats

Player	% of PA		% of Batted Balls					Out %		Runs Per Event				Total Runs vs. Avg.				
	K%	BB%	GB%	LD%	FB%	IF/F	HR/OF	GB	OF	NIP	GB	LD	OF	NIP	GB	LD	FB	Tot
Lowe D	17	5	60	17	23	.07	.10	77	80	-.00	.03	.37	.19	-13	-2	-10	-9	-34
Kuroda H	15	6	51	20	29	.08	.08	79	84	.02	.02	.36	.14	-7	-5	-2	-11	-24
Kuo H	30	7	46	20	34	.15	.07	76	85	-.02	.05	.39	.13	-7	-1	-5	-7	-21
Wade C	19	7	41	21	38	.04	.10	82	94	.01	-.02	.33	.09	-3	-6	-3	-5	-18
Broxton J	31	11	45	23	32	.09	.04	73	83	.00	.06	.34	.10	-4	-0	-4	-7	-15
Billingsley C	23	10	49	20	31	.07	.09	74	81	.03	.05	.41	.16	-4	1	-2	-8	-13
Saito T	30	9	47	17	36	.09	.03	71	82	-.01	.07	.43	.06	-3	2	-3	-6	-11
Beimel J	15	11	47	19	34	.00	.00	69	89	.08	.08	.41	-.02	2	3	0	-9	-4
Maddux G	11	3	50	19	31	.09	.13	72	94	-.01	.06	.32	.14	-3	2	-1	-2	-4
Troncoso R	24	9	61	22	18	.00	.11	74	88	.02	.04	.44	.15	-1	0	1	-3	-4
Loaiza E	9	6	37	17	46	.13	.09	72	97	.07	.08	.53	.05	-0	1	2	-3	-1
Stults E	18	8	38	22	41	.10	.14	69	89	.03	.08	.32	.18	-1	1	-1	1	-0
Park C	19	10	51	19	30	.09	.15	77	82	.04	.03	.40	.26	-1	-2	-1	4	0
Kershaw C	21	11	48	21	31	.11	.13	77	84	.05	.03	.47	.21	1	-3	4	-1	1
Johnson J	15	11	56	16	28	.19	.23	77	88	.08	.03	.57	.34	1	-0	2	2	4
Proctor S	25	13	38	21	41	.22	.17	71	80	.04	.08	.47	.29	1	1	1	3	6
Penny B	12	11	49	20	31	.07	.12	75	84	.10	.04	.44	.20	4	-0	6	2	12
MLB Average	18	10	44	20	36	.10	.11	74	84	.05	.04	.39	.18	--	--	--	--	--

Fielding Stats

Name	Inn	SBA/G	CS%	ERA	WP+PB/G	PO	A	TE	FE	Grade
Catcher										
Martin R	1238.0	0.63	20%	3.63	0.298	1042	65	9	2	C
Ardoin D	145.3	0.81	23%	3.78	0.619	126	11	1	0	--
Bennett G	54.0	0.33	0%	4.50	0.833	43	3	1	0	--
Ellis A	10.0	0.00	0%	4.50	0.000	7	1	0	0	--

Name	Inn	PO	A	TE	FE	FPct	DPS	DPT	ZR	OOZ	Grade
First Base											
Loney J	1362.0	1364	121	5	7	.991	14	2	.728	58	A+
Garciaparra	38.7	49	4	0	0	1.000	0	0	.600	2	--
Blake C	17.0	27	0	0	1	.964	0	0	.750	0	--
Sweeney M	17.0	18	1	0	0	1.000	0	0	1.000	0	--
LaRoche A	8.0	11	1	0	0	1.000	0	0	1.000	0	--
Kent J	4.0	7	1	0	0	1.000	0	0	1.000	0	--
Second Base											
Kent J	885.0	168	279	2	9	.976	25	27	.820	20	D
Dewitt B	193.7	41	62	0	2	.981	3	6	.820	4	--
Maza L	136.3	30	45	0	2	.974	3	9	.738	4	--
Hu C	108.7	15	28	1	0	.977	1	3	.818	5	--
Ozuna P	81.7	17	32	0	0	1.000	0	3	.800	2	--
Young D	16.0	3	6	0	0	1.000	0	0	.750	0	--
LaRoche A	13.0	7	2	0	0	1.000	1	1	1.000	0	--
Berroa A	12.0	1	4	0	0	1.000	0	0	1.000	1	--
Blake C	1.0	0	0	0	0	.000	0	0	--	--	--
Shortstop											
Berroa A	591.7	91	219	5	3	.975	16	23	.871	26	--
Furcal R	296.0	46	92	3	1	.972	9	8	.841	12	--
Garciaparra	238.0	29	89	1	3	.967	5	7	.823	16	--
Hu C	229.0	46	75	0	0	1.000	6	8	.884	9	--
Maza L	86.0	23	35	2	0	.967	3	3	.848	5	--
Ozuna P	6.7	0	4	0	0	1.000	0	0	1.000	1	--

Name	Inn	PO	A	TE	FE	FPct	DPS	DPT	ZR	OOZ	Grade
Third Base											
Dewitt B	727.7	58	193	3	5	.969	16	1	.711	42	A+
Blake C	469.7	27	104	0	2	.985	10	0	.720	16	F-
LaRoche A	105.0	6	25	1	0	.969	1	0	.688	2	--
Garciaparra	73.0	2	21	1	1	.920	0	0	.750	6	--
Martin R	71.0	2	21	3	0	.885	4	0	.722	5	--
Ozuna P	1.0	0	0	0	0	.000	0	0	--	--	--
Left Field											
Pierre J	622.7	125	0	1	2	.977	0	0	.895	31	--
Ramirez M	436.3	91	1	1	1	.979	0	0	.895	23	--
Ethier A	277.3	48	3	0	2	.962	0	0	.927	10	--
Young D	86.0	16	2	0	0	1.000	0	0	.765	3	--
Repko J	18.0	6	0	0	0	1.000	0	0	.800	2	--
Ozuna P	5.0	0	0	0	0	.000	0	0	--	--	--
Sweeney M	1.0	0	0	0	0	.000	0	0	--	--	--
Tiffee T	1.0	0	0	0	0	.000	0	0	--	--	--
Center Field											
Kemp M	825.7	209	10	0	1	.995	6	0	.907	44	F
Jones A	496.3	133	1	0	1	.993	0	0	.886	40	--
Pierre J	116.3	28	1	0	0	1.000	2	0	.955	7	--
Repko J	9.0	7	0	0	0	1.000	0	0	1.000	2	--
Right Field											
Ethier A	881.0	171	8	0	0	1.000	0	0	.865	30	F-
Kemp M	478.7	97	6	1	1	.981	0	0	.848	20	--
Young D	72.7	8	2	0	0	1.000	2	0	1.000	1	--
Repko J	15.0	2	0	0	0	1.000	0	0	1.000	1	--

Milwaukee Brewers

Stat Facts:

- Only 61% of Rickie Weeks' ground balls were outs, lowest rate among ML regulars
- Jeff Suppan allowed only 4 stolen bases in 11 attempts
- Mitch Stetter walked 21% of the batters he faced
- 1% of Jason Kendall's outfield flies were home runs
- 26% of Russell Branyan's outfield flies were home runs
- Prince Fielder had 10 sacrifice flies
- Mike Cameron and Bill Hall each struck out 28% of the time
- C.C. Sabathia allowed 6 home runs in 131 innings
- Eric Gagne allowed 11 home runs in 46 innings
- Brian Shouse allowed 62% ground balls
- Salomon Torres induced 15 double plays in 80 innings
- J.J. Hardy made 72 OOZ plays

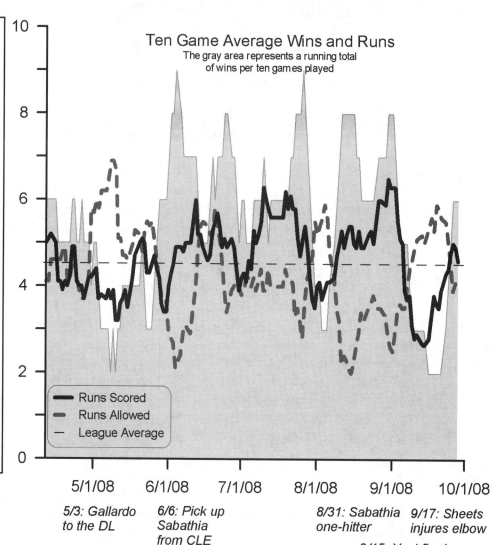

Ten Game Average Wins and Runs
The gray area represents a running total of wins per ten games played

Legend:
— Runs Scored
-- Runs Allowed
— League Average

5/3: Gallardo to the DL
6/6: Pick up Sabathia from CLE
8/31: Sabathia one-hitter
9/17: Sheets injures elbow
9/15: Yost fired as manager

Team Batting and Pitching/Fielding Stats by Month

	April	May	June	July	Aug	Sept/Oct
Wins	15	13	16	16	20	10
Losses	12	16	10	11	7	16
RS/G	4.7	3.9	5.0	5.1	5.6	3.6
RA/G	4.7	4.6	4.3	4.6	2.7	4.7
OBP	.318	.323	.322	.335	.343	.311
SLG	.392	.418	.476	.481	.449	.370
FIP	4.68	5.03	4.28	3.76	3.67	4.64
DER	.696	.698	.706	.678	.725	.697

Batting Stats

Player	BR	Runs	RBI	PA	Outs	H	2B	3B	HR	TB	K	BB	IBB	HBP	SH	SF	SB	CS	GDP	H-A	L^R	BA	OBP	SLG	GPA
Fielder P *	104	86	102	694	440	162	30	2	34	298	134	84	19	12	0	10	3	2	12	.009	.073	.276	.372	.507	.294
Braun R	104	92	106	663	454	174	39	7	37	338	129	42	4	6	0	4	14	4	13	.058	-.004	.285	.335	.553	.289
Hart C	84	76	91	657	472	164	45	6	20	281	109	27	2	5	4	9	23	7	17	-.045	.020	.268	.300	.459	.250
Hardy J	78	78	74	629	427	161	31	4	24	272	98	52	3	1	5	2	2	1	18	-.043	.070	.283	.343	.478	.274
Cameron M	74	69	70	508	345	108	25	2	25	212	142	54	1	6	1	3	17	5	4	-.055	.065	.243	.331	.477	.268
Weeks R	69	89	46	560	374	111	22	7	14	189	115	66	0	14	1	4	19	5	5	-.047	.038	.234	.342	.398	.253
Kendall J	57	46	49	587	397	127	30	2	2	167	45	50	7	13	6	2	8	3	5	-.008	.013	.246	.327	.324	.228
Hall B	46	50	55	448	323	91	22	1	15	160	124	37	2	3	1	3	5	6	4	.041	.110	.225	.293	.396	.231
Kapler G	35	36	38	245	164	69	17	2	8	114	39	13	0	1	1	1	3	1	3	.011	.076	.301	.340	.498	.278
Counsell C *	26	31	14	302	198	56	14	1	1	75	42	46	1	5	1	2	3	1	5	-.017	.029	.226	.355	.302	.236
Branyan R *	23	24	20	152	99	33	8	0	12	77	42	19	4	0	0	1	1	0	0	.141	.333	.250	.342	.583	.300
Durham R +	21	21	13	122	80	30	12	0	3	51	23	15	1	0	0	0	2	2	1	.138	.060	.280	.369	.477	.285
Rivera M	13	8	14	69	45	19	5	0	1	27	10	6	0	1	0	0	2	0	2	.020	-.097	.306	.377	.435	.278
Dillon J	9	13	6	90	60	16	3	0	1	22	21	13	0	1	1	0	1	0	1	-.115	.234	.213	.337	.293	.225
Gross G *	6	6	2	54	34	9	3	0	0	12	7	10	0	0	0	1	2	0	0	.173	--	.209	.352	.279	.228
Parra M *	5	2	6	58	44	12	5	1	0	19	18	2	0	0	3	0	0	0	3	.108	.148	.226	.255	.358	.204
Suppan J	2	2	1	63	43	7	1	0	0	8	13	3	0	0	10	0	0	0	0	.025	.132	.140	.189	.160	.125
Gwynn T *	2	5	1	49	36	8	1	0	0	9	7	4	0	1	1	1	3	1	1	-.086	-.556	.190	.271	.214	.175
McClung S	2	2	0	22	14	5	1	0	0	6	10	0	0	0	2	0	0	0	0	.190	.320	.263	.263	.316	.197
Nelson B *	1	0	0	8	5	2	2	0	0	4	0	1	0	0	0	0	0	0	0	-.154	.360	.286	.375	.571	.312
Iribarren H	1	1	1	15	12	2	1	0	0	3	3	1	0	0	0	0	0	0	0	-.142	.154	.143	.200	.214	.144
Lamb M *	1	2	0	11	8	3	0	0	0	3	1	0	0	0	0	0	0	0	0	.250	--	.273	.273	.273	.191
Gamel M *	1	0	0	2	1	1	1	0	0	2	1	0	0	0	0	0	0	0	0	--	--	.500	.500	1.000	.475

Italicized stats have been adjusted for home park.

Batted Ball Batting Stats

Player	% of PA		% of Batted Balls					Out %		Runs Per Event				Total Runs vs. Avg.				
	K%	BB%	GB%	LD%	FB%	IF/F	HR/OF	GB	OF	NIP	GB	LD	OF	NIP	GB	LD	FB	Tot
Fielder P	19	14	41	19	40	.13	.19	75	83	.08	.04	.45	.30	9	-2	3	21	32
Braun R	19	7	39	17	44	.13	.19	67	86	.01	.09	.46	.28	-7	9	2	25	29
Hardy J	16	8	48	15	36	.15	.16	68	89	.05	.08	.46	.23	-1	9	-1	9	16
Cameron M	28	12	33	22	46	.13	.20	69	92	.02	.09	.42	.26	-2	2	-1	10	9
Branyan R	28	13	22	21	57	.12	.26	85	85	.03	-.01	.44	.38	-0	-2	0	11	9
Kapler G	16	6	46	18	36	.14	.14	70	76	.01	.09	.38	.27	-3	4	-0	7	8
Weeks R	21	14	46	15	39	.16	.11	61	90	.08	.14	.32	.15	7	16	-13	-5	6
Durham R	19	12	34	19	47	.15	.09	71	80	.07	.08	.45	.20	1	1	1	2	4
Hart C	17	5	40	19	40	.05	.09	74	84	-.01	.05	.44	.16	-10	3	5	4	2
Counsell C	14	17	47	23	30	.15	.02	82	92	.14	-.00	.41	-.01	9	-4	3	-12	-4
Hall B	28	9	39	21	40	.18	.16	71	90	-.00	.07	.37	.21	-7	1	-4	-0	-10
Kendall J	8	11	46	18	37	.06	.01	76	84	.16	.04	.32	.04	9	1	-7	-17	-13
MLB Average	18	10	44	20	36	.10	.11	74	84	.05	.04	.39	.18	--	--	--	--	--

Pitching Stats

Player	PRC	IP	BFP	G	GS	K	BB	IBB	HBP	H	HR	DP	DER	SB	CS	PO	W	L	Sv	Op	Hld	H-A	R^L	RA	ERA	FIP
Sheets B	100	198.3	812	31	31	158	47	2	1	181	17	11	.706	13	7	2	13	9	0	0	0	.001	-.025	3.36	3.09	3.42
Sabathia C *	98	130.7	516	17	17	128	25	0	4	106	6	17	.708	5	1	0	11	2	0	0	0	.042	-.031	2.14	1.65	2.51
Bush D	67	185.0	763	31	29	109	48	3	10	163	29	15	.744	17	9	0	9	10	0	0	0	-.029	-.039	4.48	4.18	4.95
Parra M *	60	166.0	741	32	29	147	75	1	2	181	18	20	.649	8	5	2	10	8	0	0	0	-.056	-.038	4.93	4.39	4.21
Suppan J	49	177.7	780	31	31	90	67	7	4	207	30	27	.691	4	7	2	10	10	0	0	0	-.013	.020	5.57	4.96	5.46
McClung S	46	105.3	456	37	12	87	55	3	7	93	10	12	.710	5	4	0	6	6	0	0	1	.019	-.040	4.02	4.02	4.46
Villanueva C	43	108.3	464	47	9	93	30	1	3	112	18	7	.691	5	2	0	4	7	1	1	11	-.102	.064	4.40	4.07	4.53
Torres S	33	80.0	344	71	0	51	33	5	4	75	6	15	.700	1	2	0	7	5	28	35	5	-.034	-.029	3.94	3.49	4.10
Shouse B *	25	51.3	212	69	0	33	14	4	0	46	5	7	.713	1	1	1	5	1	2	5	15	-.117	-.122	3.33	2.81	3.77
Mota G	23	57.0	244	58	0	50	28	0	0	52	7	8	.711	4	1	1	5	6	1	4	11	.080	-.080	4.42	4.11	4.52
Gallardo Y	19	24.0	97	4	4	20	8	0	0	22	3	2	.697	0	1	0	0	0	0	0	0	-.055	-.096	1.88	1.88	4.16
Gagne E	15	46.3	203	50	0	38	22	2	2	46	11	7	.723	0	0	0	4	3	10	17	7	.066	.017	5.44	5.44	6.07
Stetter M *	15	25.3	109	30	0	31	19	1	4	14	2	2	.774	2	2	1	3	1	0	1	4	.018	-.033	3.20	3.20	4.39
Riske D	13	42.3	193	45	0	27	25	0	0	47	6	4	.689	2	2	1	1	2	2	7	11	.150	-.060	5.31	5.31	5.54
Difelice M	10	19.0	78	15	0	20	4	0	0	17	4	1	.740	1	0	0	1	0	0	0	1	-.057	-.203	3.32	2.84	4.47
Dillard T	3	14.3	65	13	0	5	6	2	0	17	2	2	.673	0	1	0	0	0	0	0	1	.134	-.087	7.53	4.40	5.16
Jackson Z *	1	3.7	18	2	0	1	2	0	0	5	0	0	.667	0	0	0	0	0	0	0	0	--	-.208	4.91	4.91	4.29
Tavarez J	1	7.3	41	7	0	10	5	0	0	13	0	0	.462	0	0	0	0	1	0	0	0	-.030	-.290	12.27	8.59	2.52

Italicized stats have been adjusted for home park.

Batted Ball Pitching Stats

	% of PA		% of Batted Balls					Out %		Runs Per Event				Total Runs vs. Avg.				
Player	K%	BB%	GB%	LD%	FB%	IF/F	HR/OF	GB	OF	NIP	GB	LD	OF	NIP	GB	LD	FB	Tot
Sabathia C	25	6	51	22	27	.10	.06	81	84	-.03	.00	.36	.09	-12	-7	-4	-15	-38
Sheets B	19	6	41	18	41	.09	.07	78	83	-.01	.03	.42	.14	-13	-4	-3	-3	-23
Bush D	14	8	41	18	41	.12	.13	78	86	.05	.02	.36	.20	-3	-6	-7	9	-8
Torres S	15	11	56	20	24	.07	.11	73	82	.08	.04	.27	.19	2	-0	-6	-3	-6
Shouse B	16	7	62	19	19	.10	.18	80	74	.02	.01	.33	.33	-2	-2	-2	1	-6
McClung S	19	14	44	18	38	.13	.10	76	86	.08	.03	.36	.16	6	-0	-6	-3	-4
Stetter M	28	21	36	16	48	.29	.12	78	87	.08	.02	.31	.17	3	-1	-4	-2	-3
Mota G	20	11	45	22	33	.09	.14	76	84	.05	.03	.30	.22	1	-2	-3	1	-3
Villanueva C	20	7	47	19	35	.07	.16	70	88	.01	.07	.37	.23	-5	5	-4	5	0
Gagne E	19	12	37	24	39	.11	.19	77	92	.06	.02	.39	.24	1	-1	2	3	5
Riske D	14	13	29	29	42	.10	.10	70	85	.11	.07	.32	.14	3	1	3	0	7
Parra M	20	10	52	22	27	.06	.14	69	85	.04	.07	.39	.20	0	9	2	-3	9
Suppan J	12	9	44	23	32	.07	.16	77	89	.09	.03	.37	.23	4	-3	10	10	22
MLB Average	18	10	44	20	36	.10	.11	74	84	.05	.04	.39	.18	--	--	--	--	--

Fielding Stats

Name	Inn	SBA/G	CS%	ERA	WP+PB/G	PO	A	TE	FE	Grade
Catchers										
Kendall J	1328.3	0.62	40%	3.85	0.332	1025	95	6	0	A+
Rivera M	127.3	1.27	11%	4.10	0.636	112	11	3	0	--

Name	Inn	PO	A	TE	FE	FPct	DPS	DPT	ZR	OOZ	Grade
First Base											
Fielder P	1383.0	1369	89	2	15	.988	17	0	.684	37	F
Dillon J	25.0	25	3	0	0	1.000	2	1	.667	0	--
Branyan R	24.0	26	1	0	0	1.000	0	0	.667	1	--
Rivera M	21.0	20	3	0	0	1.000	2	0	1.000	3	--
Nelson B	2.0	1	0	0	0	1.000	0	0	--	--	--
Second Base											
Weeks R	1056.0	256	333	7	8	.975	26	47	.807	41	B
Durham R	202.7	58	61	0	0	1.000	6	8	.836	6	--
Counsell C	112.0	16	42	0	0	1.000	3	2	.795	6	--
Dillon J	43.7	9	18	1	0	.964	3	2	.737	0	--
Hall B	32.0	3	16	0	2	.905	1	0	.833	1	--
Iribarren H	9.3	1	3	0	0	1.000	1	0	1.000	2	--
Shortstop											
Hardy J	1268.0	202	430	6	9	.977	41	40	.826	72	A
Counsell C	185.3	30	73	2	0	.981	5	7	.902	7	--
Escobar A	2.0	0	0	0	0	.000	0	0	--	--	--
Third Base											
Hall B	899.3	69	193	8	9	.939	23	1	.722	28	C
Branyan R	276.0	22	63	1	3	.955	7	0	.729	9	--
Counsell C	268.3	23	54	1	0	.987	6	0	.696	12	--
Dillon J	9.0	0	2	0	0	1.000	0	0	1.000	1	--
Lamb M	2.0	0	2	1	0	.667	0	0	.500	1	--
Gamel M	1.0	0	0	0	0	.000	0	0	--	--	--

Name	Inn	PO	A	TE	FE	FPct	DPS	DPT	ZR	OOZ	Grade
Left Field											
Braun R	1310.0	275	9	0	0	1.000	0	0	.892	69	B
Kapler G	118.3	22	1	0	0	1.000	0	0	.889	6	--
Nix L	10.0	4	0	0	0	1.000	0	0	1.000	0	--
Dillon J	9.0	1	0	0	0	1.000	0	0	--	--	--
Gross G	4.0	2	0	0	0	1.000	0	0	1.000	0	--
Gwynn T	4.0	1	0	0	0	1.000	0	0	--	--	--
Center Field											
Cameron M	1057.0	293	3	1	0	.997	0	0	.935	64	C
Kapler G	251.0	70	0	0	1	.986	0	0	.945	18	--
Gross G	98.7	28	1	0	1	.967	2	0	.958	5	--
Gwynn T	46.0	14	0	0	0	1.000	0	0	1.000	2	--
Iribarren H	3.0	1	0	0	0	1.000	0	0	1.000	0	--
Right Field											
Hart C	1376.0	302	8	2	3	.984	4	0	.890	62	D
Kapler G	66.0	9	0	0	0	1.000	0	0	.778	2	--
Gross G	6.7	3	0	0	0	1.000	0	0	1.000	2	B
Gwynn T	6.3	0	0	0	0	.000	0	0	--	--	--

Minnesota Twins

Stat Facts:
- Alexi Casilla led the AL with 13 sacrifice hits
- Nick Blackburn allowed just 2 stolen bases in 4 attempts
- The Twins turned 34 DPs behind Blackburn
- The top five Twins' starters allowed a total of just 20 steals
- None of the five had a BB% above 6%
- Boof Bonser allowed 11 stolen bases in 11 attempts
- Carlos Gomez had a .223 GPA in 614 PAs
- Gomez made 104 OOZ plays, and started 8 double plays
- Joe Mauer tied for the major league lead with 11 sacrifice flies
- Justin Morneau had 10
- The Twins had a .648 DER behind Livan Hernandez
- Delmon Young hit just 2 infield pop-ups

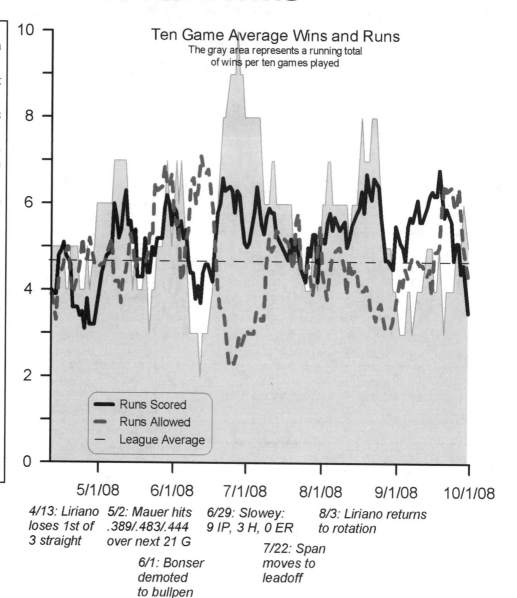

Ten Game Average Wins and Runs

The gray area represents a running total of wins per ten games played

Runs Scored
Runs Allowed
League Average

4/13: Liriano loses 1st of 3 straight

5/2: Mauer hits .389/.483/.444 over next 21 G

6/1: Bonser demoted to bullpen

6/29: Slowey: 9 IP, 3 H, 0 ER

7/22: Span moves to leadoff

8/3: Liriano returns to rotation

Team Batting and Pitching/Fielding Stats by Month

	April	May	June	July	Aug	Sept/Oct
Wins	13	15	17	15	17	11
Losses	14	13	11	10	12	15
RS/G	3.8	5.5	5.1	5.5	5.6	5.0
RA/G	4.5	5.2	4.4	4.6	3.8	5.0
OBP	.305	.341	.335	.361	.350	.350
SLG	.362	.399	.434	.441	.421	.389
FIP	4.37	4.31	4.33	4.20	3.60	5.00
DER	.687	.681	.682	.710	.692	.691

Batting Stats

Player	BR	Runs	RBI	PA	Outs	H	2B	3B	HR	TB	K	BB	IBB	HBP	SH	SF	SB	CS	GDP	H-A	L^R	BA	OBP	SLG	GPA
Morneau J *	118	97	129	712	457	187	47	4	23	311	85	76	16	3	0	10	0	1	20	-.021	.053	.300	.374	.499	.293
Mauer J *	95	98	85	633	382	176	31	4	9	242	50	84	8	1	1	11	1	1	21	.049	-.029	.328	.413	.451	.299
Young D	71	80	69	623	432	167	28	4	10	233	105	35	7	7	1	5	14	5	19	.011	.021	.290	.336	.405	.253
Span D *	65	70	47	411	255	102	16	7	6	150	60	50	3	4	8	2	18	7	3	.014	-.024	.294	.387	.432	.282
Gomez C	65	79	59	614	446	149	24	7	7	208	142	25	0	7	3	2	33	11	7	.020	.023	.258	.296	.360	.223
Kubel J *	65	74	78	517	350	126	22	5	20	218	91	47	2	0	0	7	0	1	12	.044	.033	.272	.335	.471	.268
Harris B	51	57	49	490	333	115	29	3	7	171	98	39	0	4	7	6	1	1	13	-.004	-.004	.265	.327	.394	.246
Casilla A +	46	58	50	437	287	108	15	0	7	144	45	31	0	2	13	6	7	2	8	.043	-.034	.281	.333	.374	.243
Punto N +	40	43	28	377	258	96	19	4	2	129	57	32	1	0	5	2	15	6	10	.029	-.014	.284	.344	.382	.250
Cuddyer M	36	30	36	279	195	62	13	4	3	92	40	25	4	5	0	0	5	1	7	.058	.010	.249	.330	.369	.241
Buscher B *	34	29	47	245	162	64	9	0	4	85	42	19	0	0	0	7	0	2	6	-.030	.109	.294	.340	.390	.251
Lamb M *	27	20	32	261	185	55	12	3	1	76	32	17	4	0	0	8	0	1	3	-.078	.136	.233	.276	.322	.205
Monroe C	24	22	29	179	134	33	9	0	8	66	48	16	1	0	0	0	0	1	3	.070	-.147	.202	.274	.405	.224
Everett A	14	19	20	150	100	27	6	1	2	41	15	12	1	1	6	4	0	0	0	-.026	.086	.213	.278	.323	.206
Tolbert M +	12	18	6	123	87	32	6	3	0	44	19	7	0	0	2	1	7	1	5	.036	.003	.283	.322	.389	.242
Redmond M	11	14	12	137	98	37	6	0	0	43	11	5	0	2	0	1	0	0	6	.055	-.020	.287	.321	.333	.228
Ruiz R	11	13	7	68	46	17	2	0	1	22	21	6	1	0	0	0	0	0	1	.089	.034	.274	.338	.355	.241
Macri M	5	3	4	36	24	11	1	0	1	15	10	2	0	0	0	0	1	1	0	.027	.104	.324	.361	.441	.273
Clark H *	2	0	1	8	6	2	2	0	0	4	2	0	0	0	0	0	0	0	0	.127	-.127	.250	.250	.500	.238
Slowey K	1	1	2	8	6	2	1	0	0	3	1	0	0	0	0	0	0	0	0	-.206	-.275	.250	.250	.375	.206
Blackburn N	1	0	0	3	2	1	0	0	0	1	0	0	0	0	0	0	0	0	0	-.233	--	.333	.333	.333	.233

Italicized stats have been adjusted for home park.

Batted Ball Batting Stats

Player	% of PA		% of Batted Balls					Runs Per Event				Total Runs vs. Avg.				
	K%	BB%	GB%	LD%	FB%	IF/F	HR/OF	GB	OF	NIP	GB	LD	OF	NIP	GB	LD	FB	Tot
Morneau J	12	11	43	19	38	.09	.12	76	77	.11	.03	.41	.24	9	-3	6	19	30
Mauer J	8	13	49	23	28	.04	.05	74	81	.18	.03	.40	.13	16	2	13	-2	29
Span D	15	13	54	26	20	.04	.11	73	78	.10	.07	.32	.22	7	6	2	-2	13
Kubel J	18	9	40	20	41	.05	.14	77	84	.04	.03	.38	.22	-1	-4	-1	12	7
Cuddyer M	14	11	46	21	33	.13	.05	75	83	.08	.03	.38	.13	2	-1	1	-3	-0
Tolbert C	15	6	41	30	30	.15	.00	78	87	.01	-.00	.43	.00	-1	-0	5	-5	-2
Buscher B	17	8	33	28	39	.10	.06	77	85	.03	.01	.37	.10	-1	-3	5	-4	-2
Young D	17	7	55	17	28	.02	.08	72	85	.02	.06	.47	.13	-6	6	4	-7	-2
Punto N	15	8	45	21	35	.22	.03	70	79	.05	.06	.36	.12	-1	4	-0	-7	-4
Harris B	20	9	53	16	30	.04	.07	72	75	.03	.06	.42	.19	-3	2	-4	-0	-4
Monroe C	27	9	44	16	40	.11	.17	78	85	.00	.03	.36	.26	-3	-1	-4	3	-5
Redmond M	8	5	47	28	25	.07	.00	80	86	.07	-.00	.32	.01	-1	-2	3	-5	-5
Casilla A	10	8	52	15	34	.19	.08	74	84	.08	.05	.33	.13	0	8	-8	-7	-7
Everett A	10	9	39	15	46	.11	.04	82	80	.10	.01	.30	.11	1	-3	-4	-2	-8
Lamb M	12	7	39	18	43	.12	.01	83	80	.05	.00	.33	.07	-1	-3	-3	-5	-13
Gomez C	23	5	44	17	39	.16	.05	67	79	-.03	.10	.35	.13	-14	18	-13	-11	-21
MLB Average	18	10	44	20	36	.10	.11	74	84	.05	.04	.39	.18	--	--	--	--	--

Pitching Stats

Player	PRC	IP	BFP	G	GS	K	BB	IBB	HBP	H	HR	DP	DER	SB	CS	PO	W	L	Sv	Op	Hld	H-A	R^L	RA	ERA	FIP
Baker S	90	172.3	703	28	28	141	42	2	3	161	20	16	.714	8	5	0	11	4	0	0	0	-.047	-.025	3.45	3.45	3.85
Slowey K	70	160.3	653	27	27	123	24	1	4	161	22	13	.708	4	4	1	12	11	0	0	0	-.055	-.064	4.15	3.99	3.98
Blackburn N	68	193.3	823	33	33	96	39	4	7	224	23	34	.679	2	2	0	11	11	0	0	0	-.021	-.010	4.75	4.05	4.44
Nathan J	64	67.7	261	68	0	74	18	4	2	43	5	7	.759	5	0	0	1	2	39	45	0	-.079	-.016	1.73	1.33	2.71
Perkins G *	52	151.0	661	26	26	74	39	0	3	183	25	14	.692	3	4	2	12	4	0	0	0	-.023	.052	4.83	4.41	5.24
Hernandez L	36	139.7	627	23	23	54	29	3	1	199	18	20	.648	3	4	1	10	8	0	0	0	-.033	.013	5.99	5.48	4.71
Reyes D *	33	46.3	188	75	0	39	15	2	2	40	4	11	.695	6	2	2	3	0	0	3	17	-.014	-.090	2.33	2.33	3.64
Bonser B	32	118.3	532	47	12	97	36	1	1	139	16	10	.657	11	0	0	3	7	0	2	2	-.053	-.058	6.62	5.93	4.26
Liriano F *	30	76.0	329	14	14	67	32	1	1	74	7	6	.689	6	3	3	6	4	0	0	0	-.058	-.033	4.74	3.91	3.93
Breslow C *	30	38.7	149	42	0	32	14	2	0	24	0	2	.748	0	5	3	0	2	1	2	5	-.042	-.069	2.09	1.63	2.51
Crain J	28	62.7	268	66	0	50	24	3	1	62	6	6	.690	6	1	0	5	4	0	3	17	-.064	.003	4.16	3.59	3.93
Guerrier M	25	76.3	344	76	0	59	37	9	0	84	12	4	.686	8	1	1	6	9	1	5	20	-.030	-.004	5.54	5.19	4.83
Bass B	20	68.3	303	44	0	32	22	3	3	84	11	14	.672	1	2	1	3	4	1	2	3	-.061	.031	5.53	4.87	5.35
Mijares J *	13	10.3	34	10	0	5	0	0	0	3	0	0	.897	0	0	0	0	1	0	0	2	.037	.053	0.87	0.87	2.26
Rincon J	7	28.0	133	24	0	20	16	2	2	33	5	2	.689	4	1	0	2	2	0	0	1	-.056	-.052	6.75	6.11	5.84
Korecky R	6	17.7	74	16	0	6	8	0	0	19	2	6	.690	2	0	0	2	0	0	0	0	-.026	-.036	4.58	4.58	5.38
Neshek P	6	13.3	56	15	0	15	4	1	0	12	2	0	.714	0	0	0	0	1	0	2	6	-.112	-.024	4.73	4.73	3.61
Humber P	4	11.7	50	5	0	6	5	0	1	11	4	2	.794	0	0	0	0	0	0	0	0	.116	.039	4.63	4.63	8.20
Guardado E*	2	7.0	33	9	0	5	2	0	0	12	1	1	.560	0	0	0	1	1	0	1	2	-.127	.053	7.71	7.71	4.52

Italicized stats have been adjusted for home park.

Batted Ball Pitching Stats

Player	% of PA		% of Batted Balls					Out %		Runs Per Event				Total Runs vs. Avg.				
	K%	BB%	GB%	LD%	FB%	IF/F	HR/OF	GB	OF	NIP	GB	LD	OF	NIP	GB	LD	FB	Tot
Baker T	20	6	33	21	46	.14	.10	70	85	-.00	.06	.28	.15	-10	0	-12	-1	-23
Nathan J	28	8	47	19	33	.11	.10	81	89	-.02	-.01	.28	.15	-5	-5	-8	-4	-22
Breslow C	21	9	40	19	41	.18	.00	77	82	.03	.03	.24	.01	-1	-1	-5	-7	-14
Slowey K	19	4	36	19	45	.10	.11	76	85	-.03	.04	.40	.17	-14	-3	-1	6	-11
Reyes D	21	9	60	17	23	.03	.14	73	88	.03	.05	.32	.20	-1	1	-4	-2	-5
Liriano F	20	10	42	18	40	.15	.09	70	81	.04	.07	.35	.17	-1	2	-4	-1	-3
Crain J	19	9	41	17	42	.16	.09	72	77	.04	.06	.38	.21	-1	1	-3	2	-0
Blackburn N	12	6	45	21	34	.09	.10	71	83	.04	.05	.35	.18	-6	3	3	4	4
Rincon J	15	14	40	14	46	.05	.13	65	77	.10	.09	.24	.25	2	1	-4	5	5
Bonser B	18	7	41	20	39	.09	.11	67	82	.01	.09	.38	.19	-5	7	1	5	7
Guerrier M	17	11	47	18	35	.09	.14	73	87	.06	.06	.45	.20	2	2	1	2	7
Bass B	11	8	59	17	24	.08	.18	74	73	.09	.04	.43	.34	1	2	2	7	12
Perkins G	11	6	38	22	40	.09	.12	76	85	.05	.04	.38	.19	-3	-2	9	11	15
Hernandez L	9	5	44	22	34	.07	.10	72	86	.05	.05	.44	.16	-4	6	18	3	23
MLB Average	18	10	44	20	36	.10	.11	74	84	.05	.04	.39	.18	--	--	--	--	--

Fielding Stats

Name	Inn	SBA/G	CS%	ERA	WP+PB/G	PO	A	TE	FE	Grade
Catchers										
Mauer J	1203.0	0.52	26%	4.22	0.329	831	52	3	0	B
Redmond M	253.0	0.75	14%	4.02	0.178	180	9	0	0	--
Jorgensen R	3.0	0.00	0%	0.00	0.000	1	0	0	0	--

Name	Inn	PO	A	TE	FE	FPct	DPS	DPT	ZR	OOZ	Grade
First Base											
Morneau J	1363.0	1316	89	0	4	.997	14	4	.699	22	F-
Lamb M	52.3	46	8	0	0	1.000	0	1	.833	4	--
Cuddyer M	18.0	22	1	0	1	.958	0	0	.500	0	--
Buscher B	14.0	13	0	0	0	1.000	0	0	.667	0	--
Clark H	5.0	3	1	0	0	1.000	0	0	1.000	0	--
Harris B	3.0	1	1	0	0	1.000	0	0	--	--	--
Macri M	3.0	3	0	0	0	1.000	0	0	1.000	0	--
Second Base											
Casilla A	833.7	196	247	4	8	.974	31	42	.800	15	F
Harris B	319.7	56	101	2	3	.969	11	13	.864	4	--
Punto N	215.7	54	79	1	1	.985	8	10	.760	8	--
Tolbert M	75.0	15	30	1	0	.978	4	4	.786	2	--
Macri M	10.0	1	6	0	0	1.000	0	1	1.000	0	--
Clark H	3.0	0	2	0	0	1.000	1	0	1.000	0	--
Everett A	1.0	0	0	0	0	.000	0	0	--	--	--
Buscher B	1.0	0	0	0	0	.000	0	0	--	--	--
Shortstop											
Punto N	530.7	103	187	3	5	.973	24	20	.860	15	--
Harris B	464.3	84	159	6	0	.976	13	26	.779	17	--
Everett A	364.0	61	145	4	3	.967	14	14	.854	13	--
Tolbert M	90.0	14	26	1	0	.976	3	1	.793	2	--
Casilla A	10.0	2	3	0	0	1.000	0	0	1.000	0	--

Name	Inn	PO	A	TE	FE	FPct	DPS	DPT	ZR	OOZ	Grade
Third Base											
Buscher B	519.3	37	113	5	5	.938	9	0	.688	16	--
Lamb M	458.7	41	88	2	2	.970	6	2	.602	14	--
Harris B	256.3	18	48	2	0	.971	4	0	.707	3	--
Tolbert M	89.3	9	24	4	0	.892	3	0	.655	5	--
Macri M	64.3	3	14	1	0	.944	3	0	.500	3	--
Punto N	63.0	3	16	0	0	1.000	1	0	.688	2	--
Clark H	8.0	3	2	0	0	1.000	0	0	1.000	0	--
Left Field											
Young D	1324.0	282	11	2	6	.973	4	0	.851	48	F
Kubel J	130.0	24	1	2	0	.926	0	1	.778	3	--
Pridie J	4.0	0	0	0	0	.000	0	0	--	--	--
Monroe C	1.0	0	0	0	0	.000	0	0	--	--	--
Center Field											
Gomez C	1271.0	436	9	4	4	.982	8	0	.946	104	A
Span D	116.7	34	1	1	0	.972	0	0	.821	11	--
Monroe C	56.7	13	1	0	0	1.000	2	0	.786	2	--
Cuddyer M	8.0	3	1	0	0	1.000	2	0	1.000	1	--
Punto N	6.0	1	0	0	0	1.000	0	0	1.000	0	--
Right Field											
Span D	686.7	192	5	1	2	.985	4	0	.927	39	A
Cuddyer M	501.7	123	6	0	1	.992	7	0	.901	23	--
Kubel J	238.7	74	1	0	1	.987	0	0	.878	9	--
Monroe C	25.0	5	0	0	0	1.000	0	0	.800	1	--
Pridie J	7.0	3	0	0	1	.750	0	0	1.000	1	--

New York Mets

Stat Facts:
- Jose Reyes led the majors in triples, PAs, and Outs
- David Wright's 23 LD runs above average led the majors
- Wright's LD% was 26%
- Wright made 56 OOZ plays
- Carlos Beltran made 111 OOZ plays
- Beltran stole 25 bases in 28 attempts
- Johan Santana led the NL with 234 IP and 964 BFP
- Pedro Feliciano led the majors with 86 appearances
- Oliver Perez led the majors with 105 walks allowed
- Perez's 14% BB rate tied for highest in the majors and his GB rate of 32% was lowest in the majors among 162+ IP pitchers
- Mike Pelfrey allowed only 5 stolen bases in 11 attempts
- Pelfrey induced 30 DPs

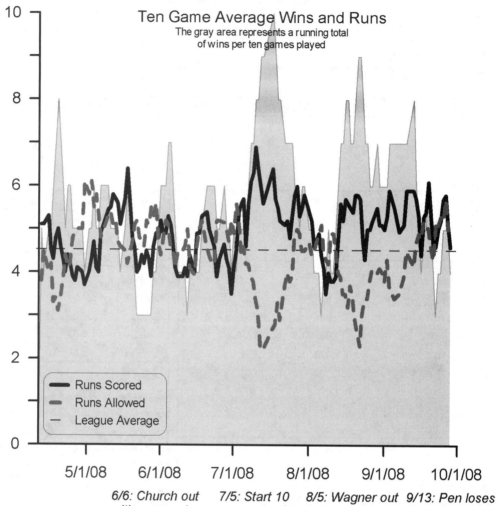

Ten Game Average Wins and Runs
The gray area represents a running total of wins per ten games played

- Runs Scored
- Runs Allowed
- League Average

6/6: Church out with concussion; OPS before: .906; .656 after

6/7: Delgado hitting .237/.320/.395; Mets 6.5 games back

7/5: Start 10 game streak to catch Phils

8/5: Wagner out for year with elbow injury

9/13: Pen loses first of 6 games down the stretch

9/27: Santana's heroic shutout not enough

Team Batting and Pitching/Fielding Stats by Month

	April	May	June	July	Aug	Sept/Oct
Wins	14	13	13	18	18	13
Losses	12	15	15	8	11	12
RS/G	4.6	5.0	4.3	5.9	4.9	5.0
RA/G	4.5	4.9	4.7	3.8	3.8	4.7
OBP	.341	.327	.325	.374	.332	.345
SLG	.371	.424	.378	.481	.430	.438
FIP	4.55	4.38	4.32	3.92	4.47	3.98
DER	.709	.701	.682	.716	.721	.666

Batting Stats

Player	BR	Runs	RBI	PA	Outs	H	2B	3B	HR	TB	K	BB	IBB	HBP	SH	SF	SB	CS	GDP	H-A	L^R	BA	OBP	SLG	GPA
Beltran C +	117	116	112	706	448	172	40	5	27	303	96	92	13	1	1	6	25	3	11	.027	.060	.284	.376	.500	.302
Wright D	117	115	124	736	457	189	42	2	33	334	118	94	5	4	0	11	15	5	15	.082	.115	.302	.390	.534	.318
Reyes J +	116	113	68	763	508	204	37	19	16	327	82	66	8	1	5	3	56	15	9	-.008	-.007	.297	.358	.475	.287
Delgado C *	106	96	115	686	453	162	32	1	38	310	124	72	19	8	0	8	1	1	16	.005	.047	.271	.353	.518	.296
Tatis F	55	33	47	306	199	81	16	1	11	132	59	29	3	3	0	1	3	0	7	.070	-.010	.297	.369	.484	.295
Church R *	46	54	49	359	243	88	14	1	12	140	83	33	3	3	1	3	2	3	9	.019	.031	.276	.346	.439	.273
Castillo L +	39	46	28	359	240	73	7	1	3	91	35	50	2	2	7	2	17	2	13	.004	.001	.245	.355	.305	.243
Easley D	35	33	44	347	246	85	10	2	6	117	38	19	0	7	2	3	0	0	15	-.061	.008	.269	.322	.370	.244
Schneider B	34	30	38	384	260	86	10	0	9	123	53	42	9	1	4	2	0	0	11	.005	.082	.257	.339	.367	.251
Murphy D *	26	24	17	151	96	41	9	3	2	62	28	18	1	1	0	1	0	2	4	-.022	-.093	.313	.397	.473	.305
Castro R	24	15	24	157	110	35	7	0	7	63	34	13	2	1	0	0	0	0	2	.021	.015	.245	.312	.441	.258
Chavez E *	18	30	12	298	205	72	10	2	1	89	22	17	3	0	9	2	6	1	6	.051	.050	.267	.308	.330	.227
Pagan A +	15	12	13	105	66	25	7	1	0	34	18	11	0	0	1	2	4	0	0	.046	-.080	.275	.346	.374	.256
Evans N	10	18	9	119	82	28	10	0	2	44	24	7	2	1	0	2	0	0	1	-.095	.185	.257	.303	.404	.244
Alou M	10	4	9	54	34	17	2	0	0	19	4	2	0	2	0	1	1	1	1	.109	.141	.347	.389	.388	.280
Casanova R +	7	5	6	61	41	15	2	0	1	20	10	6	0	0	0	0	0	0	1	-.040	.076	.273	.344	.364	.253
Anderson M *	4	16	10	151	112	29	6	0	1	38	27	9	0	0	2	2	2	1	2	-.040	.186	.210	.255	.275	.189
Cancel R	3	5	5	53	39	12	2	0	1	17	6	3	0	0	1	0	1	2	0	.062	.296	.245	.288	.347	.223
Reyes A +	3	13	3	121	88	24	0	0	1	27	20	4	0	2	5	0	2	0	2	-.053	-.077	.218	.259	.245	.183
Martinez R	2	0	3	18	13	4	3	0	0	7	3	2	0	0	0	0	0	0	1	.259	-.315	.250	.333	.438	.267
Nixon T *	2	2	1	41	29	6	1	0	1	10	9	6	1	0	0	0	1	0	0	.094	-.025	.171	.293	.286	.209
Stokes B	1	0	0	3	1	2	0	0	0	2	1	0	0	0	0	0	0	0	0	-.350	--	.667	.667	.667	.480
Martinez P	1	3	4	46	33	6	1	0	0	7	15	0	0	0	7	0	0	0	0	-.171	.077	.154	.154	.179	.117
Clark B	1	0	1	11	7	2	0	0	0	2	2	1	0	1	1	0	1	0	1	.000	-.255	.250	.400	.250	.249
Perez O *	1	2	3	67	50	6	1	0	0	7	23	4	0	0	7	0	1	0	0	-.027	.103	.107	.167	.125	.109

Italicized stats have been adjusted for home park.

Batted Ball Batting Stats

Player	% of PA		% of Batted Balls			IF/F	HR/OF	Out %		Runs Per Event				Total Runs vs. Avg.				
	K%	BB%	GB%	LD%	FB%			GB	OF	NIP	GB	LD	OF	NIP	GB	LD	FB	Tot
Wright D	16	13	36	26	38	.08	.14	71	85	.09	.06	.44	.21	12	3	23	11	48
Beltran C	14	13	45	22	33	.15	.14	75	86	.11	.04	.45	.22	12	1	15	4	32
Reyes J	11	9	44	23	33	.11	.08	70	86	.09	.09	.37	.13	4	16	10	-7	24
Delgado C	18	12	42	25	34	.12	.21	83	88	.07	-.01	.45	.29	5	-12	16	14	24
Tatis F	19	10	42	26	32	.04	.14	71	88	.05	.06	.44	.19	1	1	8	2	12
Murphy D	19	13	41	33	25	.00	.04	67	80	.07	.09	.40	.13	2	2	6	-2	8
Church R	23	10	45	24	31	.11	.18	79	81	.03	.02	.40	.29	-2	-2	3	5	4
Evans N	20	7	44	23	33	.14	.08	68	83	.00	.10	.37	.15	-2	2	1	-1	1
Castro R	22	9	36	24	40	.09	.18	79	79	.02	.01	.26	.29	-1	-2	-2	5	-0
Schneider B	14	11	53	26	21	.10	.11	82	88	.09	-.01	.38	.14	4	-7	7	-7	-4
Castillo L	10	14	66	16	18	.13	.05	77	79	.16	.02	.32	.10	9	-1	-6	-9	-7
Easley D	11	7	47	21	33	.10	.06	76	82	.07	.02	.32	.12	0	-3	-1	-4	-8
Anderson M	18	6	49	17	34	.11	.03	75	91	.00	.05	.35	.03	-2	0	-3	-6	-10
Reyes A	17	5	62	29	9	.00	.13	85	100	-.01	-.02	.20	.09	-2	-2	-2	-4	-11
Chavez E	7	6	53	19	28	.09	.00	73	79	.09	.05	.25	.07	-1	2	-6	-8	-13
MLB Average	18	10	44	20	36	.10	.11	74	84	.05	.04	.39	.18	--	--	--	--	--

Pitching Stats

Player	PRC	IP	BFP	G	GS	K	BB	IBB	HBP	H	HR	DP	DER	SB	CS	PO	W	L	Sv	Op	Hld	H-A	R^L	RA	ERA	FIP
Santana J *	135	234.3	964	34	34	206	63	5	4	206	23	12	.714	6	5	2	16	7	0	0	0	-.012	.008	2.84	2.53	3.51
Pelfrey M	80	200.7	851	32	32	110	64	1	13	209	12	30	.687	5	6	4	13	11	0	0	0	-.072	-.055	3.86	3.72	4.02
Perez O *	73	194.0	847	34	34	180		4	11	167	24	17	.721	8	1	0	10	7	0	0	0	-.015	-.088	4.64	4.22	4.69
Maine J	53	140.0	608	25	25	122	67	2	4	122	16	6	.717	7	6	1	10	8	0	0	0	.004	-.050	4.50	4.18	4.42
Martinez P	31	109.0	493	20	20	87	44	3	6	127	19	10	.668	15	2	1	5	6	0	0	0	-.058	-.015	5.78	5.61	5.17
Smith J	27	63.3	271	82	0	52	31	4	4	51	4	6	.722	6	2	0	6	3	0	3	18	-.035	-.110	3.98	3.55	3.85
Wagner B *	26	47.0	184	45	0	52	10	0	0	32	4	3	.737	0	0	27	34	0	0	1	0	-.081	.051	3.26	2.30	2.73
Schoeneweis	24	56.7	243	73	0	34	23	6	4	55	7	6	.720	2	2	2	2	6	1	5	15	-.075	-.149	3.65	3.34	4.72
Heilman A	24	76.0	356	78	0	80	46	8	9	75	10	1	.687	2	0	0	3	8	3	8	15	-.046	-.102	5.68	5.21	4.66
Feliciano P	23	53.3	237	86	0	50	26	8	3	57	7	9	.656	0	0	0	3	4	2	4	21	-.014	-.159	4.05	4.05	4.21
Sanchez D	22	58.3	254	66	0	44	23	3	3	54	6	4	.713	4	0	0	5	1	0	1	21	.021	.035	4.32	4.32	4.21
Stokes B	16	33.3	138	24	1	26	8	3	0	35	5	4	.697	3	0	0	1	0	1	3	4	.030	-.099	3.51	3.51	4.04
Figueroa N	15	45.3	211	16	6	36	26	1	2	48	3	3	.667	3	0	0	3	3	0	1	0	-.077	-.127	5.16	4.57	4.26
Vargas C	12	37.0	150	11	4	20	11	0	2	33	4	6	.735	2	1	0	3	2	0	1	1	.090	-.082	4.86	4.62	4.58
Muniz C	7	23.3	100	18	0	16	7	0	2	24	4	2	.718	0	0	1	1	1	0	1	1	-.108	-.093	5.40	5.40	5.22
Ayala L	5	18.0	78	19	0	14	2	0	0	23	3	1	.661	1	0	0	1	2	9	11	0	.013	.019	6.00	5.50	4.15
Knight B	4	12.0	57	4	2	10	7	0	2	14	0	2	.632	0	0	0	1	0	0	0	0	-.044	-.156	5.25	5.25	3.79
Niese J *	3	14.0	69	3	3	11	8	0	0	20	2	1	.625	0	0	0	1	1	0	0	0	-.193	.004	7.07	7.07	5.20
Sosa J	3	21.7	107	20	0	12	11	4	0	30	4	1	.638	0	1	0	4	1	0	0	1	-.045	-.107	9.55	7.06	5.46
Wise M	2	7.0	34	8	0	6	3	1	0	10	2	0	.652	1	0	0	0	1	0	0	1	-.043	-.045	6.43	6.43	6.06
Armas Jr. T	2	8.3	37	3	1	6	1	0	0	11	2	0	.679	1	0	0	1	0	0	0	0	--	-.229	7.56	7.56	5.24
Rincon R *	1	4.0	16	8	0	3	1	0	0	4	1	0	.727	0	1	0	0	0	0	0	1	.130	-.101	4.50	4.50	5.70
Parnell R	1	5.0	19	6	0	3	2	0	0	3	0	1	.786	0	0	0	0	0	0	0	0	.223	.154	5.40	5.40	3.20

Italicized stats have been adjusted for home park.

Batted Ball Pitching Stats

Player	% of PA		% of Batted Balls					Out %		Runs Per Event				Total Runs vs. Avg.				
	K%	BB%	GB%	LD%	FB%	IF/F	HR/OF	GB	OF	NIP	GB	LD	OF	NIP	GB	LD	FB	Tot
Santana J	21	7	41	22	36	.14	.09	73	94	-.00	.05	.41	.08	-14	-0	4	-25	-35
Wagner B	28	5	38	20	42	.08	.06	72	95	-.04	.06	.42	.03	-5	-0	-2	-7	-14
Maine J	20	12	41	20	39	.14	.10	68	86	.06	.09	.31	.14	2	4	-9	-6	-8
Smith J	19	13	63	20	18	.09	.14	80	84	.07	.02	.35	.22	3	-2	-3	-4	-6
Perez O	21	14	32	22	46	.11	.08	67	90	.07	.09	.37	.09	8	2	-3	-14	-6
Pelfrey M	13	9	50	21	30	.09	.05	76	83	.08	.03	.44	.09	3	-4	13	-18	-6
Vargas C	13	9	49	17	34	.08	.06	68	97	.07	.08	.45	.00	0	2	-0	-6	-4
Sanchez D	17	10	44	25	31	.16	.13	80	93	.06	.02	.35	.14	1	-2	2	-4	-4
Stokes B	19	6	39	24	38	.13	.09	77	87	-.01	.02	.45	.13	-2	-2	3	-2	-2
Schoeneweis S	14	11	50	19	31	.05	.12	78	85	.09	.02	.40	.16	2	-2	0	-1	-0
Figueroa N	17	13	41	21	39	.04	.04	64	85	.09	.11	.40	.06	3	3	1	-5	2
Feliciano P	21	12	53	19	27	.12	.14	68	91	.06	.07	.48	.17	1	2	2	-3	3
Heilman A	22	15	41	24	35	.13	.14	77	82	.07	.03	.42	.22	5	-3	3	1	6
Martinez P	18	10	41	24	35	.07	.13	77	80	.05	.03	.46	.23	1	-3	11	7	16
MLB Average	18	10	44	20	36	.10	.11	74	84	.05	.04	.39	.18	--	--	--	--	--

Fielding Stats

Name	Inn	SBA/G	CS%	ERA	WP+PB/G	PO	A	TE	FE	Grade
Catchers										
Schneider B	881.0	0.59	28%	4.11	0.419	741	41	4	1	B
Castro R	354.3	0.58	22%	3.68	0.229	286	19	4	0	--
Casanova R	118.0	0.38	40%	4.65	0.534	89	7	0	0	--
Cancel R	93.0	0.19	0%	4.65	0.387	81	1	0	0	--
Molina G	18.0	0.50	0%	3.50	0.500	19	0	0	0	--

Name	Inn	PO	A	TE	FE	FPct	DPS	DPT	ZR	OOZ	Grade
First Base											
Delgado C	1376.0	1237	105	3	5	.994	9	0	.750	38	C
Easley D	31.0	25	1	0	0	1.000	0	0	1.000	2	--
Anderson M	26.0	22	4	0	0	1.000	0	1	1.000	2	--
Tatis F	18.0	16	1	2	0	.895	0	0	1.000	1	--
Evans N	12.0	7	0	0	0	1.000	0	0	1.000	0	--
Phillips A	1.0	0	0	0	0	.000	0	0	--	--	--
Second Base											
Castillo L	689.7	160	186	1	5	.983	15	23	.751	16	--
Easley D	539.3	128	160	1	4	.983	11	23	.795	4	--
Reyes A	193.3	48	59	0	0	1.000	8	8	.885	6	--
Martinez R	38.0	5	11	0	0	1.000	2	0	.846	0	--
Anderson M	4.0	1	2	0	0	1.000	0	0	1.000	0	--
Shortstop											
Reyes J	1420.0	221	422	6	11	.974	48	40	.835	40	F
Easley D	44.0	7	14	0	0	1.000	0	1	.765	1	--
Third Base											
Wright D	1433.0	114	286	7	9	.962	18	3	.714	56	A
Tatis F	22.0	2	2	0	0	1.000	0	0	.000	2	--
Easley D	9.0	3	0	0	0	1.000	0	0	.500	0	--

Name	Inn	PO	A	TE	FE	FPct	DPS	DPT	ZR	OOZ	Grade
Left Field											
Tatis F	284.0	47	0	0	2	.959	0	0	.829	13	--
Murphy D	249.0	50	1	0	2	.962	2	0	.897	15	--
Chavez E	197.3	62	2	0	0	1.000	0	0	.939	16	--
Evans N	186.3	37	2	0	0	1.000	0	0	.828	13	--
Pagan A	169.7	28	0	0	1	.966	0	0	.900	10	--
Anderson M	165.7	45	1	0	2	.958	2	0	.974	7	--
Alou M	92.3	18	0	0	0	1.000	0	0	.895	1	--
Nixon T	44.3	11	1	0	0	1.000	0	0	.889	3	--
Easley D	26.0	2	0	0	1	.667	0	0	.000	2	--
Aguila C	26.0	5	1	0	0	1.000	0	0	1.000	1	--
Clark B	14.7	2	0	0	0	1.000	0	0	1.000	0	--
Phillips A	9.0	1	0	0	0	1.000	0	0	1.000	0	--
Center Field											
Beltran C	1407.0	418	8	1	2	.993	2	0	.925	111	A
Chavez E	38.3	9	1	0	0	1.000	0	0	1.000	1	--
Pagan A	18.7	8	0	0	0	1.000	0	0	1.000	1	--
Right Field											
Church R	724.0	180	7	0	1	.995	2	0	.872	50	A
Chavez E	400.0	109	4	0	1	.991	4	0	.940	31	--
Tatis F	292.7	55	2	0	0	1.000	0	0	.959	8	--
Nixon T	37.7	9	0	0	0	1.000	0	0	.875	2	--
Pagan A	8.0	3	0	0	0	1.000	0	0	--	--	--
Clark B	2.0	0	0	0	0	.000	0	0	--	--	--

New York Yankees

Stat Facts:

- Jason Giambi led the league with 22 HBP
- Derek Jeter hit a ground ball on 58% of his balls in play, most among ML regulars
- 93% of Melky Cabrera's outfield flies were outs
- Mariano Rivera struck out 12.83 batters for each one he walked, best ratio in the majors
- 28% of the fly balls off Rivera were infield pop-ups
- Andy Pettitte's -.108 R^L was lowest in the majors among 162+ IP pitchers
- Pettitte's FIP (3.74) was significantly lower than his ERA (4.54)
- Mike Mussina's FIP was exactly equal to his ERA
- Alex Rodriguez made 57 OOZ plays
- Jose Molina threw out 43% of attempted base stealers
- Cody Ransom (!) put the ball in play 31 times, and had 3 doubles and 4 home runs
- The Yankees had 9 pitchers with at least 7 starts

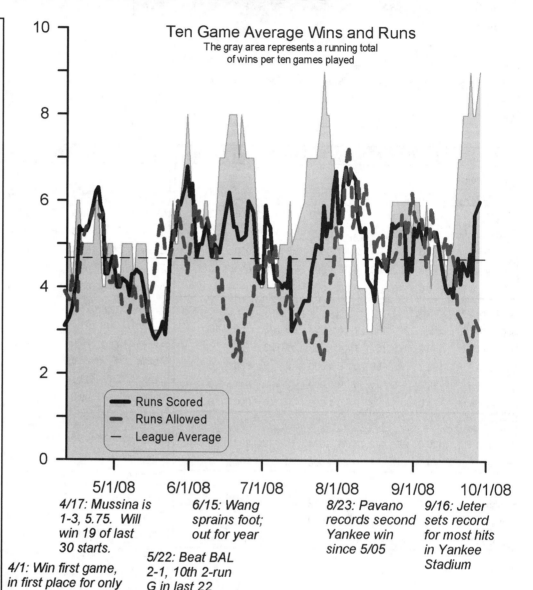

Ten Game Average Wins and Runs
The gray area represents a running total of wins per ten games played

Legend: Runs Scored / Runs Allowed / League Average

4/17: Mussina is 1-3, 5.75. Will win 19 of last 30 starts.

4/1: Win first game, in first place for only time during season

6/15: Wang sprains foot; out for year

5/22: Beat BAL 2-1, 10th 2-run G in last 22

8/23: Pavano records second Yankee win since 5/05

9/16: Jeter sets record for most hits in Yankee Stadium

Team Batting and Pitching/Fielding Stats by Month

	April	May	June	July	Aug	Sept/Oct
Wins	14	14	16	15	13	17
Losses	15	12	12	10	15	9
RS/G	4.3	4.8	4.9	5.2	4.8	5.3
RA/G	4.6	4.6	4.1	4.2	5.3	4.2
OBP	.326	.339	.358	.353	.341	.333
SLG	.411	.424	.434	.415	.447	.432
FIP	4.32	4.16	3.82	3.51	4.04	3.83
DER	.686	.699	.684	.674	.674	.683

Batting Stats

Player	BR	Runs	RBI	PA	Outs	H	2B	3B	HR	TB	K	BB	IBB	HBP	SH	SF	SB	CS	GDP	H-A	L^R	BA	OBP	SLG	GPA
Abreu B *	105	100	100	684	454	180	39	4	20	287	109	73	2	1	0	1	22	11	14	.041	-.007	.296	.371	.471	.285
Damon J *	104	95	71	623	401	168	27	5	17	256	82	64	0	1	2	1	29	8	6	.008	.054	.303	.375	.461	.284
Rodriguez A	96	104	103	594	375	154	33	0	35	292	117	65	9	14	0	5	18	3	16	.044	-.027	.302	.392	.573	.320
Jeter D	82	88	69	668	446	179	25	3	11	243	85	52	0	9	7	4	11	5	24	.001	.025	.300	.363	.408	.265
Giambi J *	79	68	96	565	352	113	19	1	32	230	111	76	5	22	0	9	2	1	6	.036	.012	.247	.373	.502	.294
Cano R *	61	70	72	634	457	162	35	3	14	245	65	26	3	5	1	5	2	4	18	.028	-.040	.271	.305	.410	.240
Matsui H *	53	43	45	378	248	99	17	0	9	143	47	38	6	3	0	0	0	0	10	-.003	.018	.294	.370	.424	.273
Cabrera M +	34	42	37	453	324	103	12	1	8	141	58	29	5	3	4	3	9	2	11	-.005	-.029	.249	.301	.341	.220
Nady X	34	26	40	247	173	61	11	0	12	108	48	14	1	4	0	1	1	1	5	.007	-.073	.268	.320	.474	.262
Posada J +	23	18	22	195	130	45	13	1	3	69	38	24	3	2	0	1	0	0	7	-.020	-.016	.268	.364	.411	.267
Betemit W +	17	24	25	198	147	50	13	0	6	81	56	6	0	1	1	1	0	1	7	.028	-.034	.265	.289	.429	.237
Gardner B *	17	18	16	141	99	29	5	2	0	38	30	8	0	2	3	1	13	1	0	-.066	.140	.228	.283	.299	.202
Molina J	15	32	18	297	219	58	17	0	3	84	52	12	0	6	8	3	0	0	9	.055	-.024	.216	.263	.313	.197
Ransom C	10	9	8	51	30	13	3	0	4	28	12	6	0	1	1	0	0	0	0	-.329	-.167	.302	.400	.651	.343
Moeller C	9	13	9	103	72	21	6	0	1	30	18	7	1	4	0	1	0	0	2	-.119	-.050	.231	.311	.330	.222
Christian J	7	6	6	43	32	10	3	0	0	13	4	3	0	0	0	0	7	1	1	.116	.198	.250	.302	.325	.217
Sexson R	5	2	6	35	22	7	1	0	1	11	10	6	0	0	0	1	0	0	1	.028	.120	.250	.371	.393	.265
Rodriguez I	4	11	3	101	81	21	4	0	2	31	15	4	1	1	0	0	4	0	6	.047	.055	.219	.257	.323	.197
Duncan S	4	7	6	65	48	10	3	0	1	16	13	7	0	0	0	1	0	0	1	.124	.145	.175	.262	.281	.188
Miranda J *	3	2	1	14	6	4	1	0	0	5	4	2	0	1	0	1	0	0	0	-.156	-.679	.400	.500	.500	.350
Ensberg M	2	6	4	80	61	15	0	0	1	18	22	6	0	0	0	0	0	1	1	-.100	-.030	.203	.263	.243	.179
Rasner D	1	0	0	3	1	0	0	0	0	0	1	2	0	0	0	0	0	0	0	-.300	--	.000	.667	.000	.300

Italicized stats have been adjusted for home park.

Batted Ball Batting Stats

Player	% of PA		% of Batted Balls			IF/F	HR/OF	Out %		Runs Per Event				Total Runs vs. Avg.				
	K%	BB%	GB%	LD%	FB%			GB	OF	NIP	GB	LD	OF	NIP	GB	LD	FB	Tot
Rodriguez A	20	13	42	18	40	.09	.24	68	80	.07	.07	.42	.38	7	4	1	33	44
Giambi J	20	17	33	17	50	.10	.19	76	84	.10	.03	.32	.29	14	-4	-10	24	25
Damon J	13	10	44	22	34	.14	.12	69	82	.09	.08	.35	.20	5	9	4	4	23
Abreu B	16	11	48	23	30	.03	.14	76	84	.07	.03	.43	.22	5	-2	13	8	23
Jeter D	13	9	58	18	24	.03	.08	68	81	.08	.07	.34	.18	3	12	-4	-3	8
Matsui H	12	11	47	19	34	.09	.10	74	74	.10	.04	.32	.23	4	0	-3	6	8
Nady X	19	7	44	22	35	.05	.18	81	84	.01	-.00	.39	.28	-3	-4	1	7	2
Posada J	19	13	40	21	40	.04	.06	75	85	.07	.02	.48	.11	2	-1	3	-2	1
Moeller C	17	11	28	22	50	.08	.03	81	85	.06	-.01	.40	.06	0	-2	0	-2	-3
Betemit W	28	4	43	25	33	.00	.11	74	77	-.06	.03	.40	.25	-7	-2	2	3	-3
Rodriguez I	15	5	63	14	24	.00	.11	80	88	.00	-.01	.41	.14	-1	-2	-2	-2	-7
Gardner B	21	7	48	17	35	.09	.00	69	93	.00	.10	.43	-.04	-2	3	-2	-7	-8
Cano R	10	5	47	19	33	.08	.08	74	85	.04	.04	.34	.13	-5	1	-2	-5	-11
Cabrera M	13	7	46	19	35	.16	.08	72	93	.05	.06	.32	.06	-2	3	-5	-14	-18
Molina J	18	6	48	19	33	.03	.04	85	87	.01	-.03	.41	.07	-4	-9	-1	-8	-22
MLB Average	18	10	44	20	36	.10	.11	74	84	.05	.04	.39	.18	--	--	--	--	--

Pitching Stats

Player	PRC	IP	BFP	G	GS	K	BB	IBB	HBP	H	HR	DP	DER	SB	CS	PO	W	L	Sv	Op	Hld	H-A	R^L	RA	ERA	FIP
Mussina M	94	200.3	819	34	34	150	31	3	8	214	17	27	.669	12	7	0	20	9	0	0	0	.003	.077	3.82	3.37	3.37
Rivera M	76	70.7	259	64	0	77	6	0	2	41	4	4	.765	6	1	0	6	5	39	40	0	.056	.030	1.40	1.40	2.13
Pettitte A *	76	204.0	881	33	33	158	55	4	7	233	19	17	.659	20	8	9	14	14	0	0	0	.019	-.108	4.94	4.54	3.74
Chamberlain	66	100.3	417	42	12	118	39	3	2	87	5	7	.672	8	4	1	4	3	0	1	19	-.028	-.033	2.87	2.60	2.66
Wang C	39	95.0	402	15	15	54	35	1	3	90	4	13	.706	8	3	0	8	2	0	0	0	.006	-.039	4.17	4.07	3.81
Rasner D	33	113.3	513	24	20	67	39	1	5	135	14	13	.670	3	3	0	5	10	0	0	0	-.027	.011	5.88	5.40	4.79
Veras J	31	57.7	253	60	0	63	29	6	3	52	7	2	.702	5	3	0	5	3	0	2	10	-.002	-.020	3.59	3.59	3.98
Bruney B	30	34.3	137	32	1	33	16	0	1	18	2	1	.812	3	0	0	3	0	1	2	12	-.049	.024	1.83	1.83	3.55
Ramirez E	27	55.3	233	55	0	63	24	2	3	44	7	5	.706	2	4	0	5	1	1	4	5	-.043	-.023	4.07	3.90	3.95
Coke P *	26	14.7	52	12	0	14	2	0	0	8	0	2	.750	0	0	0	1	0	0	0	5	-.050	.089	0.61	0.61	1.73
Farnsworth K	23	44.3	185	45	0	43	17	3	1	43	11	3	.708	5	6	0	1	2	1	1	11	.004	-.087	3.65	3.65	5.53
Ponson S	21	80.0	360	16	15	33	32	2	5	99	11	12	.681	2	3	0	4	4	0	0	0	.013	-.107	5.96	5.85	5.51
Aceves A	19	30.0	120	6	4	16	10	0	0	25	4	4	.767	2	2	0	1	0	0	0	0	-.047	-.019	2.40	2.40	4.90
Giese D	17	43.3	186	20	3	29	14	1	1	39	3	0	.734	9	1	0	1	3	0	0	0	-.084	.004	4.57	3.53	3.76
Hawkins L	12	41.0	173	33	0	23	17	3	0	42	3	6	.700	1	2	0	1	1	0	1	1	-.017	-.150	5.71	5.71	4.08
Robertson D	11	30.3	131	25	0	36	15	2	0	29	3	1	.662	4	3	0	4	0	0	0	0	.037	.025	5.34	5.34	3.43
Ohlendorf R	10	40.0	187	25	0	36	19	3	1	50	7	6	.629	0	0	0	1	1	0	0	4	-.042	-.101	6.98	6.53	4.98
Pavano C	9	34.3	154	7	7	15	10	0	4	41	5	4	.683	5	1	0	4	2	0	0	0	-.112	-.034	6.03	5.77	5.47
Hughes P	8	34.0	157	8	8	23	15	0	1	43	3	3	.652	8	0	0	0	4	0	0	0	.005	-.063	6.88	6.62	4.44
Britton C	8	23.0	105	15	0	12	11	1	0	28	4	3	.679	0	0	0	0	0	0	0	0	-.003	-.143	5.09	5.09	5.75
Kennedy I	7	39.7	194	10	9	27	26	0	1	50	5	1	.652	5	2	1	0	4	0	0	0	-.039	.128	8.39	8.17	5.55
Marte D *	7	18.3	80	25	0	24	10	1	1	14	1	0	.705	0	0	0	1	3	0	0	10	-.104	.041	5.40	5.40	2.96
Albaladejo J	7	13.7	58	7	0	13	6	0	0	15	1	4	.605	2	2	0	0	1	0	0	1	.158	-.016	3.95	3.95	3.60
Traber B *	4	16.7	80	19	0	11	7	1	2	23	3	1	.649	3	1	0	0	0	0	0	1	-.231	.203	7.02	7.02	5.69
Sanchez H	1	2.0	8	2	0	1	2	0	0	1	0	1	.800	0	0	0	0	0	0	0	0	-.353	.053	4.50	4.50	5.23

Italicized stats have been adjusted for home park.

Batted Ball Pitching Stats

Player	% of PA		% of Batted Balls					Out %		Runs Per Event				Total Runs vs. Avg.				
	K%	BB%	GB%	LD%	FB%	IF/F	HR/OF	GB	OF	NIP	GB	LD	OF	NIP	GB	LD	FB	Tot
Rivera M	30	3	55	15	31	.28	.11	77	94	-.07	.04	.31	.10	-10	-1	-10	-10	-30
Chamberlain J	28	10	52	14	34	.10	.06	73	74	.01	.05	.37	.18	-5	1	-11	-4	-18
Mussina M	18	5	48	22	30	.07	.10	73	82	-.02	.05	.36	.17	-15	3	2	-3	-13
Bruney B	24	12	43	14	44	.21	.07	76	93	.04	.06	.17	.05	0	0	-7	-5	-11
Wang C	13	9	55	22	23	.04	.06	77	89	.08	.03	.32	.07	2	-0	-1	-11	-11
Giese D	16	8	31	18	51	.10	.05	70	90	.04	.09	.37	.04	-1	1	-1	-6	-7
Aceves A	13	8	42	17	41	.08	.09	72	88	.06	.06	.25	.12	-0	0	-3	-1	-4
Ramirez E	27	12	33	22	45	.11	.12	68	94	.03	.10	.41	.13	-1	1	-1	-2	-3
Robertson D	27	11	43	16	41	.09	.10	59	93	.02	.14	.37	.09	-1	3	-2	-3	-3
Hawkins L	13	9	48	18	34	.02	.07	79	71	.07	.02	.26	.19	1	-1	-4	2	-2
Veras E	25	13	41	18	41	.06	.12	73	87	.04	.07	.38	.19	1	0	-3	1	-1
Pettitte A	18	7	51	20	29	.07	.11	73	82	.02	.06	.43	.18	-8	7	7	-4	1
Farnsworth K	23	10	39	14	47	.09	.22	65	85	.02	.10	.26	.33	-1	2	-6	9	4
Hughes P	15	10	34	27	39	.09	.07	80	82	.08	.03	.40	.14	1	-1	4	-0	4
Pavano C	10	9	40	17	42	.06	.08	61	89	.11	.13	.41	.11	1	4	0	-1	5
Ohlendorf R	19	11	47	18	35	.18	.19	66	80	.05	.09	.36	.33	1	3	-1	5	8
Kennedy I	14	14	41	12	48	.06	.08	68	70	.12	.09	.38	.25	4	3	-4	9	12
Rasner D	13	9	40	21	39	.15	.11	71	82	.07	.06	.37	.20	1	4	3	4	12
Ponson S	9	10	52	20	27	.08	.15	74	82	.13	.04	.37	.24	5	2	3	4	13
MLB Average	18	10	44	20	36	.10	.11	74	84	.05	.04	.39	.18	--	--	--	--	--

Fielding Stats

Name	Inn	SBA/G	CS%	ERA	WP+PB/G	PO	A	TE	FE	Grade
Catchers										
Molina J	737.0	0.90	43%	3.69	0.440	634	52	3	0	A+
Posada J	234.3	1.42	8%	4.65	0.538	197	7	1	0	--
Moeller C	225.0	0.88	32%	4.20	0.240	159	15	2	1	--
Rodriguez I	223.7	1.05	23%	5.63	0.322	173	14	1	0	A+
Cervelli F	13.7	0.66	0%	7.90	0.000	11	0	0	0	--
Stewart C	8.0	1.13	0%	6.75	2.250	8	0	0	0	--

Name	Inn	PO	A	TE	FE	FPct	DPS	DPT	ZR	OOZ	Grade
First Base											
Giambi J	898.0	870	36	2	7	.990	1	0	.679	22	F-
Betemit W	207.0	191	13	0	1	.995	3	1	.821	6	--
Duncan S	107.0	98	5	2	1	.972	0	1	.545	4	--
Sexson R	80.0	78	8	0	0	1.000	1	0	.429	4	--
Ransom C	42.0	47	1	0	0	1.000	0	0	.500	0	--
Ensberg M	35.0	38	0	0	0	1.000	0	0	.800	0	--
Miranda J	32.7	30	2	0	0	1.000	0	0	.750	2	--
Posada J	31.0	25	0	0	0	1.000	0	0	.750	0	--
Nady X	4.0	3	1	0	0	1.000	0	0	.667	0	--
Moeller C	3.0	4	0	0	0	1.000	0	0	--	--	--
Molina J	1.0	0	0	0	0	0.000	0	0	--	--	--
Damon J	1.0	1	0	0	0	1.000	0	0	--	--	--
Second Base											
Cano R	1376.0	305	482	4	9	.984	57	52	.809	30	F
Gonzalez A	28.0	4	7	0	0	1.000	1	0	.889	0	--
Betemit W	24.0	4	8	1	0	.923	2	0	.857	0	--
Ransom C	13.0	3	3	0	1	.857	0	0	.750	0	--
Shortstop											
Jeter D	1258.0	220	347	7	5	.979	35	31	.839	29	C
Ransom C	63.0	12	22	1	1	.944	1	3	.636	4	--
Gonzalez A	63.0	12	15	0	0	1.000	0	2	.867	1	--
Betemit W	57.0	10	19	0	0	1.000	3	2	.941	0	--

Name	Inn	PO	A	TE	FE	FPct	DPS	DPT	ZR	OOZ	Grade
Third Base											
Rodriguez A	1126.0	73	251	7	3	.970	22	1	.703	57	A+
Ensberg M	133.0	8	32	1	0	.976	2	0	.591	5	--
Betemit W	100.0	4	21	1	2	.893	3	0	.567	4	--
Gonzalez A	54.7	6	11	0	0	.944	2	0	.538	4	--
Ransom C	24.0	1	6	0	0	1.000	0	0	.714	1	--
Moeller C	3.7	0	0	0	0	.000	0	0	--	--	--
Left Field											
Damon J	659.3	155	2	0	1	.994	0	0	.917	33	--
Nady X	389.7	87	2	1	1	.978	0	0	.886	17	--
Matsui H	176.3	40	2	1	0	.977	2	0	.886	9	--
Gardner B	145.3	25	1	0	0	1.000	0	0	.920	2	--
Christian J	53.0	5	0	0	1	.833	0	0	.714	0	--
Cabrera M	18.0	4	0	0	0	1.000	0	0	.500	2	--
Center Field											
Cabrera M	973.7	272	7	2	2	.986	2	0	.938	59	C
Damon J	285.0	77	1	0	1	.987	0	0	.928	13	--
Gardner B	160.7	53	4	0	0	1.000	0	0	.976	13	--
Christian J	22.3	5	1	0	0	1.000	0	0	1.000	0	--
Right Field											
Abreu B	1310.0	270	10	0	2	.993	6	0	.872	32	F-
Nady X	50.0	10	0	0	0	1.000	0	0	.727	2	F-
Cabrera M	23.7	8	0	0	0	1.000	0	0	.875	1	--
Duncan S	23.0	4	0	0	0	1.000	0	0	1.000	0	--
Matsui H	18.0	2	0	0	0	1.000	0	0	1.000	1	--
Christian J	17.0	6	0	0	0	1.000	0	0	1.000	0	--

Oakland Athletics

Stat Facts:
- Jack Hannahan had the fewest Base Runs among ML regulars
- For the second straight year, Jack Cust led the league in both BB% and K%
- Cust walked or struck out in 52% of his plate appearances
- 31% of Cust's outfield flies were home runs
- One-quarter of Mark Ellis' fly balls were infield pop-ups, most among ML regulars
- Dana Eveland allowed the fewest home runs (10) of any 162+ IP pitcher
- Brad Ziegler induced 23 double plays in 60 innings, far and away the best rate in the majors
- 65% of the batted balls against Ziegler were ground balls
- Ziegler's FIP was 2.61 higher than his ERA, far and away the biggest differential among 30+ IP pitchers
- Base stealers went just 11-for-23 against Greg Smith
- Smith's 16 pickoffs led the majors; no one else had as many as 10

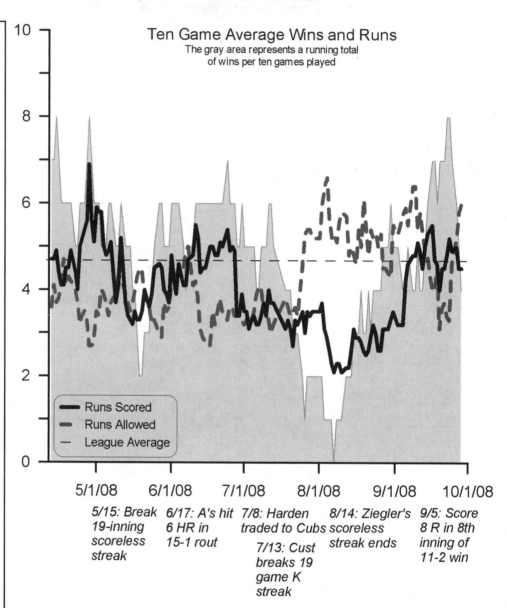

Ten Game Average Wins and Runs

The gray area represents a running total of wins per ten games played

Legend:
- Runs Scored
- Runs Allowed
- League Average

5/15: Break 19-inning scoreless streak

6/17: A's hit 6 HR in 15-1 rout

7/8: Harden traded to Cubs

7/13: Cust breaks 19 game K streak

8/14: Ziegler's scoreless streak ends

9/5: Score 8 R in 8th inning of 11-2 win

Team Batting and Pitching/Fielding Stats by Month

	April	May	June	July	Aug	Sept/Oct
Wins	17	12	16	8	10	12
Losses	12	15	10	17	20	12
RS/G	4.7	3.9	4.7	3.4	2.7	4.8
RA/G	3.5	4.0	3.4	4.4	5.4	5.0
OBP	.336	.321	.322	.302	.285	.341
SLG	.362	.376	.392	.346	.347	.392
FIP	3.62	3.53	4.13	4.73	4.62	4.46
DER	.709	.701	.739	.712	.677	.668

Batting Stats

Player	BR	Runs	RBI	PA	Outs	H	2B	3B	HR	TB	K	BB	IBB	HBP	SH	SF	SB	CS	GDP	H-A	L^R	BA	OBP	SLG	GPA
Cust J *	91	77	77	598	377	111	19	0	33	229	197	111	3	2	0	4	0	0	7	.031	.011	.231	.375	.476	.293
Suzuki K	65	54	42	588	405	148	25	1	7	196	69	44	2	11	2	1	2	3	20	.065	-.025	.279	.346	.370	.253
Barton D *	58	59	47	523	352	101	17	5	9	155	99	65	5	3	6	3	2	1	6	-.014	-.053	.226	.327	.348	.239
Ellis M	57	55	41	507	352	103	20	3	12	165	65	53	2	5	5	2	14	2	11	-.058	-.063	.233	.321	.373	.242
Crosby B	56	66	61	605	445	132	39	1	7	194	96	47	0	0	0	2	7	3	18	.032	-.002	.237	.296	.349	.225
Sweeney R *	55	53	45	433	284	110	18	2	5	147	67	38	3	3	2	6	9	1	9	-.018	.086	.286	.350	.383	.259
Brown E	46	48	59	438	322	98	14	2	13	155	65	27	2	5	0	4	4	2	16	.023	.066	.244	.297	.386	.235
Hannahan J *	40	48	47	501	346	95	27	0	9	149	131	55	4	2	3	5	2	0	5	.026	.032	.218	.305	.342	.227
Gonzalez C *	32	31	26	316	237	73	22	1	4	109	81	13	1	0	1	0	4	1	7	.010	.081	.242	.273	.361	.217
Thomas F	26	20	19	217	143	49	6	1	5	72	44	28	0	2	0	1	0	0	6	.057	-.082	.263	.364	.387	.266
Davis R	25	28	19	207	152	51	5	4	3	73	34	7	0	1	2	1	25	6	1	-.061	-.000	.260	.288	.372	.227
Buck T *	24	16	25	172	122	35	9	1	7	67	38	11	0	4	0	2	1	0	2	-.180	.083	.226	.291	.432	.244
Sweeney M	16	13	12	136	93	36	8	0	2	50	6	7	0	2	0	1	0	0	3	-.042	.017	.286	.331	.397	.253
Chavez E *	15	10	14	95	69	22	7	0	2	35	18	6	0	0	0	0	0	0	2	.017	-.062	.247	.295	.393	.236
Cunningham A	13	7	14	87	61	20	7	1	1	32	24	6	1	1	0	0	2	0	1	.085	-.087	.250	.310	.400	.245
Pennington C	12	14	9	117	77	24	5	0	0	29	18	13	0	2	2	1	4	1	1	-.019	.010	.242	.339	.293	.230
Denorfia C	9	10	9	71	47	18	3	0	1	24	16	6	0	1	2	0	2	0	3	-.035	-.145	.290	.362	.387	.265
Bowen R +	8	6	9	98	77	16	5	1	1	26	38	4	0	1	2	0	0	0	2	-.046	-.049	.176	.219	.286	.173
Murphy D	7	10	13	117	86	19	3	0	3	31	38	11	0	2	0	1	2	1	1	-.024	-.016	.184	.274	.301	.202
Patterson E	7	11	8	104	76	16	3	0	0	19	24	12	0	0	0	0	8	0	0	-.092	.034	.174	.269	.207	.176
Bankston W	5	4	4	63	47	12	3	0	1	18	15	2	0	1	0	1	0	0	0	-.059	.144	.203	.238	.305	.187
Baisley J	4	1	5	47	34	11	1	0	0	12	7	4	0	0	0	0	0	0	2	.086	-.096	.256	.319	.279	.218
Petit G	2	4	0	25	15	8	2	0	0	10	9	2	0	0	0	0	0	0	0	-.227	.024	.348	.400	.435	.295
Conrad B +	1	0	2	19	17	3	1	0	0	4	9	0	0	0	0	0	0	0	1	.261	-.138	.158	.158	.211	.126
Fiorentino J	1	0	1	1	0	1	0	0	0	1	0	0	0	0	0	0	0	0	0	--	--	1.000	1.000	1.000	.714

Italicized stats have been adjusted for home park.

Batted Ball Batting Stats

Player	% of PA		% of Batted Balls					Out %		Runs Per Event				Total Runs vs. Avg.				
	K%	BB%	GB%	LD%	FB%	IF/F	HR/OF	GB	OF	NIP	GB	LD	OF	NIP	GB	LD	FB	Tot
Cust J	33	19	41	21	39	.05	.31	79	85	.05	.02	.40	.45	9	-6	-7	26	22
Thomas F	20	14	27	21	52	.09	.07	76	86	.07	.01	.48	.11	3	-2	3	-1	2
Sweeney M	4	7	42	17	41	.16	.05	75	83	.16	.05	.40	.10	1	1	1	-2	0
Sweeney R	15	9	45	21	34	.06	.05	72	80	.06	.06	.34	.12	1	2	-1	-4	-1
Buck T	22	9	46	14	40	.09	.14	80	86	.02	.04	.50	.20	-2	-0	-2	1	-2
Pennington C	15	13	36	19	46	.11	.00	76	82	.10	.03	.41	.02	2	-0	-0	-4	-3
Suzuki K	12	9	45	19	36	.09	.05	70	86	.09	.06	.37	.07	4	5	0	-13	-4
Davis R	16	4	48	22	31	.17	.08	68	89	-.03	.10	.32	.09	-4	5	-1	-6	-7
Murphy D	32	11	38	23	39	.12	.14	79	89	.00	.03	.27	.18	-2	-1	-3	-1	-7
Ellis M	13	11	34	20	46	.25	.08	76	88	.10	.03	.39	.10	6	-4	1	-11	-8
Bowen R	39	5	43	13	43	.09	.05	74	70	-.06	.06	.41	.19	-4	-0	-3	-1	-9
Patterson E	23	12	41	17	42	.22	.00	73	86	.04	.06	.20	.02	-0	0	-4	-5	-9
Brown E	15	7	42	17	42	.19	.11	79	85	.04	.00	.39	.17	-2	-6	-4	0	-12
Barton D	19	13	35	19	46	.07	.06	79	85	.07	.02	.35	.10	5	-6	-6	-6	-12
Gonzalez C	26	4	49	18	33	.15	.07	76	80	-.05	.04	.48	.14	-9	0	-1	-6	-16
Hannahan J	26	11	37	21	42	.09	.08	83	81	.03	-.00	.40	.16	-2	-8	-3	-2	-16
Crosby B	16	8	48	16	36	.18	.05	75	85	.04	.03	.44	.09	-3	-1	-4	-14	-23
MLB Average	18	10	44	20	36	.10	.11	74	84	.05	.04	.39	.18	--	--	--	--	--

Pitching Stats

Player	PRC	IP	BFP	G	GS	K	BB	IBB	HBP	H	HR	DP	DER	SB	CS	PO	W	L	Sv	Op	Hld	H-A	R^L	RA	ERA	FIP
Duchscherer	82	141.7	557	22	22	95	34	2	8	107	11	15	.753	4	2	1	10	8	0	0	0	-.051	-.053	2.86	2.54	3.75
Smith G *	74	190.3	800	32	32	111	87	5	3	169	21	14	.734	11	12	16	7	16	0	0	0	.006	-.036	4.35	4.16	4.84
Eveland D *	67	168.0	737	29	29	118	77	2	12	172	10	30	.681	13	4	2	9	9	0	0	0	-.038	-.040	4.39	4.34	4.15
Ziegler B	59	59.7	229	47	0	30	22	3	1	47	2	23	.707	1	0	2	3	0	11	13	9	-.053	-.104	1.21	1.06	3.67
Harden R	57	77.0	311	13	13	92	31	1	1	57	5	3	.703	4	5	0	5	1	0	0	0	-.021	-.023	2.45	2.34	2.89
Devine J	49	45.7	170	42	0	49	15	2	0	23	0	6	.764	3	1	0	6	1	1	2	11	.013	-.072	1.38	0.59	1.94
Blanton J	39	127.0	550	20	20	62	35	3	1	145	12	13	.689	0	1	0	5	12	0	0	0	-.020	.072	5.24	4.96	4.26
Street H	35	70.0	287	63	0	69	27	6	1	58	6	6	.717	6	3	0	7	5	18	25	6	-.007	-.019	3.73	3.73	3.32
Braden D *	27	71.7	301	19	10	41	25	2	2	77	8	8	.680	1	2	7	5	4	0	0	0	.032	.051	4.52	4.14	4.58
Gaudin C	26	62.7	263	26	6	44	17	1	3	63	6	8	.689	1	3	1	5	3	0	0	2	-.060	.019	4.16	3.59	3.98
Casilla S	23	50.3	229	51	0	43	20	2	2	60	5	7	.639	9	0	0	2	1	2	3	7	.014	.028	3.93	3.93	4.06
Embree A *	22	61.7	270	70	0	57	30	5	2	59	8	9	.694	6	1	1	2	5	0	5	18	-.046	-.030	5.25	4.96	4.38
Blevins J *	21	37.7	156	36	0	35	13	2	3	32	2	4	.699	2	2	2	1	3	0	1	5	-.108	-.084	3.35	3.11	3.18
Brown A	18	35.0	147	31	0	28	21	1	1	23	3	5	.766	0	1	0	1	0	0	1	2	.027	.000	3.34	3.09	4.54
Gallagher S	15	56.7	266	11	11	54	36	1	2	60	7	3	.671	1	0	0	2	3	0	0	0	-.110	-.051	6.67	5.88	4.89
Foulke K	14	31.0	133	31	0	23	13	2	2	28	7	2	.753	3	1	0	0	3	1	2	8	-.038	.097	4.06	4.06	5.84
Outman J *	9	25.7	116	6	4	19	8	1	2	34	1	4	.605	1	0	0	1	2	0	0	0	-.044	-.114	4.91	4.56	3.31
Saarloos K	7	26.3	118	8	1	12	4	1	0	37	2	3	.650	1	0	0	1	0	0	0	0	.018	-.081	5.81	5.47	3.65
Gonzalez G *	6	34.0	163	10	7	34	25	1	3	32	9	1	.717	0	2	0	1	4	0	0	0	.022	-.133	9.00	7.68	7.05
Meyer D *	5	27.7	132	11	4	20	14	0	1	35	6	1	.659	1	1	1	0	4	0	0	0	.007	-.052	9.11	7.48	6.23
DiNardo L *	4	23.0	114	11	2	12	13	2	2	31	3	4	.631	2	0	0	1	2	0	0	0	.026	-.063	7.83	7.43	5.58
Calero K	2	4.7	20	5	0	7	3	0	1	3	0	0	.700	0	0	0	0	0	0	0	0	.127	-.452	5.79	3.86	2.16
Gray J	1	4.7	24	5	0	4	1	0	1	8	1	0	.588	0	0	0	0	0	0	0	0	-.152	-.080	7.71	7.71	5.59

Italicized stats have been adjusted for home park.

Batted Ball Pitching Stats

Player	% of PA		% of Batted Balls					Out %		Runs Per Event				Total Runs vs. Avg.				
	K%	BB%	GB%	LD%	FB%	IF/F	HR/OF	GB	OF	NIP	GB	LD	OF	NIP	GB	LD	FB	Tot
Duchscherer J	17	7	41	20	39	.05	.07	81	88	.03	-.00	.29	.10	-5	-9	-10	-8	-31
Devine J	29	9	39	18	43	.09	.00	78	95	-.01	.02	.30	-.06	-3	-2	-5	-10	-20
Harden R	30	10	30	19	50	.14	.06	68	91	.01	.08	.43	.05	-4	-0	-3	-9	-16
Street H	24	10	36	22	42	.14	.09	81	90	.02	-.01	.46	.11	-2	-5	2	-5	-10
Ziegler B	13	10	65	16	19	.06	.03	75	90	.09	.01	.49	.03	1	-3	1	-8	-9
Blevins J	22	10	43	18	38	.10	.06	64	88	.03	.11	.29	.08	-1	2	-3	-4	-5
Brown A	19	15	35	15	50	.04	.07	68	93	.09	.06	.28	.06	2	-0	-4	-3	-5
Gaudin C	17	8	41	20	39	.12	.09	76	87	.03	.02	.42	.12	-2	-2	1	-2	-5
Smith G	14	11	34	20	45	.14	.09	77	90	.09	.03	.36	.11	8	-3	-2	-7	-4
Eveland D	16	12	49	22	29	.09	.07	75	79	.08	.03	.33	.16	8	-1	-1	-6	-1
Saarloos K	10	3	53	22	25	.04	.08	70	91	.00	.07	.39	.08	-2	2	2	-3	-0
Embree A	21	12	45	12	44	.12	.12	67	82	.05	.07	.45	.22	1	2	-5	4	1
Foulke K	17	11	31	16	53	.10	.16	72	87	.06	.08	.30	.22	0	1	-3	4	2
Blanton J	11	7	46	20	33	.09	.08	80	83	.06	.02	.43	.16	-2	-3	8	-1	2
Braden D	14	9	38	18	44	.13	.09	70	82	.07	.06	.38	.16	1	1	-1	2	3
Outman J	16	9	40	21	40	.12	.03	68	76	.05	.07	.49	.16	-0	3	0	0	4
Casilla J	19	10	43	20	36	.14	.10	68	78	.05	.08	.42	.20	1	2	1	1	5
Gallagher S	20	14	27	26	47	.04	.09	66	90	.08	.12	.39	.12	4	2	4	-0	9
Gonzalez G	21	17	42	18	40	.00	.18	80	78	.09	.02	.53	.32	4	-2	1	7	10
Meyer D	15	11	28	15	57	.13	.13	67	76	.08	.09	.49	.27	1	1	1	7	10
MLB Average	18	10	44	20	36	.10	.11	74	84	.05	.04	.39	.18	--	--	--	--	--

Fielding Stats

Name	Inn	SBA/G	CS%	ERA	WP+PB/G	PO	A	TE	FE	Grade
Catchers										
Suzuki K	1215.0	0.53	23%	3.86	0.207	927	53	4	1	C
Bowen R	220.0	0.82	25%	4.87	0.409	147	9	0	0	--

Name	Inn	PO	A	TE	FE	FPct	DPS	DPT	ZR	OOZ	Grade
First Base											
Barton D	1121.0	1021	73	5	6	.988	19	1	.776	28	B
Bankston W	108.0	104	6	0	1	.991	0	0	.750	3	--
Sweeney M	90.0	89	11	0	0	1.000	1	0	.750	4	--
Hannahan J	80.0	82	5	0	2	.978	0	0	.857	2	--
Baisley J	33.0	37	1	0	1	.974	0	0	1.000	2	--
Bowen R	2.0	2	0	0	0	1.000	0	0	--	--	--
Brown E	0.3	1	0	0	0	1.000	0	0	--	--	--
Second Base											
Ellis M	1011.0	228	336	1	3	.993	36	51	.897	31	A+
Patterson E	169.3	48	49	1	3	.960	6	9	.773	3	--
Pennington	136.0	33	44	0	0	1.000	7	11	.769	0	--
Murphy D	61.0	12	20	0	0	1.000	1	2	.818	1	--
Petit G	39.0	7	14	0	0	1.000	1	0	1.000	1	--
Conrad B	17.0	4	3	0	0	1.000	0	0	1.000	0	--
Davis R	1.0	0	0	0	0	.000	0	0	--	--	--
Shortstop											
Crosby B	1263.0	202	384	13	4	.972	48	45	.816	43	C
Murphy D	88.0	10	27	1	1	.949	1	5	.710	1	--
Pennington	56.0	10	16	4	0	.867	1	4	.579	0	--
Petit G	28.0	7	12	2	0	.905	3	3	.600	2	--
Third Base											
Hannahan J	983.7	70	218	5	4	.970	24	1	.759	43	A+
Murphy D	143.3	12	27	1	0	.975	7	1	.733	3	--
Chavez E	130.0	12	32	1	0	.978	4	0	.676	7	--
Baisley J	79.0	6	14	0	0	1.000	2	0	.647	1	--
Pennington	64.0	8	11	0	1	.950	2	0	.889	1	--
Conrad B	33.0	1	4	1	0	.833	1	0	.800	0	--
Barton D	2.0	1	1	0	0	1.000	1	0	1.000	0	--

Name	Inn	PO	A	TE	FE	FPct	DPS	DPT	ZR	OOZ	Grade
Left Field											
Cust J	585.7	129	4	0	4	.971	0	0	.849	22	--
Brown E	413.0	89	6	1	0	.990	2	0	.852	20	--
Cunningham	150.0	41	1	0	3	.933	0	0	.868	8	--
Denorfia C	70.3	9	1	0	0	1.000	0	0	.750	3	--
Patterson E	63.0	15	0	1	0	.938	0	0	.750	6	--
Murton M	61.0	27	1	0	0	1.000	2	0	1.000	7	--
Buck T	47.0	11	1	0	0	1.000	0	0	.889	3	--
Sweeney R	43.0	12	0	0	0	1.000	0	0	.917	1	--
Murphy D	2.0	0	0	0	0	.000	0	0	--	--	--
Center Field											
Gonzalez C	528.7	176	5	0	2	.989	2	0	.957	42	--
Davis R	465.0	147	4	0	1	.993	4	0	.929	43	--
Sweeney R	362.7	95	0	0	0	1.000	0	0	.929	17	--
Denorfia C	73.7	26	0	0	0	1.000	0	0	.947	8	--
Fiorentino J	4.0	0	0	0	0	.000	0	0	--	--	--
Brown E	1.0	0	0	0	0	.000	0	0	--	--	--
Right Field											
Sweeney R	486.7	136	6	0	0	.993	0	0	.913	31	--
Brown E	433.3	111	4	0	3	.975	4	0	.904	18	--
Buck T	287.0	73	2	0	0	1.000	0	0	.949	18	--
Gonzalez C	160.7	43	0	0	0	1.000	0	0	1.000	12	--
Cust J	39.0	4	0	0	0	1.000	0	0	.400	2	--
Cunningham	18.3	6	0	0	0	1.000	0	0	1.000	4	--
Denorfia C	10.0	2	0	0	0	1.000	0	0	1.000	0	--

Philadelphia Phillies

Stat Facts:

- Chase Utley led the majors with 27 HBP
- Utley's H-A was exactly .000
- Utley made 66 OOZ plays, and turned 65 DPs
- 2% of Ryan Howard's fly balls were infield pop-ups, and 32% were home runs
- 92% of Shane Victorino's outfield flies were outs
- J.C. Romero's -.192 R^L was lowest in the majors among 40+ IP pitchers
- Kyle Kendrick's 9% K rate was among the lowest in the majors, and his 27% LD rate among the highest
- 80% of the groundballs allowed by Cole Hamels resulted in outs, tied for the highest rate in the majors among 162+ IP pitchers
- Pat Burrell walked in 16% of his PAs
- Pedro Feliz hit a line drive on just 16% of his balls in play
- Jimmy Rollins stole 47 bases in 50 attempts
- Jason Werth stole 20 bases in 21 attempts

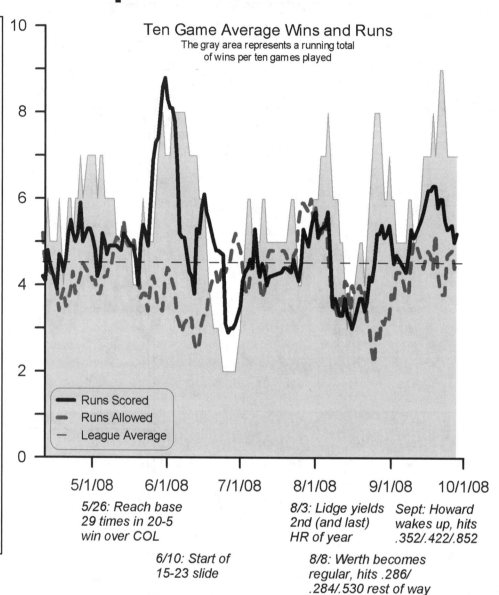

Ten Game Average Wins and Runs
The gray area represents a running total of wins per ten games played

- Runs Scored
- Runs Allowed
- League Average

5/26: Reach base 29 times in 20-5 win over COL

6/10: Start of 15-23 slide

8/3: Lidge yields 2nd (and last) HR of year

8/8: Werth becomes regular, hits .286/ .284/.530 rest of way

Sept: Howard wakes up, hits .352/.422/.852

Team Batting and Pitching/Fielding Stats by Month

	April	May	June	July	Aug	Sept/Oct
Wins	15	17	12	15	16	17
Losses	13	12	14	10	13	8
RS/G	4.8	6.0	4.3	5.0	4.0	5.5
RA/G	4.4	4.3	3.9	4.8	3.4	4.4
OBP	.335	.346	.322	.332	.322	.336
SLG	.446	.468	.394	.468	.394	.457
FIP	4.53	3.96	4.77	4.48	3.69	4.05
DER	.710	.674	.723	.692	.683	.702

Batting Stats

Player	BR	Runs	RBI	PA	Outs	H	2B	3B	HR	TB	K	BB	IBB	HBP	SH	SF	SB	CS	GDP	H-A	L^R	BA	OBP	SLG	GPA
Howard R *	120	105	146	700	469	153	26	4	48	331	199	81	17	3	0	6	1	1	11	.034	.069	.251	.339	.543	.282
Utley C *	112	113	104	707	441	177	41	4	33	325	104	64	14	27	1	8	14	2	9	0.000	.015	.292	.380	.535	.299
Burrell P	95	74	86	645	412	134	33	3	33	272	136	102	8	1	0	6	0	0	10	-.052	.038	.250	.367	.507	.286
Rollins J +	94	76	59	625	416	154	38	9	11	243	55	58	7	5	3	3	47	3	11	.058	-.006	.277	.349	.437	.261
Victorino S	84	102	58	627	422	167	30	8	14	255	69	45	2	7	5	0	36	11	8	.056	.028	.293	.352	.447	.265
Werth J	74	73	67	482	307	114	16	3	24	208	119	57	1	4	0	3	20	1	2	-.014	.065	.273	.363	.498	.282
Feliz P	47	43	58	463	333	106	19	2	14	171	54	33	3	0	3	2	0	0	14	.005	.066	.249	.302	.402	.232
Dobbs G *	37	30	40	240	163	68	14	1	9	111	40	11	1	1	0	2	3	1	4	.025	.162	.301	.333	.491	.267
Coste C	37	28	36	305	210	72	17	0	9	116	51	16	1	10	3	2	0	1	7	.056	.058	.263	.325	.423	.247
Jenkins G *	30	27	29	322	228	72	16	0	9	115	68	24	5	1	0	4	1	1	6	.024	.140	.246	.301	.392	.229
Ruiz C	28	47	31	373	266	70	14	0	4	96	38	44	6	4	4	1	1	2	14	-.045	.025	.219	.320	.300	.215
Bruntlett E	18	37	15	238	175	46	9	1	2	63	35	21	3	3	2	0	9	2	7	-.001	.076	.217	.297	.297	.204
Taguchi S	8	18	9	103	73	20	5	1	0	27	14	8	0	0	4	0	3	0	2	.099	-.088	.220	.283	.297	.197
Stairs M *	4	4	5	19	12	5	1	0	2	12	3	1	0	0	0	1	0	0	0	.050	.338	.294	.316	.706	.312
Hamels C *	3	3	3	85	59	17	2	0	0	19	29	0	0	1	8	0	0	0	0	-.005	.102	.224	.234	.250	.164
Marson L	2	2	2	4	2	2	0	0	1	5	2	0	0	0	0	0	0	0	0	--	-.375	.500	.500	1.250	.527
Bohn T	2	1	3	5	3	2	1	0	0	3	1	0	0	0	0	0	0	0	0	.033	.775	.400	.400	.600	.324
Eaton A	2	1	1	36	23	5	2	0	0	7	6	5	0	0	3	0	0	0	0	-.055	.069	.179	.303	.250	.195
Snelling C *	2	1	1	4	2	2	1	0	1	6	0	0	0	0	0	0	0	0	0	-.467	--	.500	.500	1.500	.588

Italicized stats have been adjusted for home park.

Batted Ball Batting Stats

Player	% of PA		% of Batted Balls					Out %		Runs Per Event				Total Runs vs. Avg.				
	K%	BB%	GB%	LD%	FB%	IF/F	HR/OF	GB	OF	NIP	GB	LD	OF	NIP	GB	LD	FB	Tot
Utley C	15	13	33	24	42	.12	.16	75	88	.10	.04	.42	.23	11	-2	16	16	41
Burrell P	21	16	34	20	45	.13	.19	77	88	.08	.03	.41	.28	12	-5	0	19	25
Howard R	28	12	41	22	36	.02	.32	82	84	.02	-.01	.35	.48	-3	-11	-6	44	24
Werth J	25	13	39	23	38	.10	.21	73	81	.04	.06	.39	.35	2	0	2	17	21
Victorino S	11	8	45	19	36	.17	.08	66	92	.08	.11	.46	.08	2	18	9	-14	15
Rollins J	9	10	45	24	31	.12	.08	79	81	.13	.02	.36	.17	7	-5	10	-2	11
Dobbs G	17	5	30	25	45	.07	.12	84	80	-.01	-.02	.43	.21	-4	-4	7	6	6
Coste C	17	9	38	23	39	.13	.12	76	85	.04	.04	.37	.17	-1	-2	2	0	-1
Jenkins G	21	8	44	21	35	.10	.10	77	79	.01	.03	.42	.18	-3	-2	2	-0	-4
Taguchi S	14	8	57	20	24	.00	.00	74	94	.05	.04	.38	-.05	-0	-0	-1	-5	-6
Feliz P	11	7	46	16	37	.17	.12	75	87	.06	.04	.34	.17	-1	-1	-6	-0	-9
Bruntlett E	15	10	47	20	33	.21	.04	78	93	.07	.01	.37	.02	1	-2	-1	-10	-12
Ruiz C	10	13	54	17	29	.11	.06	80	88	.14	.00	.31	.08	7	-5	-7	-10	-14
MLB Average	18	10	44	20	36	.10	.11	74	84	.05	.04	.39	.18	--	--	--	--	--

Pitching Stats

Player	PRC	IP	BFP	G	GS	K	BB	IBB	HBP	H	HR	DP	DER	SB	CS	PO	W	L	Sv	Op	Hld	H-A	R^L	RA	ERA	FIP
Hamels C *	114	227.3	914	33	33	196	53	7	1	193	28	18	.734	15	2	1	14	10	0	0	0	.002	.050	3.52	3.09	3.70
Moyer J *	84	196.3	841	33	33	123	62	4	11	199	20	21	.699	13	6	4	16	7	0	0	0	.041	-.006	3.90	3.71	4.33
Myers B	70	190.0	817	30	30	163	65	6	6	197	29	18	.686	17	3	1	10	13	0	0	0	-.068	.029	4.88	4.55	4.50
Lidge B	55	69.3	292	72	0	92	35	4	1	50	2	3	.679	8	1	0	2	0	41	41	0	.064	-.100	2.21	1.95	2.31
Madson R	45	82.7	340	76	0	67	23	4	1	79	6	9	.691	7	1	0	4	2	1	3	17	.014	-.038	3.16	3.05	3.25
Durbin C	43	87.7	365	71	0	63	35	7	4	81	5	16	.698	3	4	1	5	4	1	7	17	-.039	-.075	3.39	2.87	3.60
Kendrick K	40	155.7	722	31	30	68	57	2	14	194	23	9	.682	15	5	1	11	9	0	0	0	-.051	-.061	5.96	5.49	5.58
Romero J *	36	59.0	255	81	0	52	38	5	5	41	5	3	.761	10	2	3	4	4	1	5	24	-.017	-.192	2.75	2.75	4.47
Condrey C	31	69.0	303	56	0	34	19	8	2	85	6	10	.657	3	3	0	3	4	1	1	1	-.049	-.019	3.39	3.26	3.91
Eaton A	28	107.0	478	21	19	57	44	5	6	131	15	18	.663	4	5	0	4	8	0	0	0	.007	-.019	5.97	5.80	5.22
Blanton J	26	70.7	305	13	13	49	31	0	3	66	10	8	.726	4	0	0	4	0	0	0	0	-.027	-.044	4.58	4.20	5.10
Happ J *	15	31.7	138	8	4	26	14	1	1	28	3	0	.734	1	0	0	1	0	0	0	1	.097	-.017	3.69	3.69	4.12
Seanez R	15	43.3	189	42	0	30	25	4	1	38	2	5	.710	7	1	1	5	4	0	1	2	-.062	-.023	4.98	3.53	3.94
Eyre S *	13	14.3	53	19	0	18	3	1	1	8	1	3	.733	1	0	0	3	0	0	1	4	-.177	-.019	1.88	1.88	2.23
Gordon T	9	29.7	139	34	0	26	17	1	0	31	3	0	.667	1	0	0	5	4	2	3	14	.135	.051	5.76	5.16	4.38
Walrond L *	3	10.3	49	6	0	12	9	4	0	13	0	1	.536	0	1	0	1	1	0	0	0	.059	-.188	6.10	6.10	2.33
Swindle R *	1	4.7	24	3	0	4	2	0	0	9	2	0	.563	0	0	0	0	0	0	0	0	--	-.237	7.71	7.71	8.34

Italicized stats have been adjusted for home park.

Batted Ball Pitching Stats

Player	% of PA		% of Batted Balls					Out %		Runs Per Event				Total Runs vs. Avg.				
	K%	BB%	GB%	LD%	FB%	IF/F	HR/OF	GB	OF	NIP	GB	LD	OF	NIP	GB	LD	FB	Tot
Hamels C	21	6	40	22	39	.13	.13	80	88	-.01	.00	.34	.19	-17	-12	-7	-0	-36
Lidge B	32	12	46	22	32	.18	.05	74	83	.02	.04	.39	.10	-2	-1	-4	-8	-15
Durbin C	17	11	46	21	34	.16	.07	74	86	.06	.03	.39	.09	1	-2	-0	-9	-10
Madson R	20	7	51	19	30	.12	.09	77	79	.01	.04	.38	.18	-4	-1	-2	-3	-10
Romero J	20	17	62	16	22	.09	.13	83	86	.09	-.01	.43	.19	6	-5	-3	-4	-6
Happ J	19	11	31	27	43	.15	.09	72	87	.05	.06	.22	.13	0	-1	-3	-2	-4
Moyer J	15	9	44	21	35	.13	.10	74	88	.06	.04	.38	.15	0	0	3	-7	-3
Seanez R	16	14	47	24	29	.11	.00	82	74	.10	-.01	.37	.12	3	-3	1	-3	-3
Blanton J	16	11	40	21	39	.06	.11	75	92	.07	.03	.39	.13	2	-2	1	-2	-0
Gordon F	19	12	40	17	43	.05	.08	66	83	.07	.11	.46	.16	1	2	-0	1	4
Condrey C	11	7	54	19	27	.11	.10	74	81	.06	.04	.43	.19	-0	3	3	0	6
Myers B	20	9	47	20	32	.11	.16	74	85	.03	.04	.43	.25	-5	0	5	8	9
Eaton A	12	10	42	23	35	.13	.13	69	87	.10	.07	.40	.18	5	4	9	1	19
Kendrick K	9	10	44	27	29	.11	.14	77	88	.12	.03	.38	.21	8	-3	21	3	29
MLB Average	18	10	44	20	36	.10	.11	74	84	.05	.04	.39	.18	--	--	--	--	--

Fielding Stats

Name	Inn	SBA/G	CS%	ERA	WP+PB/G	PO	A	TE	FE	Grade
Catchers										
Ruiz C	828.0	0.86	18%	3.85	0.250	623	58	4	1	D
Coste C	612.7	0.76	15%	3.97	0.235	488	23	1	2	--
Marson L	9.0	1.00	0%	3.00	0.000	9	1	0	0	--

Name	Inn	PO	A	TE	FE	FPct	DPS	DPT	ZR	OOZ	Grade
First Base											
Howard R	1402.0	1408	101	5	13	.988	13	0	.743	32	F
Bruntlett E	16.0	18	1	0	0	1.000	1	0	.750	2	--
Utley C	14.0	16	2	0	0	1.000	1	0	.800	1	--
Coste C	9.0	7	1	0	0	1.000	0	0	--	--	--
Dobbs G	8.0	6	2	0	0	1.000	0	0	--	--	--
Second Base											
Utley C	1395.0	340	463	6	7	.984	37	65	.839	66	A+
Bruntlett E	28.0	5	8	0	1	.929	1	0	.778	1	--
Harman B	17.0	2	3	0	0	1.000	0	0	1.000	0	--
Iguchi T	9.0	1	2	0	0	1.000	0	0	1.000	0	--
Shortstop											
Rollins J	1168.0	193	393	3	4	.988	39	29	.849	57	A
Bruntlett E	279.7	39	92	2	2	.970	11	5	.837	12	--
Feliz P	2.0	1	0	0	0	1.000	0	0	--	--	--
Third Base											
Feliz P	978.3	73	223	2	6	.974	19	1	.714	27	F
Dobbs G	327.3	34	67	1	2	.971	6	1	.611	21	--
Bruntlett E	132.0	16	26	1	1	.955	1	0	.677	5	--
Cervenak M	10.0	0	0	0	0	.000	0	0	--	--	--
Ruiz C	1.0	0	0	0	0	.000	0	0	--	--	--
Harman B	1.0	0	0	0	0	.000	0	0	--	--	--

Name	Inn	PO	A	TE	FE	FPct	DPS	DPT	ZR	OOZ	Grade
Left Field											
Burrell P	1198.0	202	12	0	2	.991	2	0	.829	46	F-
Taguchi S	89.7	22	0	0	2	.917	0	0	.810	5	--
Werth J	71.3	15	0	0	0	1.000	0	0	.846	4	--
Bruntlett E	52.3	11	0	0	0	1.000	0	0	1.000	3	--
Bohn T	22.0	6	1	0	1	.875	0	0	1.000	3	--
Dobbs G	16.0	4	0	0	0	1.000	0	0	1.000	1	--
Center Field											
Victorino S	1195.0	314	7	0	2	.994	4	0	.913	83	A
Werth J	233.3	73	2	0	2	.974	2	0	.942	24	--
Golson G	13.0	2	0	0	1	.667	0	0	.500	1	--
Taguchi S	8.0	0	0	0	0	.000	0	0	0.000	0	--
Right Field											
Werth J	661.3	143	7	0	0	1.000	2	0	.898	37	--
Jenkins G	642.0	140	7	2	3	.967	2	0	.858	38	--
Taguchi S	72.0	11	0	0	0	1.000	0	0	.889	3	--
Victorino S	40.0	14	0	0	0	1.000	0	0	.900	5	--
Stairs M	16.7	5	0	0	0	1.000	0	0	.750	2	--
Bruntlett E	12.7	3	0	0	0	1.000	0	0	.667	1	--
Dobbs G	4.7	1	0	0	0	1.000	0	0	1.000	0	--
Golson G	0.3	0	0	0	0	.000	0	0	--	--	--

Pittsburgh Pirates

Stat Facts:
- Nate McLouth's H-A was exactly .000
- McLouth made 87 OOZ plays
- Freddy Sanchez had the lowest BB% among NL regulars
- Sanchez's GPA was .232
- Paul Maholm allowed just 5 stolen bases in 12 attempts
- Maholm induced 31 double plays
- Base stealers went just 6-for-12 against Zach Duke
- Duke's 10% K rate tied for lowest in the majors among 162+ IP pitchers
- Opponents attempted zero steals against Franquelis Osoria
- Xavier Nady started 10 double plays from right field
- Doug Mientkiewicz walked 14% of the time, and struck out 8%
- Tom Gorzelanny allowed 20 homers in 105 innings

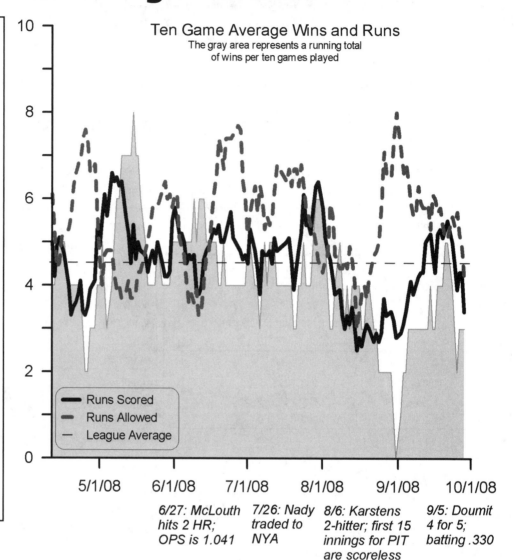

Ten Game Average Wins and Runs
The gray area represents a running total of wins per ten games played

Runs Scored / Runs Allowed / League Average

6/27: McLouth hits 2 HR; OPS is 1.041
7/26: Nady traded to NYA
8/6: Karstens 2-hitter; first 15 innings for PIT are scoreless
9/5: Doumit 4 for 5; batting .330
7/31: Bay traded to BOS

Team Batting and Pitching/Fielding Stats by Month

	April	May	June	July	Aug	Sept/Oct
Wins	11	15	12	12	7	10
Losses	16	13	15	14	21	16
RS/G	4.7	5.3	4.5	5.2	2.9	4.6
RA/G	5.9	5.0	5.6	5.8	5.4	5.1
OBP	.316	.339	.313	.340	.296	.314
SLG	.375	.445	.398	.462	.352	.387
FIP	4.80	4.38	5.60	5.05	4.92	4.29
DER	.667	.666	.694	.664	.687	.678

Batting Stats

Player	BR	Runs	RBI	PA	Outs	H	2B	3B	HR	TB	K	BB	IBB	HBP	SH	SF	SB	CS	GDP	H-A	L^R	BA	OBP	SLG	GPA
McLouth N *	109	113	94	685	440	165	46	4	26	297	93	65	11	12	5	6	23	3	5	-.000	.058	.276	.356	.497	.290
Doumit R +	80	71	69	465	306	137	34	0	15	216	55	23	4	6	0	5	2	2	10	.063	.012	.318	.357	.501	.292
LaRoche A *	79	66	85	554	369	133	32	3	25	246	122	54	7	2	0	6	1	1	9	-.018	.038	.270	.341	.500	.284
Bay J	75	72	64	459	285	111	23	2	22	204	86	59	2	2	0	5	7	0	3	.014	-.079	.282	.375	.519	.304
Sanchez F	59	75	52	608	429	154	26	2	9	211	63	21	1	4	8	6	0	1	13	-.043	.047	.271	.298	.371	.232
Nady X	59	50	57	360	228	108	26	1	13	175	55	25	1	5	0	3	1	0	9	-.054	.025	.330	.383	.535	.313
Mientkiewicz	46	37	30	334	212	79	19	2	2	108	28	44	3	2	0	3	0	0	6	.008	.024	.277	.374	.379	.269
Bautista J	40	38	44	363	249	76	15	0	12	127	77	38	4	2	6	3	1	1	10	-.040	.069	.242	.325	.404	.252
Michaels J	35	25	44	254	185	52	9	1	8	87	52	23	0	1	1	1	1	0	9	.005	-.057	.228	.300	.382	.235
Wilson J	31	24	22	330	230	83	18	1	1	106	27	13	0	5	6	1	2	2	6	.093	-.034	.272	.312	.348	.232
Gomez C	21	26	20	200	136	50	8	0	1	61	30	13	1	1	1	2	0	0	3	.010	-.034	.273	.322	.333	.233
Moss B *	21	12	23	177	126	35	10	2	6	67	45	15	1	1	0	3	0	1	2	.029	-.049	.222	.288	.424	.240
Morgan N *	18	26	7	175	118	47	13	0	0	60	32	10	0	3	1	1	9	5	0	-.019	.029	.294	.345	.375	.254
Paulino R	15	8	18	130	97	25	5	0	2	36	24	11	1	0	0	1	0	0	4	-.043	.047	.212	.277	.305	.205
Rivas L	14	25	20	223	170	45	6	2	3	64	27	13	0	1	2	1	3	2	7	.047	.100	.218	.267	.311	.202
Pearce S	14	6	15	119	83	27	7	0	4	46	22	5	0	3	0	2	2	0	1	-.142	.104	.248	.294	.422	.243
Chavez R	12	12	10	122	88	30	4	0	1	37	14	4	1	1	0	1	0	0	2	.059	-.007	.259	.287	.319	.213
LaRoche A	8	11	12	183	142	25	4	0	3	38	30	14	1	2	2	1	2	0	3	.030	-.060	.152	.227	.232	.163
Cruz L	4	6	3	74	56	15	3	0	0	18	2	3	0	2	2	0	1	1	3	.053	-.170	.224	.278	.269	.196
Bixler B	2	16	2	120	92	17	2	1	0	21	36	6	2	4	2	0	1	0	1	.025	.025	.157	.229	.194	.155
Diaz R	2	0	1	6	3	3	0	0	0	3	1	0	0	0	0	0	1	0	0	--	.700	.500	.500	.500	.357
Maholm P *	1	4	3	73	59	8	0	0	0	8	28	6	0	0	2	0	0	0	2	.024	-.099	.123	.197	.123	.122

Italicized stats have been adjusted for home park.

Batted Ball Batting Stats

	% of PA		% of Batted Balls					Out %		Runs Per Event				Total Runs vs. Avg.				
Player	K%	BB%	GB%	LD%	FB%	IF/F	HR/OF	GB	OF	NIP	GB	LD	OF	NIP	GB	LD	FB	Tot
Bay J	19	13	37	18	45	.09	.16	66	83	.08	.10	.43	.25	6	6	0	15	27
McLouth N	14	11	35	19	47	.13	.12	77	80	.10	.03	.39	.23	7	-3	0	21	25
Nady X	15	8	40	27	34	.14	.16	74	76	.05	.04	.38	.30	-0	-0	9	10	19
Doumit R	12	6	41	23	35	.07	.11	77	80	.05	.03	.41	.21	-2	-2	12	8	16
LaRoche A	22	10	37	20	43	.06	.16	78	82	.03	.02	.44	.27	-2	-5	3	19	15
Mientkiewicz D	8	14	39	22	38	.09	.02	75	83	.17	.04	.38	.06	9	-1	5	-8	5
Morgan N	18	7	50	25	26	.10	.00	66	85	.02	.12	.40	.01	-1	6	2	-6	1
Pearce S	18	7	38	17	45	.13	.11	65	94	.01	.13	.29	.13	-1	3	-3	-1	-2
Bautista J	21	11	45	16	39	.10	.14	70	88	.04	.06	.39	.20	0	0	-6	2	-4
Moss B	25	9	46	18	36	.05	.15	83	76	.01	-.01	.32	.31	-2	-3	-4	5	-4
Chavez R	11	4	41	23	36	.11	.03	79	88	.01	.02	.35	.02	-2	-1	1	-5	-6
Gomez C	15	7	44	20	36	.09	.00	75	76	.03	.04	.39	.06	-1	-0	1	-5	-6
Paulino R	18	8	43	19	38	.06	.03	73	82	.03	.05	.25	.09	-1	-0	-3	-3	-7
Michaels J	20	9	40	20	40	.07	.11	80	88	.03	-.01	.37	.16	-1	-5	-2	-0	-8
Wilson J	8	5	41	22	37	.14	.01	73	89	.07	.05	.36	.01	-1	2	3	-14	-11
Bixler B	30	8	63	11	25	.17	.00	76	80	-.01	.05	.31	.06	-2	-0	-5	-5	-12
Sanchez F	10	4	45	24	30	.07	.06	74	87	.02	.04	.33	.08	-7	-0	6	-13	-14
Rivas L	12	6	51	16	33	.14	.06	76	96	.04	.03	.37	.03	-2	-1	-3	-9	-15
LaRoche A	16	9	49	16	36	.08	.07	89	90	.05	-.05	.25	.08	-1	-6	-7	-5	-19
MLB Average	18	10	44	20	36	.10	.11	74	84	.05	.04	.39	.18	--	--	--	--	--

Pitching Stats

Player	PRC	IP	BFP	G	GS	K	BB	IBB	HBP	H	HR	DP	DER	SB	CS	PO	W	L	Sv	Op	Hld	H-A	R^L	RA	ERA	FIP
Maholm P *	86	206.3	853	31	31	139	63	2	9	201	21	31	.704	5	7	2	9	9	0	0	0	-.025	-.085	3.88	3.71	4.20
Duke Z *	51	185.0	829	31	31	87	47	1	7	230	19	13	.668	6	6	4	5	14	0	0	0	.007	-.019	5.40	4.82	4.46
Snell I	47	164.3	766	31	31	135	89	0	2	201	18	18	.644	20	4	0	7	12	0	0	0	-.004	-.038	5.86	5.42	4.64
Grabow J *	42	76.0	322	74	0	62	37	2	1	60	9	8	.737	3	2	1	6	3	4	8	16	.017	-.012	2.96	2.84	4.53
Yates T	26	73.3	331	72	0	63	41	4	2	72	6	5	.694	4	1	0	6	3	1	5	14	-.022	-.052	4.79	4.66	4.14
Capps M	26	53.7	211	49	0	39	5	0	2	47	5	4	.725	4	1	0	2	3	21	26	0	-.066	.027	3.35	3.02	3.35
Gorzelanny T	24	105.3	490	21	21	67	70	0	1	120	20	17	.681	16	4	3	6	9	0	0	0	-.093	-.052	6.75	6.66	6.42
Marte D *	24	46.7	192	47	0	47	16	1	1	38	4	3	.718	3	1	0	4	0	5	7	15	-.026	.027	3.47	3.47	3.33
Dumatrait P	23	78.7	351	21	11	52	42	2	2	82	7	9	.694	2	2	0	3	4	0	0	0	-.005	-.061	5.49	5.26	4.64
Burnett S *	19	56.7	253	58	0	42	34	3	2	57	7	8	.690	5	3	2	1	1	0	0	8	-.005	-.157	4.92	4.76	5.07
Beam T	17	45.7	199	32	0	24	20	4	2	43	6	4	.735	3	1	0	2	2	1	1	2	.001	-.117	4.14	4.14	5.04
Osoria F	14	60.7	276	43	0	31	12	0	4	87	10	12	.630	0	0	0	4	3	0	2	3	.026	-.039	6.38	6.08	5.11
Karstens J	13	51.3	220	9	9	23	13	0	0	56	7	7	.689	3	3	1	2	6	0	0	0	.122	.019	5.61	4.03	4.84
Bautista D	11	41.3	188	35	0	34	28	2	0	46	5	8	.661	6	2	0	4	3	0	1	7	-.135	-.022	6.10	6.10	5.02
Davis J	7	34.0	153	14	4	13	17	0	3	38	2	8	.661	5	1	0	2	4	0	0	0	-.092	-.027	6.35	5.29	4.97
Ohlendorf R	5	22.7	113	5	5	13	12	0	0	36	3	2	.612	2	1	1	0	3	0	0	0	.033	-.120	7.15	6.35	5.36
Sanchez R	4	13.3	57	10	0	3	6	0	1	14	0	4	.702	0	0	0	0	0	0	1	0	.014	.042	4.05	4.05	4.33
Chavez J	4	15.0	74	15	0	16	9	2	0	20	2	0	.617	3	0	0	0	1	0	2	0	-.188	.080	6.60	6.60	4.20
Taubenheim T	3	6.0	27	1	1	4	3	0	0	7	0	0	.650	1	1	0	0	0	0	0	0	--	.059	3.00	3.00	3.37
Salas M	3	17.0	88	13	0	9	14	3	2	25	5	3	.644	0	0	0	1	0	0	0	0	-.003	-.196	8.47	8.47	7.50
Hansen C	3	15.7	78	16	0	7	20	1	1	11	1	2	.755	2	1	0	1	4	1	3	0	.031	.130	8.04	7.47	6.97
Van Benschot	2	22.3	125	9	5	21	20	1	3	37	7	3	.568	4	1	0	1	3	0	0	0	.077	-.133	11.28	10.48	8.35
Meek E	2	13.0	61	9	0	7	12	2	1	11	3	4	.737	2	0	0	0	1	0	0	0	-.172	.237	7.62	6.92	7.66
Herrera Y	2	18.3	100	5	5	10	12	0	1	35	1	3	.553	1	0	0	1	1	0	0	0	-.202	-.069	9.82	9.82	4.95
Morris M	2	22.3	118	5	5	9	7	1	2	41	6	2	.585	3	3	0	0	4	0	0	0	.074	-.038	12.49	9.67	6.96
Barthmaier J	1	10.3	53	3	3	6	8	0	0	16	3	2	.639	1	1	0	0	2	0	0	0	.148	.042	10.45	10.45	8.14

Italicized stats have been adjusted for home park.

Batted Ball Pitching Stats

Player	% of PA		% of Batted Balls					Out %		Runs Per Event				Total Runs vs. Avg.				
	K%	BB%	GB%	LD%	FB%	IF/F	HR/OF	GB	OF	NIP	GB	LD	OF	NIP	GB	LD	FB	Tot
Maholm P	16	8	54	19	28	.06	.13	76	86	.04	.03	.35	.19	-2	-0	-7	-2	-12
Capps M	18	3	31	23	46	.12	.08	70	90	-.04	.08	.30	.10	-5	0	-2	-3	-10
Marte D	24	9	37	22	41	.10	.09	74	93	.01	.04	.36	.07	-2	-1	-1	-5	-10
Grabow J	19	12	40	20	41	.12	.11	82	87	.06	-.01	.41	.15	2	-6	-1	-2	-8
Yates T	19	13	48	22	30	.08	.10	76	89	.07	.04	.42	.12	3	-0	2	-6	-1
Beam T	12	11	36	13	51	.13	.09	76	80	.11	.04	.40	.20	2	-1	-4	5	2
Karstens J	10	6	42	20	39	.04	.11	74	92	.05	.04	.43	.13	-1	2	3	-0	3
Dumatrait P	15	13	42	24	34	.12	.08	79	82	.10	.02	.38	.15	5	-2	4	-3	4
Davis J	8	13	52	24	24	.04	.07	77	84	.17	.01	.41	.12	4	-1	4	-2	4
Burnett S	17	14	48	19	33	.04	.13	78	80	.10	.01	.42	.24	4	-2	0	3	5
Bautista D	18	15	39	22	40	.02	.10	67	86	.09	.08	.38	.17	4	1	1	1	7
Osoria F	11	6	50	22	28	.11	.18	68	80	.04	.08	.39	.30	-1	6	6	6	17
Duke Z	10	7	48	21	31	.08	.10	78	74	.06	.03	.38	.25	-2	-0	8	14	20
Snell I	18	12	38	25	37	.08	.09	73	84	.07	.05	.45	.17	7	1	18	2	27
Gorzelanny T	14	14	40	16	44	.05	.13	68	83	.12	.07	.43	.22	11	4	-1	14	27
MLB Average	18	10	44	20	36	.10	.11	74	84	.05	.04	.39	.18	--	--	--	--	--

Fielding Stats

Name	Inn	SBA/G	CS%	ERA	WP+PB/G	PO	A	TE	FE	Grade
Catchers										
Doumit R	909.0	0.82	18%	5.07	0.525	596	59	6	2	D
Chavez R	278.0	0.68	38%	4.76	0.453	188	23	1	0	--
Paulino R	260.0	1.07	26%	5.43	0.312	198	16	1	1	--
Diaz R	8.0	1.13	0%	9.00	1.125	5	1	0	0	--

Name	Inn	PO	A	TE	FE	FPct	DPS	DPT	ZR	OOZ	Grade
First Base											
LaRoche A	1135.0	1130	81	2	6	.993	11	2	.702	34	C
Mientkiewicz	283.3	290	19	0	0	1.000	1	0	.837	7	--
Gomez C	35.0	39	4	0	0	1.000	0	0	1.000	3	--
Doumit R	1.0	1	0	0	0	1.000	0	0	--	--	--
Second Base											
Sanchez F	1135.0	291	355	5	2	.989	43	58	.818	30	C
Rivas L	191.7	51	68	0	1	.992	5	17	.900	3	--
Gomez C	110.7	33	20	0	2	.964	1	3	.696	1	--
Cruz L	17.0	6	5	0	0	1.000	0	2	1.000	1	--
Shortstop											
Wilson J	696.3	115	277	3	2	.987	28	24	.847	39	A
Bixler B	278.0	53	121	3	5	.956	13	12	.848	13	--
Rivas L	223.0	37	70	1	5	.947	9	12	.810	7	--
Cruz L	163.3	32	61	1	0	.989	2	11	.824	7	--
Gomez C	94.3	16	34	0	3	.943	3	4	.742	7	--
Third Base											
Bautista J	726.3	45	196	3	8	.956	15	1	.691	34	C
LaRoche A	397.3	19	111	5	4	.935	19	0	.746	19	--
Mientkiewicz	244.7	24	54	2	5	.918	4	0	.690	3	--
Gomez C	85.7	5	17	0	1	.957	1	0	.667	4	--
Rivas L	1.0	0	0	0	0	.000	0	0	--	--	--

Name	Inn	PO	A	TE	FE	FPct	DPS	DPT	ZR	OOZ	Grade
Left Field											
Bay J	921.3	178	3	1	2	.984	0	0	.864	38	F
Moss B	216.3	43	2	0	1	.978	2	0	.861	12	--
Morgan N	166.7	40	0	0	1	.976	0	0	.865	8	--
Michaels J	128.7	29	0	0	0	1.000	0	0	.769	9	--
McLouth N	18.0	2	0	0	0	1.000	0	0	1.000	1	--
Pearce S	4.0	1	0	0	0	1.000	0	0	1.000	0	--
Center Field											
McLouth N	1300.0	380	5	1	0	.997	2	0	.867	87	F-
Morgan N	97.3	31	0	0	0	1.000	0	0	.913	10	--
Michaels J	57.3	22	0	0	0	1.000	0	0	.950	3	--
Right Field											
Nady X	713.7	189	10	1	1	.990	10	0	.903	31	F-
Michaels J	248.0	73	1	1	2	.961	0	0	.935	15	--
Pearce S	226.3	49	1	1	1	.962	0	0	.932	8	--
Moss B	148.0	39	4	0	0	1.000	2	0	.900	12	--
Mientkiewicz	60.0	20	1	0	0	1.000	0	0	.950	1	--
Morgan N	47.0	14	0	0	0	1.000	0	0	1.000	3	--
McLouth N	12.0	2	0	0	0	1.000	0	0	1.000	0	--

San Diego Padres

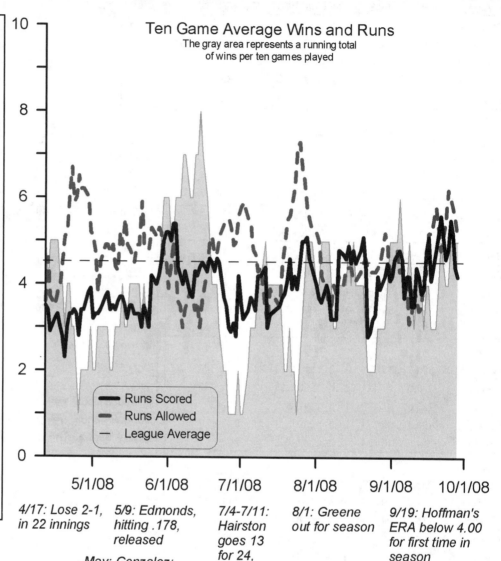

Ten Game Average Wins and Runs
The gray area represents a running total of wins per ten games played

— Runs Scored
-- Runs Allowed
— League Average

4/17: Lose 2-1, in 22 innings

5/9: Edmonds, hitting .178, released

May: Gonzalez: 29 RBI in 29 G

7/4-7/11: Hairston goes 13 for 24, 5 HR

8/1: Greene out for season

9/19: Hoffman's ERA below 4.00 for first time in season

Team Batting and Pitching/Fielding Stats by Month

	April	May	June	July	Aug	Sept/Oct
Wins	11	12	10	9	11	10
Losses	17	17	17	16	16	16
RS/G	3.3	4.0	4.1	3.9	4.2	4.2
RA/G	4.6	4.7	4.9	5.0	4.1	4.9
OBP	.299	.318	.340	.299	.317	.329
SLG	.334	.396	.420	.403	.388	.403
FIP	3.81	4.08	4.12	4.76	4.08	4.90
DER	.713	.682	.693	.682	.710	.701

Batting Stats

Player	BR	Runs	RBI	PA	Outs	H	2B	3B	HR	TB	K	BB	IBB	HBP	SH	SF	SB	CS	GDP	H-A	L^R	BA	OBP	SLG	GPA
Gonzalez A *	124	103	119	700	468	172	32	1	36	314	142	74	18	7	0	3	0	0	24	-.042	.103	.279	.361	.510	.315
Giles B *	102	81	63	653	408	171	40	4	12	255	52	87	2	2	0	5	2	2	18	-.021	.021	.306	.398	.456	.319
Kouzmanoff K	82	71	84	668	476	162	31	4	23	270	139	23	3	15	0	6	0	0	14	-.048	-.028	.260	.299	.433	.264
Gerut J *	62	46	43	356	236	97	15	4	14	162	52	28	0	0	0	0	6	4	1	-.034	-.021	.296	.351	.494	.306
Hairston S	51	42	31	362	248	81	18	3	17	156	84	28	2	3	3	2	3	1	2	.041	.048	.248	.312	.479	.283
Headley C +	48	34	38	368	248	89	19	2	9	139	104	30	1	5	0	2	4	1	5	-.052	-.008	.269	.337	.420	.279
Gonzalez E	38	38	33	353	250	89	15	0	7	125	76	25	1	2	0	1	1	3	11	.000	.030	.274	.329	.385	.265
Greene K	31	30	35	423	314	83	15	2	10	132	100	22	1	5	0	7	5	1	7	.041	-.026	.213	.260	.339	.219
Iguchi T	30	29	24	330	245	70	14	1	2	92	75	26	0	0	1	0	8	1	11	.023	-.044	.231	.292	.304	.225
McAnulty P *	22	9	13	164	107	28	7	1	3	46	41	26	2	2	0	1	0	0	0	.030	.170	.207	.341	.341	.260
Rodriguez L	20	22	12	225	154	58	11	1	0	71	13	13	0	0	7	3	1	1	9	-.012	-.061	.287	.326	.351	.255
Hundley N	20	21	24	216	152	47	7	1	5	71	52	11	0	2	0	5	0	0	1	.014	-.016	.237	.278	.359	.233
Venable W *	16	16	10	124	83	29	4	2	2	43	21	13	1	0	0	1	1	1	1	-.000	-.033	.264	.339	.391	.272
Bard J +	15	11	16	198	147	36	9	0	1	48	25	18	2	1	1	0	0	0	5	-.050	-.066	.202	.279	.270	.210
Clark T +	14	5	11	107	69	21	3	0	1	27	32	19	0	0	0	0	0	0	2	-.055	.012	.239	.374	.307	.266
Huber J	10	5	8	67	46	15	3	0	2	24	19	3	0	2	1	0	0	0	0	-.187	.050	.246	.303	.393	.255
Barrett M	8	9	9	107	79	19	3	0	2	28	16	9	0	1	1	2	0	0	4	.078	.182	.202	.274	.298	.215
Edmonds J *	6	6	6	103	76	16	2	0	1	21	24	10	1	1	1	1	2	1	1	-.132	.071	.178	.265	.233	.193
Antonelli M	5	6	3	65	47	11	2	0	1	16	11	5	1	3	0	0	0	0	1	.118	-.107	.193	.292	.281	.219
Stansberry C	4	4	2	18	10	6	1	0	0	7	3	2	0	0	0	0	0	0	0	.184	-.288	.375	.444	.438	.336
Kazmar S	3	2	2	46	31	8	1	0	0	9	14	5	0	0	1	1	0	0	0	-.060	-.163	.205	.289	.231	.204
Carlin L +	3	12	6	105	83	14	3	1	1	22	34	10	0	1	0	0	0	0	3	-.015	-.019	.149	.238	.234	.180
Ambres C	3	3	0	48	33	8	1	0	0	9	15	7	0	0	0	0	1	0	0	.007	0.000	.195	.313	.220	.213
Baek C	3	2	2	38	24	5	1	0	1	9	7	1	0	0	8	0	0	0	0	-.128	.117	.172	.200	.310	.182
Crabbe C +	3	4	2	39	28	6	1	0	0	7	6	4	0	1	0	0	1	0	0	-.073	.135	.176	.282	.206	.194
Macias D *	2	2	5	25	17	4	0	0	2	10	6	2	0	0	1	2	0	0	1	.082	.006	.200	.250	.500	.258
Germano J	2	1	1	12	5	4	1	0	0	5	3	0	0	0	3	0	0	0	0	.335	-.183	.444	.444	.556	.368
Leblanc W *	1	0	0	9	5	3	0	0	0	3	3	0	0	0	1	0	0	0	0	-.420	--	.375	.375	.375	.285
Peavy J	1	4	2	58	39	13	2	0	0	15	12	3	0	0	5	1	0	1	2	.068	.014	.265	.302	.306	.231
Myrow B *	1	1	3	24	19	3	0	0	1	6	5	2	0	0	0	1	0	0	1	.178	.190	.143	.208	.286	.180
Maddux G	1	1	2	49	37	5	0	0	0	5	14	1	0	0	6	0	1	0	0	.025	-.138	.119	.140	.119	.101
Reineke C	1	1	1	6	5	1	0	0	0	1	4	0	0	0	0	0	0	0	0	.175	--	.167	.167	.167	.127
Haeger C	1	0	0	1	0	1	0	0	0	1	0	0	0	0	0	0	0	0	0	-.700	--	1.000	1.000	1.000	.761

Italicized stats have been adjusted for home park.

Batted ball stats are listed after fielding stats.

Pitching Stats

Player	PRC	IP	BFP	G	GS	K	BB	IBB	HBP	H	HR	DP	DER	SB	CS	PO	W	L	Sv	Op	Hld	H-A	R^L	RA	ERA	FIP
Peavy J	95	173.7	709	27	27	166	59	1	5	146	17	17	.719	18	9	1	10	11	0	0	0	-.080	-.044	2.95	2.85	3.65
Maddux G	47	153.3	638	26	26	80	26	4	5	161	16	16	.705	21	3	0	6	9	0	0	0	-.073	.022	4.70	3.99	4.04
Adams M	43	65.3	259	54	0	74	19	2	0	49	7	4	.730	5	1	0	2	3	0	2	10	-.069	.011	2.48	2.48	3.11
Young C	41	102.3	434	18	18	93	48	4	1	84	13	4	.738	15	2	1	7	6	0	0	0	-.061	-.082	4.05	3.96	4.36
Wolf R *	37	119.7	522	21	21	105	47	0	8	123	14	13	.684	7	3	1	6	10	0	0	0	-.062	.063	5.19	4.74	4.35
Bell H	36	78.0	324	74	0	71	28	4	3	66	5	7	.714	10	2	0	6	6	0	7	23	-.061	.051	3.58	3.58	3.25
Baek C	35	111.0	475	22	20	77	30	2	3	118	12	11	.683	7	4	2	6	9	0	0	0	.036	-.068	4.86	4.62	4.06
Meredith C	25	70.3	302	73	0	49	24	3	1	79	6	14	.653	12	1	0	0	3	0	6	11	.014	-.068	4.35	4.09	3.86
Banks J	25	85.3	372	17	14	43	32	5	3	94	12	10	.709	17	3	0	3	6	0	0	0	-.000	-.027	4.96	4.75	5.08
Hoffman T	20	45.3	180	48	0	46	9	2	0	38	8	3	.744	3	0	0	3	6	30	34	0	-.012	-.126	3.77	3.77	3.93
Ledezma W *	18	54.3	249	25	6	49	38	2	3	49	4	3	.697	12	2	0	0	2	0	0	0	-.010	-.007	4.80	4.47	4.51
Geer J	14	27.0	117	5	5	16	9	2	0	29	2	2	.700	1	1	0	2	1	0	0	0	-.087	.150	2.67	2.67	3.76
Hampson J *	14	30.7	126	35	0	19	10	2	0	31	1	8	.677	3	1	0	2	1	0	0	0	.002	-.056	3.23	2.93	3.17
Estes S *	11	43.7	198	9	8	19	18	0	2	50	6	5	.693	6	1	0	2	3	0	0	0	-.028	-.074	5.36	4.74	5.49
Hensley C	9	39.0	173	32	1	26	25	3	1	36	2	7	.697	4	0	0	1	2	0	1	3	.021	-.040	6.23	5.31	4.30
Germano J	9	43.7	194	12	6	17	13	2	1	54	8	6	.684	9	2	0	0	3	0	0	0	.003	.041	6.39	5.98	5.63
Corey B	8	39.0	167	39	0	18	9	3	0	42	7	1	.729	2	1	0	1	3	0	2	3	-.024	.025	6.23	6.23	5.07
Tomko B	7	9.3	36	6	0	9	5	2	0	3	0	0	.864	0	0	0	0	0	0	0	0	-.030	.098	1.93	1.93	2.24
Reineke C	6	18.0	78	4	3	13	12	1	0	14	1	2	.750	0	0	0	2	1	0	0	0	.030	-.030	5.00	5.00	4.31
Falkenborg B	4	10.7	53	9	0	10	8	1	0	15	2	2	.606	1	0	0	0	1	0	0	0	-.081	.034	4.22	4.22	5.73
Rusch G *	4	19.7	92	12	0	12	11	4	0	22	2	1	.687	1	0	0	1	2	0	0	0	-.018	-.044	6.86	6.41	4.37
Thatcher J *	4	25.7	128	25	0	17	13	2	0	42	4	3	.585	1	0	0	0	4	0	3	5	-.072	.055	8.77	8.42	5.19
Leblanc W *	3	21.3	104	5	4	14	15	2	0	29	7	2	.676	1	0	0	1	3	0	0	0	-.120	-.010	8.02	8.02	7.98
Guevara C	3	12.3	60	10	0	11	9	2	0	13	2	1	.658	3	0	0	1	0	0	0	0	-.096	.087	6.57	5.84	5.23
Hayhurst D	2	16.7	84	10	3	14	10	1	0	27	2	3	.569	5	1	0	0	2	0	0	0	.052	.010	9.72	9.72	4.70
Henn S *	2	9.3	47	4	0	9	9	1	0	11	1	1	.643	0	0	0	0	0	0	0	0	-.043	-.184	7.71	7.71	5.24
Ekstrom M	2	9.7	47	8	0	6	7	1	0	14	2	2	.625	1	0	0	0	2	0	0	0	.086	-.078	7.45	7.45	6.51
Cameron K	2	10.0	46	10	0	5	6	2	0	10	0	0	.686	0	1	0	0	0	0	0	0	-.136	-.062	8.10	3.60	3.40
Wells J	1	3.0	14	2	0	2	1	0	0	4	0	0	.636	1	0	0	0	0	0	0	0	--	.056	6.00	6.00	2.87

Italicized stats have been adjusted for home park.
Batted ball stats are listed after fielding stats.

Fielding Stats

Name	Inn	SBA/G	CS%	ERA	WP+PB/G	PO	A	TE	FE	Grade
Catchers										
Hundley N	486.3	1.02	24%	4.76	0.352	366	32	4	0	--
Bard J	416.7	1.34	15%	4.26	0.281	329	20	2	1	--
Carlin L	259.7	1.11	22%	3.88	0.243	206	14	3	0	--
Barrett M	252.3	1.71	10%	4.46	0.392	205	16	2	0	--
Morton C	43.3	1.25	17%	4.78	0.831	26	5	0	0	--

Name	Inn	PO	A	TE	FE	FPct	DPS	DPT	ZR	OOZ	Grade
First Base											
Gonzalez A	1417.0	1306	130	3	3	.996	15	2	.697	35	F
Clark T	22.0	17	1	0	0	1.000	0	0	1.000	1	--
Rodriguez L	10.0	3	2	0	0	1.000	0	0	.667	0	--
Myrow B	9.0	9	0	0	0	1.000	0	0	--	--	--
Second Base											
Iguchi T	663.3	142	204	1	0	.997	19	33	.862	16	--
Gonzalez E	559.7	92	189	0	4	.986	19	16	.842	16	--
Antonelli M	137.3	38	34	2	0	.973	0	6	.806	1	--
Rodriguez L	39.0	11	10	0	0	1.000	1	2	.778	1	--
Crabbe C	29.7	4	7	2	1	.786	0	1	.444	2	--
Stansberry C	24.7	4	3	0	2	.778	0	0	.600	0	--
Kazmar S	3.0	2	2	0	0	1.000	0	1	1.000	0	--
Hairston S	1.7	1	1	0	0	1.000	0	0	1.000	0	--
Shortstop											
Greene K	934.0	146	289	5	3	.982	33	32	.835	37	C
Rodriguez L	391.3	79	121	2	1	.985	20	12	.823	16	--
Kazmar S	98.7	26	24	1	0	.980	0	3	.760	1	--
Crabbe C	18.0	3	4	0	0	1.000	0	1	.600	0	--
Gonzalez E	16.3	1	11	0	0	1.000	0	0	.917	0	--
Third Base											
Kouzmanoff	1379.0	128	277	6	5	.974	34	1	.705	42	D
Headley C	55.0	3	9	1	0	.923	0	0	.857	3	--
Gonzalez E	23.0	1	3	0	1	.800	0	0	.600	0	--
Rodriguez L	1.3	1	1	0	0	1.000	1	0	1.000	0	--

Name	Inn	PO	A	TE	FE	FPct	DPS	DPT	ZR	OOZ	Grade
Left Field											
Headley C	713.0	156	2	2	3	.969	0	0	.916	36	B
Hairston S	310.0	70	2	0	0	1.000	0	0	.921	12	--
McAnulty P	266.0	48	1	0	0	1.000	0	0	.886	9	--
Huber J	139.3	27	0	1	0	.964	0	0	1.000	8	--
Macias D	21.0	7	0	0	0	1.000	0	0	.857	1	--
Gonzalez E	7.0	2	0	0	0	1.000	0	0	1.000	0	--
Crabbe C	2.0	0	0	0	0	.000	0	0	--	--	--
Center Field											
Gerut J	605.7	189	2	1	1	.990	2	0	.932	39	--
Hairston S	378.0	114	2	1	1	.983	0	0	.900	24	--
Venable W	238.0	84	1	0	0	1.000	0	0	.981	31	--
Edmonds J	212.3	63	1	0	1	.985	2	0	.914	10	--
Ambres C	22.3	3	0	0	0	1.000	0	0	1.000	1	--
Giles B	2.0	0	0	0	0	.000	0	0	--	--	--
Right Field											
Giles B	1263.0	276	3	1	6	.976	2	0	.895	72	A
Gerut J	63.0	17	0	0	0	1.000	0	0	1.000	3	--
Ambres C	50.0	16	0	0	0	.941	0	0	.875	9	--
McAnulty P	48.3	18	0	0	0	1.000	0	0	1.000	7	--
Gonzalez E	16.7	5	1	0	0	1.000	2	0	1.000	1	--
Crabbe C	10.0	3	0	0	0	1.000	0	0	1.000	1	--
Macias D	7.3	4	0	0	0	1.000	0	0	1.000	0	--

Batted Ball Batting Stats

Player	% of PA		% of Batted Balls					Out %		Runs Per Event				Total Runs vs. Avg.				
	K%	BB%	GB%	LD%	FB%	IF/F	HR/OF	GB	OF	NIP	GB	LD	OF	NIP	GB	LD	FB	Tot
Giles B	8	14	42	21	37	.10	.07	70	81	.18	.06	.34	.15	17	5	5	2	29
Gonzalez A	20	12	43	20	37	.05	.22	78	86	.05	.01	.40	.32	3	-6	2	26	25
Gerut J	15	8	47	17	36	.09	.14	68	86	.05	.10	.41	.22	-1	7	-0	6	12
Hairston S	23	9	38	14	48	.18	.18	66	86	.01	.11	.43	.27	-4	5	-6	10	4
Venable W	17	10	49	13	37	.15	.07	64	85	.06	.11	.47	.15	1	3	-1	-1	2
Headley C	28	10	38	25	37	.01	.08	72	78	.00	.06	.40	.20	-5	0	2	3	0
McAnulty P	25	17	41	18	41	.13	.09	82	87	.07	.01	.54	.11	3	-2	0	-3	-1
Gonzalez E	22	8	47	19	33	.00	.08	74	82	.01	.04	.39	.16	-4	-1	-1	-0	-6
Barrett M	15	9	41	22	38	.07	.07	78	92	.06	.01	.26	.06	0	-1	-2	-3	-6
Kouzmanoff K	21	6	40	22	39	.06	.11	76	84	-.01	.03	.40	.19	-12	-4	4	5	-7
Rodriguez L	6	6	49	19	31	.03	.00	76	88	.12	.04	.39	-.02	-0	0	1	-10	-8
Edmonds J	23	11	28	22	49	.03	.03	89	90	.03	-.05	.33	.00	-0	-3	-1	-4	-9
Hundley N	24	6	39	17	44	.14	.09	68	90	-.02	.10	.40	.09	-5	2	-3	-5	-9
Carlin L	32	10	52	13	35	.10	.05	87	83	-.00	-.02	.34	.12	-2	-2	-4	-2	-11
Bard J	13	10	47	22	31	.13	.02	90	85	.08	-.05	.36	.04	1	-7	-0	-7	-13
Iguchi T	23	8	48	17	34	.12	.03	75	82	.00	.03	.40	.07	-4	-1	-4	-9	-19
Greene K	24	6	32	21	48	.09	.07	74	89	-.02	.05	.34	.08	-8	-2	-5	-9	-25
MLB Average	*18*	*10*	*44*	*20*	*36*	*.10*	*.11*	*74*	*84*	*.05*	*.04*	*.39*	*.18*	--	--	--	--	--

Batted Ball Pitching Stats

Player	% of PA		% of Batted Balls					Out %		Runs Per Event				Total Runs vs. Avg.				
	K%	BB%	GB%	LD%	FB%	IF/F	HR/OF	GB	OF	NIP	GB	LD	OF	NIP	GB	LD	FB	Tot
Peavy J	23	9	41	21	38	.17	.11	74	85	.01	.04	.30	.16	-7	-2	-12	-8	-29
Adams M	29	7	42	18	40	.14	.13	77	82	-.02	.03	.31	.22	-6	-2	-7	1	-14
Bell H	22	10	46	20	35	.08	.07	74	86	.03	.04	.35	.11	-2	-1	-4	-6	-13
Maddux G	13	5	49	22	29	.04	.10	77	84	.02	.03	.35	.18	-7	-4	2	-0	-9
Young C	21	11	22	25	53	.19	.11	74	87	.05	.06	.30	.16	0	-3	-4	-1	-8
Hoffman T	26	5	39	14	47	.10	.15	71	91	-.04	.06	.30	.20	-5	0	-6	2	-8
Hampson J	15	8	39	16	45	.15	.03	64	79	.04	.10	.33	.08	-0	1	-2	-3	-4
Geer J	14	8	35	28	37	.06	.06	78	93	.05	.02	.38	.03	-0	-1	3	-4	-2
Wolf R	20	11	39	24	37	.12	.12	75	83	.04	.03	.37	.20	0	-4	2	2	-1
Meredith C	16	8	67	16	17	.08	.17	71	90	.04	.06	.42	.23	-1	5	-1	-3	-1
Baek C	16	7	41	21	38	.18	.11	65	90	.02	.11	.36	.14	-4	8	1	-5	0
Corey B	11	5	43	18	38	.15	.16	77	89	.04	.03	.38	.22	-1	-1	-0	2	0
Hensley C	15	15	51	18	31	.03	.06	77	82	.12	.02	.45	.13	4	-2	0	-2	1
Ledezma W	20	16	38	21	42	.06	.07	69	91	.10	.08	.43	.06	5	1	1	-6	2
Banks J	12	9	36	22	42	.09	.11	75	92	.09	.05	.41	.13	2	-1	4	-1	4
Estes S	10	10	54	21	25	.03	.16	75	88	.12	.04	.35	.23	2	0	1	1	4
Germano J	9	7	49	18	33	.17	.19	72	89	.09	.05	.41	.27	0	1	2	4	7
Thatcher J	13	10	41	25	34	.25	.17	74	75	.09	.05	.57	.29	1	1	7	2	11
MLB Average	*18*	*10*	*44*	*20*	*36*	*.10*	*.11*	*74*	*84*	*.05*	*.04*	*.39*	*.18*	--	--	--	--	--

San Francisco Giants

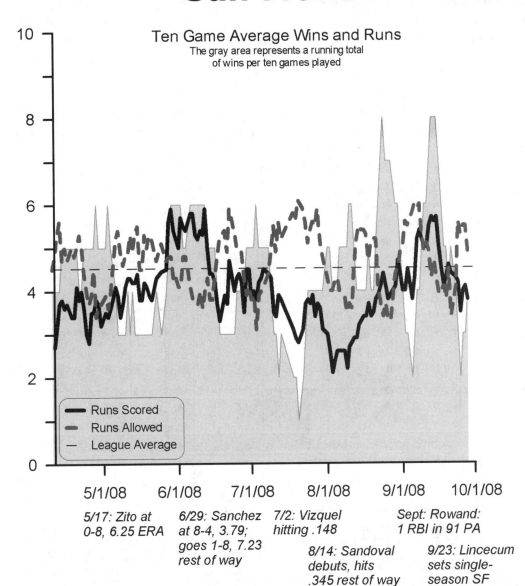

Ten Game Average Wins and Runs
The gray area represents a running total
of wins per ten games played

- Runs Scored
- Runs Allowed
- League Average

5/17: Zito at 0-8, 6.25 ERA

6/29: Sanchez at 8-4, 3.79; goes 1-8, 7.23 rest of way

7/2: Vizquel hitting .148

8/14: Sandoval debuts, hits .345 rest of way

Sept: Rowand: 1 RBI in 91 PA

9/23: Lincecum sets single-season SF K record

Stat Facts:
- Fred Lewis hit just 1 infield pop-up
- Tim Lincecum led the majors with 143 Pitching Runs Created and 265 strikeouts
- Lincecum struck out 29% of the batters he faced
- Base stealers went just 13-for-23 against Matt Cain
- Kevin Correia allowed only 4 steals in 11 attempts
- Bengie Molina tied for the ML lead with 11 sacrifice flies
- Molina put the ball in play 88% of the time
- Brian Wilson's .098 R^L was highest in the majors among 40+ IP pitchers
- Jonathan Sanchez's FIP was 1.11 lower than his ERA
- 20% of the outfield flies against Pat Misch were home runs
- Randy Winn made 70 OOZ plays in right field
- Winn stole 25 bases in 27 attempts

Team Batting and Pitching/Fielding Stats by Month

	April	May	June	July	Aug	Sept/Oct
Wins	13	10	13	8	15	13
Losses	16	17	14	16	14	13
RS/G	3.2	4.5	4.6	3.4	3.7	4.4
RA/G	4.5	5.0	4.3	5.2	4.6	4.6
OBP	.306	.333	.336	.280	.329	.334
SLG	.370	.422	.383	.321	.400	.387
FIP	4.30	4.63	3.48	4.01	4.26	4.39
DER	.679	.708	.687	.654	.690	.697

Batting Stats

Player	BR	Runs	RBI	PA	Outs	H	2B	3B	HR	TB	K	BB	IBB	HBP	SH	SF	SB	CS	GDP	H-A	L^R	BA	OBP	SLG	GPA
Winn R +	85	84	64	667	423	183	38	2	10	255	88	59	6	0	1	9	25	2	6	.001	.002	.306	.363	.426	.267
Molina B	69	47	95	569	398	155	33	0	16	236	38	19	5	9	0	11	0	0	23	-.008	-.005	.292	.322	.445	.254
Rowand A	67	57	70	611	425	149	37	0	13	225	126	44	7	14	0	4	2	4	21	-.022	.044	.271	.339	.410	.252
Lewis F *	67	81	40	521	348	132	25	11	9	206	124	51	3	0	0	2	21	7	5	.076	.021	.282	.351	.440	.265
Aurilia R	49	33	52	440	304	115	21	1	10	168	56	30	4	1	0	2	1	1	11	-.038	.074	.283	.332	.413	.250
Bowker J *	41	31	43	350	251	83	14	3	10	133	74	19	1	3	0	2	1	1	7	.004	.136	.255	.300	.408	.235
Durham R +	38	43	32	304	194	77	23	0	3	109	49	38	0	2	0	1	6	2	6	-.008	-.050	.293	.385	.414	.274
Castillo J	37	42	35	420	316	96	28	4	6	150	71	25	1	1	0	0	2	2	16	-.007	.002	.244	.290	.381	.224
Velez E +	29	32	30	292	220	72	16	7	1	105	40	14	1	1	1	1	15	6	11	-.052	-.024	.262	.299	.382	.228
Sandoval P +	23	24	24	154	101	50	10	1	3	71	14	4	1	1	0	4	0	0	6	-.058	-.122	.345	.357	.490	.280
Vizquel O +	22	24	23	300	215	59	10	1	0	71	29	24	9	0	7	3	5	4	4	.066	-.074	.222	.283	.267	.192
Burriss E +	20	36	18	274	184	68	6	1	1	79	24	23	1	5	5	1	13	5	7	-.005	-.004	.283	.357	.329	.240
Ishikawa T *	18	12	15	104	70	26	6	0	3	41	27	9	1	0	0	0	1	0	1	-.134	.112	.274	.337	.432	.257
Schierholtz	12	12	5	81	53	24	8	1	1	37	8	3	0	3	0	0	0	1	1	.167	.010	.320	.370	.493	.287
Roberts D *	11	18	9	130	86	24	2	2	0	30	18	20	1	0	1	2	5	3	0	.190	.075	.224	.341	.280	.221
Holm S	8	10	6	98	66	22	9	0	1	34	16	10	1	3	0	1	0	1	3	.149	.071	.262	.357	.405	.259
Denker T	6	6	3	42	28	9	4	1	1	18	10	5	0	0	0	0	0	0	0	.217	.033	.243	.333	.486	.269
Horwitz B	5	5	4	42	28	8	0	0	2	14	10	5	0	0	0	1	0	0	0	-.029	.075	.222	.310	.389	.234
McClain S	5	7	7	38	25	9	1	0	2	16	8	5	0	0	0	0	0	1	0	-.137	-.053	.273	.368	.485	.284
Lincecum T *	4	7	5	81	60	11	1	1	0	14	32	5	0	0	6	0	0	0	1	.003	.085	.157	.213	.200	.145
Ochoa I	4	7	3	135	100	24	8	0	0	32	28	4	1	3	7	0	0	1	3	-.025	.009	.200	.244	.267	.175
Ortmeier D	4	4	5	73	53	14	6	0	0	20	18	7	1	2	0	0	2	2	1	.100	.019	.219	.315	.313	.218
Bocock B	4	4	2	93	70	11	1	0	0	12	29	12	0	0	4	0	4	2	2	-.084	-.016	.143	.258	.156	.154
Cain M	1	3	3	72	55	7	1	0	2	14	34	4	0	0	6	0	0	0	0	.077	-.047	.113	.167	.226	.130
Zito B *	1	1	2	59	45	6	0	0	0	6	10	4	0	0	4	0	0	0	0	.056	-.052	.118	.182	.118	.110
Misch P	1	0	1	14	8	1	0	0	0	1	2	1	0	0	4	0	0	0	0	-.004	.243	.111	.200	.111	.117
Davis R	1	2	0	19	17	1	0	0	0	1	6	1	0	0	0	0	4	0	0	-.033	-.090	.056	.105	.056	.061

Italicized stats have been adjusted for home park.

Batted Ball Batting Stats

Player	% of PA		% of Batted Balls					Out %		Runs Per Event				Total Runs vs. Avg.				
	K%	BB%	GB%	LD%	FB%	IF/F	HR/OF	GB	OF	NIP	GB	LD	OF	NIP	GB	LD	FB	Tot
Winn R	13	9	51	19	30	.05	.07	72	79	.07	.07	.39	.17	2	9	4	0	16
Lewis F	24	10	54	18	28	.01	.09	68	79	.02	.09	.51	.21	-3	10	4	0	11
Durham R	16	13	44	21	34	.16	.03	71	71	.09	.06	.43	.17	5	2	4	-1	10
Sandoval P	9	3	45	26	29	.13	.06	59	88	.01	.14	.36	.07	-2	6	5	-4	6
Rowand A	21	9	49	19	32	.11	.11	74	76	.03	.04	.41	.23	-2	-0	0	4	2
Molina B	7	5	35	18	47	.04	.07	76	83	.08	.02	.40	.12	-2	-5	3	6	1
Aurilia R	13	7	41	18	41	.13	.08	72	84	.05	.06	.37	.14	-2	3	-1	-0	-1
Roberts D	14	15	50	19	31	.04	.00	82	92	.13	.01	.40	-.02	3	-1	-0	-5	-4
Burriss E	9	10	65	14	21	.09	.03	77	84	.13	.02	.47	.05	3	1	-1	-9	-5
Bowker J	21	6	37	25	38	.18	.13	78	84	-.01	.02	.37	.21	-6	-4	3	1	-6
Velez E	14	5	59	15	26	.05	.02	76	65	.01	.03	.39	.21	-3	-0	-4	1	-7
Castillo J	17	6	52	20	27	.08	.07	83	76	.01	-.02	.46	.19	-5	-10	6	-2	-11
Bocock B	31	13	51	18	31	.50	.00	78	100	.02	.02	.27	-.10	-1	-1	-4	-5	-11
Ochoa I	21	5	60	11	30	.16	.00	80	76	-.02	.02	.23	.10	-3	0	-7	-4	-13
Vizquel O	10	8	42	21	37	.08	.00	81	84	.09	.01	.27	.01	1	-4	-5	-12	-20
MLB Average	18	10	44	20	36	.10	.11	74	84	.05	.04	.39	.18	--	--	--	--	--

Pitching Stats

Player	PRC	IP	BFP	G	GS	K	BB	IBB	HBP	H	HR	DP	DER	SB	CS	PO	W	L	Sv	Op	Hld	H-A	R^L	RA	ERA	FIP
Lincecum T	143	227.0	928	34	33	265	84	1	6	182	11	27	.687	20	3	0	18	5	0	0	0	.017	.002	2.85	2.62	2.67
Cain M	98	217.7	933	34	34	186	91	9	7	206	19	14	.692	13	10	0	8	14	0	0	0	-.002	-.027	3.93	3.76	3.85
Sanchez J *	56	158.0	695	29	29	157	75	1	7	154	14	17	.672	19	3	1	9	12	0	0	0	.013	-.026	5.13	5.01	3.90
Zito B *	52	180.0	818	32	32	120	102	10	4	186	16	17	.688	6	4	2	10	17	0	0	0	.022	-.065	5.75	5.15	4.62
Correia K	26	110.0	514	25	19	66	47	3	4	141	15	10	.652	4	7	1	3	8	0	0	0	-.006	.008	6.55	6.05	5.08
Yabu K	26	68.0	302	60	0	48	32	4	8	63	3	8	.692	3	0	0	3	6	0	1	9	-.032	-.125	4.37	3.57	3.95
Wilson B	25	62.3	274	63	0	67	28	4	3	62	7	8	.663	2	1	0	3	2	41	47	0	.047	.098	4.62	4.62	3.81
Hinshaw A *	21	39.7	179	48	0	47	29	4	3	31	5	2	.705	1	1	0	2	1	0	0	4	.010	-.097	3.63	3.40	4.59
Walker T	20	53.3	226	65	0	49	21	3	1	47	7	5	.723	2	1	0	5	8	0	4	19	.054	-.122	4.89	4.56	4.14
Sadler B	19	44.3	197	33	0	42	27	4	8	34	6	3	.746	3	3	0	0	1	0	0	1	-.001	.064	4.26	4.06	5.16
Romo S	18	34.0	130	29	0	33	8	1	0	16	3	0	.819	4	1	0	3	1	0	0	5	.043	.089	3.44	2.12	3.29
Taschner J *	17	48.0	227	67	0	39	24	2	2	57	5	4	.650	6	2	1	3	2	0	4	14	.013	-.060	5.06	4.88	4.43
Misch P *	15	52.3	230	15	7	38	15	2	3	56	11	2	.718	5	0	0	0	3	0	0	0	-.083	-.019	5.85	5.68	5.40
Chulk V	10	31.7	139	27	0	16	8	2	2	33	6	1	.720	1	0	0	0	3	0	2	2	-.078	.027	5.12	4.83	5.41
Valdez M	9	16.0	69	17	1	13	7	2	2	14	1	2	.696	1	1	0	1	0	0	0	2	.046	-.131	2.81	1.69	3.70
Hennessey B	7	40.3	196	17	4	21	15	1	1	63	8	0	.629	4	3	0	1	2	0	1	0	-.041	.025	7.81	7.81	5.85
Matos O	4	20.7	98	20	0	16	9	1	1	26	3	0	.638	2	1	0	1	2	0	1	0	.062	.001	7.40	4.79	4.85
Threets E *	4	10.0	50	7	0	6	9	2	3	11	1	3	.677	1	0	0	0	1	0	0	0	.150	.078	3.60	3.60	6.30
Espineli E *	4	16.0	69	15	0	8	8	2	0	17	5	4	.750	2	0	0	2	0	0	0	0	-.192	-.127	5.63	5.06	7.39
Palmer M	2	12.7	67	3	3	3	13	1	2	17	1	2	.646	0	0	0	0	2	0	0	0	-.193	-.004	9.24	8.53	7.07

Italicized stats have been adjusted for home park.

Batted Ball Pitching Stats

Player	% of PA		% of Batted Balls					Out %		Runs Per Event				Total Runs vs. Avg.				
	K%	BB%	GB%	LD%	FB%	IF/F	HR/OF	GB	OF	NIP	GB	LD	OF	NIP	GB	LD	FB	Tot
Lincecum T	29	10	44	21	35	.08	.06	74	85	.00	.04	.40	.10	-12	-4	-8	-22	-46
Romo S	25	8	33	14	53	.09	.08	81	97	.00	.01	.40	.04	-2	-2	-4	-5	-12
Cain M	20	11	33	23	44	.10	.07	74	84	.05	.05	.38	.14	0	-3	2	-4	-5
Walker T	22	10	48	21	31	.13	.15	79	74	.03	.01	.30	.31	-1	-3	-4	3	-5
Yabu K	16	13	47	23	30	.11	.05	75	91	.10	.04	.38	.05	5	-1	2	-9	-3
Wilson B	24	11	52	19	30	.14	.11	70	85	.03	.06	.46	.20	-0	1	-0	-2	-2
Sanchez J	23	12	41	21	37	.10	.09	73	79	.04	.05	.37	.19	1	-0	-3	1	-0
Sadler W	21	18	32	21	47	.05	.12	78	91	.10	.01	.36	.13	5	-3	-2	-1	-0
Hinshaw A	26	18	25	22	53	.12	.11	58	85	.07	.15	.25	.19	3	1	-4	1	1
Misch P	17	8	44	19	36	.11	.20	77	84	.03	.03	.30	.29	-1	-1	-3	6	1
Chulk V	12	7	38	16	46	.12	.13	72	85	.06	.07	.41	.20	-0	1	-0	3	3
Taschner J	17	11	39	19	43	.09	.08	62	84	.07	.13	.35	.16	1	6	-1	1	7
Zito B	15	13	36	23	40	.09	.07	70	82	.10	.07	.31	.13	13	4	-1	-3	13
Hennessey B	11	9	37	19	44	.13	.14	53	78	.09	.19	.34	.26	1	8	0	8	17
Correia K	13	10	38	25	37	.06	.10	69	88	.08	.08	.39	.15	3	6	11	1	22
MLB Average	18	10	44	20	36	.10	.11	74	84	.05	.04	.39	.18	--	--	--	--	--

Fielding Stats

Name	Inn	SBA/G	CS%	ERA	WP+PB/G	PO	A	TE	FE	Grade
Catchers										
Molina B	1128.3	0.80	32%	4.30	0.471	987	71	4	1	A
Holm S	210.3	0.98	9%	4.71	0.813	190	5	0	0	--
Sandoval P	86.3	1.04	30%	4.38	0.730	76	6	0	0	--
Alfonzo E	17.0	1.59	0%	5.29	0.000	10	1	1	0	--

Name	Inn	PO	A	TE	FE	FPct	DPS	DPT	ZR	OOZ	Grade
First Base											
Bowker J	550.3	448	39	0	6	.988	3	0	.742	13	--
Aurilia R	477.0	384	26	1	3	.990	8	0	.719	12	--
Ishikawa T	213.3	161	20	0	3	.984	5	0	.742	10	--
Sandoval P	121.0	100	12	0	1	.991	4	0	.769	2	--
Ortmeier D	52.0	41	6	0	0	1.000	0	0	.909	2	--
McClain S	28.3	26	2	0	0	1.000	0	0	1.000	3	--
Snow J	0.0	0	0	0	0	.000	0	0	--	--	--
Second Base											
Durham R	535.3	130	129	0	3	.989	16	23	.768	8	--
Velez E	449.7	102	104	1	6	.967	10	15	.783	5	--
Burriss E	282.0	66	80	1	3	.973	3	10	.848	10	--
Denker T	70.0	19	16	1	0	.972	1	2	.813	1	--
Castillo J	51.0	8	15	0	1	.958	1	0	.923	3	--
Ochoa I	48.0	8	14	0	1	.957	2	1	.833	2	--
Aurilia R	3.0	0	0	0	0	.000	0	0	0.000	0	--
Rohlinger R	3.0	0	0	0	0	.000	0	0	--	--	--
Shortstop											
Vizquel O	657.7	108	179	1	1	.993	23	18	.868	25	--
Burriss E	315.0	50	93	3	2	.966	7	6	.772	10	--
Ochoa I	238.0	45	71	0	3	.975	10	7	.833	5	--
Bocock B	227.0	39	73	0	4	.966	12	8	.857	7	--
Castillo J	4.3	1	1	0	0	1.000	0	0	0.000	1	--
Third Base											
Castillo J	820.0	47	166	7	8	.934	17	0	.663	28	F
Aurilia R	427.7	31	67	1	4	.951	3	0	.646	11	--
Sandoval P	85.0	3	14	0	0	1.000	0	0	1.000	4	--
Rohlinger R	68.3	7	12	2	1	.864	1	0	.667	4	--
McClain S	36.0	3	8	0	0	1.000	0	0	.583	1	--
Gillaspie C	4.0	1	0	0	0	1.000	0	0	--	--	--
Denker T	1.0	0	0	0	0	.000	0	0	--	--	--

Name	Inn	PO	A	TE	FE	FPct	DPS	DPT	ZR	OOZ	Grade
Left Field											
Lewis F	905.7	178	11	0	6	.969	2	0	.907	40	B
Roberts D	205.7	54	3	0	0	1.000	4	0	.930	14	--
Winn R	107.7	30	1	0	0	1.000	0	0	1.000	7	--
Ortmeier D	80.3	13	1	0	0	1.000	0	0	.867	1	--
Horwitz B	63.3	20	0	0	0	1.000	0	0	.950	1	--
Velez E	43.3	5	0	1	0	.833	0	0	.833	0	--
Bowker J	27.0	5	0	0	0	1.000	0	0	1.000	0	--
Davis R	7.0	2	0	0	0	1.000	0	0	1.000	0	--
Timpner C	2.0	0	0	0	0	.000	0	0	--	--	--
Center Field											
Rowand A	1275.0	412	6	1	3	.991	0	0	.945	68	F-
Winn R	71.0	18	1	0	0	1.000	0	0	.833	3	--
Lewis F	69.0	16	0	0	0	1.000	0	0	.929	3	--
Davis R	22.7	6	0	0	0	1.000	0	0	.667	0	--
Velez E	4.0	3	0	0	0	1.000	0	0	1.000	2	--
Right Field											
Winn R	1108.0	309	5	0	3	.991	4	0	.945	70	A+
Schierholtz N	161.7	40	1	0	0	1.000	0	0	.960	16	--
Bowker J	91.3	22	0	0	0	1.000	0	0	.905	3	--
Velez E	44.3	8	1	0	0	1.000	0	0	.625	3	--
Lewis F	18.0	5	0	0	0	1.000	0	0	.800	1	--
Horwitz B	9.0	6	0	0	0	1.000	0	0	1.000	2	--
Ortmeier D	5.0	1	0	0	0	1.000	0	0	1.000	0	--
Burriss E	2.3	0	0	0	0	.000	0	0	--	--	--
Davis R	2.0	1	0	0	0	1.000	0	0	1.000	0	--

Seattle Mariners

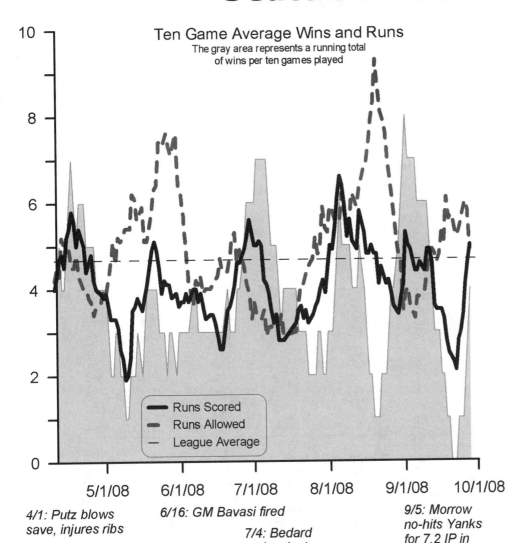

Ten Game Average Wins and Runs
The gray area represents a running total
of wins per ten games played

- Runs Scored
- Runs Allowed
- League Average

5/1/08   6/1/08   7/1/08   8/1/08   9/1/08   10/1/08

*4/1: Putz blows
save, injures ribs*

*4/25: Johjima
signs 3-year
extension*

6/16: GM Bavasi fired

*7/4: Bedard
makes last
start of year*

*9/5: Morrow
no-hits Yanks
for 7.2 IP in
first start*

Stat Facts:
- Richie Sexon's H-A of -.107 was lowest in the majors among 150+ PA players
- Yuniesky Betancourt had the lowest BB% of any regular in the majors
- Jose Lopez had the second-lowest
- Lopez made 51 OOZ plays
- 57% of the batted balls by Ichiro Suzuki were ground balls
- Ichiro stole 43 bases in 47 attempts
- Base stealers went just 6-for-13 against R.A. Dickey
- Ryan Feierabend had 6 pickoffs in 40 innings, and allowed 1 stolen base in 5 attempts
- Roy Corcoran's GB rate of 69% was highest in the majors
- Corcoran's LD rate of 10% was among the lowest in the majors
- Corcoran allowed just 1 homer in 73 innings
- King Felix batted twice: 1 sac bunt, 1 grand slam home run

Team Batting and Pitching/Fielding Stats by Month

	April	May	June	July	Aug	Sept/Oct
Wins	13	8	10	10	12	8
Losses	15	20	16	16	16	18
RS/G	4.5	3.5	4.0	4.0	4.6	4.1
RA/G	4.3	5.9	4.2	4.4	6.1	5.1
OBP	.321	.292	.324	.325	.332	.314
SLG	.396	.367	.357	.397	.427	.387
FIP	4.35	4.56	3.96	4.39	5.30	4.90
DER	.693	.665	.687	.707	.673	.678

Batting Stats

Player	BR	Runs	RBI	PA	Outs	H	2B	3B	HR	TB	K	BB	IBB	HBP	SH	SF	SB	CS	GDP	H-A	L^R	BA	OBP	SLG	GPA
Ibanez R *	109	85	110	707	466	186	43	3	23	304	110	64	11	3	0	5	2	4	13	.005	-.014	.293	.358	.479	.289
Suzuki I *	94	103	42	749	485	213	20	7	6	265	65	51	12	5	3	4	43	4	8	.010	.033	.310	.361	.386	.267
Lopez J	84	80	89	687	470	191	41	1	17	285	67	27	5	1	6	9	6	3	14	.041	.001	.297	.322	.443	.263
Beltre A	74	74	77	612	421	148	29	1	25	254	90	50	10	2	0	4	8	2	11	-.049	.099	.266	.327	.457	.269
Betancourt Y	53	66	51	590	430	156	36	3	7	219	42	17	0	2	6	6	4	4	23	.066	-.007	.279	.300	.392	.240
Johjima K	38	29	39	409	305	86	19	0	7	126	33	19	1	8	1	2	2	0	12	.021	.020	.227	.277	.332	.214
Reed J *	31	30	31	312	217	77	18	1	2	103	38	18	0	2	3	3	2	3	5	.028	.165	.269	.314	.360	.238
Vidro J +	29	28	45	330	242	72	11	0	7	104	36	18	2	0	2	2	2	1	5	.014	-.024	.234	.274	.338	.214
Cairo M	27	34	23	250	174	55	14	2	0	73	32	18	0	4	6	1	5	2	6	.035	.053	.249	.316	.330	.232
Sexson R	27	27	30	292	205	55	8	0	11	96	76	37	0	0	0	3	1	0	8	-.107	.144	.218	.315	.381	.244
Clement J *	24	17	23	224	162	46	10	1	5	73	63	15	0	5	0	1	0	1	4	-.009	-.048	.227	.295	.360	.229
Bloomquist W	24	32	9	192	123	46	1	0	0	47	29	25	1	1	1	0	14	3	1	-.018	.089	.279	.377	.285	.248
Balentien W	21	23	24	260	207	49	13	0	7	83	79	16	1	0	0	1	0	1	12	.008	.018	.202	.250	.342	.204
Lahair B *	15	15	10	150	107	34	4	0	3	47	40	13	1	0	1	0	0	1	4	-.084	.107	.250	.315	.346	.235
Burke J	9	10	8	100	72	24	3	0	1	30	7	5	0	1	1	1	0	1	3	-.016	.091	.261	.303	.326	.225
Wilkerson B	6	1	5	68	46	13	4	0	0	17	15	10	0	0	2	0	1	2	1	-.118	.237	.232	.348	.304	.240
Norton G +	6	2	4	18	9	7	2	0	0	9	4	2	0	0	0	0	0	0	0	.249	.279	.438	.500	.563	.377
Valbuena L *	5	6	1	54	37	12	5	0	0	17	11	4	0	1	0	0	0	0	0	-.003	-.122	.245	.315	.347	.235
Hulett T *	2	2	2	56	41	11	1	0	1	15	17	5	0	1	1	0	0	0	3	.006	.229	.224	.309	.306	.222
Hernandez F	1	1	4	2	0	1	0	0	1	4	0	0	0	0	1	0	0	0	0	-1.450	--	1.000	1.000	4.000	1.495
Tuiasosopo M	1	1	2	47	37	7	2	1	0	11	16	2	0	1	0	0	0	0	0	.243	-.071	.159	.213	.250	.163
Bedard E *	1	0	0	4	2	2	0	0	0	2	2	0	0	0	0	0	0	0	0	-.350	--	.500	.500	.500	.361
Morse M	1	0	0	11	7	2	1	0	0	3	4	1	0	1	0	0	0	0	0	.129	-.118	.222	.364	.333	.255

Italicized stats have been adjusted for home park.

Batted Ball Batting Stats

Player	% of PA		% of Batted Balls					Out %		Runs Per Event				Total Runs vs. Avg.				
	K%	BB%	GB%	LD%	FB%	IF/F	HR/OF	GB	OF	NIP	GB	LD	OF	NIP	GB	LD	FB	Tot
Ibanez R	16	9	41	19	40	.14	.11	71	83	.06	.06	.45	.20	2	4	8	8	22
Suzuki I	9	7	57	20	23	.14	.05	68	86	.10	.09	.35	.07	3	25	4	-20	11
Beltre A	15	8	40	22	39	.10	.15	80	87	.05	.01	.35	.22	-1	-7	2	10	5
Lopez J	10	4	44	20	36	.10	.09	67	91	.02	.09	.36	.11	-7	14	5	-8	3
Bloomquist W	15	14	56	20	24	.24	.00	66	76	.10	.10	.31	.05	3	5	-1	-6	1
Sexson R	26	13	47	18	34	.11	.20	71	88	.04	.06	.26	.29	0	1	-8	4	-3
Lahair B	27	9	43	20	38	.08	.09	68	87	-.00	.06	.36	.13	-2	0	-2	-2	-5
Reed J	12	6	52	20	28	.16	.04	73	82	.05	.06	.37	.09	-2	1	0	-8	-8
Clement J	28	9	41	18	40	.16	.10	74	84	-.00	.04	.40	.18	-3	-1	-3	-1	-9
Cairo M	13	9	49	20	31	.10	.00	72	87	.07	.07	.33	.01	1	2	-2	-10	-9
Vidro J	11	5	48	19	32	.13	.09	80	89	.04	.01	.34	.12	-3	-4	-1	-5	-13
Balentien W	30	6	47	14	39	.13	.13	73	82	-.04	.04	.36	.21	-7	-1	-8	0	-16
Betancourt Y	7	3	40	20	40	.12	.04	72	84	.03	.04	.33	.09	-6	-0	0	-10	-17
Johjima K	8	7	45	21	34	.18	.06	80	90	.09	.01	.32	.06	-0	-6	-1	-13	-20
MLB Average	18	10	44	20	36	.10	.11	74	84	.05	.04	.39	.18	--	--	--	--	--

Pitching Stats

Player	PRC	IP	BFP	G	GS	K	BB	IBB	HBP	H	HR	DP	DER	SB	CS	PO	W	L	Sv	Op	Hld	H-A	R^L	RA	ERA	FIP
Hernandez F	95	200.7	857	31	31	175	80	7	8	198	17	32	.678	19	4	1	9	11	0	0	0	.006	-.050	3.81	3.45	3.80
Rowland-Smit	54	118.3	506	47	12	77	48	0	2	114	13	12	.721	4	2	0	5	3	2	3	1	.016	.074	3.73	3.42	4.62
Washburn J *	50	153.7	675	28	26	87	50	2	7	174	19	18	.686	5	4	2	5	14	1	1	0	.043	-.057	5.10	4.69	4.78
Bedard E *	35	81.0	347	15	15	72	37	0	4	70	9	10	.716	5	1	0	6	4	0	0	0	-.035	.049	4.22	3.67	4.42
Dickey R	35	112.3	500	32	14	58	51	4	2	124	15	8	.703	6	7	5	5	8	0	0	0	.002	.005	5.21	5.21	5.24
Silva C	34	153.3	689	28	28	69	32	2	4	213	20	19	.649	8	2	0	4	15	0	0	0	-.021	-.044	6.69	6.46	4.69
Morrow B	34	64.7	265	45	5	75	34	1	0	40	10	4	.788	3	1	0	3	4	10	12	3	-.107	-.072	3.62	3.34	4.45
Corcoran R	31	72.7	316	50	0	39	36	4	2	65	1	12	.714	1	0	0	6	2	3	6	8	.045	-.033	3.84	3.22	3.74
Batista M	26	115.0	556	44	20	73	79	6	6	135	19	10	.678	19	2	0	4	14	1	4	4	.004	-.036	6.97	6.26	6.17
Green S	26	79.0	358	72	0	62	36	1	6	80	3	7	.665	3	1	0	4	5	1	4	17	-.061	-.085	5.35	4.67	3.71
Putz J	23	46.3	211	47	0	56	28	2	2	46	4	4	.645	1	2	1	6	5	15	23	0	-.062	-.029	3.88	3.88	3.75
Lowe M	18	63.7	303	57	0	55	34	0	4	78	6	9	.632	5	0	0	1	5	1	5	1	-.086	-.099	6.22	5.37	4.52
Jimenez C *	17	34.3	141	31	2	26	13	0	1	32	2	3	.697	1	3	2	0	2	0	4	4	-.038	.079	3.41	3.41	3.70
Rhodes A *	13	22.0	92	36	0	26	13	2	0	17	0	3	.679	1	0	0	2	1	1	2	13	.078	-.016	3.27	2.86	2.37
Baek C	9	30.0	127	10	1	15	13	1	0	28	6	3	.763	2	1	0	0	1	0	0	0	-.131	.081	5.40	5.40	6.03
Feierabend R	8	39.7	183	8	8	26	14	0	1	59	7	2	.607	1	4	6	1	4	0	0	0	-.100	-.031	7.71	7.71	5.35
Messenger R	6	12.7	57	13	0	7	5	1	1	16	1	1	.651	4	2	0	0	0	1	1	2	-.031	.102	3.55	3.55	4.34
Woods J *	5	19.0	87	15	0	9	11	2	1	22	5	3	.705	0	0	0	0	0	0	1	1	-.053	-.045	6.16	6.16	7.28
Thomas J *	1	4.0	22	8	0	2	2	0	0	9	0	0	.500	0	0	0	0	1	0	1	1	.246	.249	6.75	6.75	3.73
Wells J	1	5.3	30	6	0	3	6	0	0	7	2	0	.737	1	0	0	0	0	0	0	0	.022	.002	10.13	10.13	10.36

Italicized stats have been adjusted for home park.

Batted Ball Pitching Stats

Player	% of PA		% of Batted Balls					Out %		Runs Per Event				Total Runs vs. Avg.				
	K%	BB%	GB%	LD%	FB%	IF/F	HR/OF	GB	OF	NIP	GB	LD	OF	NIP	GB	LD	FB	Tot
Morrow B	28	13	33	16	51	.09	.14	75	89	.03	.04	.21	.18	-1	-2	-11	1	-12
Corcoran R	12	12	69	10	20	.02	.02	73	83	.11	.05	.36	.09	4	4	-9	-8	-8
Hernandez F	20	10	52	18	29	.08	.11	74	84	.04	.04	.42	.18	-1	-1	-2	-4	-8
Bedard E	21	12	40	17	43	.08	.10	78	82	.05	.01	.38	.17	1	-4	-5	1	-6
Rowland-Smith R	15	10	39	19	42	.15	.08	77	88	.07	.03	.42	.11	2	-1	1	-6	-5
Jimenez C	18	10	39	18	43	.19	.06	79	84	.05	.02	.54	.08	-0	-2	2	-4	-4
Green S	17	12	63	17	19	.08	.07	74	69	.07	.05	.36	.23	3	2	-3	-3	-1
Putz J	27	14	40	20	40	.10	.09	65	78	.05	.11	.32	.20	1	2	-3	1	1
Baek C	12	10	41	11	48	.13	.12	73	89	.10	.07	.50	.17	1	1	-2	1	2
Dickey R	12	11	46	17	36	.09	.11	76	86	.11	.04	.43	.17	5	1	1	3	9
Lowe M	18	13	45	21	35	.10	.09	59	81	.07	.14	.35	.18	3	8	-1	0	10
Washburn J	13	8	36	23	41	.13	.10	72	86	.07	.06	.39	.15	1	2	9	0	13
Feierabend R	14	8	38	22	40	.13	.14	70	74	.05	.09	.45	.29	0	3	5	8	15
Silva C	10	5	44	23	33	.08	.11	71	81	.04	.06	.37	.22	-4	6	12	11	26
Batista M	13	15	46	20	34	.09	.13	70	86	.13	.09	.41	.21	14	9	5	5	33
MLB Average	18	10	44	20	36	.10	.11	74	84	.05	.04	.39	.18	--	--	--	--	--

Fielding Stats

Name	Inn	SBA/G	CS%	ERA	WP+PB/G	PO	A	TE	FE	Grade
Catchers										
Johjima K	833.3	0.77	27%	4.57	0.335	632	34	7	0	B
Clement J	292.0	0.55	0%	5.05	0.709	195	7	0	1	--
Burke J	246.0	0.62	29%	4.79	0.585	181	10	0	0	--
Johnson R	64.0	1.55	9%	5.06	0.563	44	7	0	0	--

Name	Inn	PO	A	TE	FE	FPct	DPS	DPT	ZR	OOZ	Grade
First Base											
Sexson R	604.0	568	48	0	2	.997	4	0	.702	21	--
Cairo M	394.0	414	23	0	1	.998	3	0	.770	9	--
Lahair B	273.0	277	18	0	2	.993	4	1	.811	6	--
Lopez J	100.0	100	11	0	1	.991	0	0	.850	6	--
Vidro J	55.3	54	5	1	0	.983	0	0	.750	4	--
Norton G	6.0	7	1	0	1	.889	0	0	.500	1	--
Burke J	2.0	4	0	0	0	1.000	0	0	--	--	--
Reed J	1.0	2	0	1	0	.667	0	0	--	--	--
Second Base											
Lopez J	1229.0	259	468	3	8	.985	52	46	.821	51	A
Valbuena L	125.0	21	41	0	0	1.000	2	8	.721	0	--
Bloomquist	37.0	8	15	0	0	1.000	4	3	.800	0	--
Cairo M	26.0	7	10	0	0	1.000	0	2	1.000	0	--
Hulett T	18.0	4	9	0	0	1.000	0	2	1.000	0	--
Shortstop											
Betancourt Y	1325.0	237	401	9	12	.968	43	55	.799	33	F
Bloomquist	93.0	17	23	0	0	1.000	0	1	.737	5	--
Hulett T	13.0	2	1	0	0	1.000	0	0	.500	0	--
Cairo M	2.0	0	1	0	0	1.000	0	0	0.000	1	--
Valbuena L	2.0	1	1	0	0	1.000	1	0	1.000	0	--
Third Base											
Beltre A	1208.0	100	272	5	10	.961	29	0	.700	78	A+
Cairo M	112.0	13	21	1	0	.971	5	0	.704	2	--
Tuiasosopo	105.0	11	23	1	1	.944	4	0	.654	6	--
Bloomquist	7.0	0	0	0	0	.000	0	0	--	--	--
Burke J	2.0	0	1	0	0	1.000	0	0	1.000	0	--
Hulett T	1.0	0	0	0	0	.000	0	0	--	--	--

Name	Inn	PO	A	TE	FE	FPct	DPS	DPT	ZR	OOZ	Grade
Left Field											
Ibanez R	1340.0	302	9	2	3	.984	2	0	.893	43	F
Balentien W	43.0	13	1	0	0	1.000	0	0	.813	0	--
Reed J	29.7	5	1	0	0	1.000	0	0	.833	0	--
Bloomquist	17.7	3	0	0	0	1.000	0	0	1.000	1	--
Cairo M	4.0	0	0	0	0	.000	0	0	0.000	0	--
Jimerson C	1.0	0	0	0	0	.000	0	0	--	--	--
Center Field											
Suzuki I	601.7	195	4	0	1	.995	2	0	.902	38	F-
Reed J	453.7	132	1	0	1	.993	0	0	.950	36	--
Balentien W	218.7	60	0	0	0	1.000	0	0	.878	17	--
Bloomquist	161.3	48	1	1	2	.942	0	0	.875	13	--
Right Field											
Suzuki I	788.3	175	7	2	2	.978	2	0	.900	50	--
Balentien W	293.0	76	5	0	2	.976	0	0	.817	18	--
Wilkerson B	148.7	18	1	0	0	1.000	0	0	.867	5	--
Reed J	101.0	19	0	0	2	.905	0	0	.895	2	--
Bloomquist	74.3	14	0	0	0	1.000	0	0	1.000	2	--
Morse M	25.0	6	2	0	0	1.000	0	0	.833	1	--
Norton G	3.0	0	0	0	0	.000	0	0	--	--	--
Cairo M	2.0	0	0	0	0	.000	0	0	--	--	--

St. Louis Cardinals

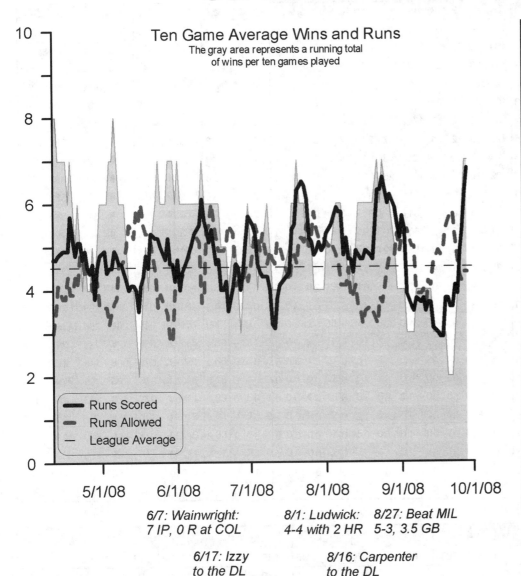

Ten Game Average Wins and Runs
The gray area represents a running total
of wins per ten games played

- Runs Scored
- Runs Allowed
- League Average

6/7: Wainwright:
7 IP, 0 R at COL

8/1: Ludwick:
4-4 with 2 HR

8/27: Beat MIL
5-3, 3.5 GB

6/17: Izzy
to the DL

8/16: Carpenter
to the DL

Stat Facts:

- Skip Schumaker's L^R of .141 was highest among ML regulars
- Albert Pujols led the majors with 133 Base Runs, a .379 GPA, and 34 IBB
- Pujols struck out just 8% of the time, far and away the lowest rate among power hitters
- Pujols hit more ground balls than fly balls
- Pujols made 52 OOZ plays
- Cesar Izturis made 58 OOZ plays
- Ryan Ludwick's GB% was lowest among ML regulars
- 21% of Ludwick's outfield flies were home runs
- Opponents attempted just 1 steal against Braden Looper
- No Cardinals pitcher allowed as many as 10 steals
- Yadier Molina put the ball in play 87% of the time
- Aaron Miles put the ball in play 85% of the time

Team Batting and Pitching/Fielding Stats by Month

	April	May	June	July	Aug	Sept/Oct
Wins	18	15	15	13	13	12
Losses	11	13	12	14	13	13
RS/G	4.7	4.4	5.0	5.0	4.9	4.8
RA/G	3.6	4.8	4.5	5.3	4.2	4.6
OBP	.374	.342	.337	.340	.357	.348
SLG	.415	.407	.447	.434	.451	.450
FIP	3.86	4.44	4.64	5.19	4.42	4.01
DER	.720	.693	.693	.670	.714	.698

Batting Stats

Player	BR	Runs	RBI	PA	Outs	H	2B	3B	HR	TB	K	BB	IBB	HBP	SH	SF	SB	CS	GDP	H-A	L^R	BA	OBP	SLG	GPA
Pujols A	133	100	116	641	356	187	44	0	37	342	54	104	34	5	0	8	7	3	16	.037	.059	.357	.462	.653	.379
Ludwick R	110	104	113	617	390	161	40	3	37	318	146	62	3	8	1	8	4	4	9	.026	-.021	.299	.375	.591	.323
Glaus T	96	69	99	637	412	147	33	1	27	263	104	87	3	3	0	3	0	1	14	-.039	-.041	.270	.372	.483	.295
Schumaker S	75	87	46	594	398	163	22	5	8	219	60	47	2	2	4	1	8	2	19	-.034	.141	.302	.359	.406	.269
Ankiel R *	67	65	71	463	313	109	21	2	25	209	100	42	3	5	0	3	2	1	8	-.028	.062	.264	.337	.506	.284
Molina Y	57	37	56	485	332	135	18	0	7	174	29	32	4	1	3	5	0	2	21	.024	.054	.304	.349	.392	.260
Miles A +	43	49	31	408	275	120	15	2	4	151	37	23	2	0	5	1	3	3	13	.024	.007	.317	.355	.398	.265
Kennedy A *	40	42	36	365	258	95	17	4	2	126	43	21	4	1	0	4	7	1	13	.037	.036	.280	.321	.372	.242
Izturis C +	38	50	24	454	317	109	10	3	1	128	26	29	1	6	3	2	24	6	6	.014	.051	.263	.319	.309	.226
Lopez F +	30	30	21	169	99	60	8	2	4	84	28	11	1	1	0	1	4	3	0	.004	-.018	.385	.426	.538	.333
Duncan C *	29	26	27	257	177	55	8	0	6	81	52	34	3	0	0	1	2	1	9	-.037	.100	.248	.346	.365	.252
Barton B	21	23	13	179	118	41	9	2	2	60	39	19	0	2	4	1	3	1	5	-.008	.010	.268	.354	.392	.263
Mather J	20	20	18	147	103	32	7	0	8	63	32	12	1	1	0	1	1	0	2	-.064	-.053	.241	.306	.474	.262
LaRue J	18	17	21	189	135	35	8	1	4	57	20	15	1	5	3	2	0	0	6	-.047	-.035	.213	.296	.348	.225
Ryan B	12	30	10	218	155	48	9	0	0	57	31	16	0	2	3	0	7	2	4	-.049	.019	.244	.307	.289	.215
Looper B	7	5	4	80	50	16	3	1	0	21	21	4	0	0	13	0	0	0	3	.009	.051	.254	.299	.333	.222
Wainwright A	4	5	6	65	45	16	2	0	1	21	20	2	0	0	2	1	0	1	0	.065	-.069	.267	.286	.350	.221
Johnson M *	2	1	2	18	12	5	0	0	0	5	2	1	0	0	0	0	0	0	0	-.072	-.505	.294	.333	.294	.228
Pineiro J	2	3	4	57	46	5	3	0	0	8	35	3	0	0	3	0	0	0	0	.079	.020	.098	.148	.157	.108
Phelps J	2	4	1	36	25	9	1	0	0	10	11	2	0	0	0	0	0	0	0	.099	.124	.265	.306	.294	.216
Washington R	2	2	3	22	17	3	2	0	0	5	6	3	0	0	0	0	0	0	1	.064	-.277	.158	.273	.263	.193
Wellemeyer T	1	2	5	72	49	9	0	0	0	9	29	1	0	0	12	1	0	0	0	.066	-.049	.155	.167	.155	.116
Worrell M	1	1	3	2	1	1	0	0	1	4	0	0	0	0	0	0	0	0	0	-1.450	--	.500	.500	2.000	.741
Parisi M	1	0	2	4	3	1	1	0	0	2	1	0	0	0	0	0	0	0	0	-.238	--	.250	.250	.500	.243
Thompson B	1	2	2	17	9	3	0	0	0	3	6	2	0	0	3	0	1	0	0	.040	.150	.250	.357	.250	.228
Garcia J *	1	0	0	3	1	0	0	0	0	0	1	2	0	0	0	0	0	0	0	.300	--	.000	.667	.000	.307

Italicized stats have been adjusted for home park.

Batted Ball Batting Stats

Player	% of PA		% of Batted Balls			IF/F	HR/OF	Out %		Runs Per Event				Total Runs vs. Avg.				
	K%	BB%	GB%	LD%	FB%			GB	OF	NIP	GB	LD	OF	NIP	GB	LD	FB	Tot
Pujols A	8	17	40	22	37	.12	.20	68	88	.19	.09	.45	.29	25	9	20	24	77
Ludwick R	24	11	27	26	47	.09	.21	71	82	.04	.07	.43	.32	0	-1	13	32	43
Glaus T	16	14	38	19	43	.10	.13	71	87	.10	.06	.44	.19	11	1	3	8	23
Lopez F	17	7	50	20	29	.08	.11	51	77	.02	.21	.32	.24	-1	11	0	2	13
Ankiel R	22	10	36	19	45	.11	.18	73	84	.03	.05	.41	.28	-1	-1	-1	16	13
Schumaker J	10	8	58	22	20	.04	.09	76	76	.09	.03	.34	.20	2	1	4	-3	4
Mather J	22	9	30	22	48	.14	.17	71	91	.02	.08	.37	.20	-1	0	-0	2	1
Miles A	9	6	54	21	25	.06	.05	72	76	.06	.05	.33	.15	-2	5	1	-4	1
Barton B	22	12	51	17	32	.09	.06	70	83	.05	.07	.48	.13	1	2	-1	-3	-1
Duncan C	20	13	42	23	36	.18	.10	75	89	.07	.03	.38	.12	2	-1	1	-4	-2
Molina Y	6	7	46	21	33	.12	.03	73	85	.13	.04	.37	.06	2	0	6	-12	-4
Ryan B	14	8	52	19	28	.11	.00	69	88	.06	.08	.33	-.01	-0	3	-2	-9	-8
Kennedy A	12	6	43	25	32	.05	.02	77	82	.04	.02	.34	.07	-2	-3	5	-8	-8
LaRue J	11	11	39	18	43	.11	.07	88	90	.12	-.04	.36	.09	2	-6	-2	-3	-9
Izturis C	6	8	47	22	31	.15	.01	73	90	.15	.05	.30	-.01	3	3	-0	-21	-15
MLB Average	18	10	44	20	36	.10	.11	74	84	.05	.04	.39	.18	--	--	--	--	--

Pitching Stats

Player	PRC	IP	BFP	G	GS	K	BB	IBB	HBP	H	HR	DP	DER	SB	CS	PO	W	L	Sv	Op	Hld	H-A	R^L	RA	ERA	FIP
Lohse K	80	200.0	839	33	33	119	49	3	3	211	18	19	.697	9	3	1	15	6	0	0	0	-.050	.019	3.96	3.78	3.92
Wellemeyer T	80	191.7	807	32	32	134	62	1	7	178	25	12	.729	7	6	2	13	9	0	0	0	.043	-.018	3.94	3.71	4.56
Looper B	68	199.0	842	33	33	108	45	1	11	216	25	26	.700	1	0	0	12	14	0	0	0	-.013	-.022	4.57	4.16	4.58
Wainwright A	61	132.0	544	20	20	91	34	1	3	122	12	11	.715	2	4	2	11	3	0	0	0	-.021	-.044	3.48	3.20	3.82
Pineiro J	42	148.7	645	26	25	81	35	0	2	180	22	18	.681	5	4	2	7	7	1	1	0	-.041	-.006	5.39	5.15	4.78
Franklin R	33	78.7	346	74	0	51	30	4	3	86	10	9	.698	2	1	0	6	6	17	25	13	.019	.014	3.89	3.55	4.66
Springer R	32	50.3	205	70	0	45	18	1	1	39	4	2	.730	1	2	0	2	1	0	2	15	.127	-.120	2.50	2.32	3.58
McClellan K	29	75.7	327	68	0	59	26	2	4	79	7	11	.684	2	1	0	2	7	1	6	30	-.053	.014	4.40	4.04	3.96
Perez C	19	41.7	177	41	0	42	22	0	1	34	5	7	.710	3	1	0	3	3	7	11	6	-.030	-.031	3.89	3.46	4.40
Thompson B	18	64.7	273	26	6	32	19	1	3	72	5	11	.682	1	1	1	6	3	0	1	1	-.034	.004	5.29	5.15	4.19
Villone R *	18	50.0	229	74	0	50	37	2	2	45	4	7	.691	0	0	0	1	2	1	2	16	-.009	-.080	4.86	4.68	4.46
Isringhausen	12	42.7	200	42	0	36	22	0	5	48	5	3	.667	6	2	0	1	5	12	19	2	.001	.089	5.91	5.70	4.94
Motte J	11	11.0	40	12	0	16	3	0	0	5	0	1	.762	0	0	0	0	0	1	1	4	.143	-.008	1.64	0.82	1.11
Carpenter C	7	15.3	63	4	3	7	4	0	0	16	0	3	.692	0	0	0	0	1	0	0	0	-.153	.088	2.93	1.76	3.07
Flores R *	7	25.7	131	43	0	17	20	3	1	34	2	1	.626	4	0	0	1	0	1	3	14	.025	.043	5.61	5.26	4.99
Jimenez K	6	24.0	114	15	0	11	15	0	1	28	5	3	.695	2	0	0	0	0	0	0	0	-.023	.066	5.63	5.63	6.99
Boggs M	6	34.0	164	8	6	13	22	0	2	42	5	5	.689	2	0	0	3	2	0	0	0	.031	-.088	7.68	7.41	6.47
Reyes A	5	14.7	61	10	0	10	3	0	0	16	2	1	.674	1	0	0	2	1	1	1	2	.001	.173	4.91	4.91	4.22
Garcia J *	4	16.0	69	10	1	8	8	0	1	14	4	3	.792	0	0	0	1	1	0	0	3	.103	-.010	5.63	5.63	7.14
Parisi M	3	23.0	121	12	2	13	15	2	0	37	2	0	.604	0	1	0	0	4	0	0	0	-.016	-.030	9.39	8.22	4.90
Worrell M	1	5.7	27	4	0	4	4	1	0	8	1	2	.611	0	0	0	0	1	0	0	0	.005	.091	7.94	7.94	5.67

Italicized stats have been adjusted for home park.

Batted Ball Pitching Stats

Player	% of PA		% of Batted Balls					Out %		Runs Per Event				Total Runs vs. Avg.				
	K%	BB%	GB%	LD%	FB%	IF/F	HR/OF	GB	OF	NIP	GB	LD	OF	NIP	GB	LD	FB	Tot
Wainwright A	17	7	46	19	35	.17	.10	77	90	.02	.04	.41	.13	-5	0	-0	-8	-13
Springer R	22	9	30	20	49	.16	.07	71	92	.02	.06	.37	.05	-1	-0	-2	-6	-10
Wellemeyer T	17	9	39	21	40	.13	.12	77	87	.04	.04	.37	.16	-3	-4	-1	-2	-9
Lohse K	14	6	46	22	32	.09	.09	77	82	.03	.03	.34	.18	-7	-3	1	-0	-9
McClellan K	18	9	48	21	31	.11	.09	78	81	.04	.01	.45	.16	-1	-4	4	-3	-3
Looper B	13	7	48	20	32	.08	.12	75	85	.04	.04	.38	.18	-4	-1	3	2	-1
Perez C	24	13	39	20	41	.04	.11	72	87	.05	.04	.43	.16	1	-1	-0	0	-1
Villone R	22	17	38	22	40	.09	.08	80	73	.09	-.01	.32	.23	5	-4	-2	2	1
Thompson B	12	8	51	20	29	.10	.07	76	77	.07	.03	.41	.19	0	-1	3	-0	2
Franklin R	15	10	43	19	38	.10	.12	74	86	.07	.04	.41	.19	1	-0	1	3	4
Isringhausen J	18	14	51	22	28	.14	.09	78	79	.08	.03	.53	.18	3	-1	5	-2	5
Flores R	13	16	51	19	31	.18	.09	65	76	.14	.11	.44	.20	4	3	1	-0	8
Boggs M	8	15	52	19	29	.11	.16	75	74	.18	.04	.36	.33	5	-0	0	5	10
Pineiro J	13	6	49	22	30	.04	.14	81	73	.03	.01	.40	.30	-5	-7	9	19	16
MLB Average	18	10	44	20	36	.10	.11	74	84	.05	.04	.39	.18	--	--	--	--	--

Fielding Stats

Name	Inn	SBA/G	CS%	ERA	WP+PB/G	PO	A	TE	FE	Grade
Catchers										
Molina Y	1002.0	0.44	31%	4.22	0.350	653	70	7	2	A
LaRue J	412.0	0.39	28%	4.24	0.306	289	16	2	0	--
Johnson M	40.0	0.45	0%	3.38	0.900	34	0	0	0	--

Name	Inn	PO	A	TE	FE	FPct	DPS	DPT	ZR	OOZ	Grade
First Base											
Pujols A	1215.0	1297	135	2	4	.996	11	4	.840	52	A+
Duncan C	142.0	143	13	0	0	1.000	3	0	.667	5	--
Glaus T	28.7	29	2	0	0	1.000	0	0	1.000	2	--
Kennedy A	18.0	23	3	1	0	.963	0	0	0.000	3	--
Phelps J	17.0	18	0	0	0	1.000	0	0	0.000	0	--
Mather J	13.0	9	1	0	0	1.000	0	0	1.000	1	--
Molina Y	11.0	13	3	0	0	1.000	0	0	.857	0	--
LaRue J	7.3	7	1	0	0	1.000	0	0	.667	0	--
Lopez F	1.0	2	0	0	0	1.000	0	0	--	--	--
Barden B	1.0	0	0	0	0	.000	0	0	.000	0	--
Second Base											
Kennedy A	635.7	144	224	3	4	.981	21	35	.881	31	--
Miles A	499.7	91	165	1	2	.988	24	22	.810	10	--
Lopez F	157.3	27	57	1	0	.988	8	7	.815	2	F-
Ryan B	149.0	23	39	1	0	.984	0	5	.763	4	--
Barden B	8.0	1	4	1	0	.833	0	0	.800	0	--
Pujols A	3.3	1	0	0	0	1.000	0	0	--	--	--
Washington	1.0	0	0	0	0	.000	0	0	--	--	--
Shortstop											
Izturis C	1001.0	170	370	5	6	.980	36	39	.869	58	A+
Ryan B	255.3	42	91	0	1	.993	10	9	.859	12	--
Miles A	172.3	32	56	1	0	.989	9	3	.857	10	--
Lopez F	25.0	3	7	0	0	1.000	1	0	1.000	0	--
Third Base											
Glaus T	1243.0	99	279	3	4	.982	24	3	.698	37	F
Lopez F	85.3	2	23	1	1	.926	2	0	.750	4	--
Miles A	61.0	2	16	0	0	1.000	1	0	.647	4	--
Washington	19.3	0	9	0	0	1.000	0	0	.750	0	--
Ryan B	19.3	2	6	1	0	.889	1	0	.667	2	--
Izturis C	15.7	3	3	0	0	1.000	0	0	.750	0	--
Barden B	7.0	0	2	0	0	1.000	0	0	1.000	1	--
Mather J	3.0	0	0	0	0	.000	0	0	.000	0	--

Name	Inn	PO	A	TE	FE	FPct	DPS	DPT	ZR	OOZ	Grade
Left Field											
Schumaker S	338.3	85	4	1	0	.989	0	0	.897	24	--
Duncan C	321.3	73	1	0	2	.974	0	0	.870	13	--
Barton B	209.0	43	2	0	1	.978	0	0	.919	9	--
Ludwick R	169.7	42	2	0	0	1.000	0	0	.921	7	--
Ankiel R	131.0	22	0	1	2	.880	0	0	.895	5	--
Mather J	124.7	30	1	0	0	1.000	0	0	.885	7	--
Lopez F	58.0	3	1	0	0	1.000	0	0	.750	0	--
Stavinoha N	53.0	9	0	0	0	1.000	0	0	.833	4	--
Miles A	26.0	3	0	0	0	1.000	0	0	1.000	1	--
Phelps J	21.0	1	0	0	0	1.000	0	0	.500	0	--
Kennedy A	1.0	0	0	0	0	.000	0	0	--	--	--
Ryan B	1.0	1	0	0	0	1.000	0	0	1.000	0	--
Washington	0.0	0	0	0	0	.000	0	0	--	--	--
Center Field											
Ankiel R	766.3	213	4	3	2	.977	2	0	.921	38	F-
Schumaker S	552.7	136	5	0	1	.993	4	0	.920	32	--
Mather J	67.0	19	0	1	0	.950	0	0	1.000	4	--
Ludwick R	64.0	20	0	1	0	.952	0	0	1.000	4	--
Miles A	2.0	0	0	0	0	.000	0	0	--	--	--
Barton B	2.0	0	0	0	0	.000	0	0	--	--	--
Right Field											
Ludwick R	962.3	231	10	0	2	.992	6	0	.918	42	D
Schumaker S	249.3	64	1	0	1	.985	0	1	.909	14	--
Mather J	64.7	17	0	0	0	1.000	0	0	1.000	7	--
Kennedy A	55.0	15	0	0	0	1.000	0	0	.900	6	--
Barton B	48.0	15	0	1	0	.938	0	0	.923	3	--
Stavinoha N	20.0	2	0	0	0	1.000	0	0	--	--	--
Ryan B	19.0	4	0	0	0	1.000	0	0	1.000	2	--
Duncan C	15.0	4	0	0	0	1.000	0	0	1.000	2	--
Phelps J	10.0	4	0	0	0	1.000	0	0	.800	0	--
Miles A	3.7	3	0	0	0	1.000	0	0	1.000	0	--
Washington	3.0	0	0	0	0	.000	0	0	--	--	--
Ankiel R	2.0	1	0	0	0	1.000	0	0	--	--	--
Lopez F	2.0	1	0	0	1	.500	0	0	--	--	--

Tampa Bay Rays

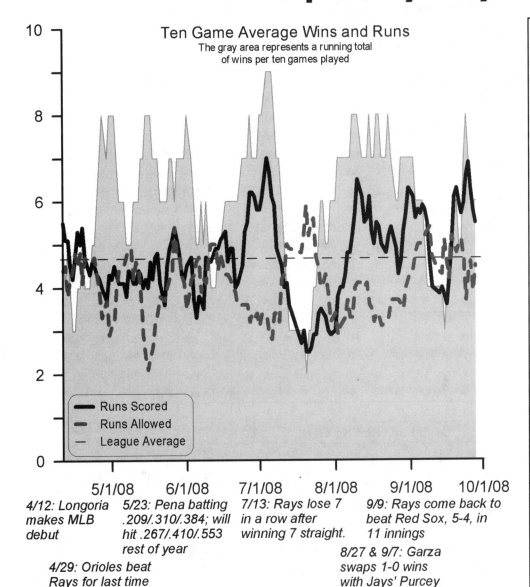

Ten Game Average Wins and Runs
The gray area represents a running total
of wins per ten games played

- Runs Scored
- Runs Allowed
- League Average

4/12: Longoria makes MLB debut

4/29: Orioles beat Rays for last time in season (Rays win next 12 games)

5/23: Pena batting .209/.310/.384; will hit .267/.410/.553 rest of year

7/13: Rays lose 7 in a row after winning 7 straight.

9/9: Rays come back to beat Red Sox, 5-4, in 11 innings

8/27 & 9/7: Garza swaps 1-0 wins with Jays' Purcey

Stat Facts:
- Jonny Gomes' ratio of fly balls to line drives was 5.6:1
- Andy Sonnanstine allowed just 1 stolen base in 4 attempts
- Grant Balfour struck out 37% of the batters he faced, by far the highest rate in the majors
- 19% of the fly balls off Matt Garza were infield pop-ups, highest rate in the majors among 162+ IP pitchers
- Akinori Iwamura grounded into just 2 DPs in 707 PAs
- Iwamura turned 71 double plays
- One-half of Carlos Pena's batted balls were fly balls, and 21% of his outfield flies were home runs
- B.J. Upton made 87 OOZ plays and had 16 assists, including 10 double plays
- Evan Longoria made 43 OOZ plays and started 25 double plays
- Carlos Pena made 44 OOZ plays and committed just 2 errors
- Troy Percival allowed just 23% ground balls and 10% line drives, and 67% fly balls

Team Batting and Pitching/Fielding Stats by Month

	April	May	June	July	Aug	Sept/Oct
Wins	15	19	16	13	21	13
Losses	12	10	10	12	7	14
RS/G	4.8	4.2	5.2	3.5	5.8	5.1
RA/G	4.0	4.0	4.1	4.1	3.8	4.9
OBP	.333	.338	.349	.311	.360	.343
SLG	.398	.402	.457	.370	.476	.424
FIP	4.10	3.94	3.84	4.34	4.17	5.00
DER	.720	.717	.706	.717	.694	.717

Batting Stats

Player	BR	Runs	RBI	PA	Outs	H	2B	3B	HR	TB	K	BB	IBB	HBP	SH	SF	SB	CS	GDP	H-A	L^R	BA	OBP	SLG	GPA
Pena C *	95	76	102	607	376	121	24	2	31	242	166	96	7	12	0	9	1	1	6	.033	.108	.247	.377	.494	.296
Upton B	89	85	67	640	415	145	37	2	9	213	134	97	4	2	3	7	44	16	13	.014	.022	.273	.383	.401	.276
Iwamura A *	82	91	48	707	463	172	30	9	6	238	131	70	3	4	3	3	8	6	2	.039	.026	.274	.349	.380	.255
Longoria E	75	67	85	508	334	122	31	2	27	238	122	46	4	6	0	8	7	0	8	-.009	-.021	.272	.343	.531	.290
Navarro D +	58	43	54	470	321	126	27	0	7	174	49	34	1	3	3	3	0	4	16	.026	-.020	.295	.349	.407	.262
Hinske E *	56	59	60	432	303	94	21	1	20	177	88	47	4	3	0	1	10	3	13	-.046	.105	.247	.333	.465	.269
Crawford C *	56	69	57	482	339	121	12	10	8	177	60	30	1	2	0	5	25	7	10	.068	.036	.273	.319	.400	.246
Bartlett J	54	48	37	494	339	130	25	3	1	164	69	22	1	9	5	4	20	6	9	.019	.104	.286	.329	.361	.241
Gross G *	42	40	38	345	237	73	13	3	13	131	75	40	0	2	0	1	2	2	6	.096	.080	.242	.333	.434	.261
Floyd C *	36	32	39	284	184	66	13	0	11	112	58	28	2	5	0	5	1	0	4	.135	.113	.268	.349	.455	.274
Zobrist B +	33	32	30	227	152	50	10	2	12	100	37	25	1	2	0	2	3	0	4	-.069	-.011	.253	.339	.505	.282
Aybar W +	32	33	33	362	251	82	17	2	10	133	44	32	3	4	1	1	2	2	7	.006	.030	.253	.327	.410	.252
Gomes J	20	23	21	177	128	28	5	1	8	59	46	15	1	7	0	1	8	1	1	.002	.027	.182	.282	.383	.225
Riggans S	18	21	24	152	109	30	7	0	6	55	30	12	0	1	2	2	0	0	4	-.029	.050	.222	.287	.407	.233
Baldelli R	11	12	13	90	60	21	5	0	4	38	25	7	0	3	0	0	0	0	1	.051	.059	.263	.344	.475	.277
Perez F +	10	18	8	72	48	15	2	0	3	26	16	8	1	1	3	0	5	0	3	-.030	.062	.250	.348	.433	.268
Ruggiano J	5	9	7	81	63	15	4	0	2	25	27	4	0	1	0	0	2	0	2	.073	-.072	.197	.247	.329	.195
DiFelice M	4	1	4	22	14	6	1	0	0	7	1	1	0	1	0	0	0	0	0	.170	.221	.300	.364	.350	.254
Haynes N *	3	3	3	47	36	10	0	0	0	10	12	3	0	0	0	0	4	1	1	.091	.007	.227	.277	.227	.183
Johnson D *	3	3	4	28	20	5	0	0	2	11	7	3	0	0	0	0	0	0	0	-.040	.138	.200	.286	.440	.241
Sonnanstine	1	2	0	9	3	2	0	0	0	2	3	2	0	0	2	0	0	0	0	-.357	.242	.400	.571	.400	.361

Italicized stats have been adjusted for home park.

Batted Ball Batting Stats

Player	% of PA		% of Batted Balls					Out %		Runs Per Event				Total Runs vs. Avg.				
	K%	BB%	GB%	LD%	FB%	IF/F	HR/OF	GB	OF	NIP	GB	LD	OF	NIP	GB	LD	FB	Tot
Pena C	27	18	32	18	50	.10	.21	74	81	.07	.04	.41	.33	11	-3	-7	27	28
Longoria E	24	10	39	20	42	.09	.21	67	86	.02	.08	.40	.31	-2	3	-2	19	19
Upton B	21	15	51	19	31	.05	.08	71	75	.08	.07	.38	.20	11	5	-4	-0	12
Zobrist B	16	12	44	13	42	.07	.16	76	85	.08	.04	.51	.25	2	-1	-1	7	7
Floyd C	20	12	51	20	29	.02	.18	78	84	.05	.03	.44	.26	1	-1	2	4	6
Gross G	22	12	40	17	43	.07	.14	65	92	.05	.11	.37	.17	1	5	-5	3	5
Hinske E	20	12	39	20	41	.08	.17	83	87	.05	-.02	.40	.26	2	-7	-1	11	4
Iwamura A	19	10	47	20	33	.09	.04	67	86	.05	.10	.42	.08	2	14	3	-15	3
Navarro D	10	8	46	23	30	.14	.06	74	86	.08	.05	.39	.09	1	2	10	-10	3
Aybar W	12	10	40	21	40	.15	.10	77	88	.09	.03	.36	.14	3	-1	0	-2	0
Riggans S	20	9	47	16	37	.10	.17	80	83	.03	.01	.39	.24	-1	-2	-2	2	-3
Gomes J	26	12	34	10	56	.13	.15	81	87	.04	.01	.44	.23	-0	-2	-6	4	-4
Crawford C	12	7	49	21	30	.07	.07	75	88	.05	.04	.40	.10	-2	-0	6	-8	-5
Bartlett J	14	6	49	21	30	.10	.01	67	83	.03	.10	.32	.06	-4	12	-2	-14	-8
MLB Average	18	10	44	20	36	.10	.11	74	84	.05	.04	.39	.18	--	--	--	--	--

Pitching Stats

Player	PRC	IP	BFP	G	GS	K	BB	IBB	HBP	H	HR	DP	DER	SB	CS	PO	W	L	Sv	Op	Hld	H-A	R^L	RA	ERA	FIP
Shields J	97	215.0	877	33	33	160	40	0	12	208	24	24	.700	7	6	1	14	8	0	0	0	-.053	-.017	3.93	3.56	3.92
Kazmir S *	81	152.3	641	27	27	166	70	2	4	123	23	8	.733	7	3	4	12	8	0	0	0	-.025	-.087	3.60	3.49	4.43
Garza M	80	184.7	772	30	30	128	59	2	6	170	19	22	.714	5	1	0	11	9	0	0	0	-.033	-.021	4.05	3.70	4.20
Jackson E	70	183.3	792	32	31	108	77	1	2	199	23	32	.692	12	6	1	14	11	0	1	0	-.025	-.010	4.47	4.42	4.96
Sonnanstine	69	193.3	819	32	32	124	37	2	5	212	21	19	.688	1	3	0	13	9	0	0	0	-.002	.017	4.89	4.38	3.98
Balfour G	62	58.3	224	51	0	82	24	1	0	28	3	2	.783	2	1	0	6	2	4	5	14	-.040	.055	1.54	1.54	2.27
Howell J *	56	89.3	370	64	0	92	39	1	4	62	6	7	.738	10	3	1	6	1	3	5	14	-.039	-.019	2.92	2.22	3.45
Wheeler D	35	66.3	264	70	0	53	22	4	0	44	10	3	.793	1	1	0	5	6	13	18	26	-.020	-.035	3.39	3.12	4.41
Hammel J	25	78.3	346	40	5	44	35	4	2	83	11	9	.705	11	1	0	4	4	2	2	1	-.040	-.023	5.17	4.60	5.20
Miller T *	19	43.3	187	68	0	44	20	1	4	39	2	7	.675	0	2	0	2	0	2	3	11	-.043	-.064	4.36	4.15	3.39
Percival T	16	45.7	194	50	0	38	27	0	1	29	9	0	.815	7	2	0	2	1	28	32	4	-.061	-.026	5.12	4.53	5.97
Bradford C	14	19.0	81	21	0	4	8	3	1	18	1	2	.746	3	1	0	1	0	0	1	5	-.047	-.130	1.42	1.42	4.44
Birkins K *	13	10.0	37	6	0	7	5	0	0	5	0	3	.800	0	0	0	0	0	0	0	0	.090	-.072	0.90	0.90	3.33
Glover G	10	34.0	160	29	0	22	18	5	1	42	3	6	.647	0	0	0	1	2	0	0	2	-.001	-.017	5.82	5.82	4.32
Price D *	9	14.0	57	5	1	12	4	0	1	9	1	1	.744	0	0	0	0	0	0	0	1	.063	-.070	2.57	1.93	3.52
Reyes A	9	22.7	96	26	0	19	10	2	1	21	2	3	.688	2	0	0	2	2	0	1	2	-.097	-.066	4.76	4.37	3.89
Dohmann S	4	14.7	66	12	0	12	7	1	0	18	2	2	.644	4	0	0	2	0	0	0	0	-.176	.081	6.14	6.14	4.59
Niemann J	4	16.0	76	5	2	14	8	0	1	18	3	1	.660	2	1	0	2	2	0	0	0	-.010	.029	6.75	5.06	5.61
Salas J	2	6.3	27	5	0	8	4	0	0	5	0	0	.667	0	0	0	0	0	0	0	0	-.084	-.134	7.11	7.11	2.60
Talbot M	1	9.7	54	3	1	5	11	0	1	16	3	2	.618	2	0	0	0	0	0	0	0	.157	-.159	11.17	11.17	9.95

Italicized stats have been adjusted for home park.

Batted Ball Pitching Stats

Player	% of PA		% of Batted Balls					Out %		Runs Per Event				Total Runs vs. Avg.				
	K%	BB%	GB%	LD%	FB%	IF/F	HR/OF	GB	OF	NIP	GB	LD	OF	NIP	GB	LD	FB	Tot
Balfour G	37	11	29	19	52	.12	.06	79	92	-.01	.03	.33	.05	-4	-3	-7	-8	-22
Howell J	25	12	54	17	30	.12	.10	78	85	.03	.02	.30	.16	-1	-3	-10	-6	-21
Garza M	17	8	42	18	40	.19	.09	72	86	.04	.05	.34	.15	-3	1	-8	-7	-17
Shields J	18	6	46	16	37	.08	.11	77	77	-.00	.03	.35	.23	-12	-4	-14	14	-16
Wheeler D	20	8	28	17	54	.11	.10	73	92	.02	.06	.29	.12	-2	-1	-7	-2	-13
Kazmir S	26	12	31	20	49	.14	.14	78	86	.03	.03	.37	.21	-2	-6	-8	7	-9
Miller T	24	13	32	25	44	.10	.04	73	82	.05	.04	.35	.11	1	-1	-0	-2	-3
Percival T	20	14	23	10	67	.10	.12	72	93	.08	.06	.40	.14	3	-1	-6	2	-2
Sonnanstine A	15	5	42	17	41	.14	.09	72	83	.00	.07	.43	.17	-11	7	-0	2	-2
Hammel J	13	11	47	21	32	.12	.14	75	84	.10	.04	.34	.22	3	-0	1	2	6
Glover G	14	12	40	19	42	.14	.07	60	79	.10	.11	.33	.19	2	3	-1	2	6
Jackson E	14	10	39	21	40	.13	.11	71	87	.08	.05	.35	.17	5	0	1	4	10
MLB Average	*18*	*10*	*44*	*20*	*36*	*.10*	*.11*	*74*	*84*	*.05*	*.04*	*.39*	*.18*	--	--	--	--	--

Fielding Stats

Name	Inn	SBA/G	CS%	ERA	WP+PB/G	PO	A	TE	FE	Grade
Catchers										
Navarro D	1011.3	0.62	36%	3.90	0.365	837	55	5	0	A+
Riggans S	343.3	0.66	4%	3.62	0.393	268	5	5	0	--
DiFelice M	54.0	1.00	33%	3.67	0.500	42	3	0	0	--
Hernandez M	33.0	0.82	0%	3.27	0.545	20	1	1	0	--
Jaso J	16.0	0.00	0%	4.50	0.563	11	1	0	0	--

Name	Inn	PO	A	TE	FE	FPct	DPS	DPT	ZR	OOZ	Grade
First Base											
Pena C	1168.0	991	106	1	1	.998	8	2	.729	44	A
Aybar W	155.0	144	11	0	0	1.000	1	0	.947	8	--
Hinske E	87.0	78	8	0	1	.989	3	0	.500	4	--
Johnson D	47.0	39	5	0	0	1.000	1	0	1.000	2	--
Second Base											
Iwamura A	1337.0	284	397	2	5	.990	33	71	.787	44	B
Aybar W	70.7	17	19	0	0	1.000	0	4	.867	2	--
Zobrist B	41.0	11	11	0	0	1.000	1	2	.889	1	--
Johnson E	9.0	3	5	0	0	1.000	0	1	.667	1	--
Shortstop											
Bartlett J	1097.0	204	309	11	5	.970	38	30	.807	44	B
Zobrist B	293.3	51	78	3	4	.949	10	11	.829	5	--
Brignac R	21.3	4	7	1	1	.846	0	3	.667	0	--
Aybar W	18.0	2	6	0	0	1.000	1	0	.714	1	--
Johnson E	18.0	4	6	0	1	.909	2	1	.833	0	--
Longoria E	9.0	0	1	0	0	1.000	0	0	1.000	0	--
Cannizaro A	1.0	1	0	0	0	1.000	0	0	--	--	--
Third Base											
Longoria E	1045.0	86	230	6	6	.963	25	0	.731	43	A+
Aybar W	358.3	29	84	1	3	.958	12	0	.700	15	--
Hinske E	49.0	1	6	0	0	1.000	0	0	1.000	0	--
Zobrist B	4.7	0	2	0	0	1.000	0	0	1.000	0	--

Name	Inn	PO	A	TE	FE	FPct	DPS	DPT	ZR	OOZ	Grade
Left Field											
Crawford C	920.7	231	2	1	3	.983	0	0	.911	47	A
Hinske E	265.0	45	2	0	1	.979	0	0	.864	7	--
Ruggiano J	94.0	23	0	0	0	1.000	0	0	.938	8	--
Zobrist B	79.3	21	1	0	0	1.000	0	0	.938	6	--
Gomes J	40.0	13	0	0	0	1.000	0	0	.923	1	--
Perez F	32.7	5	0	0	0	1.000	0	0	.750	2	--
Haynes N	12.0	2	0	0	0	1.000	0	0	1.000	0	--
Baldelli R	7.0	1	0	0	0	1.000	0	0	1.000	0	--
Johnson D	6.0	3	0	0	0	1.000	0	0	1.000	1	--
Riggans S	1.0	0	0	0	0	.000	0	0	--	--	--
Center Field											
Upton B	1248.0	378	16	1	6	.983	10	0	.921	87	C
Perez F	112.0	47	1	0	0	1.000	2	0	.971	14	--
Gross G	30.0	6	1	0	0	1.000	0	0	1.000	1	--
Zobrist B	27.0	8	0	0	0	1.000	0	0	.833	3	--
Ruggiano J	17.0	5	2	0	0	1.000	2	0	.667	1	--
Haynes N	13.0	4	0	0	0	1.000	0	0	.800	0	--
Crawford C	7.0	2	0	0	0	1.000	0	0	1.000	0	--
Johnson E	3.0	1	0	0	0	1.000	0	0	1.000	0	--
Right Field											
Gross G	761.7	183	6	0	1	.995	0	0	.943	33	B
Hinske E	339.3	88	2	0	1	.989	0	0	.916	12	--
Gomes J	125.0	25	0	0	1	.962	0	0	.808	4	--
Ruggiano J	87.0	21	0	0	1	.955	0	0	.947	3	--
Haynes N	83.0	19	0	0	1	.950	0	0	1.000	4	--
Baldelli R	29.7	5	0	1	0	.833	0	0	1.000	2	--
Perez F	17.0	1	0	0	0	1.000	0	0	1.000	0	--
Johnson E	8.0	3	0	0	0	1.000	0	0	1.000	0	--
Zobrist B	7.0	0	0	0	0	.000	0	0	--	--	--

Texas Rangers

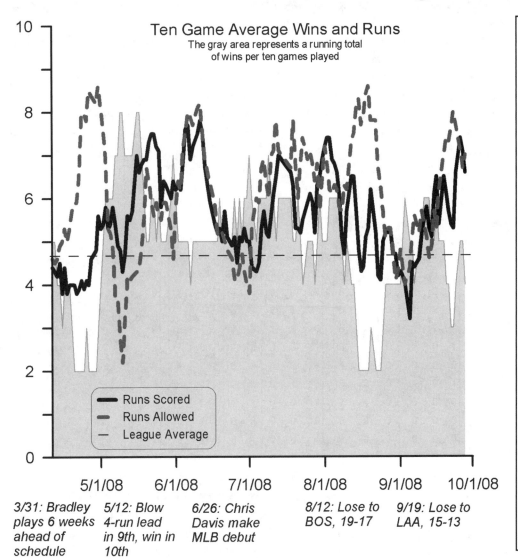

Ten Game Average Wins and Runs
The gray area represents a running total
of wins per ten games played

— Runs Scored
-- Runs Allowed
— League Average

3/31: Bradley plays 6 weeks ahead of schedule

5/12: Blow 4-run lead in 9th, win in 10th

6/26: Chris Davis make MLB debut

8/12: Lose to BOS, 19-17

9/19: Lose to LAA, 15-13

Stat Facts:

- Milton Bradley led the AL in GPA
- The Rangers' .636 DER behind Kevin Millwood was the lowest in the majors among 162+ IP pitchers
- Millwood's FIP (4.06) was more than a run lower than his ERA (5.07)
- The Rangers' DER behind Luis Mendoza was just .609
- Jamey Wright induced zero infield pop-ups
- Frank Francisco struck out 31% of the batters he faced
- Ian Kinsler turned 71 double plays
- Kinsler stole 26 bases in 28 attempts
- Kinsler had a very low strike-out rate (11%) and a high fly ball rate (43%)
- Taylor Teagarden put the ball in play 28 times, and had 4 singles, 5 doubles, and 6 home runs
- Just 2% of Josh Hamilton's fly balls were infield pop-ups
- Josh Rupe induced 22 double plays in 89 innings

Team Batting and Pitching/Fielding Stats by Month

	April	May	June	July	Aug	Sept/Oct
Wins	10	19	14	13	11	12
Losses	18	10	13	12	18	12
RS/G	4.6	5.9	5.9	6.1	5.0	6.0
RA/G	6.3	4.5	5.9	7.0	6.1	6.1
OBP	.350	.350	.346	.362	.342	.376
SLG	.430	.468	.471	.471	.444	.495
FIP	5.19	4.04	5.04	5.78	4.71	4.17
DER	.664	.701	.676	.663	.668	.661

Batting Stats

Player	BR	Runs	RBI	PA	Outs	H	2B	3B	HR	TB	K	BB	IBB	HBP	SH	SF	SB	CS	GDP	H-A	L^R	BA	OBP	SLG	GPA
Hamilton J *	116	98	130	704	443	190	35	5	32	331	126	64	9	7	0	9	9	1	8	.075	.046	.304	.371	.530	.291
Kinsler I	105	102	71	583	367	165	41	4	18	268	67	45	1	6	7	7	26	2	12	.011	-.029	.319	.375	.517	.289
Bradley M +	88	78	77	510	294	133	32	1	22	233	112	80	13	9	0	6	5	3	10	.079	.059	.321	.436	.563	.327
Young M	83	102	82	708	481	183	36	2	12	259	109	55	0	2	0	6	10	0	19	.040	.042	.284	.339	.402	.246
Murphy D *	62	64	74	454	310	114	28	3	15	193	70	31	3	0	2	6	7	2	7	.023	.050	.275	.321	.465	.253
Byrd M	62	70	53	462	295	120	28	4	10	186	62	46	3	9	2	2	7	2	10	.042	-.007	.298	.380	.462	.278
Davis C *	45	51	55	317	218	84	23	2	17	162	88	20	1	1	0	1	1	2	5	-.002	-.010	.285	.331	.549	.278
Laird G	45	54	41	381	258	95	24	0	6	137	63	23	2	6	4	4	2	4	5	-.018	-.007	.276	.329	.398	.240
Vazquez R *	44	44	40	347	218	87	18	3	6	129	66	38	3	0	5	4	0	1	4	.032	.123	.290	.365	.430	.264
Boggs B +	38	30	41	334	224	64	17	4	8	113	93	44	1	3	1	3	3	2	3	.035	.032	.226	.333	.399	.243
Blalock H *	37	37	38	281	194	74	19	1	12	131	40	19	3	2	0	2	1	0	10	.103	-.021	.287	.338	.508	.271
Catalanotto	30	28	21	278	187	68	23	1	2	99	29	20	0	6	3	1	1	1	6	-.038	.066	.274	.342	.399	.246
Cruz N	29	19	26	133	79	38	9	1	7	70	28	17	2	1	0	0	3	1	1	.020	.114	.330	.421	.609	.332
Saltalamacch	29	27	26	230	151	50	13	0	3	72	74	31	1	0	0	1	0	2	1	.028	-.150	.253	.352	.364	.242
Teagarden T	16	10	17	53	32	15	5	0	6	38	19	5	0	1	0	0	0	0	0	.106	-.135	.319	.396	.809	.369
Arias J	14	15	9	120	83	32	7	3	0	45	12	7	0	2	1	0	4	1	4	.005	.135	.291	.345	.409	.250
Duran G	12	22	16	158	115	33	6	1	3	50	32	7	0	2	5	1	1	1	4	-.022	.073	.231	.275	.350	.205
Shelton C	12	14	11	117	79	21	5	0	2	32	33	17	0	0	3	0	1	0	3	-.004	-.096	.216	.333	.330	.226
Metcalf T	8	11	14	61	45	13	2	0	6	33	12	3	0	1	0	1	0	0	2	-.062	-.180	.232	.279	.589	.265
Ramirez M	8	8	9	55	36	10	1	0	2	17	15	6	0	3	0	0	0	0	0	.234	-.128	.217	.345	.370	.241
Botts J +	6	2	5	46	32	6	3	0	2	15	18	8	0	0	0	0	0	0	0	.060	.016	.158	.304	.395	.229
Broussard B	2	8	8	89	71	13	0	0	3	22	20	5	1	2	0	0	0	0	2	.002	.041	.159	.225	.268	.163
Ellison J	1	5	2	14	10	3	0	0	0	3	1	1	0	0	0	0	0	0	0	-.218	.168	.231	.286	.231	.181
Millwood K	1	1	0	6	3	1	1	0	0	2	2	1	0	0	1	0	0	0	0	-.305	.325	.250	.400	.500	.296

Italicized stats have been adjusted for home park.

Batted Ball Batting Stats

Player	% of PA		% of Batted Balls					Out %		Runs Per Event				Total Runs vs. Avg.				
	K%	BB%	GB%	LD%	FB%	IF/F	HR/OF	GB	OF	NIP	GB	LD	OF	NIP	GB	LD	FB	Tot
Bradley M	22	17	41	25	34	.10	.22	65	79	.09	.10	.43	.37	12	7	9	17	46
Hamilton J	18	10	46	21	33	.02	.20	72	83	.05	.07	.37	.31	1	6	4	25	37
Kinsler I	11	9	32	24	43	.08	.09	72	80	.09	.06	.39	.18	3	1	12	11	26
Byrd M	13	12	46	21	33	.04	.09	72	79	.10	.06	.39	.19	6	3	5	4	19
Davis C	28	7	35	25	40	.06	.22	75	82	-.02	.05	.46	.34	-7	-1	7	14	13
Cruz N	21	14	40	22	38	.09	.23	69	83	.07	.08	.51	.38	1	1	3	7	12
Blalock H	14	7	36	21	43	.06	.11	77	86	.04	.01	.45	.18	-1	-3	6	5	6
Vazquez R	19	11	46	27	26	.07	.11	72	80	.05	.06	.34	.21	1	3	3	-1	6
Murphy D	15	7	42	18	40	.11	.12	72	84	.03	.06	.37	.21	-3	2	-3	7	3
Young M	15	8	47	23	31	.04	.07	72	84	.04	.05	.35	.14	-2	3	4	-4	1
Arias J	10	8	48	20	32	.10	.00	68	82	.08	.08	.39	.05	0	2	1	-3	1
Saltalamacchia J	32	14	31	27	42	.10	.06	72	80	.02	.07	.43	.16	-1	-0	2	-1	0
Catalanotto F	10	9	53	18	30	.08	.03	75	84	.10	.04	.50	.07	2	0	4	-7	-0
Laird G	17	8	38	22	41	.08	.06	73	85	.03	.05	.41	.10	-2	2	3	-5	-2
Boggs B	28	14	39	24	37	.06	.12	83	84	.04	-.01	.47	.19	1	-6	3	-0	-2
Shelton C	28	15	27	29	44	.11	.08	82	86	.04	-.02	.39	.11	1	-3	0	-2	-4
Duran G	20	6	39	18	43	.19	.08	79	86	-.01	.01	.45	.11	-3	-3	-1	-3	-10
MLB Average	18	10	44	20	36	.10	.11	74	84	.05	.04	.39	.18	--	--	--	--	--

Pitching Stats

Player	PRC	IP	BFP	G	GS	K	BB	IBB	HBP	H	HR	DP	DER	SB	CS	PO	W	L	Sv	Op	Hld	H-A	R^L	RA	ERA	FIP
Padilla V	61	171.0	757	29	29	127	65	4	15	185	26	22	.679	9	4	2	14	8	0	0	0	-.005	-.097	5.26	4.74	5.05
Millwood K	57	168.7	767	29	29	125	49	3	6	220	18	15	.636	26	4	0	9	10	0	0	0	-.024	.024	5.55	5.07	4.06
Feldman S	41	151.3	651	28	25	74	56	2	10	161	22	28	.706	22	5	0	6	8	0	0	0	-.009	-.021	6.13	5.29	5.41
Francisco F	38	63.3	264	58	0	83	26	2	0	47	7	1	.716	7	1	0	3	5	5	11	12	.023	.002	3.41	3.13	3.18
Rupe J	30	89.3	392	46	0	53	46	3	10	93	8	22	.691	0	1	0	3	1	0	2	2	-.001	-.021	5.24	5.14	4.99
Wright J	25	84.3	379	75	0	60	35	3	8	93	5	14	.657	9	1	2	8	7	0	6	17	.023	-.032	6.08	5.12	4.00
Guardado E*	23	49.3	194	56	0	28	17	2	0	38	3	11	.753	3	0	0	3	3	4	4	23	-.006	-.067	3.65	3.65	3.80
Harrison M *	23	83.7	372	15	15	42	31	2	2	100	12	12	.684	3	3	0	9	3	0	0	0	.003	.042	6.13	5.49	5.20
Nippert D	20	71.7	341	20	6	55	37	3	1	92	10	6	.639	5	2	0	3	5	0	0	0	-.042	.066	6.53	6.40	4.97
Gabbard K *	17	56.0	263	12	12	33	39	4	1	64	5	12	.676	2	0	0	2	3	0	0	0	.025	-.049	5.79	4.82	5.14
German F	17	21.7	93	17	0	15	13	1	0	18	0	1	.723	2	2	0	1	3	0	1	0	.091	-.097	2.08	2.08	3.51
Ponson S	16	55.7	252	9	9	25	16	0	2	71	3	7	.650	1	2	1	4	1	0	0	0	.023	-.039	5.82	3.88	4.00
Benoit J	16	45.0	209	44	0	43	35	2	0	40	6	4	.704	1	1	1	3	2	1	4	13	.005	.095	5.60	5.00	5.25
Wilson C *	13	46.3	214	50	0	41	27	2	2	49	8	6	.669	1	1	0	2	2	24	28	1	.087	.012	6.80	6.02	5.45
Madrigal W	12	36.0	154	31	1	22	14	0	0	36	4	4	.711	4	2	0	0	2	1	3	3	-.038	-.080	5.50	4.75	4.62
Loe K	11	30.7	134	14	0	20	8	1	0	36	3	3	.660	0	0	1	1	0	0	1	2	-.042	-.196	5.28	3.23	3.88
Mendoza L	8	63.3	316	25	11	35	25	4	6	97	7	5	.609	7	2	1	3	8	1	2	0	.020	.028	10.52	8.67	4.84
McCarthy B	8	22.0	93	5	5	10	8	0	1	20	3	2	.761	6	1	0	1	1	0	0	0	-.023	-.141	4.50	4.09	5.32
Hurley E	8	24.7	107	5	5	13	9	0	1	26	5	1	.734	0	2	0	1	2	0	0	0	-.052	-.010	5.47	5.47	6.03
Littleton W	6	18.0	80	12	0	14	8	0	3	18	1	4	.685	0	0	0	0	0	0	0	1	-.074	.014	6.00	6.00	4.23
Jennings J	4	27.3	135	6	6	12	18	2	1	35	8	2	.708	0	1	0	0	5	0	0	0	.098	-.046	8.89	8.56	8.02
Mathis D	4	22.3	112	8	4	9	14	2	0	37	3	7	.605	1	1	0	2	1	0	0	0	-.033	.014	8.06	6.85	5.78
Murray A *	3	7.7	38	2	2	5	3	0	0	12	0	1	.567	0	0	0	1	0	0	0	0	.136	.165	4.70	3.52	3.10
Gordon B	2	4.0	16	3	0	1	0	0	0	4	0	0	.733	0	0	0	0	0	0	0	0	.235	.322	2.25	2.25	2.73
Tejeda R	1	6.0	29	4	0	4	5	0	0	5	1	0	.737	2	0	0	0	0	0	1	0	.361	-.105	9.00	9.00	6.56
Hunter T	1	11.0	63	3	3	9	3	0	1	23	4	0	.565	1	1	0	0	2	0	0	0	-.211	-.048	16.36	16.36	7.41

Italicized stats have been adjusted for home park.

Batted Ball Pitching Stats

Player	% of PA		% of Batted Balls					Out %		Runs Per Event				Total Runs vs. Avg.				
	K%	BB%	GB%	LD%	FB%	IF/F	HR/OF	GB	OF	NIP	GB	LD	OF	NIP	GB	LD	FB	Tot
Francisco F	31	10	33	19	48	.15	.11	72	86	-.00	.08	.37	.18	-4	-0	-5	-1	-10
Guardado E	14	9	26	19	55	.10	.04	76	88	.06	.02	.34	.06	-0	-2	-2	-4	-8
Madrigal W	14	9	33	20	47	.09	.06	82	83	.07	-.00	.46	.12	0	-2	2	-0	-0
Wright J	16	11	62	20	19	.00	.08	73	74	.08	.05	.33	.21	3	4	-2	-3	1
Loe K	15	6	50	16	33	.17	.10	68	77	.02	.09	.35	.24	-1	3	-1	1	2
Hurley E	12	9	22	22	57	.09	.12	78	95	.09	.04	.46	.12	1	-0	2	1	3
Benoit J	21	17	27	17	56	.13	.10	76	84	.09	.03	.48	.16	5	-1	-0	1	4
Ponson S	10	7	57	18	25	.04	.06	70	72	.08	.07	.34	.21	0	4	-1	1	5
Gabbard K	13	15	65	13	22	.07	.11	73	79	.14	.04	.49	.20	7	2	-1	-2	6
Rupe J	13	15	49	18	33	.05	.08	70	86	.13	.04	.40	.13	9	1	0	-3	7
Wilson C	19	14	49	16	35	.04	.17	69	90	.08	.07	.52	.24	3	2	1	3	8
Jennings J	9	14	46	17	37	.13	.24	79	72	.17	.02	.32	.43	4	-1	-1	9	11
Feldman S	11	10	43	19	37	.07	.12	79	81	.10	.00	.37	.22	6	-8	1	13	13
Harrison M	11	9	40	23	36	.08	.12	76	79	.09	.03	.34	.25	2	-1	3	10	14
Padilla V	17	11	43	19	38	.11	.14	71	86	.06	.06	.39	.21	4	3	-0	9	16
Nippert D	16	11	37	24	39	.13	.12	62	85	.07	.12	.37	.19	3	7	4	3	17
Millwood K	16	7	41	25	34	.10	.10	70	85	.03	.08	.39	.17	-5	10	15	-0	20
Mendoza L	11	10	50	21	29	.08	.11	66	74	.10	.10	.39	.26	3	9	5	6	23
MLB Average	18	10	44	20	36	.10	.11	74	84	.05	.04	.39	.18	--	--	--	--	--

Fielding Stats

Name	Inn	SBA/G	CS%	ERA	WP+PB/G	PO	A	TE	FE	Grade
Catchers										
Laird G	753.0	0.87	27%	5.21	0.430	523	35	6	2	B
Saltalamacchia J	464.3	0.91	15%	5.14	0.562	345	17	9	0	--
Teagarden T	100.7	0.80	22%	4.92	0.179	67	6	2	0	--
Ramirez M	82.0	1.65	20%	7.90	0.878	56	5	1	0	--
Melhuse A	42.0	0.86	50%	6.86	0.000	18	2	0	0	--

Name	Inn	PO	A	TE	FE	FPct	DPS	DPT	ZR	OOZ	Grade
First Base											
Davis C	404.0	358	34	0	1	.997	2	1	.672	15	--
Blalock H	296.0	262	13	0	1	.996	5	0	.593	13	--
Shelton C	247.3	241	20	0	3	.989	0	1	.690	12	--
Catalanotto F	224.7	215	15	0	0	1.000	5	0	.724	5	--
Broussard B	204.0	202	22	2	0	.987	1	0	.786	10	--
Botts J	41.0	51	2	0	2	.964	0	0	.800	2	--
Ramirez M	23.0	20	4	0	0	1.000	0	0	.500	2	--
Vazquez R	2.0	2	0	0	0	1.000	0	0	--	--	--
Second Base											
Kinsler I	1064.0	292	390	6	12	.974	52	71	.801	20	F
Arias J	225.0	48	67	0	2	.983	5	12	.806	3	--
Duran G	94.0	24	22	0	0	1.000	1	1	.905	1	--
Vazquez R	59.0	20	15	0	0	1.000	0	5	.800	2	--
Shortstop											
Young M	1289.0	193	465	6	5	.984	60	50	.850	41	B
Vazquez R	138.0	23	52	1	2	.962	4	10	.837	4	--
Duran G	13.0	2	6	0	0	1.000	0	1	1.000	0	--
Metcalf T	2.0	0	0	0	0	.000	0	0	--	--	--
Third Base											
Vazquez R	533.0	30	117	3	7	.936	14	1	.645	21	--
Davis C	276.0	31	44	3	0	.962	6	0	.597	4	--
Blalock H	263.0	24	54	2	2	.951	6	0	.646	11	--
Duran G	223.0	13	45	4	1	.921	2	0	.673	8	--
Metcalf T	130.0	15	18	0	1	.971	7	0	.593	1	--
Laird G	10.0	0	3	0	0	1.000	0	0	.750	0	--
Melhuse A	6.0	1	2	0	0	1.000	0	0	.500	0	--
Shelton C	1.0	0	0	0	0	.000	0	0	--	--	--

Name	Inn	PO	A	TE	FE	FPct	DPS	DPT	ZR	OOZ	Grade
Left Field											
Boggs B	579.0	131	7	1	2	.979	4	0	.875	33	--
Murphy D	404.7	86	3	0	1	.989	0	0	.909	16	--
Byrd M	236.0	61	0	0	0	1.000	0	0	.851	21	--
Catalanotto F	168.3	29	0	0	1	.967	0	0	.694	4	--
Duran G	21.0	7	0	0	0	1.000	0	0	.857	1	--
Botts J	14.0	3	0	0	0	1.000	0	0	.750	0	--
Ellison J	11.0	5	0	0	0	1.000	0	0	1.000	1	--
Bradley M	8.0	1	0	0	0	1.000	0	0	.333	0	--
Center Field											
Hamilton J	912.0	268	3	2	3	.982	6	0	.882	73	B
Byrd M	433.0	149	4	3	0	.981	0	0	.936	32	--
Murphy D	85.0	30	0	0	0	1.000	0	0	.793	7	--
Boggs B	9.0	4	0	0	0	1.000	0	0	1.000	1	--
Ellison J	3.0	0	0	0	0	.000	0	0	--	--	--
Right Field											
Murphy D	407.3	107	1	0	1	.991	2	0	.978	20	--
Hamilton J	289.0	77	4	0	1	.988	4	0	.879	19	--
Byrd M	279.0	71	3	1	2	.961	0	0	.895	20	--
Cruz N	274.0	72	1	1	1	.973	2	0	.860	23	--
Bradley M	157.3	42	4	0	3	.939	6	0	.857	6	--
Ellison J	15.0	6	0	0	0	1.000	0	0	1.000	2	--
Boggs B	11.3	3	0	0	0	1.000	0	0	.667	1	--
Duran G	9.0	4	0	0	0	1.000	0	0	1.000	0	--

Toronto Blue Jays

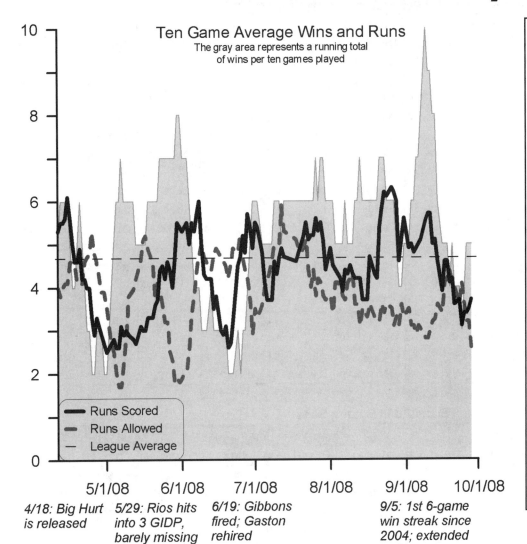

Ten Game Average Wins and Runs
The gray area represents a running total
of wins per ten games played

- Runs Scored
- Runs Allowed
- League Average

4/18: Big Hurt is released

5/29: Rios hits into 3 GIDP, barely missing fourth

6/19: Gibbons fired; Gaston rehired

7/8: McGowan fractures labrum; out for year

9/5: 1st 6-game win streak since 2004; extended to 10

9/25: Halladay wins 20th

Stat Facts:
- Roy Halladay led the AL with 140 Pitching Runs Created
- He led the majors with 246 IP and 987 BFP
- A.J. Burnett led the AL with 231 strikeouts
- Jesse Litsch allowed just 3 stolen bases in 9 attempts
- Only 6% of the fly balls off Litsch were infield pop-ups, lowest rate in the majors among 162+ IP pitchers
- The Blue Jays' highest GPA was Vernon Wells' .273
- Wells' percentage of line drives was just 17%
- Scott Rolen made 48 OOZ plays
- Lyle Overbay made 47 OOZ plays
- Shaun Marcum's FIP (4.52) was more than a run higher than his ERA (3.39)
- Scott Downs induced 66% ground balls
- Joe Inglett hit just 1 infield pop-up

Team Batting and Pitching/Fielding Stats by Month

	April	May	June	July	Aug	Sept/Oct
Wins	11	20	10	13	16	16
Losses	17	10	16	11	12	10
RS/G	4.1	4.0	4.3	4.6	5.0	4.5
RA/G	4.0	3.1	4.2	4.5	3.6	3.2
OBP	.338	.337	.342	.320	.327	.320
SLG	.360	.394	.397	.397	.414	.436
FIP	3.83	3.32	4.16	4.25	4.06	3.22
DER	.695	.730	.699	.696	.708	.708

Batting Stats

Player	BR	Runs	RBI	PA	Outs	H	2B	3B	HR	TB	K	BB	IBB	HBP	SH	SF	SB	CS	GDP	H-A	L^R	BA	OBP	SLG	GPA
Rios A	91	91	79	687	478	185	47	8	15	293	112	44	2	2	0	5	32	8	20	.016	-.025	.291	.337	.461	.262
Overbay L *	72	74	69	630	423	147	32	2	15	228	116	74	3	3	1	5	1	2	24	-.022	.101	.270	.358	.419	.261
Scutaro M	67	76	60	592	389	138	23	1	7	184	65	57	0	5	6	7	7	2	8	-.014	.011	.267	.341	.356	.238
Wells V	66	63	78	466	317	128	22	1	20	212	46	29	5	3	0	7	4	2	16	.006	.016	.300	.343	.496	.273
Rolen S	57	58	50	467	313	107	30	3	11	176	71	46	2	10	0	3	5	0	12	-.025	-.001	.262	.349	.431	.260
Inglett J *	48	45	39	385	249	102	15	7	3	140	43	28	0	4	8	1	9	2	5	.072	.013	.297	.355	.407	.257
Stairs M *	40	42	44	368	251	80	11	1	11	126	87	41	9	5	0	2	1	1	10	-.000	.038	.250	.342	.394	.248
Lind A *	38	48	40	349	242	92	16	4	9	143	59	16	3	2	1	4	2	0	8	-.013	.027	.282	.316	.439	.247
Barajas R	37	44	49	377	271	87	23	0	11	143	61	17	0	7	0	4	0	0	9	-.031	-.057	.249	.294	.410	.230
Eckstein D	35	27	23	303	195	72	18	0	1	93	27	24	1	8	9	2	2	1	6	-.048	.073	.277	.354	.358	.244
Zaun G +	32	29	30	288	194	58	12	0	6	88	38	38	1	1	3	1	2	1	6	.100	-.049	.237	.340	.359	.238
Hill A	24	19	20	229	157	54	14	0	2	74	31	16	0	3	4	1	4	2	4	.001	.066	.263	.324	.361	.232
Wilkerson B	19	20	23	241	169	45	8	2	4	69	53	25	4	1	2	5	2	3	3	.019	.019	.216	.297	.332	.212
Stewart S	16	14	14	200	142	42	4	2	1	53	18	22	1	1	0	2	3	1	8	.017	.049	.240	.325	.303	.218
Mench K	13	18	10	131	90	28	11	1	0	41	18	14	2	0	0	2	2	0	3	.097	.006	.243	.321	.357	.229
Snider T *	13	9	13	80	51	22	6	0	2	34	23	5	0	0	0	2	0	0	0	.098	.013	.301	.338	.466	.263
McDonald J	11	21	18	207	151	39	8	0	1	50	25	10	0	2	7	2	3	1	3	-.013	.057	.210	.255	.269	.178
Thomas F	8	7	11	72	53	10	1	0	3	20	13	11	0	1	0	0	0	0	3	.004	-.024	.167	.306	.333	.217
Bautista J	5	7	10	61	46	12	2	0	3	23	14	2	1	0	2	1	0	0	2	.116	.129	.214	.237	.411	.205
Thigpen C	2	2	1	21	14	3	0	0	1	6	8	1	0	1	2	0	0	0	0	-.204	.258	.176	.263	.353	.203

Italicized stats have been adjusted for home park.

Batted Ball Batting Stats

Player	% of PA		% of Batted Balls					Out %		Runs Per Event				Total Runs vs. Avg.				
	K%	BB%	GB%	LD%	FB%	IF/F	HR/OF	GB	OF	NIP	GB	LD	OF	NIP	GB	LD	FB	Tot
Wells V	10	7	47	17	36	.15	.16	70	88	.08	.06	.43	.22	-0	5	4	7	16
Rios A	16	7	41	21	38	.08	.08	76	74	.02	.03	.41	.22	-6	-4	8	15	13
Rolen S	15	12	36	21	44	.13	.08	72	85	.09	.05	.40	.14	5	-1	3	-1	7
Overbay L	18	12	44	23	33	.03	.10	81	81	.07	-.01	.43	.18	5	-11	8	1	4
Inglett J	11	8	49	25	26	.01	.04	78	84	.08	.03	.40	.09	1	-1	9	-7	2
Zaun G	13	14	44	15	40	.14	.08	74	85	.12	.04	.36	.13	5	-0	-4	-2	-2
Lind A	17	5	51	19	30	.05	.12	74	84	-.01	.04	.42	.20	-5	1	1	2	-2
Stairs M	24	13	43	20	37	.10	.13	74	87	.05	.04	.40	.19	1	-1	-1	-0	-2
Eckstein D	9	11	52	20	28	.09	.02	71	86	.14	.08	.32	.03	4	6	-2	-10	-2
Mench K	14	11	45	27	27	.15	.00	84	91	.09	-.02	.44	-.01	1	-3	4	-6	-3
Hill A	14	8	35	17	47	.18	.03	69	82	.06	.08	.36	.08	-0	1	-2	-5	-5
Scutaro M	11	10	43	23	35	.10	.05	71	92	.11	.07	.31	.04	6	7	-1	-18	-6
Stewart S	9	12	52	22	26	.07	.03	81	81	.14	-.00	.24	.10	3	-3	-3	-4	-7
Barajas R	16	6	37	17	46	.12	.09	76	84	.02	.04	.36	.15	-4	-2	-4	1	-8
Wilkerson B	22	11	47	16	36	.11	.08	79	87	.04	.02	.37	.12	-0	-2	-5	-4	-11
McDonald J	12	6	42	15	43	.13	.02	78	86	.04	.03	.31	.03	-2	-2	-5	-8	-18
MLB Average	18	10	44	20	36	.10	.11	74	84	.05	.04	.39	.18	--	--	--	--	--

Pitching Stats

Player	PRC	IP	BFP	G	GS	K	BB	IBB	HBP	H	HR	DP	DER	SB	CS	PO	W	L	Sv	Op	Hld	H-A	R^L	RA	ERA	FIP
Halladay R	140	246.0	987	34	33	206	39	3	12	220	18	26	.706	15	5	0	20	11	0	0	1	.005	.003	3.22	2.78	3.09
Burnett A	100	221.3	957	35	34	231	86	2	9	211	19	14	.672	22	9	5	18	10	0	0	0	.019	-.030	4.43	4.07	3.52
Marcum S	78	151.3	630	25	25	123	50	2	8	126	21	11	.748	5	2	0	9	7	0	0	0	-.061	-.019	3.57	3.39	4.52
Litsch J	75	176.0	735	29	28	99	39	2	8	178	20	17	.715	3	6	1	13	9	0	0	0	-.045	-.006	4.04	3.58	4.35
Downs S *	59	70.7	290	66	0	57	27	7	4	54	3	8	.734	2	0	1	0	3	5	9	24	-.054	-.033	1.91	1.78	3.19
Carlson J *	44	60.0	237	69	0	55	21	7	3	41	6	3	.763	1	3	2	7	2	2	2	19	-.099	-.010	2.40	2.25	3.55
McGowan D	43	111.3	474	19	19	85	38	1	5	115	9	13	.677	12	4	0	6	7	0	0	0	-.039	-.072	4.85	4.37	3.89
Ryan B *	34	58.0	249	60	0	58	28	3	4	46	4	5	.710	4	0	0	2	4	32	36	1	-.081	.057	3.26	2.95	3.63
Tallet B *	34	56.3	240	51	0	47	22	3	1	52	4	3	.705	6	1	0	1	2	0	0	4	.003	.000	3.04	2.88	3.55
League B	22	33.0	141	31	0	23	15	2	3	28	2	6	.724	0	0	0	1	2	1	1	5	.032	-.077	2.45	2.18	4.08
Purcey D *	22	65.0	289	12	12	58	29	0	4	67	9	4	.677	2	3	1	3	6	0	0	0	.057	.008	5.68	5.54	4.77
Frasor J	21	47.3	208	49	0	42	32	4	1	36	4	3	.736	5	2	0	1	2	0	1	4	-.036	-.095	4.37	4.18	4.39
Camp S	18	39.3	166	40	0	31	11	3	2	40	2	6	.683	3	0	0	3	1	0	0	7	-.042	-.142	4.12	4.12	3.08
Parrish J *	18	42.3	179	13	6	21	15	0	0	47	5	6	.696	2	1	2	1	1	0	0	0	-.075	.040	4.04	4.04	4.84
Wolfe B	14	22.0	86	20	0	14	6	1	0	18	2	5	.734	1	0	0	0	2	0	0	3	.010	-.052	2.45	2.45	3.82
Richmond S	12	27.0	113	5	5	20	2	0	2	32	2	4	.655	1	1	0	1	3	0	0	0	.173	-.281	4.00	4.00	3.16
Accardo J	3	12.3	56	16	0	5	4	2	1	15	1	3	.667	1	0	0	0	3	4	6	2	.115	-.047	7.30	6.57	4.20
Benitez A	2	6.3	26	8	0	9	2	0	0	4	3	0	.833	1	0	0	0	1	0	1	2	.415	-.133	7.11	5.68	7.49

Italicized stats have been adjusted for home park.

Batted Ball Pitching Stats

Player	% of PA		% of Batted Balls					Out %		Runs Per Event				Total Runs vs. Avg.				
	K%	BB%	GB%	LD%	FB%	IF/F	HR/OF	GB	OF	NIP	GB	LD	OF	NIP	GB	LD	FB	Tot
Halladay R	21	5	54	19	27	.09	.10	79	81	-.02	.02	.36	.18	-20	-8	-9	-11	-48
Marcum S	20	9	43	17	40	.10	.13	80	83	.03	.02	.29	.22	-3	-7	-15	9	-16
Downs S	20	11	66	12	22	.07	.08	80	70	.05	.01	.34	.22	0	-3	-9	-3	-16
Carlson J	23	10	34	21	45	.09	.09	85	91	.03	-.02	.40	.11	-1	-5	-2	-3	-11
Burnett A	24	10	49	19	32	.12	.10	76	79	.02	.04	.43	.22	-6	-1	-2	-1	-10
Litsch J	13	6	49	20	32	.06	.11	76	84	.03	.04	.32	.18	-5	2	-6	1	-9
Tallet B	20	10	43	22	36	.17	.06	83	81	.04	-.01	.44	.12	-1	-4	2	-4	-7
Ryan R	23	13	39	19	42	.09	.07	78	91	.05	.01	.50	.07	1	-2	1	-6	-6
League B	16	13	67	19	14	.00	.14	80	83	.09	-.00	.34	.22	2	-2	-1	-2	-4
Camp S	19	8	54	19	27	.03	.06	82	77	.02	-.01	.44	.17	-1	-2	1	-1	-4
McGowan D	18	9	41	21	38	.12	.08	74	83	.04	.05	.37	.16	-1	1	0	-2	-2
Frasor J	20	16	38	24	38	.02	.08	84	89	.09	-.00	.36	.10	4	-3	0	-3	-2
Richmond S	18	4	36	25	39	.11	.06	75	83	-.04	.03	.49	.14	-2	-1	4	-0	1
Parrish J	12	8	37	22	41	.07	.09	79	82	.08	.00	.39	.16	0	-2	2	2	2
Purcey D	20	11	32	23	45	.05	.11	62	91	.05	.12	.35	.13	1	4	-0	0	5
MLB Average	18	10	44	20	36	.10	.11	74	84	.05	.04	.39	.18	--	--	--	--	--

Fielding Stats

Name	Inn	SBA/G	CS%	ERA	WP+PB/G	PO	A	TE	FE	Grade
Catcher										
Barajas R	785.3	0.68	29%	3.32	0.264	674	47	4	0	A
Zaun G	612.3	0.76	23%	3.81	0.485	515	28	5	2	--
Thigpen C	49.0	0.92	20%	2.20	0.184	36	3	0	0	--

Name	Inn	PO	A	TE	FE	FPct	DPS	DPT	ZR	OOZ	Grade
First Base											
Overbay L	1354.0	1316	155	1	3	.997	16	1	.795	47	B
Barajas R	27.0	27	5	0	0	1.000	1	0	.500	2	--
Bautista J	27.0	29	0	0	0	1.000	0	0	.500	0	--
Wilkerson B	20.0	22	0	0	0	1.000	0	0	.500	1	--
Scutaro M	15.0	15	1	0	0	1.000	0	0	1.000	1	--
Thigpen C	3.0	1	0	0	0	1.000	0	0	--	--	--
Second Base											
Inglett J	541.3	123	176	1	4	.984	12	24	.825	12	--
Hill A	479.0	87	150	1	0	.996	12	15	.837	15	--
Scutaro M	354.3	60	126	0	1	.995	8	9	.810	13	--
Eckstein D	45.0	7	14	0	0	1.000	2	2	.846	2	--
Bautista J	16.0	2	6	0	0	1.000	1	1	1.000	0	--
Velandia J	8.0	1	0	0	0	1.000	0	0	--	--	--
McDonald J	3.0	0	0	0	0	.000	0	0	--	--	--
Shortstop											
Eckstein D	484.3	69	146	4	5	.960	14	17	.769	15	--
McDonald J	478.0	80	134	4	5	.960	15	17	.807	19	--
Scutaro M	472.3	71	165	2	3	.979	12	14	.874	21	--
Velandia J	10.0	1	1	0	0	1.000	0	0	1.000	0	--
Inglett J	2.0	0	2	0	0	1.000	0	0	1.000	0	--
Third Base											
Rolen S	1006.0	74	217	2	9	.964	13	0	.741	48	A+
Scutaro M	332.0	22	84	1	0	.981	7	0	.773	25	--
Inglett J	45.0	5	13	0	0	1.000	1	0	.833	2	--
Bautista J	40.0	5	11	0	0	1.000	1	0	.818	2	C
McDonald J	23.0	0	5	0	0	1.000	0	0	1.000	2	--

Name	Inn	PO	A	TE	FE	FPct	DPS	DPT	ZR	OOZ	Grade
Left Field											
Lind A	590.7	113	2	0	0	1.000	2	0	.889	17	--
Stewart S	310.3	56	3	0	0	1.000	6	0	.896	13	--
Wilkerson B	138.7	24	0	0	0	1.000	0	0	.800	4	--
Mench K	125.0	28	0	0	0	1.000	0	0	.923	4	--
Snider T	99.0	14	2	0	0	1.000	2	0	.923	2	--
Inglett J	73.0	15	0	0	0	1.000	0	0	.917	4	--
Stairs M	62.0	10	0	0	0	1.000	0	0	.833	0	--
Scutaro M	25.0	4	1	0	0	1.000	0	0	1.000	1	--
Coats B	23.0	6	0	0	0	1.000	0	0	1.000	2	--
Center Field											
Wells V	889.0	217	5	0	3	.987	2	0	.876	40	F-
Rios A	522.7	156	10	0	3	.982	2	0	.955	29	--
Wilkerson B	28.0	7	0	0	0	1.000	0	0	1.000	1	--
Inglett J	7.0	1	0	0	0	1.000	0	0	1.000	0	--
Right Field											
Rios A	820.0	170	4	0	1	.994	4	0	.889	50	--
Wilkerson B	336.3	77	3	0	1	.988	0	0	.926	14	--
Mench K	98.0	22	1	0	0	1.000	0	0	.900	4	--
Inglett J	87.3	14	0	0	0	1.000	0	0	.833	4	--
Snider T	60.0	11	0	0	0	1.000	0	0	1.000	0	--
Stairs M	45.0	9	0	0	0	1.000	0	0	.875	2	--

Washington Nationals

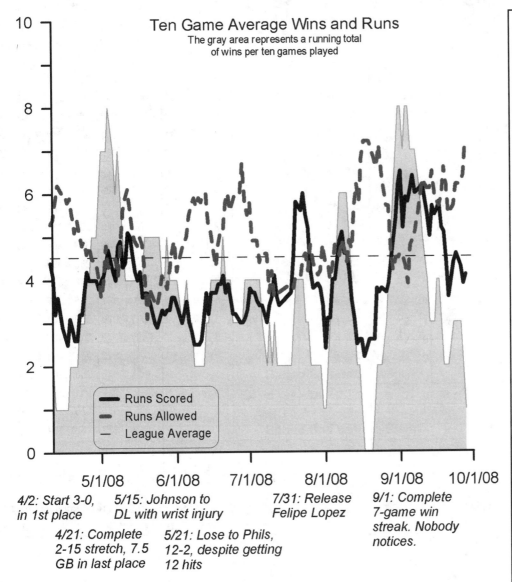

Ten Game Average Wins and Runs
The gray area represents a running total
of wins per ten games played

- Runs Scored
- Runs Allowed
- League Average

4/2: Start 3-0,
in 1st place

4/21: Complete
2-15 stretch, 7.5
GB in last place

5/15: Johnson to
DL with wrist injury

5/21: Lose to Phils,
12-2, despite getting
12 hits

7/31: Release
Felipe Lopez

9/1: Complete
7-game win
streak. Nobody
notices.

Stat Facts:

- Nick Johnson walked in nearly one-quarter of his PAs
- In 84 innings, Saul Rivera allowed 13 stolen bases in 13 attempts
- 17% of the fly balls off John Lannan were home runs, tied for the highest rate in the majors among 162+ IP pitchers
- Lastings Milledge made 81 OOZ plays
- Ryan Zimmerman made 42 OOZ plays, and committed zero fielding errors
- Jay Bergmann allowed 25 homers in 140 innings
- Cristian Guzman put the ball in play 86% of the time
- 53% of Guzman's batted balls were grounders
- Guzman's ground balls produced 15 more runs than average
- Paul LoDuca grounded into 9 double plays in 153 PAs
- 27% of the batted balls off Jesus Colome were line drives

Team Batting and Pitching/Fielding Stats by Month

	April	May	June	July	Aug	Sept/Oct
Wins	11	13	9	5	14	7
Losses	17	16	18	19	15	17
RS/G	3.7	3.9	3.3	3.9	4.5	4.7
RA/G	4.8	4.6	5.6	4.3	5.3	6.1
OBP	.311	.308	.325	.311	.333	.349
SLG	.337	.368	.371	.363	.395	.405
FIP	4.38	4.77	4.42	4.15	5.52	4.75
DER	.691	.701	.667	.685	.715	.678

Batting Stats

Player	BR	Runs	RBI	PA	Outs	H	2B	3B	HR	TB	K	BB	IBB	HBP	SH	SF	SB	CS	GDP	H-A	L^R	BA	OBP	SLG	GPA
Guzman C +	79	77	55	612	411	183	35	5	9	255	57	23	1	5	1	4	6	5	10	.037	.054	.316	.345	.440	.263
Milledge L	60	65	61	587	411	140	24	2	14	210	96	38	1	14	5	7	24	9	19	.022	-.030	.268	.330	.402	.246
Belliard R	53	37	46	337	219	85	22	0	11	140	58	37	1	3	1	0	3	2	6	-.011	.073	.287	.372	.473	.283
Harris W *	50	58	43	424	286	92	14	4	13	153	66	50	2	3	3	1	13	3	8	.002	-.001	.251	.344	.417	.257
Dukes E	47	48	44	334	217	73	16	2	13	132	79	50	1	6	0	2	13	4	10	.018	-.031	.264	.386	.478	.290
Zimmerman R	47	51	51	466	320	121	24	1	14	189	71	31	1	3	0	4	1	1	12	-.002	.043	.283	.333	.442	.258
Flores J	46	23	59	324	232	77	18	1	8	121	78	15	1	4	0	4	0	1	7	-.040	.053	.256	.296	.402	.232
Kearns A	29	40	32	357	258	68	10	0	7	99	63	35	0	8	0	1	2	2	11	.018	-.056	.217	.311	.316	.217
Lopez F +	26	34	25	363	267	76	20	0	2	102	54	32	1	2	2	2	4	5	13	-.079	.020	.234	.305	.314	.213
Boone A	23	23	28	255	185	56	13	1	6	89	52	18	1	2	1	2	0	1	8	-.044	.078	.241	.299	.384	.228
Johnson N *	21	15	20	147	87	24	8	0	5	47	25	33	4	4	0	1	0	0	2	-.028	.088	.220	.415	.431	.292
Nieves W	19	15	20	196	138	46	9	1	1	60	29	13	1	0	5	2	0	1	7	.033	.044	.261	.309	.341	.222
Langerhans R	18	17	12	139	86	26	5	2	3	44	31	25	1	1	2	0	2	0	1	-.165	-.026	.234	.380	.396	.267
Hernandez A	17	11	17	91	55	27	4	0	0	31	8	10	0	0	0	0	0	0	1	-.048	.042	.333	.407	.383	.276
Young D +	15	15	10	180	116	42	6	0	4	60	28	28	4	1	0	1	0	0	8	-.057	.078	.280	.394	.400	.275
Bonifacio E	15	26	12	174	124	39	5	5	0	54	41	14	0	0	0	3	6	4	2	.131	-.088	.248	.305	.344	.221
Casto K *	14	15	16	182	133	35	10	0	2	51	36	19	1	0	0	0	1	0	5	.011	.162	.215	.297	.313	.210
Lo Duca P	14	13	12	153	116	32	7	0	0	39	9	9	0	5	0	0	1	0	9	.016	-.030	.230	.301	.281	.203
Gonzalez A	11	9	9	54	35	17	6	0	1	26	6	4	0	1	0	0	0	1	2	-.086	.046	.347	.407	.531	.313
Pena W	9	10	10	206	161	40	6	0	2	52	48	10	0	0	0	1	0	1	5	.076	.020	.205	.243	.267	.174
Orr P *	5	10	7	79	56	19	2	1	0	23	16	2	0	1	1	0	1	0	0	.080	-.075	.253	.282	.307	.202
Bernadina R	5	10	2	86	66	16	1	1	0	19	21	9	0	0	1	0	4	3	3	-.039	-.017	.211	.294	.250	.193
Estrada J +	4	0	4	55	44	9	0	0	0	9	4	1	0	1	0	0	0	0	0	-.005	-.077	.170	.200	.170	.131
Mackowiak R	4	7	4	63	47	7	1	0	1	11	17	8	0	1	0	1	0	0	1	-.040	.172	.132	.254	.208	.165
Montz L	3	2	3	26	18	3	0	0	1	6	9	5	0	0	0	0	0	0	0	.160	-.176	.143	.308	.286	.208
Redding T	2	2	3	65	40	8	1	0	0	9	14	5	0	0	13	0	0	0	1	.013	-.029	.170	.250	.191	.159

Italicized stats have been adjusted for home park.

Batted Ball Batting Stats

Player	% of PA		% of Batted Balls			IF/F	HR/OF	Out %		Runs Per Event				Total Runs vs. Avg.				
	K%	BB%	GB%	LD%	FB%			GB	OF	NIP	GB	LD	OF	NIP	GB	LD	FB	Tot
Dukes E	24	17	47	18	35	.06	.17	71	85	.08	.07	.54	.25	6	2	3	4	15
Guzman C	9	5	53	23	25	.12	.06	67	86	.04	.09	.41	.10	-5	15	15	-13	13
Belliard R	17	12	42	23	35	.06	.14	77	85	.07	.03	.43	.23	3	-2	6	5	12
Johnson N	17	25	38	24	39	.15	.18	78	83	.16	.02	.30	.29	8	-1	-1	3	9
Zimmerman R	15	7	46	20	34	.07	.12	68	90	.04	.08	.36	.16	-2	8	-0	-0	5
Harris W	16	13	43	18	38	.12	.12	70	93	.09	.07	.40	.15	5	3	-1	-3	4
Young D	16	16	58	17	25	.03	.10	70	78	.12	.05	.35	.19	5	1	-2	-1	4
Langerhans R	22	19	44	25	31	.16	.10	86	84	.10	-.00	.48	.18	4	-2	2	-2	2
Bonifacio E	24	8	54	22	24	.04	.00	73	88	.00	.06	.49	.00	-2	2	2	-7	-4
Milledge L	16	9	45	20	35	.14	.09	75	83	.05	.03	.39	.15	-1	0	1	-5	-5
Boone A	20	8	42	20	38	.14	.10	74	83	.01	.04	.33	.18	-3	-1	-3	-0	-7
Flores J	24	6	37	25	38	.19	.10	79	81	-.02	.02	.40	.18	-7	-4	4	-1	-8
Lo Duca P	5	9	49	16	35	.18	.00	79	84	.18	-.01	.36	.02	2	-3	-1	-6	-8
Nieves W	15	7	54	20	26	.05	.03	74	86	.03	.04	.37	.06	-2	0	-1	-6	-8
Casto K	20	10	48	27	25	.19	.04	80	92	.05	-.00	.36	.03	-0	-3	2	-7	-8
Kearns A	18	12	47	21	32	.15	.10	75	94	.07	.03	.31	.10	3	-2	-4	-8	-11
Pena W	23	5	54	21	25	.11	.00	70	94	-.03	.06	.33	-.05	-5	2	-3	-11	-17
Lopez F	15	9	50	18	32	.05	.02	82	76	.06	-.02	.33	.12	1	-8	-5	-5	-17
MLB Average	18	10	44	20	36	.10	.11	74	84	.05	.04	.39	.18	--	--	--	--	--

Pitching Stats

Player	PRC	IP	BFP	G	GS	K	BB	IBB	HBP	H	HR	DP	DER	SB	CS	PO	W	L	Sv	Op	Hld	H-A	R^L	RA	ERA	FIP
Lannan J *	69	182.0	779	31	31	117	72	1	7	172	23	21	.716	18	7	5	9	0	0	0	0	.021	.016	4.40	3.91	4.84
Perez O *	56	159.7	711	30	30	119	55	4	8	182	22	14	.665	13	7	4	7	0	0	0	0	-.098	-.059	4.90	4.34	4.61
Redding T	56	182.0	791	33	33	120	65	5	7	195	27	21	.694	13	7	0	10	11	0	0	0	.048	-.013	5.44	4.95	4.92
Bergmann J	38	139.7	614	30	22	96	47	2	1	153	25	10	.697	9	1	0	2	11	0	0	0	.052	-.032	6.06	5.09	5.14
Hanrahan J	37	84.3	364	69	0	93	42	7	1	73	9	7	.699	11	0	0	6	3	9	13	3	-.046	-.000	4.27	3.95	3.66
Rivera S	33	84.0	371	76	0	65	35	2	2	90	3	9	.662	13	0	0	5	6	0	6	17	-.045	.030	4.39	3.96	3.37
Shell S	32	50.0	199	39	0	41	20	1	2	34	5	6	.771	2	1	0	2	2	2	3	7	-.033	-.082	2.52	2.16	4.12
Colome J	26	71.0	312	61	0	55	39	4	4	61	6	6	.721	8	3	0	2	2	0	2	1	.031	-.035	4.82	4.31	4.40
Rauch J	25	48.3	192	48	0	44	7	1	0	42	5	2	.721	3	0	0	4	2	17	22	0	.027	-.011	3.35	2.98	3.10
Balester C	22	80.0	358	15	15	50	28	1	6	92	12	7	.679	3	3	1	3	7	0	0	0	.022	-.008	5.96	5.51	5.14
Hinckley M *	20	13.7	49	14	0	9	3	0	1	8	0	3	.778	1	0	0	0	0	0	0	4	.049	.046	0.66	0.00	2.76
Mock G	18	41.0	180	26	3	46	23	3	0	37	4	5	.673	2	0	0	1	3	0	0	0	.044	-.020	4.39	4.17	3.69
Hill S	15	63.3	296	12	12	39	23	2	1	88	5	6	.618	8	3	0	1	5	0	0	0	-.123	.063	6.68	5.83	4.04
Ayala L	14	57.7	257	62	0	36	22	4	4	63	6	9	.672	1	1	0	1	8	0	4	19	-.055	-.006	6.40	5.77	4.45
Manning C *	14	42.0	189	57	0	37	31	2	0	35	8	4	.761	4	0	0	1	3	0	2	7	-.043	-.067	5.36	5.14	5.99
Chico M *	12	48.0	219	11	8	31	17	1	1	63	10	4	.669	2	2	1	0	6	0	0	0	-.016	.022	6.38	6.19	5.68
Martis S	6	20.7	92	5	4	23	12	0	0	18	5	1	.731	3	0	0	1	3	0	0	0	.126	-.115	6.10	5.66	5.86
Clippard T	4	10.3	48	2	2	8	7	1	0	12	2	1	.677	0	0	0	1	1	0	0	0	-.041	-.121	4.35	4.35	5.91
Cordero C	3	4.3	22	6	0	5	3	1	0	6	0	0	.571	0	0	0	0	0	0	0	1	.159	.135	2.08	2.08	2.28
Sanches B	2	11.0	54	12	0	10	5	0	1	16	2	2	.583	1	0	0	2	0	0	1	0	.116	-.004	8.18	7.36	5.38
Estrada M	2	12.7	63	11	0	10	5	1	2	17	4	1	.643	0	1	0	0	0	0	1	3	.001	-.085	9.24	7.82	7.15
Schroder C	2	5.0	27	4	0	3	6	0	0	6	2	0	.750	0	0	0	0	0	0	0	0	.234	-.038	5.40	5.40	10.80
King R *	1	6.3	33	12	0	1	4	0	1	9	1	1	.654	2	0	0	0	0	0	1	4	-.072	-.276	5.68	5.68	7.31
O'Connor M *	1	9.0	48	5	1	4	11	0	0	11	3	1	.733	1	0	0	1	1	0	1	0	.067	-.364	13.00	13.00	10.31
Speigner L	1	8.0	42	7	0	1	6	1	2	13	1	2	.625	0	2	0	0	1	0	0	0	.219	.210	11.25	11.25	7.20

Italicized stats have been adjusted for home park.

Batted Ball Pitching Stats

Player	% of PA		% of Batted Balls					Out %		Runs Per Event				Total Runs vs. Avg.				
	K%	BB%	GB%	LD%	FB%	IF/F	HR/OF	GB	OF	NIP	GB	LD	OF	NIP	GB	LD	FB	Tot
Shell S	21	11	38	17	45	.10	.09	75	96	.05	.03	.37	.08	0	-2	-4	-5	-10
Rauch J	23	4	32	23	45	.18	.06	70	88	-.05	.07	.42	.08	-5	-0	2	-5	-9
Rivera S	18	10	54	21	25	.08	.05	71	86	.05	.06	.36	.07	1	4	-1	-10	-6
Hanrahan J	25	12	43	22	36	.10	.11	71	86	.03	.08	.33	.17	-0	2	-5	-3	-6
Lannan J	15	10	54	19	27	.11	.17	79	84	.07	.01	.34	.27	4	-7	-7	5	-5
Colome J	18	14	32	27	41	.17	.07	74	91	.09	.04	.32	.08	5	-2	0	-7	-4
Mock G	26	13	45	19	36	.15	.12	67	90	.04	.09	.44	.14	0	2	-1	-3	-1
Manning C	20	16	40	16	44	.12	.15	79	90	.10	.02	.48	.18	4	-2	-1	1	2
Ayala L	14	10	43	23	34	.10	.11	77	84	.08	.03	.41	.17	2	-1	5	-0	5
Balester C	14	9	40	22	39	.14	.11	69	87	.07	.08	.40	.17	2	4	4	0	10
Redding T	15	9	40	20	40	.08	.11	72	88	.06	.06	.41	.16	1	2	5	3	11
Bergmann J	16	8	30	24	46	.13	.11	71	86	.04	.06	.40	.17	-3	-0	9	5	11
Chico M	14	8	37	23	39	.08	.17	66	84	.06	.12	.32	.25	-0	4	1	7	12
Hill S	13	8	46	25	28	.03	.08	78	69	.06	.02	.45	.25	0	-2	11	5	14
Perez O	17	9	47	20	34	.06	.13	70	83	.05	.08	.41	.22	-1	9	3	8	19
MLB Average	18	10	44	20	36	.10	.11	74	84	.05	.04	.39	.18	--	--	--	--	--

Fielding Stats

Name	Inn	SBA/G	CS%	ERA	WP+PB/G	PO	A	TE	FE	Grade
Catcher										
Flores J	673.0	0.78	19%	4.51	0.495	474	29	4	1	--
Nieves W	449.7	0.96	19%	4.60	0.460	359	31	2	1	--
Lo Duca P	161.0	0.78	7%	5.03	0.280	114	6	0	0	--
Estrada J	94.3	1.62	24%	5.15	0.191	78	8	2	0	--
Montz L	56.0	1.45	33%	5.14	0.643	44	4	0	1	--

Name	Inn	PO	A	TE	FE	FPct	DPS	DPT	ZR	OOZ	Grade
First Base											
Boone A	342.0	313	17	0	1	.997	8	0	.774	7	--
Johnson N	300.3	302	14	0	0	1.000	0	0	.818	8	--
Young D	290.0	275	15	1	6	.976	3	0	.676	3	--
Belliard R	201.0	185	14	0	2	.990	0	1	.833	6	--
Casto K	175.7	149	13	0	2	.988	2	1	.636	0	--
Lo Duca P	118.0	113	8	0	3	.976	1	0	.700	4	--
Langerhans	7.0	8	0	0	0	1.000	0	0	.000	0	--
Second Base											
Lopez F	622.7	128	196	4	6	.970	16	22	.826	5	F-
Bonifacio E	325.0	78	82	3	4	.958	10	13	.845	8	--
Belliard R	229.7	53	60	0	3	.974	6	13	.759	2	--
Hernandez A	138.0	34	43	0	0	1.000	4	4	.912	4	--
Harris W	86.3	29	30	0	1	.983	3	5	.846	3	--
Orr P	31.0	8	10	0	1	.947	1	1	.583	2	--
Boone A	1.3	0	0	0	0	.000	0	0	--	--	--
Shortstop											
Guzman C	1174.0	192	394	6	11	.972	37	35	.838	50	C
Gonzalez A	93.0	13	28	0	0	1.000	3	4	.792	4	--
Lopez F	54.0	3	21	0	0	1.000	3	1	.857	2	--
Orr P	43.0	9	10	1	1	.905	2	1	.700	2	--
Belliard R	33.0	6	11	0	1	.944	2	1	.778	3	--
Hernandez A	24.0	3	3	2	1	.667	0	0	.375	0	--
Harris W	13.0	3	2	0	0	1.000	1	0	--	--	--
Third Base											
Zimmerman	910.7	95	199	10	0	.967	24	1	.712	42	A+
Belliard R	215.3	16	40	3	2	.918	3	0	.615	8	--
Boone A	113.0	3	23	1	0	.963	2	0	.667	4	--
Casto K	103.0	12	23	0	0	1.000	1	0	.773	6	--
Harris W	44.0	0	6	0	0	1.000	0	0	1.000	2	--
Orr P	37.0	4	16	0	0	1.000	0	0	.737	1	--
Gonzalez A	11.0	1	2	0	0	1.000	0	0	.667	0	--

Name	Inn	PO	A	TE	FE	FPct	DPS	DPT	ZR	OOZ	Grade
Left Field											
Harris W	562.0	145	4	0	2	.987	4	0	.943	45	--
Pena W	408.0	99	3	0	3	.971	0	0	.881	25	--
Langerhans	141.7	26	1	0	0	1.000	0	0	.826	7	--
Mackowiak R	73.3	11	0	0	0	1.000	0	0	.714	1	--
Dukes E	57.7	16	0	0	1	.941	0	0	.882	1	--
Bernadina R	56.0	19	2	0	0	1.000	0	0	.923	7	--
Casto K	53.7	11	0	0	0	1.000	0	0	.818	2	--
Lopez F	49.0	9	1	0	0	1.000	0	0	1.000	1	--
Lo Duca P	23.7	11	0	1	0	.917	0	0	.818	2	--
Orr P	9.0	2	0	0	0	1.000	0	0	1.000	0	--
Center Field											
Milledge L	1185.0	348	1	1	4	.986	0	0	.870	81	F-
Harris W	131.3	46	0	0	1	.979	0	0	.944	12	--
Bernadina R	108.0	27	0	0	1	.964	0	0	.818	9	--
Dukes E	9.0	5	0	0	0	1.000	0	0	1.000	2	--
Right Field											
Kearns A	734.0	187	3	2	2	.979	0	0	.893	45	B
Dukes E	602.7	137	9	3	2	.967	2	0	.897	33	--
Langerhans	74.3	23	1	0	0	1.000	2	0	1.000	6	--
Mackowiak R	14.0	2	0	0	0	1.000	0	0	1.000	0	--
Casto K	9.0	4	1	0	0	1.000	2	0	1.000	2	--

Playing Time Constellations

John Burnson's Playing Time Constellations have become a staple of the *Hardball Times Baseball Annual*. John is the publisher of the *2009 Graphical Player*, featuring player profiles unlike anything you'll find in another book or on the Internet. The constellations on the following pages are just a small sample of John's work.

Elsewhere in this *Annual*, you have seen how many games each player played at each position. But the constellations tell you more: not only who played where, but when, and in what order. Take a look at the Arizona Diamondbacks constellation below. Positions are listed in the vertical axis and players are listed in the horizontal axis. Upward trajectory indicates increased playing time; downward trajectory indicates decreased playing time.

Each dot represents a month's worth of playing time for that player at that position. In each cell, the plot moves from left to right, from April to September. A dot is displayed only if the player appeared at that position that month. Cells are 150 PA tall, and each team is represented by players with at least 120 appearances last year. Players with asterisks finished the year with another team.

So, let's see what the Arizona constellation tells us about their year. Eric Byrnes started the year in left field. When Byrnes came up lame in April, Conor Jackson moved from first base to left, where he stayed for the rest of the year. Chad Tracy took over for Jackson at first, with help from Tony Clark.

On the following ten pages, you'll find similar graphs for every major league team. You'll see, for example, when the Tigers switched Miguel Cabrera and Carlos Guillen between first and third, how the Dodgers transformed their outfield throughout the year (particularly after they obtained Manny Ramirez) and the way Alexei Ramirez and Juan Uribe filled in when Joe Crede was out for the White Sox. The Playing Time Constellations are a feast for the eyes.

John Burnson is also the publisher of *HEATER Magazine*. *HEATER* is an electronic baseball magazine, published twice a week during the season, and providing the very best in fantasy baseball coverage and statistics. These graphs are only a small sample of what you can receive with a one-year subscription. To learn more (and subscribe), visit the *HEATER Magazine* website (http://www.heatermagazine.com/).

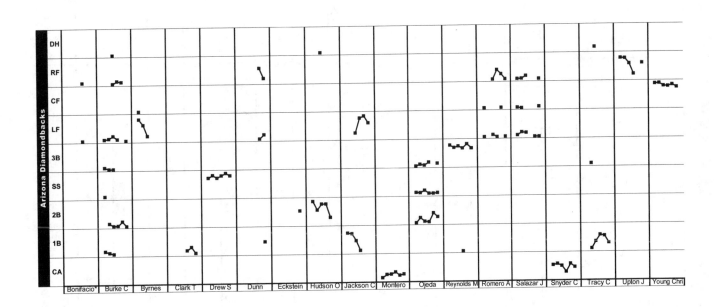

Playing Time Constellations

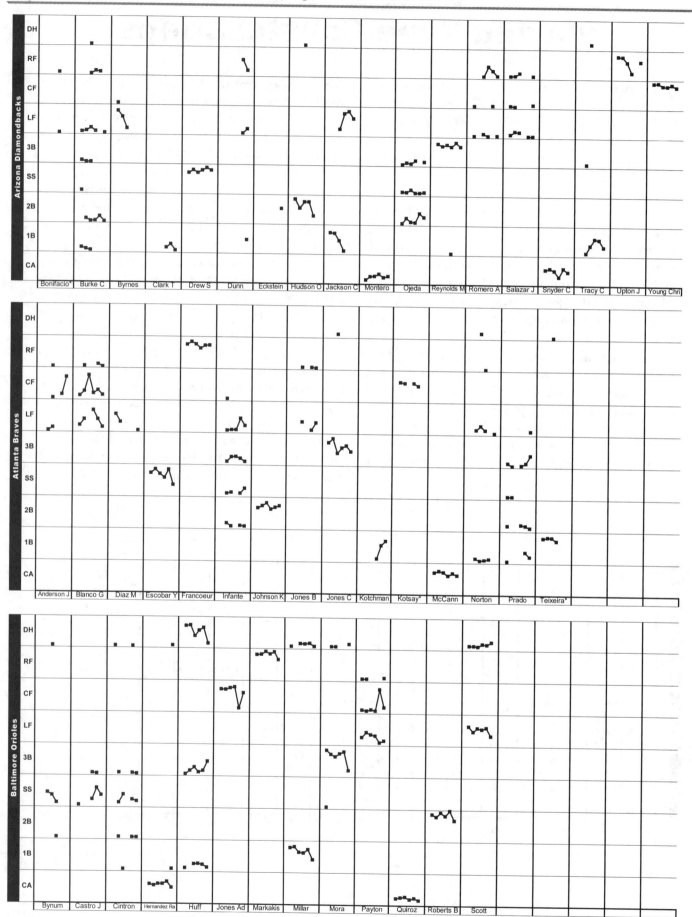

Constellations courtesy John Burnson; HEATER Magazine/Graphical Player

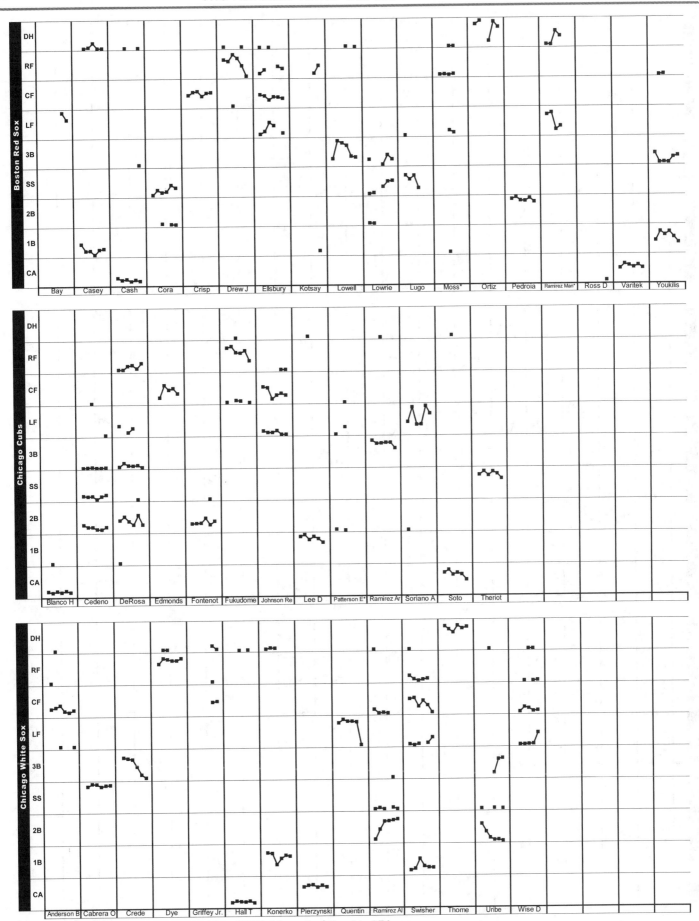

Constellations courtesy John Burnson; HEATER Magazine/Graphical Player

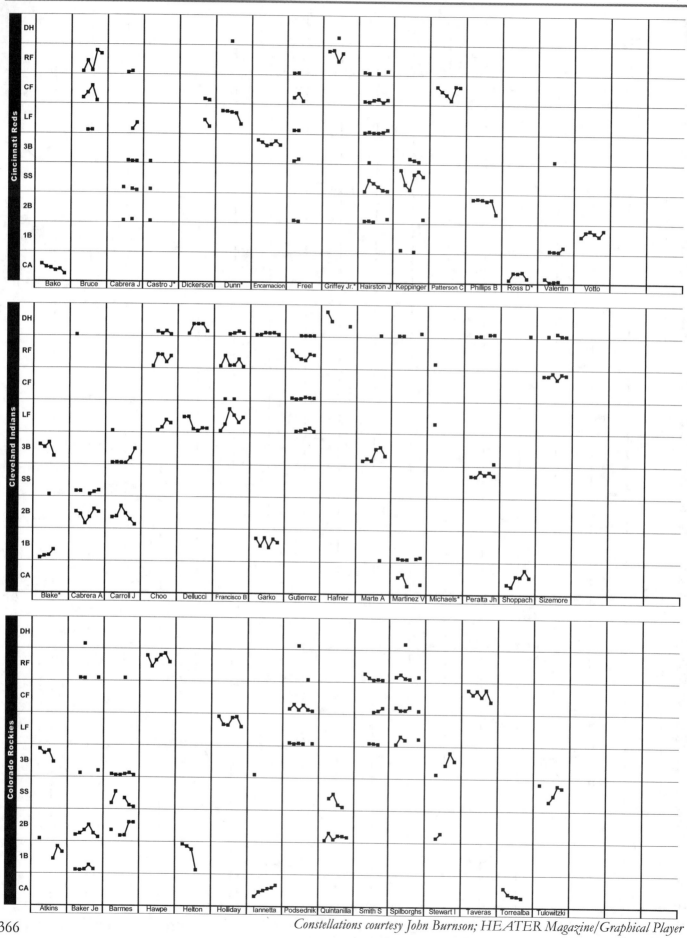

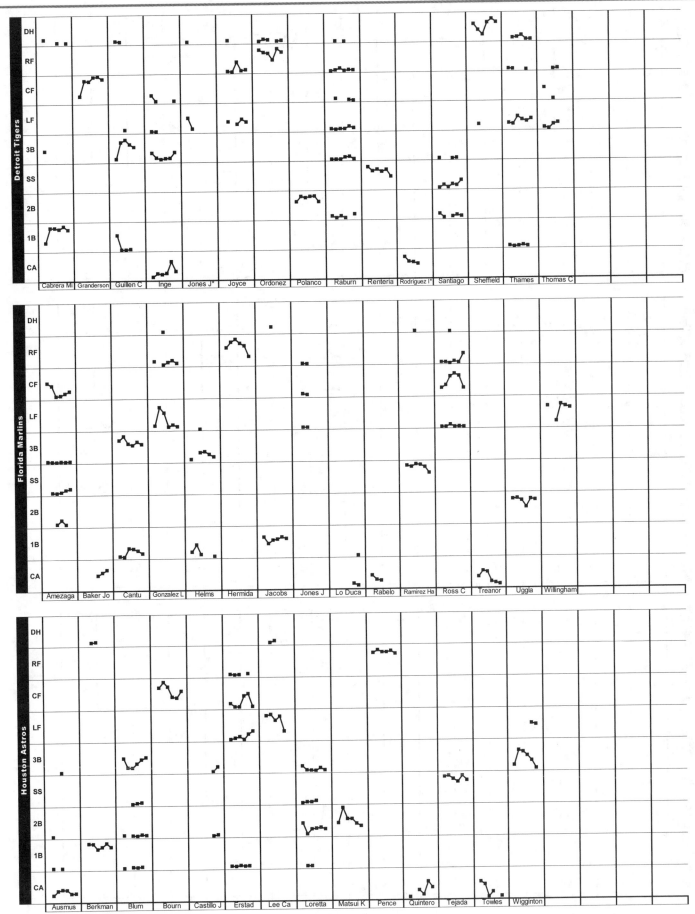

Constellations courtesy John Burnson; HEATER Magazine/Graphical Player

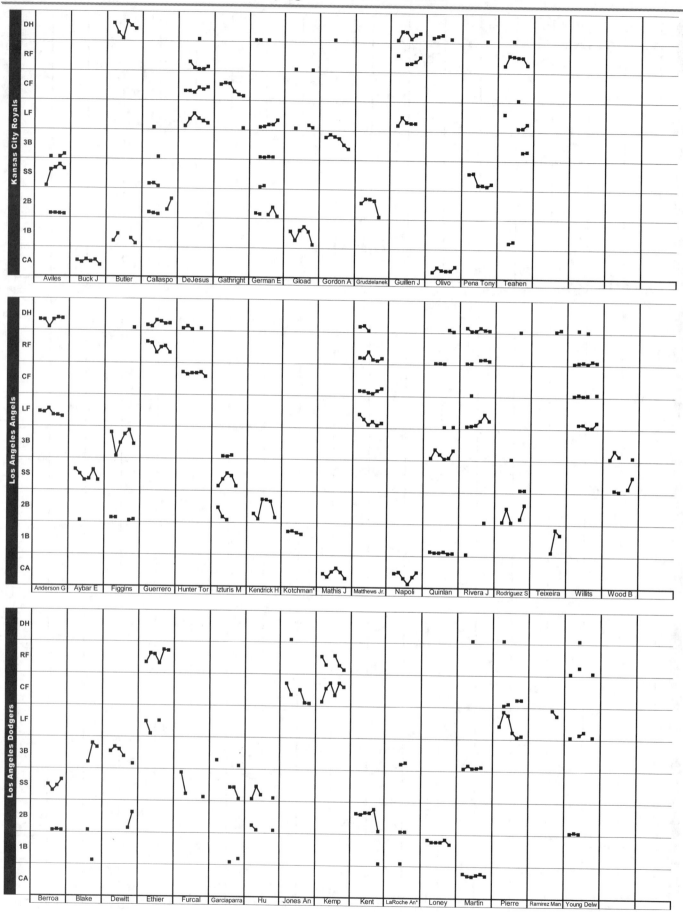

Constellations courtesy John Burnson; HEATER Magazine/Graphical Player

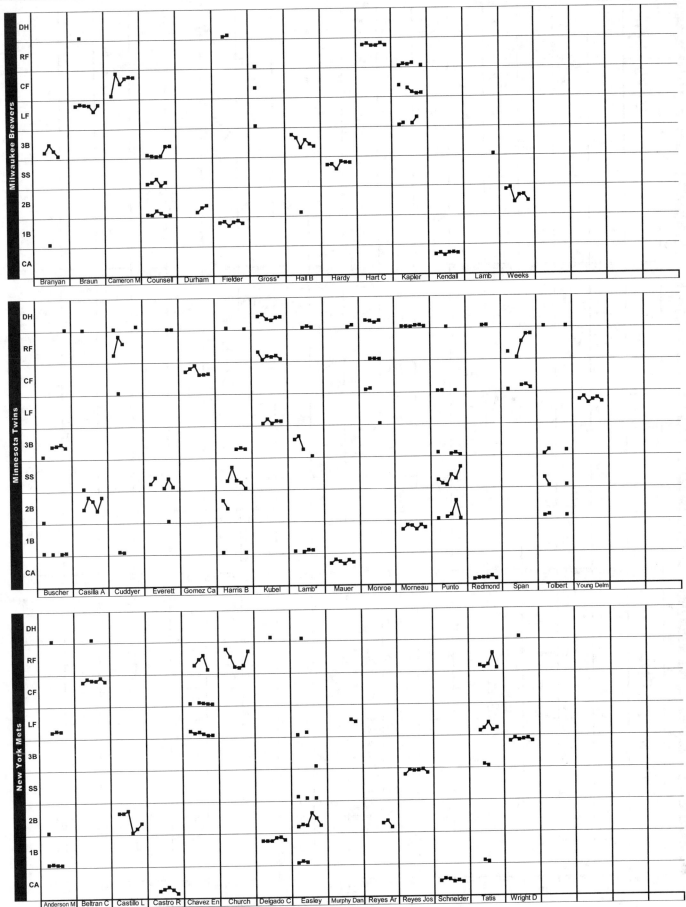

Constellations courtesy John Burnson; HEATER Magazine/Graphical Player

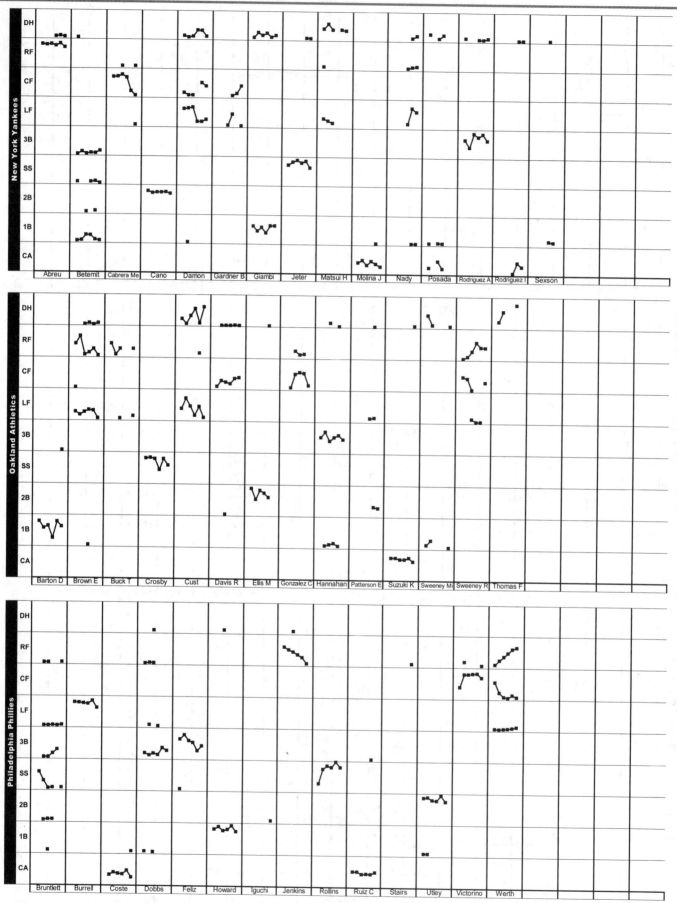

Constellations courtesy John Burnson; HEATER Magazine/Graphical Player

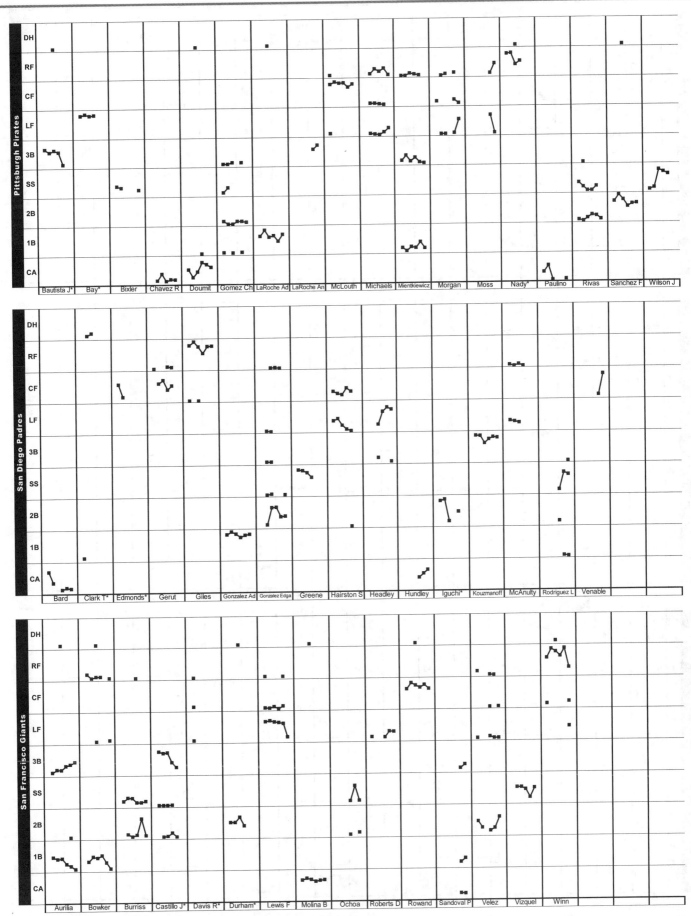

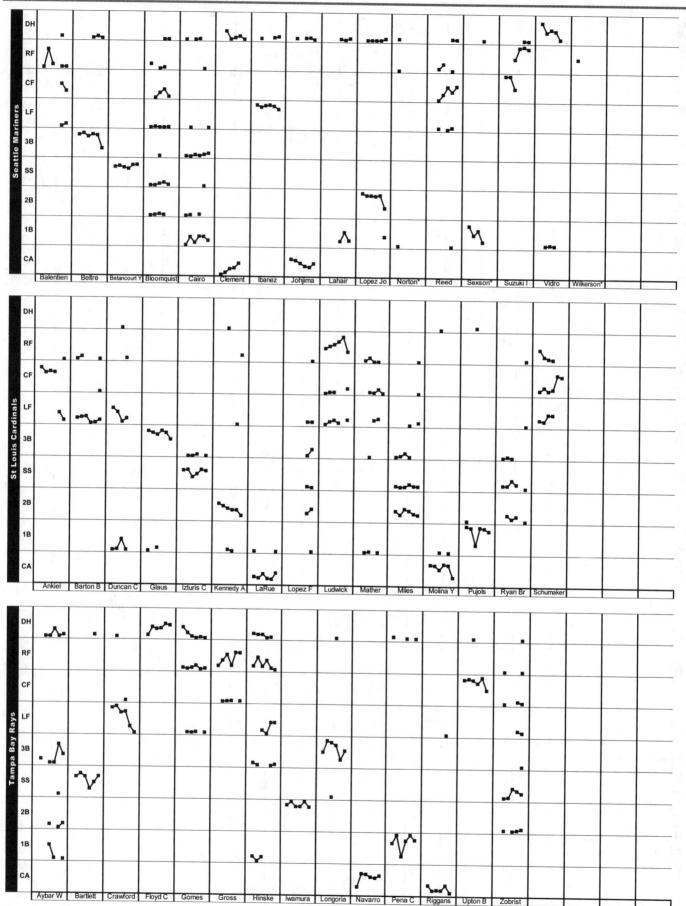

Constellations courtesy John Burnson; HEATER Magazine/Graphical Player

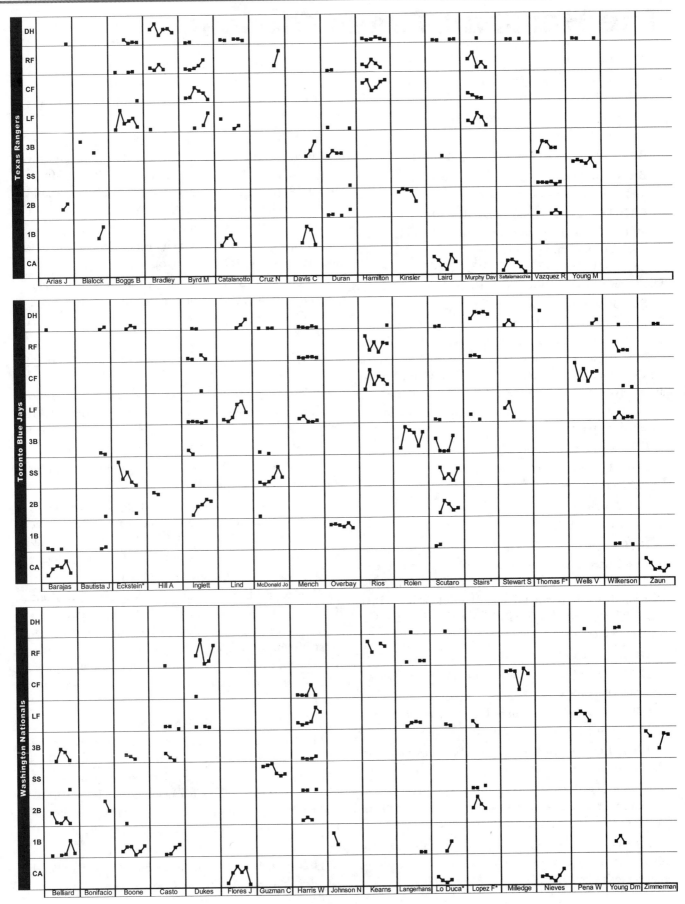

Constellations courtesy John Burnson; HEATER Magazine/Graphical Player

The Hardball Times Glossary

A: Assists. The number of times a fielder makes a throw that results in an out.

AB: At-Bats

AB/RSP: At-Bats with Runners in Scoring Position (second and/or third base)

BA: Batting Average; Hits divided by At-Bats

BA/RSP: Batting Average with Runners in Scoring Position (second and/or third base)

BABIP: Batting Average on Balls in Play. This is a measure of the number of batted balls that safely fall in for hits (not including home runs). The exact formula we use is (H-HR)/(AB-K-HR+SF). This is similar to DER, but from the batter's perspective.

BR: Base Runs, a run contribution formula created by David Smyth, which quantifies the number of runs contributed by a batter. The fundamental formula for Base Runs is (baserunners * scoring rate) + home runs. You can read more about Base Runs in Colin Wyers' article. Note that our Base Runs include an adjustment for batting with runners in scoring position and are adjusted for park.

BB: Bases on Balls, otherwise known as walks

BFP: Batters Faced by Pitcher; the pitching equivalent of Plate Appearances for batters

CS: Caught Stealing

CWS: Career Win Shares

DER: Defense Efficiency Ratio. The percent of times a batted ball is turned into an out by the team's fielders, not including home runs. The exact formula we use is (BFP-H-K-BB-HBP-0.6*E)/(BFP-HR-K-BB-HBP). This is similar to BABIP, but from the defensive team's perspective.

DP: Double Plays

DPS: Double Plays Started, in which the fielder typically gets only an assist

DPT: Double Plays Turned, in which the fielder records both an assist and a putout

ERA: Earned Run Average. Number of earned runs allowed divided by innings pitched multiplied by nine.

ERA+: ERA measured against the league average and adjusted for ballpark factors. An ERA+ over 100 is better than average, less than 100 is below average.

ExpWS: Expected Win Shares. The number of Win Shares an average major leaguer would accrue, given that player's playing time.

FB: Fly ball, as categorized by BIS's scorekeepers. Includes both infield and outfield fly balls.

FE: Fielding Errors, as opposed to Throwing Errors (TE)

FIP: Fielding Independent Pitching, a measure of all those things for which a pitcher is specifically responsible. The formula is (HR*13+(BB+HBP)*3-K*2)/IP, plus a league-specific factor (usually around 3.2) to round out the number to an equivalent ERA number. FIP helps you understand how well a pitcher pitched, regardless of how well his fielders fielded. FIP was invented by Tom M. Tango.

FPct: Fielding Percentage, or the number of fielding chances handled without an error. The formula is (A+PO)/(A+PO+E).

G: Games played

GB%: The percent of batted balls that are grounders. GB% is a better way to measure ground ball tendencies than the more common Ground ball/Fly ball ratio (G/F), because ratios don't follow normal scales (a G/F ratio of 2 doesn't equal twice as many ground balls than 1) and definitions of fly balls can be inconsistent.

GIDP (or GDP): The number of times a batter Grounded Into Double Plays

GPA: Gross Production Average, a variation of OPS, but more accurate and easier to interpret. The exact formula is (OBP*1.8+SLG)/4, adjusted for ballpark. The scale of GPA is similar to BA: .200 is lousy, .265 is around average and .300 is a star.

Grade: To help you interpret our Revised Zone Ratings, we have assigned a grade to each fielder who played at least the equivalent of 80 games or caught at least 700 innings. The grades, which are evenly distributed between "A" and "F," are based on the RZR and OOZ stats for non-catchers and stolen base stats for catchers.

GS: Games Started, a pitching stat.

H-A: Home minus Away, a stat for expressing the "home field advantage" enjoyed by each player. The exact formula is each player's GPA at home minus his GPA on the road. This is calculated for both batters and pitchers; since both tend to perform better at home, H-A is generally positive for batters and negative for pitchers.

Holds: A bullpen stat. According to MLB.com, *A relief pitcher is credited with a hold any time he enters a game in*

a save situation, records at least one out and leaves the game never having relinquished the lead. A pitcher cannot finish the game and receive credit for a hold, nor can he earn a hold and a save in the same game.

HRA: Home Runs Allowed, also a pitching stat

HR/Fly or HR/F: Home Runs as a percent of outfield fly balls. The home run totals are adjusted by the home ballpark's historic home run rates. Typically, about 11% of outfield flies are hit for home runs.

IBB: Intentional Base on Balls.

IF/Fly or IF/F: The percent of fly balls that are infield flies. Infield flies are those fly balls caught within the infield baselines.

ISO: Isolated Power, which measures the "true power" of a batter. The formula is SLG-BA.

K: Strikeouts

K/G: Strikeouts per Game, the number of strikeouts divided by total number of batters faced, times the average number of batters per game in that specific league (generally around 38 batters a game).

L: Losses

L^R: See R^L.

LD%: Line Drive Percentage. Baseball Info Solutions tracks the trajectory of each batted ball and categorizes it as a ground ball, fly ball or line drive. LD% is the percent of batted balls that are line drives. Line drives are not necessarily the hardest hit balls, but they do fall for a hit around 75% of the time.

LI: Leverage Index. Invented by Tom M. Tango, LI measures the criticality of a play. It is based on the range of potential WPA outcomes of a play, compared to all other plays. 1.0 is an average Index.

NIP: Not In Play; represents plays in which the batter didn't put the ball in play: strikeouts, walks and hits by pitch.

OBP: On Base Percentage, the proportion of plate appearances in which a batter reached base successfully, including hits, walks and hit by pitches.

OF: Outfield Flies. BIS categorizes each fly ball as an infield fly or outfield fly, using the infield baselines as the boundary, depending on where the ball would have landed if not caught.

OOZ: Plays made out of zone. A zone is defined as all areas of the field in which that fielding position successfully converts 50% of chances into outs, on average.

Op: Save Opportunities

OPS: On Base plus Slugging Percentage, a crude but quick measure of a batter's true contribution to his team's offense. See GPA for a better approach.

OPS+: OPS measured against the league average, and adjusted for ballpark factors. An OPS+ over 100 is better than average, less than 100 is below average.

Outs: Outs. Not just outs at bat, by the way, but also outs when caught stealing. Two outs are included when hitting into a double play.

P/PA: Pitches per Plate Appearance.

PA: Plate Appearances, or AB+BB+HBP+SF+SH.

PO: Putouts, the number of times a fielder recorded an out in the field. First basemen and catchers get lots of these. From a pitching perspective, PO stands for pickoffs—the number of times a pitcher picks a base runner off a base.

POS: Position played in the field

PRC: Pitching Runs Created, a stat developed by THT's David Gassko. PRC measures the impact of a pitcher by putting his production on the same scale as a batter's Runs Created. PRC is calculated by inserting the number of runs allowed by a pitcher into a league-average context, and then using the Pythagorean Formula to estimate how many wins that pitcher/team would achieve. That win total is then converted into the number of offensive runs it would take to achieve the same number of wins. The impact of fielders is separated in the process.

Pythagorean Formula: A formula for converting a team's Run Differential into a projected win-loss record. The formula is $RS^2/(RS^2+RA^2)$. Teams' actual win-loss records tend to mirror their Pythagorean records, and variances can usually be attributed to luck.

You can improve the accuracy of the Pythagorean formula by using a different exponent (the 2 in the formula). In particular, a sabermetrician named US Patriot discovered that the best exponent can be calculated this way: $(RS/G+RA/G)^{.285}$, where RS/G is Runs Scored per Game and RA/G is Runs Allowed per Game. This is called the PythagoPat formula.

PWins: Pythagorean Wins. See the previous entry.

R: Runs Scored and/or Allowed.

R/G: Runs Scored Per Game. Literally, R divided by games played.

R^L (or L^R): The difference in GPA between a player's performance against left-handed and right-handed pitchers or batters. The order of subtraction depends on the player's natural platoon split—for right-handed batters, for instance, it's L-R. You can read more about R^L in the Stats Introduction of this *Annual*. Note that, for team stats, the formula is the more common L-R for batters and R-L for pitchers.

RBI: Runs Batted In

RISP: Runners In Scoring Position

RS: Runs Scored

Run Differential: Runs Scored minus Runs Allowed

RZR: Revised Zone Rating. RZR measures how often a fielder successfully fields a ball that is hit into his zone. A zone is defined as all areas of the field in which that fielding position successfully converts 50% of chances into outs, on average. RZR differs from the original Zone Rating by removing plays made out of zone and listing them separately.

SB: Stolen Bases

SB%: The percent of time a runner stole a base successfully. The formula is SB/SBA.

SBA: Stolen Bases Attempted.

SBA/G: Stolen Base Attempts per nine innings played.

ShO: Shutouts

SLG and SLGA: Slugging Percentage. Total Bases divided by At-Bats. SLGA stands for Slugging Percentage Against. It represents SLG from the pitcher's perspective.

SO: Strikeouts

Superlwts: Super Linear Weights, an expansion of Pete Palmer's original Linear Weights formula, was created by Mitchel Lichtman. It quantifies the impact of a batter or pitcher, based on all aspects of play, including batting, pitching, fielding and baserunning. Superlwts is expressed as the number of runs better or worse than an average player.

Sv: Saves. According to MLB.com, *A pitcher is credited with a save when he finishes a game won by his club, is not the winning pitcher, and either (a) enters the game with a lead of no more than three runs and pitches for at least one inning, (b) enters the game with the potential tying run either on base, or at bat, or on deck, or (c) pitches effectively for at least three innings.*

Sv%: Saves divided by Save Opportunities

TB: Total Bases, calculated as 1B+2B*2+3B*3+HR*4

TBA: Total Bases Allowed. A pitching stat.

TE: Throwing Errors, as opposed to Fielding Errors (FE)

UER: Unearned Runs

UERA: Unearned Run Average, or the number of unearned runs allowed for each nine innings pitched.

UZR: A fielding system invented by Mitchel Lichtman, it is very similar to John Dewan's plus/minus system, except that it expresses fielding prowess in terms of runs above/below average instead of plays above/below average.

W: Wins

WHIP: Walks and Hits Per Inning Pitched, a variant of OBP for pitchers. This is a popular stat in rotisserie baseball circles.

wOBA: Introduced in *The Book*, this rate stat is similar to OPS and GPA, except that it is set to the scale of OBP.

WPA: Win Probability Added. A system in which each player is given credit toward helping his team win, based on play-by-play data and the impact each specific play has on the team's probability of winning.

WPA/LI: Literally, the WPA of a play divided by its criticality (measured by LI). This stat takes WPA and effectively neutralizes the impact of the game situation. It's another approach for judging player impact on a game—removing the game context but leaving the player's impact on scoring.

WP+PB/G: Wild Pitches and Passed Balls per Nine Innings played. A fielding stat for catchers.

WS: Win Shares. Invented by Bill James. Win Shares is a very complicated statistic that takes all the contributions a player made toward his team's wins and distills them into a single number that represents the number of wins he contributed to the team, times three.

There are three subcategories of Win Shares: batting, pitching and fielding.

We have tweaked James' original formula a bit. Details are available on our website.

WSAge: The average age of a team, weighted by each player's total Win Shares contribution.

WSAB: Win Shares Above Bench. WSAB is a refined approach to Win Shares, in which each player's total Win Shares are compared to the Win Shares an average bench player would have received.

Our research indicates that this is an important adjustment to Win Shares, because it gives greater context to the Win Shares totals. The impact is similar to adding "Loss Shares" for each player.

The bench player is defined as 70% of Expected Win Shares for all players except starting pitchers, for whom it is 50% of Expected Win Shares.

WSP: Win Shares Percentage is a rate stat, calculated as WS/(2*ExpWS). WSP is similar to winning percentage in that .500 is average, but WSP ranges above 1.000 and below .000.

xFIP: Expected Fielding Independent Pitching. This is an experimental stat that adjusts FIP and "normalizes" the home run component. Research has shown that home runs allowed are pretty much a function of flyballs allowed and home park, so xFIP is based on the average number of home runs allowed per outfield fly. Theoretically, this should be a better predictor of a pitcher's future ERA.

Who Were Those Guys?

Richard Barbieri spent his college years studying the whole range of human history. Finding that exhausting he now writes nearly exclusively about baseball which has a far shorter, but no less interesting, past. He lives in New York City.

Sal Baxamusa is a graduate student studying chemical engineering. A native of California, Sal currently resides in New England with his wife and son.

Phil Birnbaum is editor of *By the Numbers*, SABR's Statistical Analysis Newsletter. He lives in Ottawa, where he works as a software developer.

Carolina Bolado lives in New Jersey and works by day making restaurant menus available online to the masses and by night fixing punctuation on The Hardball Times' website. In the precious few hours that she is not glued to her computer, she can be found riding her bicycle, experimenting with new recipes in the kitchen, or rooting for her hometown Marlins.

A graduate of Michigan State University, **Brian Borawski** is a CPA who owns his own small business consulting practice as well as other business ventures. A lifelong Tigers fan, Brian writes about his favorite team at Tigerblog (www.tigerblog.net) and he's a member of SABR's Business of Baseball committee.

John Brattain, who will be starting his fifth season at THT, also writes for *MSN Canada* and blogs at Baseball Digest Daily. He'd like to thank his lovely wife Kelly (AKA "Shego") and his daughters Belinda and Kataryna for their patience as he monopolizes the computer. He'd like to give a shout out to the hard working editors and technical support staff at the Hardball Times for keeping him presentable.

Craig Brown is a soft-tossing left hander with a minus breaking ball. He lives in Kansas City with his wife and two daughters where he writes for Royals Authority in between soccer games and dance recitals

Craig Calcaterra is an attorney and baseball writer -- not necessarily in that order—who lives in New Albany, Ohio. His blog, ShysterBall.com, is updated daily.

Matthew Carruth works as a software engineer by day and writes for The Hardball Times, Lookout Landing, and FanGraphs by night. A graduate of the University of Pennsylvania, he also runs StatCorner.com and specializes in rooting for losing teams.

Derek Carty is currently a student in New Jersey, a die-hard Mets fan, and a fantasy baseball enthusiast. He won his first expert league in as many opportunities this year, contributed to RotoWorld and FOX Sports, and of course writes regularly for THT Fantasy Focus.

For over twenty years, Baseball Info Solutions owner **John Dewan** has collected, published and analyzed in-depth baseball statistics. He is the author of the award-winning Fielding Bible and the forthcoming The Fielding Bible—Volume II (available February, 2009). He announces his annual Fielding Bible Awards on November 1 in The Bill James Handbook and at www.fieldingbible.com.

Joe Distelheim is a retired newspaper editor who has seen Super Bowls, national political conventions, Pete Rose flattening Ray Fosse in Cincinnati, several presidents, the Delaware State Fair and more grammatical errors than Barack Obama had votes. But he never has seen his Cubs in a World Series.

Mike Fast resides in Austin, Texas, and is a semiconductor engineer and a joyful husband and father of two. He is a longtime Kansas City Royals fan whose interest in baseball has been rekindled in the last couple years by the wonders of PITCHf/x. He enjoys baseball analysis, writing for The Hardball Times, and part-time work as a baseball consultant.

David Gassko is a student in Texas. He has consulted for major league teams since 2005.

Anthony Giacalone is an independent historian living in Naperville, Illinois. He has presented numerous papers to the annual convention of the Society for American Baseball Research, some of which were even about baseball. He is currently writing a history of Dick Allen, Baseball and American society from 1955-1980.

Brandon Isleib is a Hardball Times columnist who grew up thinking baseball writers had the best job in the world and still can't find a reason to disagree. The day after he was born, Bill Wegman won his first major league game and Billy Jo Robidoux hit his first major league home run, so he's proud of the iconic successes his birth brought the Milwaukee franchise. Though originally from suburbs of Boston and Philadelphia, he currently lives in Montgomery, Alabama with his wife and their overzealous cat.

Ben Jacobs has returned to Rochester, N.Y., after a three-year absence and currently works as a copy editor at the Democrat and Chronicle. A die-hard Red Sox fan, he enjoyed being back in New York for the end of the Yankees' postseason streak.

Josh Kalk is a physics and math geek who loves to follow anything baseball related.

Rich Lederer is President and Chief Investment Officer of Lederer & Associates, a Registered Investment Adviser in Long Beach, California. He is also the co-founder and lead writer for Baseball Analysts (www.baseballanalysts.com). He is married with two adult children and writes about baseball as a diversion from the rough and tumble investment world.

Will Leitch is a contributing editor for *New York* magazine and the founder of Deadspin. He also writes a regular column for *Sporting News* magazine. He is the author of three books and lives in Brooklyn.

Mitchel Lichtman has been a professional baseball analyst for almost 20 years. He has done work for several major league teams and is the host of the sabermetric blog, www.insidethebook.com. He lives in Las Vegas, Nevada until it gets too hot, at which time he packs up and heads for the Finger Lakes region of central New York. He has degrees from Cornell University and the University of Nevada Boyd School of Law. He is an avid golfer and he and his family are owned by 2 Basset Hounds, 2 English Bulldogs and an assortment of cats.

Don Malcolm edited *The Big Bad Baseball Annual* from 1995-2001, and still has all his fingers and toes. His book on film noir, *The Dark Embrace*, will be published in 2010.

Tim Marchman has written about baseball for the *Wall Street Journal*, *Slate*, and *The New Republic*, and was the baseball columnist for the *New York Sun*. He lives in Chicago.

Jack Marshall is a professional ethicist, writer, lawyer and lifetime baseball enthusiast who lives in Alexandria, Virginia. He is president of ProEthics, a national ethics training firm, and the writer of The Ethics Scoreboard, a website devoted to ethics commentary on sports, pop culture, and politics.

ESPN.com's **Rob Neyer** has written or co-written six books about baseball.

Joe Posnanski has been writing columns for the *Kansas City Star* since 1996 and for Sports Illustrated since August. Joe has twice been named best sports columnist in America by the Associated Sports Editors. His book on Buck O'Neil, *The Soul of Baseball* won the Casey Award as the best baseball book of 2007, and his new book on the 1975 Cincinnati Reds will be published by William Morrow in Fall 2009.

Greg Rybarczyk is a former Naval Officer and current reliability engineer for a major multinational corporation. He is the creator of Hit Tracker, an aerodynamic model for recreating the trajectory of batted baseballs, with which he has observed and analyzed more than 15,000 MLB home runs and other batted balls since April, 2006. This off-season Greg is hoping to find out what the inside of his eyelids look like. He lives in the Portland, OR area with his wife and two children.

Corey Seidman is currently attending Penn State University, in the pre-law program. He covers the Phillies at Phanatic Phollow Up and is currently a writing intern at Comcast Sportsnet.

Eric Seidman is a graduate business student whose baseball analysis can be found at Fangraphs, Baseball Prospectus, and Statistically Speaking. He is also an accomplished screenwriter and a devout Phillies fan.

Sean Smith has been a fan of baseball and the Angels since 1982. He lives in Maryland with his wife, baby daughter, and two cats.

Dave Studenmund first started producing the *Hardball Times Annual* five years ago. It seemed like a good idea at the time.

Tom M. Tango (aka Tangotiger), co-author of *The Book— Playing The Percentages In Baseball*, runs the Tango on Baseball website, where you will find a large number of research pieces devoted to sabermetrics. His inspirations have been Pete Palmer and Bill James, and is thankful for the generosity of Retrosheet and Baseball1 in providing data to the public. He has worked as a consultant for major league teams in hockey and baseball. Born and raised in Canada, he now resides in New Jersey with his family.

Roel Torres grew up in Worcester, received his undergraduate degree from Harvard with Honors, and lives in Somerville, MA. He is a Featured Writer at Bill James Online.

Steve Treder, a writer for The Hardball Times since its founding, has presented papers to the Cooperstown Symposium on Baseball and American Culture, and to the SABR Annual Convention. His articles have also been published in *Nine*, *The National Pastime*, and *Outside the Lines*.

Bryan Tsao is the editor of the Hardball Times website by night. By day, he does user experience design and research for Watercooler, a startup that makes online fan communities for sports and TV fans. He is a proud alum of UC San Diego and UC Berkeley, and roots for the A's in his spare time.

Having just completed his second season at THT, **TUCK**!'s award-winning cartoons, illustrations, and comics have appeared in a diverse assortment of avenues: Notorious hockey websites, the programs sold outside St. Louis Blues NHL homegames, as well as THT's Annual and Season Previews, and a hockey trivia book. (Honorable mention placements and contributions include the Pulitzer Newspapers, Gannett Newspapers, Marvel Comics, Image Comics, and many impressive near-misses that make for entertaining happy hour conversation.) When not (literally) drawing the ire of wicked officials (both on and off the field of play), TUCK! enjoys hanging with family and friends, and playing music just too darned loud.

John Walsh is a research physicist by day, baseball researcher by night. Despite living four thousand miles from Fenway Park, he remains an avid Red Sox fan.

Victor Wang is currently a freshman at Northwestern University in Evanston, Illinois. His work has been featured in the *New York Times, San Diego Union-Tribune,* and espn.com.

Craig Wright worked 21 years in major league baseball pioneering a career that integrated science and baseball. He is the primary author of the book *The Diamond Appraised* and currently writes a baseball column under the same name. Subscription information can be found at diamondappraised. com. Craig also researches and writes *A Page from Baseball's Past,* one of the longest running pre-game radio shows in baseball history. A delightful text version of these stories, delivered to your email inbox, can be subscribed to at page-frombaseballspast.com.

Colin Wyers blogs about the Cubs at Goatriders of the Apocalypse (goatriders.org) and covers sabermetrics for Statistically Speaking (statspeak.net.) He does work out of a basement, but at least it's his own basement (although his wife and kids might argue that point).

Notes

Also Available from ACTA Sports

THE BILL JAMES HANDBOOK 2009
BILL JAMES
and BASEBALL INFO SOLUTIONS

Every year, thousands of avid baseball fans eagerly await **The Bill James Handbook**—the best and most complete annual baseball guide available. Full of exclusive stats, this book is the most comprehensive resource of every hit, pitch and catch in Major League Baseball's 2008 season. Key features include the Fielding Bible Awards, the Young Talent Inventory, and Career Data with more statistical categories than any other book.

$23.95, 520 pages, paperback
$28.95, 520 pages, spiral-bound
Available November 2008

THE BILL JAMES GOLD MINE 2009
BILL JAMES

Starting in the 1970s, a night watchman from Kansas forever changed the way that many people view baseball analysis and ultimately the game itself. In his latest work, Bill James continues that tradition with **The Bill James Gold Mine 2009**—a groundbreaking collection of original essays, statistical profiles, and hidden "nuggets" of information worth their weight in gold.

$23.95, 320 pages, paperback
Available February 2009

THE FIELDING BIBLE—VOLUME II
JOHN DEWAN
and BASEBALL INFO SOLUTIONS

First published in 2006, *The Fielding Bible* completely changed the entire perception of fielding statistics in Major League Baseball. Using the revolutionary Plus/Minus approach to fielding analysis previously available exclusively to Major League Baseball teams, John Dewan and Baseball Info Solutions have moved the conversation forward on this important and often overlooked part of the game.

$23.95, 240 pages, paperback
Available February 2009

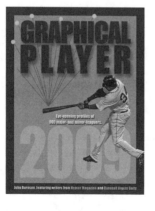

GRAPHICAL PLAYER 2009
JOHN BURNSON and WRITERS
FROM *HEATER* MAGAZINE

In *Graphical Player*, John Burnson offers a new approach to ballplayer analysis: visually analyzing charts and graphs to uncover trends and tendencies among players. With full profiles of 900 major and minor league players, key features include daily game logs (now for three years), support for point leagues (including yearly and weekly trends), and the Graphical Minors—profiles of baseball's top prospects. Burnson and his team of writers won the 2008 CBS Sportsline Fantasy Baseball League of Experts.

$21.95, 300 pages, paperback
Available December 2009

THE HARDBALL TIMES SEASON PREVIEW 2009
THE HARDBALL TIMES WRITERS

Everything you need to win your fantasy league championship is in this book, from whom to draft, what prospects to stash away for next year, and which players will cost you more than they're worth. Featuring the exclusive Hardball Times Projection System, one of the most accurate projection systems available today.

$19.95, 208 pages, paperback
Available February 2009